W9-BSH-191

GENERATIONS

THE ESPERTI PETERSON INSTITUTE CONTRIBUTORY SERIES

Eileen R. Sacco, Managing Editor

Generations: Planning Your Legacy
Legacy: Plan, Protect, and Preserve Your Estate
Ways and Means: Maximize the Value of Your Retirement Savings
Wealth Enhancement and Preservation, 2d ed.

GENERATIONS

Planning *Your* Legacy

---

*Practical Answers
from America's Foremost
Estate Planning Attorneys*

— A Special Edition —

ROBERT A. ESPERTI   RENNO L. PETERSON

ANTHONY J. MADONIA

EPI

The editors and contributors are not engaged in rendering legal, tax, accounting, and financial planning, or similar professional services. While legal, tax, accounting, and financial planning issues covered in this book have been checked with sources believed to be reliable, some material may be affected by changes in the laws or in the interpretations of such laws since the manuscript for this book was completed. For that reason the accuracy and completeness of such information and the opinions based thereon are not guaranteed. In addition, state or local tax laws or procedural rules may have a material impact on the general recommendations made by the contributing authors, and the strategies outlined in this book may not be suitable for every individual.

ISBN 0-922943-13-3

Library of Congress Catalog Number 98-074253

Managing editor: Eileen Sacco

Legal review: David K. Cahoone, J.D., LL.M.

Project manager: Christy Allbee

Marketing services: Brian Budman, George Chamberlin, Reneé Garcia, Eric Johnson, Ling Lam, Lydia Monchak

Jacket designer: Richard Adelson

Composition, design, & editing services: C+S Gottfried, http://www.lookoutnow.com/dtp

Printed and bound in Canada by Quebecor Printing

Esperti Peterson Institute Incorporated
410 17th Street, Suite 1260
Denver, CO 80202

Contents

Preface

The Esperti Peterson Institute is an innovative company that invents, inaugurates, and improves sophisticated wealth design strategies. It consists of selected members of the National Network of Estate Planning Attorneys who participate in the Institute's Masters Program. The Masters Program is a unique experience—a forum in which some of the finest estate planning minds in the United States spend 3 years enhancing their techniques in wealth design strategies. Graduates of this program are given the designation "Fellows of the Esperti Peterson Institute." Participants in the Masters Program for Attorneys *must* be members of the National Network of Estate Planning Attorneys, and many of the Institute Fellows and current Masters Program participants are contributing authors of *Generations*.

The National Network was founded in 1989 to bring estate planning practitioners nationwide closer together so that its members might collectively expand their expertise and planning horizon to better serve the estate planning needs of their clients. The Network and each of its members are:

■ Dedicated to helping families create their own legacies by assisting them to give what they have to whom they want, the way they want, and when they want and to save every tax dollar, attorney fee, and court cost possible.

■ Devoted to providing client families with sound legal alternatives for achieving their goals and to creating quality legal documents in easily understood language that will perpetuate wealth and values through succeeding generations.

Network members aspire to the highest professional standards of ethics and to behavior that lends dignity to their profession. The Network encourages professionals to work together for the benefit of their mutual clientele in order to offer the best and most effective planning possible. It believes that when professionals work together to combine their respective talents and skills—rather than compete with one another—clients and professionals alike are the winners.

The National Network and the Esperti Peterson Institute are recognized as cutting-edge institutions that have significantly enhanced the quality of estate and wealth planning in the United States. Because of the growing need for international planning, the Institute and the Network are in the process of becoming a global force in estate and wealth planning.

Generations is an important addition to the publications offered by the Esperti Peterson Institute, of which we are the cofounders and cochairmen. Written by 137 members of the National Network of Estate Planning Attorneys, it is the fifth publication in the "Contributory Book Series" that began with *Wealth Enhancement and Preservation*, and it is the second in a series of estate planning books that began with *Legacy: Plan, Protect, and Preserve Your Estate*.

Generations is an enhancement of *Legacy*, bringing the basic and sophisticated estate planning concepts originally found in *Legacy* up to date and providing a wealth of additional planning perspectives and information.

Generations is the product of extended research by the Esperti Peterson Institute. Because of many changes in the law since *Legacy* was published, including the Tax Reform Act of 1996, the Taxpayer Relief Act of 1997, and the IRS Restructuring and Reform Act of 1998, as well as new rulings by the courts, the Department of the Treasury, and the Internal Revenue Service, an update of *Legacy* was necessary. In order to accomplish this task, the Institute asked the original contributors to *Legacy* to submit meaningful revisions, and it asked additional members of the National Network of Estate Planning Attorneys to participate as new contributors in updating the information. The response was overwhelming. The new contributors were asked to submit their own responses to a minimum of 25 questions most frequently asked by their clients. They not only helped bring the law up to date but also added significant new information and different viewpoints.

Faced with such a large amount of important new research, we soon realized that including it in a second edition of *Legacy* would make the text so large that readers would be too intimidated to tackle it. In fact, the volume of new material demonstrated that there was a need for a new book that retained some—but not all—of the basic information found in *Legacy* and also covered the new, more sophisticated topics submitted by the new contributors. Thus, *Generations* is a new book which accomplishes just that.

In editing *Generations*, we were faced with the same challenges we had encountered with all the books in the Contributory Series. The responses of the *Generations* contributing authors reflected a variety of practices, levels of sophistication, and differing views. We received a great many duplicate questions, but the scope of the questions was broad and enlightening. They, once again, gave us an in-depth perspective on the diversity of estate planning needs across the United States and the variety of techniques being used to solve those needs.

As editors of a great volume of material, we had to retain its scope and reconcile diverse writing styles and views. At the same time, we wanted to ensure that the book would be readable and informative. But even that was not enough. We wanted to ensure that readers could open the book to virtually any page and find useful information. To do so, we retained a certain degree of repetitiveness so that readers would not have to go back and forth in the book to gain understanding. Anyone who reads *Generations* from cover to cover will see this repetition. Those who want to go to particular areas of interest will not.

Generations is an up-to-date, informative book that covers the estate planning topics that the clients of National Network members find especially important. It delivers a vast amount of usable estate planning information; it is a user-friendly book, not a heavy legal tome or reference book. We are very proud of the efforts of our contributory authors in bringing to you, the reader, the essence of practical planning from some of the most successful estate planning attorneys in the nation.

We especially wish to thank Anthony J. Madonia for his contributions to *Generations,* and we are honored to dedicate this special edition to him.

Robert A. Esperti
Renno L. Peterson
The Esperti Peterson Institute
October 1998

Introduction

Anthony J. Madonia

I am thrilled and honored to have the opportunity to participate in the writing of *Generations*. As an estate planning professional, I have read countless books on this subject but found none of them to be easily understandable, even though written by professionals and for professionals. I think the need for this book, *Generations,* which puts most of these concepts into a much more understandable format, is obvious. I have thoroughly enjoyed the challenge of interpreting an array of complex laws and rules and translating them into a language and format that is easy to read.

It is my hope that readers of this book will gain a real appreciation for all the laws that govern estate planning. While I believe that readers will gain some technical knowledge in this area, *Generations* was not designed to be a technical reference but a general overview of the varied subjects that it contains.

I feel that my 13 years of experience in the fields of taxation, estate planning, and business planning fully qualifies me to participate in this project. My entire professional career has been dedicated to these areas, and my focus has always been on assisting individuals in accomplishing their estate planning goals. This includes the minimization of estate taxes, legal fees, and administrative burdens. I have also assisted many business owners in the sale of their businesses or in the transfer of their businesses to the next generation of owners, and I am particularly sensitive to the needs of those people. This experience lends a unique slant to the usual concept of estate planning.

I spent 3 years at a local CPA firm in Chicago, during which time I began attending law school, and 2 years with the accounting firm K.P.M.G. Peat Marwick, where I concentrated in the areas of taxation particularly as they related to real estate investments. I have been in the private practice of law for the past 8 years, and founded my own firm in October 1995. During my entire legal career, my practice has been limited to estate planning, tax planning, and business planning, with the ultimate goal of leading business owners through the complex maze we call estate planning and into personal and financial peace of mind.

When I advise clients, the needs of the client, especially as they relate to that client's personal and financial issues, are of utmost importance. I believe that it is of paramount importance to learn everything I can about a client's personal and financial situation before rendering any advice on how to structure his or her estate or business succession plan. We do not live in a society where one size fits all, and the only way to do an excellent job of assisting clients is to learn everything that I can about each individual situation.

Often, I will work with the client's financial planner, insurance professional, and other attorneys in the course of my representation. I feel it is very important to maintain the relationships which the clients have built over the years, and I look forward to working with other people associated with each client because these professionals can add valuable input to the process. It is important to recognize that each person fills a very specific and important role in the client's life, and by working together, it can only benefit the client.

My professional goals are to build my law firm while continuing to provide the personalized, expedient, and thorough services that my clients expect and demand. As my practice becomes busier, I have added associates and support staff to assist in this process and will continue to do so in order to preserve this level of service.

Acknowledgments

I would like to acknowledge David E. Shoub, a founding member of the National Network of Estate Planning Attorneys, who introduced me to the Network in 1991. Since that time I have greatly increased my knowledge in this area and have learned about the particular sensitivities that clients face in the estate planning process. Mr. Shoub has been instrumental in helping me focus on the finer points of both estate planning and client management, and for that I am appreciative. I would also like to acknowledge Daniel F. Lisowski, who has built his air-freight operation from a three-person staff to a significant competitor in its marketplace. Dan has always been an excellent sounding board and has taken the time and extended me the courtesy of explaining some of the secrets of his success.

Finally, I am happily married to Jennifer J. Madonia. Without her encouragement and support, it would have been impossible to make the professional commitments I have made. I am very grateful for her kindness and enthusiasm. We have three wonderful children, Nicholas Anthony, Natalie Theresa, and Nathan Anthony.

∞

Anthony J. Madonia, J.D., CPA, graduated with a B.S. in accounting from the University of Illinois in 1985 and received his J.D. in 1990 from John Marshall Law School. He was a senior tax accountant with Peat, Marwick, Main & Co., a national certified public accounting firm, while completing his legal education. He is in the 3-year Esperti Peterson Institute Masters Program in Wealth Strategies Planning.

Mr. Madonia was a partner in a small law firm before establishing Anthony J. Madonia & Associates, Ltd., in 1995. Mr. Madonia's legal practice is concentrated on the areas of wealth planning, estate and income tax planning, and business law and succession planning. Mr. Madonia frequently provides educational seminars to accounting professionals, financial planners, insurance professionals, and senior citizen groups.

PART ONE

Exploring the Basics

"Estate planning" is a term that has changed dramatically over the years. At one time, it meant having a will and, if a person was married, titling property jointly with a spouse. It conjured up visions of death and dying. It suggested great wealth and expensive, wood-paneled law offices in the heart of big cities. No longer is this the case, because of a multitude of developments that have occurred in the last two decades.

Perhaps the greatest change that has taken place is the recognition by attorneys that wills and probate are no longer appropriate in most situations. These two traditional planning methods are now seen as vestiges of another era, more suited for the agricultural ways of the early and mid-1900s than for the modern, technological society in which we now live. Changing views of finance and lifestyle, developments in computers and communications, and advanced strides in medicine have made estate planning far more complex and, frankly, more important for a larger group of people than ever before. *Estate planning* is no longer just a will and jointly titled property; it is a broad field that encompasses finances, retirement planning, medical planning, charitable planning, gift planning, tax planning, and intergenerational planning. Its scope is almost daunting.

In order to make some sense out of such a broad field, our contributing authors have taken the perfectly intelligent course of beginning with the basics. To understand the many sophisticated planning techniques that abound in estate planning, one must understand the fundamentals. These include the concept of an estate, how it is planned, and the traditional methods of planning. Once you have a firm grasp of these basic estate planning concepts, the more complex methods of planning will be easier to understand and apply.

Chapter 1 is particularly significant as it addresses some of the major changes in the gift and estate tax law that were introduced in the Taxpayer Relief Act of 1997. While this legislation loosened the tight grasp of estate and gift taxes on many Americans, it also contains complex provisions that will be phased in over a long period of time. Now, more than ever, it is important to understand how these changes affect tax planning. Surprisingly, these changes mandate more, not less, planning.

Please remember as you read Chapters 1 and 2 that the concepts are basic but necessary in understanding the estate planning process. Our contributing authors have taken a huge amount of complex material and reduced it to its essence. Once you read the material in these chapters, you will have the tools for moving on to some of the most effective estate planning solutions that are now available.

chapter 1

Basic Estate
Planning Concepts

THE FUNDAMENTALS
OF ESTATE PLANNING

⚑ *What is an estate?*

There is a common misconception that "estates" are exclusive to multi-millionaires. Most people do not realize what actually makes up an estate and only have an idea about estates from watching television reruns of *Dallas,* where they see the "Southfork Ranch" estate. A residence, no matter how large or small, is part of an estate. An *estate* is, quite frankly, everything a person owns in his or her own name or owns with another person, everything payable to his or her estate, and everything controlled by that person. Your estate can comprise your residence, cash, stocks, bonds, and other investments, as well as businesses that you may own. Your estate also comprises retirement plans, such as IRAs and Keoghs, and life insurance death benefits. It even includes personal property, such as vehicles, collectibles, and other treasured items.

⚑ *What is estate planning?*

The definition of estate planning adopted by the National Network of Estate Planning Attorneys is:

I want to control my property while I am alive and well, care for myself and my loved ones if I become disabled, and be able to give what I have to whom I want, the way I want, and when I want, and, if I can, I want to save every last tax dollar, attorney fee, and court cost possible.

A good estate plan will meet this definition of estate planning.

⌁ Is estate planning just having a will?

For centuries, that is about all it was. Today, the field of estate planning has grown to be one of the most technically demanding and comprehensive areas of the law.

Estate planning is ensuring that your hopes, dreams, and concerns for yourself and for your loved ones will be accomplished if you become incapacitated or die. It is protecting you and those you love by keeping you, your family, and your sensitive business information out of probate court when you become legally incapacitated or die.

Estate planning is designing a trust agreement which contains your loving instructions for your family's continued well-being after your death and also contains provisions to eliminate estate taxes.

It can include planning for redirecting what would have been paid in estate taxes to useful charitable projects, at no net cost to you or even at a net gain—you and your heirs may have more money for yourselves than would be the case if you had left nothing to charity.

If you are a business owner, estate planning is planning for the survival of that business after your death or the efficient disposition of that business in order to use the proceeds to care for and educate your loved ones.

In this day and age, you never know when you might be sued or what the result might be, even if you have done nothing wrong. For individuals who are particularly at risk from such lawsuits, estate planning can include increased protection from creditor attack.

Through devices such as private foundations, estate planning can keep your family members together and involved for generations in community services while giving them entrée into influential circles they would not otherwise have had.

Estate planning can help you unlock the value of highly appreciated assets which have a built-in capital gain liability and devise retirement vehicles which have the benefits of qualified plans without the restrictions.

⚜ *What are some of the most common misconceptions about estate planning?*

Here are the "Great Myths," as we call them:

Myth 1: "I'm too young to worry about estate planning."
Reality: If you're young, you especially need to map out an estate plan to help *protect* your loved ones.

Myth 2: "My estate isn't large enough to need estate planning."
Reality: If your estate is fairly small, it will likely suffer a greater percentage of shrinkage from final expenses, probate costs, and so on, than will a larger estate.

Myth 3: "My estate won't be taxed, regardless of its size, because I can use the unlimited marital deduction to transfer all of my assets to my spouse tax-free."
Reality: Poorly planned usage of the unlimited marital deduction can simply postpone estate tax problems until your spouse's death. Without proper use of estate tax planning, your estate shrinkage at that time could be substantial, with your children and grandchildren feeling the losses.

Myth 4: "Most people just have a will; that's all I need."
Reality: Depending upon whose statistics you read, only about 40 to 60 percent of the population has a will, and it's true that a will is a *must* in every estate plan. But understand, a will *guarantees* the probate process. To avoid the probate process, use a funded revocable living trust as the centerpiece of your estate plan with a pour-over will as a supporting document, not the centerpiece.

⚜ *What are the traditional methods of basic estate planning?*

There are six techniques that are traditionally used in basic estate planning, and everyone, in some manner, is using at least one of these techniques. Let us briefly look at each one, along with its advantages and disadvantages.

Intestacy A majority of Americans die without a will or a trust. This is called *intestacy.* Intestacy is considered a method of estate planning because by leaving no will, a person has given the state the right to decide who will receive his or her property. Assets that pass by intestacy go through a probate process called *administration* which is almost identical to the probate process for a last will and testament.

WILL-PLANNING PROBATE A *last will and testament* is essentially a legal document that states how a person wants his or her estate distributed at death. Many people plan their estates by creating a last will and testament.

Unfortunately, wills have major disadvantages: (1) A will does *not* control how or when *all* of the will maker's property is distributed. Property owned in joint tenancy with another person, life insurance proceeds, and retirement benefits all pass outside of a will. (2) A will is not effective until the death of its maker, so it is of no help with lifetime planning. (3) Upon the maker's death, the will must be filed with the probate court, where it becomes a public document and is available to anyone who wants to read it.

Death probate is a court and administrative proceeding. It is required to manage and distribute a decedent's estate at death. Once a will enters the probate process, a person's estate is no longer controlled by his or her family. It is in the hands of the court and the probate attorneys. Because a will guarantees that a decedent's estate will go through probate, it is a very poor estate planning document for families who want to maintain control.

JOINT TENANCY WITH RIGHT OF SURVIVORSHIP There are different forms of how people hold title to property, one of which is joint tenancy with right of survivorship. The *right of survivorship* means that the survivor acquires the entire interest in the property upon the death of the other joint tenant.

Because a joint tenant's interest automatically passes by law to the surviving joint tenant at death, its ownership is not controlled by the deceased joint tenant's will. For example, two brothers, Bob and David, own a piece of property as joint tenants. Bob dies and his will says that upon his death all of his estate should go to his wife, Pat; however, because the property passes automatically at Bob's death to the surviving joint tenant, David will own the entire property and Pat will get nothing. This is only one of the many unforeseen problems that joint tenancy creates.

BENEFICIARY DESIGNATIONS Some types of property pass, at the death of their owners, to those listed in their beneficiary designations. Life insurance policies, annuities, individual retirement accounts, qualified retirement accounts, and pension plans are examples of these types of property.

The advantage of having named beneficiaries is that the property avoids probate. The disadvantage is that since the proceeds from beneficiary-designation property pass directly to the named beneficiaries and are not controlled by terms in the will, the proceeds may not pass to whom the owner wants or in the way he or she wants. Like joint ownership, beneficiary designations supersede the terms of a will.

GIFTS   Giving assets away can be a valuable part of an estate plan, but it should not be done without professional advice.

REVOCABLE LIVING TRUST   Finally, many people have living trusts, but these documents may be "bare-bones" living trusts. Bare-bones trusts often do not achieve basic planning objectives or avoid probate because their makers failed to transfer their property into their trusts. Bare-bones living trusts are usually sterile documents written in legalese and devoid of meaningful instructions for loved ones. They seldom reflect the hopes, concerns, dreams, values, and ambitions of their makers. However, when someone has a properly drafted and funded living trust, he or she can be confident that the many disadvantages of the five preceding traditional forms of estate planning have been eliminated.

THE UNIFIED TAX SYSTEM

⊿ *What is meant by a "unified" estate and gift tax system?*

The federal estate and gift tax is a *unified tax* in the sense that it is imposed upon the cumulative transfers made during life and upon death.

For many years the federal gift tax and the federal estate tax were treated separately under different schedules. Beginning with the Tax Reform Act of 1976, the federal government unified the two taxes so that they are taxed at exactly the same rates. It now does not matter whether transfers are made by gift during life or by will or trust at death; the transfers are taxed at the same rates by the same unified federal estate and gift tax schedule. However, even though the tax rates are the same, the economic effects of making taxable gifts during life and transferring property at death can be substantially different, so the term "unified" is somewhat misleading.

Federal Estate Tax

⚜ *What is the federal estate tax?*

The *federal estate tax* is a tax levied against the "right to transfer" property at the time of death. In essence, it is an *everything* tax. Any assets owned or controlled by the decedent at the time of death are included in his or her estate for federal estate tax purposes.

⚜ *At what rates are estates taxed?*

Table 1-1 shows the federal estate tax rates. Please note that these tax rates are used *before* the application of any credits.

⚜ *How are assets valued for purposes of this tax?*

The value of the assets included in the taxable estate is their fair market value at the time of the death of their owner. If there is an estate tax due, the fair market value of the assets 6 months from the date of the owner's death can be used instead as long as this "alternate" valuation decreases the amount of tax that would be due if the date-of-death value was used.

⚜ *Who is responsible for coming up with the value of the assets in an estate?*

The trustee of a living trust or the personal representative (modern name for "executor") of a will has the tasks of gathering the information that is necessary to value the estate's assets and hiring the appropriate appraisers.

⚜ *How are values actually determined for assets?*

Estates consist of many types of assets. Some are relatively easy to value, and others are hard to value. Publicly traded stocks and bonds, for example, are valued at the average of the high and low selling prices on the valuation date (if there was no trading on the valuation date, the high and low of the preceding and succeeding trade dates are used). They are easily valued by the estate's trustee or personal representative.

Hard-to-value assets such as real estate and interests in non-publicly traded businesses should be appraised by an appraiser who is specifically qualified in the valuation of these types of assets. An accurate valuation is critical because it is not uncommon for the Internal Revenue Service to dispute the value of an asset contained in a federal estate tax return.

TABLE 1-1   Federal Estate Tax Rates

If value of taxable estate is		The tax is	Of the amount over
Over	But not over		
–	$ 10,000	18% of amount	–
$ 10,000	20,000	$1,800 + 20%	$10,000
20,000	40,000	$3,800 + 22%	$20,000
40,000	60,000	$8,200 + 24%	$40,000
60,000	80,000	$13,000 + 26%	$60,000
80,000	100,000	$18,200 + 28%	$80,000
100,000	150,000	$23,800 + 30%	$100,000
150,000	250,000	$38,800 + 32%	$150,000
250,000	500,000	$70,800 + 34%	$250,000
500,000	750,000	$155,800 + 37%	$500,000
750,000	1,000,000	$248,300 + 39%	$750,000
1,000,000	1,250,000	$345,800 + 41%	$1,000,000
1,250,000	1,500,000	$448,300 + 43%	$1,250,000
1,500,000	2,000,000	$555,800 + 45%	$1,500,000
2,000,000	2,500,000	$780,800 + 49%	$2,000,000
2,500,000	3,000,000	$1,025,800 + 53%	$2,500,000
3,000,000		$1,290,800 + 55%	$3,000,000

⚑ *Who values household goods?*

Household goods, furnishings, and personal effects are appraised by those persons who routinely buy and sell such items. Household and personal effects ordinarily involve a room-by-room itemization; however, these can be grouped together if no single item exceeds $100 in value, which is rarely the case.

⚑ *How are life insurance death benefits taxed?*

There is a commonly held misconception that life insurance death proceeds are completely tax-free. This is not true. Although life insurance death proceeds are not subject to federal or state *income* tax, and they may be free from death taxes imposed by a state, they are generally not free of federal estate tax.

Any life insurance policy that is owned by the decedent or in which the decedent had any "incidents of ownership" at the time of death is included in his or her estate for federal estate tax purposes. However, if a policy insuring the life of a decedent was initially owned by an irrevocable life insurance trust or someone other than the decedent (such as the decedent's spouse or children) or was transferred by the insured more than 3 years prior to the insured's death to an irrevocable life insurance trust or another person, then the death benefit proceeds will be free of federal estate tax. (Irrevocable life insurance trusts are fully explained in Chapter 6.)

By comparison, lifetime distributions from a policy's cash surrender values are income-taxable to the extent that the amount distributed exceeds the basis in the policy (the premiums paid minus dividends). Policy loans are not taxable distributions unless the policy is classified as a *modified endowment contract.*

⚹ *What are incidents of ownership?*

Incidents of ownership are IRS-specified attributes that put policy proceeds into your estate. These attributes include the ownership of the policy, power to change the beneficiary, right to borrow against the policy, and right to surrender or cancel the policy.

⚹ *Who values life insurance?*

Life insurance is valued at the amount of the policy proceeds and is usually valued by the insurance agent of the estate or trust and the trustee or personal representative.

⚹ *Is the federal estate tax a one-time tax?*

Estate tax applies to transfers to each generation, for example, from father to son and from son to grandson.

⚹ *When is the federal estate tax due and payable?*

Subject to a limited exception, estate taxes must be paid, in cash, usually within 9 months of the person's death.

⚹ *Are there any situations in which my estate can pay the federal estate tax in installments?*

Yes. When an individual dies and his or her interest in a closely held business exceeds 35 percent of the adjusted gross estate, the executor may elect to pay estate taxes attributable to that business in installments over a maximum period of 14 years at special interest rates that are lower than those normally charged by the government for installment payments of taxes.

⚲ Does my estate have to file a federal estate tax return if it is under the current applicable exclusion amount?

If you do not use up any unified credit by making taxable gifts during your lifetime, a federal estate tax return needs to be filed only for a gross estate that is equal to or exceeds the applicable exclusion amount in effect for the year of death. (See Table 1-2.)

⚲ Can I leave money or property to charity free of tax?

You can leave any amount of money or property to qualifying charities without having to pay federal estate tax.

⚲ Are there any deductions, exemptions, or credits?

Generally, a decedent's gross estate is reduced by the following:

- Funeral and administration expenses
- Debts, mortgages, and liens
- Bequests to a surviving spouse (the *marital deduction*)
- Charitable bequests

In addition to these deductions, every estate receives a *unified credit,* the size of which varies depending on the year of death. For example, in the years 2000 and 2001, the amount of this credit is $220,550, which is a direct credit against the taxes owed on the estate of the decedent. This $220,550 unified credit is the equivalent of exempting $675,000 from a taxable estate. This means a person can pass to anyone a total of $675,000 free of federal estate tax. The unified credit gradually increases to $345,800 in 2006, which is the same as exempting $1 million from every estate.

⚲ Is there any provision of the federal estate tax law designed to give estate tax relief to the estates of owners of family businesses?

Yes, there is. In 1997, modified in 1998, an estate tax deduction was enacted for up to $1,300,000 in value of interests in a family-owned business. Since the estate tax depends on the value of all the assets included in a decedent's estate, an estate tax deduction for certain assets means that the estate tax will be lower.

Whenever the full $675,000 family-owned business deduction is used, the applicable exclusion amount is always $625,000. There is no upward adjustment in the applicable exclusion amount to parallel the phase-in of the increase in the applicable exclusion amount from $625,000 in 1998 to $1 million in 2006.

The Unified Credit

⍓ *What is the unified credit?*

Once the value of an estate is determined and all the appropriate deductions are taken, the remaining value is the taxable estate. Before the tax is finally determined, however, a credit is applied. This credit reduces the amount of the tax due.

This credit is called a *unified credit* because it can be used against taxable transfers during a person's life (lifetime gifts) and against transfers at a person's death.

⍓ *What does the term "exemption equivalent" mean?*

When the unified credit came into existence in 1982, it was a new concept in federal estate and gift taxation. The *exemption equivalent* was the dollar value of that credit. For example, the unified credit in 1997 was $192,800. This credit amount was the "equivalent" of the tax on a $600,000 estate. Here is a simple example of how the credit worked:

Taxable estate	$600,000
Tentative tax due	$192,800
Unified credit	– 192,800
Amount of tax due	$ –0–

If the taxable estate was greater than $600,000, tax was due; the unified credit did not shelter all the tax. If the taxable estate was equal to or less than $600,000, no tax was due.

⍓ *Why is the term "applicable exclusion amount" now being used instead of "exemption equivalent"?*

The Taxpayer Relief Act of 1997 changed the terminology that was used for the dollar value of the unified credit. The term "exemption equivalent" was commonly used before TRA97. Now, "applicable exclusion amount" is the term used to describe the dollar equivalent of the new unified-credit amount.

TABLE 1-2   Phase-in of the Unified Credit

Year	Unified credit	Applicable exclusion amount
1998	$202,050	$ 625,000
1999	211,300	650,000
2000	220,550	675,000
2001	220,550	675,000
2002	229,800	700,000
2003	229,800	700,000
2004	287,300	850,000
2005	326,300	950,000
2006	345,800	1,000,000

⩗ *What effect did the Taxpayer Relief Act of 1997 have on the unified credit?*

The unified credit was increased by the Taxpayer Relief Act of 1997. The new unified credit is being phased in over a 9-year period beginning in 1998. Table 1-2 shows the amount of the unified credit in each year of the phase-in and the applicable exclusion amount.

⩗ *How does the new unified-credit exemption affect my potential federal estate tax liability?*

In the interim period between 1998 and 2006, when the applicable exclusion amount is being raised from $600,000 to $1,000,000, the amount of estate tax liability will depend upon the year in which an individual dies and the net value of his or her taxable estate at that time. For example, if a person dies in 1999 with a taxable estate of $650,000 or less, no estate tax will be due.

Even though the applicable exclusion amount will gradually increase, the value of your estate will likely increase as well. Therefore, what appears to be an increase may be no increase at all after you apply a modest growth rate to your assets.

⩗ *Can you give examples that show how the phase-in of the unified credit affects estate taxes over the 9-year period?*

Table 1-3 shows the effect of the unified credit's phase-in, depending

TABLE 1-3 The Effect of the Phase-in of the Unified Credit on Various Estates

Taxable estate	Estate tax if death occurs in						
	1998	1999	2000–2001	2002–2003	2004	2005	2006
$ 625,000							
650,000	$ 9,250						
675,000	18,500	$ 9,250					
700,000	27,750	18,500	$ 9,250				
850,000	85,250	76,000	66,750	$ 57,500			
950,000	124,250	115,000	105,750	96,500	$ 39,000		
1,000,000	143,750	134,500	125,250	116,000	58,500	$ 19,500	
1,500,000	353,750	344,500	335,250	326,000	268,500	229,500	$210,000
2,000,000	578,750	569,500	560,250	551,000	493,500	454,500	435,000
2,500,000	823,750	814,500	805,250	796,000	738,500	699,500	680,000
3,000,000	1,088,750	1,079,500	1,070,250	1,061,000	1,003,500	964,500	945,000

on the year of death, for estates of different sizes. As you can see, as the amount of the unified credit increases, a greater amount of assets can be passed tax-free and the amount of estate tax decreases. In addition, the tax decrease is more significant in smaller estates because the tax liability is eventually reduced to zero for estates of up to $1 million.

⊀ I have heard that the unified credit is eliminated for larger es-tates. What is that all about?

For taxable estates over $10 million, the maximum federal estate tax bracket of 55 percent is increased by 5 percent (a 60 percent marginal rate) until the effect of the unified credit is nullified. The purpose of this approach is to phase out, and eventually eliminate, the unified credit on estates in excess of $10 million.

Unlimited Marital Deduction

⊀ How much property can I leave to my spouse without my estate having to pay federal estate tax?

The federal estate tax law permits leaving an unlimited amount to one's surviving spouse without incurring the immediate obligation to pay tax. However, to the extent that the surviving spouse owns this property at his or her death, it must be included in the surviving spouse's estate.

If your spouse is not a U.S. citizen, the unlimited marital deduction is available only for property that passes by way of a qualified domestic trust, which is explained in Chapter 3.

⊀ Why, then, can't I leave everything to my spouse and not worry about tax?

If you rely upon the unlimited marital deduction without thought, the applicable exclusion amount for the first of you to die will be wasted and result in unnecessary taxes. This happens because the marital de-duction "swallows up" the deceased spouse's applicable exclusion amount. If you take advantage of both the applicable exclusion amount *and* the marital deduction through proper planning, it is not difficult to save additional taxes. The amount of savings varies depending on the year of death. Table 1-4 shows the potential tax savings for each year as the applicable exclusion amount is being phased in.

**TABLE 1-4   Potential Tax Savings
as the Unified Credit Phases In**

Year	Applicable exclusion amount	Tax savings
1998	$ 625,000	$246,250
1999	650,000	258,500
2000	675,000	270,750
2001	675,000	270,750
2002	700,000	283,000
2003	700,000	283,000
2004	850,000	358,500
2005	950,000	409,500
2006	1,000,000	435,000

⌁ *Can you give me an example of how leaving all my assets to my spouse will cost more in federal estate taxes?*

Assume the applicable exclusion amount is equal to $1 million and you and your spouse's combined estate is $2 million. If both of you have arranged to give all your property to each other and then, after you both die, to your children, the surviving spouse's estate of $2 million will be subject to a tax of $435,000. With proper use of the applicable exclusion *and* the marital deduction, the taxes would have been zero instead of $435,000.

Gift Tax

⌁ *What is the annual gift tax exclusion, and how does it work?*

You can remove assets and the appreciation on them from your estate by making gifts of the assets during your lifetime. The federal gift tax law provides for an *annual gift tax exclusion* which allows individuals to give away tax-free a certain amount per year per person to as many persons as they wish. The annual gift tax exclusion was $10,000 for many years, but the Taxpayer Relief Act of 1997 provides that this exclusion will be indexed for inflation beginning in 1999. The annual exclusion will be increased by the amount of annual inflation but only in minimum increments of $1000, rounded down to the nearest $1000. This means that if we assume an inflation rate of 3 percent, it will take 4 years for the annual exclusion to be "kicked up" to $11,000.

⅍ Can my husband and I combine our annual exclusions?

Yes, married individuals can combine their annual exclusions; strangely enough, this is called *gift splitting*. For example, if you are married and have three children, you and your spouse can jointly give each child up to twice the annual exclusion each year. It does not matter from whose assets a gift is made. For example, if you give one child money or property that exceeds the annual exclusion and your spouse consents to split the gift on a federal gift tax return, then both your spouse's annual exclusion and yours can be applied to the value of the gift.

⅍ Are there other types of tax-free gifts that I can make in addition to annual exclusion gifts?

Yes. Payments of any amount for school tuition and medical expenses that are made directly to the school or medical provider are tax-free and are in addition to the annual exclusion.

⅍ Can I use my annual exclusion to make gifts in trust?

The annual exclusion amount is only for gifts "other than gifts of future interests in property." Gifts to a trust are gifts of a future interest and usually do not qualify. However, there are ways to qualify gifts in trust for the annual exclusion.

⅍ How do I qualify gifts in trust for my annual exclusion?

To qualify gifts to a trust for the annual exclusion, the trust must contain "demand-right" language or instructions. This means that the beneficiaries of your trust must have the current right to withdraw the money given to the trust. If they do not request withdrawal of the money within a preset period of time, the trustee will then be able to use the money as you specified in the trust and the gift will qualify for the annual exclusion.

⅍ What if my gifts to a family member exceed the annual exclusion in a given year?

If you give more than the annual exclusion amount to one person in any year, you are responsible for filing a U.S. gift tax return by April 15 of the following year.

Let's say that an individual gives $50,000 to one person in one year, and let's assume that the annual exclusion, after indexing for inflation, is $11,000. The first $11,000 is free of the gift tax. The donor must file a gift tax return by the following April 15 relative to the portion of the gift which is taxable—the remaining $39,000.

The donor does not pay gift tax on the $39,000 taxable amount, however; instead, the donor's lifetime applicable exclusion amount is reduced by $39,000. Any gift made by the donor in excess of his or her remaining applicable exclusion amount will be subject to immediate gift tax.

⚠ What does "cumulative taxation" mean?

If a taxpayer makes taxable gifts while alive, the value of those gifts is added to his or her estate at death and thus the federal estate tax that will be paid is in higher brackets. For example, suppose a mother made taxable gifts of $1 million over the years, using up her $1 million applicable exclusion amount. In the year 2007, she gave her daughter a home worth $300,000 and paid the gift tax on that gift. The mother died 20 years later with an estate of $400,000, which she left to her son. Her estate tax will be based on transfers of $1.7 million ($1,300,000 during life and $400,000 at death). Her estate will pay the federal estate tax at the $1.7 million bracket, reduced by the unified credit and a credit for the gift tax already paid.

⚠ Are gift tax rates higher or lower than estate tax rates?

They are exactly the same; that is the essence of the unified system.

⚠ I know that the federal gift tax rates are the same as the federal estate tax rates, but is the economic effect of making a lifetime gift different from the effect of having the same asset included in one's taxable estate?

While estate tax rates and gift tax rates are exactly the same, the effects of these taxes on transfers can be noticeably different. By way of example, assume that you have a piece of real estate worth $5 million. Let's further assume that you would like to transfer this real estate to your children either during your lifetime or at death and that the transfer tax (whether gift or estate tax) is 50 percent.

If you give the $5 million of real estate to your children today, the gift tax payable is $2.5 million. The effect is that you have reduced your estate by $7.5 million; $5.0 million of real estate and $2.5 million of gift taxes.

Alternatively, you could transfer the real estate to your children at the time of your death. If no lifetime gift had been made, the $7.5

million not removed from your estate during your lifetime would still be included in your taxable estate. Let's assume that your estate doubles in value to $15 million by the time of your death. The estate tax (computed at the 50 percent rate) payable at the time of your death is $7.5 million. The amount received by your children will be $7.5 million, which is $2.5 million less than they would receive if the gift (now worth $10 million) had been made during your lifetime.

Although the gift and estate tax rates are identical, the lifetime transfer produced a more desirable result.

⚘ When is a gift "complete" for federal gift tax?

A gift is complete when the donor gives up complete dominion and control over the property. The donor must give away the tree *and* the fruit that is produced by the tree before the gift is "complete" for gift tax purposes.

⚘ How do I value gifts for federal gift tax purposes?

For gift tax purposes, you must value a gift at its fair market value as of the date the gift is transferred to the recipient. The same standards for valuing an asset in an estate apply to valuing a gift.

⚘ Who pays the gift tax, the donor or the recipient?

The donor is responsible for filing a gift tax return and paying the tax. If the donor does not pay the tax, payment becomes the responsibility of the recipient. If the recipient does not, or cannot, pay the tax, the property will be used to pay the tax.

⚘ Can we review the basic methods of making gifts?

There are five basic methods of making gifts without creating a gift tax:

1. You may give unlimited amounts to your spouse during your life or at death because of the unlimited marital deduction.

2. You may give the annual exclusion amount to any person in any calendar year. If you are married, you and your spouse, by "gift splitting," may together give as much as twice the annual exclusion amount per year to anyone provided your spouse consents to the gift. A gift tax return (Form 709) must be filed for the spouse to consent to a split gift.

3. In addition to annual exclusion gifts, you may give your applicable exclusion amount, or any part of it, to any one person or to several people during your lifetime or at death.

4. You may pay school or college tuition for any person provided you pay the tuition directly to the educational institution. This, too, is in addition to the annual exclusion and the applicable exclusion amount.

5. You may pay medical bills of anyone provided you pay the sums due directly to the doctor or hospital. This is in addition to the annual exclusion and the applicable exclusion amount.

Step-Up in Basis/Capital Gain Tax

What is a step-up in basis, and why is it important?

In general terms, *basis* is your attributed cost of a particular asset. Usually this is the purchase price. Gain or loss on the sale of an asset for tax purposes is computed by subtracting your basis from the sales price. When you receive assets as a result of another person's death, your basis in the assets received is "stepped up" to the value of the assets at the date of death or, in some cases, the date that is 6 months after the date of death. This results in a very large tax savings when highly appreciated property is inherited.

For example, Mrs. A owns a stock at her death which she purchased for $1 but which is now worth $10. If she sold it for $10 while alive, she would have a $9 taxable gain. The $9 gain is the difference between the basis of $1 and the current value of $10. However, at Mrs. A's death, the stock is valued at $10 for federal estate tax purposes. In other words, the $1 basis is stepped up to the current value of $10 at her death. Therefore, if Mrs. A's heirs sell it for $10, they will pay no income tax because the stepped-up $10 basis is the same as the current $10 value.

Is there a step-up in basis on assets I give away before my death?

Under the Internal Revenue Code rules, property that is given to another has a "carryover" basis. This means that the cost basis of an asset in the hands of the recipient is the same as the cost basis was in the hands of the donor. To receive a step-up in basis, property must be included in the decedent's estate.

If my husband dies and we have jointly held property, do I get a step-up in basis?

If you purchased the property after 1966 and before 1982, you could get a 100 percent step-up in basis if your husband purchased the property himself. Outside that period, you would normally be entitled to a step-up in basis on one-half of the property.

⚛ *Are the step-up-in-basis rules different for property held in joint tenancy with right of survivorship when the owners are not married?*

Yes, they are, and they are complex. If property is held jointly between persons who are not married and one of the owners dies, there are several possible outcomes, as follows:

- If the joint owner who died paid for the entire property, the full value of the property is included in the deceased owner's estate. The property receives a 100 percent step-up in basis. For example, if Mrs. A owned stock, put it in joint tenancy with her daughter, and subsequently died, the full value of the stock would be included in Mrs. A's estate. Her daughter would then inherit the property with a 100 percent step-up in basis.

- If both joint owners contributed to the value of the asset, the value of the deceased joint owner's share is included in his or her estate. That portion of the property receives a step-up in basis. If Mrs. A and her daughter bought stock for which Mrs. A paid 60 percent and her daughter paid 40 percent, then 60 percent of the value of the stock would be included in Mrs. A's estate and would receive a step-up in basis.

- If the joint owners received the property by gift or inheritance, only the decedent's portion is included in his or her estate. For example, if three children inherited real estate from a parent and the property was jointly held by all three, one-third of the value of the property would be included in the estate of a child who dies. This one-third interest would receive a step-up in basis.

These examples represent the general rules for step-up in basis. Other consequences may occur depending on the situation. Before you make any gift, especially if it is to be titled in joint tenancy with right of survivorship, you should consult your attorney.

⚛ *What if my spouse and I own property together in a community property state?*

Community property receives a 100 percent step-up in basis on the death of either spouse. It does not matter which spouse dies first; all of the community property will receive a new basis equal to its fair market value as valued for estate tax purposes.

⚛ *If I am terminally ill, can my brother give property to me which*

I can then leave to him so that he can get a 100 percent step-up on my death?

Some individuals who know about the step-up-in-basis rules try to take advantage of them when they find that family members or friends are about to die. A person will give property to the dying person with the agreement that the dying person, in his or her will or trust, will leave that same property to the person who gave it. The result these people are looking for is a 100 percent step-up in basis.

To prevent such transactions, the Internal Revenue Code contains a provision that denies a stepped-up basis for any property which was transferred to a decedent within 1 year of his or her death and which is returned to the donor after the decedent's death.

⋙ *I own an annuity and a life insurance policy on my spouse's life. Will these items receive a step-up in basis at the time of my death?*

Generally, neither the annuity nor the cash value in the life insurance policy you own on the life of your spouse will receive a step-up in basis at the time of your death. There could, however, be an effective adjustment to basis in circumstances where your estate incurs an estate tax and these items contribute to that estate tax liability.

⋙ *Doesn't the gift of appreciated assets generate capital gain tax at the time of the gift?*

No. A capital gain is triggered only when an asset is sold. Thus, there is no capital gain tax when you make a gift of an appreciated asset, but if the recipient later sells the gift, his or her gain will be taxed.

⋙ *What is capital gain?*

Capital gain is the profit an owner realizes on the sale of investment property, such as real estate, stocks, art, or collectibles. Simply put, it is the difference between the price paid for an item and the price it is ultimately sold for.

⋙ *How did the Taxpayer Relief Act of 1997 affect capital gain taxes?*

The Taxpayer Relief Act of 1997 made major changes to the capital gain tax scheme and significantly reduced the capital gain tax rates.

Under the old law, the top tax rate for capital gains on property held for 1 year or longer was 28 percent. While the Taxpayer Relief Act of 1997 added a complex scheme for computing capital gains, it reduced the rate to 20 percent for most types of property (except art, jewelry, and other collectibles, which can still be subject to tax as high as 28 percent). For taxpayers in the lower income tax brackets, the rate is reduced to just 10 percent. For property held for at least 5 years and sold in tax years beginning after December 31, 2000, the tax rates are reduced by 2 percent to 18 and 8 percent, respectively.

The act also required a holding period of 18 months, but the period was reduced to 12 months, retroactive to January 1, 1998, in the IRS Restructuring and Reform Act of 1998.

State Inheritance Tax

⋈ *Does my estate have to pay state death tax?*

Many states have an estate or inheritance tax which is payable on the transfer of assets owned by the decedent.

⋈ *What is the difference between state inheritance and state estate taxes?*

Inheritance tax taxes the beneficiaries on the basis of the specific inheritance they receive. *State estate tax* taxes the decedent or his or her estate on the property that was owned by the decedent at death.

⋈ *Do I get credit on my federal estate tax return for my state death tax?*

Depending upon how your estate planning documents are drafted and the state in which you reside, there may be a credit for state death taxes that is taken on your federal estate tax return. If your state death taxes exceed the amount allowed as a state death credit, no additional credit or deduction is allowed.

⋈ *Do I receive an applicable exclusion amount in my state that is similar to the one offered by the federal government?*

State inheritance and estate tax laws do not necessarily follow the federal estate tax law. Some states have transfer tax credits, but others have transfer taxes that are calculated on the net estate itself without any credit. For example, in Pennsylvania a tax is payable on the net estate at 6 percent of the assets that are left to lineal descendants, such as children or grandchildren, and at 15 percent of the assets that are passing to other heirs, such as nieces or nephews.

≼ *Does the federal government share its estate tax with the states?*

In effect, the federal government shares some of its estate tax revenues with a state if the state assesses a tax. Therefore, almost every state has a *pickup tax* or a *gap tax,* which provides for the payment of a tax equal to the amount the federal government allows as a credit for state tax when the federal estate tax is paid.

≼ *I have been told that my state imposes a "widow's tax." How does that tax differ from an inheritance or estate tax?*

A *widow's tax* is an inheritance tax assessed against property passing to your spouse at your death.

≼ *Which states collect the federal estate tax credit?*

The gap tax states, those that collect just the amount of the federal estate tax credit, are Alabama, Alaska, Arizona, Arkansas, California, Colorado, Florida, Georgia, Hawaii, Idaho, Illinois, Maine, Maryland, Massachusetts, Minnesota, Missouri, Nevada, New Hampshire, New Mexico, North Dakota, Oregon, Rhode Island, South Carolina, Texas, Utah, Vermont, Virginia, Washington, West Virginia, Wisconsin, Wyoming, and the District of Columbia.

Mississippi, Montana, and New Jersey are gap tax states for property passing to spouses and/or descendants. Kentucky is a gap tax state in regard to "Class A" beneficiaries except spouses. New York will be a gap tax state by 2000 and Connecticut by 2005.

≼ *Which states charge estate taxes in addition to the amount of the federal estate tax credit?*

Ohio, Oklahoma, and Puerto Rico apply tax rates higher than the credit allowed under federal estate tax rates. New York is phasing out its estate tax, and in 2000 it will become a gap tax state.

≼ *Which states charge an inheritance tax?*

States that charge an inheritance tax calculate the tax against the value of the share that passes to *each* beneficiary. The inheritance tax states are Connecticut, Delaware, Indiana, Iowa, Kansas, Louisiana, Maryland,

Mississippi, Montana, Nebraska, New Jersey, North Carolina, Pennsylvania, South Dakota, and Tennessee.

Connecticut will phase out its inheritance tax by 2005. Kentucky imposes an inheritance tax for remote relatives and nonrelatives. Mississippi, Montana, and New Jersey impose an inheritance tax on property passing to beneficiaries other than spouses and/or descendants.

◁ *Will my estate or heirs pay tax in more than one state?*

Unlike the federal estate tax, state taxes pertain to the property within the jurisdiction of the state in which the person is domiciled. Generally, all intangible assets (stocks, bonds, securities, and interest in business enterprises) would be subject to tax in the state in which the decedent was domiciled.

If you own real estate in more than one state that has a death tax, that property will more than likely generate a tax in the state in which it is located.

Tax Planning

◁ *Why should I do estate planning—don't I have a duty to pay tax to my country?*

Consider a concept called the "hand of taxation." Count the fingers on one hand and review the following five major taxes you face:

1. Point to your thumb—you're taxed when you earn it; that's income tax.
2. Point to your index finger—you're taxed when you spend it; that's sales tax.
3. Point to your middle finger—you're taxed just because you own certain assets; that's called property tax.
4. Point to your ring finger—you're taxed when you sell something that has appreciated in value; that's called capital gain tax.
5. Point to your pinkie finger—you're taxed when you're through with it and want to give it away to someone you love either while you're alive because that person needs it more than you do or after you've died and truly have no use for it; that's called gift and estate tax.

Given all the taxes you pay, you may conclude that you have a duty to your family and loved ones to use every deduction and exemption Congress has given you to reduce federal estate tax.

⚘ *Can I take advantage of my applicable exclusion amount during my lifetime?*

In addition to using your annual exclusion, you may also give away your assets tax-free up to the amount of your applicable exclusion amount to any one or more persons however you please. To the extent that you use your applicable exclusion amount during your lifetime, your estate will not have the benefit of it on death.

⚘ *I plan to leave my property to family members or charities on my death, but should I consider giving it to them now instead?*

If you are comfortable that you will not need the property to sustain your standard of living or to meet future emergencies, you should consider this option. It will remove not only the property from your estate but, as we said earlier, the appreciation from your estate as well.

⚘ *Is removing appreciation from my estate a major issue?*

Assume that you have an asset worth $100,000 with no basis, appreciating at 10 percent per year; that your life expectancy is 21.6 years; and that you can do one of two things with that asset in a tax environment that taxes lifetime and postmortem gifts equally at 50 percent:

- *Give it to your children today:* The cost of giving it to them would be $50,000 ($100,000 × 50 percent).
- *Leave it to them in your trust or will:* The cost to them would be $400,000 because the inflationary value of the asset will be taxed at 50 percent.

⚘ *How did you arrive at these amounts?*

Under the *Rule of 72,* your asset would double in value every 7.2 years at 10 percent; $100,000 would grow to $800,000 ($100,000 × 2 in 7.2 years = $200,000 × 2 in 14.4 years = $400,000 × 2 in 21.6 years = $800,000). The estate tax on $800,000 is $400,000, which is 800 percent greater than the gift tax of $50,000.

⚘ *Should I give income-producing assets away?*

Assets which produce income are good candidates for giving because the income is removed from the tax return of the donor and put on the tax return of the gift recipient. Note that if the gift recipient is a child who is under the age of 14, this planning strategy may be defeated by the *kiddie tax,* which requires that income from the gift be subject to income tax at the child's parent's highest marginal income tax rate.

If the gift recipient is over the age of 14, a gift of income-producing property may be an opportunity to shift income to a taxpayer who is in a lower tax bracket than the gift maker.

Can I make gifts to my spouse and qualify for the unlimited marital deduction?

You have an unlimited marital deduction when making gifts to your spouse. There are no restrictions on how large these transfers can be or how often you can make them as long as your spouse is a U.S. citizen.

PROBATE

Death Probate and Administration

What are the origins of the probate process?

In our country's earlier times, a person would homestead a particular piece of land and obtain a document called a "patent," from the president of the United States, which proved that the homesteaded land was his or hers. As the people who held these patents died, a question arose as to how to remove their names from the patents and put the names of living persons on them. State legislatures had to create a system for transferring property from a deceased person to a living person while protecting family members who might have a claim or interest in the property and giving them an opportunity to be heard. The probate process was "invented" to accomplish such transfers in a fair and orderly way.

Probate also addresses the claims of a decedent's creditors. The process gives creditors an opportunity to make and prove their claims so that valid claims can be paid out of the assets of an estate before they pass to the decedent's heirs.

What is probate?

Probate is the court-supervised administration of your estate. It generally has three purposes:

1. To marshal all of your assets

2. To pay your bills and resolve disputed creditor issues

3. To oversee distribution of your estate as you directed

I know probate varies from state to state. In general, what are the mechanics of the probate process?

If you have a will, filing a petition to admit your will to probate is usually the way to initiate the probate process. If you die without a will, a petition to appoint a personal representative, sometimes called an administrator, is filed with the court. In either case, notice to all of your heirs and beneficiaries is generally required before the hearing. (A notice is often published in a newspaper of general circulation within the county of the decedent's residence.) As a practical matter, this means a delay of approximately 30 days between filing the petition for probate and having a hearing. Until the hearing and court appointment, unless action is taken to authorize the immediate appointment of a special administrator, even your named personal representative (sometimes called an executor, if male, or an executrix, if female) is not empowered to deal with your estate affairs. Once a personal representative is appointed, the court will issue documents, often called *letters of personal representative,* which serve as proof of that person's authority to take action concerning the estate. Unless you have a will which specifically relieves the personal representative from certain court-imposed duties, he or she may be required to post a bond and file an inventory of assets of the estate, as well as an annual accounting of all transactions.

Probate also involves a particular process for handling creditors. This process is designed to ensure that all creditors have notice of the death and have the opportunity to file creditor claims. Practically speaking, the process is unnecessary in the vast majority of cases since the bills and creditors could simply be paid as statements are received.

Even if all the bills and obligations of the estate are paid immediately, most probate laws require that estates remain "open" for a minimum period of time, usually 4 to 6 months, to give all creditors time to file claims against the estate. During this time, the law generally restricts the ability of the personal representative to make distributions from the estate.

The personal representative is charged with gathering all the assets of your estate so that they can be used to pay creditor claims and then the remainder can be distributed to your heirs or beneficiaries. Most states allow that estates with a limited amount of assets (for example, in California, estates consisting of personal property valued at less than $100,000) can be collected by an affidavit procedure rather than go through probate. Assets held in a living trust do not require probate administration.

⅍ What must be done to "close" a probate?

In many states, before an estate can be closed, the personal representative must file with the court an inventory of all the estate's assets with an appraisal of the value of those assets. The inventory and appraisal which are filed with the court are part of the public record. The intimate details of your estate are open to anyone who cares enough to open the court file. There is no screen to ensure that your estate records are reviewed only for legitimate purposes. If your estate is not liquid and there is a need to sell assets to pay claims or taxes, a potential buyer can inspect your probate file to gain negotiation advantage.

Once the assets are collected, the estate obligations are satisfied, and the minimum waiting period is satisfied, your personal representative can file a final accounting and petition for distribution of your estate. The details of distribution, including who will receive what, are also matters of public record.

⅍ How long does probate usually take?

Even though statutes allow estates to be closed in a limited period of time, for example, 6 months, experience demonstrates that the actual time of closure is much longer; 15 to 18 months is a realistic estimate of the time required to close an estate. In some cases it can be even longer if disagreements arise among the beneficiaries.

⅍ What is estate administration?

If a will is proved invalid or if a person dies without a will or a proper will substitute, the public, legal process which ensues is technically called *administration,* not probate. However, estate administration is equally as time-consuming and costly as probate, if not more so. Under administration, the disposition of the deceased's assets is governed by state law, not by the deceased person's desires, and thus there is greater opportunity for dispute and disagreement among heirs, family, and friends.

For purposes of this book, we'll treat the terms "probate" and "administration" as meaning the same thing. The primary difference between the two is that in probate a will has to be "proved," whereas in administration there is no will to prove.

⅍ What goes through probate, and what doesn't?

Anything you own in your own name alone or as a tenant in common with others (including community property) is subject to probate and administration. Beneficiary-designation property for which the "estate" is named as the beneficiary also goes through probate.

Property held in joint tenancy with right of survivorship (including tenancy by the entirety), property held in a living trust, or property distributed by beneficiary designations (as long as the beneficiary is not your estate) does not go through probate. Property held in a life estate, in which you are entitled to the use of the property and all its income only during your life, also does not go through probate.

⅍ What are the disadvantages of the probate process?

The disadvantages of death probate proceedings include:

LOSS OF PRIVACY   When your estate goes through probate, you lose all privacy. Your will, your assets, and your liabilities all become public record just like any other litigation at the courthouse. Con artists have been known to submit false claims against a probate estate and use the probate record to target heirs and beneficiaries for their next swindle.

WILL CONTESTS   Wills can always be contested and put aside—it happens all the time. When a will is contested, the estate is frozen and the assets cannot be transferred to loved ones. It is easy for any disgruntled heir to file a will contest since the will is already in probate court.

COSTS   The court charges the estate either a set fee or a fee based on the size of the estate. In addition, attorneys, executors, guardians, and any other fiduciaries acting within the realm of probate (or administration) charge their own fees. The total cost of probate can easily range from 3 to 10 percent of the *gross* estate—or more. For example, if a person dies owning a house that has a fair market value of $300,000 and other assets amounting to $100,000, the value of the gross estate is $400,000. A conservative estimate of the probate costs would be 5 percent of that gross amount, or $20,000. If the house was mortgaged for $200,000, the value of the *net estate* is $200,000. Thus, the probate costs would actually amount to 10 percent of the net estate!

Multiple probates   There must be a probate proceeding in every state in which the decedent owned real property.

Delays   Probate can last from several months to several years. This only adds to the frustrations and anxieties of a grieving spouse and family.

Probate has been defined as "the lawsuit you bring against yourself with your own money to benefit your creditors." This description is quite accurate, but people usually come to appreciate its veracity only after undergoing the probate of a family member or close friend.

You mentioned fiduciaries' fees. Can you give more details on this probate expense?

Two of the authors of this book, Robert A. Esperti and Renno L. Peterson, commissioned a scientific survey of probate costs for another book they wrote called *The Living Trust Revolution.* They also compared the results of this study to a 1990 report by the American Association of Retired Persons (AARP). They came to the conclusion that the at- torneys' fees for probate are usually about 3 percent of the gross estate. If the personal representative or the executor of the estate is also paid a fee, the total cost, including both sets of fees, is 5 to 6 percent of the gross estate.

Can my heirs do the probate themselves, or do they have to hire a lawyer?

They may be able to do it themselves, especially if the estate is small and there is no real estate involved. But even a modest-size estate usually requires a somewhat more formal process (even though in many states it is categorized legally as either "formal" or "informal"). In some states, the process is complicated for those not familiar with it. If that is the case in your state and if your heirs must probate your estate, they will have to hire a lawyer.

Can my agent under a durable general power of attorney settle my estate without probate?

No. By law *all* powers of attorney automatically terminate at the death of the grantor of the power.

ᕗ *If I avoid probate, do I avoid estate taxes?*

Nice try. No, your taxable estate includes pretty much everything you own at death or had too much control over. So your gross estate will include joint tenancy property (except the half owned by your U.S. citizen spouse, or any portion to which any non–U.S. citizen spouse contributed), your half of community property, the entire value of life estate property, everything in your revocable living trust, and life insurance proceeds from policies you own.

In addition, if you have the power under a trust someone else created to take some assets out of that trust for yourself, the value of those assets will also be included in your gross estate, even if you never exercised that power.

Living Probate

ᕗ *What is meant by "living probate"?*

It is possible that, prior to your death, you may become mentally disabled due to disease, stroke, or accident.

Legally referred to as a *conservatorship* or *guardianship*, a *living probate* is a legal proceeding in the probate court which is designed to protect a mentally disabled person who is unable to manage his or her financial affairs. It is the duty of the probate court to protect the disabled person's assets, creditors, and personal rights and to appoint someone to manage and assume the mentally disabled person's financial affairs.

There are disadvantages to a living probate:

IT CREATES EXPENSES   Inasmuch as it is a court proceeding, a living probate often requires the services of an attorney who will prepare the necessary court documents and make court appearances. The court may require the filing of inventories and accountings, along with periodic reports, which may necessitate the hiring of an accountant. The conservator or guardian may be required to post a bond in order to qualify for service before the court. He or she may be also required to make periodic reports to the court during the period of disability and will often utilize the services of attorneys and accountants, as well as other professionals, throughout that entire period. All these factors are very expensive to the estate.

You lose control The court will determine how your assets are to be spent for your benefit.

You lose privacy Just like a death probate, a living probate is a public proceeding which may result in a substantial invasion of privacy and loss of personal dignity.

◢ *Why can't I avoid a living probate by giving a general durable power of attorney to a trusted family member?*

Unfortunately, general powers of attorney are not always honored by banks, title companies, brokerage firms, and other financial institutions. These institutions have been increasingly fearful of the potential liability inherent in honoring such powers of attorney. Some have established their own specific requirements regarding powers of attorney. The requirements vary from one institution to another, but in general the older a power of attorney is, the less likely it is that an institution will accept it.

Also, the power of attorney, by nature, is a general one and usually gives the designated agent full power and control to do anything with the disabled party's assets. Without caring instructions on how the agent is to apply the funds, this general power can sometimes be abused.

Finally, even if you execute a power of attorney, there is no guarantee that you will not be taken before the probate court by a third party who seeks to have you declared incompetent and himself or herself appointed as your financial guardian. In such a case, your power of attorney would become useless. All too frequently, the general power of attorney causes more problems than it corrects.

chapter 2

Methods of Estate Planning

TRADITIONAL METHODS
OF ESTATE PLANNING

Ownership of Assets

What does "title" mean in relation to property ownership?

Title is the legal concept of ownership. When you take "title" to any piece of property, you specify what type of legal rights you wish to hold in the property and what legal rights others have in the same property. Title to property consists of two, often confused, subparts: legal title and beneficial title.

Legal title, quite simply, reflects who owns the property for the purposes of buying, selling, or otherwise disposing of the asset. Legal title does not, in itself, confer the right to use or enjoy the property. The *beneficial title* owner retains that right. For example, if you were to lease an automobile, the leasing company would retain legal title to the car. That is, you could not sell or otherwise transfer the car because the leasing company remains the legal owner on the formal written title to the automobile. Nevertheless you, as lessee, have exclusive beneficial, or equitable, title in the car. You, and not the leasing company, have the full right to drive, use, and enjoy the car.

35

Legal title of many assets is evidenced by a written document naming the owners and the form in which they own the asset—joint tenancy, tenancy in common, and so on. Title to real estate is evidenced by a deed naming the legal owners and describing the property. Title to stock is evidenced by a stock certificate stating in whom legal title is vested. Title to bank, brokerage, mutual fund, and IRA accounts; insurance policies; and certificates of deposit is reflected in an agreement the individual signed when he or she established the account or purchased the asset. Quite often you can determine the legal title to an asset simply by inspecting the bank or brokerage statement, the stock certificate, the insurance policy, and so on.

Beneficial title, on the other hand, is not so easily determined. By simply identifying the legal registered owner of property, one cannot be certain as to the identity of those having the right to use or enjoy the property. Fortunately, however, for estate planning purposes, you need only be concerned with what you own and in what form you own it.

⬆ *What are the most common forms or methods of owning (titling) property?*

The six most common methods of property ownership are:

- Individual (fee-simple) ownership
- Individual ownership with beneficiary designations
- Joint tenancy with right of survivorship (in some states called *tenancy by the entirety* if between spouses)
- Tenancy in common
- Trustee ownership (The trustee of a revocable living trust holds legal title to the trust property, while trust beneficiaries hold beneficial title to the trust property.)
- Community property

⬆ *Why should I be concerned about the title to my assets?*

Knowing who has the title to all of your assets is essential to successful estate planning. Title defines the legal owner or owners.

For those who use a will as the primary basis of their estate planning, title to most, if not all, of their assets usually remains in their names until death. In such circumstances, most of those assets will have to undergo probate for the title to be transferred to others.

Holding title to an asset jointly with right of survivorship with another person has traditionally served as a simple estate planning technique. When title to an asset is held jointly with right of survivorship, at death, title to the asset vests in the survivor or survivors—without probate or other proceedings. The advantage of holding title jointly with another is that doing so is inexpensive and simple. The principal danger is that it may lead to unintended and unpleasant results, such as when one of the owners dies unexpectedly and the heirs of the decedent are left with nothing. Other forms of joint ownership of title include tenancies by the entirety (a form of joint ownership for married couples in some states) and tenancies in common (in which property is held jointly, but each owner may transfer his or her part interest to third parties at death). Your attorney will suggest different planning alternatives depending upon the type of asset and how it is titled.

⚔ *What if I don't know how I hold title to my assets?*

How you hold title, or the form in which you hold title, to any asset, whether it be real estate, stocks and bonds, or automobiles, can be determined easily from documents you have. Obtaining that information is one of the first tasks in proper estate planning. For example, if you own real estate, the deed to that real estate will reveal how you hold title to it. Stock and bond certificates, or the documentation for the accounts in which you may hold those items, and the documentation for your bank accounts will reveal the forms of title. If you have questions, you should ask your estate planner to help you.

Individual ownership of property

⚔ *How does individual ownership work, and what are the advantages and disadvantages of owning property this way?*

Individual ownership, legally known as *fee-simple ownership,* means you own both legal and beneficial title to the asset. For example, if you own a bank account, stock, or a car in your sole individual name, you have both the right to control and sell the asset (legal title) and the right to spend the money in the bank account, use the proceeds from the stock sale, or drive the car (beneficial title).

Accordingly, the first advantage of fee-simple ownership is that, because you have full and exclusive ownership of the asset (legal and beneficial title), you can control and distribute the asset at your death in your will. A second advantage is that your heirs will receive a step-up in the cost basis of the property to the fair market value of the property as of your date of death. For example, if you sold this property, you would pay the capital gain tax on the difference between the cost basis and the fair market value. Cost basis is essentially the purchase price of the property, plus any improvements, less depreciation. The cost basis for your heirs, however, will be the fair market value of the property as of your date of death. A step-up in basis can result in significant capital gain tax savings to the person who inherits the property.

There are some disadvantages of individual ownership. Solely owned property may be subject to both living and death probates in the event that the owner becomes disabled and dies. This can create unnecessary expenses and delays. The public nature of the probate process may also cause problems for the owner or for the person who ultimately inherits the property.

Joint tenancy with right of survivorship

⋈ What is joint tenancy with right of survivorship property?

Most married couples own their property as joint tenants with right of survivorship, often referred to as *joint tenancy*. Frequently you will also see an elderly or infirm person name a child or close friend as a joint tenant on a bank or brokerage account to facilitate the payment of bills and expenses.

The key element in joint tenancy is its survivorship quality. The last to survive of the joint tenants receives the entire property, thus dissolving the joint tenancy and vesting both legal and beneficial title in the survivor individually. As such, joint tenancy ownership of an asset dramatically affects to whom the asset will be distributed at death.

For example, if you own real estate in joint tenancy with another person, at your death the asset will pass automatically to the surviving joint owner by operation of law.

⋈ What is tenancy by the entirety?

Tenancy by the entirety is a type of joint tenancy with right of survivorship. It is available only in some states and only between spouses.

Tenancy by the entirety's unique characteristic is that the creditor of one spouse *cannot* take any part of the property to satisfy the spouse's debt. The creditor may only be able to get a lien on the property. In some states, this creditor protection is not permanent. When the property is sold, its value may no longer be protected. However, if the proceeds are paid to an account which is also owned in tenancy by the entirety, the proceeds may escape seizure by the creditor.

Except for this creditor protection and the fact that it is available only in some states and exclusively for spouses, tenancy by the entirety is almost identical to joint tenancy with right of survivorship.

⚮ *Are there any disadvantages to owning property jointly with right of survivorship?*

Owning property in joint tenancy with right of survivorship has several drawbacks. For example, joint tenancy:

- Only postpones probate
- Supersedes your will or trust regarding distribution of the jointly held property
- Can increase estate taxes
- Can lead to capital gain tax
- May cause some children to be disinherited
- May create unintended heirs

Other problems arise if you own an asset in joint tenancy with one of your children. Joint tenancy with a child:

- Can lead to gift taxes
- Can restrict your ability to sell or transfer the property
- Subjects the property to possible claims against it by the children's creditors
- Might prevent other children from sharing in the property after your death

⚮ *Since joint ownership will pass my assets to another joint owner immediately upon my death without probate, isn't this a good arrangement?*

On the surface, joint ownership may appear to be a good and simple arrangement for one's assets since jointly owned assets will immediately pass to a joint owner free from probate. However, joint ownership can (and typically will) have a number of traps hidden within:

1. When you name a person as a joint owner of an asset, you are subjecting your asset to the liabilities and creditors of the other person. As an example, if your chosen joint owner enters into a divorce proceeding with his or her spouse, your asset may become involved in the divorce proceeding!

2. The naming of a joint owner may be construed as a gift to the

chosen joint owner at the time you name the joint owner. Thus you may be generating a gift tax obligation if the portion you transfer exceeds the gift tax annual exclusion.

3. In joint tenancy ownership with one or more persons other than a spouse, the full value of the assets will be included in the deceased joint owner's estate unless it can be proved that the other owner or owners paid for their shares in some way. When the full value of the joint property is included in one owner's estate but passes to the other owner or owners, it is the worst of all worlds: the decedent's estate has all the taxes but none of the property.

4. If you or your chosen joint owner should become mentally incapacitated, a court proceeding will likely be necessary and the court will assume the role of the incapacitated joint owner. Once the court assumes this role, any transactions regarding the joint asset instantly become subject to complex and arduous rules.

5. A joint tenancy arrangement completely bypasses any provisions you may leave in a will or a trust. This is true even if your will or trust addresses the purpose of the joint tenancy arrangement.

Is transferring property into joint ownership with my children a good way to avoid probate?

No. Transferring property to your children subjects your property to the claims of your children's creditors and could be a taxable gift.

I own joint tenancy property with my brother. Upon my death, can I leave my interest in this property to my children?

No, you cannot. A will or a trust cannot control joint tenancy property. When one joint tenant dies, the property, by operation of law, passes to the surviving joint tenant. This greatly misunderstood concept of joint tenancy causes no end of problems and heartache for families.

How can joint tenancy result in increased estate taxes?

Joint tenancy between spouses can cause increased estate taxes in taxable estates because the property automatically passes to the surviving spouse tax-free under the marital deduction. Marital-deduction property is not subject to estate tax, so the first spouse to die cannot take advantage of his or her applicable exclusion amount.

I have heard that joint tenancy can cause children to be disinherited. How can this happen?

If you and your husband own property as joint tenants and you die, he owns all the property by law. If your husband happens to remarry and puts the property in joint ownership with his new wife and then dies, she owns the property by law and your children will be disinherited. The property belongs to her, and she can do anything she wants with it.

⚜ *How can joint tenancy result in "unintended heirs"?*

Here is an example: Dad, about 62 years old, was obsessed about losing everything to a nursing home. His father had to spend his entire estate on nursing home care, and Dad was determined not to let this happen to himself. Dad focused on this to the exclusion of all other estate planning considerations.

Dad talked to a local attorney who did not have much estate planning experience. This attorney recommended that Dad transfer ownership of his home by deed to his two daughters as joint tenants with right of survivorship. Dad retained no ownership interest in his home, relying instead on the loving relationship he had always had with his daughters to allow him to continue living there as long as he could.

Both daughters were married and lived in another state. The older daughter, Ann, had one daughter, Dad's only grandchild. Ann and her husband had a well-thought-out, living trust–centered estate plan. The younger daughter, Betty, and her husband were newlyweds and had no planning. Dad liked Ann's husband but had a very bad relationship with Betty's husband.

Tragedy struck. Ann and Betty were killed in an automobile accident. You might think that since the sisters died together, Ann's joint tenancy interest in the home would go to her husband and daughter under the terms of her living trust. But there was litigation in which Betty's husband proved that the truck killed Ann first and then Betty about .02 seconds later.

The court held that the laws of joint tenancy controlled instead of Ann's trust. When Ann died, her part of the remainder interest in Dad's home passed automatically to Betty. When Betty died, her remainder interest passed by the laws of intestacy to her husband. Ann's and Betty's entire remainder interest passed by intestacy to Betty's husband, who now owns the home and can legally charge Dad rent or even evict him if he chooses to do so.

⚜ *I am single and I would like to avoid probate upon my disability or death. Why shouldn't I just retitle my home in joint tenancy with right of survivorship with one or more of my children?*

If you die first, your estate will in fact avoid probate. Of course, when

when your child later dies, the property could be part of your child's probate estate.

If your child predeceases you, the property will automatically return to you (outside of the probate system), leaving you with no provision as to where the property will ultimately go upon your death. You would be right back where you started, and by then it might be too late to do any further planning.

Also, if either you or your child is disabled and cannot handle your own financial affairs, a living probate might be required—a guardianship or conservatorship—with respect to the entire property.

Further, you might create a taxable gift when you put your child's name on the deed with you as a joint tenant. Retitling your home in such a manner is considered a gift because, among other things, after the retitling either you or your child can go to court and obtain an order to divide the property into two separate parcels. So retitling your home in joint tenancy with your child is treated the same as dividing your home into two parcels and giving one parcel to your child. Depending on the value of the property, you might be required to pay a gift tax. (Generally, if the value of a gift exceeds the annual exclusion, you will incur a gift tax. If the jointly held property is a bank account or brokerage account in street name, the gift is not deemed to have been made until the child withdraws the funds.)

Another problem with retitling your home in joint tenancy with your child is that you may lose control over your home, because your child as a joint owner must consent to any sale or transfer of the property.

Also, if your child has creditors, say, from a business transaction or from an automobile accident, you are in jeopardy of losing your home to the creditors. The child's joint tenancy ownership in the property can be taken. An even bigger problem can occur if the child gets divorced. His or her joint tenancy interest may be considered marital property under state law and, as such, be subject to the whim of the judge in dividing the marital assets.

All these rules and results are the same whether the joint tenant is your child or anyone else other than your spouse.

Before my father died, he put all his property in joint tenancy with right of survivorship with my oldest brother, with whom my father was living. My father recently died. Soon after, my brother told me that he had "done more for Dad than the rest of us had" and that he was keeping all of Dad's property instead of dividing it equally among the six children. Can my brother legally keep title to the property and not share it with the rest of us?

Probably so, unless you are willing to go to court and try to prove that your father didn't intend this result. Part of the tragedy of joint ownership is this kind of unintended consequence. Even if your brother decides to share the property with the rest of you, there can be a gift tax if the value of each sibling's share is more than the annual exclusion.

Tenancy-in-common property

≱ *What is tenancy in common?*

Tenancy in common is ownership of property between two or more people. Each of the owners owns a percentage of the property, called an *undivided interest.* An undivided interest means that each tenant in common owns a part of the property but there is no way to identify which part he or she owns.

All the owners of tenancy-in-common property have the right to use and possess the property during their lives, no matter what percentage each person owns. Unless some other agreement is reached, tenants in common may give away or sell their interest in the property. Typically, in dealing with their property, tenants in common are very much like sole owners.

They may also leave their interest in the property to anyone they choose at their death.

≱ *Does tenancy in common have a right of survivorship feature?*

No. Property owned by tenants in common does not automatically pass to the surviving owners. If you and your two siblings own a cabin in the mountains as tenants in common, you would have legal title to an undivided one-third of the cabin. Not only are you free to dispose of your interest in the cabin as you determine during your lifetime; you are also free to pass your interest at your death to your beneficiaries under your will or trust or by intestacy if you have no formal estate plan.

≱ *What are some of the advantages of owning property as tenants in common?*

Much like a sole owner, a tenant in common is considered to be in control of his or her share of the property. Each tenant has the freedom to give away or sell his or her interest in the property and to leave it to whomever he or she chooses at death.

Tenancy-in-common interests receive a step-up in cost basis for tax purposes. For example, if two tenants in common own a parcel of real estate and one dies, the decedent's interest in the property will receive a step-up in basis but the surviving tenant's interest will not.

❧ What are some disadvantages of owning property as tenants in common?

Property that is held by tenants in common may be subject to both living and death probates if an owner becomes disabled or dies. This can create unnecessary expenses and delays. The public nature of the probate process may also cause problems for the owner or for the person who ultimately inherits the property.

In addition, since a tenancy-in-common interest is freely transferable, an owner might, involuntarily, become a tenant in common with someone other than the original co-owner of the property. The co-tenants may not be able to agree regarding the management or sale of the property, creating legal battlefields over control issues.

❧ Is tenancy in common better than joint tenancy with right of survivorship?

In many respects, tenancy in common is superior to joint tenancy as a form of property ownership. Not only can you control to whom the property will pass at your death, but you can utilize estate tax planning strategies unavailable with joint tenancy property. The major pitfall with tenancy in common is that, as with individual ownership, the property may be subject to the probate process.

❧ When would you recommend that couples own property as tenants in common?

A married couple often will have one or two assets which are very valuable and which make up the bulk of their combined estate. They may be uncomfortable assigning sole ownership of the assets to one spouse or the other. In this situation, it may make sense because of estate tax planning considerations to have each of them own an undivided one-half of the property as tenants in common. This solution meets the need to allocate assets to each of them for estate tax purposes and allows them to continue as co-owners of the property.

For unmarried persons, holding their property as tenants in common rather than as joint tenants ensures that the property will pass to an owner's intended heirs rather than to the remaining co-owners.

Trustee ownership

⚱ *What is meant by "trustee ownership"?*

The form of property ownership most rapidly expanding in the estate planning field is that of trustee ownership. By establishing a revocable living trust, you can control who will receive your property at your death and avoid the probate process as well.

When you establish a revocable living trust, you will put most of your assets into that trust. A common misunderstanding is that the trust owns the property within it. This is not really true. The *trustee* of the trust holds legal title to the trust property. The trust beneficiaries hold beneficial title to the trust property. Accordingly, the trustee has the power to invest, reinvest, buy, sell, and trade the trust property (as defined in the trust agreement), while the trust beneficiaries have the right, as provided in the trust, to use the trust property and receive the income or principal of the trust.

It is both common and generally advised that the maker of a revocable living trust be the trustee and the beneficiary of his or her trust (married couples can be joint trustees and beneficiaries of a joint trust). Thus the maker alone can control both the managerial and investment decisions as trustee while using or otherwise spending the trust assets without limitation as beneficiary.

Upon the maker's death, all the trust property will pass to the beneficiaries named by the maker in the trust upon the terms and conditions that the maker chose. These trust assets are not subject to the legal hoops, costs, and delays of the probate process.

As in the case of sole ownership, the trust assets that are included in the estate of the trust maker receive a step-up in basis at death.

⚱ *Is nominee ownership the same as trustee ownership?*

A *nominee* is any person or organization that takes title to property on behalf of someone else. Nominees are sometimes used so that the real owner of the property can hold title to it in another name. For example, some people do not want it known that they hold property in trust. In these circumstances, the trustees will form a partnership to hold title to the property. The partnership is the nominee for the trust; the trust owns the property indirectly, but the partnership's name is on the title of any property.

Community property

➤ *What states require community property?*

Arizona, California, Idaho, Louisiana, Nevada, New Mexico, Texas, Washington, and Wisconsin.

➤ *What is community property?*

While the community property laws vary in each of the nine community property states, *community property* is generally defined as all property acquired by either spouse during marriage which is not considered separate property.

Separate property falls primarily into three categories:

1. Any property owned or claimed by a spouse prior to marriage
2. Any property acquired by a spouse during marriage by partition of community property, by gift, by inheritance, or by devise under a will or trust
3. Any property acquired from recoveries for personal injuries to a spouse's body or reputation during marriage, excluding any recoveries for loss of earning capacity during marriage

All earnings from personal efforts and income from community property are community property. In some community property states, income from separate property remains separate property; in other community property states, income from separate property becomes community property unless the spouses have a written agreement that such income is to remain separate property.

Spouses who own community property are deemed to be partners, each owning an undivided one-half interest in the property. In that respect, community property is much like tenancy by the entirety.

➤ *If I look at a deed or title to a car, can I tell if the property is community property?*

Not always. Community property is ownership created by law. Who owns the actual title is irrelevant. It is how and when the property is acquired that determines if property is community or not.

➤ *What is community presumption?*

All property of a marriage is presumed to be community property. This presumption can be overcome if the spouse who is asserting that property is separate property does so with clear and convincing evidence of the separate nature of the property. This evidence is usually found by tracing the property to the time it was acquired, that is, to its *inception of title.*

Separate property acquired with separate property or with the proceeds from the sale of separate property will remain separate property as long as adequate records are kept to properly trace its inception of title.

⋈ *If my spouse and I have community property, what rights do we have in the property?*

Community property is similar to property that is owned by tenants in common in common law property states. As with tenancy-in-common property, each spouse owns 50 percent of the property. This interest is called an *undivided interest* because neither spouse knows which 50 percent he or she owns. For example, if a horse is community property, one spouse doesn't own the front part of the horse and the other the rear. Each simply owns 50 percent of the whole horse.

As a general rule, if one spouse wants to give away or sell his or her interest in community property, the other spouse must approve the sale or gift. Some community property states recognize the concept of *special controlled community property,* that is, community property titled in just one spouse's name. Even though both spouses own the special controlled community property equally, the spouse whose name is titled on that particular property has sole management of and control over it. He or she may dispose of or transfer it without the agreement of the other spouse as long as doing so does not fraudulently affect the other spouse's 50 percent ownership.

A spouse can, on death, leave his or her undivided interest in community property to others by will or trust. If a child inherits his or her father's interest in community property, that child becomes a tenant in common with his or her mother.

⋈ *Are there any tax advantages to community property?*

Yes, there is one very important income tax advantage that community property has over any other type of property. At the death of one of the spouses, community property receives a 100 percent step-up in basis. This means that if a married couple bought a vacation home for $100,000 and, at the death of one of the spouses, the house was worth $200,000, the surviving spouse could sell the house for $200,000 and there would be no capital gain tax.

Let's contrast this to the situation in a common law property state.

If the home was owned in joint tenancy or tenancy in common, at the death of the spouse only one-half of the house would receive a step-up in basis. In this example, if the surviving spouse sold the house for $200,000, there would be a capital gain tax on $50,000. This is because the deceased spouse's half of the house would get a new basis of $100,000, and the surviving spouse's half would retain its cost basis of $50,000 (one-half its original cost).

⋗ *Since we are married and live in a community property state, the fact that we hold our property as joint tenants doesn't defeat the presumption of community property for estate planning and income tax purposes, does it?*

In some community property states it does. Unless provided otherwise by statute, joint tenancy and community property cannot exist at the same time on the same piece of property. This seemingly inconsistent result is a product of two conflicting types of law. Community property is a concept inherited from French and Spanish law. Joint tenancy is a concept inherited from English law. Like oil and water, they do not mix. Their legal incompatibility creates an anomaly in the law that can be rectified only by statute.

Without a law to the contrary, joint tenancy property that is owned by spouses in a community property state will lose the full step-up in basis allowed for community property. In addition, joint tenancy property passes to the surviving spouse by law; it is not subject to the control of the deceased spouse's will or trust. Community property can be controlled by will or trust and is therefore much better for estate planning purposes.

⋗ *We have been married 54 years in a community property state, and all our property is community property. Why do we need powers of attorney or a trust to handle our affairs if one of us becomes incapacitated? Can't one spouse act for the other?*

Not always. Although community property states allow either spouse, with one signature, to manage most property, this is not true for all property. Any sale or transfer of real estate or agreement to mortgage requires both signatures. Liquidating or borrowing from an employer-sponsored retirement plan [a qualified plan, such as a 401(k)] requires the consent of both spouses under federal law. If, for example, one of you becomes incapacitated and the other has to sell or borrow against real estate or tries to dip into a qualified pension plan to pay expenses, the healthy spouse will be forced to go to court for authority to sign for you if you do not have a trust or an appropriate power of attorney. In many cases, a court will stay involved to ensure the proceeds are handled properly.

⩟ *What are the three ways to change the character of community and separate property?*

COMMINGLING   If separate property is commingled with community property to the extent that, even through tracing, clear and convincing evidence of its separate nature cannot be shown, the separate property will become community property.

PARTITIONING   The laws of all the community property states allow spouses to enter into an agreement to divide (partition) their community property into separate property and to declare that certain property is separate property. The agreement must be signed and acknowledged before a notary public. It is now possible under the laws of most community property states for spouses and prospective spouses (through a prenuptial or postnuptial agreement) to agree not only to partition community property or declare the separate character of separate property presently in existence but also to partition or declare that certain property to be acquired in the future will be the separate property of a particular spouse. Thus, it is possible to agree that income from personal efforts, separate property, and property produced from separate property (such as offspring of livestock) is or will be separate property.

GIFTS   If one spouse makes a gift of either separate or community property to the other spouse, this property, and all income or property produced from it, is presumed to be the separate property of the recipient spouse. Also, gifts made jointly to the spouses from a third party are deemed to be separate property held jointly, not community property.

⩟ *What is the character of property owned by a spouse who moves from a noncommunity state to a community property state? What is the character of property acquired in a community property state by a person in a noncommunity state?*

If a spouse was domiciled in a common law state at the time he or she acquired property, the property is generally treated as his or her separate property and will remain separate regardless of whether he or she moves it to a community property state, as long as commingling does not occur. Further, if a spouse domiciled in a community property state acquires property outside the state, its character as to that spouse will be governed by the rules of the community property state. Thus, if the property is acquired with community property, it will be community property; if it is acquired with separate property or by gift, inheritance, or bequest, it will be the separate property of the acquiring spouse, as long as adequate records are kept to trace its inception of title and no commingling occurs. If a spouse who is domiciled in a common law property state acquires real estate in a community property state, the real estate will generally be deemed to be that spouse's separate property since it was acquired with separate property.

⚔ *Can spouses own community property with right of survivorship?*

The laws of most community property states allow spouses to own community property with right of survivorship. Spouses can agree between themselves that all or part of the community property which they presently have or will acquire in the future will become the property of the surviving spouse on the death of a spouse.

Such agreements avoid probate at the first death of a spouse. However, it is strongly recommended that spouses not enter into joint community survivorship property agreements for several reasons. First, the same disadvantages that characterize joint tenancy also exist with joint community survivorship ownership. In addition, such an agreement may have to be adjudicated to the satisfaction of creditors or other third parties. That is, a court hearing may be required to obtain a court order stating that a particular agreement satisfies the statutory requirements for such agreements.

Even though the surviving spouse may prevail, either with or without the necessity of a court hearing, he or she would still be subject to all the severe shortcomings of joint tenancy. Joint community survivorship property can create more problems than it can solve. Stay away from such ownership.

Wills

⚔ *What is a will?*

A *will* is any written document in which the maker states his or her intention to devise or bequeath his or her real or personal property at death. For a will to be legally enforceable, it must conform to the specific legal requirements of the state in which it is created.

The important features of a will are as follows:

- A will must be prepared and executed with the formalities required by the laws of the jurisdiction in which it is created.
- A will takes effect only on its maker's death.
- A will affects only assets which are owned by the maker alone and which do not pass to others by the operation of law or by contract (joint tenancies and beneficiary designations).

⌘ Is a will the best way to plan my estate?

There are many advantages and disadvantages to planning your estate with a will. Whether the advantages outweigh the disadvantages is a function of many personal factors: the size and complexity of your estate, the degree to which you want to ensure that your assets will, in fact, be transferred to the individuals you choose in the manner you choose, the value you place on privacy, and the importance of minimizing taxes, costs, and attorney's fees.

⌘ What are some of the advantages of a will?

The most significant advantages of will-based planning include the following:

1. *Wills avoid intestacy.* If a person dies without a valid will (or funded living trust), all of that person's probate assets will be transferred by the laws of intestacy. State intestacy laws vary considerably depending on whether the decedent is survived by a spouse, the number of children surviving the decedent, and so on. Generally speaking, however, all intestacy laws, in varying degrees and percentages, seek to provide for the decedent's spouse, children, parents, and then more remote relatives. If no individual entitled to inherit the decedent's estate is found within the time prescribed by state law, the property will revert *(escheat)* to the state.

Thus, the primary advantage of having a will is that it permits distribution of your probate estate pursuant to your wishes rather than the state's wishes.

2. *Wills permit the nomination of a personal representative and a guardian for minor children.* In addition to identifying who will receive your probate assets, a will allows you to nominate your personal representative (often referred to as your *executor* if a male or *executrix* if a female). If you do not name a personal representative, the probate court will appoint an individual (often a close family member) who may or may not be the individual you would have chosen.

In a similar vein, a will permits you to name a guardian or guardians of your children. For most people, choosing a guardian of their minor children is a carefully reasoned decision and one that is best made by the parents and not the court.

3. *Wills are easily implemented and maintained.* In most instances, creating a will is an uncomplicated event. While certain individuals wish to handwrite their own wills (called *holographic wills*) or use one of the many forms or computer software applications available to the public, most individuals engage the services of an attorney to ensure that their wills conform to the peculiarities of local laws.

Moreover, as attorneys become more technologically advanced, there is decreasing reliance on amendments, or *codicils,* to wills. Rather, once your will is part of the attorney's electronic files, the attorney often simply incorporates your intended changes directly into your will, reprints the document, and has you execute a new, updated will.

4. *Wills can provide maximum tax savings, protect your children's inheritance from their creditors, and/or establish trusts to "ease" children into their inheritance.* In theory, a "complex" will can provide many of the advantages found in a living trust–based estate plan. In fact, from a legal perspective, the actual language found in a complex will can be almost identical to the trust language of a living trust. Separate trust shares can be created for the benefit of a surviving spouse in an attempt to minimize or eliminate federal estate taxes, and separate subtrusts can be established to provide for the needs of children and loved ones.

❧ *What are the primary disadvantages of wills?*

The one overreaching caveat regarding wills is that although in theory they may provide tremendous advantages, in practice their usefulness and effectiveness often fall far short of the theoretical optimum. While wills can be effective planning tools for smaller estates, the more complex a person's affairs are, the less effective a will is in planning the estate. Here are some of the major shortcomings of wills:

1. *Wills often fail to control a great deal of the maker's property.* The greatest disadvantage of planning your estate with a will, especially if you have a larger, more complex estate, is that your will may fail to actually control the distribution of much of your property. A will controls only the property that is part of your probate estate. Your probate estate includes:

- All property that is titled in your individual name and does not have a beneficiary-designation clause
- All property that is payable to your estate or subject to a power of appointment
- Your share of any tenancy-in-common property that you own

A will cannot control your joint tenancy assets; they pass automatically to the surviving joint tenant. Nor can your will control assets such as certificates of deposit, individual retirement accounts, Keogh plans, and life insurance for which you have named your spouse, children, or other loved ones as beneficiaries.

2. *Wills offer no protection against conservatorship of the maker.* While a will can effectively appoint your personal representative and the guardians of your minor children, it cannot name or appoint an individual to protect you or handle your affairs in the event of your disability. Quite simply, your will is ineffective until after your death. Hence, should you become disabled, your financial affairs may well become subject to your state's guardianship or conservatorship proceedings.

3. *Wills do not easily cross state lines.* In order for your will to transfer the property that makes up your probate estate, it must be filed with the court in the state and county of which you were a resident at your death. While a will executed in one state is valid in another state, it will nonetheless be interpreted according to the laws of the state in which you were domiciled at your death. For example, if your will does not contain a specific clause directing that taxes be apportioned among a certain class of beneficiaries, state A may assess tax liability against each beneficiary according to the amount received by the beneficiary and state B might assess all tax liability against the "remainder" of your estate. Thus, unwittingly, by moving from state A to state B, you could shift the entire tax burden of your estate from each of your beneficiaries to just a select few who were named the recipients of the balance, or remainder, of your assets. Wills are not very portable from state to state.

4. *Wills are fully public.* Despite the fact that most people are reticent to discuss their financial affairs in public, give their latest income tax return to a stranger, or discuss their net worth or cash-flow difficulties at a cocktail party, a person who dies leaving a will to transfer his or her assets may well be exposing this very information. Quite simply, a will, all accompanying inventories, tax returns (in some states), statements of assets and liabilities, the identity of your beneficiaries, the amounts they receive, and the manner in which they are to receive your legacy typically may be filed with the probate court and open to public inspection.

No doubt, the late Jackie Kennedy Onassis had some of the finest lawyers prepare her estate planning documents. Nonetheless, because a will was the cornerstone of her estate plan, it took only a simple drive or a phone call to the courthouse to obtain a complete copy of all such information, and it was a top story on the news.

Your privacy cannot be maintained under a will, and the financial condition of your family and business can be open for inspection by anyone.

5. *Wills ensure probate.* Any asset controlled, disposed of, or transferred by a will must go through probate. Many believe that just having a will (or, more often, their *particular* will) avoids probate, but this is impossible. If your will is used to transfer any of your property, it must first be submitted to the probate court and then be administered in accordance with each and every rule inherent to your state's probate code.

6. *Wills are easily challenged.* Probate of a will provides an open door for any disgruntled heir to challenge the terms of the will.

Can you give me an example of what you mean when you say that a will does not control all my property?

Consider Mr. Smith. Mr. Smith, age 57, is married and has two children, ages 17 and 22. He and his wife have a gross estate for federal estate tax purposes of $1,592,000, of which $1,118,000 is deemed for tax purposes to be owned by Mr. Smith. Table 2-1 lists Mr. Smith's assets, as well as how he owns them.

For the purposes of this example, we assume that Mr. Smith made an appointment with a respected attorney and received a complex will that contains tax planning trust provisions for his wife and creates trusts for his children which, upon his wife's death, are designed to retain the remaining principal in trust until each child reaches the age of 35.

Mr. Smith signed his will with great peace of mind, confident that his affairs were finally in order. Assuming that Mr. Smith passes away and is survived by his wife and two children, what does his will control?

Unfortunately, Mr. Smith's will controls only the disposition of his automobile and personal property valued at $54,000! His one-half inter-

TABLE 2-1   Mr. Smith's Assets

Asset	Value	Title
Principal residence	$ 175,000	½ joint tenancy with right of survivorship with spouse
Stocks/bonds	200,000	½ joint tenancy with right of survivorship with spouse
CDs	60,000	Beneficiary designation: wife, else children
Checking account	11,000	½ joint tenancy with right of survivorship with spouse
Lincoln town car	24,000	Individually titled
Artworks and collectibles	28,000	½ joint tenancy with right of survivorship with spouse
Other personal property	30,000	Individually titled
Life insurance	225,000	Beneficiary designation: wife, else children
IRA	265,000	Beneficiary designation: wife, else children
Cabin in mountains	100,000	½ joint tenancy with right of survivorship with brother
Total	$1,118,000	

est in the family residence, his stocks and bonds, checking account, and artworks will all pass automatically to Mrs. Smith because she is the surviving joint owner. The cabin in the mountains will pass not to Mrs. Smith or to the Smiths' children but to Mr. Smith's brother, despite the fact that Mr. Smith did not name his brother as an heir in his will.

Mr. Smith's certificates of deposit, life insurance proceeds, and IRA will pass to Mrs. Smith, not by virtue of his will but by the beneficiary-designation clauses naming Mrs. Smith as primary beneficiary.

In total, not accounting for court costs, attorney fees, or taxes, Mrs. Smith will receive $1,018,000 in assets from Mr. Smith (all of his assets except for the cabin, which went to his brother), yet only $54,000 pursuant to his will. At first blush, the fact that the will did not control $1,064,000 of Mr. Smith's assets may seem moot because Mrs. Smith did receive the majority of the property her husband intended. Such a cursory conclusion is flawed.

Mr. Smith's will had federal estate tax planning provisions which sought to hold all assets for the benefit of Mrs. Smith during her lifetime, while paying her the income and, if needed for her health, education, maintenance, and support, the principal as well. By creating such a trust, the will was designed to prevent the assets from being included in Mrs. Smith's taxable estate upon her death. Nevertheless, as Mr. Smith's will failed to control most of his property, $1,018,000 was transferred outright to Mrs. Smith. Since Mrs. Smith already had assets of her own valued at $474,000 for tax purposes, her taxable estate now totals $1,492,000. If Mrs. Smith were to die in 2006 or later, this would generate a federal estate tax of $206,560. If Mrs. Smith lives for several years after Mr. Smith's death, the appreciation in the value of her estate could cause a much higher federal estate tax liability and added probate costs.

Now let us assume the same set of facts except that Mrs. Smith predeceases Mr. Smith. Her one-half interest in the joint tenancy property passes by law to her husband, thus altering Mr. Smith's federally taxable estate as shown in Table 2-2.

Now what does Mr. Smith's will control? It still fails to control a great deal of his property, and thus his intended estate plan will not be fully implemented. First, the cabin in the mountains will still pass to his brother, not his children. Second, $490,000 of his estate (again without taking into account taxes, court costs, and attorney's fees) will be transferred outright to his two children as a result of their being listed on beneficiary designations. These assets will not be held in trust for the children until they reach age 35, contrary to Mr. Smith's intentions. Moreover, if Mr. Smith dies while his youngest child is still a minor, a guardian will have to be appointed to receive that child's one-half share of the $490,000 passing outside of Mr. Smith's will. If Mr. Smith dies in 2006 or later, the federal estate tax due will be $251,400. Properly planned, the Smith estate could have been structured to avoid most, if not all, federal estate tax and probate fees.

Accordingly, if your estate planning goals are to minimize federal estate taxes, court costs, and attorney's fees, to protect your legacy from your children's creditors, or to ensure that your children receive their inheritance when they are mature and not simply of "legal age," but your estate includes assets that are owned in joint tenancy or controlled by beneficiary designations, then you need a comprehensive estate plan that controls your property in a way that will accomplish your goals.

⚄ *Is it true that if I have a will my estate will not be subject to probate?*

If you own property in your name when you die, no matter how clearly

TABLE 2-2   Mr. Smith's Assets after the Death of Mrs. Smith

Asset	Value	Title
Principal residence	$ 350,000	Individually titled*
Stocks/bonds	400,000	Individually titled*
CDs	120,000	Beneficiary designation: wife, else children
Checking account	22,000	Individually titled*
Lincoln town car	24,000	Individually titled
Artworks and collectibles	56,000	Individually titled*
Other personal property	30,000	Individually titled
Life insurance	225,000	Beneficiary designation: wife, else children
IRA	265,000	Beneficiary designation: wife, else children
Cabin in mountains	100,000	½ joint tenancy with right of survivorship with brother
Total	$1,592,000	

*Value doubled by reason of Mrs. Smith's death.

you may set forth your desires in your will, your will *guarantees* that a probate proceeding will be necessary. Every state has laws which affect the timing and manner in which your assets are distributed, and nothing you say in your will can avoid those laws.

⍩ Won't a will satisfy the definition of estate planning?

The definition of estate planning that is used by the National Network of Estate Planning Attorneys is:

> I want to control my property while I am alive and well, care for myself and my loved ones if I become disabled, and be able to give what I have to whom I want, the way I want, and when I want, and, if I can, I want to save every last tax dollar, attorney fee, and court cost possible.

Let's take a look at this definition of estate planning and see how a will stacks up.

A will does allow you to control your property while you are alive and able to do so. A will can do nothing to protect you if you are incapacitated; a will is effective only upon your death.

Does a will actually control property at death? It controls only the property that is not titled in joint tenancy or governed by beneficiary designations.

As far as giving your property to whom you want, the way you want, and when you want, the only thing a simple will can do is give property outright, which may not be in the best interest of the beneficiaries. Often it is not. In order to meet these objectives, your will would have to include one or more testamentary trusts and make sure there is no property titled in joint tenancy or passed through beneficiary designations.

As far as avoiding court costs such as probate, a will does not avoid them. A will guarantees probate as to the property it controls, so it also guarantees that there will be professional fees such as those for attorneys and appraisers. Only a will with testamentary trust provisions will provide any type of tax planning or tax savings; but such a will would have the added disadvantage of requiring continued court supervision and control until all purposes of the testamentary trust have been satisfied. For example, the court will often require the filing of annual, or more frequent, accountings that are available for public inspection.

As you can see, a will, in almost all respects, falls short of meeting the definition of proper estate planning.

⩗ *Does my will take care of transferring property that I have in another state?*

Generally, states will recognize as valid a will admitted to probate in another state. However, this does not mean that real property outside your home state will automatically transfer according to the terms of your will. Instead, a process known as *ancillary probate* or *ancillary administration* is required. Although another state will recognize and accept the beneficiary you have named, each state can determine the method and requirements for transferring real property located within its borders. Ancillary administration is a probate procedure which requires the filing of documents in the probate court of the state where the real property is located. Going through ancillary administration amounts to probating the will twice but under different requirements depending on the states involved. Sometimes taxes must be paid on the value of the property before it can be transferred to the beneficiaries.

In most instances, ancillary probate proceedings require that an attorney in the ancillary state be retained, and if the executor of the estate is not a resident of that state, he or she may be required to post a bond with the court. Needless to say, ancillary probate involves additional costs and fees, leaving even less for loved ones.

🔊 *I have homes in two states, and I spend a considerable amount of time in both. I understand that this can cause tax problems. What should I know?*

Although you may have more than one residence, you technically have only one "domicile." It is important to determine which state is considered your domicile, because it is the law of that state which will control the operation of your estate plan and the taxation of your estate. Sometimes, by putting certain language in your estate planning documents, you can select the law of another state to control the operation of those documents in order to obtain more favorable results; your advisors can assist you with the details.

The indications of domicile in a state include the following:

- You vote in that town and state.
- You spend more than half the year in that state.
- You have your major religious and other community and social activities in that state.
- You have a driver's license for that state, and you have a car registered there.
- You file an income tax return in that state.

If it is not clear from the above indicators which of the two states is your domicile, it is important that you make an informed decision and develop facts and circumstances to support your domicile in the state which you choose. Otherwise, *both* states may consider themselves your domicile and impose state death taxes on your estate.

Beneficiary Designations

🔊 *What is beneficiary-designation property?*

While you may have title to certain assets in your individual name, the very nature of an asset may dictate to whom it will be transferred at your death. For example, certificates of deposit, individual retirement accounts, and life insurance contracts typically contain a *beneficiary-designation clause,* wherein you specify who will receive the asset or the proceeds at your death. While you retain legal and beneficial title to such an asset during your life, and thus can consume the asset or change the beneficiaries, by designating beneficiaries on the asset, you are, in essence, predetermining who will take legal and equitable title to that asset at your death. As such, your will, despite its provisions, will not control the asset.

⚜ Is designating a beneficiary a good way to avoid probate?

A beneficiary designation directs the proceeds of life insurance policies, individual retirement accounts, and annuities to particular persons or entities without the need for probate in most situations. However, designating a beneficiary can lead to consequences other than probate avoidance. For example, your choice of beneficiary can have a tremendous tax consequence for the person to whom you intend to be generous! Failing to name the proper person on beneficiary designations can result in a requirement that money be paid out and taxed immediately, instead of over a much longer period. In addition, payment made directly to a person may leave your estate without funds to pay taxes or debts.

Beneficiary designations do not always guarantee the avoidance of probate or court-supervised administration. If you name your estate as a beneficiary, the proceeds will go through probate. If you name a minor as a beneficiary, a financial guardian may have to be appointed by the court to hold and invest the proceeds. Finally, if the beneficiary you name is mentally incompetent to take the property, a financial guardian will have to be appointed.

Naming a beneficiary is something that should be considered carefully and should be accompanied by expert advice.

⚜ Can life insurance policies and proceeds become living or death probate assets?

We usually think of life insurance policies as nonprobate assets. This is because a life insurance contract is a third-party beneficiary contract. Upon the death of the insured, the policy proceeds are payable by the life insurance company to the beneficiary. Probate courts usually have no jurisdiction over nonprobate assets such as life insurance, living trust assets, jointly owned assets, and retirement death benefits.

There are a number of ways, however, that your life insurance policies and the proceeds can get caught up in either a living probate or a death probate, or both. Let's explore the ways this can occur:

You fail to name a beneficiary or a contingent beneficiary. If you fail to name a beneficiary on your life insurance policy or if the beneficiary you have named fails to survive you, the insurance company will pay the proceeds to your probate estate. Most policies provide that the insured's probate estate is the final backup, or default, beneficiary when there is no named living beneficiary.

Your named beneficiary survives you, but dies shortly thereafter. Suppose you and your spouse were involved in an auto accident and you died instantly but your spouse died several days, hours, or even minutes later. If your spouse is named as the beneficiary on your life insurance, the insurance company will pay the proceeds of your policy to your spouse's probate estate. Since your spouse did survive you, your contingent beneficiaries are not eligible to receive your insurance proceeds.

Your beneficiary or contingent beneficiary is under a legal incapacity such as minority or incompetence. If your insurance proceeds are payable to a minor or to an incompetent adult (such as a brain-damaged or comatose spouse who survived the disaster that killed you), the insurance company will have to pay the proceeds to a court-appointed guardian of the minor or of the incompetent adult until he or she gains or regains legal capacity.

You become legally incapacitated, and a guardian of your estate is appointed to take control of all your assets including your cash-value and term life insurance. If you lose your mental capacity or become physically incapacitated due to age, illness, or injury, the probate court may have to appoint a guardian to take control of your assets to conserve your estate from the claims of creditors and other possible losses.

If you own cash-value life insurance, your policy will come under the control of the probate court. The life insurance company will not allow your spouse or anyone else to have access to your cash value, even if it is for your benefit, unless or until your spouse or someone else is appointed by the probate court as the conservator of your estate. Furthermore, once appointed, the conservator will have to get the probate court's permission to withdraw the cash value from the policy, plus post a bond for the amount withdrawn.

Both cash-value life insurance and term insurance carry with them very valuable policy rights which can be exercised only by an owner who is competent. If you become incapacitated, you will not be able to exercise any of these rights, such as your right to convert your term insurance to cash-value life insurance. Approximately 98 percent of all term life insurance never pays off because the policy lapses for nonpayment of premium, the term expires, or the policy is converted to cash-value life insurance. If your insurance policy lapsed or if the term of your term insurance policy expired, an insurance company would declare you uninsurable for purposes of acquiring any new life insurance on your life. If you become incapacitated, only a probate court–appointed guardian can exercise your policy rights for you, and you will have no say over how these policy rights will be exercised.

⊰ *May I leave all my life insurance benefits to my spouse?*

Many assets, such as insurance policies, individual retirement accounts, qualified retirement plans, and some bank accounts, require a beneficiary designation. When you die, these assets will be paid directly to the person you have named as your beneficiary, without having to go through probate. At least that is the way it is supposed to work.

Spouses often need help and guidance when their marriage partners pass away. Grief, confusion, and lethargy all take their toll during the period of bereavement. By leaving property outright to a surviving spouse through a beneficiary designation, you have no opportunity to provide him or her with guidance and assistance in managing the money. Often, an outright distribution creates more, not fewer, problems after the death of a spouse. At the death of one spouse, the survivor is an easy target for children, relatives, or unscrupulous people who want something. Leaving property outright makes it easier for those predators to feast.

If your spouse is disabled when you die, the court will probably take control of the funds. If your spouse dies before you, or you both die at the same time, the assets will have to go through probate so that the court can determine who will receive them.

Many people want to control how their property is to be used after they pass away. Leaving property outright to a spouse affords absolutely no control. If, for example, the surviving spouse remarries, there is no assurance that any property he or she received will ever pass to the deceased spouse's children. Or if the surviving spouse has creditor problems, any property left outright to that spouse is fair game for creditors. If control of your property or creditor planning is important to you, leaving property outright to your spouse is a mistake.

⊰ *What is a POD bank account?*

A *payable-on-death* (*POD*) designation is sometimes placed on bank accounts to direct that, at the owner's death, the proceeds are to be paid to a specific individual or entity.

What is a TOD account?

A *transfer-on-death (TOD)* designation is sometimes placed on brokerage accounts. TODs accomplish the same results as PODs but for different types of accounts.

Can POD and TOD accounts avoid probate?

POD and TOD accounts do avoid death probate. But they do nothing to avoid living probate. That is, if you are legally incapacitated, no one can touch either type of account without a court order or a specially drafted durable power of attorney.

Can't I simply designate my estate as beneficiary of my certificates of deposit, individual retirement accounts, and life insurance policies and then have my will control them?

If you name your estate as the beneficiary of these assets, your will can indeed control them. Doing this, however, does have pitfalls and generally should be avoided. By making your estate the beneficiary of these assets, you are subjecting otherwise probate-free assets to the jurisdiction and lengthy process of the probate court. In addition, these assets may be free from the claims of creditors when paid to a beneficiary other than your estate, but if your estate is the beneficiary, creditors may very well have access to these assets.

Living Wills

What is a living will?

A *living will,* or advanced medical directive, is a legal document which directs your physician to discontinue life-sustaining procedures if you are in a terminal condition or a permanently unconscious state.

It is considered a final expression of your right to refuse medical treatment which should be followed by your physician. Many people execute living wills so that family members or other loved ones are not put in the position of having to decide whether to terminate or continue life-sustaining treatment when there is no hope of recovery.

The living will is now recognized in virtually all states. Most states have very detailed laws setting forth the language that must be included in order for the document to be valid. As each state has different laws, it is a good idea to check with an attorney in your state to get more information on your state's requirements.

⚰ *Who decides whether or not to invoke the terms of my living will?*

You should be aware that most major hospitals have created "ethics" panels or independent review boards which consist of physicians, nurses, and other personnel not currently involved in the treatment of the individual in question. These panels or boards review the situation and give the treating physician(s) direction.

You should ask your local hospital (or the hospital where you may be taken if you have a severe or terminal condition) what its policies are in regard to living wills.

⚰ *How are living wills misinterpreted?*

Living wills are sometimes misunderstood as the equivalent of a "do not resuscitate" (DNR) order, which is an agreement between the patient and the physician that the patient will not be resuscitated if sudden unconsciousness occurs. This situation could occur even if there is no terminal illness meeting the narrow conditions described above for invoking the living will.

For example, a woman who had just had a hip transplant was being wheeled to the recovery room when she suffered a cardiac arrest and lapsed into unconsciousness. The hospital personnel made no attempt to resuscitate her "because she has a living will." This was an improper use of that document because a hip transplant is not a terminal illness from which there is no reasonable prospect of recovery.

⚰ *What is a power of attorney for health care?*

Beyond expressing your wishes as to life-sustaining issues, you may also express your wishes with regard to courses of medical treatment. In a *power of attorney for health care,* you name a surrogate or attorney-in-fact to make medical decisions for you if you are unable to do so yourself. For instance, if major surgery or long-term treatment is proposed and you are too ill to make your feelings known, your surrogate would invoke the power of attorney to facilitate your wishes.

⚰ *What are some of the issues that I may wish to address in my living will and other medical directives?*

Some of the issues you may want to address specifically are terminal conditions or illnesses (such as certain types of cancer, stroke, and major heart problems), vegetative states, and the types of treatments you may want to have withheld (such as tube feeding, artificial nutrition, hydration—in all their various forms). Your personal medical concerns may dictate other issues that should be included. Be sure to address quality-of-life issues and make an express statement of your desire and philosophy regarding your right to die with dignity.

It is impossible to create the perfect document when you cannot know what the specific situation will be at the time help is needed. With comprehensive medical directives, however, you should have some peace of mind that your wishes have been made known and that your desires will be carried out.

ALTERNATIVE METHODS OF ESTATE PLANNING

Why can't I just give my property away while I'm living?

There are several reasons. First, by giving your property away, you give up control of your property. Regardless of your good intentions, and the good intentions of the person you give the property to, you no longer have any guarantee that the property will be used as you wish or that the property will be used to take care of you.

If you give the property away, it becomes subject to the claims of the recipient's creditors, including his or her spouse. Also, if the recipient predeceases you, the property will pass in accordance with that person's estate planning. If no planning is in place, the property will pass to the recipient's spouse or children. If the children are minors, their share cannot be used for any purpose other than the care of the children. If the recipient divorces, his or her spouse will have a valid claim against the property.

Also, if the property you give away is valued at more than the gift tax annual exclusion, you must file a federal gift tax return and pay the appropriate taxes.

I taped the names of family members to the bottoms of different items in my home, such as lamps and paintings, to show who is to get the items at my death. Is this okay? How can I make sure that my favorite niece receives the cameo my grandmother left me?

Tape might be okay for the first relative who gets into your home after you pass away, but it would be hard to predict what the slower relatives will get! There are better ways, with appropriate documentation, of ensuring that the right individuals receive what you want them to.

Some states allow personal property to be passed by means of a *personal property memorandum.* This is a document, separate from your will or trust, in which you specifically identify the items of personal property and the individuals who are to receive the items. Your trust or will must refer specifically to the personal property memorandum, but you can prepare the memorandum at your leisure, and you don't have to sign it in front of a notary. Since you can change the memorandum whenever you want, your will or trust should state that if your heirs discover two personal property memorandums which conflict, the provisions of the one dated last will control.

If your state does not allow the use of the personal property memorandum, your attorney will draft the appropriate documentation for transferring your personal items to the individuals who should receive them.

≈ *Someone told me that a good way to avoid probate is just to sign a quitclaim deed giving my real estate to my kids and then place the deed in a safe deposit box so that they can record it when I die. Is this a good idea?*

This is a bad idea. The problem it attempts to solve (probate) may not be as bad as the ones it creates.

First, it may not be necessary (depending on your own state) to record the deed to have a completed transfer. If this is the case, your children could claim that you have actually given them title now, and they could gain control of your property.

Next, the Internal Revenue Service could claim that your children received the property as a gift from you. If your children receive property from you by gift, their basis in the property will probably be less than what it would be if they inherit the property from you. In this case, they may be forced to pay greater capital gain tax than they would if they inherit the property from you.

You are much better off creating a revocable living trust and transferring title to your real estate to the trust. In this way you retain control of the real estate during your life, your disability trustee can manage your real estate for your benefit if you become disabled, and the property can pass to your children when you die, without its having to go through probate.

≈ *My husband and I lease a safe deposit box in which we keep all sorts of things for our children and grandchildren. We have writ-*

ten a letter in which we say that everything in the box belongs equally to our children. Will this technique allow our children to receive its contents tax-free?

The Internal Revenue Service is likely to take one of two positions: (1) You have made an incomplete gift and the property will be taxed in the estate of the surviving spouse. Or (2) you owe back gift tax and interest and penalties for not filing a gift tax return.

≱ *I have a number of collectibles, including coin and stamp collections, antiques, and paintings. I have specifically listed some of these items for coverage on my homeowner's insurance policy. Would I be wise to give these items to my adult children, within the annual gift tax exclusion, under custody agreements by which they would ask me to safe-keep them in my home until my death?*

Whether this arrangement would withstand an attack by the Internal Revenue Service (for gift tax or estate tax purposes) or by creditors (for enforcement of claims against you) depends upon the answer to two questions:

- *Will your estate be filing an estate tax return?* If a federal estate tax return is filed, it is likely that the IRS will try to tax the value of the tangibles on the theory that you really did not relinquish control and that you did not make a complete gift that would remove the tangibles from your taxable estate.
- *Does your estate have obligations that can be satisfied only from the proceeds of a sale of the assets?* If, at your death, you owe money that could be paid only out of the value of the tangibles under this arrangement, your creditors will most likely ask a court to compel your personal representative to retrieve the tangibles, sell them, and apply the proceeds to the satisfaction of your debts.

Both questions might be answered differently if you should actually store the tangibles in a way that prevents you from enjoying them or if they were scheduled on each child's homeowner's policy.

≱ *If I have a Swiss bank account, will my estate have to pay a U.S. estate tax on the account?*

As long as you are an American citizen or resident of the United States, the IRS will require that the assets in the Swiss bank account be included on your federal estate tax return. The attorney and other professionals assisting in the preparation of the return cannot lawfully permit the person responsible for filing the return to omit the account.

Is there a way to eliminate the capital gain tax on the sale of a gift?

If you give property directly to charity or to one of several types of charitable remainder trusts (as discussed in detail in Chapter 8) and the recipient subsequently sells the property, you and the charity or charitable remainder trust can avoid paying the capital gain tax on the increase in value.

What is the best way to plan for community property?

If spouses are interested in acquiring the survivorship right and avoiding probate, they should seriously consider creating a revocable living trust. The revocable living trust has all the advantages of joint ownership and then some, with none of the disadvantages of joint ownership.

THE REVOCABLE LIVING TRUST

What Is a Revocable Living Trust?

Can the federal estate tax be reduced or eliminated?

There are strategies that can be used to reduce or eliminate federal estate taxes. However, many of these strategies will not always work with a will-planning probate estate plan. This is because the people who draft such plans usually do not coordinate all of the estate's assets but, rather, deal only with the property in the name of the will maker. As a result, major assets such as retirement benefits, life insurance, and joint tenancy property are not included in the plan.

You can easily design a living trust to coordinate all of your assets under one or more subtrusts and thereby take the assets into account in maximizing federal estate tax planning.

How can I make sure that my beneficiaries do not have to use their own money to pay taxes on what they inherit?

A well-drafted trust or will contains a tax apportionment clause that dictates what assets shall be used to pay the estate taxes. Typically, all estate taxes will be paid before there is any distribution to beneficiaries so that all bequests are received free of the obligation to pay additional estate taxes.

An estate tax is a tax on the transfer of assets from an estate; this is true of the federal estate tax. Some states, however, have an inheritance tax. This type of death tax is imposed on the property an heir or beneficiary receives from an estate. Planning for beneficiaries living in these states is tricky and should be addressed in the individual's estate plan.

⚜ *Specifically, what can my spouse and I do to reduce the estate tax burden on our children?*

In general, you and your advisors can create:

- Marital and family trusts in your will or living trust that will shelter up to $2 million of your property if you both die after 2006
- Irrevocable life insurance trusts to shelter your life insurance from tax
- Family limited partnerships that reduce the value of your assets for estate tax purposes
- A current program of making gifts to loved ones or charity

⚜ *How do I most effectively avoid a living and a death probate?*

Through a revocable living trust, living and death probate proceedings can be totally avoided. You may incorporate instructions into a revocable living trust which specify how your disability trustee should manage your assets if you become disabled. This simple procedure allows you to have the benefit of your assets, consistent with your directions, during the period of disability while avoiding the expense, delay, and lack of privacy imposed by the living probate process.

Similarly, a revocable living trust enables you to leave instructions for your death trustee, indicating how assets should be distributed. Because the assets are titled in the name of the trust, you avoid the expense, delay, and lack of privacy caused by a death probate.

⚜ *How can life insurance policies be totally protected from both probate systems?*

The best way to totally protect your life insurance policy and proceeds from both probate systems is to designate a revocable or irrevocable living trust as both the owner and the beneficiary of your life insurance policy.

⚜ *My husband is not well: his memory and his mental acuity have degenerated over the last several years. If I die before my husband, how can I allow him the dignity of his independence and still protect him from the problems related to his failing health?*

With a funded living trust as the center of an estate plan, a trust maker can select a cotrustee to serve with the spouse as trustees of the trust. This enables the surviving spouse to retain control and independence while having the advice and counsel of the cotrustee.

In the event that the surviving spouse's health further degenerates, the trust can provide for a smooth transition in the management of his or her affairs. For example, a son or daughter could be named to serve as cotrustee with the father. The selection of a family member provides personal consideration as well as the security of joint management for the ailing spouse.

⚑ What is a revocable living trust?

A *trust* is a contract between its maker and a trustee. In the contract, the trust maker gives instructions to the trustee concerning the holding and administering of trust assets. These instructions specify how the assets are to be held and distributed during the maker's good health, upon his or her disability, and ultimately upon his or her death.

With a *revocable living trust,* a person can be (and usually is) both the maker and the trustee. A husband and wife will often be joint trust makers and joint trustees of a joint trust.

The term "revocable" refers to a set of powers that are typically listed in the trust agreement which specify that the trust maker has the power to amend or revoke the trust. Upon revocation, the trustee is directed to return all trust assets to the trust maker. In addition to having the power to amend or revoke, the maker has the power to place assets into the trust, remove assets from the trust, make all investment decisions concerning trust assets, and control and direct all payments and distributions from the trust.

⚑ What is the difference between a revocable trust and an irrevocable trust?

As its name implies, a *revocable trust* can be revoked, changed, or amended by the maker of the trust at any time. Its maker can update it as his or her desires and the needs of loved ones change. This flexibility makes a revocable living trust an ideal foundation for almost all estate plans. A revocable living trust can be designed to control all of the maker's property, totally avoid the probate of the maker's estate, and maximize federal estate tax savings.

Irrevocable trusts, on the other hand, cannot be altered or amended without the approval of a court. Accordingly, irrevocable living trusts should be used only in certain circumstances after careful consideration and planning. Most often, irrevocable living trusts are used in conjunction with revocable living trusts to hold certain, select assets of the trust maker for the benefit of the trust maker's loved ones. If the trust maker retains no rights in the irrevocable living trust and is not a trustee or a beneficiary of the trust, the assets of the trust can be excluded from the trust maker's gross estate for estate tax purposes. This allows the trust maker to lower and, at times, eliminate federal estate taxes.

Irrevocable living trusts can be described as an advanced estate planning tool. They are most commonly used by individuals whose gross estates are taxable for federal estate tax purposes. Unlike revocable living trusts, irrevocable living trusts are rarely the foundation of one's estate plan but, rather, a supplement to it.

⚛ *What is a testamentary trust?*

A *testamentary trust* is a trust created by a will. This will-created trust designates a person to serve as trustee, names the beneficiaries of the trust, and includes directions on how assets are to be administered in the trust. The key feature of a testamentary trust is that it does not automatically take effect upon the death of a decedent; it can become effective only if the will creating the testamentary trust is admitted to probate.

Unlike a revocable living trust, a testamentary trust, in some jurisdictions, may be subject to court supervision until all assets have been distributed and all trust purposes have been completed. For example, the trust instrument that creates a revocable living trust may require that the trustee provide annual accountings of the trust's administration to the beneficiaries. In the context of a testamentary trust, the trustee may be required not only to provide the annual accountings to the beneficiaries but also to present the annual accountings for review and approval by the probate court. The presentation of such accountings for court approval necessarily involves the participation and expense of an attorney. These court expenses are normally avoided in accountings prepared for a revocable living trust.

⚛ *How does a living trust differ from a testamentary trust?*

Living trusts, also known as *inter vivos* ("during your life") trusts, are created and in force during your lifetime. You sign the trust agreement and place the assets you choose in the trust while you are alive. The trust survives both your incapacity and your death, distributing the assets of the trust during your incapacity or after your death to your loved ones in the manner you have specified in the trust agreement.

In contrast, a *testamentary trust* is created within a will and thus is not in force during your lifetime. Since a testamentary trust does not exist until the will takes effect at your death, you cannot place any assets in the trust during your life. Hence, your assets must go through the probate process before being placed in the testamentary trust.

⚘ *What is the difference between a living trust and a living will?*

A *living will* is an important part of your estate plan because it allows you to preplan for very sensitive personal issues that affect you and your loved ones. It directs your physician to discontinue life-sustaining procedures if you are in a terminal condition or a permanently unconscious state. Each state has its own statute that provides specific guidelines and language that can or should be included in your living will.

A *living trust* deals with your financial affairs rather than with health care issues. With a living trust, you can give instructions about what is to happen to your assets when you are no longer able to manage them yourself, whether due to incapacity or to death. A revocable living trust allows you to keep control over what happens with all of your assets even when you yourself are no longer able to make decisions about them.

⚘ *Isn't creating a revocable living trust just a waste of time and money if my estate is not subject to estate tax?*

Absolutely not. Your estate will pass estate tax–free on your death, but there is more to planning than taxes. In fact, many personal benefits in a revocable living trust may be significantly more important than estate tax savings. Let's go back to the beginning and look at our definition of proper estate planning:

> I want to control my property while I am alive and well, care for myself and my loved ones if I become disabled, and be able to give what I have to whom I want, the way I want, and when I want, and, if I can, I want to save every last tax dollar, attorney fee, and court cost possible.

You will notice that a lot of goals precede the concluding phrase, "and, if I can, I want to save every last tax dollar." It is those preceding goals which have priority in proper estate planning.

For many people who do not have taxable estates, a revocable living trust is an excellent planning vehicle because, among other things, it can address so many different needs. In creating a revocable living trust, you can, for example, do the following:

- You can provide for your disability by appointing someone to administer your assets while you are disabled in accordance with your detailed instructions on how to care for you and your loved ones.
- You can create a *special-needs trust* to take care of anyone in your family who may have a temporary or permanent disability or who may require special care.
- You can create a *common trust* to care for your minor children from a common pool of the estate assets, just as you would if your family were still intact.
- If some of your heirs are poor at handling money, you can arm a successor trustee with spendthrift provisions to restrain your heirs from their unwise spending or to provide protection from the claims of their creditors.
- You can delay distributions to heirs until they are mature enough to spend their inheritance wisely.
- You can avoid the public, slow, and expensive probate process.
- You can direct the disbursement of your estate in a manner tailor-made to the individual needs and capabilities of each of your heirs.
- If you have contentious family members, you can reduce the likelihood of legal conflicts among them, since a revocable living trust is generally more difficult to contest than a will.

These are just a few examples of the things you can accomplish with a revocable living trust. When you remain mindful of the real priorities in estate planning, you will never choose a planning vehicle solely on the basis of the size of your estate.

⊰ Is living trust planning a good idea for a single parent?

Definitely. In fact, it is the best overall solution to the planning problems of the single parent. How does a living trust benefit the single parent? In most respects, it offers the same advantages to a single parent as it does to a married parent. However, because there is no spouse to assist the parent if he or she becomes disabled or to provide for the emotional and financial needs of the child if the parent should die, living trust planning is particularly beneficial for a single parent. Carefully selected guardians and trustees and detailed instructions for your own care and that of your child will ensure that, no matter what life brings, your wishes will be carried out and your child provided for.

⋈ What is the income tax effect of a revocable living trust?

A revocable living trust is tax-neutral in that the trust maker is considered the owner of all trust assets during his or her lifetime for tax purposes.

⋈ What happens to the trust at the death of its maker?

At the trust maker's death, the trust may continue according to its terms or may be terminated with the trust assets' being distributed to the beneficiaries.

⋈ Can a married person create a living trust plan without the knowledge of his or her spouse?

Yes. A spouse can place separate personal property—such as bank accounts, money markets, certificates of deposit, stocks or bonds, and beneficiary designations on IRA accounts—in the name of a living trust without the other spouse's consent or signature on any of the transfer documents.

In most instances, a person would not be able to transfer joint title to real estate into his or her living trust unless the other spouse cosigned any deed that was necessary to put title into the trust.

There are two limitations on the effectiveness of creating the trust plan without the knowledge of your spouse:

1. Making maximum use of the applicable exclusion amount, which allows a married couple to leave between $1.3 million (in 1999) and $2 million (in the year 2006 and thereafter) free of federal estate tax, requires cooperation between husband and wife.
2. In most states, one spouse cannot prevent the surviving spouse from claiming the rights of homestead and of a statutory allowance for inheritance purposes, even if assets are placed in a trust.

⋈ Can I have more than one revocable trust?

Yes, you can. For instance, if you plan to be away from the office for an extended period of time, a separate revocable trust can be set up so that you can appoint someone as your trustee to handle the regular business routines of paying bills, depositing checks, and the like, while you are away. This type of trust is like a power of attorney but is safer and more restrictive.

You can also divide property among several revocable trusts and appoint a different member of the family as trustee of each trust to see how each one manages the trust property. This will give you an idea of what would happen in the event of your death. In addition, you can have the sole power to amend or revoke each trust, so that you can terminate a trust if you feel that the principal in it is being mishandled.

In some cases, spouses may each have an individual trust for separate property and a joint trust for marriage property.

✎ *I'm afraid I'll lose control of my assets if I don't own them anymore. Why do you say I won't lose control?*

First, you create a trust agreement with the help of a qualified estate planning attorney, who makes sure the document fulfills your wishes while staying within the bounds of trust law, debtor-creditor law, marital law, bankruptcy law, and tax law. Among the provisions of your trust are your instructions for the trustee in regard to managing and distributing the assets for and to your beneficiaries—you dictate the terms which the new owner of your property (your trustee) *must* obey. There is no higher duty under the law than that owed by a trustee to a beneficiary.

As if that were not enough control, you can be the sole beneficiary of the trust during your lifetime. Your trust will contain instructions on how to take care of you during a legal incapacity, and your instructions must be followed and your property used for your benefit. If you become disabled, you actually have more control over your property than you would have if you owned it outright, since without the trust your assets would be subject to a living probate.

And finally, for the ultimate in control, you can be your own trustee while you are alive and competent. You make all the decisions to buy, sell, give away, acquire, and use the property, just as you always did.

✎ *How does a revocable living trust avoid probate?*

Regardless of the specific types of property that a decedent may have, all property will be either probate or nonprobate property. Probate property is all the property that must pass through the probate process to change ownership. Nonprobate property is all the property that does not need to go through the probate process to change ownership.

Typically, probate property is property that the decedent owned in his or her own name. Nonprobate property is property that passes to a named beneficiary, such as a life insurance policy, annuity contract, certificate of deposit, or individual retirement account. It also includes property that was owned by the decedent in joint tenancy with rights of survivorship.

Property held in a revocable living trust is nonprobate property because it is not directly owned by the trust maker. Since the property is no longer owned by the maker in his or her individual name, it does not need to pass through the probate process to have the ownership changed. This transfer of ownership from the individual to the trustee of the trust is referred to as "funding" the trust.

Any time a revocable living trust is used, it is extremely important that it be funded. All assets left outside the trust may have to pass through the probate process to change ownership. Trust makers should periodically review their estate plans and their assets to make sure that they are owned correctly and that the appropriate assets are placed in the trust.

I understand that the probate process is public. If I had a revocable living trust, would everyone still know my affairs?

No. Unlike the probate process, a living trust is not public and does not warrant public attention. In some states, such as California, the trust may be open to inspection by your "heirs at law" or other "interested persons," but it does not need to be filed in the public records.

Does a living trust avoid an ancillary probate?

When a revocable living trust is properly funded, neither probate in the state of domicile nor ancillary probate proceedings are necessary because the assets are held and owned by the trust.

If my state has simplified or informal probate laws, should I still consider creating a living trust?

All states differ as to the formality of their probate laws. Many states have adopted a probate law that reduces some of the requirements of traditional probate (e.g., court hearings). Even though your state may have informal probate, certain procedures must still be dealt with, resulting in significant cost, delay, and frustration. Additionally, a probate that begins as an informal process can instantly become a very formal probate once the slightest problem occurs.

Even if your state has an informal probate process, you may own real estate in a state that has formal probate, and the probate laws of that state would apply to the real estate. A revocable living trust can avoid all probates.

⚜ *Is my living trust something that the government will shut down?*

The living trust has been authorized by common law for hundreds of years and is growing more and more popular. The trend for the federal government has been to liberalize the use of living trusts, giving them equal footing with probate estates. For example, in 1997, Congress enacted legislation allowing equal treatment of living trusts and probate estates for most income tax purposes.

State governments have followed the federal trend of enacting legislation favorable to the use of living trusts. However, there is no telling whether the states will decide to exert more control over living trusts. Living trusts expedite the transfer of wealth without the usual red tape. In the absence of any special-interest group trying to pull living trusts into the probate system, it is unlikely that state governments would want to create more probates or conservatorships; the courts are overcrowded as it is.

⚜ *Does a revocable living trust always have assets in it?*

A revocable living trust may be unfunded, partially funded with only specific assets, or fully funded. If a revocable living trust is unfunded or not fully funded, the trust maker's assets that are not held in the trust will pass to the trust in accordance with a "pour-over" provision in his or her will. These assets will be subject to probate.

⚜ *Can I keep some of my property outside of my trust?*

Yes, you can. But any such assets will have to go through the probate process which the trust is set up to avoid.

⚜ *Are assets held in a living trust protected from creditors' claims?*

Generally speaking, when assets are held in a revocable trust, they are not protected from the legitimate claims of the trust maker's creditors. This is because the maker can revoke the trust and take back the trust property at any time. The law finds that it is inequitable to allow the trust maker to have this control and full use and benefit from the trust property while denying creditors the power to compel revocation in order to satisfy their just claims.

An *irrevocable* trust may provide some creditor protection because the maker is not able to revoke the trust and get the property back. The maker may have a *beneficial interest* in the trust, such as a right to income or to principal, and that interest may be reached by the maker's creditors. However, if the beneficial interest is subject to the discretion of the trustee and the maker is not the sole trustee, creditors can be thwarted. In fact, two states, Alaska and Delaware, allow trust makers of certain irrevocable trusts to retain rights in the trust and still have the trust assets be free from creditor claims.

⚴ *Are there ways to draft my living trust so that the trust assets are less vulnerable to my beneficiaries' creditors?*

While a revocable living trust cannot protect the maker from his or her creditors, it can protect the beneficiaries from the claims of their creditors. When a special clause is inserted into the trust document to protect trust assets from claims of the beneficiaries' creditors, the trust is said to be a *spendthrift trust.*

Spendthrift trusts are not valid in all states. In addition, the mere presence of a spendthrift clause does not always ensure creditor protection. There are, however, several measures that can be taken to make a spendthrift trust less vulnerable if it is attacked by a beneficiary's creditors. For example, trust agreements may specify that the trustee *must* make distributions for the support of the beneficiary or that the trustee *may* make distributions based solely on the trustee's discretion. Courts have generally held that spendthrift trusts which *require* that distributions be made for the support of the beneficiary may be reached by creditors for support-related debts; creditors generally cannot seize assets of a spendthrift trust that allows the trustee to distribute trust assets based *solely* on the trustee's discretion.

If your objective is to protect your beneficiaries from their creditors, it is generally best to give the trustee of the spendthrift trust sole discretion as to whether or not to pay the trust's income or principal to the beneficiary, as opposed to requiring mandatory payments of income or principal to the beneficiary. Additionally, it is not advisable to name the beneficiary of the spendthrift trust as the sole trustee of his or her own trust. Doing so could invoke the *doctrine of merger* of equitable and legal title, thus allowing the beneficiary's creditors to reach the trust's assets.

Creditors could also reach the assets of a spendthrift trust if the conditions necessary for the trust to terminate have already occurred but the trust has not been terminated. For instance, if the terms of the spendthrift trust require that the trust terminate when the trust beneficiary reaches 30 years of age, a creditor of the beneficiary may require that all assets be distributed to the beneficiary when he or she turns 30. The beneficiary cannot elect to wait out the creditor. To solve this problem, you can make the term of the trust be the duration of the beneficiary's life.

⊀ Is the cost of a will or a trust income tax–deductible?

Though the legal fee for drafting a will is generally not tax-deductible, a portion of the fee for the planning and drafting of a revocable living trust generally is. The maintenance, conservation, and protection of income-producing assets is deductible, subject to the 2 percent floor for itemized deductions.

⊀ If I set up a revocable living trust, will it help me avoid taxes while I am alive?

No, a revocable living trust will not help you avoid taxes while you are alive. Because you still control all the assets, you still pay the taxes on the income from them.

⊀ My bank is currently managing my assets under a trust arrangement. Isn't the bank's document a revocable living trust?

The agreement you signed with your bank may be a revocable living trust. A legal document sets forth the conditions which determine the nature of the legal relationship. If the document describes itself as a "trust agreement" and identifies the bank as your "trustee," a legal trust relationship probably exists. Whether it is a revocable trust depends on the specific terms of the document. The phrase "revocable living trust," as used by members of the National Network of Estate Planning Attorneys, signifies a very complete statement of your intentions that includes your best thoughts on providing for yourself and your loved ones. The bank's document probably contains inadequate instructions in the event of your disability and no provisions for distribution other than to return the assets to your probate estate.

Trust documents prepared by banks for general usage are commonly known as *letter trusts*. Under these arrangements, you, as the maker, designate the bank's trust department as your trustee but retain the right to revoke the trust arrangement. You are designated as the recipient of all the income. Your estate is designated as the beneficiary upon your death. No provision is made for your disability other than the continuation of income payments to you during your lifetime.

The purpose of the letter trust is to create a specific relationship between you and the bank. The bank is not authorized to be a broker or seller of investment securities. However, the relationship created by the letter trust agreement permits the bank, acting as your trustee, to invest on your behalf and to earn a fee for doing so. These trusts are not designed for estate planning; they are designed to expedite and make easier the bank's investment of your assets.

You should consult your attorney about creating a fully developed revocable living trust as an amendment to the letter trust. In this way, your bank, continuing as your trustee, will have full instructions, in the event of your disability or death, for managing and distributing your assets.

Why do you recommend a revocable living trust as a basic strategy for proper estate planning rather than other traditional methods?

A revocable living trust–centered estate plan meets all the criteria in the definition of estate planning:

- It allows you to control all your affairs and assets during your life and after your death.
- It minimizes taxes, fees, and costs, thereby preserving your wealth.

If you procrastinate and do nothing, the courts will take control of your assets. When you die, your assets will be distributed according to state law; if you become incapacitated, they will be managed by a conservator. The outcome in either case may not be what you want.

With the traditional methods of planning, you can lose control. A will probably will not control all of your assets, and it does not avoid probate when you die. Furthermore, it provides no protection at incapacity. Joint ownership doesn't avoid probate; it just postpones it. If a joint owner becomes incapacitated, the other joint tenant could end up in the probate court. Joint ownership can also cause the unintentional disinheritance of a tenant's own family.

Beneficiary designations are not always effective either. They create problems if the beneficiaries are minors or are disabled or if they have creditor or marriage problems.

Finally, none of the traditional methods is particularly useful as a basic strategy for wealth preservation.

⅍ *If revocable living trusts are such an outstanding planning tool, why do attorneys either downplay their use or fail to recommend them to clients?*

Most attorneys are required to take basic courses in wills and probate administration in law school. Trusts are, in many instances, an elective course. Even though the popularity of revocable living trusts as a basic planning vehicle has blossomed in the last 10 years, many schools and continuing legal education programs have failed to catch up with the public demand.

Many attorneys are also reluctant to recommend this planning tool since they believe it will mean less income for them. They mistakenly believe a relatively small fee for sophisticated planning now is not enough to forgo the eventual probate estate revenue. They fail to realize that clients will complete this planning elsewhere to avoid probate and obtain all the advantages of revocable living trust planning.

Joint Revocable Living Trust

⅍ *What is a joint revocable living trust?*

A *joint revocable living trust* is a single trust created by a married couple that addresses each spouse's wishes as to his or her property. Both spouses are the trust makers, and both are almost always the trustees.

⅍ *Can spouses create a joint living trust if they own their property in joint tenancy?*

Of course. Joint trusts are good estate planning tools for married couples with joint tenancy property. However, allowing property to pass outright to the surviving spouse pursuant to the survivorship feature of joint tenancy may defeat the trust makers' planning, particularly if federal estate tax planning is implemented. With a joint trust, it is important that, during funding, the spouses "sever" the jointly held property into equal ownership between them to prevent the property from passing outright to the surviving spouse upon the first spouse's death.

⅍ *If my spouse and I choose to have a joint trust, are we able to direct the trustee to hold our separate property within the same trust?*

The creation of a joint trust to hold your assets during your lifetime does not preclude either you or your spouse from directing the trustee to hold one or more specific assets for the benefit of either spouse individually.

If individual assets are part of your joint revocable living trust, the trustee must take care to account for the assets and any income derived from them as separate income. This is particularly critical when the trustee is holding separate property for any of the beneficiaries.

Gift tax and asset tax basis issues must be considered when ownership transfers occur. Therefore, the trustee must carefully document any change of ownership from one spouse individually to the spouses jointly.

When establishing the assets in the separate name of either spouse, you must consult local law with regard to the requirements for a full transfer of the ownership rights. This transfer is more complicated in a community property state than it is in a common law state. Your attorney can advise you about the requirements for documenting transactions involving specific individual assets.

If a joint revocable living trust is established with the spouses as cotrustees, may either spouse act independently or is joint action always required?

Generally, either trustee is able to exercise the full powers on behalf of the trust for the benefit of both trust makers. Limitations requiring joint action by the trustees could be written into the revocable living trust, but such limitations make management of the trust cumbersome.

If there is a lack of trust between the spouses, they should consider having a professionally managed trust during their lifetimes or establishing separate trusts. In this way, concerns that a spouse might use the trustee relationship to take advantage of the other spouse are eliminated. A third-party trustee can also play an important role as a financial manager, record keeper, and investment advisor for your trust.

Advantages of Revocable Living Trusts

What are the benefits of a revocable living trust?

Control, cost, convenience, and confidentiality are the four primary reasons that many people turn to trust-centered estate planning.

CONTROL   A fully funded revocable living trust allows the trust maker to retain control of his or her estate planning affairs while avoiding probate and its related pitfalls.

Perhaps the most important attribute of a revocable living trust is that it allows the trust maker to retain control of his or her financial affairs even in the event of disability. Studies have shown that people are much more likely to experience a lengthy period of disability during their lifetime than they are to die suddenly without any period of disability. While a will has absolutely no effect until the will maker has died, a revocable living trust is effective as soon as it is executed by the trust maker. This means that the provisions of the trust can go into effect while the trust maker is alive, so he or she can plan for disability and other issues that may arise during life. Matters including who the successor trustees will be, how the trust maker's medical expenses will be paid, and where the maker will live and what standard of living he or she will retain during the disability can be planned and will take effect immediately upon the trust maker's disability without any need for a living probate. The people designated by the trust maker to handle such matters simply follow the directions that are included within the trust and supplemental documents, including the living will and durable powers of attorney for health care.

In the absence of proper planning, the trust maker's wishes may remain unknown and decisions affecting the trust maker may be left to chance.

COST   Because property that is held by a revocable living trust avoids probate, the cost of administering the trust estate after the maker's death is much lower than the professional fees for administering that same property in the probate process.

With a revocable trust, there is no need to retain an attorney to steer the estate through probate. The directions to the successor trustees for the administration and distribution of the trust property are in the trust document. Of course, the successor trustees may seek the advice of an estate planning attorney and a knowledgeable accountant as needed, but in most cases the assistance required from professional advisors is minimal.

Further, trust estates avoid such costs as filing fees, newspaper publication costs, and other expenses associated with the required notices, hearings, and other procedures dictated by probate laws.

The fees and costs associated with administering an estate using a revocable living trust are nominal. A trustee's fee is based upon the "going rate" of bank trust departments, and national surveys show that the average total cost of administering a revocable living trust estate is less than 1 percent of the gross value of the estate!

Let's compare the costs of probate administration with those of trust administration for an estate of $200,000. On average, the costs associated with administering the probate estate equal $14,000, of which $6000 (3 percent of the gross estate) is the probate attorney's fee, another $6000 is the executor's fee, and the remaining $2000 (1 percent) covers the filing fee, publication costs, probate bond, appraisals, and other costs—a total of 7 percent of the gross estate. Now let's suppose that the estate plan consists of a revocable living trust. The costs of administering the estate are now about $2000, or 1 percent. Use of the living trust eliminated the probate attorney's fee, probate filing fee, publication costs, and probate bond and significantly reduced the executor's fee.

Similarly, living probate proceedings are avoided with proper trust-centered estate planning in which health care agents are appointed and successor trustees are designated in the trust agreement. Living probate–related costs, including attorney fees, filing fees, costs of publication, and the like, are avoided, resulting in preservation of trust assets for the benefit of the trust maker.

CONVENIENCE   While the results of administration of a probate estate or a trust estate are the same—taxes are paid and distributions are made to the beneficiaries—the probate process is cumbersome and time-consuming in comparison to the process of administering a trust estate. The trust maker's specific directions within the trust document address the contingencies of disability and death and appoint successor trustees to carry out those directions.

Upon the disability or death of the trust maker, the successor trustees have legal control of the trust assets immediately, without involvement of any court, so the trust maker's lifetime endeavors may be continued without interruption. If the trust maker was engaged in a business enterprise, the ability to continue its operations is generally critical to the health of the business. In addition, the successor trustees carry out the administration of the trust in a timely manner, whether by creating subtrusts for the benefit of the beneficiaries or by making immediate distributions.

CONFIDENTIALITY   Trusts are private. While wills and the entire probate process are open to the public, trusts remain confidential. For many, this in itself is a compelling factor in favor of revocable living trusts.

Most of us have been reared to keep our financial matters private. It is unlikely that we would discuss our income or net worth with neighbors at a social gathering. However, if you die with a will controlling your affairs, all of your sensitive financial matters are at once open to public scrutiny. Your will and the accompanying inventory of your estate, the value of your assets, and your outstanding debts are all filed with the probate court in the county where you resided at death. Anyone, such as an intrusive neighbor or potential suitor for your business, can simply contact the court, forward a small check to cover the expense of photocopying your estate file, and receive copies of all papers filed in your estate.

Since fully funded trusts are not subject to the rules of the probate court, the inventories, notices to beneficiaries, and accountings of all assets and debts of your estate are not filed with the court and hence not open for public scrutiny.

Disadvantages of Revocable Living Trusts

⋙ *All that you've told me about living trust–centered estate planning sounds really attractive. Are there any disadvantages of a revocable living trust?*

There can be, but they are few in number, and most of these problems depend upon the state(s) in which you own real property. Even when there are disadvantages, the benefits of a revocable living trust usually *far* outweigh the drawbacks.

EXPENSE   One objection to a revocable living trust is that it is more expensive than a will. True enough in some cases. However, a living trust–centered plan is usually only *initially* more expensive than a will. Wills have been priced below cost for years by attorneys who build up huge files of wills and then reap the probate fees in years to come. Although executors do not have to use the attorneys who drafted the wills as their attorneys, most do.

The cost of a will and after-death administration through the probate process almost always exceeds, by a large amount, the cost of a funded living trust and its private after-death administration.

Reducing the cost of death administration is only one benefit of avoiding probate, and avoiding probate is only one (small) benefit of a revocable living trust.

FUNDING   Some people find it annoying to have to determine what they own and how they own it and then have to change the ownership of their property to a living trust. Yes, this can be annoying, but it has to be done only once. And if people think it is a problem for them while they are alive and well, think of what a problem it will be for their spouses or children if they become disabled or die.

The choice is this: People can either "probate" their own estates themselves or pay the courts and lawyers to do it for them after they are no longer around to answer questions such as, "Where is the deed to the house?"

Most people who have gone through the funding process, one piece of property at a time, report that they feel a great sense of relief and peace of mind, knowing that they finally have their records in order—which is actually one more advantage of living trusts.

TENANCY-BY-THE-ENTIRETY PROPERTY   If a husband and wife own property as tenants by the entirety and transfer the property into their revocable living trusts, the property is no longer tenancy-by-the-entirety property. However, for most people, the benefits of tenancy by the entirety are not that substantial.

Tenancy by the entirety is available only in some states and only between spouses. Generally, the creditor of one spouse cannot get at the house to satisfy the debt; the creditor can get only a lien on the house. But this relief is not permanent. When the property is sold, the proceeds of the property may no longer be protected. Also, if a couple's home has a large mortgage, the mortgage is probably the one debt they are really concerned about, but tenancy by the entirety will not protect their home from its own mortgage when both spouses are liable on the mortgage. If the home is close to being paid for, it is likely the couple do not have pressing bankruptcy concerns. Nonetheless, for some couples, under certain circumstances, tenancy-by-the-entirety protection might have enough psychological benefits to warrant keeping the property outside their living trusts until the first spouse passes away or until circumstances change.

There are at least two court cases, one in Hawaii and one in Missouri, which held that tenancy-by-the-entirety property, when transferred into a revocable living trust, retains its status as tenancy by the entirety for purposes of creditor protection. Make sure that you discuss with your estate planning attorney the status of the law in your state regarding this issue.

HOMESTEAD   In some states, homeowners may not be entitled to protections afforded by a declaration of homestead if they place their homes in revocable living trusts. Even in these states, however, there are often ways to title a home so that the benefits of placing the home in a living trust and the declaration of homestead can both be obtained. To what extent a declaration of homestead can protect a home, under what circumstances, and for how long are a matter of state law. Generally, like tenancy by the entirety, it is not permanent protection. And, like tenancy by the entirety, it does not protect the home from claims by the mortgage holder.

Miscellaneous issues Retirement plans and certain professional practices or franchises may require some special handling for living trusts. In some states, real estate transfer taxes may be triggered upon transfer of real property to a trust (this is very rare); the title insurance company may have some particular requirements; or real estate tax breaks available for owner-occupied residences or the elderly or disabled may not be available when real estate is placed in a trust.

If debt-encumbered property is to be held in a living trust, written assurance should be obtained from the lender that the transfer will not trigger a "due-on-sale clause" (by federal statute this cannot happen in regard to a personal-residence mortgage).

This may seem like a long list, but these issues, when they do occur, are minor and rarely outweigh the substantial benefits of a funded revocable living trust. And more and more state legislatures are sweeping away the few remaining and outmoded quirks of state law regarding living trusts.

Your estate planning attorney should guide you through any issues regarding funding your revocable living trust in your state with your particular assets.

⚜ *What are the comparative costs of a will and a living trust?*

The actual costs of wills and trusts vary from community to community. A living trust typically costs more than a will of comparable complexity, but this general rule may be different in any given community. Any cost comparison between the two must factor in the quality of the service given by the attorney, the scope of the services provided, including advice on how title to assets should be held, and the thoroughness of the planning. In addition, you should take into account the probate and administration expenses saved by using a living trust. On a national level, the cost of passing property to a spouse or from one generation to the next through the probate process can range from 3 to 10 percent of the *gross* estate. This figure includes court filing fees; executor commissions; and legal, accounting, and appraisal fees. On the other hand, the same estate plan implemented at death through a living trust typically costs from less than 1 percent up to 1½ percent of the gross estate.

As you can see, a fair cost comparison must include not just the cost of the initial documents but the total cost of passing your property to the next generation.

THE NEED FOR PROPER ESTATE PLANNING

≥\ *What happens if I do no estate planning?*

All of us have planned our estates, whether we know it or not. If you do not have a will or a living trust, the state where you live has an estate plan for you, and you are not likely to hold it in high regard.

Should you become disabled, the court, not you or your family, will choose and appoint a conservator to inventory, appraise, and manage your assets and report the information to the court. That information usually becomes part of the public record. There will be attorney and conservator fees imposed against your estate to pay for this privilege.

When you die, your estate will be subject to probate. Again, your assets will be valued and listed in the public record. Creditors will be individually notified of their right to make claims. And the administrator of the estate and the administrator's attorney will each be entitled to a fee.

Once all the creditors, your administrator, and your attorney have been paid, your assets will be distributed to your beneficiaries according to the preferences set forth in your state's statutes (the laws of intestate succession). If a share passes to your children, it will be given to them immediately and without restriction if they are 18 years of age or older. If a child is not of majority (18 to 21 years of age), a guardian and conservator will be appointed to control his or her person and inheritance until the child reaches the age of majority, at which time the child will receive his or her inheritance, or what's left of it, outright.

If a share is established for your spouse, the size of the share will depend on your state's laws and on the way your property is titled. Your spouse may get all of your estate or very little.

Some assets do not go through probate, but this might not be much better. Life insurance proceeds will pass to whomever you named as the beneficiary. If you forgot one of your children, or if your ex-spouse is still listed as your beneficiary, there may be no recourse because a beneficiary designation supersedes the state's law as to who will receive your property.

Compare this "plan" with the way in which you would like your property to be held and administered in the event of your death or disability. You will probably decide that a plan you design and control is called for.

> *Can't I simply name as beneficiary the person I want to receive my assets or put his or her name on the title with mine and be done with all of this estate planning business?*

Maybe, but not likely. It is important to analyze the nature of the assets you expect to leave behind as well as the individuals you wish to see benefit from them. For some assets, such as an account with a broker, you may not be permitted to name a beneficiary. While in some states you may do so, you need to make sure that your state allows such a beneficiary designation.

Additionally, when you retitle assets in your name and that of another person who is not your spouse, you may be making a taxable gift to that person or setting the stage for some very unfavorable income and estate tax consequences.

Further, by adding another person's name to the title of an asset, you may also be relinquishing your ability to control the asset. Once that person's name is on the title, that person has rights to the property. And so do that person's creditors. You could be subjecting your property to the other person's financial mistakes.

Other problems with this approach include the following:

- Minors cannot receive or control property that is held in their names. If you title an asset in the name of a minor or name a minor as a beneficiary, a guardian must be appointed to handle any property left to that minor. Minors generally will not receive any benefit from property left to them before they reach their age of majority, which is usually 18 years. There are some circumstances under which they will be permitted to use their property prior to age 18, but only with the court's permission.

- Disabled or incompetent beneficiaries cannot receive property directly. An incompetent beneficiary must have a guardian and conservator appointed. A disabled individual may be receiving substantial governmental assistance, eligibility for which could be needlessly jeopardized by naming him or her a beneficiary or titling assets in his or her name.

- If your spouse is not the parent of your children, even if he or she agrees on what to do with the property on your death, there is always the possibility that unintended beneficiaries will ultimately receive your property.

- Perhaps most important, you must consider yourself and your well-being. You may invest substantial time and energy in planning for your loved ones, trying to save them needless expense and red tape, but you have to take these same principles and intentions and turn them inward, toward yourself. You, too, deserve to have the best possible plan to care for yourself. Don't sell yourself short in this process.

Simply adding another's name to the title of your assets or naming beneficiaries does not ensure that any planning or real benefits will result for you. In fact, doing so may create more problems for you and your loved ones. Before taking these steps, see an expert estate planning attorney so that you can determine what your alternatives and consequences really are.

🔖 *I don't really own much. I am married, with two little kids. All that my spouse and I own is titled in joint tenancy with right of survivorship. Do we need any additional planning?*

Yes, you do. Even if joint tenancy with right of survivorship allows the surviving spouse to own assets without probate when one of you dies, it does not provide any protection for your children in the event both of you die in close proximity to one another. If you and your spouse were killed in a tragic accident and neither had a will, who would care for your children and how would they inherit your assets? Without at least a will, the probate court will choose the guardians who will care for your children, and it will choose a financial guardian for your assets. The benefits of providing for yourself in the event of disability to prevent a guardianship over your assets, and the benefits of minimizing taxes and expenses, pale in comparison to the importance and benefit of providing for the care of your minor children.

⚮ *I am single and have no children. Why do I need estate planning?*

A proper estate plan will provide for the distribution of your estate in the way *you* want after your death. Just as important, it will also provide for your care in the event that you become disabled.

One planning concept is to use your assets to do some charitable good after your death. Such charitable gifts either can be made outright upon the person's death or, in larger estates, can be held in trust in perpetuity for charitable purposes. Private charitable foundations and community foundations can retain assets after a person's death and pay the income to various charities according to that person's wishes over a period of time.

One way a single person can accomplish this is by purchasing life insurance on his or her life which would be payable to his or her trust, the ultimate beneficiary of which would be a private charitable foundation or community foundation.

⚮ *Why should I worry about estate planning if I am young and don't have a lot of assets?*

Two common excuses for avoiding estate planning are "I don't have enough assets" and "I'm too young to die." These are misconceptions that can be attributed to a lack of understanding of the consequences of failing to plan and a disinclination to recognize that some day we all die. There are many reasons why estate planning is particularly important when assets are limited.

Estate planning for even modest estates is important because of inflation. This is easily demonstrated through the use of the *Rule of 72,* which holds that 72 divided by the inflation rate equals the number of years it will take to double the size of an estate. For example, if the inflation rate is 5 percent, the rule says that the value of an estate will double every 14.4 years *just because of inflation!* If this seems unlikely to you, just consider how much you paid for your home as compared to the original cost of your parents' homes. Inflation is a certainty of life that simply cannot be ignored. The Rule of 72 does not take into account that the value of assets may grow in excess of the inflation rate. The point is that the value of your life insurance and your house, along with any other assets you may have or acquire, can be significant, especially over time.

The second reason why estate planning is important is because, according to morbidity tables (tables for disability statistics published by insurance companies), the chance of your becoming incapacitated or disabled in the next year is significantly greater than your chance of dying. The absence of an estate plan necessitates a formal, legal guardianship and conservatorship proceeding that involves court costs and the expense of an attorney and would unnecessarily tie up your assets. If you are married and your assets are titled in both your name and your spouse's, those assets will be tied up as well.

In a guardianship and conservatorship proceeding, the court seeks to protect the assets of an incapacitated person, so it requires annual accounting reports justifying the use of assets. Depending upon state law, court permission might be required for the sale of major assets. A performance bond might also be required. The cost of guardianship and conservatorship proceedings far exceeds the cost of an estate plan even for young people with small estates.

In the absence of a proper estate plan, state law determines how assets will be distributed at your death. In states where property is generally owned by married couples in the form of tenancy by the entirety or joint tenancy with right of survivorship, the jointly held property will pass automatically to the surviving joint tenant by operation of law. This may create federal estate tax problems when your spouse dies which could deprive your children of an inheritance.

In states where real property is held by spouses as tenants in common, the absence of a written estate plan results in the assets of the deceased spouse passing to the children, with the surviving spouse receiving only a partial share.

If the children are minors, they cannot hold property in their own names and a formal guardianship proceeding is necessary for the court to appoint the surviving spouse as the guardian. An expensive performance bond may also be required. Since a parent has the obligation to support the children, courts generally do not permit the parent to use the children's assets for their support unless the parent is destitute. A further complication is that the surviving spouse may be unable to handle the present house payments and desire to sell the home. With the children owning part of the equity of the home and portions of the deceased spouse's other assets, the surviving spouse may not have access to those funds to purchase a new home.

Thus, even though a person is young and has few assets now, the adverse consequences of failing to plan can be enormous.

⚭ *At what amount of net worth should I begin to consider estate planning?*

If you have assets and loved ones, you are a strong candidate for considering a revocable living trust–centered estate plan. Although a living trust can be utilized to achieve substantial estate tax savings for estates in excess of the applicable exclusion amount, tax planning is generally not the primary motivation of most clients.

Arguably, a young couple with a relatively small estate and minor children has a greater need for a revocable living trust–centered estate plan than a more affluent couple with no children. The need to provide loving and detailed instructions for the care and well-being of a minor child may greatly exceed the need to do estate tax planning.

The estate planning process should address a host of issues including planning for the trust maker's disability, providing detailed instructions for the care and well-being of the trust maker's family, preserving and expanding wealth, and, finally, avoiding probate and reducing professional fees, court costs, and tax dollars.

Attorneys often ask clients, "What is most important in your life?" Without hesitation, most clients consistently answer, "my family." Clearly, for most clients, tax planning is secondary to planning for their loved ones. The decision to embark on a living trust–centered estate plan is therefore generally not related to the size of a person's estate.

⚭ *My wife and I have about $1 million in assets. Do we need to do any estate tax planning?*

Yes. If you hold title to your assets in joint tenancy or the survivor of the two of you is the beneficiary of any life insurance, the surviving spouse will wind up owning all these assets, and you will lose some significant estate tax benefits.

For example, if one of you died in 1999, that spouse's $650,000 applicable exclusion amount will be lost unless you take steps to preserve it. If you have a combined estate of $950,000, by doing proper estate planning, you can save as much as $115,000 for the benefit of the surviving spouse.

∾ *Since the law is always changing, shouldn't I wait until I am retired to do my estate planning?*

Estate taxes are a creature of a political system that is constantly being pulled in opposite directions by two forces, those with wealth and those without it. This dynamic balance, while relatively stable for the most part, is always subject to movement toward more conservative or more liberal tax policies. It is impossible to predict how far the law may be pulled in one direction or another during any period of time.

Waiting to plan might be the best strategy if you could be guaranteed that you would live through these periods of uncertainty. Unfortunately, life is as uncertain as our political system. If your disability or death might have negative personal and financial consequences for your family, then the time to plan was yesterday.

∾ *Why is it that so many people, even many attorneys, have not availed themselves of estate planning strategies that could save money, protect their loved ones from financial disaster, keep control of their assets and distribute them in the way they want, and avoid the high costs and public scrutiny of probate?*

Statistics indicate that many attorneys do not even have wills. However, just because a person is an attorney doesn't necessarily mean that he or she has expertise in estate planning. For example, the late Chief Justice of the Supreme Court, Warren Burger, attempted to create his own will, only to have it cost his family $400,000 more than would have been paid if he had properly planned his estate.

It is important to find an attorney who is qualified in estate planning, and who will spend the necessary amount of time working with you and your family to learn your needs, values, fears and objectives.

∾ *The questions so far have involved fictional examples of why people need to do estate planning. Are there any examples of real people who could have benefited or did benefit from proper estate planning?*

Let us look at Elvis Aron Presley's estate as an illustration. When the "King of Rock 'n' Roll" died at the age of 42 in August 1977, his gross estate was valued at more than $10 million. His death probate took 12 long years to complete, and his probate file was finally closed in December 1989. A study made in 1991 by Longman Group USA, Inc., shows that Elvis's gross estate shrank by 73 percent after probate, the

TABLE 2-3   Estates of Famous Persons
Settlement Costs and Shrinkage

Name	Gross estate	Settlement costs	Net estate	Shrank
Elvis Presley	$ 10,165,434	$ 7,374,635	$ 2,790,799	73%
J. P. Morgan	17,121,482	11,893,691	5,227,791	69
John D. Rockefeller	26,905,182	17,124,988	9,780,194	64
Frederick Vanderbilt	76,838,530	42,846,112	33,992,419	56
Marilyn Monroe	819,176	448,750	370,426	55
Conrad N. Hilton	199,070,700	105,782,217	93,288,483	53
William E. Boeing	22,386,158	10,589,748	11,796,410	47
Cecil B. DeMille	4,043,607	1,396,064	2,647,543	35
Erle Stanley Gardner	1,795,092	636,705	1,158,387	35
Walt Disney	23,004,851	6,811,943	16,192,908	30
Franklin Roosevelt	1,940,999	574,867	1,366,132	30
Clark Gable	2,806,526	1,101,038	1,705,488	30
Harry M. Warner	8,946,618	2,308,444	6,638,174	26

most dramatic shrinkage among the famous people listed in the study. By the time his settlement costs were paid, about $2.8 million from the original $10 million was left as the net estate. The settlement costs reported in the study include (1) debts, (2) administrative expenses, (3) attorney's fees, (4) executor's fees, (5) state estate tax, and (6) federal estate tax. The settlement costs and shrinkage of other famous people's estates are shown in Table 2-3.

On the other hand, Andy Warhol, by planning with some of the techniques described in this text, minimized the shrinkage of his gross estate of $297,909,396 to 2.3 percent.

Groucho Marx's case gives us a graphic illustration of a *living probate* saga that a person may have to face because of his or her failure to plan for incapacity. Groucho had a will, but it did not do him any good on his incapacity. The last 3 years of his life became a living probate battle, in full view of TV cameras, as three parties vied for control over his wealth and care: his live-in friend Erin Fleming, the Bank of America, and Groucho's family. Day in and day out, he was wheeled in and out of court. There was no respect for his dignity and feelings during the lengthy and spectacular trial.

Erin Fleming went to the probate court in Santa Monica, California, to have Groucho declared mentally incompetent. Groucho Marx was indeed judicially declared incompetent in 1974. In addition, Erin Fleming was named his guardian and also his joint custodian along with the Bank of America. All the court proceedings were open to the public and were covered by the nation's media. The personal life of this famous star was fully exposed. Groucho completely lost control over what was essential to his dignity as a person, namely, his privacy, his personal decisions, and his wealth.

Finally, let us look at Karen Ann Quinlan's case. Karen Ann Quinlan was 21 years old when she slipped into a coma at a party on April 15, 1975. She became a prisoner in a helpless body supported only by medical technology. Her parents, Joseph and Julian Quinlan, decided to take her off the respirator, end her pain, and put her back in a natural state so that she could die in "God's time." However, the doctors at St. Clare's Hospital in Denville, New Jersey, refused to comply with their request because Karen was legally an adult and did not have a living will and a durable power of attorney for health care.

Joseph, her father, had to be appointed her guardian through a living probate, which lasted more than a year. The New Jersey State Supreme Court ruled unanimously in the Quinlans' favor on March 31, 1976. Karen was removed from her respirator in May 1976. When she did not die as expected, she was moved to a nursing home. Her parents never sought to have her feeding tube removed during the 9 years she lived after she was taken off the respirator. She died on June 11, 1985. During those frustrating 10 years the Quinlans had to face mounting health care costs as Karen continued to be cared for. The loss of control over their own affairs disrupted and strained the lives of the Quinlan family.

PART TWO

Planning with a
Revocable Living Trust

Our first book, *The Handbook of Estate Planning,* published in 1981, was considered cutting-edge because we wrote about the superiority of revocable living trust–centered planning over will planning and probate. A great national debate among estate planners raged for the next decade, in which we advanced our revocable living trust arguments in a number of works, including *Loving Trust, The Living Trust Revolution, The Living Trust Workbook,* and *Legacy.* Now, almost 20 years after our first book, revocable living trust–centered planning has prevailed; living trust–centered planning has supplanted will planning and probate by far as the better method of estate planning.

There has been a vast amount of material written about revocable living trusts, how they work, and how they are used in planning. In Chapters 3, 4, and 5, our contributing authors have done a monumental service by condensing a wealth of material into a comprehensive summary of some of the most important issues concerning revocable living trust planning.

Our contributors submitted more research for this text on the subjects of trustees (Chapter 4) and funding of trusts (Chapter 5) than contributors submitted for previous books. Concentration in these two areas is not a surprise. As we all become more familiar with what living trust planning is all about, we want to ensure that our legacy is protected and preserved in the manner that we have set forth. Trustees are charged with following our instructions, so it is logical that there are concerns about who should serve as trustees and what the duties and responsibilities of trustees are.

Just as important is funding a living trust. One of the results of the popularity of living trust planning is that many professionals jump on the bandwagon but they forget the rest of the band! The phenomenon that we see today is a proliferation of revocable living trusts that have not been funded or are partially funded. The result is a client who thinks he or she is protected from probate but is not. Thus a client pays for a revocable living trust–centered plan but does not reap all the benefits because the trust does not own assets. Our contributing authors are fully aware of this trend and have offered many very astute questions and answers to make the funding process understandable.

Revocable living trust–centered planning is clearly superior planning for almost all situations. It can be flexible and thorough, and it offers many safeguards to the maker and his or her loved ones. However, if revocable living trust–centered planning is not properly designed, drafted, and implemented by a competent, well-trained attorney, along with other professional advisors who understand the planning process, it will not reach its full potential. This chapter explains how a revocable living trust–centered plan can be put together in a way that makes it effective for the maker and the people he or she cares about the most.

chapter 3

Creating a Revocable Living Trust

GENERAL CONSIDERATIONS

Should we discuss our estate plan with our children?

This is a very delicate decision that will depend on your family situation, the relationship between you and your children, the relationships among your children, and whether or not your children (and perhaps their children) are treated equally.

Often the ultimate goal is to avoid hard feelings among siblings once the parents are no longer alive. If one child is given more than the others to compensate him or her for having been the parents' caregiver, the siblings should know this so that they do not accuse that child of having undue influence over your decision to give him or her more. If a well-off child is given less than his or her less fortunate brothers and sisters, the reason for this decision should be explained to clarify that it does not indicate a lack of love and affection. If one sibling gets a distribution outright while another's share is held in trust for a number of years, there will be natural resentment unless you explain why, as a parent, you feel it is best for one child to wait and the other not to wait.

A similar discussion should take place among spouses of a second marriage and the children of both marriages. If the children of the first marriage are your ultimate beneficiaries, they should know this so that they do not resent the new stepparent for "taking their inheritance."

99

⚰ *Should I coordinate my estate plan with the estate plans of other family members?*

If you anticipate receiving assets from the estate of a family member or if you contemplate making a family member with estate planning concerns a beneficiary of your plan, the other family member's estate plan must be considered in the development of your estate plan. For example, a family member with significant estate tax concerns may not want to receive additional assets from your plan. In such a case, you may wish to choose a different beneficiary or designate an additional beneficiary since that family member might disclaim the assets he or she is to receive from your plan. If you are to receive assets from the estate of a family member, you may wish to have your estate planning attorney consult with that person's estate planning attorney to coordinate efforts so that your plan is not significantly altered because of your being a beneficiary of the other family member's estate plan.

⚰ *Do I have to let my beneficiaries and successor trustees know what the terms of my trust instrument are?*

One of the many benefits of a revocable living trust is that the wishes of the maker can be kept private and need not be shared with third persons, including family members and named beneficiaries, during the lifetime of the trust maker. Similarly, because the trust is revocable, the trust maker during life can repeatedly amend the trust instrument to change the designated beneficiaries or the distributions to particular beneficiaries without the beneficiaries' knowledge or consent. After the trust maker's death, there is no requirement, as there is with a will, that the trust instrument be filed with the court or any particular authority.

As a practical matter, although the specific terms of a revocable living trust need not be disclosed to family members, relatives, or named trustees prior to a maker's death, the persons selected to serve as trustees should certainly be made aware of the existence of the revocable living trust and their designation as successor trustees after the maker's death. They can then act promptly following a trust maker's death to carry out their duties as trustees. After the trust maker's death, the beneficiaries of the trust will have a right to review the trust instrument so that they can ensure that the successor trustees properly perform their duties and make distributions to the beneficiaries as designated by the trust maker. State law may also allow "heirs at law" to review all or part of the trust to determine whether they are included in the trust.

Is there a way I can tell my children some personal things which are not included in my estate plan?

Certainly. You can write a statement of your memories, thoughts, and feelings toward them. You can keep this statement in a sealed envelope with your other estate planning documents, or your attorney may be willing to keep this envelope and give it to your children after your death. Alternatively, you can make an audiotape or videotape of yourself in which you express your thoughts and feelings to your children. Some clients do both of these things.

I've heard that everyone should have a will. Does my living trust replace a will?

Yes. A properly drafted and fully funded trust-based estate plan replaces a will. However, as a practical matter, a special will called a *pour-over will* should be a part of your revocable living trust plan. While it may not be needed if your trust is fully funded and you do not have minor children, it is an important fail-safe device should you fail to put all your assets into your living trust. A pour-over will "pours" any assets that are not in your trust at death into the living trust so that they can be controlled by the provisions of the trust.

Property subject to this pour-over will might well have to be probated. Whether it will or not depends on the type of property and its value. The vastly superior alternative to using the pour-over will and probate is to make sure that all of your assets are placed into your living trust. If that is done, the pour-over will simply "sleeps" inside the trust plan and is never awakened for use.

How long does it take to set up a revocable living trust?

Typically, it takes about 2 to 3 weeks after the initial consultation to prepare the trust documents. After the trust documents are signed, it is necessary to complete the funding documents that are used to transfer ownership of the assets to the trustee of the trust. This process can take from a few days to several months, depending on the number and types of assets. These time frames can be shortened greatly if an emergency situation exists.

When does my living trust become effective?

A revocable living trust document and all the ancillary documents created as part of a living trust–centered plan become effective when they are properly signed. In order to receive the greatest benefits from a revocable living trust, however, you must retitle your assets in the name of the trustee. (Technically, title is changed to the name of your trustee, rather than the trust itself; but this is a technicality your attorney can help you with.) If you do not accomplish this, any assets not placed in the trust prior to your death may have to go through the probate process before coming under the control of the trust.

⚜ *Will I have to record my trust at the courthouse?*

A few states require that you record a memorandum of trust or an affidavit of trust when you convey real property to your trust. Such an affidavit or memorandum sets forth certain facts about your trust. For example, you would state the name of the trust, who the current and future trustees are, and some of the powers of the trustees with respect to assets owned by the trust. Ordinarily, you would not disclose the beneficiaries of the trust, the portion of the trust property which has been designated for each of the various beneficiaries, or the provisions for distributing the trust property.

⚜ *I don't want anyone to know I have a trust. How do I keep my trust confidential?*

In certain jurisdictions where the recording authorities require that the trust document be recorded, or in the case where you do not want anyone to know that you have a living trust, you can use an additional document called a *nominee partnership* to keep your trust confidential. It acts as an agent for your trust, thereby keeping your trust confidential as an undisclosed principal.

⚜ *If the trust papers are not filed in the courthouse or other places of public record, how are they recognized as legal documents?*

Your trust is much like a contract and is governed by contract law. Since it is not a will, it is not governed by laws pertaining to wills.

When you sign your name to any contract, whether it is for the purchase of a car, an item of personal property, or similar goods, the document is generally not filed in a public forum. Without question, such contracts, once signed, are legal documents and are generally binding upon the parties who have signed them. Likewise, when you sign your trust, it becomes a binding legal document without the necessity of its being filed or made a matter of record.

≈ *What is life like after I put all my assets into a revocable living trust?*

Life goes on just as it did before. It's kind of like putting all your assets into a big box with no lid on it. You can put property in and take it out anytime you want. You have complete control. Unlike you or I, the box doesn't die or become disabled, so court involvement is not needed to carry on your affairs after disability or death. At death, the lid goes on the box and the trust becomes irrevocable.

≈ *If I am trustee of my revocable trust, do I have to have a separate taxpayer identification number and file a separate tax return for the trust?*

No. The Internal Revenue Code classifies a revocable living trust as a "grantor trust." Thus the IRS allows you to use your own Social Security number as the trust's identification number as long as you or your spouse is a trustee of your trust. If you are married and have a joint living trust, you can use either spouse's Social Security number or you can use one person's Social Security number for some assets and the other person's for other assets.

The name of your trust will be on a 1099 form showing interest or other income items, and you will report all your income on your federal income tax return (Form 1040) exactly as you did before you set up your trust. This is because the IRS still considers your revocable trust assets to be your assets.

After your death—or if you have a joint trust, after the death of one spouse—if the trust continues, it must get a separate taxpayer identification number and file a trust income tax return (Form 1041).

≈ *How long is the life of my trust?*

A revocable trust can be terminated by the trust maker at any time, and you can specify the termination provision in your trust document.

If you do not specify a time, all but six states (Alaska, Delaware, Idaho, Illinois, South Dakota, and Wisconsin) limit a trust's length of life. The limitation on how long a trust may last comes from English law and is called the *rule against perpetuities*. English courts wanted to put limits on legal instruments that affected real estate interests so they developed a common law limiting the effect of certain legal documents to a "life or life in being plus 21 years." This English common law doctrine was originally adopted by all the states. Some states, such as

Nevada and Florida, have modified the rule against perpetuities to make it less complex and more certain as to how long a trust can last.

Therefore, in a state with the common law rule against perpetuities, if you create a trust that includes a 3-month old grandchild as a beneficiary and that grandchild lives to be 90 years old, your trust could go on for 21 years beyond that—for 111 years!

ᐅᐱ *Can I change my trust provisions later on?*

Because your trust is revocable, it is a very flexible estate planning device. You may revoke, change, or amend your trust document at any time you wish during your lifetime without penalty.

ᐅᐱ *If there are subsequent changes in the law or changes in my personal circumstances, how do I know my estate plan is still valid?*

It is important for you to recognize that an estate plan is constantly changing. As circumstances in your life change, it may be necessary to amend your plan to reflect those changes. You should review your estate plan at least annually to determine whether you need to amend it. If an amendment is necessary, you should contact your attorney for an appropriate modification of the plan.

Your estate planning attorney should notify you of any change in the law that affects your estate plan and should explain how your plan is affected. The combination of review by you and review by your estate planning attorney will ensure that the plan is effective regardless of how long it may be in force.

LIVING TRUST–CENTERED PLANNING STRATEGIES

Strategies for Everyone

ᐅᐱ *What are some basic estate planning strategies that should always be addressed?*

No two individuals will have the very same estate plan. But there are strategies that we might refer to as *basic* estate planning strategies, because they are employed in most estate plans:

1. Avoid intestacy (dying without a will or living trust).

2. Avoid the probate process to the greatest extent possible, through use of a revocable living trust instead of a will and other techniques.
3. Take advantage of basic tax code provisions that significantly defer and reduce federal estate taxes.
4. Apply the annual gift tax exclusion.
5. Name proper beneficiaries for bank accounts and pension and other retirement accounts.
6. Include directions for handling your financial affairs in the event of your incapacity.
7. Where there is a family business or a family farm, include provisions to enable the business or farm to be continued, sold, transferred, or discontinued as smoothly and efficiently as possible.

It is important to remember that an effective estate plan can be achieved only after a careful and detailed review of all your specific circumstances and objectives.

⚜ *Why should I consider life insurance as part of my estate plan?*

Life insurance plays three basic roles in your estate plan:

1. It provides the funds to replace your income for your loved ones upon your death.
2. It can provide the funds to pay for estate taxes, if necessary.
3. It can replace any wealth that you might leave to a public or private charity. (This is commonly referred to as redirecting your "social capital"—or redirecting the amount of your estate that is subject to estate tax.)

⚜ *How do I make my plan flexible for changes in my circumstances?*

Change is the nature of our world. Over time, laws will change, our family situations will change, our finances will change. Flexibility in planning means two things. First, it means establishing a plan that does not *have* to be revised every time there is a change in the laws or in a family situation. Second, it means establishing a plan that *can* be revised to reflect a change in the laws or in a family situation.

A good professional estate planning attorney will be able to help you identify your goals in such a way that future changes in your family's situation can be addressed now in the plan. A good planner will know how to build flexibility into the plan.

≼ *What documents should I expect to have in my estate plan?*

At a minimum, a proper estate planning portfolio using living trust–centered documentation will often contain:

- A section for personal and family information
- A list indicating the location of original documents
- A list of the names, addresses, and telephone numbers of professional advisors and representatives
- A list of all insurance and annuity contracts which you own, so that your intended beneficiaries will not overlook these assets
- A thorough and easy-to-understand revocable living trust agreement for you; or, if you are married, one trust for you and one for your spouse or a joint trust for both of you, if appropriate
- An affidavit of trust which contains pertinent facts about your trust that can be used to prove the trust's existence while preserving the privacy of its detailed provisions
- Pour-over will(s)
- A memorandum of distribution to dispose of your personal effects (what form this takes will depend upon the state in which you reside)
- Special powers of attorney which designate agents to fund your revocable living trust with any assets that you may acquire after you are disabled and are unable to fund the trust yourself
- A durable special power of attorney for health care which grants your designated agent the power to make medical decisions on your behalf
- A living will which directs your physician as to when to discontinue life-support systems and invasive medical procedures
- Memorial instructions which contain your burial or cremation wishes and information on the type of memorial service that you would like to have
- An anatomical gift form which allows you to make a gift of all or part of your body for medical or dental education and research, therapy, or transplant procedures
- A property agreement which severs and terminates your joint tenancy interests to allow such interests to be properly transferred into your revocable living trust (and your spouse's interests into his or her trust, if applicable)
- A section in which you can insert documentation of the assets which have been transferred into your revocable living trust

- A detailed letter from your attorney setting forth complete instructions for transferring assets into your trust (*The Living Trust Workbook,* by Esperti and Peterson, Viking-Penguin, 1994, is a complete guide on the subject.)

Strategies with Prenuptial Agreements

My spouse and I have a prenuptial agreement. How does it affect our estate planning?

Any prenuptial agreement can dramatically alter or nullify an estate plan. For example, the agreement may contain provisions for the disposition of assets at death, and, if not, it probably defines property ownership—which property is considered separate and which is considered joint. In any event, a marital agreement will likely have a very significant impact on both tax and nontax estate planning, so it is essential that you provide your estate planning attorney with a copy of the agreement.

Because the terms of a marital agreement may conflict with the estate planning goals of one or both spouses, ethical considerations may require that each spouse be represented by a separate estate planning attorney.

I have substantial assets and am thinking about getting married. Could a living trust be used to keep the assets I own before my marriage segregated from property acquired by me and my new spouse during marriage?

Yes, a living trust is an excellent way to keep separate property assets, or assets acquired before a marriage, from being commingled with assets acquired during the marriage. Since the premarital assets are in a living trust, it would be impossible to commingle them with the assets acquired during the marriage unless the commingling was intentional.

To give even more protection, consider coupling a living trust with a premarital property agreement specifying that all the assets in the living trust, along with their increase in value, interest earned, dividends earned, and future appreciation, are immune from the claims of the other spouse and his or her creditors.

To properly accomplish your desire, you must discuss your state's marital property laws with an attorney who practices in this area of the law.

⅋ I am thinking about getting married. Should I consider a pre-
nuptial agreement as part of my estate planning?

Many clients find it hard to consider the need for a prenuptial agreement when they are about to be married. To them, asking their future
spouse to sign such an agreement implies a lack of trust. Consequently,
they miss an important opportunity for estate planning. Obviously, a
young couple without substantial assets usually does not need a prenuptial agreement. But when either of the parties brings significant
financial worth to the marriage or when other factors, such as the
existence of children from a previous marriage, come into play, a prenuptial agreement is particularly warranted.

A prenuptial agreement can cover a wide range of topics, from
sharing future earnings to waiving rights of inheritance to dividing
housework. The most effective prenuptial agreements result when each
party is represented in the process by independent counsel. Independent
representation reduces the chance that a party will be able to set aside
an agreement on the grounds of undue influence, mistake, or fraud.

Full disclosure of assets is also an important factor in creating a
durable prenuptial agreement. With full disclosure, the effectiveness of
a successful attack on the agreement is remote.

Strategies for Single Parents

⅋ I am a single parent with minor children. Is there special plan-
ning I should consider to take care of my children and myself?

As a single parent, it is critical that you design a plan that will designate
a guardian for your minor children and a trust for the management of
any assets they inherit. Generally, if you are divorced, the legal guardian
will automatically be the surviving parent by law. However, there are
times when the surviving parent is unwilling or unable to accept his or
her parental responsibility. Therefore, it is important to designate in
your pour-over will who you would nominate to be your children's
guardian in the event you have the right to do so. In addition, you
should choose the person or institution you believe to be the best to
serve as a trustee to manage your children's assets. For the children's best
interests to be served, select a guardian and trustees who will coordinate
their efforts to care and provide for the children.

It is equally important that you structure a plan to care for yourself
and your children in the event you become disabled. One way of doing
this is to use a power of attorney. Unfortunately, even good powers of

attorney fail because third parties, such as attorneys, banks, and lenders, can choose whether or not they will rely on the document and act on it to release assets. Thus, at the time when you need it, a power of attorney may not be effective, and then a guardianship will be required. Another negative aspect of a power of attorney is that is does not provide any direction to the agents on what action they should take; therefore, agents can make decisions according to what they deem appropriate rather than on the basis of your directions or instructions.

The most effective disability planning tool for providing for yourself and your children is a fully funded living trust. You can include instructions for the care of your children and yourself in the event you become disabled, thereby eliminating the need for a guardianship or conservatorship to manage your assets.

By establishing a carefully drafted living trust plan and transferring your assets into it, you can avoid probate and will be well on the way to implementing a comprehensive estate plan to care and provide for your children and prevent unnecessary hardships, delays, and expenses in the event you become disabled or incapacitated.

Strategies for Single Individuals

Is a living trust a good idea for someone who is single and has no children?

Yes, if you are widowed or divorced or have never married, a living trust offers protection for your estate. It can completely eliminate living probate and death probate. Further, if properly funded, your trust will ensure that your hard-earned wealth will be distributed to those you designate in the trust in the manner that you decide.

What goals should I have if I have no family?

Because more people today are choosing to remain single, and because people in general are living longer, it is becoming more common to encounter individuals who have no families. For such people, the paramount concerns are disability planning—finding the appropriate persons or financial institutions to carry out their decisions regarding disability and health care—and determining their beneficiaries.

Usually, these individuals have lifelong friends who can carry out the decisions and/or be named as beneficiaries, or they participate in worthy causes or organizations that lend themselves to charitable planning.

Strategies for Second Marriages

🔊 *I'm in a second marriage, and I want assurance that my children will inherit my assets. How can I accomplish this goal?*

First, it is important that you have a fully funded living trust–centered estate plan. In some states, a spouse's right to make a claim for a spousal share applies only to assets passing through the probate court. Therefore, in those states, if your assets are held by a living trust, you can provide for your spouse as you deem appropriate without having your plan rewritten by a statutory spousal claim.

Additionally, if you want to provide for your spouse but also want to guarantee that any assets remaining at your spouse's death will go to your children, you could include a specially designed *qualified terminable interest property (QTIP) trust* for your spouse as part of your living trust plan. Such a trust provides to the spouse during his or her lifetime all income generated from the assets held in the trust and the right to make nonproductive property productive.

If guaranteeing your children's inheritance is a central concern, an irrevocable life insurance trust can provide you with the means to pass a definitive amount of funds to your children. If such a trust is properly drafted and maintained, not only will your children receive this benefit but you also receive the benefits of not having the life insurance included in your gross estate and not having to sacrifice any applicable exclusion amount to establish it.

🔊 *I want to take care of my husband but also guarantee that my children from my former marriage are properly taken care of. What strategies can I follow to achieve both goals?*

Here are some alternatives you should consider:

1. To avoid having your children wait until both you and your husband die, consider giving them lifetime advances on their inheritance; or leave them a portion of your estate at the time of your death and the remainder after the death of your husband.
2. You can leave all or a portion of your estate in a QTIP trust. In this way, your husband gets all the income from the assets and the trust qualifies for the marital deduction; yet it preserves as much of the principal as you elect to pass to your children after your husband's death.
3. You and your husband can enter into a postmarriage agreement that clearly sets forth the rights each of you has in the other's estate.

Then you can each create an estate plan that will carry out your planning objectives and will be legally binding.

4. You can trust your husband to carry out your estate plan at his death. This alternative is fraught with danger, however, and should be avoided if you want to guarantee that your children ultimately receive a certain portion of your estate.

My children are adults, established in their careers and financially secure. What's wrong with leaving everything I own to my new spouse and stepchildren, who need it much more than my children do?

There is nothing inherently wrong with disinheriting your adult children. However, in making this choice, consider carefully the emotional and psychological consequences to your children. Even if your children do not need your money, they may feel hurt that you did not leave them an inheritance. If you do disinherit certain children, consider meeting with them and explaining why you have made this particular choice. An alternative way to address this would be to write a letter to them, delivered before or after your death.

My spouse and I each have children from a previous marriage. Are there any special planning strategies we should consider?

When both spouses have children from previous marriages, special care must be taken in the estate planning process. There is no one solution that is right for every situation. Your estate planning team needs to understand your goals and desires for all the children. If the second marriage occurs when the children are adults, the considerations are usually financial. If the children are younger, other issues are involved.

A living trust is a particularly good vehicle for making sure that each spouse's respective property is passed on to his or her own children. It allows you to tailor instructions to your trustee concerning the needs of family members, rather than turning control over to the court.

It is extremely disturbing to hear about situations in which one spouse received property from the other spouse and then left it to his or her own family to the exclusion of the predeceased spouse's children.

You can easily resolve this problem by establishing a trust for the benefit of your surviving spouse and including directions specifying that the balance of your trust estate be passed to your children. You can make whatever provisions you desire for your surviving spouse. He or she can be the trustee and have access to income and principal as you direct. However, the ultimate disposition of the trust estate remains subject to your control and direction.

⚜ *My new bride and I each have two children from previous marriages. Do we have any special estate planning needs?*

Planning for the "blended family" is among the most challenging aspects of basic estate planning. Dying with no will or a simple will almost always produces unintended consequences, frequently with disastrous results. While goal and priority setting is an important part of the estate planning process for everyone, it becomes especially important in meeting the objectives of a blended family if a proper balance between competing interests is to be achieved. Many unsuccessful second marriages might have survived, and certainly much heartache could have been avoided, if these issues had been addressed before the marriage.

⚜ *What are some of the competing interests in a blended family?*

Here are some examples of competing interests which can be present in the blended-family environment:

- Between your children and your new spouse, who is to get what, and when will they get it?
- After the death of your new spouse, will you divide your assets among your children and your spouse's children, or will you give them exclusively to your children?
- Are you leaving your property outright or in trust for the benefit of the children?
- Are you treating assets that were owned by you and your spouse at the time of your marriage the same as assets that are the product of the marriage?
- Do you wish to make gifts to your children or expenditures for their education and health during your life even if doing so means that your new spouse will have less after your death?

⚜ *How do couples in second marriages deal with these issues?*

There is no such thing as a typical answer, not even a majority answer. Experience shows that couples vary dramatically in how they strike a comfortable balance between these competing interests. Among the influencing factors are:

- The relative ages of the two sets of children

- The respective ages of the spouses
- The relative financial, educational, health, and other needs of the spouses and their respective children
- The quality of the relationship between the spouses and their respective relationships with each of the two sets of children

Strategies for Unmarried Couples

⨄ *What special challenges do unmarried couples have in planning their estates?*

The unlimited marital deduction applies only to couples deemed married under state law, making it harder to eliminate estate tax on the death of the first partner of an unmarried couple. One method of paying federal estate tax is to purchase life insurance on each person, using the proceeds to pay the estate tax.

⨄ *My partner and I are not married, but we regard each other as the equivalent of a spouse. Do we have any special planning needs?*

Because the law treats married couples differently from unmarried couples, and because society makes certain assumptions when dealing with a spouse, you and your partner do, indeed, have special planning needs. First, consider carefully what powers and authority you want to give each other during a period of mental incapacity and after death. Then ensure, through a competent attorney, that you each have legally enforceable documents granting those powers and authority. Some states have *presumptive statutes* that make this difficult because family members are favored over others.

Second, consider writing a letter to those family members who might legally or practically presume that they will be in charge of you and your affairs in the event of mental incapacity and after your death. The letter should explain what you have done and why, and it should request that they not interfere with your wishes.

⨄ *My life partner and I are concerned about what will happen should one of us become incapacitated or die. Neither of our families is truly accepting of our relationship. What can we do to protect what we have?*

The marriage contract imposes certain rights and obligations on a husband and wife. Such obligations include the duty to support each other and provide necessaries; in some states, there is protection from disinheritance, and so on. In the absence of such a marriage contract, the partners must fashion their own agreement.

These agreements are sometimes called *living-together agreements* or *prenuptial agreements.* They are enforceable as contracts provided that they are supported by "fair and adequate consideration," which, in this context, generally means that there is full disclosure between the partners. Such agreements can cover almost anything the couple considers important, such as ownership of particular items of property used in the household; how jointly acquired assets are to be divided in the event of a breakup; and each partner's obligation, if any, with respect to supporting a disabled or even unemployed partner, and for how long. Each partner should expect to carry disability income insurance and health insurance.

To protect one another in the event of incompetence or death, each of you should consider living trust–based planning, with cross designation of one another in representative capacities. This will enable each of you to retain control over your joint estate and be involved in the decision-making process. Your living trusts can also handle property distribution on death to avoid probate.

PLANNING FOR
FAMILY MEMBERS

Planning for a Spouse

Am I required by the laws of my state to leave a portion of my assets to my spouse?

The inheritance and succession statutes of most states contain a provision designed to prevent a spouse from being disinherited. Such statutory provisions, often called *elective-share statutes,* entitle a surviving spouse to a minimum distribution from the estate of a deceased spouse and can be used to override the terms of a trust or will. If you do not take this into consideration when designing an estate plan, the enforcement by your spouse of his or her elective share can significantly disrupt the settlement of your estate.

How do I determine whether I have given my spouse at least as much as the elective-share amount if I have provided for my spouse with lifetime interests in one or more trusts?

The answer to this question is a matter of state law about which you should contact an estate planning attorney in your state. However, assuming your state has an elective-share statute, your state code will generally have "commutation rules" which provide a means of valuing a spouse's lifetime interests in the marital trust and any other lifetime trust created for the benefit of a spouse.

Once you have calculated that amount, you can compare it to the elective-share amount to determine whether your spouse would be entitled to an elective-share of your estate.

If I wish to leave assets to my spouse, is there a preferred way to do so?

One of the best ways to leave assets to a spouse is through a revocable living trust. Following are some of the advantages of using revocable living trust planning:

- Probate can be avoided on the deaths of both spouses.
- A living probate can be avoided if the surviving spouse is unable to manage his or her financial affairs after the first spouse dies.
- Federal estate tax may be eliminated on the first spouse's death and either eliminated or substantially reduced on the death of the surviving spouse, depending on the size of the estate.
- A cotrustee can be named to serve with the surviving spouse and provide him or her with asset and financial management assistance.
- By leaving assets in trust, you may provide your spouse with creditor protection if the spouse is sued.
- The assets left in trust can be protected from a later, unsuccessful second marriage of your spouse. Additionally, your surviving spouse may be able to more comfortably refuse to give away assets or to loan money to other family members or friends by stating that the assets were left in trust and cannot be used for those purposes.

How much property can I leave to my spouse without incurring federal estate taxes?

You can leave an unlimited amount to your spouse without paying any federal estate taxes. Every dollar you leave to your spouse qualifies for the marital deduction, which offsets, dollar for dollar, the assets included in your gross estate. Since your gross estate minus your allowable deductions is your taxable estate—the amount on which taxes are paid—the marital deduction can effectively reduce your taxable estate to zero.

Generally the tax law allows use of the marital deduction to cancel the estate taxes on the first spouse's death, but there is a catch: Those assets which qualify for the marital deduction in the first spouse's estate will be taxable in the estate of the surviving spouse, without the benefit of a marital deduction (unless the surviving spouse has remarried).

If you leave all of your property to your spouse, your estate will not pay any estate taxes if your spouse survives you; but upon your spouse's death, the entire value of your property plus your spouse's property will be subject to estate taxes.

⅍ How can my spouse and I save on federal estate taxes by establishing a living trust?

A married couple can create a joint living trust, or each spouse can create a separate living trust. Regardless of whether one or two trusts are used, each trust provides that two subtrusts will spring to life upon the first spouse's death. These subtrusts are designed to keep the property free from estate tax.

There are a number of ways this can be done. In the most basic plan, on the first spouse's death, an amount of cash or property equal to the applicable exclusion amount passes to a *family trust* and the balance to a *marital trust*. The family trust is free of estate tax because of the unified credit; the marital trust is free of tax because of the unlimited marital deduction.

On the death of the surviving spouse, the family trust, no matter what its value, will pass free of federal estate tax to the beneficiaries. In the marital trust, the surviving spouse's applicable exclusion amount will shelter all or part of that spouse's estate, depending on the year of death and the value of the estate; and the balance will be taxed, unless the spouse leaves it to charity.

The end result? A tax savings of as much as $435,000 on an estate of $2 million. See Figures 3-1 and 3-2 for a comparison of basic two-trust planning and no planning.

⅍ How is this $435,000 of tax savings generated?

With subtrust planning, both spouses can use their applicable exclusion amounts. If they relied solely on the marital deduction, they would waste one of those applicable exclusion amounts. If the date of death is

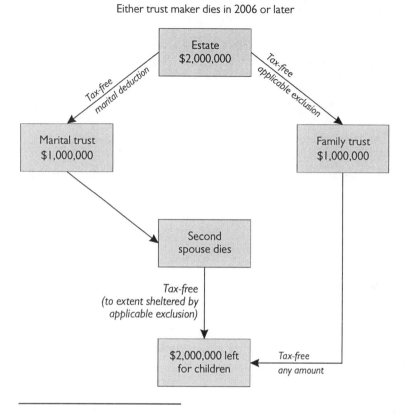

Figure 3-1 *Basic two-trust plan.*

2006 or later, the savings are $435,000. If death occurs earlier, the amount saved varies: $258,500 in 1999, $270,750 in 2000 and 2001, $283,000 in 2002 and 2003, $358,500 in 2004, and $409,500 in 2005.

⚜ *How can a marital trust qualify for the marital deduction?*

Under the Internal Revenue Code, a trust qualifies for the marital deduction if it meets certain criteria. These include:

- The spouse must have the right to all of the trust's income, paid at least annually, for life.
- The spouse must be the only lifetime beneficiary of the trust; none of the income or principal can be paid to anyone else while the spouse is living.
- The spouse must be able to direct the trustee to convert assets that do not produce income to income-producing assets.

Either spouse dies in 2006 or later

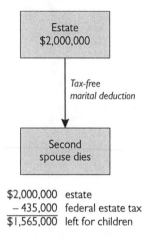

$2,000,000   estate
  – 435,000   federal estate tax
$1,565,000   left for children

Figure 3-2 *No planning.*

If these criteria are met, the trust qualifies for the marital deduction. Of course, these are the minimum requirements. The spouse can be given more rights to a marital trust, but not less.

≛ *What about a family trust? What rights must be given to a spouse?*

There is no requirement that a spouse be given any rights in a family trust. In fact, a family trust is designed so that it will be subject to estate tax at the maker's death and will not be included in the surviving spouse's estate upon his or her death. Remember, this trust's assets are sheltered from tax by the applicable exclusion amount, so even though the family trust is estate-taxable at the first spouse's death, there is no estate tax liability.

Typically, a spouse is given rights to the income and principal in a family trust. It is not uncommon for a spouse to have the absolute right to income in the family trust and the right to use the principal under certain circumstances. The family trust can be drafted liberally to allow a great deal of spousal rights, although the surviving spouse cannot have unrestricted access to the principal or the trust will be included in his or her estate. The terms of a family trust are drafted by your attorney after he or she fully understands your financial situation and your planning goals.

⚔ *As the value of the family trust grows, will any increase over the initial applicable exclusion amount be subject to estate tax at my spouse's death?*

The family trust is designed to be tax-free when the first spouse dies. The value of the family trust is equal to the applicable exclusion amount, meaning that no tax is due. If the family trust is properly drafted and administered, it is not included in the estate of the second spouse to die, regardless of how much it has grown.

⚔ *How important is the fact that the family trust, no matter how large it grows, will not be subject to estate tax when the surviving spouse dies?*

The family trust's tax-free benefit can be significant. A simple approximation of the value of the family trust in the future can be calculated using the *Rule of 72*. This rule states that if you divide 72 by the interest rate or rate of growth of an asset, the result is the number of years it takes to double that asset. For example, 72 divided by 7.2 equals 10; that is, it takes 10 years to double the asset at 7.2 percent growth. The recent equities market has produced returns in excess of 14.4 percent, which, when divided into 72, results in 5; it takes 5 years to double an asset at 14.4 percent growth. Minimal inflation of 3.6 percent divided into 72 equals 20, so it takes 20 years to double an asset at the inflation rate. If we apply the growth rate of 7.2 percent to the family trust and assume that your spouse will survive you by 20 years, the value of the family trust will double twice. The entire family trust will pass to your children free of federal estate tax, no matter how large it has grown.

⚔ *What is the best possible way to protect my estate for my children, provide for my spouse, and defer federal estate tax?*

The best approach is to create a *qualified terminable interest property (QTIP) trust* in your living trust document. A QTIP is a type of marital trust that qualifies for the unlimited marital deduction. After you are deceased, all or part of your assets passes to the QTIP trust. Your spouse is the only beneficiary of the QTIP trust, and the trust continues for his or her lifetime. Upon your spouse's death, the remaining trust assets pass to your children according to the terms of your trust. QTIP trusts are discussed in detail in Chapter 6.

➷ *What are the maximum rights my spouse can have in my family trust?*

The maximum rights a spouse can be given in a family trust without having the value of the trust included (and thus taxed) in his or her estate are the rights to:

- Receive all the income
- Receive the greater of 5 percent or $5000 of the trust's principal each year
- Receive any or all of the principal in the trustee's discretion
- Appoint the property, through a limited testamentary power, to any recipient other than the spouse's estate or the creditors of his or her estate

If you were to grant your spouse greater rights than these in the family trust, your spouse would be deemed to control the assets and, at his or her death, the full value of the trust property would be included in his or her estate for tax purposes—the very outcome you sought to avoid by using the family trust.

➷ *What are the minimum rights I can give my spouse in my family trust?*

If your spouse either consents to give up his or her rights or receives property of yours at your death that suffices to comply with your state's rules, your family trust does not have to provide for your spouse.

➷ *Will there be an income tax on the family trust's income?*

Yes, the income earned on the assets in the family trust will generate an income tax, which must be paid by the trust if the income is retained in the trust. If the income is distributed to the surviving spouse or to the children, they must report and pay income tax on the trust income at their respective tax brackets. The trust receives a deduction for the amounts distributed so that the trust income is taxed only once.

➷ *Do the assets in the family trust receive a stepped-up basis upon the death of either spouse?*

On the death of the first spouse, the assets in a family trust receive a step-up in basis because they are included in the deceased spouse's estate. However, upon the death of the surviving spouse, the assets distributed from the family trust do not receive a stepped-up basis. Since assets held in the family trust are not included in the surviving spouse's estate (they pass to the beneficiaries of the family trust free of estate tax), they do not receive a step-up in basis at the death of the surviving spouse.

Since the assets in the family trust do not receive a stepped-up basis upon the death of the surviving spouse, would we be better off to forgo the use of the family trust altogether?

You would not be better off if, on the death of the second of you to die, there is a federal estate tax due. The federal estate tax rates range from 37 to 55 percent (60 percent on estates between $10,000,000 and $21,040,000). The federal income tax rates on capital gains are considerably less at 20 percent for most assets, and they apply only to the excess of the money received for the asset over its tax basis. Even considering state income tax on capital gains, which can increase capital gain taxes by as much as 8 percent in some states, in a taxable estate you will always be better off passing property by using your applicable exclusion amount than you would be if you retained the property in the survivor's estate in order to obtain a step-up in basis at the time of the second death.

My spouse and I are having revocable living trusts drafted, and we are discussing the division of our assets between the two trusts. I am concerned about taking assets that were titled to me and transferring them to my spouse's trust. In the event of a divorce, do I retain the assets that were in my name prior to the transfer to my spouse's trust?

In most states, during a divorce proceeding, property is divided into either "marital property," which is subject to "equitable distribution" by the court, or "nonmarital property," which is not subject to equitable distribution. Generally, the manner in which assets are titled does not affect their classification as either marital or nonmarital property: the court will categorize the assets under the state's guidelines and will distribute property without regard to whose name appears on the title. Thus, whose living trust holds title to which assets is of little consequence in a divorce proceeding.

My spouse and I have an estate over $650,000. Rather than

doing a trust now, can we wait until one of us dies and set up a trust at that time?

Your question assumes that when you or your spouse dies, the survivor will have the capacity to create a trust; this may not be the case. It also assumes that you and your spouse will not die simultaneously; this, too, may not be the case. Both of these possibilities should be considered in your planning.

In addition, one of the purposes of a living trust is to preserve both spouse's applicable exclusion amounts (so that both can pass the maximum amount estate tax–free to their heirs). Since your applicable exclusion amount belongs to you, and not to your spouse, you are the only person who can make the arrangements under your estate plan to use it. In other words, your applicable exclusion amount is not an election that your spouse can make after your death. While your spouse can set up a living trust after your death, your spouse will be limited to his or her own applicable exclusion amount. Therefore, you and your spouse should establish and fund your separate revocable living trusts or joint trust while both of you are living.

≫ *I want to make sure that the money I made during my life goes to my children and not to someone my husband marries after I'm gone. What can I do to prevent that?*

You can have your attorney add a clause to your trust which, in the event of remarriage, shuts off access to the income or principal, or both, of the family trust and to the principal of the marital trust. (Remember, your husband must be able to receive all the income from the marital trust for his life in order to qualify that trust for the marital deduction.) You can also provide that if your husband's marriage ends for any reason, he can once again benefit from the provisions that were terminated at the time of the remarriage.

When you use this provision, it is important that the trustee of the living trust be someone other than your husband or that there be a cotrustee serving with your husband. If your husband were the sole trustee, he could deplete the marital and family trusts before the children knew about the remarriage provision. The children would then be at the point of having to sue your husband or possibly lose the funds.

≫ *My husband and I do not have a good marriage; we are staying married for the benefit of the children. Although we live in a community property state, I have quite a bit of separate rental* *real estate property. If something happens to me, I want to make sure the children are provided for. Can I do that?*

Yes. You can leave all your separate property in trust, with the income to benefit your children. In order to ensure that your wishes are followed, and because you may not feel comfortable with your husband as the trustee, you may want to name a corporate trustee, such as a bank trust department or an established trust company.

Planning for Noncitizen Spouses

Do I or my spouse qualify for the unlimited marital deduction if my spouse is not a U.S. citizen?

Federal estate tax law requires that a surviving spouse be a U.S. citizen in order to qualify for the unlimited marital deduction. There is a valid reason for this: Congress does not want a surviving noncitizen spouse to leave the United States with property that has never been taxed. The citizen spouse's estate still benefits from the applicable exclusion amount. The estate of the U.S. citizen decedent will have to pay federal estate taxes on everything over the applicable exclusion amount unless the surviving noncitizen spouse is the beneficiary of a special marital trust called a *qualified domestic trust (QDOT)*.

What are the requirements of a QDOT?

To qualify as a QDOT, a marital trust must meet the following requirements:

- At least one trustee must be a *U.S. trustee,* that is, a U.S. citizen or a domestic corporation. This trustee can be a cotrustee.
- A QDOT with assets over $2 million must have a U.S. bank as trustee. If it does not, a bond or letter of credit equal to 65 percent of the QDOT assets must be posted with the IRS.
- If the QDOT has assets under $2 million and has more than 35 percent of its value in non-U.S. real property, the trust must meet either the bank or bond requirement.
- The trust instrument must provide that no distribution (other than one of income) may be made from the trust unless the U.S. trustee has the right to withhold the estate tax imposed on the distribution.
- The trust must meet U.S. Treasury requirements regarding the collection of estate tax on distributions of principal.
- The decedent's personal representative of the will, or the trustee of

the decedent's revocable trust if there is no personal representative, must make an election on the decedent's estate tax return to have the trust treated as a qualified domestic trust.

■ A QDOT must be maintained and administered under the laws of a state in the United States, although the trust does not have to be in the United States.

A QDOT must constitute an ordinary trust: a trustee must take title to property for purposes of conserving it for beneficiaries.

⌲ Can my noncitizen spouse receive the trust's income?

Your spouse can receive the income, just as a citizen spouse can, and will pay federal income tax on the income he or she receives.

⌲ What happens if my spouse becomes a citizen after the date of my QDOT?

If your noncitizen surviving spouse becomes a citizen before the estate tax return is due, none of the QDOT rules will apply.

⌲ I am a U.S. citizen and have a considerable estate. My spouse is not a U.S. citizen. How can we minimize our federal estate tax costs and also avoid the inflexibility of a QDOT?

A U.S. citizen spouse may make annual exclusion gifts to his or her noncitizen spouse of up to $100,000 a year. (It is not clear as to whether the law allows this annual exclusion amount to be indexed for inflation as is the $10,000 annual exclusion.) The $100,000 annual exclusion provides a great planning opportunity. The gifts of cash can be leveraged by using the funds to purchase life insurance on your life. Life insurance is highly recommended in circumstances where one's financial objectives for a surviving noncitizen spouse cannot otherwise be accomplished without estate tax liability or the restrictions of a QDOT.

Your noncitizen spouse (or a trust you fund for his or her benefit) could purchase a life insurance policy on your life and pay annual premiums from your annual gifts of $100,000. Your noncitizen spouse (or trust) could be designated as the policy owner and beneficiary. The life insurance proceeds paid upon your death will not be part of your estate and will be totally tax free to your noncitizen spouse as beneficiary of the policy. Your noncitizen spouse could then use the proceeds as he or she desires (including purchasing assets from your estate if liquidity is needed) or take the insurance proceeds out of the United States and have no liability for the estate tax upon his or her subsequent death.

Planning for Children

⊰ *Is there a way to plan now for the maximum amount to pass to our children when the second of us dies?*

Yes. The surviving spouse's strategy for investment and distribution of marital and family trust property can be structured to pass the largest amount possible to the next generation. The decision to maximize amounts passing to children is usually made after reviewing the terms of the family trust and after the surviving spouse determines that he or she can live primarily from the income and principal from the marital trust. For example, the surviving spouse may decline to take all or part of the income from the family trust and may decide never to take distributions of principal. The surviving spouse may, instead, spend only out of the marital trust, with the goal of keeping that trust's property total under the applicable exclusion amount.

This strategy means that the family trust will continue to grow and, upon the surviving spouse's death, will pass to the children free of estate tax. The only property taxed on the second death will be the value of the surviving spouse's estate—the marital trust plus any property owned by the surviving spouse outside of the marital trust. The total of that property can frequently be kept below the applicable exclusion amount through the surviving spouse's spending and making lifetime gifts.

Minor children

⊰ *Why is planning for minors important?*

Virtually all parents want to pass their estates to their children. Unfortunately, whether assets are passed to minor children through beneficiary designations, as a result of joint tenancy, or under the terms of a simple will or bare-bones trust, the assets are often passed without adequate instructions concerning the use of the funds.

Minors cannot own and use assets. Before a minor will be able to use inherited assets, the court must appoint a guardian or conservator to manage the assets for and on behalf of the child under the direction of the court. This process can be expensive and time-consuming.

It is much more sensible to pass the assets under the terms of a revocable living trust. Parents may include instructions in the trust regarding the use of assets for the benefit of their minor children, and they may empower a trustee to handle the assets in accordance with those instructions. Parents can specify the amounts and times of distributions and may provide that the children receive their funds at different times or at different ages, depending upon the personality and character of each child.

Revocable living trust planning affords parents the opportunity to provide for individual children according to each child's unique needs and in ways that will best fulfill their desires for each child.

⅍ *My spouse and I want to ensure that if we both die unexpectedly, our minor child will be cared for according to our wishes. How do you suggest we approach an overall plan to accomplish this?*

Adequately providing for your children may be the most important estate planning issue you face. You must first decide who will be the nurturing parent or guardian for your minor child. Who would provide the best home, give the most love, and care for your child's needs? This person may or may not be the best equipped to handle financial and investment decisions. Therefore, your second decision is to select the proper person or entity that can best implement a financial plan and manage the assets you want to provide for your child.

The next step is to establish a plan which incorporates these decisions. Either a will or a revocable living trust allows you to establish a trust for the purpose of holding assets for the benefit of your minor child. The terms of the trust should provide guidance for the trustee and specify when distributions are appropriate and how they are to be made. Individualized instructions can be designed for each child. You can provide broad, general directions or very specific incentive plans which provide guidelines for college education, the purchase of a home or automobile, a wedding, or other significant events. The essential point is that you must take action and establish a plan. It can always be modified and tailored to meet specific needs over time.

⅍ *My husband and I are expecting our first child. Do we need to wait until after the baby is born to do estate planning?*

No, you can establish a plan immediately, as long as you include a provision in your plan stating that it is made in contemplation of the birth or adoption of a child or children. In fact, before the baby's birth is an ideal time to meet with your advisors to begin considering the changes that the new addition to your family will make for you personally and financially. There are decisions you will want to make about naming guardians for your child. There are decisions about the amount and type of insurance coverage you will need to provide for your child and his or her education expenses.

If you wait until after the birth of the baby, you will probably be too busy dealing with the immediate needs of your lives to find any time for addressing these important issues. Before the sleepless nights and endless diapers bombard you, take time to talk together about your goals and dreams and the way you plan to meet the needs of your little one so that you can prepare an appropriate plan. This type of planning is very positive and can provide a tremendous sense of peace and well-being.

⋈ Our children are infants. How can we make sure that we adequately provide for them?

In planning for young children, it is important to assess what their personal nurturing and parenting needs will be, as well as their financial needs, if one or both of you die. Your personal team of professional advisors can offer assistance and counseling through this process.

Most parents have thought about these issues and realize their great importance. Unfortunately, most of them exercise more caution in selecting a baby-sitter for one evening than they do in planning who will care for their children and their money if they die. This is not a deliberate failure or neglect of their children's needs. Rather, they don't plan because they believe "it's not urgent," or "it's expensive," or "it's a negative thing to think about," or because they "just can't decide who to choose." As difficult as such decisions are to address, they are crucial to the welfare of children. If planning questions go unanswered, a child's life can be completely devastated.

When children are involved, it is better to have some kind of plan than no plan at all.

⋈ What happens if I do not leave a plan for my minor children?

If you do not plan for the needs of your minor children, a court will take charge of your assets in a guardianship. Even if you nominate the guardian, it is the court, rather than the guardian, that has the final say. Not only is the guardianship process expensive, but there is no way to ensure that the court will carry out your values and desires for your children. Also, court jurisdiction and the guardianship ends when your minor children reach majority, which in most states is age 18. At this time, the children are given unconditional control of their property.

In addition, in a guardianship, the funds for each child are maintained in separate accounts. The court does not allocate more money to one child even if that child has greater needs. Thus, if one of your children has health problems or special needs and all of his or her share is used, the court cannot divert part of the funds of another child whose share is more than adequate for his or her needs. All children are treated equally, even if they have unequal needs.

☙ In planning my estate, how do I take into account the 20-year age difference between my children?

Start by asking yourself how you would treat your children if you were still alive when they are to receive their inheritances. If your oldest children have already been provided with a college education, a wedding, or a down payment on a house, would you want to make sure your youngest children have those same benefits? If your estate is measured in millions, there is enough money available for everyone. However, if you have a more modest estate, you should consider the use of a *common trust.*

A common trust, which can be incorporated into a will or a living trust, states that, on the deaths of both you and your spouse, all your assets will continue to be held in trust for the benefit of all your children until your youngest child reaches a certain age, which you designate, or until your youngest graduates from college. At that point, the common trust can be divided into separate shares for each of your children. Their separate shares can either be distributed then or continue to be held in trust and be distributed later at specified ages.

This technique allows you to make sure that your youngest children receive the same benefits that your older children received, just as you would have done if you were still alive.

☙ When should the common trust terminate?

There are many alternatives as to when the common trust terminates. One of the most common approaches is to have the trust end when the youngest child reaches a certain age, such as 23, or when the youngest child reaches a certain age or completes college, whichever occurs first. At that time, any remaining trust property is divided equally (or otherwise, as you designate) into separate shares for each child. You can instruct the trustee to distribute the property in a lump sum or in some other way, depending on the provisions in your trust.

☙ When will my children be old enough to properly manage their inheritances?

The legal age of adulthood and—unless otherwise planned and provided for by the parents—the time at which a child is entitled to receive his or her inheritance is generally the age of 18, although this age may vary on the basis of circumstance and state law. Since it is often difficult to know how well an 18-year-old will manage money, parents are sometimes concerned about a lump-sum distribution to children. In some cases, this is true even though the children are already adults at the time the estate plan is established.

In a revocable living trust, you can provide a trustee with specific directions regarding how and when distributions should be made to your children. It isn't uncommon in the situations just mentioned for parents to stretch out an inheritance over a period of years and stagger the distributions at ages 30, 35, and 40, for example. In this way, if the child mishandles the first distribution, he or she has two more chances to learn to manage the money or property responsibly. Some parents simply plan to distribute the income from the trust quarterly or annually during the child's life to ensure that the child always has access to money, but in small-enough portions that poor decision making won't wipe out the full inheritance.

Parents who have such concerns need to know that they can achieve their goal of providing support to their children without worrying that the children will accidently or purposefully undermine that goal.

Special children

⅍ *How should the needs of a special child be met?*

A family with a special-needs child faces many challenges, but perhaps none is more wrenching than trying to deal with an uncertain future and make an estate plan for that child. Parents want to ensure the financial well-being of their disabled child, and the needs of such a child may continue long after the parents are gone.

For many persons with disabilities, losing eligibility for benefits is not an option. Persons with physical or mental disabilities often rely on public benefits to pay or supplement the cost of attendant care, medical care, wheelchairs, and rehabilitation. Public benefits may also provide for other basics such as food, clothing, and shelter. Historically, families resorted to the very unsatisfactory arrangement of either disinheriting the disabled person or leaving the disabled child's share to siblings to avoid losing benefits. A much better solution is the *special-needs trust.*

The future of many essential government benefits for persons with disabilities is uncertain. There is a growing trend for the federal and state governments to provide fewer resources for persons with disabilities. Many people feel that providing for care will increasingly fall upon families, churches, and nonprofit organizations in the future.

A special-needs trust can enable a disabled person to inherit property without jeopardizing eligibility for government benefits, can coordinate the parents' estate plan so that the child will be provided for if the parents become disabled or die, and can protect the assets from the child's creditors.

To ensure that their special child will be cared for most effectively, the parents must have a carefully thought-out plan, and the plan must be flexible enough to work despite an uncertain future. A proper estate plan will focus on achieving as much independence as possible for the disabled beneficiary.

⚜ How does a special-needs trust protect my disabled son's eligibility for public benefits and still take care of his day-to-day needs?

A special-needs trust protects eligibility for public benefits by *supplementing*, rather than replacing, essential government benefits that your son may be receiving or might later be eligible for from various government assistance programs.

The purpose of the special-needs trust is to cover items that government benefits do *not* pay for: trips to visit family members, reading material, educational tools, and over-the-counter medicines are just a few of the many purchases that can be made on behalf of the beneficiary. Assets in a special-needs trust can also be used to pay for programs of training, education, treatment, and rehabilitation not covered by public benefits. The trust may also provide for certain recreation, entertainment, and consumer-goods expenses that enhance the beneficiary's self-esteem. A well-planned and well-managed special-needs trust can serve as a safety net to provide for your son throughout his life.

⚜ What specifically are "special needs"?

Special needs are any items that are essential for maintaining the comfort and happiness of a disabled person and that are not being provided by any public or private agency. Special needs include medical and dental expenses not covered by Medicaid, annual independent checkups, equipment, training, education, treatment, rehabilitation, eyeglasses, transportation (including vehicle purchase and maintenance), insurance (including payment of premiums on life insurance for the beneficiary), and essential dietary needs. Special needs may also include electronic equipment such as radios, CD players, television sets, and computer equipment; camping, vacations, athletic contests, movies, and travel; money to purchase appropriate gifts for relatives and friends; payments for a companion or attendant; and other items to enhance self-esteem.

⋈ Does the Social Security Administration allow special-needs trusts?

Yes. In 1975, the Social Security Administration established rules allowing assets to be held in trust for a recipient of Supplemental Security Income (SSI) as long as the disabled beneficiary (1) cannot control the amount or the frequency of trust distributions and (2) cannot revoke the trust and use the trust assets for his or her personal benefit.

⋈ Can the disabled person act as a trustee of a special-needs trust?

No. The whole premise of a special-needs trust is that the disabled beneficiary cannot be considered to have control over the principal or income of the trust. The assets of the trust are for the benefit of the disabled person, but he or she has no power or authority to direct the payment of funds.

⋈ Who acts as a trustee of a special-needs trust?

Families fortunate enough to have responsible, nondisabled members can name one (or more) of these family members to serve as trustee for the disabled child. Since the sibling or other relative will likely be very familiar with the needs, wants, and desires of the disabled beneficiary, proper discretionary decisions can be made for the benefit of the beneficiary.

For families that do not have such trustees readily available, the selection of the trustee becomes much more difficult. Special organizations have been formed in some states to serve as trustees for the disabled; they are designed to protect a disabled beneficiary's funds from creditors while preserving the right to receive governmental assistance such as SSI and Medicaid. Such organizations typically have a master trust and use an individual adoption agreement for purposes of implementing the special-needs trust. Depending upon the desires of the trust maker, the organization can serve as trustee of the special-needs trust, using its sole discretion for the benefit of the disabled family member, or it can invest and preserve the assets while working in conjunction with the recommendations of a contact person designated in the adoption agreement. The contact person can be a relative or friend selected by the trust maker for making discretionary decisions. Since the organization is able to pool several individual special-needs trusts, management fees are much less than would normally be charged for a private, individual trust, making smaller trusts financially viable.

Once the individual adoption agreement has been properly established, the trust maker may fund the trust currently with gifts or after the trust maker's death with life insurance, individual retirement accounts, retirement plans, or other devices utilizing the beneficiary designation.

⚜ Who can establish a special-needs trust?

Parents or other family members of a disabled child can establish a special-needs trust as part of their general estate plan. A special-needs trust can be part of a parent's living trust, or it can be a separate, *stand-alone* trust. A stand-alone special-needs trust solely for the disabled child has the advantage of being available to be the recipient of gifts from other concerned family members such as grandparents and friends.

⚜ Aren't all special-needs trusts the same?

No. A "boilerplate" special-needs trust, focusing solely on preservation of public benefits, achieves limited goals and objectives and can condemn a disabled person to a lifetime of dependence. A proper special-needs trust should focus first on the specific needs of the disabled beneficiary, needs of the family, and preservation of wealth and lastly on preservation of public benefits. Many of the public programs allow the beneficiary to own no more than $2000 in cash including SSI and Medicaid.

In some cases, a well-planned special-needs trust can enable the beneficiary to eventually become independent and no longer require public benefits. In many other cases, it allows the beneficiary to maintain a dignified quality of life while he or she remains on benefits indefinitely. If public benefits help achieve independence, the eligibility for benefits should be maintained. Benefit programs such as SSI and Medicaid allow very limited income and resources to be controlled by the disabled beneficiary.

⚜ What provisions should be considered when creating a special-needs trust?

The primary goal in creating a special-needs trust is to benefit the special beneficiary in a way that does not disrupt any government benefits that he or she may be receiving. In order to effectively accomplish this goal, the special-needs trust should address the following issues.

PROHIBITION AGAINST PROVIDING SUPPORT   If a beneficiary receives support from any source, including a trust, the amount of governmental assistance can be reduced on a dollar-for-dollar basis. *Support* includes such things as food, clothing, and shelter for the beneficiary. The trustee of the special-needs trust should be directed to provide *nonsupport* distributions.

In addition, the negative effect of providing for support items can be minimized by taking advantage of the *presumed maximum value rule.* Under this rule, if noncash distributions for support items are made, they are presumed to have a monthly maximum fair market value of $177, so the SSI benefits will not be reduced more than $177 per month. Therefore, with proper drafting, making less frequent in-kind distributions having a value well in excess of $177 each will yield a much greater benefit to the beneficiary than making smaller distributions every month. Typically, an annual distribution large enough to supplement the beneficiary's needs over the entire course of the year would provide the best benefit. For the trustee to be permitted to make distributions for support purposes, the trust should specify that the trustee has the sole discretion to determine that the government benefits available to the beneficiary are inadequate for meeting his or her basic subsistence needs.

LIMITATION ON CASH DISTRIBUTIONS   Typically, cash distributions are to be discouraged or prohibited unless special situations arise that would prevent the beneficiary from receiving the necessary benefits of the trust. For example, if the beneficiary has a terminal condition in which the life expectancy is not ascertainable (e.g., an HIV-positive diagnosis) or if there is a concern that future reductions in government support would reduce the beneficiary below subsistence-level existence, cash distributions may be desirable. If cash is to be distributed, the specific situations under which the distributions can be made should be clearly defined to minimize the amount of lost public benefits.

IDENTIFICATION OF THE NONSUPPORT PURPOSE OF THE TRUST   The trust should specify that it is the trust maker's intent to have the government benefit program provide for the supportive care and that the purpose of the trust is to provide for the nonsupport requirements of the beneficiary. The trust should further specify that it is the intent of the maker not to make the beneficiary ineligible for any existing or future benefits.

Prohibition of beneficiary directive power   The trustee should have sole discretion over distributions from the trust, and the beneficiary should not be authorized in any respect to infringe upon the trustee's discretion.

Identification of nonsupport expenses or permitted uses   If the trust maker has specific purposes in creating the special-needs trust, they can be identified. For example, the trust can direct that payments for school tuition and education may be made, and such payments will not affect benefits as long as the expenditures are not for room and board, which are considered support. Similarly, the trust can state that assets may be utilized to create burial trusts or long-term service contracts or to provide for other types of nonsupport expenses specified by the trust maker, such as the costs of attending family gatherings.

Payment of home-ownership expenses   Although a home is considered to be a "noncountable" asset for purposes of obtaining SSI or medical assistance, the payment of real estate taxes or a mortgage could be deemed to be a contribution toward housing and result in a loss of benefits. However, by making use of the rule that in-kind distributions have a presumed maximum value of $177 per month, mortgage obligations or real estate taxes for an entire year could be paid in a single month to minimize the impact of the loss of benefits. Non-interest-bearing loans are not counted as either income or assets as long as the funds are expended in the month received, and distributions could be made to correspond with the due date of real estate taxes or home repairs.

Through a properly prepared special-needs trust, a trust maker can significantly increase the quality of the disabled loved one's life and minimize or eliminate any loss of government benefits to which the beneficiary is entitled.

⋙ *What assets can be held in a special-needs trust?*

Any kind of asset may be held by the trust, including cash, personal property, or real property. Often, no assets are put into the special-needs trust until the death of the trust maker, in which case the trust is an "empty shell" waiting for a future event. It is prudent, but not required, to place some assets into the trust and begin using the trust immediately.

⚜ *Can a special-needs trust be the recipient of insurance proceeds?*

Yes, funding a trust with life insurance is often ideal if the primary objective of the trust is to provide for a child upon the death of his or her parents. It is often desirable for concerned family members to make the special-needs trust the recipient of life insurance policies.

The special-needs trust could be an irrevocable life insurance trust to hold the insurance policy and ensure that the insurance proceeds are not taxed to the trust maker's estate.

⚜ *Can additions be made to a special-needs trust?*

Yes. Additional property may be added to the trust at any time by the trust maker or any other person except the disabled beneficiary. Additions may be made as gifts during life or as bequests through wills or living trusts, life insurance policies, employee benefit plans, or retirement plans.

⚜ *Does every person with a disability need a special-needs trust?*

Absolutely not. This sort of planning is appropriate if (1) the beneficiary lacks the capacity to manage his or her financial affairs or (2) maintaining eligibility for public benefits is essential or will enhance the person's standard of living. There are many persons with disabilities who do not receive benefits and have no impediment preventing them from managing their financial affairs.

⚜ *One of our children is not disabled but does have a number of psychological and social problems. How can we make sure that this child will be properly cared for after my spouse and I are gone?*

One of the greatest strengths living trusts have is their flexibility: the trust maker can include customized language that describes in detail his or her wishes. Certain legal language can be inserted that enables the trustee to personally care for a child.

In your case, including information particularly unique to your child would be most helpful to the successor trustee, such as the child's likes, dislikes, habits, and routines, his or her personal strengths and weaknesses, legal entities or agencies that interact in supportive roles to benefit the child, previous problems and how they were resolved, ways in which you wish the trustee to spend "discretionary" money on behalf of your child, and other related information. You can also make arrangements with a particular provider of benefits and record them for the trustee so that he or she can provide the same level of care, concern, and love for your child as you would if you were still living.

Adult children

⬩ *Do I have to distribute my assets equally to my children?*

Parents often struggle with the decision of whether or not to distribute their assets equally to their children. Despite what some people may believe, children are not all equal and usually they should not be treated as equals. Facts and circumstances surrounding a particular child will determine how you will distribute assets, if any, to that child or to his or her beneficiaries. This can be particularly troublesome if there is a family business and not all family members are active in the business.

You should distribute your assets to whom you want, when you want, and in the amounts that are appropriate considering all surrounding issues. You might consider what may be *equitable* for your beneficiaries rather than constraining yourself by arbitrary notions of equality: equitable may end up being equal, but equal is not always equitable.

Your decision on how to distribute your children's shares to them upon your death should take into consideration such factors as each child's age, health, ability to make financial decisions, family circumstances, and situation with creditors. Basically, you should look at what each child truly needs or may need and plan in the most loving and realistic way you can for that child.

⬩ *Should I give my adult children their inheritance all at once or over a period of time?*

Although your natural inclination may be to give your adult children their inheritances outright, that may not be the best or wisest course of action for them. A well-thought-out series of subtrusts in your living trust can provide for the specific needs of your children. Leaving property to your children in trust can often protect them from their own inexperience with money, from their inability to make wise decisions, from their creditors, or from a divorcing spouse. Adult children who do not have experience with large sums of money are often overwhelmed when they receive an inheritance. They may make some poor choices and come to realize, too late, that their inheritance has gone to poor investments and frivolous spending.

Perhaps an adult child is easily influenced by friends and family and can't say "no" when asked for a handout. Perhaps he or she has a drug or alcohol problem and a large "windfall" will only increase his or her ability to satisfy the dependency. Or perhaps, at the time of your death, one of your children may have the misfortune of being in the middle of a nasty divorce or a lawsuit.

By using trusts, you can plan for all these situations very specifically if they currently exist, or you can plan in anticipation of the possibility of those problems and provide some protection for your children if it is later needed.

How do most people leave instructions for their adult children?

They create a subtrust for each child's share within their living trust document.

Can we leave our property equally to our children but structure the terms and conditions of each of their trusts differently?

This is a common and effective planning strategy. You can provide detailed instructions in each child's trust which specifically meet your hopes, concerns, dreams, values, and aspirations for that child and which specifically address your assessment of that child's strengths and weaknesses.

How can I prevent squabbles among my children?

By doing good planning! Family squabbles are more likely to occur when people do not leave instructions which make their intentions clear. If your instructions are complete and give a clear indication of your intentions, there will be less likelihood that your children will argue over different interpretations of the instructions.

There is nothing wrong with adding language to your estate plan which describes your intentions. The problem with many "cookie-cutter" documents is that no specialized language is added. A good estate planning professional will be able to help you identify your hopes, concerns, and desires and properly incorporate them into your planning documents.

Won't we be unreasonably dominating our children from the grave if we leave our property in trust for them?

You have hopes, dreams, and aspirations for your children while you are living; why should they change when you are dead?

Distributions from the trust should be based upon each child's individual ability to manage and conserve money and the dynamics of each child's marriage situation. However, many parents do not like to restrict one child's access to assets while giving the other children full access. Frequently, the practical solution they arrive at is to determine the strategy for the least responsible child and then apply it uniformly to all their children.

⋟ *What options do I have regarding the distribution of assets?*

Once you've decided on the terms for dividing the inheritance into each child's own share or trust, you have the following additional options to consider:

- Whether or not the trust income will be periodically distributed, and if so, when
- When the trust principal (trust assets) will be distributed
- The degree of permitted discretionary distributions by the trustee

⋟ *What income taxes do trusts pay?*

Table 3-1 shows the income tax rates for income retained by trusts. When a trust distributes net income, the trust receives an income tax deduction. This means that the trust or estate does not pay tax on net income it distributes; the tax is paid by the beneficiary recipient.

⋟ *Should a trustee accumulate income or distribute it?*

If the income accumulated by the trust is insignificant, it may be beneficial to let the net income accrue and be distributed along with the principal of the trust. If there is significant net income generated by the trust, it is generally beneficial to pay the net income to the child since the child is most likely in a lower tax bracket and thus will be taxed on the income at a lower rate than the trust would be.

Distribution of net income helps the child learn how to manage money and makes the child less dependent on receiving principal distributions. Once you make the decision to pay income to the children, the next decision is how often it should be paid.

⋟ *How frequently should income distributions be made?*

While once-a-year payments might encourage the child to learn to budget, such an approach may be somewhat extreme. Ideally, monthly income is preferable; however, most stock dividends are paid quarterly. It is administratively difficult to receive income, determine the prorated expenses, and process the checks every month. Arguably there might

TABLE 3-1 Income Tax Rates for Trusts
(tax years beginning in 1999)

If taxable income is		The tax is	Of the amount over
Over	But not over		
$ –0–	$1600	15.0%	$ –0–
1600	3800	$240 + 28.0%	1600
3800	5800	$856 + 31.0%	3800
5800	7900	$1476 + 36.0%	5800
7900	–	$2232 + 39.6%	7900

be a breach of fiduciary duty if the trustee was slow in making monthly distributions. It might be more feasible to provide for distributions at least quarterly; this would still give the child an opportunity to learn budgeting.

≼ *Should we give our trustee the authority to make discretionary distributions of trust principal?*

The pressure to make periodic distributions of principal is somewhat alleviated if you give the trustee the authority to make interim distributions for legitimate reasons.

Frequently, the trustee is given the authority to make distributions for the "health, education, maintenance, and support" of the child. These are known as the *ascertainable standards* in the Internal Revenue Code. Collectively they provide for a beneficiary's all-encompassing needs. Thus, the trustee, in his or her discretion, could pay for a child's major medical needs. Similarly, the trust could provide the trustee with a standard for discretionary distributions. For example, some parents prefer a conservative standard which requires the existence of a genuine need, while others prefer a more liberal standard which allows financial assistance for such matters as the purchase of a residence, a business, or any other extraordinary opportunity.

≼ *Do discretionary distribution plans provide built-in creditor protection?*

Yes. Because the distributions are in the trustee's sole discretion, payments do not have to be made when a beneficiary's creditors are making demands or lurking nearby. The trustee, who should be an independent trustee rather than a beneficiary or family member, can retain the funds in the safety and protection of the trust.

⚄ *Are there many strategies for multiple distributions?*

There are as many strategies as there are inventive parents and grandparents. In general, however, if a child has not reached middle-age maturity or does not have a track record to demonstrate financial responsibility, it might be appropriate to use a minimum two-stage distribution, 5 years apart, with quarterly payments of net income throughout the period of the trust. In this way, the child can learn from mistakes he or she makes from the first distribution and hopefully be more responsible with subsequent distributions of principal.

For the same reason, staggered distributions are also appropriate if the trust assets are significant. Distributions typically begin when the child reaches a certain age (usually at age 30 or 35) or on the death of the surviving parent, and they continue at specified intervals over a predetermined period of years. For example:

> Distribute 25 percent of our daughter's share to her on the death of the survivor of us, and distribute the balance in three additional distributions at 5-year intervals from that date.

⚄ *If I set up a revocable living trust and I want my children to be beneficiaries of the trust, can I provide that distributions to my children be made directly to revocable living trusts set up by them?*

Yes, you can. Doing so makes a great deal of sense because it allows their inheritance to be governed by their own set of instructions. The inheritance will then be protected from a living probate and a death probate.

⚄ *Is there a general approach that most people use in planning for responsible adult children?*

Usually the children are named as their own trustees in a cotrusteeship with others whom they can name and replace—subject to standards (this "creditor-proofs" the trust estate). In this way, adult children can receive what they want from their trusts whenever they want it.

⚄ *Can we provide for our children's retirement years through trust planning?*

Parents can sometimes reasonably predict that their children will frivolously waste the distributions. A strategy you can use in this situation is to provide the net income to the children and give authority to the trustee to make discretionary distributions of principal with the final distribution at age 55 or later. In other words, the assets are used to ensure the children's retirement.

⚜ *I'm afraid my children will not save properly for retirement. I'd like them to receive part of my estate immediately upon my death, but is there any way I can make sure that most of what I leave them is retained for their retirement?*

Yes. You can design the distribution pattern from your trust to help your children in their retirement years. You could give your trustee instructions to hold some or all of the principal of the trust until your children reach retirement age. This does not need to be an all-or-nothing provision. If you wish the children to have access to a portion of your estate immediately upon your death, you may provide that instruction, with the remainder to be held in trust until the children's retirement age.

⚜ *How can I protect my son from himself? He is terrible with money, and I'm afraid he will squander his inheritance.*

Because such an adult child is likely to squander or lose money immediately, an outright distribution is out of the question. However, most parents love their children regardless of the shortcomings they may have, and most parents want to help their children with their resources rather than simply disinherit them.

A *lifetime trust* can provide that your son will be taken care of from his share of your estate for his lifetime under definite instructions that take into account the difficulties he is having during life.

An *incentive trust* can provide that your son must alter his behavior in order to receive distributions from the trust.

⚜ *My son has a drug addiction. Can I put a provision in my trust that prevents him from accessing any of the trust assets unless he passes a drug test?*

Absolutely. Your attorney can draft your trust to your specific requests. A typical provision of this nature will allow money to be spent on your son's behalf for rehabilitation but will not allow the trustee to disburse funds unless your son passes a drug test. You may also want to include periodic distributions based on the results from follow-up drug testing.

If you want to provide for your son upon your death but are concerned about the possibility of drug or alcohol abuse, you need only to leave appropriate instructions in your trust document. For example:

> Under normal circumstances I would like my son to have all of the income and whatever principal is necessary to provide him with his every need, as long as it is reasonable.
>
> However, if my trustee knows or has reason to suspect that my son is dependent upon or has a problem with drugs and/or alcohol, then my trustee, in my trustee's sole and absolute discretion, may withhold both income and principal distributions until my son is evaluated for drug and alcohol abuse.
>
> If it is determined that my son has a drug or alcohol abuse problem, my trustee shall offer my child the opportunity to enter a treatment program to be paid for from the assets of my son's trust.
>
> If my son refuses to seek treatment which in the reasonable discretion of my trustee is warranted and proper, my trustee may withhold payments of both income and principal from my son's trust until he proves to the satisfaction of my trustee that he no longer has a substance abuse problem.

❧ *Can I provide for the costs of food, shelter, and medical care without giving the funds directly to my addicted daughter?*

In order to ensure that the payments are used for the benefit of your daughter, as opposed to her using the trust disbursements to further her habit, the trustee could make all mortgage or rental payments directly to the mortgage company or landlord. Similar arrangements could be made for medical expenses, food, clothing, and expenditures for other basic necessities.

❧ *How can I leave my assets to my children without squelching their incentive to be responsible and to grow and develop?*

To promote gratitude and philanthropy, you could leave a portion of your estate to a charitable foundation and name your children as trustees. To give them an incentive to provide for themselves and their families, you could match their earnings, dollar for dollar, or double their annual incomes when they hit some income milestone such as $100,000.

❧ *I want my children to lead productive, hardworking lives which contribute to our society. How can I build incentives into their*

inheritance without being overly controlling or just giving them too much money?

There are a number of approaches you might consider:

- *Opportunity funding:* You may instruct your trustee to create or buy an "opportunity" for a child. The benefits to the child will occur primarily if the child successfully develops the opportunity.
- *Testamentary charitable foundation:* You may want to create a trust or foundation in your living trust that springs to life after your death and directs that, under certain guidelines, your children assist in the philanthropic endeavor of giving away the income of the trust. This strategy not only encourages children to look beyond themselves but also enhances their personal and social status in their communities.
- *Staggered distributions:* You may simply want to stagger distributions to the children at certain more mature ages or after certain periods of time. A second- or third-chance formula allows your children to have resources left if they fail to handle their first distributions wisely.
- *Trustee discretion with criteria:* Your trustee can hold a child's share for life with the discretion to make certain distributions. You can set any number of specific criteria for the exercise of that discretion, such as liberal or conservative standards for distributions, and you can suggest or direct under what circumstances that child's trust principal should be distributed.
- *Milestone incentives:* You may condition distributions from your trust on your children's reaching certain milestones which can either be clearly defined or be left to the discretion of your trustee.

The opportunities for creating incentives for your children are almost endless; however, you must also be sensitive to the risks of overcontrolling. With the assistance of an experienced, knowledgeable estate planning team, you can create the structures which encourage the desired outcome without the negative responses.

How can I make sure that only my children receive their inheritance?

In your living trust, you can create at your death a trust share for each child so that a child's spouse, or ex-spouse, or even a child's creditors cannot get to the trust-share property.

The trust will contain instructions that all trust shares are created only for the children and their beneficiaries. There will also be *spendthrift* provisions stating that distributions are to be used only for the child's health, support, maintenance, and education expenditures and that on the beneficiary's death, the proceeds of his or her trust share will pass directly to grandchildren and others. Spendthrift provisions protect the beneficiaries from the claims of their creditors and from their own attempts at improper actions with regard to the trust's income or principal.

⍶ *We have been very fortunate in that all our children's marriages look sound today, but so much can happen, and divorce is so common. Can we protect our legacy from going to a child's spouse in a divorce?*

If you choose to leave your property in trust for your children rather than making an outright distribution, you will provide some divorce protection in most states. Unlike an outright distribution, property held in trust for a beneficiary is not owned by the beneficiary; it is owned by the trust. Because it is not owned by the beneficiary, the trust property is generally not subject to the claims of creditors or claims resulting from a divorce proceeding. However, there are exceptions to this general rule. Most states have given judges of family courts broad power to attach property if justice requires. For example, it may be extremely unjust to deny a nonbeneficiary spouse a portion of trust property if doing so would impoverish that spouse. In some states, the family court might exercise its equity powers to invade the trust.

Having an independent trustee distribute the trust property in accordance with an ascertainable standard or specific guidelines will provide more protection against a beneficiary's divorce than would be the case if the beneficiary is the sole trustee with broad powers to demand principal.

⍶ *I have eight children, four of whom help me operate my dairy farm. The assets of the dairy farm account for 90 percent of my $2 million estate. I want the four who operate the farm to receive it, but I also want the other four to receive an equal share of my estate. Is there a way to accomplish this?*

This is a very common agribusiness situation. Life insurance made payable directly to the noninvolved children or payable to a trust for their benefit can go a long way toward equalizing the children's shares.

A trust agreement can be structured so that it pays the proceeds to these children free of federal estate tax.

> *How can our family's vacation retreat be made available to all our children without unfairly burdening any one of them with the cost of upkeep and taxes?*

Family retreats (cottages, camps, cabins, etc.) are often the most cherished of estate assets; their use by family members can have a positive effect on family dynamics after parents are gone. However, leaving a share of the cottage, along with its proportion of the upkeep and taxes, to each child may place a burden on some of the sibling owners and may make it difficult for them to equitably divide the use of the retreat.

Creating a *family-retreat subtrust* in your living trust can afford a workable alternative to dividing the interest among your children. In the subtrust, you can name all the children as trustees and create a fund for maintaining the property regardless of its use.

> *If someone named in my trust agreement dies before me, how does this affect my revocable living trust?*

The death of a named beneficiary generally has no legal effect upon the validity of the revocable living trust. If a beneficiary dies before the trust maker, any trust provisions pertaining to that person will generally lapse and the distribution that would have been made to that person will be distributed as otherwise designated in the trust instrument. If appropriate care has been taken in drafting the trust, it will designate who is to receive a specific bequest of property if a particular named beneficiary dies before the trust maker. In addition, as long as the maker is still alive, he or she is free to amend the trust instrument to account for the death of a beneficiary.

> *If my trust gives a distribution to a beneficiary and gives that person the power to appoint the distribution by a trust, does the property in the distribution go through probate?*

No, the property goes directly from one trust to another if the power of appointment is exercised.

> *If my trust gives a distribution to a beneficiary and gives that person the power to appoint the distribution by a will, does the property in that distribution go through probate?*

Yes, the property will go through probate on the death of your beneficiary if the power of appointment is, in fact, exercised in his or her will.

Planning for Grandchildren

✍ We would like to leave our assets to our children to provide for the education of their children (our grandchildren) at least through graduate school. But we are a little afraid that our children will not use the inheritance for that purpose. Is there a way to ensure that our wishes are carried out?

Yes. You can leave your assets in trust, with the income and principal to be used as needed for the education of your grandchildren. You can also provide that after the last grandchild has been educated, the remaining principal is to be given to your grandchildren. If you were to pass the excess to your children, there could be generation-skipping transfer tax consequences.

✍ One of my sons is not married, and he'll probably never get married. Can I prepare my estate so that anything I leave him will go to my grandchildren after he dies?

Absolutely. The ability to accomplish this is one of the great benefits of leaving property to your children in trust. By leaving property to your son *in trust,* rather than through an outright distribution, you can specify that he has use of the property during his lifetime and that, when he dies, it passes according to your instructions to your descendants.

Planning for Other Family Members

✍ How can I provide for my surviving widowed mother?

You can establish a separate trust with your mother as the primary income beneficiary. The trust's terms could allow the trustee to use the principal, if necessary, for the health, maintenance, and welfare of your mother during her lifetime. Any assets remaining after the death of your mother could be distributed to your other surviving family members.

It is not wise to combine trust assets for your parent with trust assets for your surviving spouse and children. The trustee may be unreasonably criticized for exercising discretion in providing too much income or principal for any particular family beneficiary. Your trust should have explicit instructions as to how the income and principal of the separate trust are to be used.

USING POWERS OF APPOINTMENT
FOR TAX PLANNING

⚑ *What is a power of appointment?*

A *power of appointment* is a legal instrument that authorizes a person to designate who will receive property. This power is given by one person to another person. For example:

> Ralph gives his son, Dave, the power to designate which of Ralph's grandchildren will receive Ralph's property 10 years after his death.

Ralph is the *giver* of the power, and Dave is the *holder* of the power. Dave has the right to *appoint* which of Ralph's grandchildren will receive Ralph's property.

Powers of appointment are very important and are frequently used by attorneys in planning the estates of their clients.

⚑ *What is a general power of appointment?*

A *general power of appointment* is a legal instrument that authorizes the power holder to direct property to anyone, including the holder, his or her creditors, his or her estate, or the creditors of his or her estate.

⚑ *What is a testamentary general power of appointment?*

A *testamentary general power of appointment* is a legal instrument that comes into effect at the death of the holder and is generally exercised in a will or trust. The document giving rise to the power may specify how and where it is to be exercised.

⚑ *What is a limited power of appointment?*

A *limited power of appointment* is any power which is not a general power. In other words, a limited power enables the holder to transfer property to anyone *other than* the holder, the holder's creditors, the holder's estate, or the creditors of the estate.

A limited power of appointment can be crafted so that the holder may use it only to vary the timing or the proportion of distributions to a class of individuals or to specifically named individuals. For example:

> I give my son the power to distribute this property to or for the benefit of his children, outright or in trust, in equal or unequal shares among those children as he shall exclusively determine.

In this example, the property must pass to the grandchildren, but the son can leave out one or more of his children or distribute the property equally or unequally either outright or in trust. The power does not give the son the right to leave the property to his spouse, a charity, or friends or to use it to pay his creditors.

✍ What is the tax effect of giving someone a general power of appointment?

When a person has a general power of appointment over property, the property will be included in that person's taxable estate for federal estate tax purposes. Practitioners often use general powers in planning clients' estates when they wish to place, or "trap," specific property in one beneficiary's taxable estate. In contrast, a limited power of appointment has no tax effect; the property is not included in the holder's estate because the power is limited in its scope.

✍ Should I give my child a general power of appointment?

Parents usually give a general power of appointment over the property they leave to a child to make sure that, when the child dies, the property will not be subject to a generation-skipping transfer tax. Frequently, if the child has a small estate, the child's applicable exclusion amount will wipe out the tax on the inherited property when it passes to his or her children.

Ironically, if the property were to pass straight from you to your grandchildren without being included in your child's estate, it could be subject to the horrendous 55 percent flat generation-skipping tax on gifts to grandchildren in addition to federal estate tax on the child's estate.

PLANNING FOR DISABILITY

✍ Who should plan for disability?

Everyone. Not only all single people—unmarried, divorced, or widowed—but also married people should consider disability planning. Married people, usually assuming that their spouses will be there for them, often do not consider what would happen if their spouses become disabled as well or die suddenly.

Disability Planning
with Traditional Techniques

≥ᴪ *Why can't I just rely on my family to take care of me?*

Since World War II, relocation of families is commonplace: grown children move away to pursue careers or get transferred around the country; parents move south or west to enjoy their golden years after retirement. As a result, many parents and children today reside great distances from each other.

A widely dispersed family is not a problem as long as everyone is healthy. Unfortunately, while advances in medical care keep people alive longer and life expectancies are increasing, the quality of one's life may suffer. It is not unusual now for people to become physically disabled, mentally disabled, or both. If there is a capable spouse, he or she will care for the other spouse and make the health care and living decisions.

What happens if there is no competent spouse and no effective planning is in place? The courts will decide. A judge will appoint a guardian who will be responsible for making the living, financial, and health care arrangements for the incompetent person. The courts usually follow a system of priorities in making guardian appointments: spouse, adult children, parents, siblings, and so on. So if you have not chosen who your guardian will be, you may end up with a person you do not want. For example, if you have no spouse or your spouse cannot serve, the court might appoint your adult child to be your guardian. But you might not want your child, who perhaps is not yet 25 and lives hundreds of miles away, to be making decisions about your life, especially if the child lacks mature judgment. You might prefer a brother or a sister. However, if you have failed to do disability planning, the court will decide for you.

≥ᴪ *Who decides how I am to be cared for if I become disabled and have no formal planning in place?*

Most people have firm ideas about how they would like to be cared for during their disability. However, if they have not left instructions, how they want to be cared for and how they are actually cared for may be entirely different. For example, a great majority of people want to remain in their homes if they become disabled. If possible, they would like to stay in familiar surroundings where they are comfortable. Their next choice is to go to an attended health care facility that is homelike but meets their medical needs. As a last resort, people agree to be placed in nursing homes. Unfortunately, without disability planning, an individual does not have any say about his or her care; the decisions are left to the mercy and judgment of a court-appointed guardian.

⚜ Are there different kinds of guardians?

Yes. In most states, there are two types of guardianships. There is a "guardian of the person," who makes health care and other personal decisions, and there is a "guardian of the property," sometimes called a *conservator*, who makes financial decisions. Both are court-appointed and subject to the court's supervision.

⚜ Will putting our assets in joint tenancy solve the living probate problem?

Placing assets in joint tenancy is not a satisfactory solution. Upon the disability of one of the joint tenants, the asset is frozen because the sale of the asset requires the signatures of both joint tenants.

⚜ Who should be the beneficiary of my disability insurance?

If you have disability insurance personally or through work, your trust should be the beneficiary so that the proceeds of the policy will not have to go through a living probate.

⚜ What is a power of attorney?

A *power of attorney* is a written instrument by which you appoint another person to perform certain specified acts on your behalf. This document gives power to a designated agent, called an *attorney-in-fact*— hence the name, "power of attorney."

There are two basic types of powers of attorney: the *general*, which grants the agent power to deal with all your assets and to take any action on your behalf; and the *special*, which allows the agent to perform only certain acts or to control specific property.

Most people believe that a power of attorney may be used only if the person granting the power, who is called the *principal*, becomes incapacitated. In fact, a traditional power of attorney automatically becomes invalid upon the incapacity or death of the principal. However, in all states both general and special powers of attorney can be made *durable*; that is, they can be written to remain valid even if the principal becomes incapacitated or incompetent. A power of attorney is durable only when it specifically states that it is to continue upon the legal incapacity of the principal.

When prepared, executed, and used correctly, the durable power is a highly effective financial management instrument and should be part of every estate plan.

◄ *What are the risks and benefits associated with creating a durable power of attorney?*

The risk of granting a durable power of attorney is that the person you name as power holder may either be dishonest or have bad judgment. If the power holder is dishonest, he or she could use the power to gain control of your assets and then abscond with them. If the power holder has bad judgment, he or she could mismanage your assets or make poor decisions. The important point here is that a general power of attorney is only as good as the agent holding the power. Be sure to name honest and responsible people or financial institutions as your power holder.

Now for the benefits: In terms of being prepared (and that is what estate planning is all about), it is good to have someone who can transact your financial matters for you if you are unable to do so for any reason. Professional advisors may differ on whether it is better to have a general durable power of attorney, which would allow someone to transact any business activity for you, or better to have a special durable power of attorney, which would allow someone to transact only specific business matters for you or would be effective only under certain circumstances, such as your disability. Consequently, you should discuss powers of attorney with your advisors so that you can decide which type is best for you.

◄ *When should I sign a durable power of attorney?*

You should sign a durable power when you are healthy, competent, and able to make your own decisions. This will alleviate much of the difficulty that could arise if you should become incapable of making these decisions.

◄ *Must third parties honor powers of attorney?*

In the absence of a state law to the contrary, there is little that can be done to force a third party to accept a power of attorney. Many banks will require that you fill out their forms to authorize your agent to write checks on your account. If you do not have their forms, you are out of luck. In addition, the IRS generally will not honor a power of attorney if the power does not specify the tax number and tax year at issue.

Even in states which require that a third party accept a power of attorney, there are enforcement problems. For example, if the law states that a person must accept a valid power of attorney but that person refuses to do so, the effort of going to court to enforce the law makes little economic sense. Also, the time it would take could result in a financial or other loss.

◢ Can I give a power of attorney to an agent to create a trust on my behalf?

State laws differ on this issue for a number of reasons, and they also differ as to whether or not the agent can create a revocable or an irrevocable trust. Some states will permit it if the power of attorney clearly states that the agent has such power; other states will not permit it at all on the basis of public policy, even though the power of attorney clearly authorizes it. Your estate planning attorney can give you the answer to this question for your state.

◢ If my mother gives me a general, broad durable power of attorney, can I make lifetime gifts of her assets after she becomes incapacitated?

IRS private letter rulings, federal case law, and the common law of most states indicate that if the giver of the power wants the agent to make gifts, the power of attorney must clearly spell out that authority. Powers of attorney that do not specify this authority are routinely challenged by the IRS, and any gifts made under such circumstances have been included in the deceased power giver's estate for federal estate tax purposes.

◢ If I become disabled or incapacitated, how can I make changes in my estate planning documents to meet the requirements of new tax legislation or family requirements?

If your state's laws allow it, you should execute a durable power of attorney or some other special power of attorney stating that your agent has the power to make changes in your estate planning documents such as living trust agreements, stockholder's agreements, partnership agreements, voting agreements, and management agreements that control estate planning entities or family enterprises. The power of attorney must grant authority specifically to make anticipated possible revisions or must set conditions under which such revisions will be necessary. It should also provide that in the event that such authority does not specifically exist, your attorney-in-fact may petition a court having jurisdiction for permission to make such changes.

☙ *Will the Social Security Administration recognize a power of attorney?*

The Social Security Administration does not recognize powers of attorney for the purpose of dealing with Social Security accounts. The administration recognizes only an individual who is appointed through the representative-payee designation process.

☙ *Does a power of attorney help avoid probate on my death?*

A power of attorney does not allow you to avoid probate. Regardless of whether or not you have a power of attorney, if you do not have a fully funded revocable living trust, your assets will pass through probate in order to be retitled in the name of your heirs or testamentary trustees.

Disability Planning with the Revocable Living Trust

☙ *Can a living trust–centered plan help in my disability planning?*

You can incorporate your disability planning into your revocable living trust. If your trust is properly funded, there will be no need for a court to appoint a guardian for your property since your successor trustee will function in that capacity.

☙ *Can my living trust provide for my disability?*

Current statistics tell us that over one-third of us will be disabled for 6 months or longer at some point in our lives. As a result, comprehensive disability instructions in a revocable living trust are tremendously important.

With proper planning, you can provide for the uninterrupted administration of your affairs without the cost, delay, public exposure, court supervision, and accounting that accompany a conservatorship. This is the lifetime equivalent of avoiding probate on death.

Through a revocable living trust, you can designate a trustee to administer your trust and its assets in the event of your disability. You can retain control over your estate by including detailed disability instructions, and you can even define the conditions under which you will be deemed disabled.

⫘ *I am blind. My daughter's name is on my checking account, so she can write and sign checks for me, but I would like her to be able to handle all my affairs. Can I do that safely with a living trust?*

Yes. You can name your daughter as a cotrustee, thus providing her with the same authority as you have in regard to trust assets. To be safe, you can also set out detailed instructions (which you cannot normally do in a power of attorney or in the typical joint checking account), such as requiring that any significant transfers of assets, which you will define while you are living, must be done by both trustees, not just one.

⫘ *What is the most important matter I should consider in my disability planning?*

Of utmost importance is the proper selection of your disability trustee: Who do you want to control your assets and make decisions as to their investment and use? Who will have the authority to write checks, sell assets, invest income, or cash checks in order to pay the ongoing expenses of your care or the upkeep of your residence?

You should select someone who will be loyal to you in handling your assets, is adequately prepared to deal with the investment and tax issues that may arise, and is able to dedicate the time needed to follow through on the responsibility. Both you and the person you designate must also be aware of the responsibility inherent in managing the financial affairs of another person, including the possibility of surcharges and lawsuits for mishandling the account.

⫘ *Please give me some examples of how I can plan for disability with a living trust.*

A well-drafted trust document will include instructions as to how the disability trustee should use the assets of the trust. A typical provision is any one of the following:

1. Provide for me only.
2. Provide for me and my spouse.
3. Provide for me, my spouse, and any children who may be dependent upon me for support based solely on needs or in a specified order of priority.
4. Provide for me and anyone else who may be dependent upon me for support, such as my parents.

Of course, you can set forth your own specific limitations or exceptions.

≥ *How does the disability trustee of my living trust get the authority to act in the event that I am disabled?*

As with nearly all aspects of a revocable living trust, the disability trustee gets his or her authority from the trust document. In a properly drafted living trust there will be specific definitions of what constitutes a disability. For instance, the trust may define "disability" in any one of these different ways:

1. If two licensed physicians say that I am unable to care for myself or my financial affairs, that is a definition of my disability.
2. If my doctors and family cannot agree that I cannot take care of myself or my financial affairs, and my loved ones ask a probate court to determine my competency, and the probate court determines I am not competent, that is a definition of disability.
3. If I am missing or have been kidnapped or otherwise held against my will, that is also a definition of my disability.

In the event of a disability as defined by the trust, your disability trustee gives an *affidavit of trust* to third parties or institutions, demonstrating that he or she is authorized to act on your behalf.

≥ *Can I create enough flexibility to enable my trustee to handle unforeseen circumstances?*

In your trust, you can include instructions for the trustee in regard to specific instances and provide general guidance in the event of unforeseen circumstances. You may, for instance, provide that some of your assets be used for your benefit and for gifts to loved ones during your lifetime or for improvements to your property.

≥ *Why is having a successor trustee under a trust better than having an agent with a durable power of attorney?*

In the event of your disability, the power and authority granted to your successor trustee is limited and controlled by your specific instructions in your trust agreement. In contrast, a power of attorney provides the agent with unlimited power.

In addition, trustees are governed by fiduciary law to act in good faith on behalf of the trust beneficiaries and can be held liable if they do not follow your specific instructions. Agents under a power of attorney are not always governed by such fiduciary law and may not be held liable to the same extent for their actions.

In the event of your death, the successor trustee can continue in that capacity to carry out your instructions as set forth in the trust. Any power of attorney, whether durable or not, by law automatically terminates at your death. Therefore, after your death, your agent under a power of attorney no longer has authority to act on your behalf.

↠ I own and operate my own business. How can it function during my disability?

You can name successor trustees in your living trust whom you authorize and direct to run the business in your absence. Dedicated employees are often named in this regard.

↠ Can I update my disability instructions?

Of course. In fact, it is quite common to do so. For example, you may want to include a preference for certain nursing home care or home health care should you require it.

↠ If I become disabled and my family does not approve of the disability trustees listed in my trust, can the family fire them and take control of my affairs?

Family members would not have the power to terminate the trustees. They would have to bring a lawsuit—most probably in your county's probate court—to have the trust set aside, and this is enormously difficult to do.

The court would be restricted to deciding two issues: (1) Were you competent when you signed your trust? Arguments over whether or not you are disabled would be moot: if you aren't disabled, you control your trust anyway; and if you are disabled, the trust's terms are operational. (2) Are your successor trustees competent to act in their fiduciary capacity?

If the answers to these questions are yes, the court will have no right to interfere with your planning.

Health Care Powers of Attorney

↠ What is a durable power of attorney for health care?

A *durable power of attorney for health care* is an important part of disability planning. It is a legal instrument by which you designate an agent to make health care decisions for you in the event that you are unable to do so for yourself. By this means, you are able to appoint as your agent someone who you are confident will carry out your wishes.

In the health care power, you can inform your agent of your preferences regarding issues of health care that are important to you, such as home care, life support, and pain management.

Although a health care power does not directly affect your assets, it is still an important estate planning tool. It is a gift to your loved ones that enables them, when faced with difficult decisions, to know that they are carrying out your wishes.

⚑ Who should be my health care agent?

Here are some characteristics you may want to consider when deciding whom to name as the agent in your health care power of attorney:

- *The ability to engage or draw out busy health care professionals:* Communication is essential for gaining information; having a medical background helps with this process but is not essential.
- *The ability to command attention and respect:* A person with this quality is more likely to be included in decision making.
- *Leadership abilities:* A respected leader among family members can instill unity and confidence.
- *Time to devote to this task:* Busy executives or people with many responsibilities are not always capable of devoting the time needed.
- *Geographical proximity:* Having an agent who is not far away is advantageous, but this is not as important as the above characteristics.

Having more than one person acting simultaneously as an agent is not recommended in most cases. It is hard enough to get overburdened medical staff and physicians to spend time explaining options and care alternatives to one person. Forcing them to work with a committee is almost impossible.

It is also important for you to discuss your health care desires with your health care agent before disability occurs. Your agent needs to hear from your lips and see in your eyes that the choices being made are truly your choices and that you believe your health care decisions are a matter of personal dignity and control. Having this knowledge will greatly ease your agent's burden of making difficult health care decisions.

⚑ I have a will that contains instructions for my health care and my burial. Why do I need additional documents?

A will generally has no validity until after you die and it is submitted to, and accepted by, the probate court. This is well after it is needed to provide health care or burial instructions. While your instructions on these subjects will not necessarily be ignored, you are presenting them in a highly unusual form which could impede the very purpose you intended. Also, in some states, there are prescribed forms or witnessing formalities for health care and burial instruction documents that your will may not satisfy. It is better to let the will serve its intended purpose—the appointment of a personal representative and guardian for minors, and the distribution of your property—and have separate, properly drafted documents specifically dealing with health care and burial.

Living Wills

⚰ *What is a living will?*

A *living will* is a directive to your physician which states that you do not want "extraordinary means" employed to keep you alive should you be in a terminal condition or a permanently unconscious state. This will not only relieve your family or trustee of the burden of applying to the courts to make this decision but also relieve your family from having to make this decision at all.

This decision also affects your overall estate plan because you cannot estimate the length of time or the cost of employing "extraordinary means" until you succumb to your final illness or injury.

⚰ *Where should I keep my original living will, and who should receive copies?*

Your original living will should be kept in a safe place that is easily accessible at all times (not a safe deposit box, which cannot be opened at night or on weekends). Be sure someone in your family or a close friend knows where your living will is located and that he or she has ready access to it in case of an emergency. You may wish to give copies to family members, friends, and your attorney or clergy.

There is at least one national service, Advance Choice DocuBank, that will keep copies of these important records for you, allowing access 365 days a year, 24 hours a day. Upon notification, it will fax copies of your living will and other health care documents to whatever hospital needs them.

Because doctors are required to follow your directive and exercise the living will immediately upon the determination that death is imminent, it is not recommended that you provide your doctor with a copy of your living will until you are to be admitted to a hospital. Once the living will is provided to a hospital, it becomes part of your medical record. It is generally more comfortable if a family member waits a day or two to make sure that the doctor's determination of imminent death is correct before he or she and the hospital exercises the authority provided under the living will. Your family will generally know you best and will be able to determine what your desires are or are not at this time when it is most important.

⚜ How long is my living will valid?

Your living will is always valid as long as you signed it voluntarily and do not rescind it or declare it void. If you decide at any time to revoke any portion of the living will, communicate this to your attending physician immediately and retrieve and destroy all copies given to others. Then execute a new living will.

DISINHERITING A FAMILY MEMBER

Disinheriting a Spouse

⚜ Is it possible to disinherit a spouse?

It is very difficult and almost legally impossible in the United States to completely disinherit a spouse, especially a wife. A number of states still provide a wife with a *dower interest* in her husband's assets, even if his trust, will, or other documents left nothing to her. In many states, a husband or a wife is entitled to an *elective share,* which is a percentage of the estate. Election of a wife's dower interest or a spouse's elective share can be devastating to estate plans as far as estate and gift taxes are concerned. Therefore, careful planning should be made when attempting to disinherit a spouse.

A few states allow a spouse to disinherit a surviving spouse by using a revocable living trust. However, a prudent estate design should not be based on such a legislative provision, which could be repealed or amended at any time. Nevertheless, if the death of the disinheriting spouse is imminent and transferring assets to a trust can be accomplished without a fraud upon that spouse, it may be possible to disinherit the surviving spouse.

☙ *Can a spouse be disinherited in a prenuptial agreement?*

A properly executed prenuptial agreement can and commonly does delineate each spouse's rights to the other spouse's property on death. A prenuptial agreement can include waivers of dower, elective share, homestead, and other property rights that would be held by a surviving spouse in the absence of such an agreement.

☙ *Can a spouse be disinherited in a postnuptial agreement?*

A *postnuptial agreement* is a marital agreement made by spouses after they are married. In most states, but not all, these agreements are just as valid as premarital agreements, although a court may scrutinize them more closely if undue influence is suspected. Thus a validly executed postnuptial agreement can be used to disinherit a spouse if both spouses are willing and if full disclosure is made regarding all the assets owned by both spouses. Just as for a prenuptial agreement, it is essential that each spouse have a separate lawyer to ensure that neither spouse is taken advantage of.

☙ *Can I disinherit my spouse if we own property jointly?*

You cannot disinherit your spouse in regard to any property titled jointly with him or her. Such joint property will be distributed in accordance with the title to each particular asset. The surviving spouse will receive outright ownership of those joint assets along with responsibility for any liens or encumbrances on them.

Changing jointly titled assets to your sole ownership will require your spouse's consent and signature.

☙ *What inheritance rights does a spouse have in a community property state?*

In community property states, assets brought to the marriage and assets inherited during the marriage and not commingled with the community property estate remain the separate property of the deceased spouse. They do not become part of the community property that is divided equally between the spouses when one spouse dies.

☙ *My spouse has failed to support me for many years. We are living together but maintaining separate finances. May I disinherit my spouse in favor of my children or other relatives and friends?*

State statutes almost always provide that if the spouses were living together at the time of death, the surviving spouse has specific statutory rights to a share of the deceased spouse's estate. If, however, they were not living together and one abandoned the other, disinheritance might be allowed depending upon state law. You should see an attorney for an explanation of the specific statutes in your state.

Disinheriting a Child

⊁ *Can I disinherit one or all of my children?*

Yes, you can. While some states allow disinheriting a child by merely not leaving any assets to him or her, other states require that the child be mentioned to indicate that you have not merely forgotten the child.

⊁ *What are the potential consequences of disinheriting a child?*

Disinheriting a child requires very deliberate and careful thought. The emotional and financial consequences of that decision can be enormous, for both the parent and the child. When a parent wishes to disinherit a child, there is often great sadness and pain around the decision. It is a symptom of a poor relationship, and the parent is at a loss for anything else to do. The decision to disinherit a child should not be an impulsive reaction to a situation. A thorough understanding of the circumstances surrounding the decision is critical and slowing down the planning process is often the most appropriate course to ensure that the best decision is made. Alternatives that might heal the wounds and lessen the pain should always be explored. Are there other options available that might meet your interests?

An important reason for all this deliberation is to make sure that the parent's wishes will stand up to any contest. Showing that the parent made a reasoned and knowing decision is critical to withstanding a contest.

⊁ *I love my child, but she has emotional problems and addictions. I feel that I must disinherit her or else I will only magnify her problems and those of my other children. What else can I do?*

Although there are ways to disinherit a child, it sounds as though you really want to give your daughter a share of your estate but don't know how to accomplish this without creating a problem for her as well as the other heirs. Rather than disinherit your daughter, you can provide a framework for managing her inheritance without giving her any funds outright and without wreaking havoc on your other children. This requires your determining what and how much of the assets your daughter will receive and designing an appropriate structure to hold her share.

One planning option would be to designate that any share you give to your daughter is to be held in a lifetime trust under terms and guidelines for distribution which you provide in your trust agreement. These distribution instructions could be liberal or conservative. They could include incentive provisions to urge your daughter to seek treatment for her problems. Depending on the nature of the assets and the size of your estate, another option may be to establish a family limited partnership combined with a specially designed trust to hold any partnership interests given to that child.

There are planning strategies available which will allow you to design the appropriate plan to meet your needs and those of each of your children. With a little forethought and planning, you can accomplish your goals without having to take the extreme step of disinheriting your daughter.

⅍ *We have carefully considered all the alternatives and have decided that it just wouldn't be fair to our other children to leave an inheritance to our son after all the grief he has caused us. How do we disinherit him?*

If, after careful thought and consideration, you still desire to disinherit your son, there are three strategies to consider.

The first is to use a living trust as the vehicle of choice for estate planning. A living trust is much harder to contest than a will because a will starts out in the probate court, where it is very easy to initiate a contest. Since a trust does not require court supervision to be effective, it is more difficult to bring the contest before the court.

If you live in a state that requires that you name the disinherited child, one method is to acknowledge the existence of your son by awarding him a nominal amount, such as $1.

The last important strategy to consider is leaving your son enough to make a contest more risky for him. If you leave him nothing, he has nothing to lose by contesting except, of course, attorney's fees, which may or may not be a significant barrier. You can also combine a reduced inheritance with a "no-contest" provision which specifies that if your son contests the trust and loses, he gets nothing—not even the reduced inheritance. The likelihood of a contest under these terms is substantially reduced. While no-contest clauses (also known as *in terrorem* clauses) are not valid in every state, they still may be an effective deterrent to a lawsuit.

⋙ *How can I prevent my disinherited child from successfully contesting my planning?*

It is wise to anticipate such a challenge and to take measures to prevent it from being successful. A primary basis for challenging an estate plan is that the decedent did not have the requisite testamentary intent due to his or her incapacity or mistake or that he or she was under undue influence or duress. The challenger must prove that the lack of testamentary capacity existed at the time the decedent executed the trust or will.

If you are able to create a record establishing your proper capacity at the time you sign your estate planning documents, your trustee or executor will be better equipped to defeat such a challenge. There are a number of ways to do this:

■ Have a psychiatrist, a psychologist, or your attending physician examine you and give a written opinion regarding your sanity. Such a report—if it is contemporaneous with the signing of the estate planning documents—is likely to carry far more weight than anecdotal testimony made many years in the future.

■ Amend your plan on a frequent basis, with each amendment reincorporating the disinheritance language. In this way, a child who later challenges the plan will have to prove that you lacked testamentary capacity not only when you signed the last amendment but when you signed each of the preceding amendments as well.

■ Have a retired judge question you—for the record—about your understanding of your disinheritance wishes.

■ Videotape the signing of your estate planning documents. A word of caution, though: Although a good presentation on videotape can prove to a later court that you were competent, not everyone leaves the impression of being a Hollywood movie star. You should critically evaluate your "star appeal" before committing to a videotaped signing ceremony.

While these approaches may seem like overkill, they work well and should be employed in particularly difficult family situations.

ULTIMATE-REMAINDER PLANNING

❧ What is ultimate-remainder planning?

Ultimate-remainder planning is the process of deciding what to do with your estate should all your beneficiaries predecease you. Unless you specify who is to ultimately receive your property after your death *and* the deaths of all your named heirs or beneficiaries, your state's *descent and distribution statute* (referred to as the "laws of intestacy") will control who receives your assets. Every state has this statute, which originated in English common law, and all the states' versions are amazingly uniform.

Distribution entails creating and following family trees. The statutes generally provide that in the absence of planning, property shall pass to spouses, children, and their descendants. In their absence, the assets will pass to ancestors, siblings, and then descendants of siblings.

❧ What ultimate-remainder strategies do most people use in their planning?

Most people use one or a combination of the following strategies:

- I leave my property to my family in accordance with my state's descent and distribution statute.
- My estate shall be divided into two equal shares: one for my family and one for my spouse's family, both of which shall be distributed by the laws of intestacy in my state.
- I name specific relatives or friends to receive my property in specific dollar amounts or percentages, or both.
- I leave my property to designated public charities.
- I create a testamentary charitable foundation in my living trust and leave my property to it.

No matter what alternative you choose, a well-drafted estate plan should always address the contingency of having no heirs. If it does not, it is incomplete.

chapter 4

Trustees and Guardians

TRUSTEES

Duties of a Trustee

△ *What is a trustee?*

A *trustee* is a person or a licensed corporation that owes a special duty of care to the beneficiaries of a trust.

△ *What is a cotrustee?*

A *cotrustee* is a person or corporate fiduciary that is currently serving as trustee with one or more other trustees.

△ *What is a successor trustee?*

A *successor trustee* is a trustee who takes over for a previous trustee when that trustee is no longer able to perform the duties of a trustee, for whatever reason. Usually the trust maker names successor trustees in the trust agreement.

It is common to have two or three successor trustees acting at once. Theoretically, there is no limit to the number of successor trustees you can have acting at the same time but, as a practical matter, having too many can be costly and cumbersome.

⌘   What is a trust protector?

A *trust protector* is a person or corporation that, depending on the terms of the trust, has authority to oversee the trustees, to change provisions of the trust, to veto acts of the trustees, and, in general, to ensure that the trust is being property administered.

⌘   What does the term "fiduciary" mean?

The word "fiduciary" comes from Roman law and is derived from the same word as are "fidelity" and "faith." A person who is a fiduciary has been put in a position requiring him or her to be faithful and trustworthy. A trustee is the ideal example of a fiduciary. When a trustee controls trust assets, he or she must be faithful to the beneficiaries by performing the trustee's duties in their best interests, and in accordance with fiduciary law, as he or she carries out the terms of the trust agreement.

⌘   What is the primary function of my trustees?

The primary job of your trustees is to follow your instructions. That is why the instructions in your trust must be clear and well written. If your instructions are sparse, incomplete, or ambiguous, your trustees will have to rely on their own judgment. The result may be that what you intended may not happen, defeating the main purpose of your trust.

⌘   Can the successor trustee that I appoint in my revocable living trust control how my assets will be distributed?

Your revocable living trust should contain very specific instructions as to how your trust assets will be distributed. Your trustee is merely an agent whom you appoint and who has the duty to carry out your instructions. In law, the agent is known as a *fiduciary*. In essence, a fiduciary is a person who is entrusted with the assets of another and who is obligated to carry out the direction set forth by the person entrusting those assets. Fiduciaries cannot derive personal benefit from assets entrusted to them. Therefore, the instructions set forth in your revocable living trust must be followed by your trustee and cannot be changed by your trustee. Any deviation from your instructions will subject your trustee to personal legal liability.

⌘   Does my trustee have to file an accounting from time to time with my beneficiaries?

In most states, an accounting to trust beneficiaries is required periodically. Regardless of state law, it is a good idea for the trust agreement to provide for an accounting to beneficiaries.

⚜ Can the trustee, acting in his or her capacity as trustee, amend my trust?

In general, no. Under ordinary circumstances, your trustee cannot amend the trust but must work with what he or she has. Under extraordinary circumstances, it might be necessary for the trustee to bring an action in the appropriate court asking to reform the trust in some pertinent aspect to correct an obvious oversight or omission which would defeat the intent of the trust maker.

⚜ Can you summarize the general duties of trustees?

Each state has statutes that detail the powers and duties of a trustee in carrying out the management of the trust estate. It may be necessary for the trustee to seek professional management or investment advice if such expertise is not within the trustee's experience. Some of the general duties of a trustee include:

- Preparing a complete inventory and valuation of the trust assets
- Obtaining a federal tax number from the IRS
- Paying applicable expenses (medical, funeral, etc.) and taxes (federal estate tax, if applicable, and inheritance tax)
- Dividing and allocating assets to the subtrusts created in the trust if required by the terms of the trust
- Distributing assets according to the directions of the trust
- Preparing accountings as may be required

⚜ Can my trustee delegate some of his or her duties to others or appoint a temporary or substitute trustee?

Your trustee can do these things if the trust agreement authorizes them.

⚜ Do my trustees put my trust property in their individual names?

Trustees do not have equitable or real title to your property; they have legal title in accordance with their responsibility of prudently managing your property for the benefit of your trust's beneficiaries. That is why they hold property in their names *as trustees* rather than individually.

⚜ Can my trustees appropriate my property for their own use if they are not beneficiaries of my trust?

Trustees are charged with the highest duty and responsibility imposed by law in carrying out their functions. They are absolutely prohibited under the law from using trust assets or income for their personal use, enjoyment, or benefit.

⚜ How does the law measure the performance of trustees?

Each state has statutory guidelines governing a trustee's responsibilities, and these guidelines vary from state to state.

Recently, some states have adopted the *prudent investor rule,* a model rule requiring that the trustee use reasonable care, skill, and caution in investing and managing trust assets. The investment decisions and actions of the trustee are judged in terms of the trustee's reasonable business judgment regarding the expected effect on the portfolio of investments as a whole given the facts and circumstances existing at the time of the decision or action. It is important to note that the prudent investor rule is a test of the trustee's conduct and not of the resulting performance of the investments.

Under the prudent investor rule, the trustee has certain duties. The trustee has the duty to review the portfolio assets at the time he or she receives control of the trust assets. The trustee has the duty to diversify the investments of the portfolio unless it is reasonably believed that diversification would not be in the best interests of the beneficiaries. In exercising his or her investment powers and duties, the trustee must pursue an investment strategy that considers both the ability of the investments to produce income and the safety and preservation of capital.

Although the laws that govern the responsibilities and conduct of trustees are precise, they simply boil down to using common sense and good judgment. In many cases, that will mean consulting a professional advisor for guidance. Making your chosen trustees aware of what responsibilities lie ahead is a good first step toward achieving proper administration of your trust property when you are no longer able to do so due to your incapacity or death.

⚜ Who looks over the trustee's shoulder?

As with any trust, the trustee of a revocable living trust has a legal duty to do two things: to follow the rules set down by the trust maker and to act in the best interests of the beneficiaries. In normal circumstances there will not be anyone looking over the trustee's shoulder. And this is what most people want—that the trust operate or distribute after they are gone with no outside interference.

If you have an unusual situation in which a successor trustee does not follow the rules or does not act in the best interests of the beneficiaries, anyone hurt by that trustee's actions can ask the local court with jurisdiction over estates and trusts to review what the trustee has done.

⚛ *What if my trustees make mistakes and lose my funds?*

If they make mistakes which are proved to be costly to the trust or its beneficiaries, trustees are liable to the beneficiaries for those mistakes. However, whether or not the funds are collectible is another matter.

⚛ *How can I protect my beneficiaries from the mistakes of a trustee?*

Name a corporate fiduciary as a cotrustee. By law, corporate fiduciaries are liable for their mistakes and, as such, can be collected against. They must post all of their assets as their bond for the faithful performance of their duties.

Characteristics of Trustees

⚛ *What characteristics should a good trustee have?*

A good trustee should:

- Be honest and trustworthy
- Have the ability to make and handle investments
- Be financially accountable for any mistakes he or she makes
- To the extent possible, be situated in the area where your beneficiaries and your assets are located
- Have good relationships with the beneficiaries
- Be likely to survive you
- Be someone who you feel confident will manage your affairs wisely

⚛ *What kinds of questions should I ask myself when assessing potential trustees?*

You should ask yourself a great number of questions when selecting trustees:

- Are they free of monetary problems of their own?
- Have they demonstrated financial managerial ability?
- Do they have any history of substance abuse?
- Do they know the beneficiaries well?
- Are they reliable?
- Do they have the required specialized skills to manage my assets?

- Have they demonstrated problem-solving ability?
- Are they the right ages?
- Are they likely to be available when needed?
- Will they seek and utilize professional assistance when circumstances require it?
- Will they accept the appointment?

≪ Is there any requirement that my trustee have any particular abilities, education, or training?

The selection of a duly-qualified and honest trustee is one of the most important decisions to be made in the creation of a trust. This is because the trustee is the person with the primary responsibility for carrying out the trust maker's wishes to the best of his or her ability. As a result, someone who is familiar with the trust maker and his or her desires regarding how assets should be invested and how and when assets should be distributed may serve a valuable role as a trustee. Guidance and specific instructions in these areas can be included in the trust instrument.

Because the trustee will be expected to make investment decisions and will be required to account for all financial transactions involving trust assets, it is helpful if a person serving as trustee has some degree of financial knowledge and ability. Many times a person having all the desirable characteristics of a good trustee may not be available. For this reason, a trust maker may wish to consider appointing one or more persons as cotrustees. Using this "team" approach allows the individual strengths and abilities of the cotrustees to be combined to best carry out all aspects of the trust administration.

Who to Name as Trustee

≪ How do I decide who should be my trustees?

To answer this question, you must first understand in what instances, and for what stages of a trust, trustees are chosen. Trustees need to be supplied upon the occurrence of the following events:

- Creation of the trust
- Disability of a trustee
- Death of a trustee
- Resignation or termination of a trustee
- Creation of subtrusts within a trust

Usually the trust maker names himself or herself to be the initial trustee and, if married, names the spouse as cotrustee. The trust contains instructions as to who should take over the trusteeship upon the disability, death, resignation, or termination of a trustee. The trust can even name different trustees for the subtrusts that are created within the original trust.

Designating the successor trustees, those who will succeed the trust maker after his or her death or disability, can be a tough problem, and many people spend a great deal of time agonizing over the decision. Often, however, there are simple solutions to naming successor trustees. First, you want the best assurance that your wishes and desires will be carried out. Therefore, your wishes, desires, goals, and aspirations should be specified in great detail, if necessary, in order to guide the successor trustee. It is a trustee's specific role, by law, to carry out his or her duties under the trust document for the benefit of the named beneficiary.

Second, the successor trustee should be a responsible person whom you have confidence in. Usually people look to close members of the family, such as adult children, parents, siblings, aunts, and uncles. If there are no close family members, they often look to close friends. Consider how much confidence you have that the person will carry out the duties.

Once you have narrowed your list of candidates, discuss the trusteeship with them. Do not just name someone without discussing it with him or her in advance. Some people, while honored by your confidence, just might not want the duties and responsibilities. Or they might be on the verge of a major life change such as taking a new position that requires them to move far away from you. If this happens and they are in line to serve, they may decline when the time comes. In this case, if there are no other successor trustees or some mechanism for naming them, the court will appoint a successor trustee. This would be disadvantageous and time-consuming and would defeat some of the benefits of having a trust.

❧ Can I be the trustee of my own living trust?

This is commonly done. However, if you become disabled or die, it will be easier to continue the affairs of your trust if you had a cotrustee serving with you who can continue to carry out your trust instructions in your absence. At the very least, you should provide for a series of successor trustees who will assume the duties after your death or upon your disability.

Should a trustee also serve as my personal representative (executor)?

Your executor is responsible for handling the probate administration of your estate, including distribution of all your probate assets. It is important to have someone who will follow your written instructions as set forth in your estate planning documents. Likewise, you will want someone who will give appropriate attention to any of your personal property items that have a high sentimental value even though they may not have a high economic value.

If you have a living trust–centered estate plan, it is good practice to have the trustee also be your personal representative. A trustee who is a family member or close friend is often a good choice.

Family members as trustees

What are the advantages of family-member trustees?

- They will often serve for little or no fee.
- They are free from corporate technicalities which can slow down decisions and actions.
- They are usually known, trusted, and loved by trust beneficiaries.

What are the disadvantages of family-member trustees?

- They often make decisions on an emotional basis rather than an objective one.
- They may have a lack of expertise.
- They may not have the financial resources to cover mistakes.
- They may die, become incapacitated, become greedy, or even file bankruptcy.

Can I name more than one of my children as trustee?

Yes. This is often a wise choice. Many people recognize that the differences in their children can be strengths when the children work together. For example, the child with a big heart and the child who is an efficient or analytical manager may be much more effective as a trustee team than either child could be by himself or herself.

Naming more than one child as a trustee also helps alleviate the chance that a sibling or a deceased sibling's child will feel controlled by another family member. Naming cotrustees also reduces the chance of real abuse. An individual can convince himself or herself of just about anything, but when a person must justify actions to siblings or convince them of the wisdom of those actions, it is much harder to fool himself or herself.

≫ *I want my children to share equally in my estate. If I make one of them the trustee, won't that child have an unfair advantage?*

Be careful not to confuse duty and responsibility with privilege. Being a trustee is a duty and responsibility; it can also be hard work. A trustee has a fiduciary duty to the other beneficiaries, not a privileged access to funds. If anything, a trustee must be much more circumspect and careful when distributing to himself or herself.

To ensure that your children share equally in the estate, it is important that the trust provisions clearly indicate your desire. Having cotrustees, including a corporate fiduciary, will also help ensure fairness in the distribution of funds.

≫ *My spouse and I must decide on successor trustees and on guardians for our minor children. While we trust and love our in-laws, each of us would prefer to name people from his or her side of the family because we fear that our children will become distanced from the side that is not actively involved with them. What can we do to ensure that our children remain close to both sets of aunt and uncles?*

Choosing the guardian who will have parental rights for small children and choosing the successor trustee who will have control over the trust assets are often the most difficult personal choices to make in the estate planning process. Deciding which side of the family should be given this control can bring the planning process to a standstill.

As to successor trustees, it may make sense to appoint two people, one from each side of the family, to act as cotrustees. Even if trust is not an issue, having cotrustees is a good way to keep both sides of the family actively involved in the lives of your children.

With respect to guardians, many states allow for only one guardian to serve, so the appointment of "coguardians" is not possible. If that is the case in your state, it makes sense to choose the best available guardian and discuss your concerns with that person.

Corporate trustees

≫ *What are the advantages of corporate trustees?*

Corporate fiduciaries have several advantages:

- They act objectively and follow trust instructions without emotion.
- Managing trusts is their business; they do it professionally day in and day out.
- They have investment, tax, and estate administration expertise.
- They don't die or become incapacitated, and if they go out of business, their obligations will be assumed by another corporation.
- They are highly regulated by government agencies.
- They have the resources to cover errors and mistakes.

❧ What are the major disadvantages of corporate trustees?

- They charge fees for what they do.
- Because they are supposed to make decisions on an objective and unemotional basis, they are often thought of as being mean-spirited and uncaring.
- They are not always the best choice for an estate that consists mainly of real estate and/or a family business.

❧ Do I have to name a corporate trustee for my living trust?

Everyone has heard at least one horror story about a bank that didn't follow the instructions in a trust. In reality, most corporate trustees go out of their way to meet both the intent of the instructions of the trust maker and the state's fiduciary law. The benefits of having a corporate trustee can often outweigh the disadvantages. One approach is to name an individual whom you trust and who has an emotional understanding of your beneficiaries to make the nonbusiness judgments that your trust needs and name a corporate cotrustee to make investment decisions and handle government reporting.

❧ What happens to my trust if a bank is trustee and the bank fails?

When a bank is trustee, it is merely holding your assets in its fiduciary capacity. If the bank fails, those assets are not subject to claims by either depositors or creditors of the bank. Instead, the regulating authority, usually the state bank examiner, the Federal Reserve Bank, or the FDIC, arranges to have another financial institution in the geographic area take over the trustee responsibilities of the failed bank.

Even though the bank fails, your trust doesn't. The new trustee will continue to manage your trust assets in the same manner as did the failed trustee. If your trust was invested in various stocks, bonds, and mutual funds, those same stocks, bonds, and mutual funds will now be managed by the new trustee. Your trust remains completely intact as long as the value of the investments remains intact.

⊷ *Are there corporate trustees that are not banks?*

Many brokerage firms have established or are establishing trust departments or trust company subsidiaries. If you are comfortable with your broker, he or she may be able to continue to help in the investment decisions concerning your money after your death by using the brokerage firm's trust company.

Professionals as trustees

⊷ *Can I name my financial advisors and planners as cotrustees?*

Although commonly done, this has a single significant disadvantage: If advisors make their living selling investments or services, state law may preclude them from selling to a trust under which they serve as trustees.

⊷ *Is there any way that I can name my financial advisor and allow her to sell to the trust?*

You can include instructions stating that you want her to be able to sell or charge for her investment advice but that she cannot participate in any decisions with other cotrustees whenever she has a conflict of interest.

⊷ *Can we appoint our attorney to be a successor trustee of our living trust?*

You can name anyone you want to be a successor trustee; however, most attorneys will respectfully decline. Attorneys are not in the business of acting as trustees, and you may be better served by using the attorney's services as an advisor.

Cotrustees

⊷ *In what circumstances do most people need cotrustees?*

Many people want to name as a successor trustee a loving family member who is not good with money or investments but who is trustworthy and personally close to the trust's beneficiaries. In such instances, naming a trusted accountant or a corporate fiduciary as a cotrustee can shore up the individual's weaknesses while still making his or her many strengths available to your beneficiaries.

≈ *Why do you feel so strongly that having cotrustees is beneficial?*

A combination of several individuals or professional trustees is beneficial for a great many reasons that center around qualifications and balance. Also, it is prudent to have trustees watching trustees for the benefit of the trust beneficiaries.

≈ *Whom should I name as a cotrustee with me?*

If you are married and each of you has his or her own trust, it is common practice to name the other spouse as a cotrustee. If you and your spouse have a joint trust agreement, typically both of you will act as its initial trustees.

If you are single and have children, you should consider naming one or more of them. If you do not have children, or you have children but would prefer they not serve, then consider a close friend, relative, or professional advisor. If you would like professional money management, you can consider naming a corporate fiduciary. Of course, if you do, there will be trustee's fees, but they may well be worth what you pay if the services provided meet your needs.

≈ *Can my children be cotrustees with me?*

Children are commonly named as cotrustees, but seldom named as sole trustees, of their parents' living trusts.

≈ *If I name more than one trustee, who controls?*

This depends solely upon your trust instructions. You can provide for a majority vote, or you can provide otherwise. Your instructions could specify that, after your death or disability, your spouse must agree or that he or she must carry the vote of at least one other trustee to block a specific action or to institute a certain action.

≈ *If my spouse and I are cotrustees of our joint living trust, do we both have to sign everything?*

Most couples want each spouse to be able to act without the consent of the other. You can include a provision in your trust that allows either spouse to act as trustee in the administration of the trust.

Successor trustees

≈ *If I am living but unable to manage of my assets, how will the successor trustee of my living trust step in to take over?*

Your revocable living trust should define how you want this process to occur. One frequently chosen method is to have a family member or trustee obtain written opinions from two physicians indicating that the trust maker is no longer able to handle his or her financial affairs. As the trust maker, you can design the trust so that the disability trustee assumes responsibility when it best suits your needs. This is the benefit of a living trust plan versus a court-ordered guardianship.

At some point in time you may decide that you no longer want to be responsible for managing day-to-day business transactions. You may resign as trustee and allow a successor to assume the duties outlined in the trust.

As the trust maker, you control the entire process through the terms you establish in your trust.

Will there be a problem if the person I select as successor trustee is not located in my state?

If you become disabled or die, your trustee must carry out the instructions of your trust. Your instructions may require your trustee to deal with your financial institutions, creditors, or purchasers of your assets. Certainly, it will be easier if your trustee is located in the same geographic area as your residence. However, such logistical hurdles are only one factor in determining your trustee. Your paramount concern in choosing a trustee should be whether the appointed trustee will have the ability to make logical decisions on discretionary items and whether your trustee will closely follow the instructions you leave. In our modern era of communications, logistical hurdles can usually be surmounted with only mild inconvenience.

Additionally, in your revocable living trust document you can allow your trustee to delegate certain duties so that your trustee will not have to be personally present for many transactions.

How will my successor trustees know what to do in order to make my plan work?

Many people choose to have their children or other family members, rather than a professional trustee, serve as successor trustees of their trusts on either death or disability One problem with choosing family members as successor trustees is that most people have never served as a trustee before and don't understand what they need to do to accomplish the trust maker's objectives. Therefore, it is important that you select an estate planning attorney who will help educate your successor trustees as to what will be required of them when they serve in that capacity.

⊁ *What if someone we have named as a successor trustee doesn't want to serve?*

You cannot force a person or an institution to act as your trustee, so you should name alternatives in case one of your choices refuses or cannot serve.

⊁ *What kind of problems would there be if one of the trustees I named is involved in a divorce or other legal problems while he or she is serving as a trustee?*

A trustee of a trust is not an owner of the assets that are inside the trust. The trustee is a manager or agent. Therefore, a trustee's divorce or other legal proceedings involving his or her personal matters are not related to the trust and should not, in any way, jeopardize the assets that are owned inside of your revocable living trust.

A spouse as successor trustee

⊁ *If my living trust becomes an irrevocable trust at my death, does that interfere with the ability of my spouse to buy and sell and manage the assets in my trust?*

You would simply name your spouse as trustee of the trust with the power to manage, add, or remove trust property as conditions warrant.

⊁ *Can my spouse be the sole trustee after my death?*

You can name your spouse as the sole trustee of the marital trust and the family trust after your death. However, there has been significant professional debate over naming a spouse as sole trustee of the family trust. If the family trust principal distribution to the spouse is not limited by the *ascertainable standards*—health, education, support, and maintenance—as required by the IRS, the risk of naming your spouse as the trustee of the family trust is that the entire amount of the trust will be included in your spouse's estate. This could result in as much as an extra $435,000 in federal estate tax. We believe it to be a risky practice from a tax standpoint for a spouse to be the sole trustee of the family trust and would strongly recommend that a cotrustee be used.

As for naming your spouse as the sole trustee of the marital or QTIP trust, there will be no estate tax problem. That trust will be included in the spouse's estate no matter who is named as trustee.

There are a number of reasons for naming a cotrustee with your spouse in both the marital and the family trusts. When a husband or a wife dies, the surviving partner is usually at a loss in many ways. Putting him or her in a position to make all the financial decisions alone, without any help, can be a burden and often results in poor decisions on the part of the vulnerable and bereaved spouse.

It may be wiser to give your spouse some assistance by naming one or more cotrustees. This can relieve some of the burden of decision making, but it does not have to mean a loss of control. You can always give your spouse the right to remove a trustee and replace that trustee with the next person you have chosen.

In addition, having your spouse serve as a cotrustee, rather than the only trustee, offers some creditor protection to the assets you left in trust for your spouse.

> *Should I name a bank or trust company as sole trustee over my spouse's marital and family trusts?*

Most spouses do not want to have their affairs managed by a corporate entity over which they have no control, but many trust makers do want the benefits offered by professional trustees. You could name your spouse as a cotrustee of your marital and family trusts with the corporate trustee and provide that your spouse can terminate the corporate trustee and then name another fiduciary in its place.

> *Why would I give my spouse the right to fire a corporate fiduciary?*

Experience has taught most practitioners that if a spouse—or any other beneficiary for that matter—is "locked into" a trustee, it is likely that the trustee will not be very responsive to the needs of the beneficiary.

> *If I allow my spouse to terminate a trustee, can I provide a list from which the replacement must be selected?*

You can specify the precise replacement or furnish a list from which the replacement can be selected.

Successor trustees for children

> *Should I name the same trustees for all of my children?*

This would be wise when there is a common trust for children or grandchildren. Once you create the separate shares for each child, you can name the same trustees for all the children or different trustees for each child.

≫ *Should I name my children to be trustees of each other's trusts?*

It is generally not a good idea to put one child in charge of another child's inheritance even if they get along famously. There are certain things you can do in estate planning that bring families together upon death, while other things can pull them apart. This is one of the things that can pull them apart. In most circumstances siblings should not be each other's trustees.

≫ *Can I name my adult son as the trustee of his own trust?*

This is commonly done with adult children, but you should name at least one other person or institution as a cotrustee with the child. By naming an independent trustee, you creditor-proof your son's trust.

≫ *How does a cotrustee "creditor-proof" my son's trust?*

A properly drawn trust is generally not subject to the claims of creditors unless the sole trustee is also the sole beneficiary. If your son is sole trustee of his own trust and gets into financial or legal difficulties, creditors can obtain and execute judgments against him. If your son is a cotrustee of his trust and resigns, a creditor would have a difficult task in asserting rights against the trust or the remaining trustee.

≫ *Whom should I name as trustee of an adult child's trust?*

You should name a trustee team that will take into account the child's needs and your wishes for his or her success and happiness. You might not want to name the same trustees for a spendthrift child as you would for an accomplished professional or executive child whose trust needs protection only from creditors and a potential divorce.

≫ *What kinds of trustees can help my spendthrift child?*

Corporate fiduciaries and certified public accountants make excellent cotrustees for spendthrift children.

Compensation of Trustees

≫ *Is a trustee entitled to be paid for his or her services? If so, how is an appropriate trustee's fee determined?*

There is no requirement that a trustee be paid for providing services, but a person or entity designated to serve as trustee will not be required to serve for free if the trustee does not choose to do so. Instead, the person or entity is always free to decline to serve as a trustee. In many instances, family members will be designated to serve as trustees, and even if a reasonable fee for their services is provided by the trust agreement, they may choose to waive their right to receive the fee. On the other hand, if the trust administration is expected to extend over a lengthy period of time, even a family member serving as a trustee may become resentful if he or she is forced to spend large amounts of time administering the trust without compensation.

Most corporate trustees, such as banks and private trust companies, have published fee schedules which usually include an annual fee based on the percentage of assets under administration, plus minimum fees for trusts with assets valued at less than certain amounts. Corporate trustees will gladly provide their fee schedules to potential customers.

There is no requirement that an individual serving as a trustee receive the same compensation as that charged by a corporate trustee. In many cases, a trust agreement may provide that the trustee will simply receive "reasonable" compensation. As a general rule, the fees charged by corporate trustees in like circumstances will be considered as evidence of what constitutes "reasonable" compensation.

If a trust agreement does not contain a specific formula for the calculation of a trustee's fee, the trustee will generally be empowered to decide what fee the trustee considers to be reasonable. If the beneficiaries, or any other party in interest, consider the trustee's determination to be unreasonable, a legal action may need to be filed to have a court determine the reasonableness of the fee charged by the trustee. Such uncertainty and the possibility of litigation can be avoided if a specific formula defining the trustee's fee is included in the trust instrument.

Is it necessary for me to leave money to my trustee?

It is not necessary to leave a gift to your trustee in order for your trustee to be compensated. Your living trust document can have a provision stating that your trustee be reasonably compensated for his or her time and effort.

Should I compensate family members?

While family members are often willing to serve without compensation, the duties of a trustee are significant and your trustee may spend considerable time on carrying out the instructions set forth in your trust.

Ill feelings can arise if the person shouldering this burden is not fairly compensated.

⚜ *I want to make my brother a trustee under my trust, but I do not want him to be a beneficiary. Can I provide that he gets a fee for his services as trustee? If so, what should that fee be?*

Your brother need not be a beneficiary in order to be your trustee. Although in many cases a family member acting as trustee will waive the fee for his or her services, every trustee is entitled to be paid. You can specify the amount of the fee payable for the services your brother renders as trustee, or you can provide a formula based on the fees for reasonable and necessary services that are charged by professional trustees in the locality. In addition, your brother can be reimbursed for any necessary expenses incurred in connection with the administration of your trust.

Fiduciary bonds

⚜ *What is a fiduciary bond? Is a successor trustee required to obtain such a bond?*

In probate proceedings, a court generally has the discretion to require that an administrator or executor obtain an appropriate fiduciary bond to protect the heirs of the estate if the administrator or executor absconds with assets or otherwise breaches his or her fiduciary duty to the probate estate. Although many wills provide that a person named as an executor *not* be required to post such a bond, in a probate proceeding the court can overrule the wishes of the decedent and require the posting of a fiduciary bond in an amount it believes necessary.

In the case of a revocable living trust, a trust maker likewise has the discretion to designate whether or not a trustee must obtain a fiduciary bond as a condition of qualifying as a trustee. As a matter of course, it is rare that a trust maker requires a bond. Usually, the successor trustees are family members or corporate trustees.

⚜ *What are the advantages and disadvantages of requiring a fiduciary bond?*

The advantage of requiring the posting of a fiduciary bond is that the beneficiaries are protected financially if the trustee misappropriates or otherwise absconds with trust assets. One of the disadvantages of requiring such a bond, however, is the cost associated with purchasing the bond. This cost includes an annual premium that will be due each year that the bond is in effect. The premium amount generally varies, but it is based on a percentage of the assets being administered in the trust or the probate estate. In addition, before issuing a fiduciary bond, a surety company will generally require that the trustee provide detailed financial statements and either personally guarantee or pledge collateral to guarantee the repayment of any monies expended by the surety if the trustee in fact breaches his or her fiduciary duty. The requirement that a trustee post a fiduciary bond could therefore disqualify a person from serving as a trustee if the person cannot satisfy the financial requirements imposed by the surety for the issuance of the bond.

Removal of Trustees

⅍ *What are grounds for removing a trustee if the trust instrument contains no specific provision for removal?*

Even if a trust instrument does not define the circumstances under which a trustee can be removed, a court can exercise its discretion to remove a trustee if the trust or trust property is in jeopardy. Recognized grounds for removing a trustee include the trustee's nonresidence in or absence from the jurisdiction if the trustee's presence in the jurisdiction is necessary for the administration of the trust; antagonistic or hostile relations created by conflicts between the trustee's individual interests and the interests of the beneficiaries; situations in which a trustee's insolvent financial condition jeopardizes the administration of the trust funds; or situations in which the trustee lacks personal competence to administer the trust by reasons of ill health, intemperance, mental infirmity, old age, or dishonesty.

Similarly, a trustee may be removed in the court's discretion for misconduct and mismanagement in execution of the trust, including abandonment or neglect of the trust, disobedience as to court orders, failure to pay principal or income when due, failure to file an oath or give security, improprieties with respect to investments, commingling of trust funds with nontrust assets, and filing of defective reports and accounts.

As a general rule, a trustee of a revocable living trust is not initially subject to court supervision. If grounds exist for removal of a trustee, the beneficiaries would have to initiate legal action for removal if the trustee fails to resign voluntarily at their request. Courts are generally reluctant to remove a trustee who is specifically designated by a trust maker because they naturally want to give great weight to the faith placed in the trustee by the trust maker.

How difficult is it to remove or change the person or entity designated to serve as a trustee?

In the case of a revocable living trust, the trust maker retains during his or her lifetime the right to amend the trust, so the designation of trustees can easily be changed at any time by a simple amendment to the trust instrument. After the death of the trust maker, however, unless the trust instrument specifically grants the beneficiaries, or some other person, power to change the person designated as trustee, the beneficiaries may have to take legal action if appropriate grounds for removal exist and the trustee refuses to resign. A provision granting the beneficiaries the power to force the removal or change of a trustee under specific circumstances could save time and expense.

In general, should my beneficiaries be allowed to remove a trustee that I have named in my trust agreement?

It is not a good idea to have a trust that does not provide some method for removing a trustee. Matters change over time and it is entirely possible that a particular trustee may become inadequate.

If the beneficiaries are not satisfied with a trustee's performance, they should be allowed to fire the old trustee and hire a new one. When this happens, the next person you named on your list of successor trustees in the trust agreement becomes the new trustee.

In the event that the list of named trustees runs out, it is customary to provide in the trust agreement that a court can be allowed temporary jurisdiction over the trust for the sole purpose of appointing a new trustee. Courts usually appoint corporate trustees under such circumstances. This method prevents the beneficiaries from "trustee shopping" (constantly hiring and firing trustees until they find one that meets their needs or does what they want), since continually going to court would be expensive and unproductive. At the same time, it does enable them to remove a trustee who is unsatisfactory.

If a court is named to appoint a trustee, won't my trust be back in probate?

Yes, it will, but only for the limited purpose of appointing a new trustee if your instructions so provide.

POUR-OVER WILLS

If I have a living trust, do I still need a will?

Yes, you need a special type of will called a *pour-over will* for two reasons. The primary purpose of this type of will is to "catch" any assets that you own at the time of your death that are not controlled by other means such as by your living trust, a beneficiary designation, or joint tenancy with right of survivorship. The pour-over will merely states that all assets held by the decedent which pass through probate shall "pour over" to the trust maker's living trust, which defines the distribution plan in detail.

The second purpose of a pour-over will is to appoint a guardian for minor children. Your revocable living trust governs how funds will be managed for a minor beneficiary and designates the trustee who will manage those funds, but guardians should be named in your will. Even when all assets have been transferred to the trust maker's living trust, a pour-over will may have to be probated for the sole purpose of appointing the legal guardian of a minor child. However, this type of probate is usually relatively simple, without the costs and delay that a full probate of assets can create.

If I have a pour-over will, does it have to be probated when I die?

All wills go through probate; however, a will probates only the assets it controls. If your living trust is fully funded so that your pour-over will controls no property, the probate process is not necessary unless it is used to appoint the legal guardian of a minor child. If you fail to transfer your assets to your living trust, your pour-over will is designed to fund the trust for you; unfortunately, the assets it controls must go through the probate process.

Why should I appoint the guardian for my minor children in my will rather than in my trust?

Using a trust instead of a will to appoint a guardian does not provide any greater control over the appointment.

There is, however, an advantage to using a will to appoint a guardian for minors. Most states require that any document relevant to such an appointment be filed in the courts for judicial review and approval. If you use your trust document to appoint the guardian, you will have to file the trust with the court, thereby destroying the advantage of privacy generally afforded by a trust. Therefore, it is always preferable that the appointment of a guardian for minors be made in the pour-over will.

⚕ *Am I required to write a new pour-over will and trust each time a child or grandchild is born or adopted?*

You can provide in your trust agreement for a gift to a class of individuals which will remain open until the distribution puts the gift into effect. In this manner, children born or adopted into your family after you prepare your will and trust are automatically included in your plan.

GUARDIANS

⚕ *Is it important to name a guardian for my minor child?*

Absolutely. By doing so, you can ensure that the potential guardians have the same family values as you do and thus that your child will be raised the way you want him or her to be raised. It is imperative that you receive the consent of your child's potential guardians before naming them in your estate plan, since no one can be forced to serve as a guardian for your minor child. Naming primary and successor guardians will greatly reduce the possibility of family feuds regarding your child's care.

⚕ *Whom should I select as guardians for my minor children?*

This is usually the most difficult question for couples to answer. Not knowing whom to select as a guardian is quite often the reason they put off estate planning.

Guardians are appointed by the surrogate or probate court judge. The judge will usually follow the wishes of the deceased parent, but the overriding concern of the court is the best interests of the child or children.

Factors to be considered in selecting a guardian are:

1. *The age of the children and the age of the guardian:* It may not be fair to either the children or the guardian to ask older or elderly grandparents to raise very young children.
2. *The guardian's home:* If you have more than one child, should they stay together with one guardian? Will the guardian have a home

large enough to accommodate his or her existing family plus the new wards? Is provision made in your will or trust to provide the guardian with additional funds to enlarge his or her home or purchase a larger home? Should this money be paid back at a later date for the benefit of your children?

3. *The guardian's values and lifestyle:* Does the guardian have the same values you have? Will the guardian raise your children the way you would have? Does the guardian have a stable marriage? Will your children get along with the guardian's children?

4. *The management of your children's assets:* Should the guardian of your children also manage their money? Parenting qualities and money management abilities do not necessarily go hand in hand. It may be best to avoid a possible conflict of interest or the potential for abuse of discretion by having someone other than the guardian manage your children's assets.

Once you have selected a guardian for your children, remember that the guardian you choose today may not be the correct choice as the guardian's family situation changes and as your children get older. The choice of guardian should be reviewed periodically. If a change is necessary, a new will should be prepared.

≽ *Should the guardian of my child be the same person as her trustee?*
Although this is frequently done, it can be problematic. Most professionals would recommend that you name the child's guardian as a cotrustee rather than sole trustee. Alternatively, you need not appoint the guardian as trustee in any form. You have chosen your child's guardian because of his or her tremendous capacity for love and affection. The abilities which enable the guardian to nurture your child are not necessarily the abilities that make someone a good trustee. You want the guardian to focus exclusively on child rearing, and this is best accomplished by having someone else handle the financial matters. This approach will lessen the guardian's burden and provide an extra layer of fiduciary protection for minor children who cannot protect themselves.

If you choose to name the guardian as trustee, naming a cotrustee to serve with the guardian will eliminate the chance of malfeasance. Just as important, a cotrustee reduces the chance that other family members will challenge your guardian's motives when he or she is making expenditures on your child's behalf. Some expenditures such as summer camp, sports activities, vacations, or home computers could appear to benefit the guardian as much as the child. A cotrustee can help the guardian determine the appropriateness of an expenditure and deflect the jealousies or well-intentioned meddling of family members.

⚜ *Is the court obligated to follow our appointment of guardian in our wills if we die while our children are minors?*

Generally, the court will defer to your nomination unless the person designated is determined to be unfit (e.g., because of a drug or alcohol problem). The court may also designate someone other than the person nominated in your wills if there has been a significant change in his or her circumstances (e.g., divorce or a move to another state) since the nomination was made. The court may also give some weight to the wishes of your children, especially if they are old enough to participate in the proceedings.

⚜ *How can we prevent a certain relative from trying to get custody of our children (and their money) in the event of our premature deaths?*

You can specify in your pour-over will that the individual be ineligible to serve as guardian.

⚜ *My spouse and I are taking a short vacation and leaving our minor children with family members. Our concern is that, if one of our children is injured or becomes seriously ill while we are away, the family members would not be able to direct medical care for that child. Is there any way to appoint a temporary guardian for minor children?*

Some states now allow the appointment of a *short-term guardian,* who can be appointed by either parent of the child. The short-term guardian is authorized to serve as guardian immediately upon execution of the short-term guardian document, so there is no need to go into probate court and have a judge appoint the guardian. The short-term guardian usually may serve for a limited period of time, such as 60 days. Thus, parents can authorize a family member or friend to care for their minor children during the parents' period of absence.

In states that do not allow for short-term guardians, parents should have their attorney prepare a short power of attorney that authorizes a relative or friend to act on behalf of their minor children if there is a medical emergency.

chapter 5

Funding and Maintaining a Revocable Living Trust

FUNDING YOUR REVOCABLE LIVING TRUST

The Funding Process

🔊 *Is there anything I must do after I've signed my trust documents?*

Revocable living trusts are valid as probate-avoidance mechanisms only if they are properly "funded." For your property to avoid probate, all of your assets (if possible) should be owned by your trust or your trust should be the beneficiary of any property that requires beneficiary designations. But be careful when you fund your trust: Not all assets should be held in a revocable living trust, so professional advice is a must.

🔊 *What is meant by "funding" a revocable living trust?*

Funding a living trust means changing ownership of your assets to the trust or naming the trust as the beneficiary of assets such as qualified retirement plans or life insurance policies. Since the trust controls only the assets which are titled in its name or are paid directly to it by beneficiary designation, assets left outside the trust may have to go through probate at the time of your death.

⚛ What is meant by "fully funding" a living trust?

Fully funding a living trust means completing the process of transferring ownership of *all* appropriate assets to your living trust or changing beneficiary designations as appropriate to reflect your living trust as the beneficiary.

Keeping your living trust fully funded is an ongoing process. As you acquire new assets, you must place them into the living trust by retitling them to the name of your trust or they may pass through probate. However, once you complete the initial transfer process, placing assets into your trust as you acquire them requires only a small amount of effort to reap huge benefits and safeguards.

⚛ What activities are necessary to accomplish trust funding?

Trust funding is similar to probate except it is done while you are around to help answer questions, gather documents, and express your wishes. Here is a summary of what is generally required in funding a trust:

- Gathering detailed and accurate information regarding how you currently own each of your assets
- Deciding how each asset should be owned, such as in the husband's trust, in the wife's trust, and in what percentages
- Deciding who should be the beneficiary and contingent beneficiary under each insurance policy and each retirement plan (There are many variations, all of which have significantly different legal and tax implications.)
- Preparing the various documents required to change ownership or beneficiary designations to the trust
- Consolidating all the information about your assets in a user-friendly source

⚛ Can you give me an example of funding?

Suppose you created the Jane Smith Living Trust, dated January 22, 1999, and you are the initial sole trustee. The property that is currently titled in your name will be retitled to read:

> Jane Smith, Sole Trustee, or her successors in trust, under the Jane Smith Living Trust, dated January 22, 1999, and any amendments thereto.

This retitling of your assets enables your successor trustees to deal with the property, according to your instructions, in the event of your disability or death.

In practice, using the full name, as shown above, may be cumbersome. It may not fit into certain computer software programs used by brokerage houses or public agencies. To abbreviate, you could use the following:

Jane Smith, Trustee, u/a dtd 1/22/99

This is sufficient for purposes of holding title in the name of the trust, since it identifies the current trustees and refers to a particular trust document ("u/a" is an abbreviation for the words "under agreement").

⚜ *Do I transfer my debts into my trust?*

When you put your property into your trust, you generally do not have to put your debts into it; they are unaffected by the transfer of the property. However, there are some debts that you must be careful of.

Debts usually come in two types: secured and unsecured. *Secured debts* are those that attach to property. Examples of secured debt are a mortgage on real estate or a security interest in property that has been financed. In some cases, transfer of the secured property may require permission of the creditor, but the debt will travel with the property into your trust. *Unsecured debt,* such as credit card debt, does not attach to a particular asset. Unsecured creditors look to the debtor for payment; they are not particularly concerned with how property is owned.

No matter what kind of debt you do have, you are still just as liable for it when it is transferred to your trust as you were before the transfer. Living trusts are not designed to relieve anyone of his or her just debts.

⚜ *If I transfer my assets to my living trust, can anyone legally challenge those transfers?*

Transferring your assets to your living trust will not leave them any more vulnerable to challenge from others than they might have been before the transfer. Their title, and your right to ownership, will be no less secure if the assets are held by your revocable trust than if they had remained in your own name. However, always work with your attorney to ensure that the funding of your assets to your trust is appropriate to your situation.

⚜ *I am reluctant to transfer my assets out of my name and into the trust. By transferring them, won't I be losing them?*

Since deeds and other types of transfer documents are required to show that ownership of an asset is held by a revocable living trust, many people fear they are losing control in some way merely because there is a transfer occurring. In fact the opposite is true. By transferring assets to a living trust, the trust maker is able not only to continue controlling the assets as always but also to control their management through the terms of the trust in the event of his or her disability or death.

During the trust maker's life, a living trust uses the trust maker's Social Security number. Any income earned on trust assets is reported on the trust maker's individual tax return. The trust maker can add or remove property at any time and change or amend the trust at will. The trust maker totally controls the trust and its assets. Therefore, there is no reason to fear the transfer of assets into a revocable living trust. Such a transfer can help the trust maker by protecting assets if he or she becomes disabled and by providing assurance that assets will be distributed to loved ones according to the wishes of the trust maker upon his or her death.

I've heard that funding a revocable living trust makes estate planning more difficult and time-consuming. Is this true?

This view is often promoted by will-planning probate practitioners as a reason to avoid living trust–centered estate planning. Interestingly, funding your trust is one of the major *advantages* of living trust–centered planning.

The argument that funding a living trust makes estate planning more difficult and time-consuming runs counter to both legal and common sense. If it is indeed so difficult to locate and transfer assets during your lifetime, how can the process be more easily accomplished after your death, without *your* assistance—without the help of the person who owned the assets and knew more about them than anyone else? Most people do not have their financial paperwork well organized at the time of their death or disability. This results in a legal "scavenger hunt" on the part of those left behind. The time it takes to locate assets is often a major cause of delay in the average probate estate.

It's only human to procrastinate. Few people look forward to the paperwork involved in retitling their assets into the names of their trusts. However, many people go through the funding process, sometimes with the assistance of an attorney or financial advisor, and most have accomplished the complete funding of their trusts with little, if any, hassle.

With your participation, problems that loom today can be solved easily. Without your participation, those same problems can cause lengthy delays, costs, and aggravation for your loved ones.

The title to real estate is often illustrative of the difference between funding your trust while you are capable and allowing the judicial system to do so after you are incapacitated or deceased. For example, a person may believe that real estate is owned by a partnership, when in fact the land was never deeded to the partnership but remains in the individual name or joint names of one or more of the partners. This mistake in ownership is quite common, and it will cause massive partnership and tax problems that will probably not be solved to anyone's satisfaction after a partner's death.

≈ *Is there a simple way to determine what methods should be used to place my various assets into my trust?*

Most assets have some sort of paperwork which indicates their owner for legal purposes. As a general rule of thumb, the same paperwork which originally conveyed those assets to your name will be used to reconvey them to your trust. Most law firms that regularly prepare living trusts can provide you with letters of instruction that will assist you with the paperwork.

≈ *Do I have to show my bank, broker, or anyone else a copy of my trust when funding it?*

When transferring assets to your revocable living trust, more often than not the transferring agents need to see certain information from your trust to help them make the transfer. They need to know that the trust exists and that you have actually signed the trust. They need to know the names of the trustees and cotrustees and what powers they have. They also need to know the name of your trust and the date it was executed or last amended.

However, your trust is and should remain a confidential document. In a well-drafted estate plan, an *affidavit of trust* should be available in lieu of your actual trust document. It is a shortened version of the essential elements of the trust and suffices as a substitute document without disclosing the private information contained within the actual trust document.

Costs of Funding

≈ *Are there additional costs to funding a trust during my lifetime as compared to retitling the assets after death?*

Usually, there are some costs for transferring assets into a living trust.

These costs are almost always far less than the costs that would be incurred after your disability or death without living trust planning.

Your advisors, especially your attorney, can help fund your trust. For example, most brokerage houses will handle the retitling of your stock certificates to your living trust at no charge if the shares are transferred into a *street name* account (a single account that holds all of your securities with that particular company) or at a nominal cost if you wish to continue to hold the individual certificates. In addition, most full-service financial institutions or brokerage houses will transfer certificates from street name back to your name at no additional cost.

Your attorney should prepare all documentation for transfers of real estate, personal property, business interests, and most other assets that are not publicly traded. In fact, it is a good idea to have your attorney review, and perhaps supervise, all transfers into your trust, even if other advisors participate. By having your attorney supervise the process, you will be assured that the funding is done correctly for your particular plan. The fee your attorney charges, which is usually very reasonable, is a small price to pay for the peace of mind that comes with knowing your trust has been properly funded.

Time Involved in Funding

⚜ *How long should it take to transfer my assets into my revocable living trust?*

The amount of time it takes to fully fund a revocable living trust depends on a number of factors. Ideally, the assets should be funded as soon as possible after the trust signing in case of a sudden death or disability. However, the number of assets you have, as well as the types of assets being funded, will affect how long it takes to fund the trust. Barring unforeseen circumstances, your trust should be fully funded within 90 days of the trust signing. To meet this deadline, you must be actively involved in the funding process.

⚜ *Are there any assets that take a substantially longer time to fund into my trust?*

Yes. Certain assets take a substantially longer time to fund than other assets. Generally speaking, you can expect out-of-state property, time-shares, and U.S. savings bonds to take additional time to fund. The institution where an asset is held will also make a difference in the time required for retitling. Some institutions are notorious for taking more time than others to fund assets into a trust.

Incomplete Funding

⅍ *If I must have a pour-over will anyway, why do I need to transfer my assets into my living trust?*

One of the reasons you did living trust–centered estate planning was to avoid the probate process. The pour-over will is intended to go through probate only if a guardian must be appointed for a minor child or there are assets which you forgot to title in the name of your living trust. If you do not transfer all your assets to the living trust, you are subjecting your heirs to the process you were attempting to avoid and all its attendant problems: the will may be attacked and even defeated by challenges from disgruntled heirs; creditors will have to be satisfied first and foremost before any distributions are made to loved ones; and ancillary administration may be required to transfer property in other states

Ultimately, if you do not transfer your assets into your living trust, you fail to take advantage of the many safeguards and benefits offered by a living trust–centered plan. You increase the expenses as well as the hassles and heartaches that your loved ones may have to face through probate. You potentially sacrifice the plan you hoped to establish because it may be rewritten by your spouse, a disgruntled heir, or a hungry creditor.

⅍ *If all my assets are titled in the name of my living trust, how do they avoid probate upon my death?*

Remember that one of the main purposes of the probate process is to transfer title from the decedent to his or her heirs. Let's look at what happens upon death: An individual might have two types of assets— probate assets and nonprobate assets. *Probate assets* are subject to the jurisdiction of the surrogate, common, or probate court system, depending upon the state of the decedent's domicile (or the location of real estate if it is in a different state), so that title can be changed from the name of the decedent to the name of his or her heirs.

Nonprobate assets are not controlled by a court. Assets such as life insurance, pension benefits, IRAs, annuities, and similar property "pass by contract": the benefits are paid upon death to the beneficiary designated in the applicable contract. No probate is needed. Real estate or other property held as joint tenants with right of survivorship passes "by operation of law": when one of the joint owners dies, the owner who survives automatically owns the entire property. Probate is not needed to pass title on the first death.

Assets already titled in the name of a living trust are nonprobate property. Assets that name a living trust as the beneficiary are nonprobate property to the extent the proceeds from the property pass to the trust. The property in the living trust is held, administered, and distributed according to the terms of the trust agreement and thus avoids the judicial process of retitling.

◆ If I create a revocable living trust, can I keep assets in my own name and have them transferred to my trust at death without going through probate?

In some states certain kinds of assets can be owned in your own name and be transferred to your living trust at death without going through the probate process. For example, many states allow you to own bank accounts with a *payable-on-death* (*POD*) designation to a named beneficiary. In these states, all bank checking, savings, and money market accounts can be owned by you with the designation payable on death to your living trust. Many states have also adopted a *transfer-on-death* (*TOD*) designation for stocks and brokerage accounts. Therefore, in these states, it would be a good idea for you to own your stock or brokerage accounts with a TOD designation to your living trust so that your trust will be funded with these accounts at your death.

In Ohio, and in a number of other Uniform Probate Code states, subchapter S corporation stock or stock in a professional corporation can also be owned with a TOD designation without causing you to lose your subchapter S election.

Check with your attorney to see if your state allows these types of designations. If it does, this may be one method of funding part of your revocable living trust.

Other kinds of assets, including life insurance, annuities, and retirement plans, provide for beneficiary designations in all the states. As long as your living trust is designated as the beneficiary, the proceeds from these assets will be distributed to your trust at death without going through probate.

◆ Can I sign my living trust and leave my assets titled in joint tenancy with my spouse?

How assets are titled is critical to the proper planning and signing of your estate documents. For example, if you have a perfectly drafted living trust that contains an "A-B," or marital-family, subtrust provision, you and your spouse could lose massive federal estate tax benefits if you continue to hold your assets jointly. This is because the joint ownership property rules of your state will override the federal estate tax planning contained in your trust. When you die, your jointly held property will be automatically transferred to the surviving owner and thus will not be controlled by the tax instructions in your trust.

The pitfalls of holding assets jointly with right of survivorship can best be explained through an example: Assume that Bill and Mary own their house, their cars, and their other major assets as joint tenants with right of survivorship. Additionally, they have a well-drafted testamentary trust will or a living trust with A-B trust estate tax provisions. When Bill dies, these jointly held assets automatically pass to Mary. Mary now owns the property outright. Bill's trustee or executor collects the rest of Bill's property, which Bill owned in his name alone. Because a preponderance of Bill's property is in joint tenancy and automatically vests in Mary outside of Bill's will or trust, Bill's estate is unable to take advantage of Bill's applicable exclusion amount. When Mary later dies, the entire value of all the assets which Mary and Bill formerly owned as joint tenants is included in Mary's gross estate for estate tax purposes. Mary can transfer her entire applicable exclusion amount to her children free from estate taxation, but the rest is taxed.

Had Bill and Mary owned their property individually, rather than jointly with right of survivorship, each of them could have transferred the entire value of their respective applicable exclusion amounts to their children (a total of $2 million in 2006) without incurring any estate tax liability, and they could have saved as much as $435,000 of unnecessary estate tax.

⊀ *My wife and I have a combined estate that is well over $1.2 million and growing. We own all our property jointly with right of survivorship, and we do not live in a community property state. We each recently created a living trust with a bypass trust and a pour-over will. Do we have all the documents we need?*

You probably have excellent documents, but they are currently useless from a federal estate tax planning standpoint. The estate planning documents you describe anticipate that property owned at your death will go through probate and then "pour over" into your living trust. The terms of your living trust will govern the distribution of your assets to your heirs and other legatees.

Probate, however, applies only to property owned by you at your death. Property held jointly with right of survivorship is not owned by you at death but, rather, by the surviving joint tenant. Accordingly, since all of your property will automatically pass to your wife if you should be the first to die, there is nothing in your estate to probate or for your trust to control. Since there is nothing to probate, there is nothing to pour over into your living trust; therefore, no property will go into your bypass trust.

Because of the increase in the applicable exclusion amount by the Taxpayer Relief Act of 1997, the way you and your wife currently have your assets titled can cost your heirs as much as $435,000 in unnecessary federal estate taxes, depending on when you die. Also, since the survivor's assets will have to go through probate, your joint estate will further shrink by the amount of the probate costs. You and your wife could avoid all these costs by properly retitling your assets to transfer them into your respective living trusts.

Allocation of Assets

≥\ *How do we fund a joint trust with our jointly held property?*

Each of your respective assets is contributed to the trust and listed on a schedule to the trust document. Jointly held property contributed to the trust is listed as belonging to each spouse equally, with 50 percent going to each spouse's schedule.

Practitioners vary on how they fund a joint living trust. One school of thought advocates first converting the jointly held property to tenancy in common and then conveying each spouse's tenancy-in-common interest to the joint trust. Another school of thought believes that the conversion to tenancy in common is a wasted step and that the jointly held property can be transferred directly to the trust. This group believes that the conveyance to the trust automatically converts the property to tenancy in common (50-50 ownership between the spouses) and destroys the survivorship feature. Regardless of which funding technique is followed, the use of a joint trust is ideal for spouses who own their property in joint tenancy.

≥\ *How does a married couple decide which marital assets will be funded into the husband's trust and which marital assets will be funded into the wife's trust?*

The objective in funding a trust for a married couple is to allocate or reposition assets in a way that satisfies their respective ownership needs and desires while minimizing the effect of income and estate taxes on the couple and their children. In addition, liability concerns are often addressed as part of the allocation of assets in the funding process.

What are the determining factors in funding the spouses' respective trusts?

There are four main factors to be considered.

THE PSYCHOLOGICAL FACTOR Many spouses feel that all their marital assets are marital property and that both spouses have equal rights and ownership to all these assets. Others feel that some assets are more clearly associated with one spouse than the other. For example, a wife who has inherited property from her parents, such as a family vacation home, may feel stronger emotional and legal ties to that property than her husband does. Or a husband whose hobby is investing in the stock market may have a desire to maintain control over the couple's brokerage accounts. These and similar factors need to be taken into consideration when allocating assets between the spouse's respective trusts.

THE PREDETERMINED OWNERSHIP FACTOR Another consideration is whether there are significant qualified retirement plan assets that by their nature have a predetermined ownership. Qualified retirement assets must be owned by the plan participant. Any other arrangement will result in the premature payment of income taxes. Couples with large concentrations of assets in qualified plans should consult their advisors because the rules governing the lifetime and after-death use of qualified plan funds are enormously complicated.

THE CAPITAL GAIN FACTOR Yet another concern when allocating assets between the spouses is the age and health of each spouse. Is it likely that one spouse in particular will die before the other? If so, have any of the properties appreciated in value? This determination is made by looking at the cost basis and fair market value for each of the spousal assets. If there is appreciated property, the spouses will want to consider a transfer of the appreciated property to the trust owned by the ill spouse in order to obtain a step-up in basis for the appreciated property.

This technique can yield significant capital gain tax savings for the surviving spouse. However, asset transfers within 1 year of death will not receive a stepped-up tax basis.

THE LIABILITY FACTOR Does one spouse have greater exposure to liability claims as a result of his or her occupation or of the type of property that he or she owns (e.g., rental real estate or a business that deals in hazardous materials)? If so, it is important to make sure that assets necessary for the family's basic needs are not jeopardized. For this reason, it makes sense to have the spouse who is not exposed to the claims own the bulk of the family assets if the marriage is stable and the spouses are comfortable with that arrangement.

In some cases, couples may own some assets which create liability exposure and other assets which do not. In this situation, it is often appropriate to have one spouse own all the high-liability assets and to have the other spouse own the "clean assets."

Couples who have significant assets and are concerned with liability issues may also want to consider employing more sophisticated asset protection strategies such as family limited partnerships or offshore trusts.

Responsibility for Funding

⚜ *Who is responsible for funding my trust?*

Funding a revocable living trust is the responsibility of the trust maker and his or her advisors. While the attorney who drafted the trust should take the lead in funding it, the trust maker should help in every way to furnish evidence of ownership of all assets and to supply any other information. Doing so will make the process go faster and will reduce the cost of funding. Other advisors such as the accountant, life insurance professional, and financial advisor should also work with the attorney in their areas of expertise so that all funding is coordinated.

⚜ *What if I don't want to involve myself in the funding process?*

If you do not wish to actively participate in the funding process, you can delegate the process to others. Through a specially designed limited power of attorney, other individuals can do everything necessary to transfer assets to your trust *without* obtaining any control whatsoever over your assets. Thus, you can offer your heirs the chance to do the funding paperwork for you now rather than after your death. Alternatively, you can pay someone to help with the transfer process. Either way, you can supervise the process; in stark contrast, you will have no control if your assets are transferred by the probate process.

⚜ *What are the advantages of having my attorney do the trust funding?*

Most people who desire to fund their own trusts start with good intentions but fail to follow through and ensure that the funding is complete and correct. There are many benefits of having your attorney fund your revocable living trust. A good estate planning attorney will have a system in place for funding trusts quickly and accurately. If the attorney funds trusts on a regular basis, he or she will be able to identify possible problems with the assets before starting the process. Often the attorney will already have solutions or will have established relationships in the business community to solve any such problems. In addition, the attorney will be able to verify that all assets were in fact retitled and that each was done correctly.

To some people, convenience is the primary motivation for having attorneys fund their trusts. Most people have busy schedules which make funding their own trusts a nuisance. The idea of having someone else complete their funding is appealing. In other instances, individuals may not want the responsibility or may have physical limitations which prevent them from funding their own trusts.

⋈ Can my financial advisor fund my revocable living trust?

Many states have legal and ethical restrictions that prohibit or limit financial advisors' degree of participation in the funding process. For example, many states have ruled that people other than attorneys who advise clients on how assets should be titled are engaging in the unauthorized practice of law. However, financial advisors can assist in the funding process. This should always be done under the direction and control of an attorney.

Transferring Specific Assets

Bank accounts

⋈ Do I have to transfer my checking account to the trust?

If you do not transfer your checking account to your trust, it will become a probate asset at the time of your death. If your successor trustee is not a signatory on the account, he or she will not be able to access the funds until the account is probated and transferred to the trust. Unless your state allows POD or TOD designations, you should transfer all bank accounts to your trust.

For such transfers, most banking institutions simply require that you sign a new signature card showing the ownership of the account in the name of the trust. There do not have to be any outward changes with respect to the account. In other words, you can continue to use your same checks and there is no necessity for you to sign the checks as "Trustee."

I was advised that I have to have a checking account outside of my revocable living trust to avoid gift tax complications. Is this still the case?

At one time, a gift made directly from a revocable living trust to a third party was included in the trust maker's estate if the maker died within 3 years of making the gift. If you anticipated making gifts from your trust, you may have been advised to maintain an account in your individual name so that you could transfer assets from your trust to yourself as an individual before you made the gift.

The Taxpayer Relief Act of 1997 now provides that gifts made from a revocable living trust are complete when given. Thus, even gifts made from a trust within 3 years of the date of death are not included in the trust maker's estate for estate tax purposes. Therefore, it is no longer necessary to maintain an individual checking account for purposes of making gifts of revocable living trust property.

If my checking account is in the name of my trust, do I lose any benefits in the account that I would have retained by keeping the account out of my trust?

Accounts that are titled in the name of an individual revocable trust are treated the same as an individual account of the trust maker. The FDIC will provide insurance coverage for these accounts up to $100,000 per individual trust. If a husband and wife title their joint accounts which they use for their sole benefit in the name of their joint revocable trust, they are also afforded coverage up to $100,000. Also, if very specific regulations of the FDIC are met, it is possible to expand the coverage to include the trust beneficiaries if they are the trust maker's spouse, children, or grandchildren. In this instance, coverage could be afforded up to $100,000 per beneficiary in addition to the standard coverage. If the size of the accounts is such that suitable insurance coverage is not available through the FDIC, additional coverage can be obtained simply by utilizing additional financial institutions that are insured by the FDIC.

Some banks or financial institutions do not treat revocable living trust accounts the same as individuals' accounts. There may be a loss of ATM privileges or of special senior citizen account privileges, or the bank may require new account numbers. The reason for the distinction is usually only a matter of the particular bank's policy. Your estate planning attorney will be able to identify which institutions have these policies.

≥ *My husband and I have a joint banking account. We tried to retitle it so that one-half of the account would be in each of our living trusts as tenancy-in-common property. The bank says that we cannot do this. Is it correct?*

There is no legal reason why the bank cannot do what you want to do. Practically speaking, however, a bank is entitled to establish whatever operating rules it wants, and your bank may have a policy not to title an account as tenancy in common when the account holders are not individuals. However, the person you are dealing with at the bank may be unfamiliar with living trust planning. You may need to go up the bank's management chain until you find someone who can alter the bank's policy for you; you may even find that the problem is not a matter of bank policy at all

If this approach does not produce satisfactory results, there is another solution frequently used by married persons. If you are both trustees of each other's trust, you could put the account into one trust or the other, and specify that either trustee alone has the power to write checks, make withdrawals, and obtain information about the account. Assuming you have balanced your other assets properly between the two trusts, this arrangement should work in exactly the same way as would having your respective trusts hold the account as tenants in common.

≥ *If my bank won't let me put words of ownership on my account, how do I hold title in the manner that I choose?*

Most institutions use the "check-off system" to determine how title is held. Often there is only room for a minimum number of words or names, and several small boxes with four or five letters to designate how property is held. There may be one box with the letters "JT" or "JTROS" and another with "Trst" or "Trtee." If you do not check any box, and there are two or more names, it is presumed that you hold title as tenants in common. If you check the JT box, it is presumed that each of you is an equal owner of the account and that each has the right of survivorship as a joint tenant.

If you check the Trst or Trtee box, you are holding the account as a trustee. If you want to put a bank account in your trust, you must check this box. Unless the name of the trust or the beneficiary appears on the document, the bank cannot determine who is the beneficial owner of the account. Often a bank will require some evidence of a trust document or the name of the beneficiary.

Some accounts come with a blank called "Beneficiary." Such designations serve to pass title to the account at the time of your death, bypassing your estate.

Certificates of deposit

⚜ *How do we transfer our CDs into our living trust?*

You take your affidavit of trust to the institution that issued the CDs, give it to your banking representative, and request that the bank transfer them into the name of your trust.

Retirement plans

⚜ *Should I change the ownership of my IRA, 401(k) plan, and other qualified retirement plans to my trust?*

No. If you do this, all the income tax you have been deferring while putting money in the plan will become due. IRAs, 401(k) plans, and other qualified plans should not be retitled to the name of your trust.

⚜ *Can I change the beneficiary of my IRA, 401(k) plan, and other qualified retirement plans to my trust?*

Congress wanted to encourage the development of retirement plans for people to use during their retirement years. It did not intend that these plans become wealth-accumulating devices and be left to subsequent generations. So it loaded the legislation with complicated rules and penalties, including significant penalties regarding early distributions, designated beneficiaries, and minimum distributions.

The beneficiary of your qualified plan or IRA depends on your particular planning goals. Your spouse or your trust can be named. However, if you name your trust, you should follow a series of requirements to qualify your trust as a *designated beneficiary.* It is very important that your attorney advises you on the different alternatives you have when it comes to retirement plans. One of the keys to an estate plan that will meet all your objectives is properly coordinating it with your retirement plan.

Stock

≥\ *How do I transfer my publicly held securities if I have the certificates in my possession?*

If you hold the individual certificates, you need to contact the transfer agent and get a blank transfer form. You complete the form and have your signature guaranteed, and then you send the form and the certificate to the transfer agent. As discussed earlier, it may be easier to have the transfer done by a stockbroker and have the stocks placed in a street-name account.

If you have a reinvestment account with the company, you may be able to return the stock certificates to it for deposit in your reinvestment account. Then you can transfer that account to your trust.

≥\ *I own some shares of stock which are publicly traded and which I have pledged as collateral for a loan at the bank, and the bank holds the certificates. How can I get those shares transferred into my trust?*

Under most circumstances the bank will deliver the certificate to your attorney or your broker long enough for the new share certificates to be issued in the name of the trust, with the understanding and condition that they will be returned to the bank.

≥\ *Should I transfer my Section 1244 stock to my living trust?*

If you own stock in a small-business corporation which is qualified under Section 1244 of the Internal Revenue Code, that stock should *not* be transferred to your trust.

In general, if the business represented by Section 1244 stock is sold at a loss or liquidated at a loss, a Section 1244 shareholder may deduct the loss from his or her ordinary income up to $50,000 per year ($100,000 for married couples filing a joint return).

If Section 1244 stock is transferred to a living trust, the Section 1244 ordinary-loss treatment will be lost, and the losses incurred will be deemed to be capital losses, which are only deductible against capital gains or up to $3000 per year against ordinary income.

≥ *Should I transfer my stock certificates to my living trust if they are subject to a restriction agreement?*

Transfers of stock in closely held corporations, regardless of whether they are regular corporations, S corporations, or professional corporations, may be subject to restrictions imposed by agreement or by statute. It is important that you have your attorney evaluate these restrictions to determine if they preclude you from transferring your certificates to your living trust or if advance approval is needed from other persons or entities.

≥ *Can my S corporation stock be held in a revocable living trust without breaking the S corporation election?*

Since a living trust is a grantor trust under the Internal Revenue Code, it may hold S corporation stock without adversely affecting the S election.

≥ *Should I transfer my stock options to my living trust?*

Transferring your stock options to your living trust may generate an income tax on the difference between the option price and the value of the stock at the time of transfer. The stock option plan may also prohibit such a transfer. Many practitioners believe that the preferable approach is to wait until you exercise your option and to allow all holding-period requirements to expire before transferring your stock into your living trust.

Because of the different types of stock options and the many different provisions of stock option plans, it is imperative that you work with your attorney and company to determine when and how you should fund your trust with stock options.

Partnership interests

≥ *Do partnership interests present difficulties in the retitling process?*

Most partnership agreements require the permission of all the general partners in order for an individual partner to transfer his or her partnership interest. This requirement is designed to prevent a *stranger* from becoming a party to the partnership, but it inadvertently slows down the innocent attempts of trust makers to convey their partnership interests into their revocable living trusts. The correspondence or telephone calls required to explain the situation both to the other partners and to the partnership's legal counsel take time and cost money.

Real estate

⚑ *What are the pros and cons of placing real estate into my living trust?*

Generally, transferring real estate into a living trust is a tax-neutral event because a living trust is a *grantor trust*—an extension of the individual. In a vast majority of states, no tax is incurred upon the transfer, and the property continues to have the same tax basis. Generally, *ad valorem* tax issues such as homestead exemptions remain unaltered, but you should always review this with your attorney. In some states, homestead exemptions may be affected by transfers to a living trust, but this is highly unlikely.

Like any other asset held by a living trust, real estate held in a living trust avoids probate both upon death and in the event of a disability. An added benefit occurs when real property located in another state is held by a living trust because, upon the trust maker's death, the unnecessary expense of ancillary administration is avoided.

Regarding the transfer of the trust maker's personal residence to a living trust, the federal Garn–St. Germain Act mandates that for mortgages obtained through federally chartered or insured financial institutions, the transfer can occur even if there is a mortgage on the property. However, in the event that the trust maker wants to transfer commercial property to a living trust, it is important to seek approval from any lender that holds a mortgage in order to prevent the lender from considering the transfer a violation of the "due-on-sale clause" in the deed to secure debt or in the mortgage instrument. Generally, this is not difficult to obtain, and doing so is recommended in order to prevent any miscommunication or difficulty with the lender in future transactions. Unfortunately, many mortgagees are now charging for the time spent in reviewing documents or in retaining counsel to review documents.

In states where the transfer of assets to living trusts is relatively new, it may be prudent to notify your lender before the property is transferred to your living trust in order to avoid any possible problems in the future. This is particularly important if you have an equity line of credit or if you are considering refinancing the loan with the same lender.

⋈ *How do I transfer my real estate to my revocable living trust?*

Title to real estate is transferred by means of a deed from the existing owners to the trust. Each state has very specific rules with respect to the drafting of deeds, and the advice of your estate planning attorney should be enlisted to ensure that the title is properly transferred.

To avoid errors in transfer, it is advisable to have an updated title search performed to ensure that an accurate legal description is utilized and that the proper owners are identified. If an improper legal description is utilized, a cloud can be placed on the title of record, which can cost many times the cost of the title search to have corrected. The same is true of proper current owners; if a deed is prepared that is not correct as to who owns the property, title can also be clouded.

⋈ *What kind of deed should I use to transfer my real estate into my living trust?*

Most states provide for three types of deeds:

- *Quitclaim,* by which you say that you do not warrant that you own all or any part of the property, but whatever is yours, you are transferring
- *Special warranty,* by which you warrant not only that you own the property but also that you have not caused any clouds or liens on the title other than what is specified in the deed
- *Warranty,* by which you warrant that you own the property and that title is marketable in accord with other warranties, usually spelled out in the statute that authorizes this deed

Before transferring real estate, you should check with your attorney or a title company, because the type of deed to use is the one that is best recognized by the company that will issue title insurance on the property.

⋈ *Should the deed transferring title to my revocable living trust be recorded?*

Typically, it is a good idea to record the deed immediately. Deeds held for recording after a death or disability occurs may become lost or be destroyed and may not be valid in some states. In addition, if legal descriptions are found to be inaccurate when deeds are recorded at a later date, it is much more difficult to correct the title issues since the grantor is not available to execute affidavits or other documents needed to clear the title.

Another concern with an unrecorded deed is that the trust maker may sell parcels included in the description of the unrecorded deed. When the deed transferring title to the trust is later recorded, there may be a cloud on the title because the deed includes property that the trust maker no longer owns. Recording the deed immediately upon transferring title to the trust appears to be the best practice.

⋙ Can I transfer my house to my living trust without losing any federal tax benefits?

A transfer to a revocable living trust is an income tax–neutral event. The Internal Revenue Service recognizes that, in effect, there has not been a true conveyance of your property since the control of the property and the beneficial right to receive the rights and profits from the property have not been transferred. The property starts in your individual name and is moved to your trust name very much like moving coins from your left pocket to your right pocket; it never leaves your person for tax purposes.

⋙ Does transferring my principal residence to my revocable living trust affect my right to use the $250,000 capital gain exclusion?

No, the exclusion of capital gains is not forfeited if the residence is transferred to a revocable living trust. The exclusion is $250,000 for an individual and $500,000 for a married couple who sell a residence they have lived in for at least 2 out of the last 5 years. If the residence is owned for less than 2 years, a pro rata portion of the exclusion is available. For example, if a married couple sells their residence after 18 months, the exclusion amount is $375,000.

There is an additional matter to consider before making the transfer. If, after your death, your trustees place your residence into a family trust, your spouse cannot take advantage of the exclusion; but if your residence is placed in the marital trust, your surviving spouse can take advantage of the exclusion. This issue may be of minor concern because of the stepped-up basis the residence will receive after your death.

⋙ Should I be concerned with state tax issues when transferring real estate to my living trust?

You should always consult with your attorney before transferring real estate to the name of your living trust. Tax issues vary from state to state and can sometimes lead to unwanted consequences.

🔊 *If my residential property is in my trust, am I able to refinance it?*

After property has been transferred to a revocable living trust, a problem sometimes arises when the owner wants to refinance the home or get a home equity loan. The lender may want assurances that the trustee has the ability to encumber the trust property.

There are two possible solutions to this dilemma. You could provide the lender with a copy of the trust agreement or affidavit of trust to assure the lender that the trustee has the power to encumber the property. Alternatively, if you want to keep your documents private, you could take the property out of the trust, allow the lender to secure the debt against the property, and then put the property back into the trust.

🔊 *When I purchased my home, I put my children's names on the deed jointly with right of survivorship with mine, so that it would go to them at my death. We agreed that the house is to remain solely mine until I die. If I decide to put the home in my living trust, will I need my children's permission to transfer the title to my trust?*

Yes. By putting your children's names on the deed, you made them part owners of your home. You will need their consent to transfer title to a revocable living trust that is in your name alone.

🔊 *We live in a community property state and want to transfer to our joint trust commercial real estate that has a mortgage with a due-on-sale clause. Is there any way to do this without notifying the lender?*

Some community property states permit the transfer of property to a joint trust through a marital property agreement which is used as a substitute for a deed. A petition would have to be filed with the probate court at the time of the first death, but the transfer of the real estate to the trust at that time is considered a nonprobate transfer. If these special circumstances do not exist in your state, you should obtain permission from the mortgagee.

🔊 *What effect does the transfer of my real estate to my revocable living trust have on my title insurance coverage?*

Since title insurance coverage under an owner's title insurance policy does not extend to the insured's successors in interest, the trust may not be covered under the title insurance issued to the individual grantors. Upon request and the payment of a fee, the title company should be willing to issue an endorsement changing the name of the insured to the trust.

The title insurance company will usually insist upon doing a new search for liens or judgments before issuing the endorsement. Many people creating a trust do not want to incur the cost of updated title insurance. Not having the trust covered by title insurance is usually not a concern, since the title insurance policy continues to cover the grantors of the deed, who are also the trust makers and the owners on the policy that has been issued. If a title defect existed on the date the title policy was issued, that policy will still cover the grantors. Defects arising after the title policy was issued will be beyond the coverage of the policy regardless of whether the trust maker or the trust holds title.

≥ Can we lose the benefit of creditor protection if we transfer our real estate to a living trust?

While many other assets such as publicly traded stocks, bonds, bank accounts, and tangible property can be easily transferred to a revocable living trust, real estate has certain peculiarities which require closer scrutiny before the property is transferred.

In some states there are safeguards against claims of creditors when property is held by husband and wife as tenants by the entirety. These safeguards may be lost if the property is conveyed into a living trust. Many states have homestead exemptions which protect the family home from the claims of creditors. The homestead exemption may be lost in some jurisdictions through trust funding.

It is therefore important that you seek the advice of your attorney before transferring real estate to the name of your trust.

≥ Should I change the ownership of environmentally contaminated real estate to my living trust?

Real property that is contaminated not only pollutes the environment but can "pollute" your trust as well. If contaminated property is in the name of your living trust, your total trust assets are at risk of being used to pay for any resulting environmental liabilities and your trustee is *personally* at risk under federal law for the costs of cleaning up the property and paying damages claimed by third parties.

It is absolutely essential to consult an attorney with specialized knowledge of both environmental legislation and estate planning before transferring your contaminated property to your living trust.

⚔ *Can I have my local attorney transfer real estate that I own in other states to my trust?*

The mechanics of transferring real estate vary widely among the states. The use of counsel in the state where the property is located is necessary to confirm that the form of deed used will be acceptable to the title companies and will meet the various recordation requirements of the particular jurisdiction.

Vehicles

⚔ *Is there any advantage in placing a mobile home into a living trust?*

Yes, the same advantage you will have in placing any personal property in a living trust. Many people do not understand that if you rent the space where the mobile home is parked, the mobile home is not real property, like your house. It is personal property, like your car.

The reason for placing it in a living trust is the combined benefit of disability planning and probate avoidance. If you title your mobile home in the name of your living trust, your disability trustee will be able to take care of it if you should become disabled. Also, when you die, your death trustee will be able to pass the title of the mobile home to your heirs without going through the probate process.

In order to change your mobile home's title to your living trust, you should find out who registers titles to mobile homes in your state. In many states, you can change the title to a mobile home at the same place that you change the title to an automobile: the county clerk's office in the county where the mobile home is located.

⚔ *If I don't put my vehicles in my living trust, will they go through probate?*

This depends upon state law. For example, the Michigan vehicle code allows any individual to transfer up to $60,000 worth of motor vehicles to a spouse or children without the necessity of probate. The small-estate statutes of many states accomplish the same result as the Michigan statute. It is therefore important that you ask your attorney what your state's law is before you make this funding decision.

Livestock

🖎 *I am a rancher. Can I put my cattle into my living trust?*

Yes. If your livestock carries a brand, the ownership of the brand should be transferred to the trust. This is usually done by a written assignment. If the cattle are not branded, you can transfer them by an unbranded-cattle bill of sale, with the trustee of the trust as purchaser.

🖎 *How do I retitle my horse to the name of my trust?*

In order to transfer ownership of a registered thoroughbred horse, you will need to transfer the title on the back of the Jockey Club registration certificate. Many other breeds of horses also have registration certificates as evidence of title, and transfer of ownership to your living trust can be accomplished by making the transfer on the certificates.

Personal property

🖎 *How do I transfer assets that do not have formal titles?*

Assets that do not have formal titles, such as furniture, furnishings, silverware, china, collectibles, and so on, are conveyed to trust ownership by a general bill of sale or assignment. There is no need to do a detailed inventory of your personal property.

🖎 *How do I transfer my art collection to my living trust?*

If there are personal collections of substantial value, such as coin, stamp, or art collections, most practitioners tailor specific assignment documentation to convey them into the trust.

Miscellaneous assets

🖎 *How do I transfer promissory notes or installment contracts to my living trust?*

Promissory notes and installment contracts are transferred to your living trust through a written assignment prepared by your attorney.

Life insurance and annuities

🖎 *Should life insurance be owned by my revocable trust?*

When the value of an estate is such that it will be taxed, ownership of life insurance by the insured's revocable trust will only add to the estate value and increase the estate tax burden. In such cases, it may make sense to employ an irrevocable life insurance trust as the owner of the policies. If you do not use an irrevocable life insurance trust and your policy has a cash value, your living trust should be the owner *and* the beneficiary of the policy. If you become disabled, this allows your trustee to "control" the policy so that the cash value can be accessed.

In cases where the estate asset values are low, and there is little danger that the estate will be subject to estate taxation now or in the future, it makes sense for you to continue to own your life insurance and make your living trust the beneficiary of your policies.

⋈ *Who should be the beneficiary of my life insurance policies if I have a revocable living trust?*

Many people fail to realize that their life insurance is controlled by the beneficiary designation and not by their will or trust. Therefore, it is vital that the beneficiary designations of life insurance policies dovetail with the overall estate plan.

If you were to name your spouse as the beneficiary, and your spouse received the assets directly, he or she would have to transfer the insurance proceeds to his or her trust. If your surviving spouse died or became disabled without having transferred the proceeds, a probate situation would be created.

Perhaps more important is the necessity of ensuring that liquid assets are available for funding the family trust. This trust is created for the benefit of the surviving spouse, and the successor trustee determines which assets are to be placed into it. The surviving spouse typically receives the income from the family trust, so having the cash from the life insurance available to be placed into the family trust, where it can be used for investment purposes, could maximize the income available to the surviving spouse.

The most efficient way to coordinate the distribution of insurance proceeds with the overall estate plan is to name the revocable living trust as the beneficiary of the life insurance proceeds. In this way, further coordination with the life insurance policies would not be required.

⋈ *If I make my living trust the beneficiary of my life insurance policy, will the proceeds be subject to creditor claims in the same way they would be if my estate were the beneficiary?*

In virtually every state, the proceeds will not be subject to the claims of your creditors if you name your living trust as the beneficiary of your life insurance. To fully protect the proceeds from the claims of creditors, your living trust should contain a spendthrift clause.

My IRA owns an annuity. Should I change the ownership of my annuity to my living trust?

If the annuity is a "retirement-type" annuity, that is, one owned by a 403(b) plan, an IRA, or any qualified retirement plan, you should *not* change the ownership to your living trust.

Should I change the ownership and beneficiary of my regular annuity to my living trust?

If your annuity is *not* a "retirement-type" annuity—that is, it is not part of a retirement plan—you *may* change the ownership of the annuity to your living trust without adverse tax consequences. IRS regulations allow for tax-deferred treatment of an annuity of this type as long as it is owned by a "natural person." A properly drafted revocable living trust qualifies as a natural person. However, some older annuities issued before October 21, 1979, will lose their special step-up-in-basis feature if you transfer title to a living trust.

Naming your living trust as the beneficiary of the annuity will allow the proceeds to be distributed in accordance with the instructions in your living trust and will facilitate federal estate tax planning.

If you are married, you may not want to name your living trust as the beneficiary of the annuity. To do so will preclude your spouse from continuing the annuity as a tax-deferred investment after your death. This tax-deferred advantage is available only to a surviving spouse.

MAINTAINING YOUR
REVOCABLE LIVING TRUST

Funding

How can I ensure that my living trust stays fully funded?

Most lawyers provide instruction and forms to assist trust makers with their ongoing funding. Some even have formal programs to ensure full funding year to year. These funding programs also help trust makers keep their trusts up to date regarding changes in the law and changes in family and financial matters.

⚶ *Is there a penalty if I take something out of my living trust?*

You can put assets into your trust and take assets out of it without incurring a penalty or tax of any kind.

⚶ *If my assets are titled in the name of my trust, do I need anyone else's permission to access them?*

If you are your own trustee, you are not restrained in any way as to how you use, manage, invest, or handle your trust assets. Accordingly, you control the assets that are titled in the name of the trust in the same manner that you controlled them prior to putting them into your trust.

⚶ *How do I get assets out of my living trust?*

You retitle the assets in your name through the same procedures that you used to place them into the trust. Real estate is deeded, investment accounts are retitled, partnership interests are reassigned, and so on.

⚶ *Once my assets are funded into my trust, can I sell any of the assets?*

Once you create your living trust and name yourself as the trustee, you have the authority to sell any or all assets.

⚶ *Once my revocable living trust is completed, do I need to see my attorney whenever I buy an asset?*

After you complete your revocable living trust and fund it with all your major assets, you must remember to title in the name of your living trust any major assets which you acquire in the future. In most instances, you will be able to have the asset titled in the name of your trust on your own. On a few occasions, however, you may want the advice of your attorney.

⚶ *I'm planning to sell real estate that is in my trust. Will the buyer's attorney want to know about my trust?*

Yes. The buyer's attorney will want to know that your trust exists, that it owns the property being sold, and that the trustee has the authority to sell the real estate. Your affidavit of trust provides this information.

⚛ *If I put all my assets into my trust, can I borrow against those assets to get a loan?*

A properly written living trust will always allow you to pledge trust assets as collateral for your borrowing.

Creditor Protection

⚛ *Can I avoid creditors or nursing home care costs with my revocable living trust?*

As the trust maker, you retain the right to control, amend, and revoke the trust at any time. There is no protection from creditors or nursing home care costs.

⚛ *Will placing all my assets into a trust protect me from creditors?*

You cannot create a living trust for your benefit to avoid your creditors during your lifetime. Upon your death, however, a living trust, in forty-four of the states, completely cuts off the claims of your unsecured creditors. In California, Massachusetts, Michigan, New Jersey, New York, Oregon, and Florida, creditors' claims are not severed after the trust maker's death. In these six states, creditors of the trust maker can prevail upon the trust to the extent of the trust maker's interest in the trust, just as they can against any other estate.

⚛ *Can my living trust cut off the claims of my beneficiaries' creditors?*

If properly drafted, your living trust can protect your beneficiaries from their creditors through state laws called *spendthrift statutes.* Spendthrift provisions in a revocable living trust insulate trust funds from the claims of your beneficiaries' creditors.

Tax Reporting

⚛ *Will the change in the titles of my assets after they are transferred to my revocable trust affect how I report my income taxes or make my income tax reporting more complicated?*

Transferring your assets to your living trust will not change how you report your income taxes and will not make reporting more complicated. Your living trust is your alter ego. You continue to keep your books and records in precisely the same manner that you did before the trust's creation.

❧ Will there be any gift tax consequences as a result of my putting property into my living trust?

Funding a revocable living trust does not generate gift taxes, and you do not need to file gift tax returns.

Amending and Reviewing the Trust

❧ After I sign my trust, can I change it?

The revocable living trust is a very flexible document. You may change, amend, or revoke the trust at any time during your life provided you have the mental capacity to do so.

❧ Do I have to renew my living trust, or is it permanent?

You are not required to renew the trust instrument on a regular basis or to sign it again after its original execution.

A properly drafted revocable living trust will provide for a number of contingencies so that you do not have to amend or change the trust instrument each time there is a change in your assets or family situation. However, if there is a significant change in the amount or value of the assets you placed in the trust, you may need to reevaluate tax consequences and review other choices you made in the original trust instrument. You may have to amend the trust instrument if you change your mind about how your property should be distributed after your death, if a person you designated as a beneficiary or as a trustee predeceases you, or if you decide to change a provision.

❧ Will I have to amend the trust when my daughter, who is a beneficiary, gets married and changes her name?

No, you will not. She is still named as your child in the trust, and her marriage will not change her status as a child or a beneficiary.

❧ If I want to change my distribution pattern, say, by reducing a gift to my niece, do I have to redo my entire trust?

No. You simply execute an amendment to your trust revoking the section or clause pertaining to your niece and replacing it with your new wishes.

You should not attempt to change your trust by yourself (e.g., by crossing out the old clause and writing in your new instruction). A written amendment prepared by an attorney is generally necessary to properly change the provision of any trust document.

≫ *If my successor trustee dies before me, do I have to do another trust to name a replacement? If so, will it cost the same as the original trust?*

You can have your attorney make a simple amendment to your existing trust. The fee for this service will probably be not much more than the value of 1 or 2 hours of the attorney's time.

≫ *Once I have signed my estate plan and funded my living trust, do I need to be concerned about changing it in the future?*

Absolutely! You should discuss with your estate planning attorney how you will stay in touch with one another to ensure that your plan remains current with respect to any major changes in your life (you might win the lottery), family situation, or the law. You may want to ask your attorney how he or she will contact you if there is any significant change in the law that might affect your plan and if there is any new development in estate planning that could improve your plan.

On your part, you must keep your attorney informed of any major change in your financial or family situation that would alter your plan, such as a death or divorce in the family. Overall, it is important that you and your estate planning attorney talk about these issues so that you are both comfortable that there is a process by which your plan will always reflect your current estate planning goals.

≫ *It's quite possible that my wife and I may relocate within the next few years. Will we have to replan our entire estate with an attorney in our new home state?*

The U.S. Constitution guarantees that full faith and credit must be given in any state to any living trust agreement that was valid in the state in which it was created and executed. Thus, if your trust is valid in the state in which you signed the document, it will continue to be valid should you relocate to another state. It will generally not need revision to carry out your wishes, regardless of where you live. It is always a good idea, however, to check with a qualified estate planning attorney to see if any aspects of *state* law in your new home state will affect your plan made in another state. This is especially true if you relocate to a community property state from a separate property state, or vice versa.

States do have different requirements with respect to pour-over wills, living wills, durable powers of attorney for health care, and other documents. It is imperative that you have an attorney in your new home state review those documents to make sure that they comply with the laws of that state.

◢ Do I have to redo my entire estate plan to take advantage of the changes in the Taxpayer Relief Act of 1997?

It depends. Here are some guidelines that you should follow:

- If you are the owner of a small business, you should have your plan reviewed. The new law offers some excellent estate tax relief.
- If your plan has not been reviewed in the last year or so, a visit to your estate planning attorney is appropriate.
- If your plan provides for a marital trust and a family (bypass) trust, it should be reviewed. Some trusts and wills are drafted in such a way that they cannot automatically take advantage of the increases in the unified credit. You need to make sure your plan does.

◢ How do I know if I have financially outgrown my current estate planning?

Many people set up an estate plan today, not realizing that as their assets grow, they may outgrow their current planning. Therefore, it is imperative that you select an attorney who will track the growth of your estate and counsel you on a regular basis in order to determine if you have outgrown your planning and if any additional planning is required.

◢ My trust was done by my brother-in-law, who is an attorney but not an estate planning attorney. Should I have it reviewed?

It is always a good idea to have your estate plan reviewed periodically for any changes in your family, your assets, or the law. If your plan was prepared by an attorney who does not specialize or have expertise in estate planning, odds are that the plan you have is probably a "one-size-fits-all" type of trust and may not take advantage of the most recent law. Further, non-estate planning attorneys do not have the experience in the field to be able to counsel you on other planning tools that might be available for your situation.

Proper planning strategies are important so that your wants, wishes, and aspirations are optimally addressed in your plan. Your brother-in-law is probably a very professional attorney and as such should have no problem with bringing in a qualified estate planning attorney. Most qualified estate planning attorneys are more than willing to work with your trusted family attorney.

❧ How can I tell if my plan is good or bad?

Good or bad is not really the question. You should be able to sit down and picture in your mind how you want your estate handled during your disability or after your death. Read your trust and its associated documents. This may be difficult. If you cannot understand the documents, neither will your family upon your disability or death. The documents should be fairly easy to read and use. Hard-to-understand documents can create additional legal fees for interpreting and administering them. The fact is, a trust can accomplish complex objectives and still be reasonably understandable.

Is your estate organized so your family can find the important documents easily? Have you done a pour-over will, special durable powers of attorney, a health care power of attorney, and a living will? If you have questions on any one of these areas or any other part of your plan, you should have your plan reviewed and corrected as needed.

❧ What happens if I need to change my estate plan and my attorney is no longer in business or is not available to help me?

Once you have taken the time to establish a relationship with a qualified estate planning attorney, it is unfortunate and uncomfortable to have to change attorneys and start that process all over. We all know how we hate to change an accountant, doctor, or any other professional whom we like and trust.

From the technical perspective, a properly drafted estate plan can be reviewed and amended by any qualified estate planning attorney. From a practical standpoint, however, you are better served by working with someone who understands you and your family and is familiar with the documents you already have. Additionally, attorneys generally do not like working with documents prepared by others and often recommend redrafting such documents so that they are comfortable with them and sure they are correct. This costs the client time and money.

When you first seek out an estate planning attorney, try to determine if he or she will be there in the future. Questions about how long the firm has been in business at that location and how long the attorney intends to practice are certainly appropriate.

Selecting an attorney who is a member of a large organization offers an advantage in this regard. For example, members of the National Network of Estate Planning Attorneys have a shared philosophy and base their planning documents on similar principles. Thus, if your planning is done by a Network attorney and you are later forced to begin a new relationship, another Network attorney will be familiar with the form and content of the documents you already have and will understand the process you have been through. The transition should be as painless as possible when changing professionals.

⚎ *How much will it cost to maintain my estate plan?*

Since a living trust does not require income tax returns or any extra filing fees, there are no mandatory ongoing costs. However, it is a good idea for you to make sure your plan is up to date. The cost of keeping a plan current depends on how often you meet with your attorney and the work that needs to be done. Usually, any fees associated with maintaining an estate plan tend to reduce the costs upon death or disability. You and your attorney should discuss the costs of maintaining your plan. Some attorneys have formal maintenance programs that trust makers can sign up for; others are more informal. In any event, you should know what your attorney's billing approach is for maintaining your plan.

Miscellaneous Postsigning Matters

⚎ *Where should I keep my estate planning documents?*

The answer to this question depends upon how many sets of documents you receive from your attorney and in what form you receive them.

Generally, the trust maker receives two sets: a complete set of original documents in one or more binders (including a duplicate copy of the pour-over will), which can be kept in his or her home or office, and an unbound set of original documents (including the original pour-over will), which can be kept in a safe place such as a safe deposit box, home safe, or office vault.

The best place to keep your documents is someplace where they will be safe and where they can be easily located when they are needed by you, your family, or your authorized agents after you are disabled or deceased. Your attorney should also keep a copy in case your sets are lost or destroyed.

⚑ Whom do I notify after I have completed my living trust documents?

You should inform your successor trustees that you have signed your trust and, in most cases, you should provide them with a copy of the trust documents and, later, with copies of amendments if you change your trust. In more sophisticated plans where tax planning has been accomplished, you should advise your accountant that you have done your planning.

⚑ Is the cost of my estate plan deductible on my federal income tax?

Pure estate planning fees are not a deductible expense. However, a substantial part of the estate planning attorney's work involves tax planning and lifetime asset management planning that protects and conserves income-producing property. These additional components of the fee may be deductible depending upon your individual tax situation.

The percentage of the estate planning fee that will be deductible will vary from attorney to attorney and from person to person, depending on the nature of the work performed.

⚑ What do I need to substantiate the deduction?

Your attorney should provide you with a detailed invoice differentiating the tax-deductible items—tax planning and preparation of documents, and his or her advice for the management and conservation of income-producing assets—from the nondeductible items.

It is also a good idea to have an accompanying letter from your attorney explaining how he or she arrived at the allocation between deductible and nondeductible expenses.

⋈ *If something goes wrong with my estate plan and my heirs are monetarily harmed, is my attorney liable?*

If your estate plan is completed by a qualified estate planning attorney, mishaps are a rarity. However, since attorneys are human, mistakes can happen. An estate planning mistake will typically lead to monetary loss.

In almost all instances, your attorney will carry malpractice insurance for every client. The amount of coverage will usually cover any mishap. Your attorney should be happy to disclose to you the amount of malpractice insurance he or she carries.

PART THREE

Wealth Strategies Planning

Chapter 6: Advanced Estate Planning Strategies

Every time the law changes—and our income, estate, and gift tax laws get more complex—new planning opportunities arise, existing strategies become more important, and others fall by the wayside. It is sometimes amazing how much creativity comes from the estate planning community as times and laws change.

Chapter 6 is an excellent survey of the most timely and relevant estate planning techniques available. Our contributing authors address a wide range of topics that will affect almost all individuals and families with taxable estates. While there are a number of questions and answers devoted to the new estate and gift tax provisions of the Taxpayer Relief Act of 1997, many more are devoted to advanced strategies that have evolved over the last few years, either because of new laws or new ideas.

There are three topics of particular interest in Chapter 6. The first is irrevocable trusts. Irrevocable trust planning, which has always been important, now has even more significance in planning. With

225

the increase in the tax-free amount that can be used during lifetime or death, once called the *exemption equivalent* but now known as the *applicable exclusion amount,* have come more opportunities in using irrevocable trusts. Also, specialty trusts such as grantor retained annuity trusts and grantor retained unitrusts have gained new stature in planning as practitioners develop new planning ideas and see more applications for their use.

Another topic of particular interest is family limited partnerships. Their effectiveness has caused great consternation at the Internal Revenue Service, but, in spite of IRS attacks, these business entities remain viable methods for controlling property and passing wealth to other generations. This chapter has an abundance of information about what they are and how they are most effectively used.

Finally, Chapter 6 includes information about viatical settlements, which enable the elderly and terminally ill to use life insurance proceeds before death. These settlements are widely misunderstood and underused, but they have a great deal or relevance in a surprising number of planning situations.

Chapter 7: Asset Protection Planning

One of the greatest challenges facing many of us is the management of risk. We can all do a pretty good job of protecting ourselves from risk in those areas over which we have control, but in our litigious society much of our risk is not controllable.

For the most part, we use traditional forms of risk management. We buy property and casualty insurance on our cars and other possessions; we buy life and disability insurance; and we set up corporations, limited liability companies, limited partnerships, or other organizations that separate business risk from personal risk.

Risk management, of course, is asset protection. We want to protect ourselves, our families, and our property from the uncertainties of life as much as we can. This type of protection is no longer optional; it is part and parcel of the estate planning process.

Asset protection is not a new concept. Corporations, one of the oldest types of business arrangements, dating back centuries, were invented to limit liability. Insurance of every kind is a direct result of individuals' and businesses' attempting to reduce risk and protect assets.

In Chapter 7, our contributing authors have submitted questions and answers that succinctly and thoroughly explain the many facets of asset protection planning. The chapter is an excellent survey of why asset protection is important, what can and cannot be done in asset protection planning, and the consequences of using the many asset protection techniques.

Of special importance is the section at the end of the chapter on abusive asset protection and tax schemes. Because of the importance of asset protection, a number of dishonest promoters have entered the field. Their promises and solutions are not only unscrupulous but also potentially criminal in nature. All consumers who are thinking about asset protection or tax planning should be aware of these scams so that they do not get ensnared in severe legal and tax difficulties.

Chapter 8: Charitable Planning

Charitable giving has always been a fundamental and integral aspect of estate planning. Most people who plan have a strong sense of family and community and are therefore inclined to make charitable gifts a part of an overall estate plan.

This sense of charity was reflected in the questions and answers provided by a number of our contributing authors. They address a broad spectrum of charitable planning, with an emphasis on charitable remainder trust planning.

It has been our experience that more proficient estate planning attorneys have a good deal of knowledge about charitable planning. This knowledge is extremely important given the complex nature of the charitable giving provisions of the Internal Revenue Code.

Charitable planning is not an area that should be approached lightly. There are a myriad of planning issues that must be considered when doing charitable planning, including control; income, gift, and estate tax ramifications; current finances; future income and principal needs; the extent of your charitable inclination; and the types of property you own.

Chapter 8 gives an excellent overview of these issues and discusses many ways to deal with them. It also provides a number of examples which will help you visualize these charitable concepts.

Chapter 9: Business Planning

This a practical chapter that differentiates between the benefits and detriments of the many different forms of business organization. It takes a fresh look at many of the "givens" of business organization and provides questions and up-to-date answers that may surprise you.

The questions and answers in Chapter 9 emphasize the *limited liability company* as a form of business organization that is new and exciting to many people. Not surprisingly, little emphasis is given to the regular, or C, corporation as a viable business alternative as compared to limited partnerships, subchapter S corporations, and limited liability companies.

Business continuity and the manner in which business owners can protect and perpetuate their business holdings through stock redemption, entity purchase, cross-purchase, and wait-and-see agreements are discussed at length. Each is compared to the other and in light of what you might wish to accomplish in planning to maintain the value of your business after you are no longer able to serve it.

The questions and answers in Chapter 9 center on the "best ways" you can structure your business agreements to protect your loved ones and business associates upon your retirement from the business or upon your disability or death.

There are a surprising number of questions and answers on the precise procedures and methodologies that should be used to receive accurate appraisals of business interests for purposes of enacting gift and business continuity programs. There are also a number of helpful tips on the dos and don'ts of properly selling your business.

chapter 6

Advanced Estate
Planning Strategies

IRREVOCABLE TRUSTS

⅍ *What is an irrevocable trust?*

An *irrevocable trust* is a trust that cannot be changed or amended by its maker after it is signed. Irrevocable trusts are used to make gifts to others—the trust beneficiaries—"with strings attached."

When making gifts to children or grandchildren, parents and grand-parents can either give funds directly to the beneficiary or place the funds in trust, accompanied by a set of written instructions. These instructions are the strings attached to the gift.

Gifts in trust enable the donor to control the use for which the gift is intended.

⅍ *Why would I want to create an irrevocable trust?*

If one of your goals is to reduce your estate tax exposure or make current gifts with strings attached, an irrevocable trust may be the way to plan. Irrevocable trusts can be used to make annual exclusion gifts and taxable gifts. They can be used to make gifts of specific types of property, such as a residence, and they can be used to make gifts of principal while allowing the maker to retain the income for a period of years. They can provide a charitable deduction at the time of funding if the ultimate

beneficiary is a qualified charity, and they can be used to skip generations, lasting literally hundreds of years. Irrevocable trusts offer many
alternatives for tax planning.

✄ *What do I have to give up in order to get the tax benefits of an irrevocable trust?*

In an irrevocable trust, the assets are held under a trust agreement that
cannot be amended or revoked. Once the trust is funded, the value of
the assets, and their growth, is not included in your estate for federal
estate tax purposes. To keep the trust's assets out of your taxable estate
and keep the trust's income out of your taxable income, you have to
give up the power to revoke or amend the trust, and you also have to
give up the right to subsequently designate—outside of the trust's instructions—to whom or in what amounts trust income or principal is
to be paid.

In addition, you can't keep the power to vote stock in a "controlled"
corporation—a corporation in which you and related persons have 20
percent of the voting power—or the stock will be included in your
estate.

There are several types of irrevocable trusts, some of which may be
designed so that you may serve as trustee. These will be discussed later
in this chapter.

✄ *Why would I want to set up a trust in which I relinquish total control?*

You don't really give up total control. You establish the ground rules in
the trust document, through your instructions, and you appoint the
trustees to enforce those instructions.

✄ *What's the difference between an irrevocable trust and a revoca-ble living trust?*

The major difference is reflected in the name—you can't keep the power
to "revoke" or change the terms of an irrevocable trust. If you could,
the trust property would be treated for tax purposes in the same way
as your revocable living trust property: it would be included in your
taxable estate.

A revocable living trust is like a will in that it can be changed or
amended, canceled, or revoked at any time without the requirement of
a reason for doing so. An irrevocable trust is nothing more than a
complete and absolute gift which is made with strings attached. You

can place the contingencies, requests, and prohibitions you wish into your irrevocable trust terms, but you cannot retain the right to change or alter it after you execute it.

⚶ *What are demand-right trusts?*

To understand demand-right trusts, you must first understand the gift tax annual exclusion. Since 1982, the federal gift tax law has allowed individuals to exclude from the gift tax the first $10,000 given in any year to any person. In the Taxpayer Relief Act of 1997, this $10,000 amount was indexed to inflation for gifts beginning in 1999.

To qualify for the annual exclusion, the gift must be a gift of a present interest. A *present interest* is defined as the "unrestricted right to the use, possession, or enjoyment of property or the income from property."

For example, if you give one of your children $10,000, whether in cash or by transferring assets into the name of the child, so that you have no further control over the property, you've made a gift of a present interest, which qualifies for the annual exclusion. But suppose you give the cash or assets to a conventional irrevocable trust of which your child is the only beneficiary, which calls for the trustee to hold the trust assets during the child's lifetime and make payments from income or principal as needed for the child. In this case, you have not given a present interest—you have made a gift of a *future interest,* and the transfer to the trust will not qualify for the annual exclusion unless the transfer is accompanied by "demand rights."

A *demand right* in estate planning is normally a right given to beneficiaries of an irrevocable trust to demand up to an amount that is the lesser of the beneficiary's share of the contribution made to the trust or the annual exclusion. The beneficiary can then make a "demand" for his or her share of the contribution within a certain period of time (usually 30 to 45 days). This demand right qualifies the gift as a gift of a present interest for purposes of the annual exclusion. The shortest time that the tax court has approved for the demand right is 15 days.

Of course, your purpose in setting up your irrevocable trust will be undermined if your beneficiary—your child or grandchild—actually exercises his or her power to withdraw what you give to the trust. While the demand right must give your beneficiary the legal right to demand a withdrawal, in the usual family situation all that is required is to explain to the beneficiary that your overall estate plan, and the family's best interest, will be served by his or her not exercising the demand right. However, it is important that there is no agreement preventing the beneficiary from exercising a demand right; the beneficiary must have the legal right to make the demand if he or she so desires.

⚕ What's a Crummey Trust?

A *Crummey trust* is an irrevocable trust with demand rights in it. There is nothing crummy or shabby about a demand-right trust. The name "Crummey" trust comes from a tax court case which approved the use of a demand right to make a gift to a trust eligible for the trust maker's gift tax annual exclusion.

⚕ Can a demand right be given to a minor beneficiary?

The demand right can be given to a minor beneficiary through his or her guardian. In most states, a minor's parent is the natural guardian of the minor, and legal appointment of a guardian will not be required to make the demand right effective. If you have minor children and make gifts to an irrevocable trust on their behalf, your spouse, as their natural guardian, has the legal power to exercise or refuse to exercise the demand right on their behalf and qualify the demand right for tax purposes. But you need to make sure that your trust document properly provides for the giving of reasonable written notice to the minor's guardian and that your trustee carefully follows the prescribed procedure.

⚕ When I die, is my irrevocable trust a part of my estate for federal estate tax purposes?

Only the assets you own or have an interest in at your death are a part of your estate for federal estate tax purposes. When you transfer assets to your irrevocable trust, you have made a gift of those assets, and you no longer have title to them. Therefore, any assets owned by the trust will not be included in your estate. You must be cautious, however, since there are a few types of assets which can be brought back into your estate if you are not careful. Many traps like these exist, which is why you must work with a qualified professional.

⚕ What happens if a beneficiary who has a demand right dies before I do?

If a demand-right beneficiary predeceases the trust maker, the beneficiary's share of contributions made to the trust before the beneficiary's death is held and distributed according to the trust maker's instructions.

≥ Can creditors attack my irrevocable trust?

You may not create a trust and place your assets beyond the reach of your existing creditors to defraud them in the case of an existing obligation or requirement. If, however, in good faith you place assets into a trust in which you are not a beneficiary or potential beneficiary, and you are subsequently sued by a future creditor, such a creditor will generally be prohibited from accessing the trust or the gifts you made to it.

In some states, including Alaska and Delaware, it is possible to create a trust that allows the maker to have some rights in the trust and still prevent creditors from taking the assets in the trust. These asset protection trusts are highly specialized and should be drafted only by highly skilled estate planning attorneys. (Asset protection trusts are discussed in greater detail in Chapter 7.)

≥ What types of investments can the trust own?

The trust may own all types of assets. You can specify or list which assets it can own, refer to the state statute that lists those assets, or combine both in your trust instructions.

≥ Do I have to file a gift tax return when I create my trust?

You will be required to file a gift tax return in any of these situations:

- If you transfer property to your irrevocable trust that results in the use of your applicable exclusion amount or creates a gift tax liability
- If you are electing to gift-split with your spouse
- If you wish to allocate any of your generation-skipping transfer tax exemption to the gift

≥ What happens to my property after I place it in an irrevocable trust?

The trust is administered according to your instructions and, in their absence, by the discretion of the trustees you have named.

≥ Can I remove assets from an irrevocable trust once I have put them in it?

Once you place the assets in an irrevocable trust, you no longer have any control over them. Since you should not be the trustee of an irrevocable trust that you establish, you can have no authority to remove assets.

❧ What if I place a term life insurance policy in an irrevocable trust?

If you place a term life insurance policy in an irrevocable life insurance trust or if the life insurance policy is placed there when purchased by the trust, you can, in effect, remove the policy by discontinuing the gifts to the trust. If there are no other assets in the trust, the trustee will not be able to pay the life insurance premiums, so the policy will lapse. However, if you use a whole life policy that has an automatic premium loan provision or use a universal life insurance policy that has cash value, you may not be able to let the policy lapse until the cash value has been used up.

❧ Why shouldn't I be a trustee of my irrevocable trust?

To keep the trust assets outside of your estate and avoid federal estate and gift tax on those assets, neither you nor your spouse should be a trustee of the trust.

❧ Can I terminate the trustees?

You can provide instructions in your trust document as to how trustees are to be hired and fired. You cannot directly retain the hiring and firing rights as doing so would place the assets right back in your or your spouse's taxable estate.

❧ How many trustees will I need for my irrevocable trust?

You may appoint as many trustees as you wish. The number of trustees you choose will be the number that your best judgment indicates you need. You should take into consideration the purposes for which you have created the trust and the assets that are to be managed by the trustees.

❧ How is the fee for my trustees determined?

Most institutional trustees charge a percentage of the value of the assets in the trust as an annual fee for acting as trustee. The fees charged by corporate fiduciaries approximate 1 percent of the assets they manage, but this amount varies widely depending upon geographic location.

≥ *If my children cannot get along with the trustees in the future, can they change trustees?*

You should consider including a provision in your trust document which authorizes your beneficiaries to terminate the services of a trustee and to appoint a successor or a different trustee when your beneficiaries so desire or according to standards that you set forth for trustee removal and replacement.

ESTATE FREEZE STRATEGIES

Irrevocable Life Insurance Trusts

Features of an ILIT

≥ *I thought that my life insurance will go to my children tax-free when I die. Why do I need to include it in my estate planning?*

Life insurance does go to the beneficiaries free of *income* tax. However, if you own the policy when you die, the proceeds will be included in your estate and be subject to *estate* tax. "Ownership" of a policy includes, among other powers, having the right to change the beneficiary or having the right to borrow against the policy.

The way to avoid estate tax on your insurance proceeds is not to have the policy included in your estate. If the policy is owned by your children, directly, or by an irrevocable trust for their benefit, the proceeds of the policy will not be included in your estate.

≥ *What if I don't own my insurance but control it through someone else?*

Your life insurance will be included in your taxable estate as long as you possess any *incidents of ownership* for federal estate tax purposes.

≥ *What are incidents of ownership?*

Any rights, privileges, or access to life insurance policies or cash values are considered incidents of ownership. Therefore, the insured cannot retain any rights in the policies, such as to borrow the cash value or to change the owner or the beneficiary of the policies. The Internal Revenue Code provides that if the insured retains any rights in the policies, the proceeds will be included in his or her gross estate, no matter who owns the policy.

⅍ *What is an irrevocable life insurance trust?*

An *irrevocable life insurance trust* (*ILIT*) is an irrevocable trust that is created to own and be the beneficiary of life insurance policies on the trust maker's life. Properly drafted, it does not allow the insured to retain any incidents of ownership in the policies.

⅍ *Why would I want to have an irrevocable life insurance trust?*

Here are some reasons why you might want to consider including an ILIT in your estate plan:

1. The death proceeds of life insurance held in an ILIT are not included in the estate of the insured or the insured's spouse.
2. An ILIT provides estate liquidity.
3. With demand-right provisions, the gifts to an ILIT can qualify for the annual gift exclusion.
4. Properly structured, an ILIT can be used to make increased transfers to grandchildren free from the generation-skipping transfer tax.
5. The assets held in an ILIT are protected from the creditors of the donor and the beneficiaries.
6. An ILIT can be structured to take advantage of the laws in jurisdictions other than the home state of the maker.

⅍ *Since life insurance proceeds avoid probate, why shouldn't I just use the policy to provide for my loved ones instead of using an ILIT?*

Most people select the beneficiary of their life insurance policies with little thought or planning. As the years go by and changes take place, the insured rarely reviews the policies' beneficiary designations.

Many times, leaving life insurance directly to loved ones means a serious loss of control over the death proceeds. The following issues are not addressed when using only a life insurance beneficiary designation:

Minor children   If the money goes to minor children, they are too young to legally control it. But who will? What can the minor's money be used for? Is the money to be equally split for each child? What if the children have different needs?

Adult children   If you leave a lump sum of your money to an adult child, can he or she handle it? A large lump sum could destroy a young adult's work ethic and perhaps his or her life. A lump-sum payment to your adult child is also exposed to his or her spouse and creditors.

Spouse If your life insurance names your spouse as a lump-sum beneficiary, you lose control of the money. If you want the money to go to your spouse and then to your children, what happens if your spouse gets the money and then remarries? Without a premarital agreement, the new spouse has significant rights to your money. If your spouse dies before your "replacement," he or she will have a right to an elective share of up to 50 percent of your spouse's estate, even if your spouse's will gives it to your children. What if your surviving spouse does not know how to handle money or becomes incapacitated? Without planning, the money may end up in a bad investment or in a guardianship or conservatorship proceeding. Finally, leaving your life insurance directly to your spouse can be financially devastating because it can lose the benefit of the applicable exclusion amount and be fully subject to federal estate tax when your spouse subsequently dies.

⋈ *Why can't I just have my children own the insurance on my life?*

If using life insurance to provide the liquidity to pay estate taxes, you are strongly advised to hold the policy in an irrevocable life insurance trust. Compared with outright ownership of the policy by children, the irrevocable trust offers flexibility and safety in a number of ways:

- Minor children cannot own a policy.
- Adult children do not always act in a coordinated, timely, and responsible manner when called on to pay premiums to keep the policy in force.
- Even when adult children are responsible, a misfortune such as a lawsuit, bankruptcy, divorce, or death may put the policy at risk.
- If one of your children predeceases you, that child's interest in your life insurance policy will pass to someone else in accordance with the provisions of his or her will or revocable trust. The new owner may not be a family member and could possibly change the beneficiary designation or make other modifications that you would not find acceptable.
- Assuming the policy is kept in force by the children until your death, there is no assurance that all the children will act in concert to use the proceeds to provide the liquidity needed for paying the taxes on your or your spouse's estate.

- Outright ownership of a policy by children precludes the use of generation-skipping transfers and thus may unnecessarily subject unexpended proceeds to estate tax in the children's estates.

⚜ When should I use an irrevocable life insurance trust as an estate freeze strategy?

If you are single and the total value of your estate, including the full death benefit of your life insurance policies, exceeds the applicable exclusion amount ($650,000 in 1999; $675,000 in 2000 and 2001; $700,000 in 2002 and 2003; $850,000 in 2004; $950,000 in 2005; and $1 million in 2006), you should meet with your estate planning attorney to discuss using an irrevocable life insurance trust.

If you are married and the total value of your estate, including the face value of your and your spouse's life insurance, exceeds your combined applicable exclusion amount ($1,300,000 in 1999; $1,350,000 in 2000 and 2001; $1,400,000 in 2002 and 2003; $1,700,000 in 2004; $1,900,000 in 2005; and $2,000,000 in 2006), you should meet with your estate planning attorney to discuss using an ILIT.

⚜ How much control can I retain over my ILIT?

An ILIT does allow gifts with strings attached. However, if you as the insured retain too many strings, your estate could get entangled. It is therefore critical that you use a well-qualified and experienced attorney, as well as a life insurance professional, when creating the ILIT and when acquiring the life insurance. You should name a professional trustee for implementing the proper procedures and instructions of the ILIT.

⚜ I have an ILIT now, but it allows the trustee to pay some of the expenses in my estate when I die. Will this provision cause the life insurance proceeds to be included in my estate?

While it is true that a properly created ILIT will remove life insurance proceeds from the gross estate of an insured, many ILITs contain provisions which either allow or require the trustee to pay taxes, debts, obligations, liabilities, or administrative expenses of the insured or of the insured's estate. Such a provision in an ILIT is a fatal flaw and should be avoided.

A properly drawn ILIT will allow the trustee to lend money to, or buy assets from, your estate. In this way, cash is moved to your estate to pay taxes, debts, obligations, liabilities, and administrative expenses without causing the life insurance proceeds to be included in your estate.

🔖 *Can you summarize how I make gifts to my ILIT and how the trust pays the life insurance premiums?*

1. You and your professional team design your ILIT.
2. Your attorney drafts the ILIT, which you then sign.
3. After this, either the trustee purchases a life insurance policy on your life or you transfer an existing policy to the ILIT. If you transfer an existing policy to the trust, you must live 3 years from the date of the transfer to keep the policy proceeds out of your estate.
4. You make gifts to the trust to cover the amount of the policy premiums.
5. The trustee sends a notice to the trust beneficiaries (usually either children or grandchildren) stating that you made a gift and that they have the right to withdraw their share of the gift.
6. If they do not withdraw their gifts within a specific time (usually 30 to 45 days), the trustee will keep the gift in trust.
7. The trustee uses the money to pay the policy premiums.

You do not own the policy; the trust does. After your death, the death proceeds are not subject to income or estate tax, and the terms of the trust dictate when and how the proceeds will be paid to your beneficiaries.

🔖 *What are some of the provisions that need to be in an ILIT to ensure maximum flexibility?*

1. The trustee should have the power and responsibility to pay the insurance policy premiums.
2. The trustee should be given the right to engage in legal proceedings, if necessary, to collect policy proceeds.
3. The trustee should be given the authority to purchase additional policies.
4. The trustee should be authorized (but not directed) to voluntarily lend trust principal to the trust maker's estate or the maker's spouse's estate or to purchase assets from the estate of either the maker or the maker's spouse.
5. The maker should be prohibited from having any rights of any kind over life insurance on his or her life.
6. The trust beneficiaries should be given the present right to take annual exclusion gifts upon notification by the trustee of these rights of withdrawal.

7. The trust should authorize a pour over of the life insurance proceeds to the maker's living trust or estate if for some reason the proceeds are included in his or her taxable estate.

Can I provide that after my death my spouse be cared for in my ILIT's terms and still avoid estate tax on my spouse's subsequent death?

You can provide for your spouse in your ILIT precisely as you would provide for your spouse in the family subtrust of your living trust. There are a number of alternatives that are possible. For example:

> I want my trustee to pay my spouse all of the trust income and whatever he or she needs from the principal in the trustee's discretion.
>
> I want my trustee to provide for the needs of my spouse.
>
> I want my trustee to provide for the needs of my spouse and children.
>
> I want my trustee to provide for the needs of my spouse, children, and grandchildren.
>
> I want my trustee to provide for the needs of my spouse, children, grandchildren, my parents, and my spouse's parents.

Can my spouse and I sign a joint ILIT as well as separate ones?

Yes, joint ILITs are used when both spouses wish to be insured on a last-to-die basis. Individual ILITs are used when one or the other spouse has life insurance on his or her life.

Can my spouse and I use one trust for all our life insurance policies?

You can if neither of you is a beneficiary of the trust. If you want your spouse to benefit from a policy on your life or if you want to benefit from a policy on your spouse's life, the life insurance policies on one or the other of your lives must be owned by your respective individual ILITs.

On the basis of your experience, do you have any particular cautions concerning ILITs?

Do not write the checks for life insurance premiums to the insurance company. If you do, you may defeat your planning. Write your checks to your ILIT; then let the trustee deposit the money in the trust checking account and write the check on the trust's account to the life insurance company.

Care should be taken to ensure that the bank account owned by the ILIT trustee is used exclusively for the purposes of your depositing the gifts and the trustee's paying the insurance premiums.

Trustees of an ILIT

My husband wants to set up an ILIT. We would prefer that someone in the family be the trustee. Is this all right?

You can name a family member as the trustee of your ILIT as long as you closely follow a few rules. The primary rule is that the person whose life is insured with the life insurance owned by the trust cannot be the trustee of the trust. If your husband acts as the trustee of the trust, he would have incidents of ownership in the life insurance policy. This would cause the proceeds of the life insurance policy to be included in his estate on his death and would negate the reason for having set up the trust in the first place: to remove the proceeds of the life insurance from your husband's estate.

Not only should your husband not act as trustee, but he should not be able to remove and replace a trustee. Although in a recent case the courts decided that an insured could remove a trustee of the trust and replace the trustee with a *corporate* trustee, you should decide at the creation of the trust who is to be trustee.

The best trustee for an ILIT is a professional trustee, such as a bank or other corporate trustee, or a CPA. Adult family members may be trustees, but consider having a professional trustee as a cotrustee with them because of the technical nature of an ILIT.

Is there a way I can have the best of all worlds, family trustees now and then a corporate trustee later?

Many trust makers include provisions in their trust agreements for family members to serve as trustees during the trust makers' lifetimes because the life insurance proceeds are not paid to the trusts until after the makers' deaths. At that time, when sophisticated trust administration and investment management is needed, the trust provides that a corporate trustee be appointed successor trustee.

It makes even more sense to name your accountant as the cotrustee during your lifetime to assist your family trustee in paying life insurance premiums, filing any required income tax returns, and sending required notifications to trust beneficiaries.

My bank trust department prefers not to have investment man-

agement responsibility for the life insurance policy to be acquired and maintained in my proposed ILIT. Can you recommend a suitable alternative?

Most bank trust departments do not have the actuarial skills necessary to monitor life insurance policies held in ILITs to ensure that the premium deposits are sufficient to keep the policy in force through age 100. In the event that the policy lapses prematurely and coverage terminates, the bank trust department could possibly be held liable to your heirs for the amount of the death benefit, which could be millions of dollars.

One arrangement that most bank trust departments find acceptable is to have the trust agreement name a family member as the trust "investment advisor" with regard to life insurance policies that are acquired and maintained within the trust. Some state laws expressly authorize this technique. Since the investment advisor would have sole responsibility for management of the life insurance policy, the bank trust department can totally avoid the liability for a life insurance policy that fails before the date of the death of the insured. When the policy death benefits are paid to the trust as beneficiary, the bank trust department is there to provide its unique skills for proper administration and investment management of those proceeds.

Who buys the life insurance on my life or my spouse's and my lives?

The life insurance is purchased by the ILIT's trustees.

Who actually owns the life insurance policies?

An ILIT, through its trustees, is both the owner and the beneficiary of life insurance policies it owns on the trust maker's life.

Who is responsible for collecting my life insurance proceeds?

Your ILIT trustees have this responsibility for policies owned by your ILIT.

How can I be sure that my trustees will coordinate the insurance proceeds between the respective trusts?

Properly drawn ILITs provide that, following their makers' deaths, their trustees will be the same as the trustees of the makers' living trusts. Having the same people or institutions serving in both fiduciary capacities makes good planning sense and eliminates communication and coordination oversights.

Demand-right notifications

⚜ *How do my beneficiaries even know that I am making gifts to an ILIT?*

Your trustee should give them formal notice in a *demand-notice letter,* stating that you have made a gift to the trust and that they have a certain amount of time to demand their shares of the gift. If they do not make such a demand within that time period, their right to demand automatically lapses and the trustee is free to use your gifts to make the premium payments.

⚜ *My husband set up an ILIT and made me the trustee. How important is it that I send out the letters?*

The purpose of setting up an ILIT is to make gifts to the trust with no gift tax liability and then to remove the proceeds of the life insurance from the insured's estate.

Making sure that the beneficiaries of the trust have actual notice of the gifts made to the trust for their benefit is critical. Only when the beneficiaries have such notice can they decide whether to leave the gift in the trust or demand that the trustee give it to them. The Internal Revenue Service looks for evidence that beneficiaries of an ILIT had a prearranged understanding with the trust maker not to remove or demand the gifts. If there is no proof that the beneficiaries had notice of the gifts, the IRS could successfully argue that they had no meaningful opportunity to demand the gifts. If the IRS finds this, it can "pull back" into the estate the value of all the gifts your husband made to the trust, and then his estate will need to pay the tax on these gifts at his death.

Tax issues of ILITs

⚜ *Must my ILIT file a federal income tax return?*

Unlike a revocable living trust, an ILIT is a separate entity for tax purposes. For this reason, the ILIT trustee should file for a federal taxpayer identification number for the ILIT by using IRS Form SS-4.

An ILIT must file federal income tax returns if its gross income exceeds $600 in any year. This should not present a problem to most ILITs because the cash value, or inside buildup in the policy, is not taxable income until it is withdrawn in excess of the policy payments.

⋈ *Can my ILIT pay my estate taxes directly to the government?*

By law, your ILIT cannot pay the estate tax directly, but it can buy assets from or make loans to your living trust so that its trustees will have the necessary liquidity to pay the taxes.

⋈ *What is the maximum amount I can contribute gift tax–free each year to an ILIT that names my three children as the only beneficiaries?*

You can contribute up to three times your annual exclusion amount and up to your maximum available applicable exclusion amount. When joined by your spouse, you can double these limits. This assumes, of course, that you make no other gifts to your children and that your ILIT is drafted to maximize the annual exclusion amount.

⋈ *I'd like to set up an ILIT, but I don't want to lose the opportunity to give money to my children so that they can use it now, while they need it. Can I do both?*

You can make gifts to an ILIT and make other gifts to your children if you want to. Let's examine how this might work. If you are considering creating an ILIT, then someone has probably talked to you about the benefits of investing in life insurance to pay estate taxes when you die. This is an excellent strategy; you can make gifts to your children in a trust, and the trust will then invest in life insurance on your life.

The amount you give to this trust is a function of the annual premium on the life insurance your advisors have suggested would be right for you and your family. If the annual premium divided by the number of trust beneficiaries is less than the gift tax annual exclusion for each beneficiary, you can make additional gifts to your children of the difference between the per-beneficiary premium amount and the annual exclusion. However, the trust must be carefully structured to reach this result, so you must work with a qualified attorney.

To maximize the amount that you can give to your children and grandchildren, you should consider naming as many beneficiaries in your ILIT as you can. For example, you can make the beneficiaries of an ILIT "my children and their descendants." As long as your insurance premiums remain constant, as your children have more children, your annual "per-beneficiary" gift to the ILIT goes down. Then you will be able to increase the amount of your additional gifts to one or more of your children or grandchildren.

Be sure you are working with someone who knows how to draft this type of flexibility into your trust. There are some generation-skipping transfer tax issues that must be considered.

Another option might be to make gifts and "use up" some, or all, of your applicable exclusion amount. There is nothing inherently wrong with doing this. The applicable exclusion amount gives you a great deal of leeway in the amount of gifts that you can make without paying gift tax.

Discuss with your professional advisors the ways you can make gifts. They can lead you through the pros and cons of what would be best for your family's situation.

⅍ *Should I use my applicable exclusion amount for life insurance premiums in excess of my annual exclusion, or should I use it for other purposes?*

The answer depends on your other circumstances. However, using your applicable exclusion amount to purchase life insurance is generally a wise decision, since the death proceeds are usually far greater than the total amount of premiums to be paid over your lifetime. This is especially true if you do not live a long life.

When life insurance premiums are paid from a person's applicable exclusion amount, professionals refer to the transaction as "leveraging the client's credit" because the life insurance proceeds are far greater than the premium amount against which the applicable exclusion amount will be applied.

⅍ *How can I maximize the leverage of my unified credit? I understand that the Taxpayer Relief Act of 1997 increases my unified credit.*

Your unified credit equivalent, called the applicable exclusion amount under the new tax law, increases from its current level of $650,000 in 1999 as follows: $675,000 for 2000 and 2001; $700,000 for 2002 and 2003; $850,000 for 2004; $950,000 for 2005; and $1,000,000 for 2006 and thereafter.

Assuming that you and your spouse are in good health and are currently 65 years of age, you can convert one of your $1 million applicable exclusion amounts (for year 2006 and thereafter) into what would be equal to a $12 million tax-exempt estate.

Let's assume your total estate is $13 million. If you give $1 million to an ILIT to pay the premiums on a high-quality $6 million second-to-die life insurance policy, your heirs could then receive the $6 million proceeds income tax– and estate tax–free, based on current investment, expense, and mortality assumptions. They use the $6 million of life insurance proceeds to pay the tax due on your remaining $12 million estate instead of using part of your estate to pay the taxes. Thus, your $12 million estate passes to your heirs completely intact.

⚜ Is there a way that I can multiply the number of beneficiaries of my ILIT in order to have more available annual exclusions?

Yes. An ILIT can be drafted to include what are known as *contingent beneficiaries*. These are beneficiaries who will benefit from the life insurance policy owned by the ILIT only if a primary beneficiary is not alive at the time the policy matures. Contingent beneficiaries are usually grandchildren. An ILIT that is drafted this way is sometimes called a *Cristofani trust,* after the famous case in which this technique was first approved by the tax court. This technique is aggressive; but, in the right situations and if done properly, it will have powerful results.

⚜ I've heard of a $5000 gift limitation when it comes to ILITs. What is that about?

In addition to the annual exclusion gift limitations, there is another limitation that may apply to ILITs. This limitation is called the *5-and-5 limit.* When a beneficiary of an ILIT declines to withdraw his or her share of the contribution made to the trust by the donor, the situation is known as a "lapse." Upon a lapse, that beneficiary is, in effect, making a gift of the amount allowed to lapse to the other beneficiaries of the trust! The result can be that the beneficiary is involuntarily forced into using up part of his or her lifetime applicable exclusion amount.

This adverse result applies only to lapse amounts over the greater of $5000 or 5 percent of the value of the trust. It is for this reason that some planners advise limiting gifts to ILITs to no more than $5000 per beneficiary per year.

Skilled attorneys can draft around the 5-and-5 problem by using, when appropriate, separate shares within the ILIT for each beneficiary or "hanging powers" that allow a beneficiary to use up the full amount of annual exclusion gifts over a period of time.

⚜ I have a piece of real estate worth $5 million which should be worth $10 million by the time I die. I've heard that the transfer

costs of a gift during lifetime are less than those of a gift or bequest at death. Could an ILIT produce an even more attractive result?

A gift transferred during lifetime will be less expensive than a gift at death, especially if the gift is anticipated to appreciate in value. If you transfer a $5 million gift of real estate to your children today, the gift tax, computed at the highest possible rate of 55 percent, will be $2,750,000. The total amount transferred from your estate will be $7,750,000.

Alternatively, if you do not make the lifetime gift and the real estate goes to your children at your death, the $7,750,000 not removed from your estate during your lifetime will be included in your taxable estate and will have doubled in value to $15,500,000 by the time of your death. The estate tax, at 55 percent, will be $8,525,000. Thus, the amount left for your children will be $6,975,000, which is $3,025,000 less than the amount they will receive if you make the gift during your lifetime. The total transfer cost under this scenario is $8,525,000. These comparisons are outlined in Table 6-1.

However, for a cost of only $900,000—assuming both you and your spouse are 65 years of age and in good health, and based on current investment, mortality, and expense assumptions—a second-to-die policy could be purchased in an ILIT that would produce a death benefit of $5,500,000. That $5,500,000 could be used to pay the entire estate tax due on the real estate if it increased in value to $10,000,000. Rather than pay a total gift tax transfer cost of $2,750,000 to protect the ultimate inheritance of $10,000,000, you could use only $900,000 to produce the same result as well as retain the ownership of the real estate for the rest of your life. Please notice that, in general, the total transfer tax cost of a large gift during lifetime is approximately 35 percent of the assets transferred. The estate tax at the time of death consumes 55 percent of the assets to be transferred. The best result in this example can be achieved by making gifts to an ILIT to purchase the death benefit. The total transfer cost represents only 9 percent of the ultimate $10 million value of the real estate transferred to your children.

The results of this type of analysis can vary depending on the assumptions made for how fast assets will grow in value. Also, age and health affect the cost of life insurance. However, when planning, it makes a great deal of sense to consider this planning alternative.

≫ *I want to transfer marketable securities to my ILIT to provide the funds to pay for the annual premiums on trust-owned life insurance policies on my life. However, I do not want the trust*

TABLE 6-1   Transfer Cost Comparison

Action	Lifetime gifts	Transfer at death	ILIT
Real estate gift	$ 5,000,000		
Gift tax at 55%	2,750,000		
Total expense	7,750,000		
Net gift to children	5,000,000		
Growth	10,000,000		
Amount in taxable estate		$ 7,500,000	
Future growth		15,500,000	
Estate tax at 55%		8,525,000	
Net amount to children		6,975,000	
Future value of real estate			$10,000,000
Estate tax at 55%			5,500,000
Life insurance premium			900,000
Death benefit			5,500,000
Net gift to children			10,000,000
Total transfer tax	2,750,000*	8,525,000†	900,000‡

*Transfer tax at 35 percent   †Transfer tax at 55 percent   ‡Transfer tax at 9 percent

beneficiaries, my children, to have to pay the income tax on the income generated by the securities each year. Is there any way to avoid this problem?

The Internal Revenue Code classifies an ILIT as a "grantor trust" if the provisions of the trust permit the trustee to pay for life insurance premiums on your life or the life of your spouse. During your lifetime, the taxable income of a grantor trust is taxable to you each year; you pay the taxes on income you do not receive. Neither the beneficiaries nor the trust will have to pay the income tax generated by the securities held in trust. This is good gift and estate tax planning because your payment of the tax bill for your beneficiaries is not included in the calculation of your taxable gifts.

Disadvantages of an ILIT

🔊 *Are there disadvantages to using an ILIT?*

While ILITs are a safe and attractive means of transferring assets and providing liquidity, their main disadvantage is their irrevocability. If circumstances change beyond what you envisioned in your trust instructions, the results could be less than you expected since you are incapable of changing the terms.

⚜ Can an irrevocable trust ever be changed or revoked?

A trustee of an irrevocable trust who is neither the maker nor a beneficiary can be granted authority under the terms of the trust instrument to make limited amendments to the trust agreement. These amendments are generally limited to technical items arising from changes in the law or inadvertent errors in drafting.

An irrevocable trust can be revoked only under special circumstances. These circumstances usually arise when the trust's purpose cannot be accomplished, such as when the trust is for a disabled child and the child has a medical recovery, when a child is discharged in bankruptcy, or when a change in the tax law makes the trust useless. To revoke an irrevocable trust, the trustee petitions a court having jurisdiction after giving notice to all persons who may be affected by any change in the trust. The court may grant to the trustee and the beneficiaries the right to completely revoke the trust and distribute the assets as provided in the trust instrument.

⚜ What should I do to reduce the risk of wanting to change the terms of my ILIT at a later date?

It is very important that your long-term needs and objectives are assessed before establishing an ILIT. Working with highly experienced advisors will help you understand the ramifications of the terms of your ILIT. Your advisors can also build as much flexibility as possible into your trust.

If you determine at a future date that you do not want to keep the insurance, you can effectively revoke the trust by stopping gifts to the trust so that the trustee will not have funds for paying the premiums. If the terms of the ILIT itself are no longer acceptable to you, it is possible to establish a separate irrevocable trust with favorable terms. Then, depending on the terms of the original trust, the new trust may be able to purchase the policy from the old trust. This is a highly technical and complicated procedure requiring special legal expertise, so your attorney and other advisors must be well versed in this area of the law. Done incorrectly, the proceeds from the life insurance may be subject to income tax and possible federal estate tax. Thus, even when all factors are favorable, this is a solution that should be attempted only if no other recourse is acceptable or sufficient.

⚖ *Isn't there any other way around this "changing-circumstance" problem?*

Many practitioners invoke the equitable doctrine of *trust reformation,* which provides that a court can reform or change an irrevocable document if the change is consistent with the intent of the trust maker at the time the document was created. It is not difficult for judges to invoke this doctrine at the request of an ILIT's counsel when the circumstances are compelling and when no one will be hurt by the reformation.

The insurance

⚖ *Is it a good idea to transfer existing life insurance policies into my ILIT?*

It is rarely a good idea to transfer existing policies into an ILIT if the maker is insurable. If the insured owns the policy, he or she has an incident of ownership in it. The Internal Revenue Code provides that if the insured transfers any incidents of ownership in existing policies and subsequently dies within 3 years of the transfer, the entire proceeds are included in his or her estate.

Furthermore, transferring an existing policy to an ILIT constitutes a gift. The value of the policy for gift tax purposes is "the interpolated terminal reserve value, plus unused premium." The interpolated terminal reserve value includes not only the cash value of the policy but also, among other things, the value of having an insurance company legally obligated to pay a death benefit upon the insured's death. By having the ILIT trustee acquire a new policy, the insured will not be making a gift of an insurance policy with an interpolated terminal reserve value.

⚖ *If I have group term life insurance at my place of employment, is there any way to keep the proceeds from being included in my estate if I die while still empoyed?*

You can have your group term life insurance policy and all incidents of ownership assigned to an irrevocable life insurance trust. But be careful: You must be sure to also assign your rights to convert the group term policy to an individual policy. This often-overlooked benefit is considered to be an incident of ownership and, if not transferred, could be used to pull the life insurance proceeds back into your estate.

⚜ *After I assigned my group term life insurance policy to my ILIT, my employer changed the master insurance carrier on the policy. If I assign the new policy to my ILIT and I do not survive 3 years, will the policy proceeds be brought back into my estate?*

No, not if the new arrangements are identical in all relevant aspects to the employer's previous arrangements.

⚜ *Can my trustee purchase term insurance for my ILIT?*

Your trustee is free to purchase term, whole life, variable life, universal life, or any other form of life insurance for your ILIT. There are reasons for the purchase of each, and your trustee should coordinate the necessary decisions with the trust's insurance advisor and attorney.

⚜ *Our attorney has advised us to establish a joint ILIT funded with a "second-to-die" insurance policy. We'd like to know the cost of the insurance before we set up the trust. What can we do?*

Keep in mind that the purpose of an ILIT is generally to pay the estate tax that arises on the death of the surviving spouse or to provide replacement funds for the beneficiaries after taxes are paid. A last-to-die policy is a perfectly designed product for these situations.

Second-to-die life insurance is also far less costly than life insurance that is purchased on the life of any one spouse or policies purchased separately on both spouses' lives.

⚜ *Why should I go to the time and expense of establishing an ILIT, only to find out that I am uninsurable?*

Most people are justifiably reluctant to go to the time and expense of establishing an ILIT until they know whether they are insurable and at what cost. For this reason, they frequently sign insurance applications before their trusts are drafted and signed. This exposes the insurance proceeds to taxation if the insureds die within 3 years.

To avoid this dilemma, you can have someone else sign the insurance application as the proposed owner. Adult children, close relatives, or a business partner all have a potential insurable interest in the trust maker and could sign the application.

Once the insurance underwriting is completed, and you complete and sign your ILIT, the policy can be reapplied for by the ILIT trustee without concern for the 3-year rule.

⋇ *How much should I rely on a life insurance illustration at the time that I purchase the insurance policy owned by my ILIT?*

A life insurance illustration is not the policy. The total cost and benefits of a policy today will depend upon such variables as investment yields, administrative expenses, mortality costs, and the number of policyholders who will cancel their policies in the future. Ultimate policy performance has little to do with the illustration.

Policy illustrations, historically, have been useful only as road maps to assist buyers in understanding how their policies might perform. In the past, life insurance companies have emphasized the importance and certainty of projected policy values. However, the companies created policy illustrations that were too optimistic or even exaggerated. Purchasers relied on the illustrations, not understanding that the illustrations were not promises but were merely guesses created by the insurance companies. Consumers were outraged when actual policy performance failed to meet the projections.

Abuses have occurred with the use of illustrations because there are few regulations to control exaggerated policy illustrations and some life insurance companies and their agents have not always fully disclosed the optimistic assumptions made in the illustrations. Consequently, some insurance buyers have been led to believe that the best policy to purchase was the one with the largest promises or projections. Today, only a few states have adopted legislation to control or standardize illustration practices and assumptions.

Therefore, you should work only with a competent insurance professional, whose credentials are known to you, along with a qualified estate planning attorney and, if appropriate, a financial advisor and an accountant. If there is any doubt about the illustration, always seek a second opinion.

⋇ *What is "wait-and-see" life insurance?*

Wait-and-see life insurance is an alternative to an irrevocable life insurance trust. A husband and wife each purchase life insurance on the other's life. The husband's living trust owns the policy insuring the wife's life, and the wife's living trust owns the policy insuring the husband's life.

Now, assume the husband dies first. The full death benefit on the husband's life will be paid to the wife's living trust for her use.

The insurance policy on the wife, which is owned by the husband's revocable trust, is allocated after the husband's death to his family trust (or bypass trust, as it is sometimes called) rather than to the marital trust. The family trust is then the owner and the beneficiary of the policy.

The family trust, which is the trust that receives the applicable exclusion amount, is sheltered from estate tax on the death of the husband and on the wife's subsequent death. When the policy on the wife is allocated to the husband's family trust, it is generally valued at its cash value (called the *interpolated terminal reserve value*) rather than its death benefit value. For example, if the cash value of the policy is $100,000 and the death benefit is $1 million, it is the $100,000 value that is counted toward the husband's applicable exclusion amount. If the applicable exclusion amount on the husband's death is $650,000, his family trust would hold the insurance policy on the wife's life, valued at $100,000, and other assets worth $550,000.

When the wife subsequently dies, the $1 million death benefit from the policy on her life will be paid to the husband's family trust as the beneficiary of the policy. Because the family trust is not subject to estate taxes on the wife's death no matter what its value is, the life insurance proceeds and the remainder of the assets held in the husband's family trust will not be subject to estate taxes on her death. The result is that one spouse's life insurance proceeds are not subject to federal estate tax. However, when the husband died, the proceeds of the policy on his life were payable to the wife's living trust. To the extent that these proceeds were not spent by the wife during her life, they *are* included in her estate at her death.

Another benefit of wait-and-see life insurance is that insurance companies sometimes offer the surviving spouse, at the death of his or her spouse, the option of increasing the death benefit of the policy owned by the family trust after the first spouse's death. A decision can be made at that time as to whether more life insurance is needed.

✍ *What are the disadvantages of wait-and-see life insurance?*

It is possible that the value of the surviving spouse's policy will be greater than its cash value. For example, if the surviving spouse is not insurable because of health reasons, and death is imminent, the IRS rules would require a valuation of the policy that would approach its death benefit value.

Once the policy is in the family trust, the premiums will still need to be paid. Since all the assets in the family trust are estate tax–free, it is not wise to use these assets to pay the premiums unless there are no other assets available.

Generally, if a spouse has no other assets, he or she will want to have access to the assets in the family trust. However, with a wait-and-see life insurance trust, the spouse can have no direct access to the family trust. If the spouse does have access, the entire death benefit, on the second spouse's death, will be included in his or her estate and taxed.

If the cash value of the policy grows to more than the applicable exclusion amount (as adjusted by the Taxpayer Relief Act of 1997), there will be estate tax due on the first spouse's death. Even if the cash value is less, it is still eating up the very valuable applicable exclusion amount. With an irrevocable life insurance trust, if it is established and maintained properly, none of the applicable exclusion need be used.

The death proceeds of the first spouse to die will be included in his or her estate, to the extent they are not used, when that spouse dies. With an ILIT, all life insurance proceeds are estate tax–free. With wait-and-see life insurance, only one spouse's death benefits escape federal estate taxation.

Finally, a drawback of wait-and-see life insurance occurs if both spouses die before the policy on the first spouse to die is contributed to the family trust. In this case, the death proceeds from both policies will be included in the spouses' respective estates, and estate tax will be due. Had the policies been in an ILIT, none of the proceeds would be included in either spouse's estate.

⚜ *Is there any way for my beneficiaries to use the cash value of the life insurance before my death?*

Yes. You can give the trustee the flexibility to make loans from the cash value of the policy. The trustee can then lend the funds to the trust beneficiaries or even distribute them. Only certain types of insurance have cash value, and some severely restrict the terms of loans. Your professional advisors can help you make these choices.

⚜ *I'd like to buy a large amount of life insurance for my ILIT, to cover estate taxes, but I'm concerned that I'll lose control over the cash value and be unable to help if one of my grandchildren has a special need. Is there a way for my family to retain access to the cash surrender value of the policy despite the fact that the trust is irrevocable?*

A properly drafted ILIT may grant the trustee a power of distribution over trust assets. The trustee could be, for example, your oldest child, and that child could transfer part or all of the assets of the trust to other members of your family. Note that your oldest child, as the power holder, could not exercise the power in favor of himself or herself (except as necessary for his or her health or maintenance in reasonable comfort), his or her creditors, his or her estate, or creditors of his or her estate. Thus, if one of your grandchildren had a special need, say, because of a medical condition, this power of distribution could be exercised by the trustee to transfer part or all of the cash surrender value of your policy to or for the benefit of that grandchild.

⚜ *How can I purchase a large life insurance policy in an irrevocable life insurance trust (which would require an equally large premium deposit) and still keep the value of the gifts that I make to the trust to a minimum for gift tax purposes?*

There are three ways that you can support a large life insurance policy in an ILIT and still keep the value of your gifts to the trust, which are needed to support the premium deposit schedule, to a minimum for gift tax purposes.

One alternative is to pay the premium each and every year for the rest of your life. The longer the period over which payments are made, the lower they are. Frequently, people choose to consolidate the premium to a shorter period of time to "get it out of the way." Under this method, the amount of each payment is much larger, creating greater exposure to a gift tax liability.

Second, consider purchasing a second-to-die policy covering the lives of you and your spouse. The amount of the annual premium will be less than the premium on a policy insuring one life alone.

Third, consider paying the premium deposits on the life insurance through a split-dollar agreement. This arrangement is frequently used to help shareholder-employees of a corporation pay for the life insurance held in their ILITs. Since the corporation pays the majority of the annual premium, the amount of the gift that you make to the trust each year for the balance of the premium is reduced. This technique is also becoming popular in the family setting, where a family member (instead of a corporation) pays the majority of the annual premium, thus reducing the gift component of each premium payment.

In any event, make sure that your ILIT uses demand-right powers where possible so that each gift you make to the trust to support the premium deposit schedule will qualify as a present-interest gift eligible for the gift tax annual exclusion.

≱ *What exactly is a split-dollar agreement?*

A *split-dollar agreement* is an arrangement that separates the ownership of a life insurance policy's death benefit from the ownership of the side fund, or cash value. Thus, one party can own the cash value and another can own the death benefit. A split-dollar agreement is an excellent opportunity to further increase or leverage the gift, estate, and genera-tion-skipping tax advantages of an ILIT.

≱ *How can I reduce the cost of gifts and increase the leverage gener-ated by the gifts through a split-dollar agreement and an ILIT?*

This arrangement requires that the insured employee's corporate em-ployer advance most of the premiums on a life insurance policy each year. The corporation will recover these amounts at the insured's death or the policy's surrender (if earlier).

In a non-split-dollar scenario, the total policy premium which is paid by the insured to the trust each year is the measure of the gift to the trust for gift tax purposes. With a split-dollar arrangement, the measure of the gift is the "economic benefit" (the IRS's Table PS-58 cost for a single-life policy or Table 38 rate for second-to-die policies), which represents only a tiny fraction of the annual premium of the life insurance policy. The insured contributes only the economic-benefit portion of the premium to the ILIT each year. Since the value of the gift to the trust each year is reduced from the full policy premium to the economic benefit of the arrangement, the leverage potential of the transaction is greatly enhanced.

For example, even if the gross premium is $20,000 per year, the reportable PS-58 costs or Table 38 costs may be only $1000 for that year. The amount of the taxable gift would be reduced from $20,000 to $1000. This creates a tremendous amount of gift tax and generation-skipping transfer tax leverage.

≱ *My investment counselor says I should not lock my life insurance into an irrevocable trust. But my estate planning attorney says I would benefit from an ILIT. Why am I getting two different opinions?*

Different opinions come from different perspectives and often from different bases of knowledge. That is the reason why a team of profes-sional advisors coordinating their efforts is so valuable; you can get a variety of views on the same issue, and new insights and planning can take place.

The correct answer for you depends on your personal goals and objectives. Furthermore, the two positions are not mutually exclusive. You can own some life insurance in your name so that you can access its cash values as you deem appropriate. Such a policy will increase the size of your estate for calculating estate taxes, but that is the price of total access and control over the policy.

However, if your primary purpose in purchasing insurance is not to access cash but to pay estate taxes or provide benefits federal estate tax–free to your loved ones in the event of your death, an irrevocable life insurance trust is the best way to accomplish those goals.

Perspective changes the way an issue appears. For example, when you look at an elephant, it makes a world of difference if you look at it from the front, the rear, above, or below. From all directions it is an elephant, but your viewpoint may dramatically alter the action you take to avoid being trampled by the elephant. This is true with the directions given to you by professional advisors. The most important advisor is the one who coordinates the others on your team to offer all the perspectives and get all the advisors to see from one another's viewpoint so that you have the best estate plan for your needs and goals.

International ILITs

Can international trusts be used to hold my life insurance?

The law does not require that ILITs be domestic trusts. As long as a foreign trust meets all the necessary requirements of a domestic ILIT, the same tax result will occur.

Are international trusts more favorable than domestic ILITs?

International insurance trusts may be more favorable under some circumstances due to certain exceptions under the Internal Revenue Code. Although the policy proceeds are income tax–free, any buildup of assets within a domestic insurance trust after the life insurance policy proceeds are received will be subject to income tax if the trust income is not distributed to the beneficiaries annually.

What are the benefits of using international variable insurance products for estate planning?

There is a growing desire among many affluent individuals to be able to control the investments within their policies rather than have the insurance companies invest their money. Internationally, most insurance companies let policyholders have substantially greater input in the determination of how the funds are invested. Because of this added flexibility, some investors elect to purchase their life insurance offshore.

⚜ *How do I find and choose an international insurance company?*

Most international insurance companies do not market their services within the United States. This is not only because of the regulatory issues faced by carriers operating in the United States but also because international insurance companies would lose substantial tax benefits if they operated within the United States.

Because foreign insurance companies are adamant about not soliciting U.S. business, it is usually necessary for prospective policyholders to travel abroad to establish their offshore portfolios. Although this may be inconvenient, the benefits of using international insurance products are often substantial.

Grantor Retained Interest Trusts

⚜ *What are grantor retained interest trusts?*

Grantor retained interest trusts are special irrevocable trusts that allow the trust maker (the grantor) to make gifts of property while retaining the property's use and enjoyment or an income interest in the property for a term of years.

⚜ *What are the different types of grantor retained interest trusts?*

There are basically three types:

- The grantor retained income trust (GRIT)
- The grantor retained annuity trust (GRAT)
- The grantor retained unitrust (GRUT)

⚜ *Why are grantor retained interest trusts used?*

These special trusts are used to substantially reduce the value of the asset being transferred to the trust by delaying the use, enjoyment, or income flow of the asset for a specific term of years. The Internal Revenue Code specifically allows a gift to be reduced by the value of the grantor's retained income or use of the property.

As long as the grantor lives to the completion of the term of years, the value of the asset, plus its potential for future appreciation in value, will be removed from the grantor's estate for a much lower gift tax value. If the grantor dies before the expiration of the term of years, the value of the asset at the grantor's date of death is included in his or her estate. In effect, the grantor's estate is no worse off than if the grantor retained interest trust had never been established and the asset had never been given away by the grantor.

⋟ Why would I use a grantor retained interest trust?

If a person has an asset that is appreciating in value, good estate planning may indicate that the asset be given away to eliminate the potential estate taxes that could result if the asset is retained and continues to appreciate. However, this asset could be providing housing or income that the owner cannot or does not currently want to give up. Furthermore, the gift tax cost of giving the asset away may also be too high.

A GRIT, GRAT, or GRUT can offer an excellent solution. With these trusts, the person can give the asset to the trust while retaining possession and enjoyment of the income from the asset for a term of years. At the end of the term, the asset can be distributed to the remainder persons either outright or in trust at its then fair market value without any further gift tax cost.

⋟ How do grantor retained interest trusts lower the value of a gift?

Since possession and enjoyment of the asset or the income from the asset is not received by the intended beneficiaries until the future, the fair market value of the gift is discounted for gift tax purposes. The amount of the discount depends on several factors:

- The grantor's retained term of years
- The age and life expectancy of the grantor
- The value attributed to the possession and enjoyment or the percent of income retained by the grantor
- An interest factor that the IRS publishes monthly, which is the assumed rate of return of the trust assets (This rate is sometimes called either the *Section 7520 rate*, after the Internal Revenue Code section under which authority is granted to use the rate, or the *AFR*, which stands for "applicable federal rate.")

Basically, the higher the value of the income interest retained by the grantor and the longer the term of the trust, the less the value of the remainder interest passing to the beneficiaries; consequently, the gift amount and the gift tax will be lower. As long as the grantor outlives the income term, the present value and all future appreciation of the trust property is removed from the grantor's estate at a lower gift tax cost.

⚖ Can we use our applicable exclusion amount?

The gift to a grantor retained interest trust must first be applied against your applicable exclusion amount. You will not have to pay any gift tax unless you have exhausted your applicable exclusion amount in making prior gifts or the value of the gift to the grantor retained interest trust exceeds your remaining applicable exclusion amount.

⚖ Is appreciation in the value of the asset still subject to federal estate tax?

All appreciation in the value of the asset after the time the grantor retained interest trust is established is removed from the grantor's estate provided the grantor survives the initial term. Transferring an asset to a grantor retained interest trust freezes the value of the asset at its value at the time of the transfer.

⚖ Will my beneficiaries lose the step-up in basis on the asset if it is in a grantor retained interest trust?

Yes. Your beneficiaries assume your original basis in the asset in the trust. They will pay tax on the appreciation of the asset in excess of your original basis at the capital gain rate when and if they sell the property.

If the property is not in a grantor retained interest trust and is still includable in your estate, your beneficiaries will pay the estate tax of between 37 and 55 percent on the value of the property at your date of death and the tax will be due 9 months later. They will, however, receive a step-up in basis.

⚖ Do GRITs, GRATs, and GRUTs offer any creditor protection?

Assets placed in a GRIT, GRAT, or GRUT have been given away by the grantor. If there is no fraudulent intent to hinder or delay the ability of known creditors to collect, the assets in the GRIT, GRAT, or GRUT are out of the reach of the grantor's creditors. However, the grantor's retained interest could be reached by his or her creditors. Thus, a creditor could capture the income or could use or rent the property during the term, but once the term expires, the property then passes free of the creditor's claims to the remainder persons.

If the remainder person's interest is not retained in trust after expiration of the term, the property could be subject to claims of the remainder beneficiary's creditors. This is why it is always a good idea to either have the assets continue to be held in the same trust or have them transferred to a separate trust, created by the grantor, for the benefit of the remainder persons. The remainder persons could even serve as trustees or cotrustees of either trust at that time.

⚜ *Who should be the trustee of a grantor retained interest trust?*

During the initial term, the grantor may be the sole trustee of the grantor retained interest trust, with complete control over the trust and the trust property. If desired, the grantor may also designate a cotrustee to serve.

After the initial term, the grantor cannot be a trustee of the grantor retained interest trust. However, the grantor may designate in the trust agreement a chain of trustees to serve in the event of his or her disability during the initial term and during his or her lifetime after the initial term.

Grantor retained income trusts

⚜ *What exactly is a grantor retained income trust?*

There are three main types of grantor retained income trusts:

- The qualified personal residence trust (QPRT)
- The tangible property GRIT
- The non-family-member GRIT

Qualified personal residence trusts

⚜ *What is a qualified personal residence trust?*

A *qualified personal residence trust (QPRT)* is an irrevocable trust to which a person (grantor) transfers his or her personal residence, retaining an interest for his or her personal occupancy and use for a period of years, after which the residence passes to the beneficiaries of the trust, either outright or in trust.

⚜ *What is the purpose of a qualified personal residence trust?*

By placing your residence in a QPRT, you can reduce its value for federal gift tax purposes and eliminate its value from your estate for federal estate tax purposes while still retaining the right to enjoy and live in the home.

≫ *What residences qualify for a QPRT?*

A *personal residence* of the grantor is either:

- The principal residence of the grantor
- Another residence considered to be used for personal purposes (e.g., a vacation home)
- An undivided fractional interest in either of the above

To qualify for a QPRT, the residence must be occupied by the grantor as a residence. Recent letter rulings by the IRS also permitted residences with other structures such as small guest houses or coach houses to qualify.

≫ *Can we transfer our house on our working farm to a QPRT?*

You can establish a QPRT for your house but only if you can separate the house from the farm. This will require a survey and title work.

≫ *If my house has a mortgage on it, can I transfer the house to a QPRT?*

Yes, but if you keep paying the mortgage, the IRS may take the position that you are making a taxable gift to the QPRT every time you make a mortgage payment. It would be preferable to pay off the mortgage before you transfer the property to the QPRT.

≫ *Do I have to have an appraisal?*

Yes. Otherwise, the IRS may scrutinize the transaction and later successfully dispute the value used. It is important to retain an appraiser who has good credentials.

≫ *Can you give me an example of how a QPRT saves federal estate or gift tax?*

A father, age 65, has a home with a fair market value of $500,000. He transfers the home to a QPRT and retains the right to live in the home for 10 years, with the remainder interest going to his children. Assuming an 8 percent applicable federal interest rate, the present gift value of the remainder interest to the children is $170,600. At the end of the trust's initial term, the value of the residence has increased to $1 million.

By means of the QPRT, the father gave the home to his children, reduced the size of his estate by $1 million, used the home for 10 additional years, and utilized only $170,600 of his applicable exclusion amount by transferring ownership to his children.

ᴁ *Will an outright gift of my residence accomplish almost the same tax consequences?*

If you give your home directly to your children, two things will happen immediately:

- You will lose the legal right to continue to live in your home.
- The house will be valued at full fair market value for gift tax purposes rather than at the discounted rate permitted to the QPRT.

ᴁ *What happens if the donor dies before the initial term is completed?*

The fair market value of the home is *included* in the donor's estate as if the trust never existed.

To protect against this risk, the grantor may purchase life insurance in an amount equal to the projected taxes on the residence.

ᴁ *Who's entitled to the income tax deduction for the property taxes?*

Because the QPRT is a "grantor trust" under the Internal Revenue Code during the initial term, the grantor is treated as the owner of the property for federal income tax purposes. If the grantor pays the real estate taxes on the residence, the grantor is entitled to the income tax deduction for such taxes.

ᴁ *Who pays expenses of the house during the trust's initial term?*

During the initial term of the trust, the grantor typically pays the normal and customary expenses of repair and running the house.

ᴁ *Can the residence be sold during the initial term of the QPRT?*

Yes. However, if it is sold, there are several alternatives as to what may occur:

- You can create the trust so that it will dissolve upon the sale of the trust property and the proceeds will be distributed to you.
- You can specify that your trustee acquire another residence for you, of your choice, with any excess proceeds from the sale of your original property to be placed in a grantor retained annuity trust

account which will pay an annuity to you until the end of the initial term. At the end of the initial term, both your new residence and the capital in the grantor retained annuity trust account will become the property of your beneficiary.

■ You can specify that if another residence is not purchased, the cash will be held in a separate grantor retained annuity account which will pay an annuity to you until the end of the initial term. At the end of the initial term, the capital in the grantor retained annuity trust account will become the property of your beneficiary.

■ The trust can also prohibit the sale of the residence during the initial term without the consent of the grantor.

Your attorney can help you determine the best structure for your particular situation.

If I put my primary residence in a QPRT and the residence is sold during the initial term of the trust, am I entitled to the $250,000 exclusion on the sale?

If your residence is sold during your retained term of years, you, as the grantor, are entitled to the exclusion of up to $250,000 of gain from the sale of a principal residence.

Can a QPRT residence be rented to others during its initial term?

A residence in the trust cannot be rented full-time. During the initial term of the QPRT, the grantor must use the house more than 10 percent of the amount of days rented or a minimum of 2 weeks per year, whichever period is longer.

When do the trust beneficiaries get the use of the residence?

The beneficiaries, usually family members, have the right to possess the home only after the retained personal-use period of the donor has expired.

What if my spouse and I want to live in our residence after the initial term has expired?

If you want to continue to live in the house after the initial term has expired, you will need to pay the remainder beneficiaries—usually the children—a fair market value rent. A provision allowing you to rent the home after its initial term should be in the QPRT document.

⚡ *Can you summarize the benefits and drawbacks of a QPRT?*

A QPRT provides a number of tax benefits to its maker:

- The donor can transfer the ownership of the personal residence to his or her beneficiary in the future without paying taxes on the appreciation of the residence.
- The residence is transferred today at a discounted value from its appraised value for gift tax purposes.
- The donor is allowed to live in the house.
- The value of the house is removed from the donor's taxable estate.

There are two potential disadvantages to using qualified personal residence trusts:

- The grantor must survive the personal-use period, or the value of the home will be included in his or her estate.
- The beneficiaries do not receive a step-up in basis on the gift of the home and thus may pay a higher income tax when the home is sold.

Tangible property GRIT and non-family-member GRIT

⚡ *What is a tangible property GRIT?*

A *tangible property GRIT* is a trust that holds only tangible property. Tangible property is property that is not subject to depreciation or depletion, such as undeveloped land or a painting. Intangible property such as stocks, bonds, and interests in partnerships cannot be held in a tangible property GRIT.

In a tangible property GRIT, the grantor transfers property to a trust for a term of years and is allowed to use the property during this term. At the end of the term, the property goes to the trust's beneficiaries, who are almost invariably children. The value of the gift is the fair market value of the tangible personal property less the value of the grantor's being able to use the property for a term of years. As you can imagine, valuing the use of property for a term of years is very difficult. Thus, these special GRITs are not used very much by tax practitioners. The restrictions on the types of assets that can be used and the methods that have to be used to value those assets make these trusts impractical for most people.

≫ *How does a non-family-member GRIT work? Should I consider using one?*

The non-family-member GRIT is a vestige of a former tax loophole, the statutory GRIT. In the statutory GRIT, the grantor could transfer income-producing property to a trust for a term of years. The grantor retained the income during the term, but at the term's end, the beneficiaries owned the property. Because there were no rules about what was income-producing property, these tax devices were easily—and frequently—abused.

Congress legislated nearly all statutory GRITs out of existence in 1986; it left only one type, the non-family-member GRIT. Non-family-member GRITs work the same as statutory GRITs except that none of the grantor's immediate family can be beneficiaries. Evidently, the thinking of Congress was that it is less likely for grantors to be so generous with non-family-members.

Family members are considered to be the grantor's spouse; any ancestors or lineal descendants of the grantor or the grantor's spouse, and their spouses; and the brothers and sisters of the grantor, and their spouses. Thus nieces and nephews qualify, as do cousins and more remote family members.

Non-family-member GRITs should be considered by single persons or those generous folks who want to benefit people outside of their immediate families.

Grantor retained annuity trusts and grantor retained unitrusts

≫ *What is a grantor retained annuity trust?*

A *grantor retained annuity trust (GRAT)* is an irrevocable trust into which the grantor transfers appreciating or income-producing property in exchange for the right to receive a fixed annuity for a number of years. When the term of the trust ends, any remaining balance in the GRAT is transferred tax-free to named beneficiaries.

≫ *What are some of the advantages and disadvantages of a GRAT?*

It is possible to produce significant transfer tax savings with a GRAT if the average rate of return and growth of the property in the GRAT over its term is greater than the discount rate used to value the grantor's retained interest in the GRAT.

If the return generated exceeds the annuity percentage, the additional income and appreciation will be accumulated for the remainder beneficiary without additional gift taxes.

If the grantor dies during the term of the GRAT, a portion of the GRAT may be excluded from the grantor's estate.

A disadvantage of a GRAT is that if the trust property does not generate enough income to pay the required annuity, there has to be an invasion of principal and the remainder beneficiary can receive less than the full amount of the initial gift. In addition, the annuity amount that is being paid from the trust to the grantor during the annuity term is actually being returned to the maker's estate; if it is not spent, its value is included in the maker's estate. Usually, this retained amount is not significant compared with the value that is being excluded from the maker's estate, and the maker desires to use this income.

⅍ Can you give me a simple example of a GRAT?

Sure. Let's assume that you own stock in an S corporation that you would like to give to your children. The stock is valued at $1 million, and the distribution you receive each year from the stock is $80,000. You would like to retain the income for 10 years (you are 55) and then let your children have the stock. Let's further assume that the current interest rate published by the IRS is 6.8 percent. The amount of the gift is $460,920, which is derived from the U.S. Treasury tables. The gift represents the value of the stock ($1 million) less the present value of the annuity interest you retained, taking into account your probability of dying during the annuity term of the trust. The value assumes that the stock will pay out an income of 6.8 percent (the AFR), but the income being paid out is 8 percent.

As you can see, the value of the gift is discounted by over 50 percent; you get to keep the income for 10 years; and, if you live the full 10 years, the value of the stock, and its appreciation, is eliminated from your taxable estate.

⅍ What is a grantor retained unitrust?

A *grantor retained unitrust (GRUT)* is a trust in which the grantor retains a qualified unitrust interest, consisting of an irrevocable right to receive a fixed percentage each year of the net fair market value of the trust assets, which is determined annually.

◈ *How do GRATS and GRUTS differ?*

In a GRAT, the grantor retains either a fixed dollar amount *or* a fixed percentage of the revenue from the assets of the GRAT, based upon the *original value* of the assets as of the start date of the trust term. In a GRUT, the grantor retains a fixed percentage of revenue from the assets of the GRUT, based upon the *annually recomputed value* of the assets of the trust.

In a GRAT or a GRUT, the amount of revenue must be paid to the grantor regardless of how much or how little income is produced from the trust assets. In years when the income from the assets in the trust is less than the required revenue payout amount, principal must be used to make up the shortfall to the grantor. In years when the income from the trust assets exceeds the required revenue payout amount, the trust has to distribute only the required amount, but the grantor will still pay income tax on all the income. The excess income is retained by the trust and becomes principal.

◈ *Why would I use a GRAT rather than a GRUT?*

Generally, a GRAT is more useful than a GRUT. Because a GRAT has a fixed income amount, the assets need to be valued only once, when the trust is formed. A GRUT's payout is based on a percentage of the value of the assets as determined each year. This means that if you are funding the GRAT with hard-to-value assets, such as real estate or non-publicly traded stocks and partnership interests, an appraisal must be performed each year. This can be expensive and administratively complex.

In addition, for most situations, a GRAT results in a lower gift. This is because there is always the possibility that the GRAT will be totally used up. The asset is valued once, and even if the asset value decreases, the same annuity must be paid each year. A GRUT can never be exhausted, because the income payout is based on the value each year. Assuming the asset is always worth something, income will always be paid out.

Self-Canceling Installment Notes

◈ *What is a self-canceling installment note?*

A *self-canceling installment note* is a promissory note given by a buyer to a seller that calls for installment payments of principal and interest over a set period of time. It also provides that if the seller dies before all the payments under the note have been made, the remaining payments will be canceled and the buyer will owe nothing further.

≱ How does a self-canceling installment note work as an estate freeze strategy?

The unpaid balance owed to the seller at the time of the seller's death is not included in the seller's taxable estate. Thus, if a parent sells her business to her children in exchange for a self-canceling installment note and dies soon after the sale is completed, the parent's taxable estate will not include either the value of the business or the remaining balance owed by the children at the time of the parent's death.

≱ What are the main disadvantages of a self-canceling installment note?

Such a note must include an extra premium to compensate the seller for the possibility that the seller will die before all payments are received. The installment payments are therefore greater than those under a note having the same terms but without the self-canceling feature.

The risk premium may be either an increase in the principal amount of the note over the business's fair market value or an increase in the interest rate to be paid by the buyer on the unpaid principal.

If no risk premium is added to the note, the IRS will consider that a gift has been made by the seller to the buyer.

≱ Are self-canceling installment notes frequently used?

Because of the perceived cost of the risk premium, use of self-canceling installment notes has not caught on as a viable tax planning strategy. However, it is a technique that should be considered in a variety of situations.

Private Annuities

≱ What is a private annuity?

A *private annuity* is an agreement under which an owner transfers an asset to a buyer—the obligor—in exchange for the buyer's promise to make fixed periodic payments to the seller—the annuitant—for the rest of the seller's life. When the seller dies, the buyer's obligation to make payments ends.

⚰ *Why are private annuities used as an estate freeze strategy?*

By using a private annuity, the annuitant is able to remove the asset in its entirety from his or her estate while retaining a fixed income stream for the rest of his or her life.

⚰ *How is the amount of the annuity payment determined?*

The amount of the annuity payment the buyer must pay to the seller is determined by the fair market value of the asset and the life expectancy of the seller. Specifically, the payment is calculated on the basis of two variables:

- The number of years the annuitant is expected to live, according to the IRS tables
- The interest rate that must be charged, which is equal to 120 percent of the federal midterm rate in effect for the month in which the annuity is being valued

⚰ *How does a private annuity differ from a self-canceling install-ment note?*

Unlike a self-canceling installment note, a private annuity carries no upper limit to the amount a buyer may have to pay to fulfill his or her obligations. That is, if the seller/annuitant lives significantly beyond his or her life expectancy, the buyer will have to continue making install-ment payments until the seller's death.

There is also no limitation on the ability of a buyer to resell the purchased asset soon after acquiring it from the seller. In intrafamily transactions, the deferral of capital gains otherwise available in install-ment sales (including self-canceling installment sales) will be lost if the asset is sold by the buyer within 2 years of the date of the transaction. No such acceleration of gain occurs if the buyer in a private annuity transaction resells the acquired asset.

A private annuity must be unsecured, whereas a self-canceling note may be secured by collateral.

⚰ *What is the disadvantage of a private annuity?*

A private-annuity obligation is extinguished on the death of the annui-tant. If, however, the annuitant turns out to have the longevity of Me-thuselah, the private annuity will backfire and the cost to the buyer will be far more than the savings in federal estate tax.

Family Limited Partnerships

Features of family limited partnerships

❧ What is a family limited partnership?

A *family limited partnership* (*FLP*) is a limited partnership in which all the partners are family members or entities created by or owned by family members. A limited partnership is a common business entity that consists of at least one *general partner* and one *limited partner*. A general partner, who can own as little as 1 to 2 percent of the partnership interests, has the entire right to manage the business and can be held personally liable for partnership debts. A limited partner has no right to participate in managing the partnership business and has limited liability for partnership debts.

❧ Who are the general partners of an FLP?

The general partners are almost always parents or grandparents, or corporations, limited liability companies, or management trusts controlled by those individuals.

❧ Why would anyone want to create a corporation, limited liability company, or management trust to be an FLP general partner?

By law, a limited partnership dissolves upon the death or disability of its general partner. Using these entities provides continuity within the partnership if such an event occurs. They are also used to create an additional layer of protection from the claims of aggressive judgment creditors.

Using a corporation as a general partner also provides income tax planning options. The corporation may charge fees and receive income for management of and duties performed for the FLP. This shifts some of the income from the limited partnership to the corporate general partner. The corporation can then use the income to pay salaries or set up retirement and other tax-advantaged plans such as welfare benefit trusts, defined-benefit plans, and medical reimbursement plans. As a result, the family is able to shift income from higher to lower income tax brackets and, at the same time, set up retirement pension plans for family members who are employees of the corporate general partner.

❧ Who are the limited partners?

The limited partners are often children and grandchildren of the general partners, irrevocable trusts created by the senior family members for the benefit of junior family members, or revocable living trusts created by senior family members as part of their own estate planning.

Can I make my minor children limited partners in an FLP?

Yes, but it might be a good idea to hold their partnership interests in some kind of trust. It is difficult for minors to own property directly.

How can an FLP separate income and equity interests in the partnership assets from the managerial control over those assets?

Limited partnership statutes in all fifty states specify that this must be the case. These statutes not only allow parents and grandparents to give away massive amounts of equity but also allow them to continue to manage that equity.

Is the general partnership interest considered a security, registered or unregistered?

A general partnership interest, in either a general or a limited partnership, is usually not considered a security because a general partner normally takes an active part in the management and control of the partnership assets. When a general partnership in fact is organized and functions as a limited partnership, the partners rely upon the managing general partner to promote their interest and they have no legal right to control the activities of the partnership. Such an interest may then be considered a security.

Gift and estate tax issues of FLPs

How can I use an FLP for giving property to my children?

Typically, you, the parent, will be the general partner, and you will also be the initial limited partner. You will then make gifts of limited partnership interests to your children. There are several advantages to making gifts of limited partnership interests:

1. The general partner retains complete control over the business even if the children hold all the limited partnership interests.
2. The general partner can receive partnership income as payment for management services and as a "special allocation" of partnership income.
3. The limited partnership interests are valued at a discount, usually

at least 25 percent, from their pro rata share of the assets inside the partnership.

4. The FLP offers asset protection for the individual partners.

⚜ *How does an FLP help reduce the value of an estate?*

The FLP helps in reducing the value of the parents' estates by qualifying for various "valuation discounts."

The federal estate and gift tax is a tax on the transfer of property during the owner's life or at his or her death. The tax is based on the fair market value of the property transferred. *Fair market value* is the value at which property would change hands between a willing buyer and a willing seller, both having full knowledge of all relevant facts and neither being under any compulsion to buy or to sell. In determining the fair market value, a willing buyer will demand certain discounts in the value of property that cannot be readily sold or that the buyer cannot control.

In creating an FLP, the parents transfer assets that they fully control in exchange for a small, usually 1 or 2 percent, general partnership interest and a 99 or 98 percent limited partnership interest. Thereafter, the parents no longer own the assets outright; they own their general partnership interest, which gives them total control, and a limited partnership interest, which lacks marketability and control.

In determining the fair market value of the limited partnership interest, a willing buyer would demand a discount for lack of marketability and a discount for lack of control. The amount of each of these discounts needs to be determined for gift tax valuation purposes. This determination should always be made by a qualified business appraiser. The discounts will usually range from 25 to 60 percent.

Let's assume a couple transfers $15 million of securities and real estate to an FLP in exchange for a 1 percent general partnership interest and a 99 percent limited partnership interest. After a qualified appraisal, it is determined that the limited partnership interests should have a combined 40 percent discount for lack of control and marketability. This means that, immediately after the transfer, there is a $6 million reduction in value. With a gift and estate tax rate of 55 percent, there would be a potential tax savings of $3.3 million.

Thus, the family limited partnership allows the parents to reduce the size of their estate by making gifts of limited partnership interests and by qualifying for valuation discounts.

 ⚑ *Do gifts of limited partnership interests qualify for the gift tax annual exclusion?*

They have qualified since the inception of the gift tax. However, in a private letter ruling, the IRS has taken the position that a limited partnership interest does not qualify for the annual exclusion because the general partner has discretion as to when and if distributions are made. A private letter ruling has no force in the law and cannot be relied upon, but it shows the direction the IRS is moving in. Most practitioners feel that the IRS cannot win this issue, but until a court decides the issue, or Congress clarifies the law, or the IRS withdraws its position, there is a degree of uncertainty in the law.

 ⚑ *Can gifts be made in more than one year?*

Gifts of limited partnership interests can be made as often as and in whatever amounts the general partners wish. They can be made in a single year or over a number of years.

 ⚑ *What if we are setting up a family limited partnership only to reduce our estate taxes—won't the IRS see through it?*

It does not matter if the principal reason for establishing an FLP is to reduce tax liability, as long as there exists a business, investment, or financial reason for using that type of entity. Courts have made a determination that the IRS cannot disregard the existence of a partnership if the partnership is formed for business, investment, or financial reasons.

 ⚑ *What are some of the reasons I can set forth in my partnership agreement to satisfy the business-purpose requirement for my FLP?*

Your partnership will need to have a purpose such as:

- Managing and/or developing real estate and other assets
- Protecting partnership assets from the claims of creditors
- Providing a reasonable and smooth economic arrangement among the members of your family to maintain the partnership assets in the family
- Ensuring family harmony by providing that any dispute will be resolved by arbitration rather than going through the court system
- Preventing assets of the family from being taken through the probate court system on the death of a family member

- Providing for smooth succession and control of your family's assets
- Consolidating family assets which are held in fractional interests
- Creating an orderly and consolidated management system for all assets held by the partnership

Can an FLP help avoid probate and state death taxes?

It can, but only if structured properly. If the FLP owns passive real estate investments, including land, vacation homes, or rental property outside the state of residence, costs associated with out-of-state probate may be saved. Also, if the state of residence does not have an inheritance tax, the basic inheritance tax of the other states in which the FLP assets are situated may be avoided in certain instances through the use of an FLP.

However, it is important that the partnership interest be held in the owner's revocable living trust. If it is not, the partnership interest, rather than the assets held in the FLP, will be subject to probate.

Can an FLP disqualify my estate from special-use valuation?

In order to qualify for the installment payment of estate taxes, your closely held business or farm must be at least 35 percent of your total estate. Caution must be taken when transferring such interests to your FLP.

A transfer by a parent or grandparent to an FLP could potentially disqualify the estate from special-use valuation. It is therefore important that your attorney or accountant make the appropriate calculations prior to the transfer of special-use property to an FLP.

Valuation of partnership interests

Who appraises the partnership interests for purposes of the discount?

A qualified appraiser must appraise the value of the partnership assets and then the value of the limited partnership interests in terms of restrictions under state law and in the partnership agreement. These appraisals, while related, are not the same. The former involves the value of the assets held in the FLP, and the latter involves the value of the ownership interests in the FLP as an entity.

Can the two appraisals be completed by the same individual or company?

Yes, they can, although not always. There are a number of nationally known appraisal firms that can appraise virtually any kind of asset and the applicable discounts in an FLP. However, in some cases, the person who appraises the value of the partnership assets will be a specialist in the valuation of those particular assets (e.g., a commercial real estate professional specializing in appraising rural office buildings will be used if such buildings are part of the FLP's holdings or business). A person specializing in business valuation may then be used to establish the discounted value of the limited partnership interests.

✎ *Why are interests in FLPs much less valuable than syndicated partnerships?*

There are several basic differences between an FLP and a publicly traded or widely held syndicated partnership:

1. *The general partner's experience in operating and administering a business entity:* FLPs do not designate professional managers as general partners; rather, the general partners are the current owners of the asset, the persons who are forming the partnership.
2. *Asset risk:* Syndicated partnerships hold many assets; therefore, they are able to spread the risk of the assets within the confines of a widely held partnership base. The asset and geographic market risks found in FLPs typically are absent in syndicated partnerships.
3. *The distribution of cash prior to the partnership's liquidation:* An investor in a syndicated partnership usually expects current income in the form of cash distributions based on the partnership's operations. In contrast, an investor in an FLP is aware that the current income, if any, can be only enough to cover his or her portion of the tax liability. The expected return on an investment in an FLP is more remote than it is on an investment in a syndicated partnership.
4. *The lack of an organized secondary market for FLP interests:* One would be hard-pressed to find a buyer who is willing to buy a limited partnership interest that has many inherent risks without any assurance of income distributions or the return of his or her capital.

✎ *Is the IRS likely to challenge an FLP?*

The IRS does not like family limited partnerships when used to obtain large discounts in the value of an estate, thereby saving estate and gift taxes that would otherwise be due. The IRS admits that valuation discounts of FLPs are legitimate, but it still challenges them in many situations. A challenge is most likely if the FLP is created just before death. Forming an FLP 2 days before death or when the parent is incapacitated invites the IRS to attack the partnership as solely a scheme for avoiding tax.

ᴁ Might the laws which favor family limited partnerships change in the near future?

Since the IRS does not like the substantial estate and gift tax savings realized through the use of FLPs, it is possible that legislation in the future could limit the estate tax savings. However, you must remember that there are many advantages to the FLP, and it is unlikely that all the advantages will be taken away in one fell swoop. For instance, the creditor protection afforded by FLPs is created by state law and cannot be easily affected by federal law changes. Also, the ability to give shares of the partnership to children and relatives without giving up control of the assets within would survive any change in the law on valuation of partnerships for gift tax purposes.

Income tax issues

ᴁ Does the FLP provide any income tax savings?

It can. A partnership is a tax-reporting entity but does not itself pay taxes. All tax attributes of the partnership flow through to the partners according to their respective partnership interests. Each partner then reports his, her, or its share of the partnership's income, gains, losses, deductions, and credits. Therefore, with an FLP it is possible to split the income, gains, losses, deductions, and credits produced by the various investment assets in the partnership among the family members or family entities that are the partners. This may reduce the overall tax burden by spreading the tax attributes to partners with varying exemptions and tax brackets.

Furthermore, any management fee paid to the general partner for its services is considered earned income, even though the income produced by the assets may have been portfolio or passive income. This earned income can be used by the general partner as the basis for making contributions to qualified retirement plans or IRAs and for providing other employer-provided fringe benefits.

ᴁ Do my children or grandchildren pay taxes on partnership income that is not distributed to them?

Partners pay income tax on their share of the partnership's income whether or not it is distributed to them. Therefore, in the normal course of managing the partnership business, most general partners make distributions to their limited partners equal to the limited partners' income tax liability.

⅍ Does my FLP have to have its own federal identification number for income tax purposes?

Although the partnership itself does not pay federal income tax, it does need a federal tax identification number and a partnership return must be filed.

⅍ Are the costs of preparing a family limited partnership deductible?

There are some deductions that may be taken:

- Expenses for the collection or production of income or for the management, conservation, or maintenance of property held for the production of income and tax planning under Internal Revenue Code Section 212 are deductible subject to a minimum requirement of 2 percent of adjusted gross income.
- A partnership's organization expenses may be amortized over not less than 60 months.

⅍ When we give limited partnership interests to our children and grandchildren, what is their cost basis in the interests?

The interests given by parents retain the parents' income tax basis. Unlike assets the parents leave at death, the FLP interests do not receive a stepped-up basis to date-of-death value. When the limited partners—children and grandchildren—sell their interests at a later date, there will be capital gain tax due if the sales price exceeds their parents' and grandparents' basis in the interests.

⅍ How do I know whether capital gain tax planning is more important than federal estate and gift tax planning?

Calculations can easily be made comparing the effect of losing the step-up in basis with the effect of getting the assets out of the taxable estates of the parents or grandparents. In such comparisons, the numbers almost always show that the estate tax savings with an FLP far outweigh the potential capital gain tax savings without an FLP.

Funding an FLP

⧫ *What assets can and cannot be contributed to an FLP?*

Other than personal-use assets, such as a personal residence, most investment assets can be put into an FLP. Even family businesses can be contributed to an FLP. Closely held corporate stock of a family corporation can also be put into the partnership.

The following types of assets generally should *not* be used to fund FLPs:

- Stock options
- Annuities
- IRC Section 1244 stock
- Professional corporation or association stock
- Potential liability-producing assets
- Assets with debt in excess of adjusted basis
- Personal-use assets

IRAs and other qualified retirement plan assets, as well as S corporation stock, should never be contributed to a partnership of any kind.

⧫ *In funding an FLP, are there any other potential traps that I should be wary of?*

There are several other funding complications of which you should be aware before creating an FLP:

- Immediate gain will be recognized if your debt on property contributed to the FLP exceeds your basis.
- You cannot transfer installment notes into an FLP and immediately give the limited partners their interests without triggering income tax.
- You cannot transfer land with a mortgage or trust deed that has a due-on-sale clause without the consent of the lender.
- A transfer of property to an FLP may be subject to a transfer tax in some jurisdictions (e.g., the state of Washington).
- Transfer of property into an FLP may cause a revaluation of the property for property tax purposes.
- Capital, as distinguished from personal services or labor, must be a material income-producing factor within the FLP in order for it to be recognized for income tax purposes.
- You should not transfer annuities to an FLP unless the partnership

will hold the annuities as a nominee for the benefit of the annuitant under a nominee or special-allocation agreement that allocates all tax attributes of the annuity to the annuitant.

⚖ *Do we pay tax when we fund our FLP?*

No gain or loss is generally recognized to the partnership or the partners on the transfer of their property to the partnership in exchange for a partnership interest. Be careful, however, if you transfer property subject to a mortgage. If the mortgage is greater than your tax basis of the asset, the excess will be taxed.

Using an FLP to hold life insurance

⚖ *Can an FLP hold life insurance on the life of the general-partner parents or grandparents?*

An FLP offers a meaningful alternative to the irrevocable life insurance trust and may in many instances be superior to it.

If the partnership is the owner of life insurance on the life of a general partner and most of the FLP's ownership interests are in the hands of the children and/or grandchildren, the life insurance proceeds attributable to their limited partnership interests will not be taxed in the estate of the general-partner parents or grandparents.

⚖ *What advantages does an FLP have over an ILIT when it comes to owning insurance?*

The FLP is flexible and, unlike the ILIT, can be amended to meet changing needs and family conditions. The insured can retain control of the policy if he or she also controls the FLP as general partner.

Since the FLP is run by the general-partner members of the family, there is no need to seek out and appoint outside trustees. Money to pay for the policy premiums can be contributed to the FLP by either the general or the limited partners, or if there are sufficient earnings in the FLP, the partnership can pay for the premiums out of current earnings and avoid any demand-right issues. At the death of the insured, the FLP receives the proceeds from the insurance policy income tax–free and can use them in the same manner as they are used in an ILIT.

⚖ *Does a general partner have incidents of ownership in the life insurance policy that is payable to the FLP? Would that make*

the policy proceeds includable in the estate of the insured general partner?

The U.S. Tax Court has held that a general partner is not considered to have an incident of ownership in an insurance policy on his or her life that is owned by the partnership. Only the value of the general partner's prorated interest in the FLP is included in his or her estate.

Miscellaneous FLP issues

⌲ *Can you provide an FLP example that illustrates everything you've been telling me so far?*

Consider the following example:

- Parents contribute vacant real estate holdings appraised at $2 million to an FLP in exchange for a 2 percent general partnership interest and a 98 percent limited partnership interest.
- A qualified business appraiser applies a valuation discount of 40 percent on the limited partnership interests for lack of control and lack of marketability.
- The 98 percent limited partnership interests originally valued at $1,960,000 are thus discounted to a value of $1,176,000.
- The parents give their limited partnership interests to the children.
- No gift tax is due because the value of the gifts is less than the parents' combined applicable exclusion amount.
- The parents are able to maintain control over the real estate portfolio. The amount of the discount—$784,000 in this example—totally escapes federal estate and gift taxes.
- The appreciation attributable to the limited partnership interests in the vacant lots will not be taxed in the parents' estates.
- Interests worth $1,960,000 before discount were transferred to the children. If the interests appreciate at the rate of 7.2 percent per annum, at the end of 10 years the interests will double in value to $3,920,000.
- The parents will have removed $3,920,000 worth of real estate from their estates at a current value.

⌲ *Can you give another example of how an FLP works?*

Assume the following:

- You are 74 years of age, your spouse is 72, and you have five children. You have a $5 million estate that consists of $500,000 in bonds and publicly traded stocks and a $4.5 million farm.

■ You will be in the 55 percent marginal estate tax bracket on the death of the surviving spouse and wish to reduce your potential federal estate taxes.

■ Your assets are appreciating at 5 percent per annum; you expect to live for 14.4 more years, during which time your assets will double in value, to $10 million.

■ On your death at that time (assuming your spouse has predeceased you), the taxes on your $10 million estate—even with a bypass family trust in a living trust–centered estate plan—will be $4,465,000.

Now let us see what will happen if you create an FLP:

■ You and your spouse form an FLP that has a 1 percent general partnership interest and a 99 percent limited partnership interest.

■ The two of you transfer the farm into the partnership and get all the partnership interests—both the general and the limited—in return.

■ There is no income tax generated by your funding of your partnership.

■ The two of you no longer own the farm, but you own the partnership which owns the farm.

■ You hire an appraiser to value the farm, which she values at $4.5 million.

■ You hire a partnership valuation specialist who appraises the limited partnership interests at a discounted value of 60 percent of their real worth (a 40 percent discount).

■ The 99 percent limited partnership interest is now worth $2,673,000.

■ You begin a program to give the limited partnership interests to your children—99 percent of the partnership—while keeping the 1 percent general partnership interest.

■ On Christmas Day of the first year, you and your spouse begin your gift program:

　You give your five children $2 million worth of the limited partnership tax-free because of your combined applicable exclusion amount.

　Since each of the children is happily married, you give each couple $40,000 (a total of $200,000) without tax because of your collective annual exclusions, assuming, of course, that the IRS is wrong about limited partnership interests not qualifying for the annual exclusion and assuming the $10,000 amount has not been adjusted for inflation.

Since you have ten grandchildren, you give an additional $200,000 of partnership interests to them as well ($20,000 each).

- You make additional gifts of $273,000 on New Year's Day, a week later.
- You have now completed your program of giving away most of your farm, worth almost $4.5 million, at absolutely no tax cost.
- As the FLP's general partners, you and your spouse still run the farm. You still control the assets and the income it generates.
- You receive a salary from the partnership for managing the partnership's affairs as general partners.
- Nothing has changed except that you have achieved massive federal estate and gift tax savings.
- On the death of the survivor of you or your spouse, the survivor's estate will consist of only 1 percent of the family farm and the stocks and bonds.
- Only the 1 percent FLP interest and the stocks and bonds will be taxed.

⩗ What can we do about protecting our portfolio, which is outside of our FLP?

In the above example, you and your spouse will have a stock and bond portfolio of $1 million that will generate $345,800 in estate tax on the death of the surviving spouse. If the partnership purchases a $350,000 last-to-die life insurance policy on both spouses' lives, the policy will pay 99 percent of its proceeds tax-free to the partnership. You have now covered the remainder of your tax liability.

⩗ Can I change or revoke a family limited partnership agreement after it is initially established?

An FLP agreement can be changed unless the original agreement prohibits amendments. In this respect, an FLP is similar to a revocable trust. The difference is that, for an FLP, the permission of all the partners is usually required to make changes. You must only change your partnership agreement with the assistance of your attorney, as any changes may affect its ability to protect your assets and receive discounts.

Care should be taken before revoking an FLP. A revocation could cause negative income tax ramifications. If contributions to an FLP are made properly (and with the assistance of your attorney), there are generally no tax ramifications on the contributions to the partnership. However, once the property is contributed, there may be negative tax consequences should you terminate the partnership and distribute the property to the partners. For instance, if you contribute property with a low cost basis and then decide to terminate the partnership, it is possible that the distribution will trigger a capital gain tax you would otherwise not have to pay. You should use a family limited partnership only if you feel confident that you will stick with the benefits that this type of ownership provides.

Once we have placed assets into an FLP, how do we get money out of the partnership?

There are five ways that money can be distributed from an FLP:

1. The general partners are entitled to receive a reasonable fee for managing the FLP. If the general partner is a corporation, the corporation can pay salaries to officers and employees of the corporation.
2. The general partners may authorize pro rata distributions of partnership income or principal to the general and limited partners.
3. The FLP may make loans to any of the limited partners. The loans must be allowed by the FLP agreement.
4. Specific items of income or gain may be specially allocated to one or more specific partners.
5. The FLP can be terminated by consent of the general partner and all the limited partners, allowing each partner to receive his or her pro rata share of the partnership assets.

Isn't an FLP relatively complex? How do I go about creating one and ensuring that it is done correctly?

The family limited partnership is a separate business entity and must be maintained as such. It has its own taxpayer identification number and must file its own tax return each year. Once you set up an FLP, you will have the added cost of the annual tax return preparation. In addition, many states have franchise fees which must be paid to the state government for the privilege of using the limited partnership entity.

The FLP is an advanced estate planning and asset protection strategy. In using this strategy, you should work closely with your attorney, financial planner, and a certified public accountant who has experience in tax accounting for partnerships. Unless you are experienced with business entities and comfortable complying with the numerous laws that apply to them, you should rely on your advisors to see to all the details.

The bottom line: If you do not want to rely on your advisors, and do not want the complexity of another business entity, a family limited partnership may not be for you. On the other hand, if you are motivated to save every last dollar of estate tax and are willing to rely on your advisors, an FLP can offer substantial advantages, especially if keeping your assets from potential creditors is important to you.

Gifts

Use of the annual exclusion and the applicable exclusion amount

⚹ *Should I utilize my applicable exclusion amount during my lifetime or upon my death?*

Many people have the misconception that it is best to "save" their applicable exclusion amount until their death. However, a more powerful leveraging technique is to utilize it during your lifetime. If you use your applicable exclusion amount by making lifetime gifts, the value of the gifts will appreciate in the recipients' hands and not in your taxable estate.

Between real investment growth and inflation, the value of the gift at your life expectancy should be substantial: under the Rule of 72, the value of your gift will double every 7.2 years at 10 percent; if your life expectancy is 21 more years, a $1 million gift will be worth $8 million in the hands of the recipients at the end of that time. Assuming an applicable 55 percent federal estate tax rate, you would have to leave over $17.7 million to provide your heirs with the same value.

⚹ *Should parents always give property away instead of dying with it?*

No. Whether to give property away or bequeath it depends on a family's specific situation, assumptions about future facts and law, and the form of the gift. Nontax considerations may very well be much more important than tax-saving considerations. Serious gifts should be made only with the advice of a qualified estate planning attorney.

⚖ *Why should I consider annual gifts as part as my estate planning?*

Making gifts is one of the most powerful estate planning strategies at your disposal. You can give to any person, in any year, an amount equal to the gift tax annual exclusion, without incurring any gift taxes. Under the Taxpayer Relief Act of 1997, the annual exclusion amount of $10,000 will be indexed for inflation, in $1000 increments. This is effective for gifts made in a calendar year after 1998. However, if the amount of the inflation adjustment is less than $1000, the law calls for rounding down to the next-lowest multiple of $1000. For example, if the inflation adjustment is 9.9 percent, the amount of the annual exclusion will remain at $10,000 rather than being increased to $10,990.

Gifts reduce the taxable amount of your estate and allow any appreciation to accumulate in the estate of the recipient. There is also a fundamental difference between the calculation of estate taxes and gift taxes, even though the rates appear to be the same.

Gift taxes are calculated on the actual amount of the gift. For example, assume you are in the 50 percent gift and estate tax bracket. The tax on a $10,000 gift would be $5000, or a total cost to you of $15,000 for making the gift.

Estate taxes are calculated on the *gross* amount of the estate. To get the same $10,000 into the hands of your beneficiary after your death, you would have a cost of $20,000: $10,000 for the estate tax and $10,000 for the gift. The transaction cost is $5000 higher if the disposition is from your estate rather than from you as a gift.

You should also be aware that when you make a gift, the recipient continues with your tax basis in the property. For example, if you make a gift of stock with a present value of $10,000 and a cost basis of $1000, the recipient has to recognize $9000 of gain if he or she sells the property at present value. If the transfer occurs at death, the cost basis increases to the value at death, so if your heir then sells the stock for present value, there is no gain. However, when you compare the capital gain rate at 20 percent with the effective estate tax rates starting at 37 percent, it usually makes more sense to make the gift and pay the capital gain tax.

⚖ *I am a widow, retired and living a pleasant life. I've heard about the annual exclusion and would like to give my grown children some money this year. Should I make gifts to them?*

Maybe. First consider your present and future needs and the total sum of your assets. After you do this, it would be a good idea to discuss the amount and the timing of the potential gifts with your estate planning attorney and financial planner. They will want to discuss the practicality of the gift and your emotional comfort in making gifts. They will also review and discuss your current cash flow and asset base, as well as your future needs. Your estate tax situation is also an important consideration in determining whether you should make gifts.

Once you and your advisors accomplish this analysis, you should know with a great deal of certainty whether making gifts is appropriate. More importantly, you will have peace of mind from knowing that you have made a good financial and practical decision.

⚜ Do I have to file a gift tax return when I use any part of my applicable exclusion amount?

You must file a federal gift tax return, but no payment will be due.

⚜ Does the Internal Revenue Service have any time limits for challenging the valuation of gifts?

If a gift is made from a donor to another person in excess of the annual exclusion in any year, a gift tax return must be filed with the Internal Revenue Service following the same time schedule as is required for the filing of income tax returns. In the past, the Internal Revenue Service was able to challenge the value of gifts following the donor's death, even if those gifts were made many years before the death of the donor. While no extra gift tax could be collected on any revalued gifts, because of a loophole in the law, the IRS could use revalued gifts to increase the size of the taxable estate. The result was a higher estate tax.

Having, in essence, an unlimited statute of limitations was deemed by Congress to be inherently unfair to taxpayers. In order to provide additional protection to the taxpayer, the Taxpayer Relief Act of 1997 established strict limits on gift revaluation by the IRS. The IRS is now prohibited from revaluing gifts for estate tax purposes if a proper gift tax return was filed and 3 years have lapsed from the date the gift return was due or filed, if filed late. However, the gift must have been adequately disclosed on the gift tax return. If the gift was not adequately disclosed, the 3-year statute of limitations does not apply and the IRS will be able to challenge the value of the gifts, just as it has been doing. The 3-year statute of limitations applies to gifts made after August 5, 1997.

✎ *Is it true that I can't make gifts just before I die?*

This is a common misconception. Many people believe this because, before the Economic Recovery Tax Act of 1981, all gifts made within 3 years of the donor's death, except those qualifying for and not exceeding the annual gift tax exclusion, were included in the estate of the donor. Now this "3-year rule" covers only a few types of gifts.

The major gift included in the 3-year rule is a gift of a life insurance policy. If you give away a life insurance policy and then die within 3 years of the transfer, the death benefit of that life insurance policy will be included in your estate for estate tax purposes.

Another type of gift covered under the 3-year rule is the payment of taxes on a gift. In most cases, if you make a gift to someone and then pay gift tax, the tax is not considered another gift on which you need to pay taxes. However, if you make the gift and pay the taxes within 3 years of your death, the taxes you paid will be included in your estate.

Gift strategies

✎ *Is there a way that I can start giving interests in my rental properties to my two children but still keep control over the properties and keep at least some of the income for myself?*

Absolutely. There are several ways this can be done. You can simply start giving your children undivided fractional interests in the real estate each year, using your annual exclusion amounts. However, this is an unwieldy way to make the gifts, as you have to pay for recording new deeds each year. Also, if you give away more than 50 percent, you lose control over the property.

Another way to accomplish this goal is to put the rental properties into some sort of business entity and then give your children interests in that entity. The best solution is to use a family limited partnership in which all the partners are members of your family. Each year you can give your children partnership interests within the annual exclusion, but you still retain complete control over the operation of the rental properties and still retain the right to receive all or part of the income.

✎ *Can I make gifts directly from a revocable trust?*

Before the Taxpayer Relief Act of 1997, annual exclusion gifts made from a revocable living trust to a third party within 3 years of the date of the death of the trust maker were added back to the value of the trust for determining estate taxes owed. Now, under the 1997 act, annual exclusion gifts made from a revocable living trust are treated as though they were made directly by the maker. In the past, many estate planning advisors directed trust makers to remove the assets from the trust before making gifts. This two-step procedure for gift making is no longer necessary. This change applies to persons dying after August 5, 1997.

    Is there a way to hold my assets in a revocable trust and continue my gift planning in the event of my disability?

Through special drafting in your revocable living trust, you can provide that, in the event of disability, your trustees may make distributions to your agents under a *limited durable power of attorney* specially designed for making gifts. When a distribution is made from your trust to your agent, no gift occurs.

Your limited durable power of attorney should be drafted to be effective only upon your disability. It generally should restrict the power to give to favor only the persons and organizations you want to receive your assets. Your power of attorney should specifically authorize various formats under which gifts may be made (e.g., outright or in trust).

In addition, if you envision large transfers, as may be the case if you desire to use your applicable exclusion amount during your lifetime, you should take care to require a *special independent agent* (usually a certified public accountant or corporate fiduciary) to approve any transfers before the gifts are made. This assures you that an independent party will review your situation and determine whether the transfers are, in fact, a good idea under the circumstances.

    Since there is an unlimited gift tax exemption for tuition and health care in addition to the annual exclusion, and there is no present-interest requirement, can't I set up a trust to be used only for those purposes and contribute any amount to it I want, free of gift tax?

Unfortunately, the IRS nixed this idea in its regulations on the grounds that, because the transfer is not directly to the educational institution or health care provider, it does not qualify.

    I don't have much to give now, but I want to do something special for my church. What can I do?

You can make a gift of life insurance and tailor the amount of the death proceeds to the amount of monthly premiums you can pay. To accomplish this, you would name your church as the beneficiary of the life insurance policy. If this is done properly, you will be entitled to deduct the premium payments on your federal income tax return.

International gift planning

🔊 *Is a resident alien subject to the same gift tax rules as U.S. citizens when making gifts of property situated in the United States?*

Noncitizen residents of the United States do not have any unified credit available for lifetime gifts. Any gift exceeding the annual exclusion is a taxable transaction requiring a gift tax return and payment of the gift tax.

🔊 *What happens if a foreign nonresident parent makes a gift to a child living in the United States?*

If a foreign parent makes a gift to a child who is a citizen or resident of the United States, the gift is generally not subject to gift tax. This rule applies if the gift is made from property situated outside the United States and the non-U.S. citizen parent is not a U.S. resident.

However, caution must always be used in international estate planning: While the above rule may apply for a donor from one country, it may not apply for a donor in another country that has an estate tax treaty with the United States.

Under the Small Business Job Protection Act of 1996, all gifts of foreign property over $10,000 made by a foreign person to a U.S. citizen or resident alien must be reported to the IRS. Noncompliance with this requirement can result in a penalty of 5 percent of the amount of the foreign gift for each month in which the failure to report continues, not to exceed 25 percent of the aggregate amount of the gift.

🔊 *What happens if this same noncitizen-nonresident parent makes a gift of property situated in the United States to his or her child?*

The rules change in this situation. When a nonresident parent makes a gift of property situated within the United States, the gift is subject to the standard estate, gift, and generation-skipping transfer taxes.

According to tax law, property situated within the United States would include all real property, stock issued by U.S. corporations, and domestic bank accounts.

⚰ *What happens if the same parent dies, leaving the child a vacation house on Martha's Vineyard in his or her will?*

If the house is worth over $60,000 at the parent's date of death, estate taxes will be owed to the IRS. Any value in excess of $60,000 is subject to U.S. estate tax at graduated rates beginning at 26 percent.

Generally, noncitizen-nonresident parents are entitled to a unified credit of only $13,000. This permits an individual to shelter the first $60,000 of U.S. property from U.S. estate tax (rather than the applicable exclusion amount of $1 million allowed to a citizen's or resident's estate beginning in 2006).

Sometimes, a tax treaty obligation requires that a nonresident alien be treated the same as a U.S. citizen or resident for unified credit purposes. In these situations, the credit allowed is the greater of $13,000 or the full amount of the unified credit prorated on the basis of the ratio of U.S.-owned property to worldwide property. In other words, a foreigner gets only a portion of the full unified credit, based on the percentage of the value of his or her U.S.-owned property in relation to his or her worldwide assets.

PLANNING FOR SPOUSES

QTIP Trusts and Estate Planning

⚰ *What is a QTIP trust?*

"QTIP" stands for "qualified terminable interest property." In a nutshell, a *QTIP trust* is an estate planning device which allows you to obtain a gift or estate tax marital deduction while providing your spouse with full income and limited principal rights in your property.

⚰ *How does it work?*

The most well known type of QTIP trust is established as part of a will or trust. It generally provides that a deceased spouse's property will continue in or be transferred to a trust for the benefit of the surviving spouse. If the trust meets certain requirements, and if the person filing your estate tax return makes the election on the return, the property in the trust will qualify for the unlimited estate tax marital deduction.

There will not be any estate tax on property transferred into the QTIP trust at the first spouse's death. While the surviving spouse is still alive, the trustee of the QTIP trust must distribute the income from the trust to the spouse. The spouse may have access (either partial or complete) to the trust principal during his or her lifetime under the standards that are set forth in the deceased spouse's trust instructions.

When the surviving spouse dies, the property which is then in the QTIP trust will be taken into account in computing that spouse's estate taxes. The remaining trust property—after estate taxes are paid—is then distributed to whoever is named as the remainder beneficiaries in the trust document.

⚜ *How do I qualify my spouse's trust for QTIP treatment?*

Four requirements must be met in order for a trust to qualify as a QTIP trust:

- The trustee of the QTIP trust must be required to distribute the net income of the QTIP trust to your spouse at least annually.
- The QTIP trust must be invested in income-producing property, or the spouse must have the power to require the trustee to convert non-income-producing property to income-producing property.
- During your spouse's life, your spouse must be the only current beneficiary of the QTIP trust.
- The executor of your estate must make the appropriate election on your estate tax return.

An examination of the QTIP's name reveals a lot about what it does. "Qualified" means that assets left to such a trust qualify for the unlimited marital deduction from federal estate taxes. This is a critical provision because no estate taxes are due if the marital deduction applies. "Terminable interest" means that the trust will dictate who ultimately receives the property after both spouses pass away. This feature ensures that your intended ultimate heirs, usually your children, are protected. If your surviving spouse remarries, his or her spouse could otherwise be entitled to a portion of your estate. Furthermore, since the assets are controlled by the trustees, there is less danger that an elderly person will be talked out of his or her inheritance by predatory persons.

⚜ *Why must the QTIP trust be invested in income-producing property?*

Without this requirement, one spouse could defer taxation without giving the surviving spouse any real benefit from the property. Investments in non-income-producing property are permitted only with the approval of the beneficiary spouse.

⚜ *Are QTIPs appropriate for every married estate?*

Although QTIP trusts are popular, they are not appropriate for every estate. Some people prefer QTIP trusts over other marital deduction devices because a QTIP trust provides the surviving spouse with income during his or her life and can still restrict that spouse's ability to get to the trust principal. Many people will not wish to restrict that right when planning for a spouse.

⚜ *Why might I want to restrict my spouse's right to principal?*

There are many reasons why a spouse might not want his or her surviving spouse to have access to the trust principal. You may be concerned that your surviving spouse might remarry a person who is after his or her inheritance. A QTIP trust can ensure that your spouse will be taken care of during his or her lifetime and, after your spouse's death, that your children or grandchildren will receive an inheritance that was not depleted by a new spouse.

QTIPs are frequently used in second marriages. In the classic example, one spouse of the second marriage wants to take care of the other spouse on death but also wants to make absolutely sure that the children from his or her first marriage inherit the estate. The QTIP ensures that the hoped-for result will become a reality.

The specific terms would be something like the following:

1. Pay all of the income to my surviving spouse for the rest of his or her life. *[In order to qualify for the unlimited marital deduction as set forth in the Internal Revenue Code, the surviving spouse* must *have the right to receive all of the income at least annually from a regular marital trust or from a QTIP trust.]*
2. My trustee has the discretion to make the principal available to my surviving spouse if my spouse needs it for health, education, maintenance, and support.
3. If my surviving spouse remarries, he or she will continue to receive the income from the QTIP trust but will lose all right to principal during the period of the remarriage.
4. If my spouse becomes single again, go back to my instructions in paragraph 2 above.
5. On my spouse's subsequent death, my children will receive whatever is left in my spouse's QTIP trust.

≫ *Can I give my spouse discretion regarding distribution of the QTIP property on his or her death?*

A QTIP can give a spouse a limited power of appointment to decide who gets the principal, or it can provide that the assets pour over into another trust (created on the death of the spouse) to be held for other beneficiaries such as children or grandchildren.

≫ *How does a limited power of appointment work?*

The QTIP provides that your spouse can leave the property to a class of beneficiaries—such as children, grandchildren, descendants—in whatever amounts or proportions that he or she chooses. This enables your spouse to monitor the behavior of members of the class and make decisions based upon that behavior that will affect their inheritance.

≫ *When is this device most useful?*

A limited power of appointment is especially helpful when there are young children, whose adult behavior and personalities are not yet known, or mature children whose behavior and relationships to their parent or stepparent are in question.

≫ *Can my children receive principal distributions while my spouse is receiving the income?*

The marital deduction will be disallowed if any part of the principal benefits anybody other than the surviving spouse during that spouse's lifetime.

≫ *Are there any problems with QTIP planning?*

When property passes to a QTIP trust for a surviving spouse, he or she may want as much income as possible, while the remainder beneficiaries want to inherit as much principal as possible. This situation can put the children and the parent at odds with each other.

≫ *How does the trustee resolve this conflict in interests?*

The trustee must be fair to both the surviving spouse and the remainder beneficiaries in exercising his or her fiduciary responsibility and must invest the trust funds for both reasonable income and capital appreciation requirements.

≥ *What is the number-one problem with QTIP planning in second marriages?*

If the QTIP provides for the needs of a stepparent from trust principal, any such distribution will come directly out of the pockets of the step-children and they will have a strong interest in obtaining, reviewing, questioning, and even challenging the distributions made to the surviving spouse.

If the surviving spouse is a trustee, this fiduciary duty will place the spouse in an awkward position and exacerbate the conflict. This planning arrangement may not be good for family dynamics.

≥ *Are there other problems with QTIP planning in second marriages?*

In a remarriage situation, the spouse and the children may be of the same generation, so the likelihood that the children will predecease their stepparent is statistically very realistic. In effect, this disinherits the children of the first marriage if they do not survive the stepparent.

≥ *What alternative do I have for taking care of both my current spouse and the children I have from a prior marriage immediately upon my death?*

You can use the unlimited marital deduction through a QTIP to pass property tax-free to your spouse upon your death if you predecease your spouse, and you can provide life insurance coverage through an ILIT for the benefit of your children. In this way, your children will not have to wait until your spouse dies to receive their inheritance; your gift of life insurance will pass upon your death directly to the children from your irrevocable life insurance trust.

Lifetime QTIP Trust Planning

≥ *Together, my husband and I have an estate of $2 million, but his share of our property is only $300,000. Is there any way to ensure my husband's estate will be able to use the maximum applicable exclusion amount if he dies first and to also ensure that all my property will go to my children after we are both gone?*

Yes. In your present situation, if your husband dies before you do, only $300,000 will be included in his estate. Since your husband's taxable estate is less than the applicable exclusion amount, the benefit of the full exclusion amount will be lost. This will, of course, generate unnecessary taxes. For example, if your husband dies in 2006 and leaves the $300,000 to his children, there will be no tax because the applicable exclusion amount will be $1 million. If you die immediately thereafter, your estate will be $1.7 million, resulting in a federal estate tax of $300,000.

By using a *lifetime QTIP trust,* you can make a tax-free gift to your husband but control the use of that gift. The value of the QTIP will be included in your husband's taxable estate and not yours. Thus, if your husband dies before you do, the value of the QTIP plus the value of your husband's other assets will allow full use of his applicable exclusion amount. And you can provide that when you are both gone, the property remaining in the QTIP trust is to go to your children.

Let's say that you create a lifetime QTIP for your husband and give him $700,000. The terms of the QTIP allow your husband to have the income from the trust assets, but on his death the assets in the QTIP must be held in a trust for you, while you are living, and then be paid to your children when you die. If your husband dies in 2006 or later, $1 million will be included in his estate, $300,000 of which is his own and $700,000 of which is held in trust for you and your children. No tax is due because of the $1 million applicable exclusion amount. If you die immediately thereafter, your estate is also $1 million, which passes tax-free to your children, along with the $700,000 in the QTIP trust. By using the lifetime QTIP, you are able to transfer your $1.7 million tax-free—a savings of $300,000 in federal estate tax.

⚼ How does this lifetime QTIP work?

Generally, for a gift to your spouse to not be subject to gift tax, it must be a gift with no strings attached. However, a QTIP trust is an exception to the no-strings rule. A QTIP trust is a trust for the benefit of your spouse but over which your spouse has less than complete control.

The minimum rights which the trust must provide to your spouse are that your spouse (and only your spouse) is entitled to all the trust income, at least annually, and that your spouse has the right to require that the trustee make the trust property productive of income. You can provide that you, and not your spouse, specifies to whom the remaining trust property will go upon your spouse's death.

The property you give to the trust is considered a gift from you to your spouse, so it will be excluded from your estate and included in your spouse's estate. Thus, your spouse's applicable exclusion amount will be applied to this property and any property he or she owns. Planned properly, all property subject to tax at your spouse's death will be sheltered by your spouse's applicable exclusion.

What if my husband and I divorce? Will he still be able to use the lifetime QTIP trust that I set up for him?

Your lifetime QTIP must last for the life of your spouse. It makes no difference if your marriage ends. Therefore, this technique is often used in long-term second marriages or in second marriages with large estates.

Are the rules for a lifetime QTIP trust basically the same as the rules for one that is set up for death?

For the most part, yes. The most notable difference is that a lifetime QTIP trust cannot be used for the benefit of a noncitizen spouse. There are some other differences, so make sure you meet with your estate planning team to determine if they might affect your planning goals.

PLANNING FOR MINORS

How can I make gifts to my minor child?

Under the Uniform Gifts to Minors Act (UGMA) and the Uniform Transfers to Minors Act (UTMA), you can set up an account at a bank for the benefit of your minor child and make various irrevocable gifts to the account while your child is a minor. Gifts to these types of accounts automatically qualify for the annual exclusion for gifts. During your child's lifetime, monies from the account can be used for the child's health, education, maintenance, and support. However, you cannot use the funds in the account to relieve your obligation to support the child.

Depending upon what state you live in, your child will automatically have legal access to the account upon reaching the age of 18 or 21. This can be of concern to parents because a child may not be mature enough to properly deal with a large sum of money at that age.

Why should I establish a trust for my minor children when I could simply transfer assets to a custodian under the Uniform Gifts to Minors Act or the Uniform Transfers to Minors Act?

Establishing a custodian to benefit your minor children under UGMA or UTMA could lead to unintended or unwise consequences. Under UTMA or UGMA, all assets transferred to the custodian become the property of the minor when he or she reaches 18 (21 in some states), regardless of whether the young person receiving the assets is emotionally mature enough to manage them properly. By using a trust rather than UTMA or UGMA, you can control how or when assets will come under the control of the young beneficiary.

⅏ *My state allows me to set up an account for my disabled child under the Uniform Custodial Trust Act. Is this wise?*

Rather than setting up such an account, you should consider creating a *supplemental-needs-only trust*. The income and principal of a supplemental-needs trust are not taken into account for purposes of determining whether the beneficiary is entitled to receive governmental assistance for basic health needs. A supplemental-needs trust can be a highly effective means of planning for a disabled adult child.

Your estate planning attorney can help you design trusts that specifically meet the particular needs of your family situation and ensure that your disabled child will be provided for under all circumstances likely or even unlikely to arise.

⅏ *How does a gift in trust to a minor qualify for the annual exclusion?*

Internal Revenue Code Section 2503(c) provides a means by which parents and grandparents can give property to minors in trust and still have the entire gift amount qualify for the annual gift exclusion. Such a gift is called a *2503(c) trust*. For a gift to conform to Code Section 2503(c), three requirements must be met:

- The trust property and the income derived from it can be spent by or for the benefit of the minor child before the minor reaches the age of 21.
- When the minor reaches the age of 21, all remaining property must pass to him or her.
- If the minor dies before age 21, all remaining property must pass to the minor's estate or be subject to the minor's power to appoint

the property (to himself or herself, his or her estate or creditors, or the creditors of his or her estate).

You can create a trust, subject to the above requirements, that can receive your gifts, hold the property for the benefit of your minor child, and still qualify for the annual gift exclusion.

⚜ *Can gifts made to a child's 2503(c) trust remain in trust past the child's twenty-first birthday?*

Yes. There are two ways that a 2503(c) trust can continue after the child turns 21. The trust will still qualify for the exclusion as long as the child has the right to compel the distribution of the trust under either of the following terms:

- At any time after reaching the age of 21.
- During a limited period after reaching 21. After this period, if the right is not exercised, the trust continues under the terms set forth by the trust maker.

Generally, if the trust maker wants the trust to continue past the child's twenty-first birthday—which is almost always the case—the latter approach is used.

⚜ *What are the instructions in a 2503(c) minor's trust?*

Almost all 2503(c) minor's trusts provide the following instructions:

Use both the income and principal of the trust for the health, education, maintenance, and support of my child.

Before making any distributions to my child, see if my child has any other sources of income or support, such as grants, scholarships, or other forms of income.

My primary objective in establishing this trust is to provide a college education for my child. If my child does not immediately attend college after graduation from high school, my trustee may withhold the distribution of both income and principal in my trustee's sole discretion, until my child elects to further his or her education.

When my child obtains a college degree, my trustee shall distribute the remaining trust income and principal to my child. If my child does not obtain a college degree, my trustee shall hold both income and principal until my child reaches age 35. My trustee shall, however, have the power to make discretionary payments of both income and principal in the event of an opportunity or expense deemed by my trustee to be in the best interests of my child.

❧ Can I create a 2503(c) trust for multiple beneficiaries?

No. You must create a separate 2503(c) trust for each intended beneficiary. Each trust is a separate taxpayer and must have its own tax identification number and file a separate tax return.

❧ Is there any reason I should choose a 2503(c) trust over a simple UGMA or UTMA custodial account?

If you are custodian of the UGMA or UTMA account, all the assets in the account will be includable in your estate if you die before they are distributed to your child. Furthermore, the assets in the custodial account will count against the child if he or she applies for financial aid at a college. A properly drafted 2503(c) trust avoids both of these problems.

❧ Is there some other way I can create a trust for my minor child and still qualify for the annual exclusion?

You can create a *demand-right trust* for your minor child. This is essentially an irrevocable trust created by one or both parents for the benefit of their minor child.

There is a strict procedure for making gifts to a demand-right trust that must be followed in order to qualify the gifts for the annual exclusion: The trustee must immediately notify the minor beneficiary—through the child's legal guardian—that a gift has been made to the trust and that the beneficiary has a specified period of time (typically 30 to 45 days) to demand a distribution from the trust in the amount of the gift. If the specified number of days lapses, the gift made to the demand-right trust will stay inside the trust and continue to be governed by its terms.

An irrevocable trust with a demand-right provision is an important part of proper estate planning for anyone who wants to put money aside for a minor child, does not want the property to be taxable in the giver's gross estate, yet wants to retain some control over the child's use of the property after the child reaches the age of 21.

❧ Are there income tax benefits to 2503(c) or demand trusts?

These trusts were traditionally used to shift income to children or grandchildren in lower income tax brackets. However, under the "kiddie tax" provisions of the Tax Reform Act of 1986, this is no longer allowed for a child under the age of 14 if his or her income exceeds a nominal amount. This amount was $1400 in 1998.

≈ When a Section 2503(c) minor's trust is used, are there any traps for the unwary?

Care must be taken that the trustee does not make payments of expenses for the beneficiary that would, under local law, be considered a discharge of a parental support obligation. If such power is granted to the trustee or if the trustee makes such payments, the trust's income is taxable to the beneficiary's parents.

≈ What type of assets would be good as gifts to a minor's trust?

Gifts of variable life insurance to a minor's trust may be particularly appropriate. The capital appreciation inside the insurance is not income. The cash value, which is often substantial with this type of insurance, can be borrowed from the insurance policy for expenditures. If it is desirable to maintain the death benefit, the loan can be repaid over time with additional gifts. Many such policies are using very competitive mutual funds as investment options. To keep the cost of insurance down, a grandchild's parent's life might be insured rather than the grandparent's life.

PLANNING FOR GRANDCHILDREN

≈ What is the generation-skipping transfer tax?

A basic premise of the federal estate tax is that wealth will be taxed as it passes from one generation to the next. In transfers from parent to child, from child to grandchild, and from grandchild to great-grandchild, the federal estate tax is imposed upon each transfer.

To avoid the consecutive imposition of the federal estate tax, affluent persons established trusts for the benefit of successive generations. These trusts paid income to the intermediate generation and distributed principal to the successive generation. Historically, the federal estate tax was avoided if the lifetime beneficiaries did not have sufficient rights which would cause inclusion of the property in their estates.

In order to stop persons from circumventing the federal estate tax by such devices, Congress established the *generation-skipping transfer (GST) tax* in 1986. This tax is imposed on many transfers which avoid the normal parent-to-child-to-grandchild transfer of assets.

⚜ How much is the GST tax?

Congress chose to deal harshly with attempts to skip a generation of taxation. The penalty is very stiff: 55 percent of the property which skips a generation of taxation.

⚜ Is there an exemption amount for the GST tax?

Congress did provide that every person may designate up to $1 million of property as exempt from this tax. Under the Taxpayer Relief Act of 1997, for all years after 1998, the $1 million GST exemption will be increased by the amount of annual inflation but only in minimum increments of $10,000, rounded down to the nearest $10,000. This means that if we assume an inflation rate of 2.5 percent, after the first year of indexing, the GST exemption amount will be $1,020,000 (without the rounding down it would be $1,025,000).

The GST tax applies whether gifts are made during life or at death. A tax return must be filed and an election made to use the GST exemption. Using the exemption can be quite complex, so competent advice on GST options and effects is absolutely necessary.

⚜ Is taking advantage of the GST exemption important?

When multigenerational planning is employed, the results can be astounding. It is important to understand that property placed in a trust which is properly designated as free from generation-skipping tax can remain free from GST tax regardless of who is the beneficiary. An example may help explain the importance of this distinction.

Assume that at his death, a father leaves $1 million to his daughter. The daughter invests the property for 20 years at a 7 percent rate of return. The daughter dies in the twentieth year, leaving the property to her son. Over the 20 years at a growth rate of 7 percent, the $1 million grows to $4 million. After paying estate taxes on this property, the grandson has $1.8 million to invest. If the grandson also invests at 7 percent and lives for another 20 years, he will have $7.2 million, subject to a 55 percent tax at his death, or just over $3 million for the next generation. If the father in our example instead elects to leave the $1 million in a well-designed trust that is exempt from GST taxes, at the end of his daughter's life there would still be $4 million in trust; but because the daughter does not own this property—the trust does— it is not subject to estate tax. Now the trustee has $4 million to invest for the grandson. Twenty years later, at the grandson's death, there will be $16 million in the trust for the next generation. Within two generations, the difference between the well-planned estate and the unplanned estate is nearly $13 million.

⚐ How is a generation-skipping transfer determined?

A generation-skipping transfer is a transfer to a *skip person,* that is, a person who is more than one generation below that of the transferor. It is easiest to determine a skip person within the family tree. A transfer to a grandchild is a transfer to a skip person, because the child of the transferor is omitted, or "skipped."

⚐ How are transfers measured when they're not going to grandchildren?

When transfers are made outside the family, generations are measured in years, using the transferor's age:

- Persons who are less than 12½ years younger than the transferor are in the transferor's generation.
- Persons between 12½ and 37½ years younger than the transferor are in the transferor's children's generation.
- Persons more than 37½ years younger than the transferor are skip persons.

⚐ Upon what transfers is the GST tax levied?

It is levied on any transfer which is made to a skip person *and* is any of the following:

- *A taxable termination:* This occurs when a beneficiary's (typically a child's) interest in a trust expires or terminates and thereafter only skip persons have an interest in the property.
- *A direct skip:* This is any transfer which is made directly to a skip person and which is subject to federal gift or estate taxes.
- *A taxable distribution:* This is any distribution from a trust which

is not a direct skip or taxable termination and is made to a skip person.

⚅ How can I get a GST exemption and still have to pay federal estate tax?

If you left property directly to a grandchild and there wasn't such a thing as the GST tax, you would pay estate tax on the transfer—just like you would on the transfer to a child—from 37 to 55 percent. This is exactly what happens when you leave property to a grandchild and qualify for the GST exemption.

If you did not qualify for the GST exemption, you would pay GST tax at the top marginal bracket of 55 percent and then pay another estate tax on the transfer to your grandchildren.

⚅ I intend to leave one-third of my property to each of my two living children and the remaining one-third to my deceased son's two children (my grandchildren). Do I have to pay GST tax?

Since your son is deceased at the time you make the transfer, your grandchildren will "move up" to the generation of your deceased son and the transfer will not be subject to the GST tax.

⚅ Are there ways to soften the harshness of the generation-skipping transfer tax?

Your estate planning attorney can explain a number of softening techniques, including:

- Allocation of the GST exemptions to both spouses
- Early allocation of the GST exemption to a trust so that the appreciation or increase in the value of trust assets will magnify the benefit of the exemption
- Careful use of a general power of appointment
- Careful use of a special power of appointment
- Careful use of sequential powers of appointment

⚅ Is the GST exemption available for gifts as well as for federal estate tax?

Yes, it is available for lifetime gifts as well as for gifts at death.

❧ *How is the GST exemption allocated?*

For lifetime transfers, the allocation is made by an election on the federal gift tax return for the year in which the transfer was made. With respect to transfers at death, the allocation is made on the federal estate tax return.

❧ *What are the tax advantages of utilizing the GST exemption?*

While generation skipping was historically a tool only for the very wealthy, the Tax Reform Act of 1986 has created an opportunity for everyone to utilize this technique to save substantial taxes. With proper planning, once you transfer assets and designate them as exempt under the generation-skipping exemption, the assets plus all income and appreciation attributable to them are not taxed in the estate of the child.

❧ *What should a couple do to ensure that each spouse can take advantage of his or her individual exemption from the GST tax?*

If one spouse has assets worth less than the GST exemption, and the other has assets worth more than the GST exemption, steps should be taken to increase the size of the less wealthy spouse's estate to ensure that his or her estate can also utilize the full GST exemption. A transfer of assets between spouses may be made by outright gift or by trust.

❧ *Where can I create my GST trust?*

You can create a trust specifically for GST purposes in your will or living trust or as a separate irrevocable trust.

❧ *How can my spouse and I utilize both of our GST exemptions?*

A person must be deemed the "transferor" of property to qualify for the GST exemption. This may pose a problem with the typical estate plan created by a married couple. Such a plan generally allocates the applicable exclusion amount (up to $1 million in 2006) to a family trust, with the remaining balance to a marital trust. The property in the family trust is deemed that of the decedent, and thus the decedent qualifies as the "transferor" for GST purposes. However, the assets in the marital trust are deemed those of the surviving spouse, so he or she is now the "transferor." The decedent's remaining GST exemption may be lost.

To fully utilize both exemptions, a special election may be made as to part of the marital trust. In our example, the unused GST exemption of the first spouse to die is placed in its own trust, called a *reverse QTIP.* The property in the reverse QTIP is treated as belonging to the decedent rather than the surviving spouse for GST tax purposes but as belonging to the surviving spouse for estate tax purposes. Thus, the decedent remains the transferor of the property for GST tax purposes and, by making the proper allocations, can utilize his or her entire GST exemption. On the death of the surviving spouse, both spouses have utilized their maximum exemptions, totaling over $2 million.

⚓ Can a trust which is separate from the living trust qualify for the GST exemption?

Practitioners often create a separate irrevocable life insurance trust for GST purposes. If the trust is funded with life insurance, only the insurance premiums apply toward the GST exemption. Note that a spouse should not be named as a beneficiary of a GST trust that is created to own life insurance on the life of the other or both spouses.

⚓ Can I use a GST exemption with my revocable living trust and still allow my children to use the property?

Yes, you can. One commonly used technique is to divide the transferor's property into equal shares for his or her children. Each child's share is then divided into exempt and nonexempt trust shares. The exempt portion of each share represents the transferor's pro rata proportion of his or her GST exemption amount.

The trustee can be directed to sparingly use the property in each child's exempt share for the benefit of that child whenever the assets in the nonexempt share are not sufficient to adequately provide for the child. Whatever assets are left in the child's exempt share at that child's death can pass to that child's children without being subject to estate tax or generation-skipping tax.

⚓ Are there any nontax advantages to using generation-skipping trusts?

Placing property in trust for children and grandchildren provides several nontax benefits for your children and grandchildren. These include:

- Your descendants' trust property will not be distributed to their spouses on divorce or death.

- The trust property is not subject to the claims of the beneficiaries' creditors.

Is there a way that I can give money to my grandchildren for their education but not create an income tax problem for my children?

Yes, you can use a GST-exempt demand-right trust. You can establish a trust that will hold funds for your grandchildren's education. Your children can be the trustees, or you can appoint a third party such as a bank or trust company. Each year you and your spouse can contribute the annual exclusion amount to each grandchild. The trust can be designed to establish a separate account for each grandchild. In this manner each grandchild will have a set amount of money for his or her education, and the gifts qualify for the annual exclusion and are not considered to be GST transfers. Thus you get the best of both tax worlds: no gift tax and no GST tax.

The trust can provide for the distribution of any funds not used for education in the manner and at the age that you feel is appropriate. As a matter of fact, you can be pretty much as creative as you want in the trust's instructions, ensuring that you can leave a lasting legacy for your grandchildren. It is very important, however, that you work with highly experienced advisors, especially your attorney, so that the terms of the trust allow for use of the annual exclusion for gifts and for GST transfers.

What is a dynasty trust, and why would I want to use one?

A *dynasty trust* is a trust that passes "life interests" in property for as long as the state law allows. By not having the ownership interest pass to each generation and be taxed in each respective estate, one can pass assets to future generations while minimizing gift, estate, and generation-skipping taxes.

How long can a dynasty trust last?

State statutes generally provide that a transfer of a property interest in trust will not be valid unless it vests within the time of a life or lives in being plus 21 years. This is the classic *rule against perpetuities.*

Can the limitations of the rule against perpetuities be avoided?

A dynasty trust can be drafted so that the class of beneficiaries is so large that it maximizes the applicable period. For example, the class could be all the descendants of John D. Rockefeller living at the time he dies and the trust becomes irrevocable.

⚲ *How long is the common law perpetuities period as compared to the Uniform Statutory Rule against Perpetuities period?*

The common law period can last for the selected lives in being at the time the trust is created plus 21 years after the expiration of those lives. In a Uniform Statutory Rule against Perpetuities (USRAP) state, the period lasts for the lives in being plus 21 years or for 90 years.

Six states—Alaska, Delaware, Illinois, Idaho, South Dakota, and Wisconsin—have abolished the rule against perpetuities. If a dynasty trust is established in one of these states, it can last until the principal is exhausted. If you wish to take advantage of these states' laws, you should name a corporate fiduciary within their borders as trustee of your dynasty trust.

⚲ *What types of trusts can be utilized as dynasty trusts?*

Generally, a dynasty trust can be created as an irrevocable trust or as part of a revocable living trust, which will become irrevocable upon the death of the trust maker.

⚲ *How do I create a dynasty trust within my revocable living trust?*

Your revocable living trust can provide that, at your death, an amount equal to your available unused GST exemption is to be segregated into a dynasty trust for the benefit of your descendants. The portion of your estate in excess of the available exemption will be transferred to beneficiaries using traditional estate planning concepts.

⚲ *What is the procedure if I use an irrevocable trust as a dynasty trust?*

If you establish an irrevocable trust as a dynasty trust during your lifetime, you will file a gift tax return and allocate part of your available GST exemption to your gift to the dynasty trust. However, if your spouse is a beneficiary of the trust during your lifetime, no allocation of the GST exemption may be made to the trust until the death of either you or your spouse.

⚲ *If my wife and I leverage our combined GST exemption by purchasing a second-to-die life insurance policy in a dynasty ILIT,*

**TABLE 6-2   Death Benefit from
$2,000,000 Second-to-Die Policy**

Current age	Combined GST exempt premium	Second-to-die death benefit in dynasty ILIT*
55	$2,000,000	$20,000,000
65	2,000,000	12,000,000
75	2,000,000	7,000,000

*Based on current investment, expense, and mortality assumptions.

what is the total value that can be created for the benefit of my grandchildren?

Assuming that you and your spouse are in good health, and based on current investment, expense, and mortality assumptions, Table 6-2 shows the amount of death benefit that can be generated from a $2 million second-to-die policy at various ages. Regardless of your current age, the death benefit generated and transferred tax-free to your grandchildren will be a significant multiple of your combined GST exemption.

⋈   *What are the advantages of an international dynasty trust?*

The benefits of creating dynasty trusts internationally are greater flexibility, more efficient income tax treatment, and the ability to accommodate several nationalities of trust makers and beneficiaries.

⋈   *Do dynasty trusts generally appreciate or depreciate in value over the generations?*

Let's assume that you purchase a $1 million life insurance policy and successfully qualify it for GST treatment to keep it federal estate–tax free intergenerationally. Under the Rule of 72, your trust estate would compound and grow in both tax-free and taxable environments. The comparative values in 100 years are shown in Table 6-3.

⋈   *My family has a vacation cottage that has been in the family for two generations. I would like my children and grandchildren to have use of the property but also want to ensure that it continues down the family line. How can I accomplish this?*

You should consider an irrevocable *legacy trust.* You can establish the

TABLE 6-3   Appreciation of $1 Million Trust Estate

Interest rate, %	Years to double	Number doubles	Value in 100 years*	
			With no tax	With tax†
10.0	7.2	14	$13,780,612,340	$565,091,240
7.2	10.0	10	1,045,871,999	42,887,289
5.0	14.4	7	131,501,258	5,392,373
3.6	20.0	5	34,353,860	1,408,723

*Assumes four generational deaths in 25-year intervals and no income taxes for either calculation.
†Assumes 55% federal estate tax rate.

trust in one of the six jurisdictions that do not have a rule against perpetuities—Alaska, Delaware, Idaho, Illinois, South Dakota, and Wisconsin. That will allow the trust to remain in effect for an indefinite period of time.

If the cottage is not located in one of these six states, you should then create a limited liability company to hold the cottage. Transferring the cottage to the limited liability company helps ensure that your state's perpetuities law will not apply and the law of the state you chose will. You should then transfer your interest in the LLC to the trust.

The trustee of the trust should be a resident or a corporate trustee situated in the state you chose. You can name other trustees to be cotrustees with the resident trustee.

Once the trust has the property, it can be used by your family for generations and never be subject to estate tax. If you want the trust to be able to pay the operating expenses of the vacation home, the trustee can obtain a life insurance policy on your life or that of you and your spouse. After your deaths, the funds from the policy will be available to maintain the trust and perhaps add other items to it for the benefit of future generations.

VIATICAL SETTLEMENTS

⤷ *My husband has been diagnosed with a terminal illness. He has a paid-up $1 million whole life insurance policy that we had*

*planned to surrender in favor of a survivorship policy to be pur-
chased by the trustee of an irrevocable life insurance trust. Now
we don't qualify for such a policy, and it's too late to transfer the
existing policy since it's unlikely that my husband will survive 3
years. Any suggestions?*

You might consider a viatical settlement. "Viatication" (or sale) of a
policy in cases where the insured has been diagnosed as terminally or
chronically ill is an attractive option since passage of the Health Insurance Portability and Accountability Act of 1996. That legislation provides that the entire proceeds of the *viatical settlement* (a percentage of
the death benefit) can be received by a terminally or chronically ill
individual free of any federal income tax. This effectively removes the
life insurance from the estate for federal estate tax purposes since viatication is considered an exchange for value. Furthermore, the proceeds
can be used for a policy on the life of the surviving spouse, as gifts to
children and other family members, for uninsured medical expenses, or
many other purposes that suit the individual situation.

⚑ *What is the definition of terminal or chronic illness?*

A *terminal illness* is defined as an illness that a physician certifies as
being likely to cause death within 24 months of certification. A *chronic
illness* is defined as an illness that renders the individual permanently
or severely disabled. The percentage of the policy proceeds (the viatical
settlement) that is actually paid out will depend on the projected life
expectancy of the insured, the cost of future premiums, whether there
are outstanding loans against the policy, and interest rates.

⚑ *What types of insurance can be viaticated?*

Virtually any type of policy can be viaticated—whole life, term, variable, universal, or group.

⚑ *When was the concept of viatical settlements first utilized?*

The viatical settlement concept is actually centuries old. The term "viatical" comes from the Latin viaticum, which means "provisions for a
long journey." In recent times, the concept began to be used in the early
1980s in conjunction with the AIDS epidemic, but it was largely un-
regulated. Today viatical settlements are available in all fifty states and
are being regulated by many state insurance departments in conjunction
with the Viatical Settlements Model Act and Model Regulations, which

were adopted by the National Association of Insurance Commissioners in 1994.

✑ I'm 75 and in good health. Is there any way that I can make use of the viatical settlement concept?

With the maturing of the viatical settlement concept, underwriters have found that terminal or chronic illness may not be needed to make this concept work. Existing viatical settlement companies have developed precise mortality tables for seniors which allow the companies to offer the insured more than he or she would get if the policy was merely cashed in or surrendered. The income tax treatment is not the same as it is with the terminal or chronic illness scenario, but the proceeds receive capital gain treatment rather than being taxed as regular income. For example, the difference between the income tax basis (premiums less dividends and distributions) and the cash surrender value would be taxed as ordinary gain, but to the extent the proceeds from the viatical settlement exceed the cash surrender value, the gain should be treated as capital in nature.

chapter 7

Asset Protection Planning

THE PURPOSE
OF ASSET PROTECTION
ESTATE PLANNING

⚞ *What is asset protection?*

Asset protection is nothing more than positioning your property in such a way that it will not be subject to the whims of a potential plaintiff in a lawsuit. Surprisingly to most people, corporations, limited partnerships, and trusts are nothing more than asset protection devices. They were invented to protect individual assets in one way or another.

A good asset protection plan allows an individual to keep control over assets which might otherwise be subject to court control because of the actions of a plaintiff. Without such a plan, a defendant can virtually be held hostage to the extortionate demands of some plaintiffs and their attorneys. An asset protection plan, if properly set up, will avoid this and put the potential defendant on a level playing field with the plaintiff.

⚞ *Is asset protection aimed at reducing or eliminating legitimate debts?*

No, not at all. If you owe someone a legitimate debt, asset protection planning will not relieve you of the obligation of paying the debt. If you voluntarily incur the debt and then place your assets offshore, or in some other kind of vehicle, the transaction will be seen as fraudulent. Our law does not allow you to break it and then turn around and benefit by your unlawful act.

⚖ What is the objective of asset protection estate planning?

Your primary line of defense for protecting your assets is and always should be your personal liability insurance coverage, including malpractice insurance if you are a professional such as a doctor or a lawyer. Your insurance provides you not only with liability coverage but also with competent legal representation coverage.

Just because someone is competent and careful doesn't mean that he or she will not be sued. We live in a litigious society where a person's competence is no longer as important as who can be blamed for someone's misfortune. Typically, juries like to blame the professional or businessperson because he or she has wealth, income-producing capacity, and insurance.

We spend a lot of time on building and learning how to build our fortunes; unfortunately, we spend very little time—and very little is ever taught—on the subject of protecting our fortunes from creditors. Asset protection planning has as its objective the protection of a family's property and income from the attacks of gold-digging plaintiffs or creditors.

⚖ Why should I engage in asset protection estate planning?

Besides the obvious reason—to protect the assets that you have worked so hard to earn—you should engage in asset protection estate planning for the following reasons:

To ACHIEVE PEACE OF MIND   You can practice your chosen occupation or profession without the constant worry of losing everything if you are sued. With a clear mind you can do a much better job and be less likely to make mistakes.

To AVOID PROBATE AND ESTATE TAXES   A by-product of a well-designed asset protection estate plan is an estate plan that is also designed to avoid living probate, death probate, and estate taxes through the use of various trusts and other traditional estate planning tools.

To SAVE ON LIABILITY AND MALPRACTICE INSURANCE   With your assets protected from the reach of creditors, you will not need to carry as much insurance coverage. You could probably reduce your coverage to the minimum amount necessary to retain your privileges and still maintain the legal representation coverage. The cost of obtaining the asset protection estate planning can, in most cases, be recovered in the first year or within a few years by the savings in premiums. A further bonus is realized when such insurance premium savings continue year after year. It is never advisable to go completely bare of any liability coverage.

TO REDUCE SETTLEMENT AMOUNTS AND THE NUMBER OF LAWSUITS
By judgment-proofing your assets and reducing your liability coverage, you will cause potential plaintiffs to either terminate plans for litigation or settle within your reduced liability coverage. Just think, if we all made ourselves judgment-proof and reduced our liability coverage, the number of lawsuits and the dollar amount of settlements could decline and liability insurance rates would perhaps be more affordable again.

TO PROTECT AGAINST EXEMPLARY DAMAGES   Exemplary, treble, or punitive damages are not covered by your liability insurance. The theory is that a person who commits a wrongful act should be punished and made an example of; as a practical matter, some juries like to take from a rich defendant and give to a poor plaintiff. This is what is commonly referred to as the "deep-pocket" or "Robin Hood" syndrome!

TO PROTECT AGAINST BANKRUPTCY OF INSURANCE CARRIERS   There is no guarantee that your liability insurance is going to be there when you need it. People all over the country are realizing this unfortunate fact as more and more liability insurance carriers are filing for bankruptcy. What is even more unfortunate is that some people learn this fact after they have had claims filed against them. If your liability insurance is presently your only asset protection, you should do some serious thinking. We're experiencing a trend in the insurance industry which indicates that not only is liability coverage becoming unaffordable but some day such coverage may not even be available at any cost.

TO GAIN STRATEGIC BARGAINING POWER   An asset protection estate plan increases the likelihood of negotiating a favorable settlement.

Vince Lombardi, the famous football coach of the Green Bay Packers, was a great believer in running the ball rather than passing it. It is said that he believed that only three things could happen when passing the football—and two of them were bad. The same can be said for creditors when faced with a proper asset protection plan: four things can happen—and three of them are bad for the creditors:

1. They could settle for the amount offered.
2. They could lose and get nothing.
3. They could win, but the award could be less than the amount offered by the insurance carrier as a settlement.
4. They could win, and the award could be equal to or greater than the insurance coverage; however, due to the unavailability of leviable assets, they will probably be able to obtain only the amount of the insurance coverage and then only after a long, drawn-out court battle months or years down the road. Furthermore, the contingent percentage fee the creditor's attorneys charge will usually be a higher percentage if they have to pursue litigation.

By settling for the amount offered, creditors will be the winners, and they will get their money a lot sooner, especially in light of the time value of money. This strategy enhances the defendants' bargaining position, in effect leveling the litigation playing field. It works best if liability insurance can be used as the proverbial carrot at the end of the stick to entice the plaintiffs to settle for the amount offered by the defendants.

The concept of the contingent fee gives plaintiffs the "I've got nothing to lose" attitude. This attitude makes for an unbalanced litigation playing field against defendants, who start off as losers since they must pay hourly fees and retainers to their lawyers. Asset protection estate planning creates an incentive for plaintiffs to settle early to save litigation costs and time and to ensure at least some settlement amount.

⚖ Are any assets exempt from creditors?

By statute, most states and the federal government have defined certain assets as "exempt" from execution by creditors, including the Internal Revenue Service. *Exempt assets* are those assets that a person is entitled to keep even if the person files bankruptcy or if judgment creditors attempt to seize a person's assets to satisfy a judgment. The amount and type of assets that qualify as exempt vary from state to state. However, state law does not define which assets are protected from execution by the IRS; these assets are specifically defined by federal law.

⚖ If I have an umbrella policy, do I need to be concerned about liability?

Yes. We know a liability insurance professional who serves as a consultant to major corporations regarding their liability insurance. He also evaluates umbrella policies. He literally finds pages of matters that are not covered by insurance policies. We do not advocate dropping liability coverage if you implement a creditor protection strategy such as a family limited partnership. However, the liability policy becomes merely your first line of defense.

⚄ Can't I just create an irrevocable trust to protect my assets?

Many asset protection techniques involve an irrevocable trust. However, transferring assets to an irrevocable trust does not always protect the assets. First, an attorney must properly draft the trust with special language regarding the disposition of the assets. Second, you cannot create such a trust "in contemplation of a lawsuit." If you have already been sued or if you know you will or think you will be sued, you may not "hide" your assets in a trust. Third, you cannot name yourself as beneficiary and trustee of such a trust. The IRS and courts look at the amount of control you still have over the assets in determining whether or not they are "yours." Exceptions to this rule include charitable trusts, qualified personal residence trusts, and children's trusts (where you are not a beneficiary), but all must again have special language as to who may receive distributions.

FRAUDULENT CONVEYANCES

⚄ Why is planning in advance so important? What is a fraudulent conveyance?

You might compare planning for asset protection to buying insurance on your boat. You cannot legally insure the boat after it has sunk. In fact, you can't buy insurance after the engines have quit and you are taking on water. To carry the analogy even further, you can't even buy the insurance when the boat is fine if you are out on the ocean in the midst of a raging storm. You need to insure your boat while your boat is ship-shape, the seas are calm, and there is no storm on the horizon.

Fraudulent conveyance laws vary from state to state, but they always have the same general goal: to prevent people from making transfers with the intention of hindering, delaying, or defrauding present or subsequent creditors. Present creditors are pretty easily ascertained. Questions usually arise about which "subsequent," or future, creditors are protected by fraudulent conveyance laws. Did the individual doing the estate planning make the transfers with the intent to hinder, delay, or defraud future creditors?

Fraudulent conveyance laws are not designed to protect everyone who could someday be a person's creditor. They pertain only to those creditors that a person harbored an actual fraudulent intent against on the date of the transfer or those creditors whose rights a person acted against with reckless disregard after conveying assets. For example, an attorney who conveys all of his assets to an offshore asset protection trust, cancels his malpractice insurance, and then constantly practices law while in a drunken stupor has probably made a fraudulent conveyance as to those clients he harms with his legal advice.

It clearly is *not* a fraudulent conveyance when a transfer is made by a person who has no pending or even threatened claims or has no reason to believe that legal problems will develop in the future, but simply wants to plan for his or her family's future well-being. It clearly *is* a fraudulent conveyance when an individual makes a transfer just before filing for bankruptcy or divorce or immediately after being sued for malpractice. In between these two extremes lies a large gray area of interpretation.

Our common law seems to favor the free alienability of property, which means that a person can dispose of his or her property as he or she sees fit, including selling it; giving it to children, spouses, charities, or trustees; or burning it.

The fraudulent conveyance laws do not pertain so much to who receives the property but, rather, to the intent of the person who is making the transfer. In one of the most famous cases in this area, the court stated that planning for a future "what if" is permissible as long as the "what if" is a mere possibility rather than a probability.

If a transfer or conveyance is found to be fraudulent, the remedy serves to "unwind" the transfer so that the asset is again available to the judgment creditor.

🔌 *What are some actions that show that a conveyance is fraudulent?*

Most states have adopted a version of the Uniform Fraudulent Transfer Act or the Uniform Fraudulent Conveyance Act. These statutes define as *fraudulent conveyances* not only transfers of assets made with an intent to hinder, delay, or defraud a person's creditors but also transfers of assets made for less than reasonably equivalent value if the transfer renders the person making it insolvent. The person making the transfer is viewed as "insolvent" (1) if the person's assets after the transfer are less than his or her liabilities, (2) if the person's assets are unreasonably small in relation to his or her business, or (3) if the person intended, believed, or reasonably should have believed that he or she would incur debts beyond his or her ability to pay as they became due. In effect, these statutes permit a creditor injured by a fraudulent conveyance to have the conveyance set aside so that the transferred asset can be attached and sold by the creditor.

◢ Is it a fraudulent conveyance if a person transfers title to assets to family members as a method of avoiding probate and estate taxes?

Transferring title to assets to other family members is certainly an appropriate method of avoiding probate of the transferred assets and avoiding having the assets included as part of a person's estate for estate tax purposes. However, if the transfer of assets is made with an intent to hinder, delay, or defraud creditors or if it renders the transferor insolvent, the transfer may later be attacked as a fraudulent conveyance. This is so even if the primary intent and motivation of the transferor was estate planning, not avoiding payment to creditors.

◢ What if I'm already involved in a lawsuit?

Under the fraudulent conveyance rules, if you are currently involved in a lawsuit, you will not be able to set up an asset protection trust. This is the general rule unless the maximum potential of the claim is less than your entire net worth. In this situation, it may be possible to transfer some of your assets while still leaving enough to honor the existing claim.

This can be a very tricky issue, so you should obtain proper legal advice.

◢ What is the difference between fraudulent conveyance and fraud?

As explained above, fraudulent conveyance involves transferring assets to avoid or delay paying a legitimate debt. *Fraud*, on the other hand, is defined by *Black's Law Dictionary* as an "intentional perversion of the truth for the purpose of inducing another in reliance upon it to part with some valuable thing belonging to him." Although the terminology is similar, there is typically little relationship between the two offenses.

⚖ *Is it appropriate to sell nonexempt assets and invest the proceeds in exempt assets?*

Although a number of courts have recognized the legitimate goal of maximizing the amount of a person's exempt assets as defined by statute, a significant number of courts have recognized that the conversion of nonexempt assets into exempt assets can be viewed as evidence of "bad faith" or of an actual intent to hinder, delay, or defraud creditors. In deciding this issue, the courts focus on the timing of the asset transfers in relation to a bankruptcy filing by the transferor or in relation to actions taken by the transferor's creditors, the amount of assets transferred, and the source of the funds used to purchase the nonexempt assets that are converted into exempt assets.

⚖ *Can I sell my nonexempt assets and give the proceeds to my family members or friends?*

As long as nonexempt assets are sold for reasonably equivalent value and without an actual intent to hinder, delay, or defraud creditors, nothing prohibits a person from selling nonexempt assets even if the person is insolvent or contemplates filing bankruptcy in the future. However, the person making the transfer will have to account for the proceeds of the sale, and the separate act of giving the proceeds to family members or friends can itself be challenged as a fraudulent transfer that may be set aside.

DOMESTIC PLANNING
FOR ASSET PROTECTION

Life Insurance Policies and Annuities

⚖ *Are life insurance proceeds, disability proceeds, and annuities protected from creditors?*

In virtually all states, proceeds paid at death to named beneficiaries of life insurance or annuity policies are protected from the claims of the insured's creditors. Some states also exempt life insurance proceeds from the claims of the beneficiaries' creditors. Disability insurance benefits are likewise protected.

Although the states vary on this issue, the cash value of life insurance may also be exempt from creditors. The theory behind this exemption is that if cash values could be taken by creditors, the insurance companies would reduce the death benefits payable by the cash values removed. Since the proceeds of the death benefits are exempt, the cash values should also be exempt to protect the full payment of the proceeds by the insurance companies.

Generally, exemption of the cash value of life insurance applies only if the insured owns the policy. A trap for the unwary can be cross-owned life insurance between spouses: if a husband owns life insurance on his wife and the husband is successfully sued, his creditor could take the cash value of the life insurance he owns on his wife.

States specifically disallow protection of the cash value of policies purchased to defraud existing creditors. In other words, if a person purchases a large life insurance policy in an attempt to put cash out of the reach of creditors who are seeking to recover mature claims, the statute will not protect the cash value.

In a few states, including Florida and Texas, the cash value of annuities, variable life insurance, and variable annuities now enjoys the same full creditor exemption as the cash value of life insurance.

🔏 *Is the life insurance policy held in my ILIT protected from my creditors?*

If your life insurance is held in an ILIT, a creditor would be unable to force an action or obtain any type of order which would require that the income or dividends from the policy be paid to the creditor.

Qualified Retirement Plans and IRAS

🔏 *Are qualified retirement plans and IRAs protected from claims of creditors?*

One of the best places to shield assets is within your own retirement plan or plans, such as a corporate pension or profit-sharing plan. Qualified plans are exempt from the claims of creditors under a 1992 Supreme Court decision. The Court held that state laws exempting qualified plan assets from claims of creditors in bankruptcy are valid. The Court also held that the provision of the Employee Retirement Income Security Act (ERISA) of 1974 exempting qualified plan assets from creditors' claims in bankruptcy is also valid.

Many states also have laws protecting qualified plan assets from the claims of creditors. In these states, the plan assets are sheltered from creditors even if the owner of the account declares bankruptcy.

As long as assets remain in a qualified retirement plan, they are exempt; but as benefits are paid, they can be subject to claims. A court cannot, however, force you to take a lump-sum distribution at retirement; therefore, the creditor has to wait until you retire and until each installment is paid. It is arguable, however, that installment payments from a qualified plan are a substitute for wages and salary and that those states prohibiting garnishment of wages or salary might give the same protection to these installment payments.

Additionally, if a judgment has been rendered against an individual, that individual can continue to contribute to the plan; however, if the sponsoring corporation is also liable, the courts may be able to limit future contributions.

⚑ What is the best way to provide creditor protection for my IRA and Keogh plan?

The issue of whether IRA and Keogh plan assets are subject to creditors' claims is, to a great degree, state-specific and, to a lesser degree, unsettled. While public and private pension plans are exempt from creditors' claims (with the notable exception of court-ordered alimony or child support claims), IRAs and Keogh plans are not always exempt under state law.

If you live in a state that does not provide protection, here are a few things you can do for added safety:

- Make another person, even your spouse, a cotrustee of the plan.
- Be sure that your plan has clear spendthrift language, that is, language that prohibits creditors from taking plan assets.
- Consider joining with other, similar small businesses in your area to create a group pension plan with several principals. This action could provide your Keogh with the same protection as an ERISA plan.
- Avoid unreasonably high balances—those which may be considered in excess of what is reasonably needed for retirement.
- Avoid frequently using the account for personal loans.
- Avoid exercising individual, unlimited, and complete control over the fund.

⚑ If a plan participant dies before retirement, will the benefits paid to a beneficiary be exempt from the participant's creditors' claims?

If a retirement plan provides for a preretirement death benefit, the plan is akin to a life insurance policy, and like life insurance proceeds, the retirement plan death benefit proceeds will be exempt from the claims of the participant's creditors.

≫ *I am married, and I have children from a previous marriage. How can I ensure that my children will ultimately benefit from my retirement plan assets while still allowing my spouse to use the assets during her lifetime?*

There is a technique which comes from Internal Revenue Code Section 401(a)(9). This Code section allows a person to create a "retirement" trust for his or her qualified retirement plans. This type of trust must:

1. Be created before death.
2. Be irrevocable.
3. Name an easily identifiable beneficiary (i.e., not "my heirs").

Once created, you name your trust as the beneficiary of the qualified retirement plan. You may name your spouse as the beneficiary of the retirement trust and your children as beneficiaries after the spouse's death. When you die, the distributions from your plan can be recalculated on the basis of your spouse's life expectancy. Then, at your spouse's death, your children will receive what's left.

The assets are protected for you during your life because they are in qualified retirement plans. They are protected for your spouse because they are in an irrevocable trust, and they are protected for your children because they will not be subject to a spousal rollover (in which your spouse could name anyone he or she wanted as beneficiary).

≫ *I am thinking about creating a Roth IRA. Will it be creditor-exempt?*

Creditor exemption for IRAs is governed by state law. If asset protection is important to you, you should find out from your attorney if your state exempts Roth IRAs from creditors. If your state does not, then you might consider some alternative planning.

Title to Assets

Beneficiary designations

≫ *If I title all my property in my name and also state that the property is payable on death to my nephew, can I keep my credi-*

tors from reaching the property during my life and from reaching it in the hands of my nephew after my death?

The law of your state should be considered before you use the payable-on-death (POD) technique. Some states allow only certain kinds of property (e.g., bank accounts or investment securities) to be titled in your name and designated POD to another person. POD titling does not protect your assets from your creditors while you are alive, and you should not be surprised if creditors follow POD-titled assets into the hands of your nephew after your death.

Trustee ownership

If my spouse and I place our assets in a revocable living trust, does that protect our assets from our creditors? What about after one or both of us dies?

If you and your spouse place your assets in a revocable living trust, your creditors will be able to attach your assets just as if the assets were not held in a trust. If you look at things from your creditors' point of view, it is easy to see why the law so provides.

You and your spouse, as makers of the revocable living trust, retain the power to alter, amend, or completely revoke the trust at your leisure. You can even serve as the trustees of your own trust. In short, you can do anything with the trust property after you put it in the trust that you could have done before you put it in the trust. Because you retain so much control over the property in the revocable living trust, the trust is ignored and you and your spouse are still considered the "owners" of the property for creditor purposes. It would be unfair for the law to allow debtors to hold large amounts of property in trusts over which they retain complete control and yet deny creditors access to that property.

Most well-drafted revocable living trusts provide that if the maker of the trust dies, the trust becomes irrevocable. Most states' statutes and case law provide that once the trust becomes irrevocable, the rules applicable to revocable trusts no longer apply and assets in the trust can then be protected from creditors. There are laws with respect to fraudulent transfers and laws with respect to transferee responsibility as related to tax and certain other liabilities, and these should be taken into account to determine how much protection the then-irrevocable trust provides.

After the death or deaths of the makers, a revocable living trust can help protect assets in a majority of states. You should seek competent legal advice about the law in your state as it relates to using a revocable living trust for protection of assets after your death.

Tenancy by the entirety

> ⚝ *I understand that in my state real estate that is held by my spouse and me in tenancy by the entirety is not subject to the claims of our creditors and we thereby have some protection for our home or other real estate. Is this true?*

In most states a home or other real estate held by spouses as tenants by the entirety is protected from the claims of each spouse's separate creditors but is *not* protected from the claims of both spouses' joint creditors. Therefore, if you alone are the debtor or if your spouse alone is the debtor, your tenancy by the entirety real estate is protected. But if both you and your spouse are liable for the same debt or if you and your spouse grant a mortgage or other interest in the real estate, your jointly held property is not protected.

This protection is available only to property held jointly by a husband and wife. If you hold property jointly with a person other than your spouse, this protection is not available. Also, in some states, you must clearly show that you and your spouse intend to own property in tenancy by the entirety. If the title to the property merely states that you and your spouse own the property as joint tenants with right of survivorship, the protection given to tenancy-by-the-entirety ownership may not apply; if one spouse has a creditor, that creditor may be able to seize all or part of the property.

> ⚝ *If my spouse and I transfer our home or other real estate to a joint revocable living trust or to separate revocable living trusts for each of us, will we lose the protection of tenancy by the entirety?*

A revocable living trust has many advantages, including probate avoidance and full use of both of your applicable exclusion amounts for federal estate tax purposes. However, if you and your spouse transfer tenancy-by-the-entirety property to a joint revocable trust or to two separate revocable trusts, then, in some states, the creditor protection offered by tenancy by the entirety might be lost.

In many states, whether or not real estate is available to a creditor is determined by how the property is recorded in the office which maintains real estate title and other records. So, if real estate is recorded in the name of husband and wife as tenants by the entirety, the rights of the creditor might be hampered or possibly totally cut off with respect to that real estate. This may not be so with property titled in the name of a revocable living trust.

One way to have your cake and eat it, too, is to leave the title recorded in your names as tenants by the entirety and to formally execute either a deed that is not recorded in your county or, better yet, a joint declaration of trust ownership, which is then available for recording when appropriate. However, the mere existence of the unrecorded deed or joint declaration of trust ownership may technically eliminate the creditor protection created by tenancy-by-the-entirety ownership. You must analyze your particular state's laws and use the best arrangement to accomplish your specific needs.

Community property

⊰ *What is community property?*

In the nine community property states, spouses own most of the assets of their marriage as community property. *Community property* is all property of a marriage other than separate property. *Separate property* is any property acquired before the marriage, or any property acquired during the marriage through gifts, inheritance, bequest, recovery for personal injuries, or partition of community property. The community property system has far more tax and nontax planning advantages than the common law property systems found in the forty-one noncommunity property states, which are called common law property states.

Unfortunately, community property ownership does not protect assets from the claims of either spouse's creditors. The *separate* property of the nonliable spouse is, however, exempt from debts and tort claims of the liable spouse's creditors.

⊰ *How can we protect assets in a community property state?*

Because community property is subject to the claims of creditors of either spouse, in some instances it may be a good idea either to partition community property into separate property before a claim arises or to have one spouse give his or her property to the other spouse, thereby making the property the other spouse's separate property. Remember, separate property includes property acquired by gift.

Partitioning property is accomplished by a written document which identifies the asset being partitioned and which states the mutual intent of the husband and wife to partition the property. After the partition agreement has been signed, the husband owns his part of the asset as his sole separate property and the wife owns her part of the asset as her sole separate property.

This technique cannot be used in all community property states, so always confer with your attorney before partitioning community property.

⩗ *Are there any problems with partitioning or giving away community property?*

There are potential problems associated with both of these strategies:

■ A surviving spouse's separate property will not get a step-up in basis to fair market value at the death of the first spouse to die. (Only the deceased spouse's property gets the step-up in basis.) A surviving spouse's interest in community property will get a step-up in basis on the death of his or her spouse.

■ Once given away or partitioned, the property is the separate property of each spouse. A divorce court cannot order a spouse to transfer the separate property back to the spouse who gave it away or convert the property back to community property.

■ If one spouse dies and leaves his or her separate property to the surviving spouse in a will, the surviving spouse becomes the full owner of the property and that property is then subject to his or her creditor claims.

■ If there are too many assets in one spouse's name, creditors can easily argue that the "rich" spouse is really just holding those assets as the trustee of a *constructive,* or *resulting, trust* for the benefit of the "poor" spouse. Since a resulting or constructive trust is an unwritten revocable trust created by a person's actions, such a trust does not protect the assets of its maker. The debtor spouse's creditors may break this trust and have access to its assets.

⩗ *Can these problems be overcome?*

While the loss of a 100 percent step-up in basis on the death of the first spouse to die cannot effectively be overcome, the other problems can be by using a *community property asset protection trust.*

⁂ I live in a community property state. In my profession, I have a great deal of exposure to frivolous lawsuits. Can I create some kind of community property asset protection trust?

Yes. In a community property asset protection trust, one spouse, as trust maker, transfers legal title to some or all of his or her separate property assets to an irrevocable trust. These separate property assets may be separate assets that were previously acquired or separate assets that were recently acquired by a partition of community property or by a gift from the other spouse.

Either spouse (or both) may be named as the trustee of the asset protection trust. The trustee owns and controls the legal title to all trust assets. The nontransferring spouse is then named as the life beneficiary of the trust and, as such, will own a life estate or beneficial title to the assets for life. Beneficial title is the right to use and enjoy the property.

After the beneficiary spouse is deceased, children or others (the remainder persons) become the beneficiaries. Their beneficial title can remain in trust for their lives or can be distributed to them upon their attaining a certain age of maturity. The surviving spouse can remain as trustee and continue to be in control of the assets of the trust.

Assets can be added to the trust by any person at any time through lifetime transfers or by a will or a trust at death.

The key provision which protects assets in an asset protection trust is the *spendthrift provision*. However, the spouse who owns the separate property assets and is the maker of the trust will not qualify for protection from creditors under the spendthrift provision of the trust. This is why the spouse transferring the separate property is not a beneficiary of the asset protection trust. Trust assets are, however, protected from the creditors of the other spouse, who did not own or transfer the separate property assets to the trust and who is the life beneficiary of the trust.

Both spouses can be trustees of the asset protection trust provided successor trustees are named in the trust document. If a potential liability suit arises, the spouse who transferred the assets to the trust can resign as trustee in favor of the other spouse or a successor trustee.

Gifts

⁂ Can I protect my assets by giving them away?

Giving your assets away is one of the quickest and easiest ways of disposing of assets and protecting them from your creditors. However, the transfers should occur before any creditor claim or possible claim, or you risk having the transfers considered fraudulent. If they are deemed fraudulent conveyances, the recipients can be forced to give the gifts to your creditors. Thus, if you have no liability or malpractice claims or alleged claims against you, right now is the best time to make gifts.

There are, however, several problems associated with giving property away through a direct gift:

- You lose control and, perhaps, enjoyment of the asset you give away.
- If the value of the gift in any year to any one person exceeds the annual gift tax exclusion, you must file a federal gift tax return and claim a portion of your applicable exclusion amount. Once your applicable exclusion amount is exhausted, you will have to pay gift tax.
- There is a risk that the recipient of your gift might lose the asset to his or her creditors or to his or her spouse in a divorce action.
- If the recipient of your gift is a minor, he or she cannot own or control property. This makes it very difficult for anyone to do anything with such property.

The solution to all these problems is to make gifts through a well-drafted irrevocable trust.

Domestic Trusts

Is there an asset protection trust that I can create that is for my benefit and protected from my creditors?

The laws in all the states do *not* allow a person to set up a trust, name himself or herself as a trustee and beneficiary, and avoid creditors. The wisdom of this rule is obvious because otherwise trust makers facing significant liability could simply transfer all their assets into trusts for their own benefit.

However, in 1997, Alaska enacted a trust act that significantly increases the asset protection aspects of self-settled trusts (a trust in which you are the maker and the beneficiary). Under this act, you can transfer assets to an irrevocable trust set up in Alaska, and your creditors would be unable to make claims against those assets (even though you are the beneficiary).

There are certain requirements for creating this type of trust:

1. The assets must be located in Alaska (i.e., in a bank, brokerage, or trust company in the state of Alaska).
2. An Alaska domiciliary must administer the trust.
3. You, as the maker, may not give yourself the power to revoke the trust.
4. The trustee must have sole discretion to make or withhold distributions to you.

Even with the restrictions imposed on the Alaska trusts, they are one of the few ways to protect your assets without giving them away entirely. But be aware: The Alaska trust does not allow the maker to have unfettered control of the assets, even though it does offer asset protection.

⚂ Is an Alaska trust an ironclad asset protection plan?

Unfortunately, no. The Alaska trust statute does prohibit levying (enforcing judgment) against trust assets for judgments against the maker-beneficiary, but it does not remove the trustee from the personal jurisdiction of any federal court, anywhere in the country.

A federal court could still order an Alaska trustee to hold up distribution of any assets and to even transfer assets to the custody of the court. Refusal to comply could subject the trustee to contempt proceedings by the court. Remember, the true purpose of asset protection is not to cheat creditors to whom the maker owes legitimate debts but to create a level playing field against the predatory tactics of unscrupulous plaintiffs and their lawyers.

⚂ Does any other state have an asset protection trust law similar to Alaska's?

Yes, Delaware has enacted a similar statute.

⚂ Can I create a trust that allows me to give my house or vacation home away to keep a creditor from getting it?

You can create a qualified personal residence trust (QPRT) for your home or a vacation or second home, provided you actually use the home as a partial residence. The real estate is transferred into a trust which is created generally for a term of years. The longer the term of years, the smaller the gift to your children (who are usually the beneficiaries of the QPRT). Upon the expiration of the term, you no longer own the house, although you may rent it from the trust as long as you pay fair rent.

Most commonly, people create QPRTs for estate tax planning— there is potentially a large sum which could be saved on estate taxes. Additionally, in most states, your homestead is already protected under statute from creditors' taking it; thus the need for this type of trust for a homestead is not great (except for estate tax savings, if any). However, A QPRT should be considered by those who have more than one house, whether for vacation or partial residence anytime during the year, and face future exposure to lawsuits and creditors.

⅍ *Can my revocable living trust protect my assets?*

No, but if your trust has "spendthrift" provisions in it, your trust may be able to protect your beneficiaries' inheritance from their creditors. A *spendthrift trust* is a trust which, by its terms, imposes a restraint upon the voluntary or involuntary transfer of the interest held by a beneficiary in the trust.

The purpose of a spendthrift trust is to protect a particular beneficiary's inheritance from his or her own improvidence. The beneficiary cannot force the trustee to make distributions upon demand. Similarly, creditors of the beneficiary cannot attach the assets held in the spendthrift trust for the beneficiary or force their early distribution to pay the beneficiary's debts. Creditors can, however, attach assets once they have been distributed to a beneficiary, even if the assets were distributed from a spendthrift trust.

⅍ *What if the beneficiary of a spendthrift trust files bankruptcy?*

Bankruptcy law specifically recognizes that if a debtor is a beneficiary of a spendthrift trust that is enforceable under applicable nonbankruptcy law, the restriction on the transfer of the beneficial interest held by the debtor is enforceable in the bankruptcy case. Consequently, if the debtor is named as a beneficiary in a validly created and funded spendthrift trust, his or her interest in that trust will not be included and administered as an asset of the debtor's bankruptcy estate.

If the beneficiary received distributions from the spendthrift trust before filing bankruptcy, any such distributed assets he or she holds as of the bankruptcy filing date will be included in his or her bankruptcy estate.

🔌 *Can I use an irrevocable life insurance trust for asset protection?*

An irrevocable life insurance trust (ILIT) is a very effective asset protection tool. Assets that you place into the trust during your lifetime will be protected from your creditors as long as you have not violated any applicable fraudulent conveyance statutes. Additionally, since the life insurance policy death proceeds will be payable to your ILIT instead of outright to individuals, the ILIT, if drafted properly, will provide excellent asset protection for the beneficiaries of the ILIT during their lifetimes.

🔌 *I want to establish a college fund for my children, and I also want to ensure that if I am sued or go bankrupt, the funds I set aside for my children will not be reached by my creditors. Any suggestions?*

One of the best estate planning tools for accomplishing your objectives is a lifetime irrevocable trust for each of your children. After you create the trusts, you can make gifts of cash or other assets to the trusts subject to the annual gift tax exclusion.

It is best, for purposes of asset protection, to appoint a disinterested, nonfamily third party to serve as trustee of these trusts while your children are minors. The assets that you place in the children's trusts will be totally protected from your creditors and even from a bankruptcy court provided the trusts are properly drafted and you do not make transfers of gifts to the trusts that would violate your state's fraudulent conveyances act.

🔌 *Can I put corporate assets into a children's trust to protect those assets?*

Yes. You can achieve excellent results by having irrevocable children's trusts own valuable patents, trademarks, copyrights, licenses, and distribution agreements, as well as any other type of valuable asset that you want to protect.

With this strategy, the children's trust would lease the needed assets to the corporation. However, the lease agreement must be for the same rental amount and under the same terms as those that would apply if the assets were being leased by an independent third party.

Family Limited Partnerships

🔌 *What is a family limited partnership?*

The term "family limited partnership" does not appear anywhere in the state statutes or in the Internal Revenue Code, but such partnerships are formed under the same statutes and same requirements as those governing any other limited partnership. A *family limited partnership (FLP)* is a limited partnership that is owned by and consists predominantly of family members or family-controlled entities, such as trusts, corporations, or LLCs, that serve as the general partner and the limited partners. An FLP is used to restructure the ownership of a person's assets in a manner that maximizes the preservation and use of the assets during the person's lifetime. It also maximizes the value of what an individual can leave to his or her heirs or other beneficiaries. Family limited partnerships are discussed in detail in Chapter 6.

☙ What asset protection does an FLP offer?

The limited partnership interests cannot be seized by the creditors of the limited partners. Thus the limited partners will not lose their interest in the partnership assets.

A *charging order* is the exclusive remedy available to a creditor who has a judgment against a limited partner. The charging order is served upon the general partner, instructing the general partner to forward any distributions to the creditor instead of the limited partner. The general partner has complete control over distributions; if the general partner makes no distributions, which is the right of the general partner, the creditor has no recourse. In addition to this rather precarious position, the creditor has another burden: The IRS has held that a person or entity holding a charging order must pay income taxes on the partner's share of the partnership's income, whether the funds are disbursed or not. Thus the creditor could have to pay income tax on income earned by the limited partnership but never distributed. For these reasons, creditors generally prefer to settle their claims, even for pennies on the dollar, rather than obtaining a charging order.

☙ Will a family limited partnership provide any asset protection in the event of divorce?

It depends on how the partnership agreement is drafted. However, if drafted properly, a limited partnership interest might be protected against the risk of divorce. The partnership agreement can provide that in the event of an involuntary transfer as a result of a divorce decree, the partnership will trigger a buyout provision under which the other partners can buy the interest at its fair market value. The fair market value of a family limited partnership interest is usually less than the underlying asset value, so the divorced partner is somewhat protected.

In community property states, when a limited partnership interest is given to a person, it is separate property. The partnership agreement may be drafted with provisions that a limited partnership interest is separate property and free from the community property rules, although state law will control this issue. Always work with your estate planning attorney to ensure that your FLP is correctly drafted for your state and for your particular situation.

≫ *As a professional, I'm concerned that the assets I've accumulated could be subject to seizure in a lawsuit. How can I prevent that from happening?*

You can create a limited partnership to hold your assets. The general partner will have to be someone other than you to protect the assets from collection by the judgment creditor. If you are a limited partner, the best that a creditor can do is step into your shoes through a charging order. In that case, the general partner would not authorize distributions, so the creditor would receive phantom income from the partnership and would be required to pay income tax on it without having the cash flow that created the tax.

The general partner should be a corporation or perhaps an offshore trust. This should insulate the assets from any attempt by a creditor to collect after a lawsuit. However, you need to be aware that courts in the United States are finding new ways to reach assets that were once thought safe from creditors.

≫ *What are the advantages of using a family limited partnership for asset protection?*

In many states, there is a creditor protection advantage when property is owned by husband and wife. This type of property ownership is called tenancy by the entirety. If someone sues only the husband, or sues only the wife, and obtains a judgment against only one of them, property owned by both of them will be unavailable to the judgment creditor. However, if someone sues both of them, all their assets will be subject to being lost. Couples who have established family and marital trusts in their wills or revocable trusts, planning to ensure that their applicable exclusion amounts will pass estate tax–free, may be unwilling to split their property between the husband's trust and the wife's trust in order to ensure that the trusts will be funded at death and the contemplated estate tax savings realized. Their unwillingness stems from their fear that they will be giving up the creditor protection that holding property as tenants by the entirety provides. But if they do not split their property, they will lose as much as $435,000 to estate taxes on the second spouse's death.

The family limited partnership provides a solution to this dilemma. By first contributing their assets to the FLP, receiving partnership shares in return, and then having the partnership shares owned by their respective trusts, couples can have much better creditor protection than they would as tenants by the entirety and can ensure that their planning will save $435,000 in estate taxes.

Although the initial fees for setting up a family limited partnership are more than those for other kinds of planning, most clients see the costs of FLPs as no more than additional liability insurance premiums.

⋬ Isn't an FLP just a form, available to anyone?

An FLP, as a limited partnership, is expressly authorized by Subchapter K of the Internal Revenue Code. Every state has a Limited Partnership Act that regulates the operation of limited partnerships established within its borders. Like all partnerships, an FLP must obtain a federal ID number and must file a partnership income tax return (Form 1065) each year.

To be effective, an FLP must be carefully drafted by an attorney who is very knowledgeable not only about partnership law but also about partnership income tax and estate tax issues. Specialized language is essential to ensure the effectiveness of an FLP. If not drafted correctly, an FLP will not offer any creditor protection or accomplish any other estate planning objectives.

In addition to knowing partnership law, an attorney engaged in creating FLPs must also understand *fraudulent conveyance laws*. These are laws that exist in every state to give creditors rights in property that is conveyed with the intent of defrauding, hindering, or delaying legitimate creditor claims. If these laws are not followed, it is possible for a creditor's attorney to reach partnership assets in spite of the protections offered by an FLP.

An FLP is a complex planning strategy that should be initiated and implemented only by a qualified attorney.

Corporations

⋬ Can corporations be used as an effective asset protection tool?

Yes. A corporation is often a very practical and usable asset protection tool.

If one or more individuals establish a legal corporation according to the laws of the state of their residence or the laws of the domicile of the corporation, the corporation forms a legal barrier between the assets owned by the individuals and the corporation's creditors. If the corporation is sued, the individual stockholders' personal assets are not reachable by the corporation's creditors.

To be effective, this strategy may require the creation of several corporations in combination with trusts to create multiple legal barriers. Doing business with the public as a corporation is far more preferable than conducting business as a sole proprietor or as a general partnership as far as asset protection is concerned.

All factors, both tax and nontax, must be considered when deciding whether to use one corporation or multiple corporations to provide asset protection. It is important that you seek advice from your tax attorney as well as your other advisors before establishing a corporation.

Since I have a good business liability insurance program, why do I still need to incorporate my small business for asset protection?

Liability insurance is a must in these litigation-happy days, but no amount of insurance can protect against all possible claims. The corporate structure is a separate entity, or person, which simply provides an extra blanket of protection for your assets. You should remember, however, that if you create the liability personally, even if you were conducting your corporation's business, your corporation will not protect you against a personal judgment. That is why it is simply good business to have the protection of both personal liability insurance and a corporation.

Furthermore, the limited liability of a corporation extends to matters involving contracts and creditors' claims. New technology or discoveries could make your product or service obsolete overnight, leaving your business in financial difficulty. There could also be a significant downturn in business which might affect the value of your inventory. Every business owner should consider some form of limited liability coverage for his or her small business.

My friend and I want to go into business together and form a corporation. To get started, I intend to contribute some real estate to the new corporation and my friend will be contributing some fairly valuable equipment. Is there a way that we could protect these assets from the corporation's creditors in case the business fails?

Yes, there are several ways that you can protect the valuable assets you and your friend intend to contribute to your new business. First of all, you and your friend could simply lease the land and equipment to the corporation. If the business fails, it will stop making lease payments, thereby entitling you and your friend to reclaim your property.

Additionally, other corporations could be formed to own the property, and those corporations could lease the land and equipment to the corporation under which you will be conducting your business. Various types of trusts, limited partnerships, and limited liability companies could also own the valuable assets, with leases going to the new business venture.

No matter which of these scenarios you choose, if you structure them properly and follow the legal formalities required by state law in maintaining the entities as totally separate, the assets you and your friend now own will not be reachable by creditors of the new venture if it fails.

⋇ *If I create a revocable living trust, will it still be necessary for me to keep my corporation for personal liability purposes? Won't my living trust protect my assets from creditors?*

No. Your revocable living trust offers you, as the maker, virtually no personal liability protection because the trust is revocable and totally in your control. If it is under your control, creditors can ultimately control the property in your living trust.

You should keep the corporation, but you should talk with your estate planning attorney about the possibility of having a revocable living trust for estate planning and a separate, irrevocable trust for other assets you care to protect, not so much for yourself but for others.

OFFSHORE PLANNING
FOR ASSET PROTECTION

⋇ *What is offshore planning?*

In its simplest form, offshore planning is one more method of asset protection. Asset protection is maintaining control of what you have accumulated and ensuring that your family and loved ones will benefit from it in the long run. Its purpose is to avoid losing your hard-earned wealth to a catastrophic creditor, an irate troublemaker, an unplanned business reversal, or the IRS or some other government regulatory bureaucracy. It is planning in advance against a future catastrophe.

Buying insurance is one form of asset protection. So is proper estate planning through various trusts or a family limited partnership. By definition, *offshore planning* is international estate, business, tax, and investment planning under the laws of a jurisdiction that you find to be more advantageous than your own country's laws. People in Europe, the Middle East, or Asia who plan under the laws of the United States are doing offshore planning. For U.S. citizens, offshore planning means making use of the laws of a country other than the United States.

⍋ *Why do people use offshore planning?*

The motivations for going offshore are as many and varied as the people who choose to do so. Some people have chosen offshore planning because:

- They live in a country with an uncertain political future.
- They live in a country with forced heirship laws that would prevent them from distributing their wealth the way they choose.
- Their professional liability insurance has become more and more expensive for less and less coverage.
- They are general partners and therefore liable for the mistakes of all the other partners.
- They want to protect an expected inheritance.
- They are afraid of becoming targets of new legislation or of arbitrary decisions of regulatory agencies.
- They prefer to avoid asking their future spouses for a premarital agreement, or they would like to supplement such an agreement with added protection.
- They want to lower their high financial profile by using the confidentiality afforded by offshore planning.
- They want to protect their assets from litigious predators.
- They want to take advantage of certain offshore financial instruments that will afford them additional avenues of income tax deferral and estate tax avoidance.

⚜ Why should U.S. citizens consider using offshore planning?

With the ever-expanding theories of liability in domestic litigation and the ever-expanding global economy, U.S. citizens have become very interested in exercising their right to move a portion of their wealth offshore not only to protect that wealth from lawsuits and creditors but also to take advantage of making foreign investments, which they could not otherwise do because of the constraints of U.S. securities laws.

⚜ Who uses offshore planning?

Offshore planning is widely used by many prestigious U.S. corporations and banks. Some of the best-known names in the Fortune 500 do much of their business and banking outside the United States. Sears, McDonald's, IBM, Boeing, and Dow are among the hundreds of overseas players. Banks as large as Chase and Citibank make a good share of their profits outside the borders of our country.

Some corporations, such as Dow, have their own offshore banks which provide another profit center, as well as allow them to obtain favorable interest rates on loans and protection from currency fluctuations. Business enterprises from manufacturers to medical schools find it advantageous to locate on foreign soil. An inordinate number of ships, for example, are registered in Liberia and Panama.

Noncorporate users are often individuals of high net worth, but not always. Different people have different motivations for "going offshore." In spite of the "jet-set" image of offshore planning, many middle-class professionals and businesspeople make use of it as well.

⚜ What are the advantages of offshore planning?

One of the big benefits of offshore planning is confidentiality. Many people are simply tired of the lack of privacy in one's business and financial affairs in the United States. If you know where and how to look, you can find out dozens of things about someone through a simple search of public records. However, in many of the popular offshore financial centers, there are strict privacy laws that protect the customers of offshore institutions. Many of these jurisdictions make it illegal for an employee or officer of the bank, for example, to reveal that someone even has an account there, let alone any of the details of that account. Many jurisdictions back up their laws with criminal penalties for any institutional employees who violate them. This prevents information from getting to government agencies, competitors, and predators.

For many people, protection of their assets from the groups just mentioned is more important than privacy concerning the assets. They find themselves in positions of vulnerability and high liability and fear losing the nest egg that they have worked a lifetime to earn. They go offshore to build a hedge of protection around the things they own to preserve them for the ones they love.

◿ *Isn't going offshore a bit of overkill?*

The value of an offshore strategy is, primarily, that it keeps the trustee from the power of a domestic court and, to a lesser extent, that it keeps assets from the grasp of the "professional" plaintiff. Courts derive their power to compel citizens to do something through a legal concept known as *jurisdiction.* Jurisdiction is nothing more than the *power* of a court to compel a person (trustee) to do something. Even if the judge is wrong (which happens more than many would like to think), the domestic trustee of a trust must follow the judge's decision. If the trustee disregards a judge's court order, the court can punish the trustee. Even if the court order is later determined to be in error, refusal to obey can result in contempt, which translates to jail or a fine.

A trustee located in a foreign country managing a trust set up in that country is not within the power of a stateside court and is thus not obliged to obey such a court's order. Conversely, if a court in the trustee's country orders the trustee to do something, the trustee must obey the order or will be in contempt of that court.

◿ *Is this type of offshore planning legal?*

Of course it is. There are places on your tax return to report income from foreign trusts. But engaging in offshore planning does require that you broaden your thinking. You must stop seeing estate, business, tax, and financial planning parochially and start acting as an international person. Just as you can travel to other countries, work in other countries, carry on business in other countries, buy things from other countries, and vacation in other countries, you can also do planning in other countries.

A person doing offshore planning is much like a business located in Illinois deciding to incorporate in Delaware because advantageous laws exist there for corporations.

That's not to say that no one has ever used international planning in an illegal way. But international treaties and agreements are making it harder and harder to do so. Offshore planning does have an exotic mystique about it, brought on by books and movies about drug runners, smugglers, money launderers, and mob guys. Even though these are the types of people who get all the press (when they get caught), international finance and planning is a completely legitimate multibillion-dollar industry that quietly goes about its business 365 days per year, year after year.

In the real world of international planning, the offshore institutions that you work with are as likely to check you out before accepting you as a client as you are to check their references. They are very careful to involve themselves only with legitimate businesspeople and investors and to avoid any contact with the criminal element.

⅍ *What are some of the laws I should be aware of in using offshore planning?*

There are a few federal laws that pertain to offshore planning, most of which carry criminal penalties of fines and jail time if violated. Your best prevention against violating any of the laws mentioned below is to work with a qualified estate planning attorney and other qualified advisors who are conversant with the laws and experienced in their application.

- *Bankruptcy Reform Act of 1994,* revised Section 152 of Title 18 U.S.C. and added Section 157 entitled "Bankruptcy Fraud": Under these sections, a person who individually or on behalf of a corporation makes false or fraudulent representations, or knowingly and fraudulently transfers or conceals any of his or her property or that of the corporation, is subject to fine and/ or imprisonment.
- *Crime Control Act of 1990:* This act provides for criminal penalties for any person trying to place an asset beyond the reach of the FDIC or the RTC.
- *Money Laundering Control Act of 1986:* Enacted to help fight the war on drugs and drug traffickers, this act was broadened, in 1988, to also include financial crimes. It provides for severe fines and/or prison terms for people who conduct a financial transaction designed to evade the payment of federal income taxes, to conceal the nature, source, ownership, or control of the proceeds gained from an unlawful activity, or to avoid federal currency reporting laws.
- *Internal Revenue Code Section 7206(4):* This section provides that a person who conceals property to defeat the assessment or collection of a tax is subject to fine and/or imprisonment.

⚞ *What is "money laundering," and is it connected to asset protection?*

Money laundering is simply the depositing of money from illegally obtained sources, such as illegal drugs. Usually, the money is taken through a series of transactions, making it difficult to trace, with the idea of removing the criminal taint so that it can be used for lawful purposes. Because of the criminal nature of its origin, no income taxes are paid on these funds. Trusts, corporations, and bank accounts can all be used as vehicles for money laundering.

Offshore trusts, or as they are more preferably known, *international asset protection trusts (IAPT),* are a legitimate method of protecting assets from lawsuits which are being filed every day against honest citizens for claims of questionable merit. For people whose assets are *not* illegally obtained, there is no element of money laundering.

Most offshore jurisdictions which are acceptable for the creation of offshore trusts are signatories to money-laundering treaties, and a reputable trustee is no more eager to manage laundered money than is any other honest citizen.

⚞ *Aren't people who do offshore planning just trying to cheat others and avoid paying their debts?*

This is difficult to answer. Motives are always behind all human behavior. Whether something is dishonest or not often depends on the motive of the person doing the act. If a person's motive in doing offshore planning is to cheat or defraud others, then, yes, he or she is trying to cheat others, and such people and those who assist them run the same risks as anyone else who breaks the law.

"Asset protection planning" does not mean depriving legitimate creditors of the ability to collect honest debts. Rather, it means discouraging the predatory plaintiff and his or her attorney who are simply using a lawsuit as a form of pressure to profit from their irresponsible behavior. In this context, engaging in such planning is no different than using various estate planning techniques for reducing or avoiding estate taxes, which is perfectly legal.

Not reporting income is illegal and is punishable just as any other crime is. A reputable asset protection attorney will not assist anyone in the commission of a crime, since to do so could subject the attorney to criminal prosecution and disbarment. When you meet with your attorney to begin offshore planning, do not be surprised if he or she asks you many questions about your personal affairs, particularly any possible lawsuits either pending or about to be filed, and past tax liabilities, as these are often signs that a client wants to "hide assets," which is illegal.

Jurisdictions for Offshore Planning

⋈ *What countries are commonly used for offshore planning?*

The United States is used as an offshore center for citizens of other countries. For U.S. citizens, there are a number of offshore choices: Andorra, Anguilla, Antigua, Aruba, Australia, Bahamas, Barbados, Barbuda, Belize, Bermuda, British Virgin Islands, Cayman Islands, Cook Islands, Costa Rica, Cyprus, Gibraltar, Grenada, Guernsey, Hong Kong, Ireland, Isle of Man, Jersey, Labuan, Liechtenstein, Luxembourg, Madeira, Malaysia, Malta, Marshall Islands, Mauritius, Monaco, Montserrat, Nauru, Netherlands Antilles, Nevis, New Zealand, Niue, Panama, St. Kitts, Seychelles, Singapore, Switzerland, Turks and Caicos, and Vanuatu.

You can see that offshore jurisdictions are in all parts of the globe, including the Americas, Europe, Asia, the Far East, the South Pacific, and especially the Caribbean.

A few of these have become more popular because of legislation which serves to clarify their rules of asset protection and provide certainty about what to expect within their jurisdictions. For these reasons, some of the most popular countries include the Bahamas, Barbados, Belize, Bermuda, the Cayman Islands, the Cook Islands, Cyprus, Gibraltar, Mauritius, Nevis, and the Turks and Caicos Islands.

⋈ *What are some factors that I should look for in choosing an offshore site?*

The foreign jurisdiction that you choose should have the following factors:

- Well-defined, established, protective, and favorable asset protection laws
- A good reputation in the business world generally
- Economic and political stability

- The availability of excellent support services, such as communications, attorneys, accountants, and financial advisors
- A policy of refusal or reluctance to recognize the judgments of a U.S. court without the retrial of the case in the foreign jurisdiction's court, along with a more stringent burden of proof on a plaintiff
- Statutes of limitations that bar action in the foreign jurisdiction's courts if the occurrence giving rise to the U.S. litigation is beyond a certain, relatively short, time period
- Prohibition of contingent fees, along with a requirement that a plaintiff must post a bond for a defendant's legal fees
- A less stringent (than the U.S.) fraudulent transfer law that overrides the statute of Elizabeth (the common law fraudulent conveyance statute)
- Spendthrift trust laws which allow the maker's interest in the trust to be protected from claims of creditors
- Favorable tax laws imposed upon foreign investors

I understand that I should be looking for a country that has an "antiduress" clause in its trust laws. What is an antiduress clause, and what is its function?

Generally, with a domestic trust, the court has jurisdiction over the trust maker. In many cases, the court can simply order the trust maker to have the trustee convey to the maker sufficient assets for paying off a judgment. While the judge may not have jurisdiction over the trustee, he or she does have jurisdiction over the trust maker. Once the trust maker instructs the trustee to convey the assets to him or her, the creditor can obtain those assets.

If the trust maker fails to instruct the trustee to convey the assets, the court may hold that the disobedient trust maker is in contempt of court. The can lead to quasi-criminal consequences that the trust maker would generally like to avoid—*like going to jail!*

A number of offshore jurisdictions have enacted *antiduress statutes.* Under these statutes, if a U.S. court attempted to reach assets of an offshore trust by ordering the maker to instruct the trustee to return funds to the United States, the trustee could not comply because the trust maker would be acting under duress. Antiduress statutes define "duress" as, among other things, acting under the compulsion of a court or a court order. Since no federal or state court has jurisdiction over the trustee or the assets of the trust, the antiduress clause presents an enormous obstacle to recovery by a judgment creditor.

How do I go about doing offshore trust planning?

Offshore trust planning is a relatively new and highly specialized area of the law. You should seek out an attorney who is thoroughly familiar with offshore trusts and jurisdictions and who has contacts with foreign banks and facilitators. If you cannot find such an attorney, contact your financial advisor, accountant, or banker for a reference. Also refer to Appendix A of this text for suggestions on finding an estate planning attorney. That attorney may be experienced in providing this type of service or may be able to refer you to another attorney.

What costs should I expect to encounter in offshore planning?

Depending upon your choice of planning tools, you should expect to pay between $15,000 and $50,000 (or a small percentage of the assets) for legal fees and setup costs, along with annual maintenance fees of approximately $2000.

The Offshore Asset Protection Trust

What is an offshore asset protection trust?

An *offshore asset protection trust,* also known simply as an *offshore trust,* is typically an irrevocable, tax-neutral grantor trust. It is considered by many specialists in the field to be the most powerful strategy available for protecting assets from judgment and tort creditors.

How does an offshore trust insulate assets from creditor attack?

An offshore asset protection trust is established in an offshore jurisdiction, though the assets can remain in the United States under the indirect control of the trust maker. The trust protects assets because the foreign jurisdiction will generally not recognize a judgment from a U.S. court, and the foreign trustee can refuse to turn over assets even if a U.S. court orders it to do so.

Offshore trusts make use of two unique provisions:

1. The power to remove the trust to a different jurisdiction and

appoint a substitute foreign trustee if a claim on trust assets is made in the original jurisdiction

2. The requirement by the foreign jurisdiction that a creditor relitigate its lawsuit in every new foreign jurisdiction in order to get a judgment in those foreign jurisdictions

A creditor who obtains a U.S. judgment has several hurdles to overcome to attach the assets in the trust. Procedurally, the creditor has to file a brand-new lawsuit in the foreign jurisdiction. Also, the creditor has to prove that the statute of limitations did not expire (usually 1 to 2 years from trust creation) and that the creditor has standing to sue.

Most other countries do not allow contingent-fee litigation, so the creditor has to retain a foreign, non-contingent-fee lawyer and pay a legal-fee retainer. In some countries (those based on the English model) the creditor-plaintiff must post a cash payment with the court to cover the defendant's legal fees and court costs in the event that the plaintiff loses.

It will likely take several years for the creditor to get the case to trial. Even then, should the creditor overcome all these hurdles, the foreign trustee could change the *situs* of the trust (the trust's jurisdiction and where the assets are held), so the creditor might have to start all over again in another jurisdiction.

All these factors make it very expensive and uncertain for a creditor to attack trust assets, so they have the end result of shielding assets from creditors.

⚜ How does an offshore asset protection trust work?

The key to an offshore asset protection trust is that, once ownership of the assets has been transferred, neither the trust maker nor the trustees can be forced to repatriate the assets for the benefit of creditors. Therefore, a properly drafted offshore asset protection trust should contain language requiring that the trustee ignore instructions that are given to the trustee under duress, such as under a court order from a foreign jurisdiction.

Any asset can be transferred into an offshore asset protection trust, either directly or by transferring shares of a limited partnership which owns the asset. However, liquid assets which can be physically relocated are best. That is because courts are unlikely to give up control over a fixed asset, such as real estate, that lies within their jurisdiction.

The main reason the offshore asset protection trust works is that it places assets under the control of a trustee in a jurisdiction that does not recognize judgments awarded in the United States by U.S. courts. It works because of legislation and statute, not because your assets are "hidden." If a judgment is entered against you in a lawsuit, you will be asked under oath to disclose your assets. If you attempt to "hide" your assets, you will likely be committing perjury. Indeed, if you attempted to hide assets from, say, the IRS, you could be faced with criminal charges. Offshore planning works, ultimately, because it is based on sound legal principles. It serves to discourage a litigant from filing suit in the first place, and if a suit is filed, it encourages early and fair settlements.

⚚ What are the objectives of an offshore asset protection trust?

An offshore asset protection trust has a number of objectives, including:

1. To separate an individual from assets that creditors could take under the laws of the United States
2. To ensure that the assets are safe and secure and are under competent and reputable management
3. To allow assets to revert back to their owner when creditor exposure has subsided
4. To prevent additional estate, gift, income, and excise tax exposure
5. To be free of any violation of criminal laws, tax laws, or bankruptcy laws
6. To allow the maker to direct investments and change trustees
7. To be part of an overall comprehensive estate plan which is coordinated with the maker's other assets and estate planning
8. To put the maker in a position that allows him or her to honestly inform a court of law that he or she has no power or authority over the trustee and, because of this lack of authority, possesses no legal ability to comply with the court's orders
9. To create a situation in which assets can be moved, sold, invested, managed, or distributed by the trustee even though the maker is under court order or other constraints that prevent the maker from doing so personally
10. To allow the trustee to easily change the situs of the trust in the event of the commencement of litigation in the foreign situs or for any other legitimate reason

⬩ *What are the typical provisions of an offshore asset protection trust ?*

Offshore trusts often have the following provisions:

- Irrevocable for a term of years (with or without provisions for extension of the term, if creditors are still a problem), with a reversion to the maker, if he or she is living, at the end of the term
- Flight from the non-U.S. jurisdiction to another if creditor action is threatened
- Beneficiaries other than the maker, including the maker's spouse, children, friends, other relatives, and charities
- Discretionary spray or sprinkle powers over income and principal to the various beneficiaries, but if income and principal are not distributed, the funds will accumulate and can eventually revert back to the maker at the end of the term
- Addition or deletion of beneficiaries by the maker as long as he or she is not the sole beneficiary
- Shortening of the term of the offshore trust if the maker dies and the assets can be governed by his or her domestic estate plan

⬩ *It sounds like an offshore asset protection trust is much like a revocable living trust. Is that true?*

In many ways an offshore asset protection trust is much like a revocable living trust. For example, both can avoid the costs and time delays of probate, both can provide for administration in the event of the trust maker's disability, both can maintain confidentiality, both can aid in planning for estate taxes, and both can contain specific provisions about distributing assets to heirs. One big difference between the two trusts, however, is that the offshore trust can offer creditor protection for the trust maker during his or her lifetime, while the revocable living trust cannot.

An offshore asset protection trust should always be integrated with the trust maker's overall estate planning. A person should have an offshore trust and a revocable living trust, plus other planning tools, for a truly effective estate plan.

While the two types of trust are similar, they have different estate planning functions. An offshore asset protection trust's main objective is to protect assets from egregious creditors; a revocable living trust's primary objectives are to care for the maker if he or she is disabled, to reduce federal estate taxes, and to ensure that after the death of the maker the trust property will be managed, administered, and distributed according to the instructions in the trust.

☙ *If an offshore asset protection trust is truly irrevocable, how do I ever get the assets back?*

Offshore asset protection trusts are designed in such a way that you and your beneficiaries may receive the assets back at any time. The irrevocable nature of the trust is for your protection. Depending on the jurisdiction used, both the maker and the heirs may be allowed to be beneficiaries of the trust. Trust laws do vary, so a proper investigation of a specific jurisdiction's treatment of this issue should be made.

☙ *Are offshore asset protection trusts guaranteed to work every time?*

There are very few guarantees in life. The same is true for offshore asset protection planning. Such variables as a person's individual situation, the types of assets held by the offshore asset protection trust, the quality of the drafting of the trust document, the skill of the attack and the defense of the trust, the quality and soundness of the law of the particular foreign jurisdiction, and many other factors affect the viability of any offshore plan using an asset protection trust.

Most offshore planners agree that offshore planning "works" if it leaves their clients better off than they would have been without the planning. That standard is virtually always met.

☙ *Can you give me an example of a situation in which an offshore asset protection trust would be effective?*

To demonstrate why the offshore asset protection trust encourages settlement or avoids litigation altogether, let's look at a typical lawsuit against a person who has used offshore planning in the Bahamas. The Bahamas is a very popular offshore center because of its proximity to the United States and easy access via a short flight from Florida.

In our example, George Upright, a prominent businessman, has fired an employee for dishonesty. An overzealous attorney has convinced the employee to sue her former boss for discrimination, with one-third of the settlement to be given to the attorney in fees. The jury compares the poor, unemployed worker to the successful business owner and decides George deserves to pay because he has more. In spite of any evidence to the contrary, the jury finds for the plaintiff and awards $20,000 in actual damages and $3 million in punitive damages.

George carries $1 million of liability insurance coverage in an umbrella policy, but finds out it does not include punitive damages. George mumbles something about being covered when you fall off the roof but not when you hit the ground. After the judgment is handed down, the opposing attorney takes George's deposition, under oath, to determine where all of George's personal assets are located. George states that he has a checking account containing approximately $5000 and a savings account containing approximately $50,000 in the name of his revocable living trust. He also has a car and some personal effects. The lawyer finds out that the home George lives in is owned by his wife's revocable living trust, so it is unavailable to satisfy the judgment. Everything else, totaling approximately $2 million, is owned by an offshore asset protection trust in the Bahamas which George established about 3 years ago.

The aggressive plaintiff's attorney decides to go after the offshore trust. When he does, he trips over a whole series of barriers:

- First, the attorney finds out that Bahamian courts will not recognize a judgment handed down by a foreign court, so he must initiate new proceedings in the Bahamas.
- Since the attorney is not licensed to practice law in the Bahamas, he must retain Bahamian counsel. He wonders if the client can foot the bill for the Bahamian attorney since he, the U.S. attorney, is being paid on a contingency basis and hasn't been paid yet himself.
- The Bahamian attorney points out that the Bahamian court is unlikely to find that the plaintiff has a jurisdictional basis to bring the suit because neither George nor the assets he owns outside the offshore asset protection trust are within the Bahamian jurisdiction.
- Next, the attorney decides to sue the trustees, which would allow the Bahamian court to have jurisdiction. However, he finds there are no filing, registration, or disclosure requirements for trusts established in the Bahamas.
- George Upright, the defendant, is very cooperative and tells the attorney the name of the trust company which is acting as trustee of his offshore trust. However, because of very strict secrecy laws which apply to banks and trust companies and their employees, officers, lawyers, and accountants, the attorney is finding it very hard to gain enough information on which to formulate a claim.

- The U.S. judge issues a court order requiring that George Upright instruct the trustee to disclose all requested information about his offshore asset protection trust. George complies with the court order. The only problem is that the trust states that the trustee cannot obey any instructions from the trust maker that are given under duress. The trustee is bound by fiduciary law, a law higher than the court's order, to follow those instructions in the offshore asset protection trust.

Then the attorney finds out that because he represents a foreign plaintiff with no Bahamian assets, the court will require a substantial cash payment to George as a security deposit in the event George prevails in the case.

The litigant has to overcome all these barriers before she can even bring a case against George in the Bahamas. Now, if the plaintiff were a large corporation with lots of money and a very emotional CEO who was out to get George (instead of a person with few resources), it might actually be able to clear all these hurdles with money, patience, and persistence.

If the plaintiff does clear all the preliminary hurdles to bringing a lawsuit against the offshore asset protection trust, she is still met with some final barriers, such as:

- Actions can be brought only by actual creditors who had claims that existed at the time George set up his offshore asset protection trust and that were known about by George.
- The creditor has the burden of proving that the claim existed and that George knew about it when he established his offshore asset protection trust.
- Regardless of the above, the action has to be brought within 2 years of the date that the offshore asset protection trust was set up.

So even after clearing the preliminary hurdles, the litigant still fails to reach the offshore asset protection trust because George established the trust more than 2 years ago. Also, even if the trust was set up less than 2 years ago, the creditor could never establish that she had a claim against George at that time and that he knew about it. Finally, even if all the above factors are met and the creditor is successful, the transfer of assets to the offshore asset protection trust can be set aside only to the extent necessary to satisfy the claim. The balance of the assets in the offshore asset protection trust remain intact.

It is easy to see why the plaintiff's attorney in George's case would recommend a reasonable out-of-court settlement when faced with the daunting prospect of litigating the case (especially on a contingent-fee basis) in a foreign jurisdiction.

⅍ *What happens if the creditor is willing to litigate the matter all over again?*

In most offshore jurisdictions, you can have a trust protector who has the ability to change the trustee and the situs of the trust. If the creditor gets into court, the trust protector establishes a new trust in another jurisdiction and removes all the assets to the new jurisdiction. This will cause the creditor to start over again. In some offshore jurisdictions, there are time periods within which the creditor must bring the action after receiving the judgment. It is possible to keep the creditor at bay for years using this strategy.

⅍ *I have been wrongly sued by a former business partner. My insurance won't cover the claim, and I'm afraid the litigation will be very expensive. In addition, the IRS has recorded a tax lien against me as the result of an audit of a limited partnership in which I was an investor. I just received a $1 million inheritance, and I want to protect it by placing it into an offshore trust. Do you see any problems with this?*

Yes. The transfer you are contemplating would be fraudulent in regard to both your former business partner and the IRS. The Uniform Fraudulent Transfer Act, adopted in one form or another in each of the fifty states, provides that a transfer made by a debtor is fraudulent as to any creditor

> if the debtor made the transfer either (*a*) with the actual intent to hinder, delay, or defraud the creditor, or (*b*) without receiving a reasonably equivalent value in exchange for the transfer, when the debtor was engaged or about to engage in a business or transaction for which the remaining assets were unreasonably small or when the debtor intended to incur debts beyond his or her ability to pay them as they became due.

A transfer may also be considered fraudulent if the debtor did not receive a reasonably equivalent value for the transfer and if the debtor was insolvent at the time of the transfer or became insolvent as a result of the transfer.

As you can see, since your contemplated transfer to an offshore trust is done for the purpose of hindering future collection actions by your former business partner and by the IRS, the transfer would be fraudulent as to them and, thus, your transfer to an offshore trust would be voidable by them. The only appropriate and defensible time to engage in asset protection planning with an offshore trust is a time when you owe no substantial debts or obligations. If you wait until potentially devastating claims are already brought against you, your available options will be severely limited.

⌐ *How can I use an offshore trust in connection with a family limited partnership?*

Generally, there is no significant sacrifice of control or of access to property when an FLP is used with an offshore trust. All your bank accounts, stock brokerage accounts, real estate, and other significant assets are placed into a domestic FLP. You then transfer your FLP interest to the offshore trust. You retain control over your property as the general partner of the domestic FLP, while the offshore trust owns virtually all the partnership interests.

If there is an attack on the structure by a creditor, the FLP can then distribute its assets and personal property to an offshore account that has been established in the name of the trust. This feature provides the ultimate protection for family assets since the account will not be subject to the jurisdiction of the U.S. court judgment.

Assets in an offshore trust

⌐ *Are the assets placed in an offshore trust actually in the foreign country?*

Often these assets are not even located in the foreign country where the trust is. Many trusts set up in the Bahamas, Cook Islands, Caymans, Costa Rica, Barbados, Belize, and so on, have a bank in one of these jurisdictions that acts as trustee, but the assets themselves may be located in England, Switzerland, or even the United States! The trustee doesn't even have physical possession of these assets.

⌐ *Can an offshore trust protect real estate and other assets that are located in the United States?*

One of the advantages of an offshore trust is that no federal or state court can obtain jurisdiction over the person of the foreign trustee or the assets located in the foreign country. Jurisdiction is nothing more than the power of a court to adjudicate a dispute and compel the people involved to abide by its decision.

Jurisdiction is exercised primarily in two ways, in personam or in rem. *In personam* (personal) jurisdiction is the court's power over a person to make that person comply with the court's order. *In rem* (property) jurisdiction is the power of the court to control a particular piece of property, such as real estate or a bank account.

When a court exercises personal jurisdiction, it is ordering someone such as a trustee to surrender assets in a trust. Disregard or violation of a court order by someone over whom the court has personal jurisdiction can result in that person's being held in contempt of court, which can lead to imprisonment, fine, or both.

When a particular piece of property is within the power of the court to seize, all control over that property is at the mercy of the court. Obviously, it is easy to move money and investments offshore, but real estate cannot go anywhere. While the courts are not supposed to exercise jurisdiction over real estate owned by a foreign entity, they may choose to do so anyway.

People who want to protect real estate will sometimes borrow against their equity and use the proceeds to purchase investment assets which are then held by the offshore trust. This approach should be carefully thought out before doing it, as it involves placing a mortgage on the real estate.

Can an asset protection trust own S corporation stock?

Subchapter S elections are available for any domestic corporations whose stock is owned by an offshore asset protection trust that is a grantor trust.

Tax issues of an offshore trust

What are the income tax ramifications of an offshore asset protection trust?

A properly drafted offshore asset protection trust is a grantor trust under the Internal Revenue Code. A *grantor trust* is a trust whose income, loss, deductions, or credits are reported on the maker's income tax return rather than on a return filed by the trust itself. This means that the asset protection trust is income tax–neutral; it does not change the income taxation of the assets within it.

Under the grantor trust rules, if the maker is one of the trustees of the offshore trust, the trust need not obtain a U.S. taxpayer I.D. number; instead, the maker's Social Security number will be used.

⚜ *Am I required to pay federal income tax on income earned on assets in an offshore trust?*

Yes, you are required to pay federal income tax on assets which are in an offshore trust. The U.S. income tax system taxes income "from all sources, wherever derived," thus including offshore assets. Offshore trusts are not intended to save federal income tax. In fact, the Internal Revenue Service is increasing the number of agents whose only function is to locate foreign assets of U.S. taxpayers and verify that any income from these assets is properly reported

⚜ *If my business is involved in international operations, can I save taxes by having it held in an asset protection trust?*

The simple ownership of an international business corporation (IBC) within an asset protection trust provides no tax benefit to an individual. Congress has enacted several antiavoidance rules that specifically address the ownership of foreign corporations. These corporations, generally known as *controlled foreign corporations,* are fully taxed on their worldwide operations. Therefore, except at the corporate tax level, there are no major tax advantages of holding an IBC within a typical grantor-type asset protection trust.

There are several variations of the foreign corporation rules, so before you initiate any type of foreign business operations, regardless of their purpose, a complete analysis of the issues should be done by a competent international corporate tax attorney.

⚜ *What are the estate and gift tax consequences of an asset protection trust?*

Because the trust's assets revert to the maker at the maker's death or under certain other circumstances, the trust assets will be included in the maker's gross estate for federal estate tax purposes. All the assets in the trust receive a step-up in basis upon the maker's death. For these reasons, there is no gift tax consequence when the maker contributes assets to the offshore trust.

⚜ *Isn't there an excise tax for transferring appreciated assets to a foreign trust?*

There used to be a 35 percent excise tax for contributions of appreciated assets to an international trust. This tax was repealed by the Taxpayer Relief Act of 1997 and replaced with a provision that requires the recognition of all gain on property that is transferred to a foreign trust. The tax result is the same as it would be if the property were sold at its fair market value on the date of transfer. This provision took effect on August 5, 1997.

Neither the excise tax nor this new provision affects asset protection trusts that are grantor trusts. However, if a foreign trust loses its grantor trust status, the new tax provision will be immediately triggered.

⚜ *Do I have to report the creation of my trust to the IRS?*

Yes. When you create any foreign trust, you are required to file certain IRS forms within 90 days of creating the trust. In fact, for contributions of appreciated assets to the trust, you are required to file another form on the day of the transfer. Failure to file these forms can subject you to fines, penalties, and/or imprisonment.

⚜ *You say that I have to notify the government if I create an offshore trust. What happens if the government is my creditor?*

Asset protection trusts work against government agencies as well as private creditors. However, they must work within the rules, just as U.S. citizens must. Asset protection trusts cannot be used to avoid current tax liens, current EPA liabilities, or any other government claim against you. The government has worked closely with foreign jurisdictions, so you should not assume that all assets will be out of the reach of the U.S. government. It does have a substantial amount of power to seize your assets.

Most people who initiate asset protection planning are not concerned about normal governmental interference in their lives. They are usually more concerned with frivolous lawsuits and other miscellaneous legal actions against them.

⚜ *Is it important to file all the papers necessary in establishing an offshore trust?*

Absolutely. While an offshore trust is a tax-neutral entity, filing requirements cannot be ignored. The Small Business Job Protection Act of

1996 strengthened the reporting requirements for offshore trusts, and these requirements should be complied with by the maker. Compliance with these requirements, or the creation of an offshore trust, does not subject the maker to any higher taxes than he or she would otherwise have, just more paperwork.

The IRS has taken the position that taxpayers who create trusts in countries having stringent bank secrecy laws can expect little sympathy if it is discovered at a later time that there was no reporting or payment of income taxes on the assets held in the foreign bank. Some of the provisions of the Small Business Job Protection Act of 1996 appear to unduly conflict with certain privacy rights protected by the U.S. Constitution, although at this writing there does not seem to be any direction as to what a court might do. The safest bet is to comply with all statutes and to comply with the law, since the purpose of an offshore trust is not to evade taxes but to protect assets from unscrupulous plaintiffs and their attorneys.

◣ *I've heard that as long as a trust maker doesn't bring the money back into the United States, it is not taxable by the IRS. Is this correct?*

No. The fact that there is no tax treaty or information sharing between the United States and a foreign jurisdiction does not excuse a U.S. citizen or resident alien from his or her legal responsibilities to report the income and pay taxes on it.

Trustees of an offshore trust

◣ *Who should be the trustee of my offshore trust?*

You should name both a U.S. individual or corporate trustee and a reputable foreign professional corporate trustee. You can name one or more foreign trustees, but most people are more comfortable with having at least one U.S. trustee.

◣ *Should I use a bank or an individual as an offshore trustee?*

Many foreign jurisdictions have stricter banking laws than the United States. Misappropriation and malfeasance (dishonesty by a trustee toward a beneficiary) not only is a crime in many jurisdictions but can result in a bank's having its charter revoked as well as in criminal sanctions, including imprisonment and fines levied personally against principals. Further, in many foreign countries, if there is a complaint about a particular banking institution, it can usually be resolved much quicker than it could be under the U.S. banking system.

Many offshore jurisdictions are seeking to encourage the offshore trust business as a major revenue-producing source. They would have much to lose and nothing to gain if they did not severely punish malfeasance by members of the very industry that is to produce the revenue.

Because of the strict foreign banking laws, a bank is highly preferable to an individual for the role of trustee. You should seek out an attorney and other advisors who are knowledgeable about foreign banking laws and offshore planning so that you can identify the countries and trust companies that would be suited to your particular situation.

⅍ How do I choose an international trustee?

After choosing the offshore jurisdiction you prefer, you should interview different trustees to determine what services they can provide. Many are very sophisticated and assist their clients in almost any financial transaction. Others only passively hold their clients' assets and provide very few managerial services. Although you may pay a bit more for the services of the former, the money is well spent, especially since the latter type of trustee might frequently need to refer you to more "experienced" institutions. Just as in the United States, you get what you pay for; the cheapest trustee is not necessarily the best one for your situation.

⅍ How are my assets protected from the trustee?

Many individuals appoint a *trust protector* to oversee the activities of the trustee. The trust protector can be either an individual or a group of individuals and corporations. The trust protector is often authorized in the trust document to fire the trustee if the protector deems this necessary. Most jurisdictions have specific legislation addressing this issue. In fact, in several jurisdictions, you can give the trust protector almost any power. This allows you to provide several layers of safety regarding your foreign trustee.

In general, you must feel comfortable about dealing on an international basis. If you are more concerned with the credibility of the trustee than the threat of a lawsuit, you shouldn't proceed with this type of planning. In the worst-case scenario—a lawsuit in the United States—it may be necessary that the foreign trustee hold title and have full control of the assets within the trust. Again, if you are not comfortable with this, you should not initiate this type of planning.

⚜ How can I be sure that the trustee won't run off with the assets I place in the offshore trust?

Obviously, there is no guarantee that a trustee, anywhere, won't run off with the assets of a trust. In the United States, this risk is usually protected by a bank's assets, the FDIC, and the general integrity of the bank. Basically, the same holds for an offshore bank, except that it is not covered by the FDIC. The FDIC is really not a guarantee of trustee behavior; it is insurance for bank deposits.

You should do the same investigation of an overseas trustee as you would with any domestic trustee: know who you are dealing with. You can directly contact a bank in a foreign jurisdiction and talk to the principals firsthand, or you can work through an attorney who has offshore experience as well as contacts with reputable offshore banking institutions and money managers. Either way, you should be satisfied and comfortable with the trustee whom you select.

⚜ I would like to have a little more control over my offshore trust and my trustee. How can I accomplish this?

Some offshore asset protection trusts provide for a *trust advisory committee*. The trust maker will usually be the chairperson of the committee. The committee may:

- Render nonbinding investment advice
- Change the foreign trustee and U.S trustee as long as a replacement foreign trustee is named
- Name replacement committee members and remove members

Your participation on this committee should be suspended any time a creditor is a threat. In addition, international trustees are often directed by your instructions as set forth in a document sometimes known as a "letter of wishes." In it, you can request that the trustee invest the trust assets in a certain way or make distributions in a particular manner consistent with the terms of the trust. If the trustee does not want to follow these instructions or desires, he or she can be removed by the protector or trust advisors, or both.

An Offshore ILIT

↘ *Is there a vehicle that can serve to protect my wife's and my assets from judgment and tort creditors and at the same time afford us considerable estate tax savings?*

You can create an offshore asset protection trust which will also serve to own and be the beneficiary of a second-to-die life insurance policy on both of your lives. This policy will fund the trust on the death of the surviving spouse. The proceeds will be used to provide the liquidity to pay any estate taxes due at that time. This trust, known as an *offshore ILIT*, is useful for several reasons:

1. It allows you to obtain favorable insurance rates from reputable offshore insurance companies.
2. It saves you costs by combining the benefits of two planning tools (the offshore asset protection trust and the ILIT) in one vehicle.
3. It allows you to obtain optimum asset protection benefits for all noninsurance assets that are transferred to the trust (usually not to exceed your applicable exclusion amount) and for all remaining assets even if a portion of the trust's funds are used to finance the payment of the taxes. (*Note*: The payment of taxes is achieved by purchasing illiquid assets or by lending to the estate or trust.)

Foreign Bank Accounts

↘ *Can't I just establish a foreign bank account to provide asset protection?*

Foreign bank accounts may seem to be an exotic way of protecting assets, especially if the account is in a country which jealously protects the secrecy of its depositors. The big problem with this method is that a judge can easily order you to return the funds to the United States if a creditor learns of the foreign account.

To maintain the privacy of a foreign account and protect the secrecy of its assets, you must cheat and lie and even commit tax fraud. While it is not a crime to have a foreign account, it is a crime to lie about its existence, especially to a court or to the IRS. In fact, Form 1040 of the federal income tax return requires that foreign bank accounts be disclosed on its Schedule B.

As Sammy Davis, Jr., used to say, "Don't do the crime if you can't do the time." Therefore, you should rule out this method as a legal means of protecting your assets from creditors.

Offshore Annuities

⋈ *Is there a way that a U.S. citizen can utilize offshore planning to gain current income tax benefits?*

A nice way to obtain international diversification and tax-deferred benefits is through the use of an offshore annuity. Offshore annuities have essentially the same advantages as their U.S. counterparts. You obtain tax deferral on the income earned until you start withdrawing the funds. In addition, offshore annuities provide privacy, international diversification, the flexibility to choose which investments are subject to the annuity, and protection from judgment creditors.

Expatriation

⋈ *What is expatriation?*

Expatriation is the process of giving up citizenship in one's native country and becoming a citizen of some other country.

⋈ *How does someone give up his or her U.S. citizenship?*

The person first finds another country that will accept him or her as a citizen, based upon the person's ancestry or willingness to contribute to the local economy through business or investment. When all the arrangements are made, the person simply walks into the U.S. consulate, turns in his or her passport, and formally renounces his or her citizenship.

⋈ *Why would someone give up his or her U.S. citizenship?*

The primary nonpolitical reason that people give up their U.S. citizenship is to avoid what they consider confiscatory tax policies of the government. In spite of all the offshore and domestic tax and estate planning that can be done, the United States is still one of the few countries in the world that taxes its citizens on everything they own and earn worldwide, regardless of where they live.

The only way to avoid global taxation is to *not* be a U.S. citizen. Just living abroad will not make any difference.

Most people who take this step are, naturally, individuals who have a lot to lose because of the size of their wealth. Some pay so much in income taxes that they can't enjoy the lifestyle they prefer. Others cannot bear the thought that the government's estate taxes will take more than half of what they have worked so hard to accumulate, especially after it was already taxed once at the income tax level. Others see property ownership rights diminishing under U.S. law and fear an uncertain economic future.

One of the most famous expatriates is John Templeton, the mutual fund manager. He gave up his U.S. citizenship and moved to the Bahamas, where there is not only no income or estate tax but no tax of any kind! It is estimated that when he sold his company in 1992, he saved more than $100 million in capital gain taxes.

Another well-known example is John Dorrance III, an heir of the Campbell Soup fortune. Because he became a citizen of Ireland, his heirs will be subject to only a 2 percent estate tax instead of the 55 percent U.S. estate tax. Since his estate is estimated at over $1 billion, the savings for his family could amount to over half a billion dollars!

Obviously, these expatriates and others who move to countries that have no taxes are also saving a fortune in income taxes over the years. If they were to keep investing in the United States through normal channels, they could pay more each year in their 39.6 percent federal income tax bracket than many people earn.

✎ What are some of the estate and gift tax consequences of giving up U.S. citizenship?

The old law, pre-1996, stated that if an individual terminated his or her U.S. citizenship within 10 years of death and it could be shown that he or she did so to avoid U.S. estate and gift taxes, then estate tax will be due on death. In addition, the same look-back period applied to gifts made within 10 years of expatriation.

Before 1996, the IRS had to establish on a reasonable basis that a reason for expatriation was the avoidance of taxes. Once it established this basis, the burden was on the executor of the estate to prove that tax avoidance was not a principal purpose for expatriation.

In 1996, the law was tightened on the issue of expatriation. Generally, the new law states that an individual who leaves the United States is "presumed to have a principal purpose to avoid taxes" if his or her income is greater than $100,000 or if his or her net worth as of the date of expatriation is greater than $500,000. The IRS no longer has to establish that a person left the country for tax purposes; the rules are automatically applied. An executor no longer has the ability to contest the IRS determination of tax avoidance, as it is clearly written into tax law!

⚖ *Does this provision apply to green-card holders?*

The law passed in 1996 extends the expatriation laws to long-term residents of the United States whose residency is terminated. This rule applies to individuals who were green-card holders for at least 8 years before terminating their green-card status.

In the past, many green-card holders avoided becoming citizens because of the imposition of U.S. taxes. Now, they are basically in the same boat as a U.S. citizen.

ABUSIVE ASSET PROTECTION TRUSTS

⚖ *I attended an estate planning seminar recently where the speaker discussed the use of a "pure-equity trust" to avoid paying income tax and protect all one's assets from creditors. Does this trust work, and if it does, why isn't everyone using it?*

The easiest answer to this question is the old proviso, "If it sounds too good to be true, it probably is." Some people are truly convinced that the "pure-equity trust" (also called a "constitutional trust," "business trust," and similar names) is perfectly legal, and they can even cite court cases to support their point. Until recently there has not been much in the way of convincing evidence to show that such trusts are fraudulent and that the IRS will disallow them and assess penalties and interest against their makers.

Thankfully, the IRS has issued IRS Notice 97-24, which specifically acknowledges that this trust is an "abusive trust arrangement" and is illegal no matter how you go about it or what you call it.

⚖ *I've just learned, through the Internet, about a type of trust that totally avoids all income, gift, and estate taxes and is totally private—even the IRS can't find out what's in the trust. I'm*

thinking about putting my assets into this kind of trust. What do you think?

Using such a "trust" is the same as handling radioactive material and not worrying about getting radiation poisoning. Be aware that various types of so-called trusts—known as "Rockefeller trusts," "constitutional trusts," "common law trusts," and the like—are not the kinds of trusts that reputable estate planning attorneys produce. They are documents which con men produce, and they are becoming more prevalent. Indeed, use of these fraudulent trusts has become such a problem that the Internal Revenue Service is now taking an aggressive stand against them. All individuals who are involved and have such trusts will come under IRS scrutiny. And it appears that the IRS has never lost a case when challenging any of these trusts. A bogus document does not become legitimate simply by calling it a trust.

   🖎 *Some of these claims sound a little like those described previously in this book. How can I distinguish a fraudulent or abusive trust from a legitimate trust?*

Typically, fraudulent trusts are offered by nonattorneys who promise clients that they are creating a special "secret, elite trust," only known about and used by the wealthy and powerful, in order to eliminate *all* taxes. They are usually promoted with promises of tax benefits and no meaningful change in the makers' control over their assets, even though the trusts are irrevocable and all the makers' assets must be assigned to the trusts.

Typically, promoters make one or more of the following claims as to what the trust can do:

- Eliminate all estate and gift taxes.
- Allow income tax deductions for personal expenses paid on behalf of the maker by the trust.
- Allow depreciation for the maker's house and furnishings.
- Give a stepped-up basis for property transferred to the trust.
- Reduce or eliminate self-employment taxes.
- Reduce or eliminate income taxes, including capital gain taxes.
- Shelter all assets from the claims of creditors, even though the maker has full use of the assets.

None of these claims is true.

Typically, these trusts employ a method of hiding the true ownership of the assets they hold. These arrangements can utilize more than one irrevocable trust, each holding different assets of the taxpayer. Sometimes a foreign or charitable type of trust is involved, although with a charitable trust, there is personal use of the assets in some manner.

The abusive trust usually has the original owner of the assets maintaining control over the assets after they are transferred to the trust. The owner retains true control over the financial benefits of the trust. The trust may have a trustee, who will be the promoter or a friend of the maker, who simply carries out the instructions of the maker. Sometimes, the trustee gives the owner checks that are presigned by the trustee.

⚕ What are the consequences of setting up an abusive trust?

Currently, pure-equity trusts, constitutional trusts, and all other such trusts are being characterized by the IRS as "abusive trust arrangements." Under a program called National Compliance Strategy, the IRS is currently investigating these types of trust arrangements and subjecting the promoters and involved taxpayers to civil and criminal penalties. A national coordinated enforcement initiative is being made to catch the abusive trust schemes.

The IRS easily attacks the validity of these trusts by using legal principles applicable to trusts. Substance over form always controls taxation. For example, if personal expenses (education, personal travel, maintenance of residence) are being deducted, the IRS characterizes the whole operation as a "sham transaction." In addition to being fraudulent, abusive trusts are expensive. Many of them are sold by fly-by-night operations that charge between $5000 and $10,000 to create a trust. Remember, when the IRS starts investigating the taxpayers who made these trusts, the promoters will be long gone with no forwarding addresses, leaving their victims to fend for themselves against the IRS.

⚕ How can I dissolve my pure-equity trust and get control of my assets back?

This question is very important. It is not likely that the trust can be dissolved, because it is irrevocable. We have been successful in court by proving fraud in the making of such trusts. This approach is very expensive and time-consuming, and it does not always turn out the way you want.

Taking assets out of the trust is usually the better way to get control of them. Usually, these trusts are so poorly drafted and implemented that a good estate planning attorney can determine a sound legal basis for gaining control of the trustees and removing the assets from the trust.

Even if either of these techniques is successful, there are still tax consequences. The IRS will require the payment of back taxes and will almost always assess penalties and interest.

⚜ *If these trusts are not legal, why do people use them?*

Promoters sell these trusts by using various deceptive tactics, such as telling prospective customers that the U.S. Constitution gives them the right to make this type of trust to avoid income and other taxes. They tell their customers that attorneys are not needed and will only cause problems. Information is handed out stating that these trusts avoid all estate taxes as well as probate and will pass assets to heirs according to the maker's wishes. Lastly, they are sold as creditor protection trusts that will make the assets invulnerable to creditors and judgments. None of these statements is true.

chapter 8

Charitable Planning

CHARITABLE GIVING

⋇ *Why does a person give to charity?*

Many people give to charity because they are philanthropic. They feel they can benefit society by giving to organizations they believe in.

⋇ *I am mostly interested in giving assets to my children and other members of my family. Why should I consider charitable planning?*

If a combination of your and your spouse's estates creates a taxable estate, and you do not do any charitable planning, you will nevertheless be a philanthropist. Your charity of choice will be the federal Treasury, and your charitable beneficiary will be government largess. You will, in effect, be an involuntary philanthropist.

You have the choice today to decide whether you will be a voluntary philanthropist or an involuntary philanthropist. You have no ability to name a bridge or to put your name on a pothole or on a jet for the military; Congress will use its judgment in determining how to spend up to 55 percent of your estate, and it won't even say "thank you."

By designing a charitable estate plan, you can decide to whom your funds will be distributed and for what benefit or purpose, and you can retain the right to add or remove charities until your death. You can become a voluntary philanthropist rather than an involuntary philanthropist.

⋆ *I paid taxes on my money when I made it, and I do not want to pay another dime to the government. Will charitable planning help me?*

Yes. It can get your money where you want it to go; keep succeeding family generations involved in its disbursement; provide you with major capital gain, ordinary-income, and estate tax savings, and heighten your and your loved ones' lives.

⋆ *Can I actually "make money" by giving to charity?*

If you plan your charitable gifts wisely, the combination of tax savings and financial benefits can make your charitable sacrifices pleasurable and beneficial for you and your family. The key is to plan your gifts carefully and properly.

⋆ *If I give property to charity, won't I be disinheriting my children?*

Charitable planning often focuses on giving away that part of a person's capital that would not have been passed to his or her heirs anyway. There are two types of individual capital: personal capital and social capital. *Personal capital* is the portion of your estate that you control and can pass to your heirs. *Social capital* consists of the assets you cannot pass on to heirs—capital which will be paid in taxes unless you direct it instead to charities of your choice.

Many families who engage in charitable planning are not giving away their personal capital but, instead, are controlling and redirecting their social capital, which will otherwise go to the state or federal government.

Traditional estate planning has focused entirely on personal capital and ignored social capital. With inadequate or no planning, as much as 55 percent of a family's assets may be lost to taxes; this means that in many estates 100 percent of the planning effort is focused on only 45 percent of the estate's assets.

Few people believe that the government is doing a good job of directing how our taxes—our social capital—are being spent. Unfortunately, few people know that through creative estate planning it is within their power to control how their estate tax dollars will be spent. It is possible for people to keep all of their social capital in their own community, to be spent according to their own values, instead of sending it to the government.

Quite often, by focusing some attention on controlling social capital, you can significantly improve your financial well-being, increase the capital being passed on to your heirs, and guarantee that 100 percent of your social capital is spent on causes and organizations which you believe are worthwhile. Furthermore, you have the option, if you are insurable, of creating a wealth replacement trust to purchase life insurance on your life that will replace the wealth you redirected to charity (which otherwise would have gone to the government).

Planned charitable giving can—with tax benefits—generate additional spendable income which you can leverage by purchasing life insurance through an irrevocable life insurance trust, replacing the value of the assets you give to charity, and passing those assets on to your heirs completely free of estate and gift taxes.

⚜ *There are so many charities. How do people decide which one to benefit?*

One of the greatest philanthropists in history was Andrew Carnegie, the steel magnate. He said, "The main consideration should be to help those that help themselves; to provide part of the means by which those who desire to improve may do so; to give those who desire to rise the aid by which they may rise."

Whichever charities you choose, you are in a better position than the government to determine what needs to be done with your social capital.

⚜ *I would like to make a gift to charity but do not have the financial means available. Are there any alternatives?*

Outright gifts during life can be made only by persons who can afford to do so. However, charitable giving can include split-interest trusts.

INTER VIVOS SPLIT-INTEREST CHARITABLE TRUSTS

⚜ *What are split-interest trusts?*

Split-interest trusts are special irrevocable trusts which provide a benefit both to charity and to noncharities—the donor and his or her family members. These trusts provide that their income and principal are to be distributed or split between these two different types of beneficiaries.

Split-interest trusts have gained popularity because they can satisfy personal financial needs as well as philanthropic desires. The most commonly used split-interest trust is the charitable remainder trust. A less frequently used split-interest trust is the charitable lead trust.

Charitable Remainder Trusts

Features of CRTs

⅍ *What is a charitable remainder trust?*

A *charitable remainder trust (CRT)* is an irrevocable trust created for the purpose of holding assets given to the trust by a donor during the donor's lifetime or upon the donor's death.

A CRT is a split-interest trust in that its donated assets are shared between noncharitable beneficiaries and charitable beneficiaries. Typically, a CRT is designed to pay income to one or more noncharitable trust beneficiaries (usually the donor and the donor's spouse) for life or for a term of years, after which the remainder of the trust assets are paid to or held for qualified charitable beneficiaries.

The percentage of income that must be paid annually to the noncharitable income beneficiaries cannot be less than 5 percent of the value of the trust assets. There is no limit as to the number or type of income beneficiaries (individuals, corporations, trusts, etc.), except that at least one income beneficiary *must* be a taxable entity and that unborn individuals (such as grandchildren not yet born when the trust is created) do not qualify unless the trust's duration is limited to a term of years.

A CRT can continue for the lifetimes of the persons selected as income beneficiaries or for a term of years not to exceed 20. When the last income beneficiary dies or the term of years expires, all assets remaining in the trust must be distributed to one or more charities, called *charitable remaindermen.*

⅍ *How does a CRT work?*

To understand how a CRT works, let's look at an example of a typical situation in which a CRT is used:

> Mr. and Mrs. Hastings have stock for which they paid $10,000. The stock has grown in value over the years and is now worth $110,000. The

stock pays them a dividend of $1500 per year, which is a 1.36 percent return. Mr. and Mrs. Hastings are each 61 years old. Their total estate is large enough for this stock to be taxable in their estate at a 50 percent marginal tax rate.

If the Hastings sell the stock, they will have a capital gain of $100,000 ($110,000 sale price – $10,000 basis). Their federal capital gain tax rate is currently 20 percent. Accordingly, if the Hastings sell the stock, they will pay a $20,000 capital gain tax, leaving them with only $90,000 ($110,000 sales price – $20,000 tax) to invest. If they invest the $90,000 and receive a 7 percent return, they will receive $6300 in income.

Instead of selling the stock, the Hastings can create a CRT and donate their stock to it. The CRT then sells the stock. Since the CRT is charitable in nature, it pays no capital gain tax. Accordingly, the trust now has $110,000 to invest.

The Hastings can write into the trust that they want a 7 percent annual income from the trust. They will then be receiving $7700 per year in income. This income will continue to be paid to the Hastings or, after one of them dies, to the surviving spouse for life. Upon the death of both Mr. and Mrs. Hastings, the balance of the funds in the CRT will be paid to a charity which Mr. and Mrs. Hastings designate.

When the trust is signed and the Hastings contribute their stock to it, they are making a charitable contribution of a portion of the value of the stock. The value of the charitable deduction that the Hastings receive is the original value of the gift less the present value of the income going to the Hastings on the basis of their actuarial life expectancies. In the case of the Hastings, they receive a charitable deduction of $23,770 (based on a 7 percent rate from IRS tables for the month of contribution), which will save income tax of $9508 (assuming a 40 percent tax rate).

Since the stock is now in an irrevocable trust, the $110,000 has been removed from the Hastings' estate for estate tax purposes, thus saving $55,000 in estate taxes ($110,000 × 50 percent marginal estate tax rate). Upon the death of both Mr. and Mrs. Hastings, the remainder of the proceeds in the trust will go to the charity or charities of their choice.

⚜ Can someone with a modest estate benefit by creating a CRT?

A CRT can provide substantial benefits to persons with modest estates. Generally, individuals with smaller estates desire to maximize the income provided by their investments, and they can do so by using a CRT to convert highly appreciated but low-income-producing assets into investments which will provide a substantially greater income. At the same time, they will not lose a significant portion of the investments to capital gain taxes.

⋇ *Are there any restrictions with respect to the amount of remainder interest that is given to the charity at the termination of a charitable remainder trust?*

The Taxpayer Relief Act of 1997 requires that the value of the charitable remainder, with respect to any transfer to a CRT, be at least 10 percent of the net fair market value of the property transferred to the trust on the date of contribution. If the transfer fails the 10 percent test, the trust may be reformed, amended, or constructed in such a way as to reduce the payout rate or term of the trust in order to meet the test.

If an additional contribution is made to a CRT created before July 28, 1997, and it does not meet the 10 percent requirement, that contribution will be treated as if it had been made to a new trust that does not meet the 10 percent requirement but it will not affect the status of the original CRT.

⋇ *Are there drawbacks to using a charitable remainder trust?*

The major drawback of a CRT is that, after the deaths of the trust maker and his or her spouse, the property remaining in the trust generally goes to charities rather than to the maker's children. However, this need not be an obstacle for you. First, your children (and grandchildren) may have already received or be receiving substantial gifts from you. Second, if you wish to provide additional distributions for these beneficiaries, you can do so through life insurance and keep that insurance free of estate or gift tax.

⋇ *If I put property in a CRT, will I lose control over it?*

Yes and no. Whether you keep your property in your name or contribute it to a CRT, you will totally control the property and may make decisions regarding it. However, once you fund your CRT, you will no longer have control over your property as owner but will have control over it as trustee of the trust. As trustee, you can make *all* decisions as to how the trust's assets are invested.

⋇ *What are the major advantages of a CRT?*

A CRT is exempt from income, capital gain, gift, and estate taxes. The donor receives income and estate tax deductions for contributions to the CRT based on the remainder value.

⅍ *Can you give me an overview of the benefits of a CRT to the donor?*

You must want to make gifts to charity. A CRT is not a tax shelter that you invest in to make a return. A CRT is first and foremost a method to benefit charity. If that is your intent, a gift to a CRT gives you, as the donor, the following benefits:

- You receive a current charitable income tax deduction for the present value of the remainder interest, that is, the portion which will go to the charity.
- Your assets are transferred to the CRT and may be subsequently sold without the imposition of federal income tax on any gain realized.
- The noncharitable beneficiaries may receive more income after the transfer than the asset was earning before the transfer.
- You can retain control over the designation of the charity that is to ultimately receive the remainder.
- If you are the trustee, you may control the investment of the CRT's assets.
- You can receive recognition during your lifetime for a generous gift to charity.

⅍ *What types of assets are the best to give to a charitable remainder trust?*

The best assets to give to a CRT are highly appreciated assets in which the maker has a low basis. If an individual sells these assets without using a CRT, the gain on the sale will be subject to capital gain tax.

An additional advantage of transferring to a CRT highly appreciated assets which make up a major portion of an individual's estate is that doing so allows the tax-free diversification of a person's portfolio (so that all his or her eggs are not in one basket) and, at the same time, often permits an increase in the level of income produced.

⅍ *What kind of property can be contributed to a charitable remainder trust?*

A wide variety of assets are suitable for contribution to a charitable remainder trust. Safe assets include cash, publicly and privately owned stock, debt-free real estate, and most tangible personal property such as antiques and stamp collections.

Some assets create tax problems or cannot be used at all. Examples of these types of property are active trades or businesses, professional corporation stock, S corporation stock, debt-encumbered property, master limited partnership interests, and property which has environmental problems covered by federal or state regulations.

≱ *Since the Taxpayer Relief Act of 1997, are there any types of property that are more beneficial than others to contribute?*

Yes. One of the major factors leading some taxpayers to contribute highly appreciated assets to charity is the desire to avoid the capital gain taxes that would be incurred on the sale of such assets. Now that Congress has lowered the capital gain rate to 20 percent on most appreciated property, the benefit of capital gain tax avoidance, while still substantial, is not as great as it was in the past.

Congress did not, however, lower the capital gain rate on contributions of tangible personal property, such as coin collections and antique car collections. Therefore, the capital gain avoidance benefit might be greater if the contributed property consisted of appreciated tangible personal property, as opposed to appreciated stock. This benefit, however, must be weighed against certain limitations on the amount of the deduction that is applicable to contributions of tangible personal property if the property is unrelated to the charity's tax-exempt purposes.

≱ *Can my CRT receive my retirement benefits?*

You may not transfer your interest in a qualified retirement plan or an IRA into a CRT during your lifetime; however, you may name your CRT as the death beneficiary of your qualified plan or IRA. A qualified plan and an IRA are excellent assets to make payable to a CRT at your death (a *testamentary transfer*) because the CRT can receive distributions from the plan or IRA and offset the income taxes due with available charitable deductions.

Qualified plans and IRAs are unique assets that may be taxed at over 80 percent at the highest tax brackets. When the owner of the plan or IRA dies, the value of the assets in the plan or IRA is subject to estate tax and the noncharitable recipient of income from the plan or IRA is subject to income tax on the distributions received. People are invariably shocked when they discover that what they viewed as a significant asset in their estates will be decimated by taxation and, consequently, that very little of this asset will ultimately be passed on to their heirs.

A testamentary transfer of the benefits from a qualified plan or from an IRA into a CRT allows you, as the trust maker, to direct where and how your *social capital* (the substantial amount which would have gone to the IRS as taxes) will be spent. It allows your surviving spouse to receive a fixed percentage of the CRT for his or her life, with income tax payable only on the amounts actually distributed to your spouse.

Before designating a CRT as the beneficiary of your qualified plan or IRA, you must consider that your surviving spouse will lose the right to principal from the plan or IRA after it is transferred. Your surviving spouse's financial needs, security, and level of comfort must all be considered in determining if qualified plan or IRA benefits should be contributed to a CRT.

⚰ *I have highly appreciated assets I would like to transfer to a CRT. They are, however, mortgaged. Can I still transfer them to the CRT?*

The short answer is no. Mortgaged assets are not generally suitable, especially if you are liable for the mortgage debt. You may realize taxable income and, at the same time, disqualify the CRT from the tax-exempt status you are hoping to give it. You can, however, consider partitioning the property or paying it off by using a swing loan. *Partitioning property* means that you divide the property into pieces, keeping the mortgage on the piece that you do not put into a CRT but freeing up another piece that can be contributed to your CRT free from the mortgage.

⚰ *Can I use a CRT to increase my income?*

Because a CRT is exempt from capital gain taxes, it sometimes makes sense to contribute highly appreciated property, such as stock, to a CRT that provides you with a lifetime income. When the property is sold by the CRT, no capital gain taxes are paid, leaving a much larger principal base from which to generate an income.

⚰ *For how many years can a charitable remainder trust be in existence?*

The length of time a charitable remainder trust can remain in effect depends upon the identification of the income beneficiaries. If the income beneficiaries are named individuals, the trust can continue for the lifetime of the named individuals. If the income beneficiaries are parties other than individuals, such as other trusts, the term of the trust must be stated in years for a period not to exceed 20 years.

⚖ *In what situations can a CRT be a useful planning tool?*

A CRT is a great way to accomplish at least two, and maybe three, estate planning goals with one tool:

1. A CRT enables you to convert low-basis, low-income investments to higher-income, diversified investments without paying capital gain tax.
2. A CRT enables you to make gifts to charitable organizations that are important to you.
3. When combined with life insurance planning, a CRT enables you to pass on the value of your estate to your children and other beneficiaries with no estate tax due.

The choice, when using CRT planning, is not whether to direct your assets to your children or to a charity but, rather, whether to direct your assets to the government in estate taxes or to a charity. Therefore, the only question is whether you want to maintain control over what is done with your assets after your death. If they go to the government in estate taxes, you lose control. If they go to charitable organizations which you have chosen, you retain control over what happens with and to them.

⚖ *When does it make sense to use a CRT?*

A CRT is a sensible option when you:

- Have specific highly appreciated assets that you would like to sell without paying capital gain tax
- Want to diversify your entire portfolio without paying capital gain tax to do so
- Need to increase your income
- Want to benefit charitable causes after your death with dollars that would otherwise go to the government

Trustees of CRTs

⚖ *Whom should I name as the trustee of my CRT?*

Most trust makers name themselves and their spouses.

⚜ *Are there instances when I shouldn't act as my own trustee?*

There are three instances when it may not be advisable for you to do so:

1. When an asset whose value is hard to determine or questionable is being transferred to the trust
2. When a determination is made to distribute income to the income beneficiaries (the trust makers) from a variable annuity within a trust
3. When the terms of the trust authorize the trustee to "spray" or "sprinkle" income to the trust beneficiaries at the trustee's discretion

In any of these circumstances, trust makers serving as trustees must name an *independent special trustee* to sell the hard-to-value assets or to make the annuity distribution decisions. The independent special trustee, as the name implies, must be independent; this trustee cannot be related to or controlled (including employed) by the trust makers.

As to other assets and for other trust actions, the trust makers may continue to act as sole trustees. Once the special assets are transferred, sold, or valued by the independent special trustee or the withdrawals from the annuity are approved, the trust makers may again act as sole trustees.

⚜ *Can I be both the sole lifetime beneficiary and the trustee of my CRT?*

If you designate yourself as trustee and sole lifetime beneficiary, the trust property in the CRT will initially be included in your estate for tax purposes. However, you will receive a deduction for the amount passing to charity. Since all of the trust property will pass to charity upon your death, there are no adverse tax consequences to being both sole lifetime beneficiary and trustee.

⚜ *Can I give assets to a charitable remainder trust but still retain control over the investment decisions?*

You can retain complete control over decisions on how the property is to be invested.

Making changes to CRTs

⚜ *What if I want to change my charitable trust after I have signed it?*

Since a CRT is irrevocable, there are limits on your ability to change it once you have signed it. You can, however, by including appropriate language in the trust document, reserve certain rights such as the rights to fill trustee vacancies, change trustees, change charitable beneficiaries, and revoke noncharitable income interests.

⚜ Can the charitable remainder beneficiaries of my CRT be changed later?

Yes. Even though a CRT is irrevocable, your CRT can be drafted to allow you, your trustee, or even other income beneficiaries to change the charitable remainder beneficiaries of the trust at any time before the death of the last income beneficiary. A change in charitable beneficiary is made by a written document.

Income beneficiaries of CRTs

⚜ Whom can I name as the income beneficiaries of my CRT?

You can name yourself, your spouse, your children, or your grandchildren; a significant other; or multiple beneficiaries in a myriad of combinations.

⚜ Can I name a trust to be the income beneficiary of my charitable remainder trust?

In 1997, the IRS pronounced that a trust cannot be a CRT income beneficiary unless the trust's sole purpose is to receive and administer distributions for an incompetent beneficiary's benefit.

Taxes and CRTs

⚜ If I give appreciated assets to a CRT, can I avoid paying capital gain taxes when those assets are sold by my trustee?

Yes, although in a technical sense you are not *avoiding* capital gain tax but *deferring* it. A CRT must realize capital gains when selling appreciated assets. This means that the trustee has to maintain records that track any gain on the sale of assets by the CRT, but the gain is not recognizable by the CRT since the trust is exempt from income tax (as long as it doesn't have unrelated-business income).

However, the CRT's untaxed gain may be taxed to you in the future, as the income beneficiary of the trust, but only to the extent that the required income distributions to you exceed the ordinary income earned by the CRT, and then only at capital gain rates. However, the benefit you derive from delaying the taxes that you would have paid had you sold your appreciated assets and been subject to an immediate tax is considerable.

☙ What are the federal estate tax consequences of creating a CRT during my lifetime?

If you create a CRT during your lifetime and direct that the income payments be made to you for life and thereafter to your spouse for life, with the remainder passing to a specified charitable organization, then, in addition to the income tax deduction, there are beneficial gift and estate tax consequences, as you have made two gifts:

- A gift of the survivor income interest to your spouse, which qualifies for the gift tax marital deduction
- A gift of the remainder interest to charity, which qualifies for the gift tax charitable deduction

The value of the trust assets will be included in your estate, but your estate will have both a marital deduction for the value of your spouse's survivor income interest (if he or she survives you) and a charitable deduction for the value of the remainder passing to charity, so the trust assets will not be subject to estate tax.

☙ Why isn't the CRT property taxed in the estate of the maker?

Because a CRT trust maker retains the right to the income until death, it is included in the trust maker's gross estate for estate tax purposes. However, since all the remaining property will be distributed to charity, the value of the property is deducted from the gross estate before calculating the taxable estate.

☙ What if the income beneficiary is not the trust maker?

If someone other than the trust maker is the income beneficiary, none of the remaining property in the CRT is included in the trust maker's gross estate for estate tax purposes. This is because the trust maker had already given away all interests in the property before his or her death.

☙ What are the gift tax consequences of setting up a CRT?

The gift to the CRT consists of two parts: a gift to the income beneficiary and a gift to a charity. If the income beneficiary is the trust maker or his or her spouse, there is obviously no gift tax. If the income beneficiary is someone other than the trust maker's spouse, such as the trust maker's child or parent, the gift is taxable.

The value of the gift is determined by calculating the present value of the income stream given, taking into account the income beneficiary's life expectancy (from IRS tables), the specified payout percentage, and the applicable federal rate of interest specified by the IRS for the period in which the gift to the CRT is made. The gift of the remainder interest to a charity is not subject to gift tax.

♨ If my spouse is an income beneficiary, will he have to pay gift tax?

If you name your spouse as an income beneficiary, there will be no gift tax due because of the unlimited marital deduction.

♨ What are the tax results if I name my children as the successor income beneficiaries of my CRT?

If the trust maker names a child as the initial or successor income beneficiary—the person who receives income after the deaths of his or her parents—a taxable gift has been made to the child equal to the value of the child's life interest. If the gift is after the deaths of the child's parents, it is categorized as a gift of a future interest. This gift will not qualify for the annual exclusion, and gift tax will be due if the calculated tax is not offset by the trust maker's lifetime unified credit.

This potential tax catastrophe can be avoided if the trust maker reserves the testamentary right to revoke the child's right to future payments and accelerate the charitable remainder. Since the trust maker has retained the power to change the successor interest, the gift to the child is incomplete for gift tax purposes, and no gift tax will be due. It is unimportant whether or not the trust maker actually exercises the right to revoke the successor interest; the mere fact that he or she has the right to do so is sufficient.

♨ What are the income tax consequences of setting up a CRT?

In the year in which you establish a CRT, you receive an income tax deduction for a charitable gift.

- The gift is the present value of the remainder interest that will pass to charity when the income term is ended.
- The amount of the charitable deduction is the present value of the remainder interest.

When the income interest is for your life, the length of the term is determined actuarially, on the basis of your present age and IRS life expectancy tables. The older the income beneficiary is at the time the CRT is established, the smaller the value of the income interest going to the noncharitable beneficiaries and the larger the value of the remainder interest going to charity—which creates a larger charitable gift deduction.

⋙ *When I give assets to my CRT, how will my income tax deduction be calculated?*

The amount of your tax deduction for gifts made to your CRT is determined by calculating the present value of the remainder interest that your CRT will distribute to charity. The calculation of the present value of a future interest is somewhat complicated and takes into account the following five factors:

1. The fair market value of the property you are giving to the trust (adjusted for the amount of any ordinary-income, short-term gains, or recapture attributable to the property)
2. The type of trust you've created, that is, an annuity trust or a unitrust
3. The number of years before the charity will receive its remainder interest, based upon actuarial tables if the trust was created for the lifetime of the income beneficiaries or upon the term of years specified in the trust
4. The payout rate which you've established to provide for the income beneficiaries
5. A floating interest rate published each month by the IRS

⋙ *Is there a limit to the amount of the tax deduction that I can claim in any year?*

Yes. The limit is usually determined by three factors:

1. The type of assets you give to your trust (i.e., cash, long-term or short-term appreciated property, property having recaptured depreciation or depletion, or ordinary income property)
2. Your adjusted gross income
3. The type of charity that is the charitable beneficiary of the CRT (i.e., public charity or private foundation)

⋙ *What if I can't use all of the tax deduction in the year I make the gift?*

If the full amount of the tax deduction cannot be used in the year you make the gift to the trust, you can carry it forward and deduct it in the 5 years following the year of your initial gift.

⋙ *What are the limitations on gifts to public charities?*

If a charity is a *public charity,* such as a nonprofit school, church, or hospital, and you are making an outright lifetime gift of cash, you may deduct up to 50 percent of your contribution base (your adjusted gross income, without regard to net-operating-loss carrybacks).

Thus, if you have a contribution base of $50,000 and make a $25,000 cash gift to a public charity, you may deduct the entire $25,000 in the year of the gift. If you give $30,000, you may deduct only $25,000 in the year of the gift and carry over the additional $5000 for up to 5 more years. Because of the 50 percent limit, public charities are often referred to as "50 percent–type organizations."

However, even when you are making a contribution to a 50 percent–type organization, if your gift consists of stock, real estate, or other capital assets you've owned for more than 1 year (long-term capital gain property), your deduction is, in general, limited to 30 percent of your contribution base.

⋙ *What are the limitations on gifts to 30 percent–type organizations?*

In general, a charity that does not qualify as a public charity is labeled a "30 percent–type organization"; a private foundation is the most prominent example of this class. The ceiling on deductibility for gifts to such organizations is 30 percent of your contribution base. Thus, if you have a contribution base of $50,000 and give a $25,000 cash contribution to a private foundation, you can deduct only $15,000 in the year of the gift and carry over the remainder for up to 5 additional years.

Deductions for gifts to 30 percent–type organizations, including private foundations, are further diminished when the property given is something other than cash or ordinary-income property. For example, if you give stock or real estate that you've owned for more than a year to a private foundation, your deduction is limited to 20 percent of your contribution base and may be further limited to your tax basis (typically, what you paid for the property).

There are a few exceptions to the above classifications. For example, some private operating foundations, supporting organizations, pass-through foundations, and pooled-fund foundations are 50 percent–type organizations for some income tax deduction purposes.

The deduction rules are complex and interrelated. Only the high-lights have been touched upon here. It's extremely important to consult with a knowledgeable professional before making any substantial chari-table contribution.

🔺 *Does the trust have to pay income tax on income it does not distribute?*

A CRT is a nontaxable entity unless it generates unrelated-business taxable income (UBTI). Therefore, it does not normally pay income tax.

Types of CRTs

🔺 *Are there different types of charitable remainder trusts?*

Yes. There are three primary types of CRTs:

- *Charitable remainder annuity trust (CRAT):* The CRAT pays a fixed amount, at least annually, to the income beneficiaries on the basis of the initial value of trust principal contributed to it.
- *Charitable remainder unitrust (CRUT):* The CRUT pays a fixed percentage at least annually to the income beneficiaries but is val-ued every year to determine the amount to be distributed.
- *Charitable remainder unitrust with net income makeup provisions (NIMCRUT):* The NIMCRUT pays income just like a CRUT, but it allows the income beneficiary to defer current payments to be paid later out of the trust's income.

🔺 *What is the difference between a charitable remainder annuity trust and a charitable remainder unitrust?*

The primary difference between a CRAT and a CRUT is the method used to calculate distributions to the income beneficiaries.

Under a CRAT, the annuity amount (distribution for the first year and each successive year) is based upon the initial value of the assets contributed to the trust. Since revaluation of the trust assets is not allowed, no gifts can be made to the CRAT after the date of the initial contribution.

With a CRUT, the unitrust amount (the annual distribution to the income beneficiaries) must be based upon the value of the trust assets determined annually, usually at the beginning of the year. Consequently, the amount of the distribution to income beneficiaries can fluctuate depending on the value of the trust assets.

⚘ How is the payout amount from a CRT determined?

The trust maker transfers the property to be donated to the trustee in exchange for the trustee's agreement to pay a stream of income to the income beneficiaries for their lives or for specific periods of time. The amount of income to be paid is expressed as a percentage of the trust property (the minimum amount by law that must be taken is 5 percent).

If the trust is a CRAT, the payout amount is specified as a percentage of the value of the donated property at the time it is given to the trust. Unless and until the trust property is completely depleted, a trust maker will always receive the specified payout amount, even if the trust earns a lesser amount of income and the trustee is required to invade principal to make up the amount distributed.

If the trust is a CRUT, the payout is specified as a percentage of the value of the trust property as determined annually. If the trust property appreciates in value, the payout amount will also increase; if the property decreases in value, the payout amount will become smaller.

⚘ I understand that there are some new laws about CRTs. What are they?

There are two changes:

- The payout rate cannot be greater than 50 percent.
- The amount going to the charitable beneficiary (and the available charitable deduction) cannot be less than 10 percent of the fair market value of the property originally donated.

The 50 percent payout change was initiated to stop the perceived abuses by wealthy taxpayers who were using the system to avoid capital gain taxes while pocketing most of the money that Congress contemplated would go to charity.

The 10 percent requirement is simply the flip side of the same coin: Congress wanted to make sure that the remainder interest ultimately passing to charity would be at least 10 percent of the amount originally contributed to the CRT.

The second limitation means that certain taxpayers who want to create CRTs cannot do so because they are too young or because current interest rates are too low.

Charitable remainder annuity trusts

🖎 *I heard that the law just changed on charitable remainder annuity trusts. Do they still work?*

Yes, they still work.

🖎 *What is a charitable remainder annuity trust?*

A *charitable remainder annuity trust (CRAT)* is a type of CRT in which the income—called the *annuity amount*—paid to the income beneficiaries of the trust each year is equal to a fixed amount. This amount, which can be expressed as either a specified dollar amount or a percentage of the initial fair market value of the trust, is chosen by the trust maker before the trust is drafted. The annuity amount for a CRAT must be at least 5 percent of the initial fair market value of the trust.

Because the income paid to an income beneficiary is based upon the initial value of the trust, the income paid remains constant regardless of whether the value of the trust increases or decreases. For example, if a trust maker creates a $100,000 CRAT and chooses an annuity amount of $8000 (whether expressed as an actual dollar amount, $8000, or as a percentage, 8 percent, of the initial fair market value of the trust), the annuity amount remains a constant $8000 per year.

Also, if the CRAT does not earn enough income in a year to pay the annuity amount, capital gains or principal must be used to make up the difference.

🖎 *What are the payout limitations on a charitable remainder annuity trust?*

The annual income the CRAT pays must be at least 5 percent each year of its original principal amount but not greater than 50 percent of its originally contributed principal amount. (Congress was concerned that without this limitation, the CRAT could eventually run out of money and the charity would ultimately receive nothing.)

🖎 *How are these calculations made?*

All CRT calculations are based upon life expectancy tables issued by the Internal Revenue Service, interest rates prevailing at the time of the contribution, and the age of the noncharitable lifetime beneficiary or the term of the CRAT, whichever is applicable.

☠ What is the 5 percent probability test?

A CRAT is not valid if there is a greater than 5 percent probability that the payments to the noncharitable beneficiary (usually you and your spouse) will exhaust the CRAT assets before the deaths of those beneficiaries. This probability is calculated on the basis of the annuity amount, the age or ages of the noncharitable beneficiaries, and an assumed rate of return (geared to the federal government's borrowing rates).

☠ Is a CRAT often described as a "guaranteed-income trust"?

Yes. The reason for describing this trust as a *guaranteed-income trust* is that the amount that will be paid monthly or quarterly each year is determined at the time the trust is set up. In that sense, the income is guaranteed under the terms of the trust.

☠ Can I specify as high an annual payout as I want?

No. The new law makes it clear that you are limited to a 50 percent income interest based upon the initial value of the trust.

☠ In simple terms, in what situations is a CRAT useful?

A CRAT is useful if you believe that the trust assets will depreciate rather than appreciate over time, or if you simply do not want the market risk that they might do so.

☠ If the property I contribute to my CRT loses value, will the charitable beneficiaries have to continue my payments?

No. It sounds like you're confusing a CRT with a charitable gift annuity, which we discuss later.

The trustee of your CRT is obligated to pay you the required income amount and must do everything possible, including selling the property in the CRT, to produce that amount. However, the charitable remaindermen have no obligation to pay you anything.

☠ Can you summarize the financial requirements that the terms of a CRAT must meet?

The requirements now are:

- The CRAT must pay at least 5 percent annually to the income beneficiaries.
- The CRAT cannot pay more than 50 percent annually to the beneficiaries.
- There cannot be a greater than 5 percent chance that the assets within the CRAT will be exhausted before the trust term ends.
- The CRAT must have a minimum charitable remainder of 10 percent of the trust's initial fair market value.

Charitable remainder unitrusts

⋈ *What is a charitable remainder unitrust?*

A *charitable remainder unitrust (CRUT)* is a type of CRT in which the income paid to the income beneficiaries of the trust is equal to a fixed percentage of the annual fair market value of the trust. This percentage, which must be at least 5 percent and not more than 50 percent, is chosen by the trust maker before the trust is drafted.

Although the percentage chosen by the trust maker remains fixed, the amount to be paid—called the *unitrust amount*—to the income beneficiaries will vary depending on the fair market value of the trust each year. As the fair market value of the trust assets increases, so will the income (unitrust amount) paid to the income beneficiaries. Likewise, as the fair market value of the trust assets decreases, so will the unitrust amount.

Here is an example of how this works: If a trust maker creates a $100,000 CRUT and chooses an 8 percent payout rate, the unitrust amount for the first year is $8000. If the value of the trust in the second year rises to $110,000, the unitrust amount will be $8800. If the value of the trust in the third year falls to $90,000, the unitrust amount will be $7200.

If the trust does not earn enough income in a year to pay the unitrust amount, capital gains or principal must be used to make up the difference.

⋈ *Is there a simple way to explain CRUTs?*

A CRUT's income beneficiary receives a stated percentage of the value of the trust assets each year based on current value. If the principal goes up (inflation or real growth), the income interest goes up accordingly. If the principal goes down (deflation or poor investing), the income interest goes down accordingly.

⋈ *Do the assets of a CRUT have to be valued each year?*

Because a CRUT pays the unitrust amount to the income beneficiary on the basis of a fixed percentage of the value of the principal determined annually, the assets need to be valued annually. If the value is readily ascertainable, such as with publicly traded securities, no appraisal is required. For hard-to-value assets such as real estate or closely held business stock, a qualified appraiser must value the assets.

⋈ *Can a CRUT be created in a will or trust to take effect upon my death?*

Yes. This is a sophisticated technique that allows estate and wealth strategies planners to reduce estate taxes, benefit charity, and provide an income interest to children.

⋈ *Are there limits on the percentage a charitable remainder unitrust can pay out?*

Yes. There are three limitations:

- CRUTs have long been required to pay out a minimum of 5 percent to noncharitable beneficiaries.
- The percentage payout of a CRUT created after June 18, 1997, cannot exceed 50 percent.
- The present value of the charitable remainder interest, determined at the time of the contribution, cannot be less than 10 percent.

⋈ *What about CRUTs that were drafted before the new law took effect?*

CRUTs existing before June 19, 1997 (as to the 50 percent limitation), or before July 29, 1997 (as to the 10 percent limitation), continue to be valid, regardless of whether they satisfy the new requirements.

However, new contributions made to an existing CRUT will fail if these requirements are not satisfied after the respective effective dates.

⋈ *Does the 10 percent requirement apply to a CRUT drafted to take effect after my death?*

The 10 percent requirement does not apply to testamentary CRUTs contained in wills or living trusts executed prior to July 29, 1997, if the maker of the will or trust dies before January 1, 1999, or modifies the document before that date. Thereafter it applies.

≌ In simple terms, what is the advantage of a CRUT over a CRAT?

A CRUT gives income beneficiaries more income in periods of inflation, rising markets, and rising trust values.

Charitable remainder unitrusts with net income makeup provisions

≌ You mentioned a variation of the CRUT called a NIMCRUT. How does this work?

The *charitable remainder unitrust with net income makeup provisions (NIMCRUT)* is a special type of CRUT. The unitrust amount of a NIMCRUT is calculated by the trustee in the same manner as that of a CRUT. However, if the NIMCRUT does not earn enough income in a year to pay the unitrust amount, because the payment is limited to the income actually earned by the trust, then principal is not used to make up the difference. Instead, the trustee keeps track of any income shortage which occurs in one year and makes up that shortage by distributions of income in future years when trust income exceeds the unitrust amount. This is called the *makeup provision* of the NIMCRUT.

The makeup portion of a NIMCRUT works like an IOU. When the trust earns less income than the payout rate, the trust owes the income beneficiary more than it can pay and the shortfall is accounted for as part of the makeup account.

For example, let's assume that a trust maker creates a $100,000, 8 percent NIMCRUT. In year 1, the trust earns $8000 and pays $8000 to the beneficiary. In year 2 (assuming the $100,000 does not change in value), the trust earns $7000 ($1000 less than the required payout rate of 8 percent) and pays $7000 to the beneficiary. In year 3, the trust earns $7000 (again $1000 less than the required payout rate) and pays $7000. The makeup account at the end of year 3 equals $2000. In year 4, the trust earns $10,000, and the payout to the beneficiary is $10,000: the $8000 unitrust amount plus the $2000 makeup from years 2 and 3.

≌ Can a NIMCRUT defer income I would otherwise receive to a date when I'm in a lower income tax bracket?

An advantage of the NIMCRUT is that it allows an income beneficiary to defer trust income until he or she needs it. The deferred income can grow inside the NIMCRUT on a tax-deferred basis.

One method used to achieve this deferral of income is to have the trustee invest in a variable annuity. Because a NIMCRUT does not recognize income produced in a properly designed variable annuity until the annuity income is actually distributed to the trust, there is no income tax liability for the amounts not taken.

The income beneficiary's ability to defer income inside a NIM-CRUT while it grows on a tax-deferred basis, and the trust's ability to avoid recognizing undistributed annuity income as trust income, makes a NIMCRUT a very powerful retirement planning vehicle.

⅍ *In simple terms, what is the advantage of a NIMCRUT over a CRUT?*

A NIMCRUT:

- Allows the trust principal to grow by the amount of the retained income
- Creates higher streams of income in subsequent years
- Defers the receipt of income from current income taxation

⅍ *Is the IRS contesting the use of NIMCRUTs?*

The Internal Revenue Service has not been pleased with these vehicles and has been investigating them for some time. It appears that the IRS is continuing its investigation into CRTs that control the flow of income to the trust's beneficiary. However, given its current workload, many professionals believe that the IRS is not likely to issue its final findings until the year 2000 or later. At that time it seems very likely that the IRS will apply its rules *prospectively* rather than retroactively, so we appear to be in a NIMCRUT safe harbor.

Creditor protection with CRTs

⅍ *Can a CRT help me protect my assets from prospective creditors?*

Although seeking creditor protection is usually not a primary reason for creating a charitable trust, a CRT does provide the same type of creditor protection as any irrevocable trust provides. Since you have irrevocably transferred your property out of your name to another legal entity, a creditor cannot take that property. However, in most states, a creditor can take your right to the income from your charitable trust.

There are some methods that can be used to decrease the exposure of your income interest to creditors. One is using a NIMCRUT. In a NIMCRUT, since income can be deferred, it is possible to invest in assets that create no income for the creditor to take. You can then negotiate with the creditor and perhaps settle for pennies on the dollar while your IOU makeup account continues to build. After settling, you can have access to the amounts owed to you by the NIMCRUT when the NIMCRUT can generate that income.

If creditor protection is of great importance to you in the utilization of a CRT, it would be prudent for you not to serve as your own trustee.

≈△ *Can I make my CRT part of my will or trust so that it is funded only at my death?*

Yes, you can create a *testamentary CRT.* If you fund the CRT at your death and leave instructions that your spouse is to receive income for life from the trust, the assets passing to the trust will be included in your estate for tax purposes. However, your estate will have a marital deduction for the value of your spouse's income interest and a charitable deduction for the value, at your death, of the remainder interest, which will ultimately pass to charity. The result is that the assets included in your taxable estate are offset by the marital and charitable deductions: no tax will be due.

Wealth replacement planning

≈△ *How can I take advantage of the benefits of a CRT without reducing my children's inheritance?*

There is an often-used planning solution for those who want to take advantage of the significant tax savings that a CRT can provide but are concerned about leaving assets to a charity on death instead of to their children. The solution is to replace some or all of the value of the assets going to charity with life insurance owned in a wealth replacement trust.

A *wealth replacement trust* is an irrevocable life insurance trust which is created for the purpose of owning a policy insuring your life or a policy insuring the lives of you and your spouse (called a *survivor* or *second-to-die policy*). You can use the income tax savings from contributions to your CRT and the increased income produced by the CRT to pay a portion or all of the cost of the life insurance required to fund your wealth replacement trust.

Since the life insurance proceeds received by your children as beneficiaries of a properly created wealth replacement trust are not taxable to your estate, your children receive the full value of the proceeds.

⁂ I like the concept of a CRT but don't want to reduce my children's inheritance. What can I do to maximize their inheritance, contribute to charity, and minimize my taxes?

There are ways that you can achieve all your goals. Let's assume that you own a $1 million piece of real estate with a cost basis of zero. If you sell the property outright and pay income tax on the capital gains at 20 percent, you have $800,000 left. If you reinvest that $800,000 in an investment that yields 10 percent interest, your income will be $80,000 annually. Let's assume that you live on that interest income every year. At your death, 20 years later, the $800,000 principal is included in your estate and your estate tax bracket is 55 percent. After payment of the taxes, your family reaps the benefit of $360,000 on your original $1 million piece of property.

Now let's assume you create a CRT and transfer your $1 million piece of real estate into it. You will receive a substantial income tax deduction for your contribution to the CRT, which may put money in your pocket immediately.

The property is subsequently sold for $1 million. Because the property is in the CRT, you do not pay income tax on the capital gains. You and your spouse are the income beneficiaries of the trust. As trustee of the trust, you reinvest the entire $1 million at 10 percent, yielding $100,000 annually, $20,000 per year more than if you had sold the property outside the CRT; and over the next 20 years you will have increased your income stream by $400,000. After the deaths of both you and your spouse, the charity receives the $1 million.

We know that the value of your estate will be diminished at your death. The question is whether your children will receive $360,000 from your $1 million property or receive nothing because the property went to charity.

In our example, you, as trust maker, increased your annual income stream by $20,000 annually and received a substantial benefit from the charitable income tax deduction. You can use a fraction of this increased income or use the funds generated by your income tax deduction to pay the premiums for a $1 million life insurance policy to be held in a wealth replacement trust. Because the wealth replacement trust, not you, owns the policy, at your death the entire $1 million will be distributed to your children—estate tax–free.

This is truly a win-win situation:

- You receive a substantial income tax deduction.
- You increase your annual income stream.

- Your children receive $1 million free of income, gift, and estate tax.
- The charity or charities of your choice receive $1 million.
- The value of the property is excluded from your estate.

⚵ What is the best way to have wealth replacement life insurance as part of our CRT plan?

A second-to-die life insurance policy for husband and wife trust makers works particularly well for this purpose. The trust maker, perhaps using some or all of the income taxes saved in the year of the gifts, arranges for life insurance which will be payable to the children or for their benefit. The best way to accomplish this is to have the policy owned by someone other than the trust makers, such as the children or an irrevocable trust for the benefit of the children and other family members. That will keep the insurance proceeds out of the estate of the insured. If premiums will need to be paid on the policy in future years, the trust makers can give the money for this to the owner of the policy, using the $10,000 per donee annual gift tax exclusion.

⚵ Must I fund my wealth replacement trust with life insurance?

No, a wealth replacement trust can hold investments other than life insurance. However, since the purpose of a wealth replacement trust is to replace family wealth which would otherwise be depleted by estate taxes or charitable gifts, investing in life insurance ensures that a minimum fixed amount will be available regardless of when the insured dies.

There is no way to know how much growth securities will provide. We can assume certain rates of growth from a well-balanced portfolio of securities, but that growth occurs over time. Also, any gain on the sale of the securities will generate tax which will deplete the principal.

The growth in a life insurance policy occurs income tax–free. Additionally, the death benefit in excess of the cumulative premiums paid is not taxable income, thus providing an investment premium. Finally, life insurance will pay the face amount of the contract immediately.

Life insurance provides a specific amount of death benefit, adding stability to your planning.

Charitable Lead Trusts

⚵ What is a charitable lead trust?

A *charitable lead trust (CLT)* is another type of trust—created by the provisions of the Internal Revenue Code—that allows for charitable giving.

The CLT has charitable income beneficiaries and, typically, family members as noncharitable remaindermen beneficiaries.

⚑ Are there different types of charitable lead trusts?

A charitable lead trust is similar to a CRT in that it can be structured as either an annuity trust or a unitrust:

- *Charitable lead annuity trust (CLAT):* Under a CLAT, a fixed percentage of the original contribution is paid to a charity or charities each year, with the balance usually passing to children or grandchildren.
- *Charitable lead unitrust (CLUT):* With a CLUT, a percentage of the value of the assets is paid to a charity each year, so the assets must be valued annually to determine the amount to be paid to the charity. The balance, again, is usually paid to children or grandchildren.

⚑ How do the different types of charitable lead trusts operate?

If the return on the investment of the CLAT exceeds the amount paid to the charity, the remainder beneficiaries will ultimately receive more than the original contribution to the lead trust. On the downside, if the investments perform poorly, the amount of assets going to the remainder beneficiaries could be less than the initial distribution to the trust, since the trust principal must be used to make the annuity payment.

The annuity amount to be paid to the charity each year is established at the time the trust is created, and no additional assets can be contributed to the annuity trust during its term.

The CLUT pays a percentage of the fair market value of the trust assets to the charity each year, and the assets must be revalued each year to determine the contribution to charity. If the assets in the trust are hard to value, such as real estate or the stock of closely held corporations, it would be better to use a CLAT than a CLUT. CLUTs are best utilized to hold assets that are easy to value and are liquid.

In addition to the type of assets to be contributed to the CLT, factors to consider in determining whether to use a CLAT or a CLUT include:

- The charitable donation desired
- The desired size of the taxable gift to be distributed to the remainder beneficiaries when the trust terminates

- The rate of return the trust anticipates receiving
- Applicable interest rates

✍ With a charitable lead trust, can I name someone other than myself to receive the remainder?

Yes. In fact, in almost all cases, the recipient of the remainder of a charitable lead trust is someone other than the trust maker. One of the primary benefits of a charitable lead trust, after charitable giving, is that it removes property from the maker's estate and passes it to the maker's heirs at a future date. The value to the trust maker is that the assets are valued for gift tax purposes as the present value of the remainder interest to be transferred in the future (i.e., the present value of the assets minus the present value of the charitable income interest). It is always much less than the fair market value of the assets at transfer.

✍ We regularly give substantial amounts to charity out of our current income. Is there a way that we can make these gifts more tax-efficient and make a gift to our children as well?

People who regularly make gifts to charity should review charitable lead trust options:

- Under a *charitable lead annuity trust,* a fixed dollar amount is given to charity annually for the term or life specified. If the income from the trust is insufficient to make the annual charitable payment, the shortfall is taken out of the principal of the trust.
- Under a *charitable lead unitrust,* a fixed percentage of the fair market value of the trust assets is paid to the charity each year. Even if the assets in the trust grow in value, the charity receives the same percentage of the increase in assets.
- At the expiration of the term of years or at the death of the trust maker (whichever was specified in the document), all the assets in the charitable lead annuity trust or unitrust will be returned to the donor or to whomever was specified in the trust—almost always children or grandchildren—when it was established.

Thus, with a charitable lead trust, you can continue making regular contributions to charitable causes and ensure that the trust assets remaining after the set term, or at your death, will go to your children or grandchildren at less than fair market value.

Because the heirs have no immediate right to the assets in a charitable lead trust but, rather, are entitled to those sums only at the expiration of the term or the death of the maker, there is a substantial discount in the value of those assets for federal gift tax purposes. Discounts are generated because of the period of time during which the assets will be used for charitable purposes rather then being available to heirs.

The Internal Revenue Service publishes tables that show what the current fair market value of the assets might be, depending upon the age of the trust makers or the term of years of the charitable income interest, the income payment rate, and the federal interest rates in effect when the trust is funded.

⚲ Can you give an example of how a charitable lead trust works?

Let's use an example of a charitable lead annuity trust. The maker is a 60-year-old male who contributes $1 million to a 15-year annuity trust. Assuming that the annuity rate is 8 percent per year, the charities will be entitled each year to receive the sum of $80,000. Based on government tables and current federal applicable rates, the present value of the gift of what's left of the $1 million—which the heirs will receive in 15 years—is $252,592.

Thus, if you were the taxpayer in this example, you would be able to transfer $1 million in assets (plus any growth or appreciation on those assets or less any advance of principal) to your children and pay transfer tax based on only its $252,592 present value.

If the $252,592 gift can be covered by your unified credit amount, there will be no gift tax. You will have passed $1 million plus its appreciation and less the required income payment to your children at a cost of $252,592 of your applicable exclusion amount.

While the value of the gift will be added back for purposes of computing estate taxes on your estate (whether your death occurs during or after the 15-year trust term), only the value at the time the trust was created, $252,592, is added back, regardless of whether the $1 million of assets has appreciated since the time of the trust's creation. Further, any gift tax paid will be a credit against the eventual estate tax payable.

⚲ How are charitable lead trusts taxed?

Charitable lead trusts are subject to the general tax rules governing the treatment of all trusts. The trust is taxed on all its income, but it is entitled to all available deductions, including a deduction for any amount of gross income, without limitation, which is paid for the charitable purpose. Thus, the trust ordinarily would have little or no taxable income.

⚓ What is the difference between an inter vivos CLT and a testamentary CLT?

An *inter vivos* CLT is an irrevocable trust established during the trust maker's lifetime to provide a charity with income, discount remainder gifts to children and grandchildren, and generate income tax deductions.

A *testamentary* CLT is created in a will or revocable living trust and does not become active until after the will or trust maker's death.

⚓ What are the benefits of creating a testamentary charitable lead trust rather than creating one while I am alive?

The first benefit of a testamentary CLT is its flexibility. Because a will or revocable living trust can be changed or revised at any time before the maker's death, the charitable beneficiaries can be changed at any time.

The second benefit is its power to eliminate any federal estate tax liability regardless of the size of the trust maker's estate.

⚓ What factors must be considered in drafting a testamentary charitable lead trust?

Careful drafting of your will or revocable living trust, along with several factors that your testamentary trustees will consider, can eliminate all federal estate taxes. Factors that your trustee will consider are:

- The term of years of the annuity payment
- The value of the assets contributed to the CLT
- The percentage used to calculate the annual annuity payment to charity
- The interest rate assumption as determined by the IRS
- The calculation of the estate tax charitable deduction received at death as a result of the CLT

⚓ How can I eliminate, or "zero-out," all estate taxes using a testamentary CLT?

By mathematical calculation, it is easy to determine the length of time the trust income must be given to charity to make the remainder interest passing to children valueless for federal estate tax purposes. This period depends on a host of factors.

⅃ *Are there any disadvantages in using a testamentary CLT?*

Yes. The income amount of a CLT must be paid even in years when the income produced by the trust is inadequate. In such years, therefore, the trustee will have to spend trust principal in order to meet the income payment requirements.

⅃ *Are there different types of testamentary charitable lead trusts?*

Testamentary CLTs can be either charitable lead annuity trusts or charitable lead unitrusts, just like their inter vivos counterparts.

⅃ *When should one or the other be used?*

A testamentary CLAT should be used when you are creating a trust for the benefit of children as beneficiaries, and a testamentary CLUT should be used for the benefit of grandchildren as beneficiaries. (There are highly technical reasons for this dichotomy that are outside the scope of this book.)

⅃ *Can you summarize the benefits of a testamentary CLT?*

The testamentary CLT eliminates death taxes, benefits your favorite charities, and ultimately passes the balance on to children or grandchildren with little or no federal estate tax.

CRT versus CLT

⅃ *What do charitable remainder trusts and charitable lead trusts have in common?*

Both CRTs and CLTs:

- Were created by Congress in the Internal Revenue Code
- Are irrevocable split-interest trusts composed of an income interest and a remainder interest
- Have charitable beneficiaries and noncharitable beneficiaries
- Rely on common calculation tables in the Internal Revenue Code and on fluctuating interest rates

⅃ *What are the major differences between charitable remainder trusts and charitable lead trusts?*

In many respects, the CRT and the CLT are exact opposites of one another.

Although both result in gifts being made to charity, they differ substantially with respect to the timing of the gifts. In a charitable remainder trust, the charity receives the principal of the trust at the time the trust terminates—typically at the death of the trust maker and his or her spouse. In a charitable lead trust the principal reverts to the trust maker's family—typically children and grandchildren—at discounted values for gift tax purposes. Table 8-1 highlights the features of both.

⋟ *What are the major planning benefits of charitable remainder trusts and charitable lead trusts?*

A charitable remainder trust is typically beneficial if you want to:

- Create an income stream for yourself and your spouse.
- Diversify your portfolio and sell appreciated assets without paying capital gain taxes.
- Create income tax deductions.
- Save federal estate tax.

A charitable lead trust is often beneficial if you wish to:

- Benefit charity while you are alive.
- Transfer remainder interests to children and grandchildren at discounted gift tax values.

TABLE 8-1 Comparison of CRTs and CLTs

Features	Charitable remainder trust	Charitable lead trust
Specified income distributed	To you or family	To charity
Principal ultimately distributed	To charity	To you or family
Elimination of capital gain taxes on sale of assets	Yes	No
Income tax deduction for funding	Yes	Perhaps
Income from assets to charity	No	Yes
Federal estate tax savings	Yes	Yes
Federal gift tax savings	Yes	Yes
Ability to change charitable beneficiaries	Yes	No

- Create income tax deductions.
- Save estate tax.

✍ *What factors should I consider in deciding whether to utilize a charitable remainder trust or a charitable lead trust?*

The major factor is determining your planning motives:

- If you wish to keep the income from your assets, pass the balance to charity, and replace that balance tax-free with a wealth replacement trust, the charitable remainder strategy fits you well.
- If you wish to donate current income streams to charity and pass the principal balance in later years to children and grandchildren at discounted values for federal gift tax purposes, the charitable lead trust is for you.

OUTRIGHT GIFTS TO CHARITIES

✍ *What is the simplest and most common way to make a gift?*

The simplest way to give to a charity is to make an outright gift. Outright gifts can be made either during a person's lifetime or at death.

Donors of charitable gifts generally receive tax benefits. The availability and amount of those benefits depend on several factors, and the charitable gift must be properly structured to maximize the tax advantages. Some of the factors to be considered are:

- The type of property given (e.g., cash, stock, real estate, short-term or long-term)
- The nature of the charitable organization
- The value and tax basis of the gift
- The potential giver's contribution base (adjusted gross income, without regard to net operating loss)
- The charitable deduction interplay among other charitable gifts made in the same year or "carried over" from prior tax years

✍ *What is the tax difference between a charitable lifetime gift and a charitable gift at death?*

A charitable gift made during life has greater tax benefits because the donor can take an income tax deduction and the full value of the property is excluded from his or her estate. If the charitable gift is made at death, the full value of the property is also excluded from the decedent's estate, but the decedent does not reap the benefit of the income tax deduction. However, the decedent did have the use of the property until death, which he or she would not have had if the lifetime gift had been made.

🔊 *Are there any percentages or other limitations on the amount of property that can be left to charity at death?*

No, there are none.

Gift Annuities

🔊 *Is there a simpler way than using a CRT to receive an annuity and an income tax deduction?*

You might want to consider a *gift annuity.* A gift annuity has many of the same tax and economic consequences as a charitable remainder annuity trust, without the trust.

The concept of a gift annuity is simple: You transfer cash or other property to a charitable organization, which promises to pay you an annuity. The annuity is expressed as a percentage rate of return on investment, that is, on the value of what you transfer to the charitable organization. Normally, the annuity is to be paid to you for your life or to you or your spouse for as long as either is living.

If the amount you contribute or the value of the property you transfer to a charity is greater than what it would cost you to purchase a commercial annuity contract from an insurance company, the excess that you pay, as determined by IRS tables, is a charitable contribution for which you are entitled to a charitable deduction for income tax purposes.

In addition to this benefit, the balance of the value of the cash or other property that you transfer, over the calculated amount of the charitable contribution, is treated as being invested in the annuity. A portion of each annuity payment that you receive is treated as a tax-free return of capital (until you have recovered all of your investment in the annuity contract).

If you use appreciated property to purchase the annuity, you realize a taxable gain which (assuming the annuity interest is not assignable, except to the issuing charitable organization) is prorated over the annuity payout period until the total gain has been recognized. Here is an example:

You transfer stock that you bought for $100,000 and is now worth $500,000 to a charitable organization (such as a college) in exchange for the college's promise to pay a 6 percent annuity of $30,000 per year to you or to your spouse if he or she survives you. You and your spouse are each 60 years of age. You will (on the basis of current IRS tables) get an income tax deduction of $159,317 for the year you purchase the gift annuity—a potential income tax savings of $63,727 at a 40 percent combined tax rate.

Each $30,000 annual annuity payment will be taxed as $18,330 ordinary income, $11,501.39 capital gain, and $168.61 tax-free return of principal.

It is important to realize that a gift annuity is an unsecured obligation of the charitable organization. The specific cash or other property you transfer in exchange for the annuity is not segregated in trust to pay the annuity; the organization and its general assets stand behind the annuity. Therefore, you should consider purchasing a gift annuity only from a well-established, financially solid charitable organization.

You can purchase gift annuities that defer the commencement of the annuity payout. You might want to purchase an annuity now, obtain an income tax deduction now when your income is high, and defer the beginning of the annuity payments until your retirement. The results may be surprising!

In terms of the example above, if your annuity is to begin 5 years after the date you purchase it, your income tax deduction will increase to $260,816 (a potential tax savings of $110,970) and each $30,000 annual annuity payout will be taxed as $21,580 ordinary income, $8,075.27 capital gain, and $1,344.73 tax-free return of principal.

Life Insurance

⋑ *What are the pros and cons of gifts of life insurance to charities?*
Making charitable gifts of life insurance is an excellent way for a donor to greatly leverage his or her ultimate charitable gift. There are three general ways a donor can give life insurance to a qualified charity:

1. In most states, a charity can own and be a beneficiary of a life insurance policy on a donor's life. The donor gives the yearly premium dollars to the charity so that the charity can pay the premiums. This method has the advantage of providing the donor with an income tax charitable deduction for the premium dollars. The disadvantage is that the charity owns, and therefore controls, the insurance policy.

2. A donor can own a policy and name a charity as beneficiary of the policy. The advantage is that the donor has full control of the policy. The disadvantage is that the premiums are not income tax–deductible. The benefit proceeds payable to the charity on death will qualify for the estate tax charitable deduction.

3. Life insurance can be used in conjunction with a CRT. A trust maker can fund a CRT with an existing life insurance policy and receive a charitable contribution deduction based upon the fair market value of the policy. A trust maker can also establish a charitable remainder unitrust and give the premium dollars to the trust each year. The trustee could use these contributions to purchase a life insurance policy on the trust maker's life. The trust maker will receive a charitable contribution deduction for the additional yearly contributions to the trust.

Although a CRT can be an excellent vehicle for effecting charitable giving with life insurance, caution should be used when planning with life insurance inside a CRT. An individual should consult closely with his or her attorney and insurance professional to make sure that the use of life insurance inside the trust is a sound investment, that the insurance contract is properly funded to the trust, that the proper type of CRT is being used, that cash-value invasions or loans from the policy will not be needed or used, and that his or her state permits a trust or charity to be the owner and beneficiary of a life insurance policy.

I have old insurance policies that no longer fit my estate plan. Are there any advantages to giving them to charity?

Giving the life insurance to charity could be a smart thing to do:

- You will get an income tax deduction for the replacement cost of the policies (if paid up) or the "interpolated terminal reserve" (something more than cash surrender value), but the deduction cannot exceed your cost (i.e., the total premiums you've paid). Loans against the policy would, of course, reduce the amount of the value and therefore the amount of the deduction.
- In addition, you'll receive an income tax charitable deduction for any premiums you pay in the future.

To qualify for these charitable contribution deductions, you must be sure to properly transfer all incidents of ownership to the charitable organization.

If your employer has a group term life insurance plan under which the company pays all the premiums, the first $50,000 of coverage is provided to you income tax–free. You are taxed for any insurance coverage in excess of $50,000 on the basis of values published by the IRS. However, if you designate your charity as the beneficiary of any portion of the insurance in excess of $50,000, you will not be required to pay income tax on the value of that excess coverage. In addition, if your family's needs should change, you can revoke the designation of the charity and restore your family as beneficiary.

᷉ *When should I think of making a gift of a life insurance policy?*
Many families buy insurance when they are young for the purpose of providing cash benefits in the event of a premature death. While this is a common planning strategy, it does not reflect a family's changing needs over time. If you have old policies that were purchased in amounts smaller than your planning now requires, you have an excellent opportunity to make gifts of those policies to charity.

Buying a new policy to make a gift to charity is less effective because the guaranteed return rate on a policy is frequently less than what the charity could earn on the gift if you gave it to the charity directly as part of an endowment program.

DIRECT BEQUESTS

᷉ *I want to remember my college when I die, but I don't want to get involved in any extra documents. Is there a simple way to do this?*
The simplest way to remember an institution, whether it be an educational, a medical, or some other charitable institution, is to leave a bequest upon your death. The bequest can take several forms. A *cash bequest* provides that your college receives a specific dollar amount. You can also give tangible property such as a residence or a piece of artwork. A *residuary bequest* allows your college to receive everything after estate expenses and specific bequests have been made. You can leave the remainder of a retirement plan to your college. You might want to consider a *contingency bequest,* which would allow your college to receive your assets only in the event of the death of other beneficiaries. This is also called ultimate planning.

CHARITABLE BENEFICIARIES

Charities

Do all charitable organizations qualify as such for income tax purposes regarding charitable gifts?

Only certain charities qualify as charities under the Internal Revenue Code, so it is important to determine whether or not the organization you are interested in qualifies as a charity for income tax purposes. To do so, you should contact the charity and ask if it is qualified under the Internal Revenue Code and has received confirmation of its qualification from the IRS. You should also ask the charity to send you a copy of its latest IRS qualification letter.

You can also examine IRS Publication 78, *Cumulative List of Organizations,* which lists most qualified organizations and is updated annually. You can find this publication in your local library's reference section or call the IRS tax-help telephone number for your area.

What is a community foundation?

A *community foundation* is a public charity with special status under the Internal Revenue Code. Generally it focuses on a specific geographic region. It can serve as a grant maker to other charities within a community. Its strongest point is that it is not linked to one specific charity. It is usually very flexible in meeting the needs of the community and the needs of the donor.

A community foundation relies on endowed funds which are permanently available to provide to charities each year. Most charitable organizations, such as United Way, are dependent on many small contributions each year from many contributors. In fact, many community foundations help support local United Way organizations. An advantage of a community foundation is its flexibility in working with your tax advisors without trying to advance its own particular charitable cause.

Many people, if they have the choice, would rather leave their money to charity than to the Internal Revenue Service through estate taxes. A community foundation can be an excellent place to "park" funds which can then be directed and redirected each year by the donor and his or her family.

What is a donor-advised fund?

A *donor-advised fund* is a special fund set up within a community foundation. The donor donates a sum of money to the community foundation as a permanently endowed fund. Each year the income earned by the endowment is available to contribute to charities in the community or region which the foundation serves.

In many community foundations, the donated funds can be used to benefit charities on a national basis as well. Community foundations allow the donor of the funds, and his or her family, to direct the income from the endowment each year. This gives the family control over the money they have "given away," which makes giving much more appealing.

Can I create a testamentary gift to a community foundation on a donor-advised basis in which the foundation looks to my children or grandchildren for direction?

The assets which ultimately go to charity can still be under the control of your surviving family members. This can be structured in the original grant of the deed of gift, or it can be accomplished by making the community foundation a beneficiary of a CRT or private testamentary charitable foundation (most will be drafted under the Internal Revenue Code as "supporting organizations") you create in your will or trust.

In fact, a private foundation can be structured so that your children, by performing necessary services to the charity, may receive reasonable compensation for their services. This is an enormously complicated area of the tax law and should be done only with an attorney who specializes in this area.

Foundations

Can I leave my assets to charity, have my children and their descendants manage and distribute them—and take a salary for doing so—and replace their value tax-free in my children's trusts?

In short, yes. However, it takes a lot of detail work to ensure that this arrangement will operate as it is intended, so it must be structured properly.

Can I do so only upon my own death, or can I arrange to have it done after the death of my spouse?

You can do so after either death by the terms of your will or living trust.

⩗ *Can I accomplish the same thing while I'm alive?*

Yes. In this case, you can do so either by creating a trust or by creating a nonprofit corporation.

⩗ *What kind of charitable vehicles can I create?*

You can create a family foundation as either a private *operating foundation,* a private *nonoperating foundation,* or a *supporting organization.*

Regardless of your choice, your children and their descendants can direct charitable distributions of your family's foundation income and principal if that is your desire, and they can also receive reasonable fees for their services in addition to being reimbursed for all expenses they incur in carrying out your charitable purposes.

This is basically nothing more than after-death or testamentary family foundation planning.

⩗ *What does this kind of planning do for my children?*

Sometimes it is best to give children control of wealth rather than giving them the wealth outright. In this way they can live lives of *significance* in addition to affluence.

In short, testamentary foundation planning can empower children and their descendants within their communities and can give purpose to their lives.

⩗ *How does a family foundation work, and how much money do I need to set one up?*

A *family foundation* is what the tax law refers to as a "private foundation." The usual planning technique is to have a CRT pay its funds into a family foundation created in the trust maker's will or trust.

The children of the trust maker are usually on the foundation's board of trustees, and their job is to decide which charities are to receive the income donations each year in accordance with the instructions left by the trust maker.

What the size of your estate has to be in order to justify this planning is purely subjective, but a general standard of tax specialists is a minimum of approximately $500,000.

⩗ *Does a private foundation pay income taxes?*

A nonoperating private foundation is subject to an annual excise tax of

2 percent on its net investment income. If it makes $100,000 of income on a principal of $1 million, the tax would be $2000.

It is also subject to a 15 percent excise tax on any shortage if it fails to make "qualifying distributions" (which include reasonable expenses of administering the foundation) each year equal to 5 percent of the fair market value of its assets (computed for the preceding year). This simply means that if the trustees don't distribute 5 percent of the principal each year, the tax will be assessed.

How does a private foundation get recognized by the Internal Revenue Service?

A private foundation must obtain recognition of its tax-exempt status by formal application to the IRS. It must also file an annual income tax information return and make its financial statements available for public inspection. In addition, it must furnish certain information to the attorney general of the state in which it operates.

Do private foundations really last forever?

They can last in perpetuity, or they can last for shorter periods of time if so desired.

Should I establish a private foundation during my lifetime or after my death?

You can set up a private foundation during your lifetime, or you can provide in your will or living trust that it be established following your death.

If you establish a nonoperating private foundation during your lifetime, you can obtain an income tax deduction for contributions to it of up to 30 percent of your adjusted gross income in the year of contribution if your gift is made with cash or up to 20 percent if your gift consists of other property (stock, real estate, partnership interest, etc.) held for more than 1 year. Contributions exceeding the deduction limits in any year may be carried over for up to 5 succeeding tax years.

While the income tax deduction limits that apply to gifts to most private foundations are more stringent than those that apply to gifts to public charities (such as most colleges and universities, churches, hospitals, community foundations), a nonoperating private foundation qualifies for estate tax and gift tax charitable deductions in just the same way as any public charity does.

For example, you can leave all of your estate to a nonoperating private foundation and receive a charitable contribution for the entire value of your estate, thereby reducing the estate tax to zero. You can make an unlimited amount of gifts during your lifetime to a nonoperating private foundation without incurring any gift tax or using up any of your gift and estate tax unified credit.

🖎 *It sounds like a private foundation creates a lot of administration without providing some of the significant tax benefits of a public charity. Are there different types of foundations that may make this administration worthwhile and increase my income tax deduction?*

The combination of the administrative burden and the limitation on income tax deductibility tends to discourage widespread use of the private foundation for charitable giving, unless the amount of assets involved and the desire for control—and family involvement—are viewed as being significant to the would-be founder.

One variation of the private foundation is the *private operating foundation.* This is a foundation which directly conducts exempt activities rather than merely making payments to others for carrying out these activities. For example, a private operating foundation might be established to operate an art museum or a historic residence or to provide activities for elderly citizens of the community.

Since the operating foundation functions somewhat like a public charity, it qualifies for favorable income tax deductions for the contributor: 50 percent of the contribution base, and fair market value deductibility of up to 30 percent of the contribution base for long-term capital gain property. In a sense, it is also free of the 5 percent minimum-distribution requirement because its distributions are made directly in carrying out its operating-foundation activities.

🖎 *I'd like a larger income tax deduction than a private foundation will give me. Besides, I'm not sure my family will be comfortable with the administrative requirements of a private foundation. Isn't there anything simpler that will provide a better income tax deduction and still give me a degree of control?*

A considerable amount of control, though less than that afforded by private foundations, can be achieved through use of a *supporting organization.* This is a charitable corporation or charitable trust established by a donor which is organized and operated "exclusively for the benefit of, to perform the functions of, or to carry out the purposes of" one or more specified public charities.

As the donor, you or you and your family can have a significant representation on the governing board of the supporting organization. However, your family members or other "disqualified persons" cannot directly or indirectly have 50 percent or more of the voting power of the governing board or a veto power over the actions of the organization. Also, you or your spouse cannot retain the right to specify who will receive the income or principal from a contribution.

While you may continue to have, directly or through your family or other persons, a very substantial influence in the affairs of the organization, a supporting organization is recognized as a public charity. Accordingly, it provides the higher income tax deduction limits (50 percent of the contribution base for cash gifts, and fair market deductibility of gifts of long-term capital gain property of up to 30 percent of the contribution base) that regular public charities (colleges and universities, churches, etc.) provide to their donors.

≈ *I've heard of organizations similar to private foundations that can be set up so that a wealthy donor may not only benefit a particular public charitable organization but also provide input and management. Is this true?*

You are probably referring to a supporting organization. The advantages of using supporting organizations are as follows: The excise taxes that may apply in a private foundation generally do not apply; the highest charitable deduction is available (50 percent versus 30 percent of AGI); the family name can be carried on within the supporting organization; they are perpetual; the deduction for contributed property is at its fair market value, unlike contributions to private foundations where deductibility is limited to the cost basis except for marketable securities; and the supporting organization is not required to meet public support tests.

≈ *Can you give an example of how a supporting organization might be structured?*

A supporting organization can be established as a corporation or as a trust.

Typically, a trust will be established with several trustees. For example, a supporting organization may have nine trustees, four of which could be family members. Five trustees cannot be family members, nor can they be employees of the donor.

⋈ What does the supporting organization have to give to charity?

The trust agreement can list any number of charities which the supporting organization foresees that it might possibly support in the future. However, of that number, there must be at least *one* charity which is "attentive" to the supporting organization. The rationale behind this requirement is that the attentive organization will be watching over the supporting organization in lieu of the IRS.

In order to minimize the impact the attentive charity has on the supporting organization, many donors name a small local charity with a small budget and donate at least one-third of its budget. The same would be true if the income from the supporting organization supported a specific annual fund-raising event of the local symphony or a specific chair at a university.

After the funding of the attentive public charity, the remaining income, capital gains, and principal can be distributed to any other charities which are listed in the supporting organization's documents.

Because capital gains can be held instead of distributed each year, the principal should grow, allowing a larger amount to go to charity every year for many years to come. This is a wonderful legacy to leave to your community.

⋈ How does a supporting organization differ from a donor-advised fund?

With a donor-advised fund, the donor contributes all the assets to a community foundation. That foundation then manages the money or has outside money managers manage the money. Each year the community foundation requests the donor's input on deciding which charities will receive the income from the endowment.

With a supporting organization, the organization itself decides which of the supported charities will receive the income from the supporting organization's assets, keeping in mind that a certain amount of the income will need to go to charities which are "attentive" to the supporting organization's support. The supporting organization makes its own investment decisions, and many times the same investment managers who manage the donor's own assets also make the supporting organization's investment decisions.

CHARITABLE PLANNING STRATEGIES

⚐ *What type of CRT is best for me?*

There is no "one-trust-fits-all" CRT. The type of trust a particular individual needs depends on his or her financial requirements.

It is very important to "crunch the numbers." Your planning team should carefully analyze these considerations, and advise you regarding the type of CRT that best effectuates your planning goals. Although the type of trust you choose will depend on your particular situation, the characteristics of each of the major types of CRT (CRAT, CRUT, and NIMCRUT) generally lend themselves to different planning objectives. For example:

- A CRAT is often used by trust makers who are concerned about the possibility that the principal of the trust might decrease and who want to guarantee that they will receive a certain amount of income from the trust. The disadvantage of a CRAT is that it is not inflation-proof. A $2000 distribution from a CRAT 10 or 20 years from now will almost certainly be worth much less than a $2000 distribution today.
- Trust makers who are concerned about inflation often use a CRUT, since the distributions from a CRUT are based on a percentage of the trust, valued annually.
- Trust makers who wish to defer income use a NIMCRUT. A NIMCRUT, especially when invested in a well-designed variable annuity, allows the trust maker to defer income until he or she needs it. A NIMCRUT can also maximize the amount of the ultimate charitable distribution because it allows tax-deferred accumulation of value.
- In some situations, a person may be better off with more than one CRT. A CRAT might be used to guarantee an income flow; a CRUT, to shelter capital gains and provide an inflation hedge; and a NIMCRUT, to defer income until retirement.

CRTs are versatile planning techniques that can address a number of different, even conflicting, needs.

⚐ *I'm 60 years old. Should I consider a CRAT or a CRUT?*

Which one is best for you depends on your needs and objectives, as well as on your assessment of the future of the economy.

If you're optimistic and believe that the economy and the stock market will continue to grow in the future, and that future inflation will reduce the value of today's dollar, you might decide that your best choice is a CRUT.

For example, let's assume that you make your charitable gift by transferring stock worth $500,000 to a CRUT and that you specify a unitrust income amount of 6 percent.

If the value of the stock never changes (highly improbable), you will continue to receive $30,000 per year (6 percent of $500,000). If the assets in the trust rise to $600,000 in value, your annual income will also rise, to $36,000 per year. But if the assets in the trust decline in value to $400,000, your annual income will be reduced to $24,000 per year.

Your contribution will have these economic and tax effects:

- The trustee can sell the stock and reinvest 100 percent of the proceeds without the burden of a capital gain tax either to you or the CRT. In contrast, if you were to sell the stock yourself to reinvest in higher-yielding investments or assets that you feel have better future prospects, your $500,000 stock would shrink by $80,000 after you pay the capital gain tax (at the current 20 percent rate) on the $400,000 appreciation, leaving you with only $420,000 to reinvest.

- Your 6 percent unitrust amount is twice as high as the dividends you are now receiving from the stock. Your income from the CRUT may be higher yet in the future if your optimistic expectations for the economy and stock market are accurate (or, of course, lower if the assets decline in value).

- Assuming you create and fund the CRUT during your lifetime, you'll be entitled to an income tax deduction for the year you make the contribution for the value of your gift of the remainder interest to the charity. The exact amount of the deduction depends on interest rates published monthly by the IRS (which are based on how much the government has to pay on its borrowings). If the published interest rate is 7 percent and your spouse is also age 60, you'll be entitled to an income tax deduction in 1998 of up to $126,940, which translates into $50,776 of potential income tax savings if your combined federal and state income tax effective rate is 40 percent. There are limits on how much deduction you can take in a given year. These limits are geared to your income level, and deductions in excess of the annual limit can be carried over to the next 5 years.

■ The assets in the CRT will not be subject to federal estate or gift tax at any time.

If you are not too optimistic about the economy and the stock market, or you simply want to assure yourself of a fixed, never-changing, annual payment, you may prefer the CRAT. If you contribute your stock to a CRAT, specifying a $30,000-per-year annuity amount (6 percent of the $500,000 initial value of the stock), the trustee of the CRAT must pay you or your spouse, as long as either of you is living, a fixed annual payment of $30,000 regardless of what happens to the value of the trust's assets or the income they generate. You'll forgo the possibility of increasing annual payments with rising stock levels and inflation, but you'll lock in the fixed payment rate you specify in the CRAT document.

■ You'll also get a larger income tax deduction from a 6 percent CRAT than you would from a 6 percent CRUT under current interest rates. By contributing your stock worth $500,000 to a CRAT and specifying a fixed 6 percent annuity amount as long as you are living, you'll be entitled to an income tax deduction in the year of the gift of up to $159,317, which translates into a potential income tax savings of $63,727 (assuming a 40 percent combined federal and state effective rate). At your age, the CRAT will provide almost $13,000 more in tax benefit than the CRUT. The result would be different at any other age, payment level, and IRS rate applicable at the time you make your contributions. (For example, with a 7½ percent payment at your age under the current IRS rate, the tables are turned: a CRUT would produce a larger deduction than a CRAT.)

■ Since your contribution is appreciated stock, your tax deduction will be limited to 30 percent of your adjusted gross income. If your adjusted gross income is $150,000 in the year you make the gift, you can deduct $45,000 on your tax return for that year and carry over the balance for up to 5 more years.

With the help of your estate planning team, you should weigh the flexibility and probable (based on historical results) economic advantages of a CRUT against the fixed income of a CRAT, consider the estimated income tax deduction that will be available and usable by you if you create and fund your CRT during your lifetime, and decide which arrangement will be best for you.

Income Strategies

⚹ I'm 70, and my major asset is farmland that is appreciating quickly. I'd like to leave this land to a charity when I die, but I have to count on a certain amount of income for the remainder of my life. Would a CRT be right for me?

If you are interested in the advantages of a CRT but need a guaranteed income, you might want to consider a CRAT. Here is an example of how a CRAT could work for you:

- You establish a CRAT by placing the farmland with a fair market value of $1 million into a CRAT. The trustee sells the land and invests the proceeds in income-producing bonds.
- Your CRAT provides that 6 percent of the initial value of the trust amount will be paid to you annually for your life. You will receive $60,000 per year for life even if the principal of the trust decreases in value. For example, if the million-dollar portfolio drops by 50 percent to $500,000, you will still receive $60,000 a year, which is now 12 percent of the principal.
- The trust avoids paying capital gains when it sells the farmland; you have generated guaranteed income that the farmland would never have provided; you have an immediate income tax charitable deduction; you have reduced the size of your estate, thus saving estate taxes; and you have fulfilled your charitable desires.

⚹ My husband and I are thinking of doing a charitable remainder trust, but we're concerned that we won't be able to take enough income from it because of the new 10 percent–to–charity requirement. Are there any ways to get around this problem?

There are at least four ways that would allow you to use the CRT and increase your income:

1. *Divide the property into two portions.* You and your husband should create separate charitable remainder trusts with the maker as the only income beneficiary. Using a single life-expectancy table instead of the joint table, each of you will be entitled to a higher payout than the two of you could receive jointly. The potential disadvan-

tage of this method is that when the first spouse dies, the survivor will receive only the income stream from the survivor's CRT.

2. *Transfer all the property to the older spouse.* The older spouse would then create a CRT for his or her life only. Upon death, the income stream completely stops. This will give you the highest payout. Use a portion of the extra income to purchase a life insurance policy on the older spouse. Hold the policy in an irrevocable trust for the younger spouse and the children. This will provide the younger spouse with income should the older spouse die first.

3. *Transfer the property to one spouse, who can then fund the trust and name both of you as income beneficiaries.* If the two of you live to expectancy, you will both enjoy the income for your joint lives, but the payout will be slightly lower if it is calculated on both lives rather than one.

4. *Establish the trust for a term of years.* You may establish a charitable remainder trust for a term not to exceed 20 years. This should enable you to increase the payout rate on the trust while keeping the remainder interest above the 10 percent requirement. You'll have to run numbers to see if you can make this term-of-years trust work for you.

≤∆   *I have heard that I can use a NIMCRUT as a strategy to provide for my retirement. How do I do that?*

Let us assume that you have been setting aside money in your qualified retirement plan and you are concerned that this will not give you enough income at retirement. You are comfortable putting aside an additional amount per year over and above what you are contributing to your qualified retirement plan. You would like in some way to give something back to your community after the deaths of you and your spouse.

You should consider establishing a charitable remainder unitrust with net income makeup provisions so that you will be able to create a source of additional retirement income. You can then make contributions each year to the NIMCRUT, and you will receive an income tax deduction based on the amount contributed each year to the trust. The deduction is calculated using your life expectancy, the payout rate you specify, and the IRS rates that apply each year you make your annual contribution. The charitable remainder unitrust is not a qualified retirement plan and, therefore, not subject to the ERISA rules, such as the limits on annual additions to qualified plans, the pre-59½ penalty tax on withdrawals, or the minimum required distributions beginning after age 70½.

✎ I like the idea of limiting the CRUT payment each year to the income actually earned by the NIMCRUT. I don't need the extra income, and I think I'll be better off with the increasing value of the assets. However, in 10 years, when I retire, I may want a larger income. Can the CRUT payout percentage rate be increased when I reach retirement age?

No. The annual CRUT payout percentage rate is specified in the document, and that percentage cannot be changed. Nevertheless, a NIMCRUT may still give you the result you want. A NIMCRUT offers important planning possibilities if you do not require substantial income return from the CRUT presently or in the near term but anticipate having a more substantial income requirement in later years.

If you establish a NIMCRUT, your trustee could invest in a variable annuity to provide for your deferred income requirements. Alternatively, during the next several years before you reach retirement age, your trustee could invest in growth assets, typically paying low dividends, and you would receive only the net income actually generated by the trust. As you reach or approach retirement age and have a greater need for income, the trustee could then shift the investments in the NIMCRUT to high-income investments and pay you this enhanced income in your retirement years.

Here is an example of how this works:

> You own $500,000 worth of stock, producing $15,000 in annual dividends. You contribute the stock to a NIMCRUT, specifying a 6 percent unitrust amount. Your NIMCRUT limits the trustee's payment distribution to the trust's actual net income. Since the contributed stock pays only a 3 percent dividend, the trust at the outset would be generating a payment deficit to your makeup account at the annual rate of $15,000. In 10 years the value of the trust assets might increase to $750,000, resulting in a $22,500 actual annual income to you (assuming the assets continue to earn a 3 percent dividend rate). Over the 10 years, the NIMCRUT may have built up a deficit, or "IOU," of around $187,500 in the makeup account. By converting the trust assets into bonds producing 8 percent on the $750,000 of assets, the trustee could "pump up" the payout to you to $60,000 per year in your retirement years, until the deficit is paid off (in perhaps 12 years), after which the annual payout

would be reduced to the specified 6 percent of the trust's asset value at that time ($45,000 per year if the value remains constant).

As discussed earlier, the Internal Revenue Service is not completely happy with this strategy but is unlikely to take a formal position with regard to it until 2000 or after. And even if the IRS takes an adverse position, it is most likely that it will be prospective rather than retrospective.

    How a NIMCRUT's income is calculated is very confusing to me. Can you give me another example?

In a NIMCRUT, the payout amount is specified as the lesser of the percentage amount or the income actually earned by the trust. However, in any year when the income earned is less than the specified percentage, the difference between the two is kept track of in a "makeup account." In any subsequent year, if the trust's income is greater than the specified percentage, the excess income is also distributed, up to the balance in the makeup account.

Thus, if a trustee uses an investment strategy for growth rather than income, the amounts distributed from the trust will be minimal or nonexistent and the makeup-account balance will grow. In subsequent years, when the trustee switches to an income rather than a growth investment strategy, the income stream will be greater (since the trust property will have grown) and excess income can be distributed to use up the balance in the makeup account.

A NIMCRUT is a win-win strategy for both the trust maker and the charitable beneficiary. The trust maker/trustee has great flexibility in investment strategy, and the charitable beneficiary will always get at least as much as it would have received under a straight-payout charitable remainder unitrust.

Funding Strategies

    I am not liquid, but I'm interested in giving to charity and I own a corporation that has substantial assets. Is there a way I can use these assets to give to charity and get personal charitable deductions?

There are a number of ways that you can use corporate assets for charity and receive personal deductions.

One option is a *charitable stock bailout.* You would contribute shares of your stock to a qualified charitable organization either by direct gift or through a charitable trust. Then, according to a nonbinding plan, the charity may offer to sell the shares back to the corporation at fair market value. It is absolutely essential that there is no requirement that the charity sell the closely held stock back to the corporation.

From a practical standpoint, however, there are few charities that will be interested in holding closely held stock over a long term. Most charities need cash to carry out their charitable activities, and since the stock is not marketable and has no immediate potential benefit to the charity, an offer for sale makes imminent sense.

⚒ *Why is this beneficial to an owner of a closely held regular or C corporation?*

A charitable stock bailout offers a shareholder the opportunity to obtain a personal tax deduction for a charitable contribution made with corporate dollars.

If the corporation is 100 percent owned by the shareholder-donor, then once the shares are repurchased by the corporation, the shareholder is in the same position with regard to his or her 100 percent ownership of the corporation. In addition, the charity receives cash that was trapped inside the corporation without its being taxed as a dividend at the shareholder's tax rate. Further, the donor receives a full fair market value deduction, limited of course by the standard deduction limitations pertaining to charitable contributions.

⚒ *Who determines the value of the stock for this purpose?*

It is essential that a qualified business appraiser determine the value of the shares for purposes of both the charitable deduction and the purchase price of the shares if and when the corporation decides to purchase the shares from the charity.

⚒ *Is there a better way to reduce my estate taxes in this situation than by simply giving shares in my corporation to a charity? I'm afraid that my children are not going to get enough. Wouldn't it be better to just give them the corporation?*

You should consider using a separate irrevocable life insurance trust owning life insurance on your life. You can arrange a payment plan that will involve your corporation's paying the premium, while the proceeds will ultimately pass tax-free to your children or to trusts for their benefit.

⌘ *For the charitable stock bailout, does it matter whether the corporation is a C corporation or an S corporation?*

As of January 1, 1998, a charity is an eligible shareholder of an S corporation. However, the benefits of this technique are more pronounced when it is applied to a regular C corporation.

⌘ *What are the benefits of using this technique with a charitable trust?*

The most significant benefit is that the trust can sell the stock back to the corporation—without paying capital gain taxes on the appreciation of the stock—so that the resulting cash can be invested in a higher-yielding, more liquid portfolio.

Just as in any other charitable trust, the charitable trustee may not be under any express or implied obligation to sell or exchange the property. If the trustee is under an express or implied obligation to sell, the capital gain tax would be accelerated and the donor would be required to pay the tax just as if he or she had sold the assets ahead of time.

This technique further accomplishes the donor's charitable intentions by allowing a remainder interest to be passed on to his or her ultimate charitable beneficiary while the donor maintains an income interest during the term of the trust. Lastly, it provides an immediate income tax charitable deduction for the donor.

⌘ *If a charitable remainder trust owns stock in a corporation operating an active trade or business, is this a problem investment?*

This is not usually a problem as long as the charitable remainder trust is treated like any other minority shareholder under the statutes of the jurisdiction in which it is created.

⌘ *Is it true that a charitable remainder trust cannot have unrelated-business taxable income?*

There is nothing that prohibits a charitable remainder trust from receiving such income, but the consequences can be disastrous.

⌘ *What exactly is unrelated-business taxable income?*

Congress did not want charitable organizations to compete with other types of entities that are subject to income taxation and thus to make money in a business manner for which they would not have to pay taxes. In its view, that would be going too far.

Therefore, Congress provided that a tax-exempt organization would be taxed, just like any other taxpayer, on net income derived from regularly carrying on any trade or business not directly related to the organization's nonprofit purpose. Such income is called *unrelated-business taxable income (UBTI)*.

For example, net income earned by a church from operating a bike shop would be a classic case of UBTI. This is a rather obvious example, and it is understandable why Congress placed this limitation on tax-exempt organizations.

What is not so obvious, and trips up unsuspecting charitable organizations, is an ordinary investment that may throw off UBTI. Examples include a publicly traded master limited partnership or real estate investment trusts.

⩍ What are the adverse consequences of UBTI for a charitable remainder trust?

A charity earning UBTI is taxed on that income just like any other taxpayer would be taxed on that income.

A charitable remainder unitrust or annuity trust, however, loses its tax-exempt status on *all* its income for any year in which it receives UBTI, regardless of whether the amount is very small or was inadvertently incurred. This is a serious consequence, potentially exposing the trustee to liability. If the UBTI is received in the same year that a highly appreciated asset in the trust is sold, the entire appreciation, which otherwise would escape taxation, will be subject to taxation—even if the trust received only a single dollar of UBTI.

If a primary motivation in creating a CRUT or CRAT is to avoid imposition of capital gain tax on the sale of a highly appreciated asset, the donor's entire purpose could be frustrated by needlessly incurring UBTI.

Income Tax
and Capital Gain Tax Strategies

⩍ The city is starting to encroach on my farm property, and the real estate taxes have gotten too high because of increased assessments. How can I sell my farm without paying capital gain taxes?

There is an answer to your dilemma. If you want to continue farming, you can find a new farm to purchase and enter into a tax-free exchange. This will result in your owning a new farm and deferring your capital gain taxes into that farm. The capital gain taxes will not have to be paid until the new farm is resold. If the new farm is ultimately passed on to your beneficiaries at the time of your death, the capital gain taxes will never have to be paid.

Assuming you are ready to retire from farming, you can utilize a CRT, contribute the property to it, sell the property as trustee—without any capital gain taxes—and live on your contractual income right. You will get an income tax deduction for the transaction equal to the present value of the remainder interest your trust gives to charity, and you can carry it forward for an additional 5 years so that it can offset the taxability of your income earnings. You can use excess cash to purchase a last-to-die life insurance policy insuring you and your spouse, owned by an irrevocable life insurance trust, and replace—tax-free—the inheritance that would otherwise go to your children and be reduced by federal estate or gift taxes.

My stock presently pays a 3 percent dividend, and my proposed CRUT will pay me 6 percent. How will I be taxed on my annual income from the CRUT?

How you will be taxed on your annual income depends on how the trustee generates the funds to make the payment. In the worst case, you'll report the income you receive as ordinary income and pay tax based on the amount you are paid. Alternatively:

- If the trustee sells the stock you contribute and reinvests it in U.S. bonds paying exactly 6 percent, you will be taxed on the 6 percent rate you actually receive. The CRUT is income-tax exempt and won't have to pay income tax on its capital gains, so it can reinvest the full current value of the stock.

- If the trustee reinvests in corporate bonds paying 7 percent, you'll still be taxed only on the 6 percent annuity payment you actually receive.

- If the trustee keeps most of the stock you contribute to the CRUT but sells just enough to generate the difference between the stock's 3 percent dividend and your 6 percent payment, your actual tax burden will be somewhat reduced because your 6 percent annual payment will then be part ordinary income (3 percent) and part capital gain (3 percent).

- If the trustee sells your stock and reinvests in tax-exempt bonds, some of your 6 percent annual payment will be reported and taxed as ordinary income (to the extent that the trust received dividends or other ordinary income), some will be taxed as capital gain (until the gain is "used up"), and the balance will be tax-exempt income.

Estate Tax Strategies

⅍ Will a CRT save me federal estate taxes?

Yes. It will avoid them entirely if the principal passes to charity after your and your spouse's deaths.

⅍ I have a $1 million IRA. Can I leave it to a CRT?

Yes, you may name your CRT as the beneficiary of your IRA, and you should consider doing so.

If you name your children as the beneficiaries of your IRA, at the time of your death federal estate taxes as high as 55 percent will be paid on your IRA of $1 million. As much as $550,000 can be lost in estate taxes, leaving a balance of $450,000 to your children.

There is also going to be an additional income tax imposed (income in respect of a decedent) on your $1 million IRA. After applying the credit given for estate taxes paid, an additional $180,000 of income tax would be payable, leaving only $270,000 for your children. Assuming an 8 percent annual income yield, your children would receive only $21,600 per year.

⅍ Can a CRT help protect my IRA funds for my spouse as well?

Yes. Under the right circumstances, naming your CRT as the beneficiary of your IRA can be a planning tool for the protection of your spouse.

If you name your spouse as the beneficiary of your IRA, the $1 million benefit would qualify for the estate tax marital deduction. Therefore, no estate tax would be paid at the time of your death. However, if any proceeds remained at the time of your spouse's subsequent death, estate tax would be due and payable at that time.

You should seek advice from competent professionals before you elect to use this technique, as it could produce results you do not want.

⅍ How can I leave my IRA to a CRT and help my spouse?

The proceeds will not be subject to federal estate tax. Assuming an 8 percent annuity is paid by the charity to your surviving spouse during his or her lifetime, your spouse will enjoy $80,000 per year just as if you left it to him or her, and the remainder will thereafter pass to charity rather than to the government.

Wealth Replacement Trust Strategies

I like the idea of a wealth replacement trust, but now that I am retired, I'm not sure I have the cash to give to the trust. What can I do?

Sources of income often overlooked are:

- Cash from the deductions created on your income tax returns for making a contribution to a CRT
- The cash value of old life insurance policies that can be rolled tax-free into newer policies that may be less costly

Outright-Gift Strategies

I want to make a donation to my favorite charity. I have some highly appreciated stock worth $100,000 that the charity suggests I donate, but I really like this stock, so I'm reluctant to give it away. Does it make any difference if I donate the stock or give the charity $100,000 in cash?

Give the stock to charity, and use the $100,000 to repurchase it. There will be no capital gains on the sale of the stock by the charity, you will receive a $100,000 income tax deduction, and you will still have your favorite stock in your portfolio.

I have some stock that has a big loss, and I intend to give it to charity. Is there anything I should consider?

Yes. You should consider selling the stock, taking a capital loss deduction against any capital gains you have and some ordinary income, and giving the sale proceeds to the charity. You will get the same charitable deduction you would have received if you had donated the stock; however, you will also realize a capital loss deduction.

Is there a way to use the charitable remainder unitrust to reduce the taxation on my IRA assets?

You can make a testamentary beneficiary designation of your IRA to a CRT which would operate for the benefit of your children. This will allow them to avoid immediate income in respect of a decedent and will pay them an income for up to 20 years that will be greater in value.

The value of the estate tax you would have to pay to make this gift would be reduced by the present value of the remainder gift to charity.

chapter 9

Business Planning

TYPE OF ENTITY
AND ESTATE PLANNING

Sole Proprietorship

What is a sole proprietorship?

A *sole proprietorship* is a business owned by an individual proprietor and created without formal filing requirements (there are some very limited exceptions in a few states).

What are the estate planning considerations of a sole proprietorship?

A sole proprietorship is not generally conducive to tax planning, liability planning, or business succession planning, and it offers no liability protection. A sole proprietorship exposes the proprietor's personal assets to business creditors and business losses; it does not limit that exposure to the sole proprietor's investment in the business.

A sole proprietorship cannot survive the death of its owner, but a sole proprietor may leave his or her business *assets* by will or trust to relatives or employees.

What are the planning weaknesses of a sole proprietorship?

There are three planning disadvantages to a sole proprietorship:

425

- Unlike a corporation or other legal entity, a sole proprietorship offers the owner no liability protection.
- It is not suited for business succession. Typically, when the sole proprietor passes on, the business dies with him or her.
- It severely limits tax planning opportunities that are available with other business structures.

Regular Corporations

🖎 *Are there any estate planning benefits to incorporating?*

Incorporating affords creditor protection through limited liability and ensures the perpetual existence of the business, both of which are pluses to an estate plan. Corporate shares of stock are easily given to others, and corporate management structures are complementary to succeeding generations.

S Corporations

🖎 *What is an S corporation?*

An *S corporation* is formed like a regular corporation. The major difference between an S corporation and a regular, or C, corporation is that, under the Internal Revenue Code, "a small-business corporation" may elect not to be taxed at the corporate level but, rather, to have the corporation's income and losses pass through to the shareholders and be taxed to them.

S corporation income is passed through to the shareholders proportionate to their ownership of the corporation's shares. Thus, an S corporation is a tax pass-through business entity for federal income tax purposes, much like a sole proprietorship or partnership.

🖎 *If my living trust owns subchapter S stock after my death, will the S election be disqualified?*

A revocable living trust which is owned by an individual who is a citizen or a resident of the United States qualifies to own S corporation stock because it is a "grantor trust."

Another type of trust, called a *qualified subchapter S trust (QSST)* can also hold S corporation stock. A QSST must provide that all its income will be distributed to one income beneficiary; that no one other than the income beneficiary will be eligible for distributions during his or her lifetime; that the income interest terminates on the earlier of the income beneficiary's death or the termination of the trust; and that the trust principal is distributed to the income beneficiary if the trust terminates during his or her lifetime. A husband and wife can qualify as one income beneficiary.

A QSST may not allow payment of principal to anyone other than the income beneficiary even if the trust first disposes of the S stock. If a QSST is created, notice containing the following must be given to the Internal Revenue Service:

- Name, address, and taxpayer identification number of the current income beneficiary, the trust, and the corporation
- Identification of the election under the Internal Revenue Code
- Specification of the date on which the election is to become effective
- All information necessary to show that the current income beneficiary is entitled to make the election

Professional Corporations

As a doctor, do I gain any tax advantages, or other advantages, by operating as a professional corporation?

Yes, there are still a few tax and legal advantages to the professional corporation. The largest tax advantage comes from the ability to deduct the employee benefits paid to yourself, such as medical and disability insurance, pension plan contributions, and medical reimbursement plan payments. While you will incur payroll taxes on the salary paid to yourself, these deductions generally offset the payroll tax burden.

Does a professional corporation shield me from liability?

A professional corporation does not shield you from your professional or malpractice liability, but it does shield you from lawsuits against the corporation which do not relate to your malpractice. It also protects you from the malpractice of other practitioners working with you.

Can a professional corporation help with succession planning?

Since succeeding shareholders must be licensed to practice in your field, a professional corporation is rarely of help to family members.

General Partnerships

What is a general partnership?

A *general partnership* is a venture for profit between two or more people.

It can be created by an oral or a written agreement between the individuals, or legal entities, who agree to participate in the partnership.

⚗ *What are the estate planning attributes of a general partnership?*

Each partner is authorized to totally bind the partnership in business transactions. The partners are jointly and severally liable for the acts of the partnership and each other and, in essence, have unlimited personal liability to the partnership's creditors.

From a tax perspective, a general partnership is a flow-through entity. Any loss or profit will flow through to the partners on the basis of their ownership in the partnership.

If the partnership agreement does not specify to the contrary, a general partnership will be automatically dissolved upon the death of any partner.

⚗ *Can my attorney structure a general partnership other than the way my state's law says it has to be structured?*

Yes, your attorney can prepare a written partnership agreement that can be specifically tailored to the partners' wishes. However, it cannot limit the liability of the partners or change the partnership's flow-through nature for income tax purposes.

Limited Partnerships

⚗ *What is a limited partnership?*

A *limited partnership* is a partnership that has both general and limited partners. The general partners control *all* the business operations of the partnership, while the limited partners have no control of the partnership's business operations and have very limited or no voting rights.

⚗ *What are the estate planning concerns with a limited partnership?*

A limited partnership is a flow-through entity: its profits and losses flow through to the general and limited partners in accordance with their proportionate ownership percentages.

The general partners have full responsibility for the limited partnership's debts, liabilities, and obligations. They have unlimited liability with respect to partnership creditors.

The limited partners are not responsible for the debts, liabilities, and obligations of the partnership. Their losses are limited to the amount of their respective investments in the partnership.

Family Limited Partnerships

⋨ *What is a family limited partnership?*

In a *family limited partnership* the general and the limited partners are family members or family-controlled entities such as closely held corporations, limited liability companies, or trusts for family members.

⋨ *What does a family limited partnership do to further my gift and estate tax planning?*

It allows you to make gifts to family members at discounted values for purposes of federal estate and gift taxes, while maintaining your control—as general partner—over the assets owned by the partnership. Specifically, parents and grandparents can:

- Transfer significant percentages of their ownership interests to other family members and still maintain control of the partnership's affairs
- Make all management decisions, receive compensation for making those decisions, and do so with as little as 1 percent or less of the partnership's ownership
- Give limited-partner interests to succeeding generations at discounted values often averaging 30 to 50 percent of fair market valuations
- Protect family members from the claims of partnership creditors

⋨ *How does a family limited partnership accomplish my estate planning goals?*

Parents usually receive a token 1 percent general partnership interest in the new partnership, but that 1 percent constitutes 100 percent control of the partnership and its assets. They also initially receive a 99 percent limited partnership interest that has no voting or other control over the partnership.

The parents will then make periodic annual gifts of their limited partnership interests within their gift tax annual exclusion or combined applicable exclusion amounts—$1.3 million in 1999—to reduce the size of their estates to significantly below their fair market values.

⋈ *Is it easy to make limited partnership gifts?*

Gifts of limited-partner interests are easy to make because fractional or partial interests can easily be given away.

Limited Liability Companies

⋈ *What is a limited liability company?*

A *limited liability company* (*LLC*) is a hybrid business entity that possesses certain attributes associated with corporations and certain attributes associated with partnerships.

Instead of having partners or shareholders, the LLC has members. Members enjoy limited liability status regardless of whether or not they participate in the day-to-day affairs of the business. This means that LLC members can participate in the management and control of the business without risking their personal assets to liability as a result of the acts of others.

A limited liability company is generally treated as a partnership for purposes of federal and state income taxation. Because partnerships are not subject to corporate income tax, an LLC offers the limited liability of a corporation without the additional level of income taxation associated with regular corporations.

Most states have only recently adopted limited liability company statutes. Because the LLC is a recent phenomenon as a business entity, the case law concerning limited liability companies is in its infancy. It is, therefore, often difficult to determine its general legal or tax consequences in unique situations.

It appears that more and more people are choosing limited liability companies as the preferred business entity and that the future looks fairly assured for the LLC as an alternative to incorporation.

⋈ *What can an LLC do for me?*

An LLC is a noncorporate business entity which provides its owners with limited liability, flow-through tax treatment, and operational flexibility. It reduces the paperwork associated with incorporation, and it simplifies tax planning.

⋈ *What are an LLC's advantages from an estate planning perspective?*

An LLC is a desirable business structure because of the flexibility it offers to the professional estate planner. For example, unlike subchapter S corporations, there are no restrictions on the number of participants, and complex trusts may become members. Other advantages of the LLC include:

- The avoidance of S corporation restrictions on trust provisions after the trust maker's death
- Basis adjustments that are not available to S or C corporations
- The ability to distribute appreciated property to members without triggering gain to the members or income to the LLC
- The ability to discount minority member interests just like limited partnership interests for both gift and estate tax planning purposes

BUSINESS CONTINUITY PLANNING

Reasons for Continuity Planning

⚜ *What planning concerns should I have as a business owner?*

The primary planning concerns for all business owners, particularly those who are nonrelated owners of the same business, are:

- Ensuring a market to purchase their stock or other business interest at retirement, at death, or upon substantial disability
- Providing funds for the purchase of the business interests from the principals
- Keeping "unwanted partners" such as competitors or nonessential family members from becoming business partners.

In addition to dealing with the above concerns, family business owners must make plans to effectively continue the operations of the business, designate business successors, provide surviving spouses and children with sufficient assets, and provide sufficient liquidity for the payment of estate tax obligations so that the business will not have to be liquidated to pay those taxes at a severely discounted price.

⚜ *Is there really a need to continue a business?*

In most family businesses, the business is built upon the personality, marketing/sales, and operational talents of its principals. The absence of a principal creates a void. While the grief-stricken family seeks to fill that void, customers will have anxieties and major concerns and often go elsewhere.

Postdeath or postdisability problems are often complicated by internal family rivalry and disputes as to the ownership, control, and operation of the business. In many states, unless specific authorization is provided to operate a business, the executor (or agent under a power of attorney) can only wind down the business.

☙ What is business continuity planning?

Business continuity planning is strategic planning to ensure that the business continues under responsible management to produce profits and maintain equity values for family members and charitable beneficiaries.

☙ How can I make advance plans for the designation of my business successors?

If more than one child will be involved in the family business, one of the most important issues you should resolve is that of management roles and control. Advance decisions could mitigate or avoid the problem of dissension among children, which could destroy the business and adversely affect the harmony of the family unit. Whether children will be involved or not, advance planning should also include such issues as:

- Leaving other or replacement assets, including the benefits of life insurance trusts, to create equality among the children
- Avoiding a disproportionate estate tax burden upon the children who do not receive the business
- Providing necessary legal authority to continue the business
- Determining how business decisions will be made and who will make them
- Instituting early involvement of family members in customer public relations
- Providing for funds such as "key-person" insurance to provide needed capital during the intergenerational business hiatus

☙ Should I let my family members take over my business?

It depends on what your goals and objectives are. If family members are active in the business and doing a good job of running it, the answer is obviously yes. If, however, they are uninterested, passive inheritors, you might consider the following:

1. Passive owners are often inept owners who will not be likely to attract or keep good management.
2. If you have good managers, it is likely they will want assurances that at some point they will have a meaningful ownership stake in the business after you are gone. If not, they will likely leave for a better equity opportunity elsewhere.
3. Your family's financial security might be better served if you sold the business and had the more liquid proceeds invested and managed by professionals.
4. You might be happy with a more diversified portfolio that did not include your business interests and headaches.

⚖ *Does my family really want to continue the business?*

This is an obvious question that many people forget to ask themselves as they ponder various succession alternatives. You should meet with each of your family members and ask the following questions:

- Are you interested in working in the business?
- Are you capable of running it or handling various senior management functions?
- Are you interested in learning about it?
- Would you enjoy hiring and overseeing capable professional managers?
- Do you foresee problems with the business if something happens to me?
- What would you advise me to do with the family business?

You may be surprised at the answers you get.

⚖ *How can I provide for the protection of my spouse with the business assets?*

The small-business owner frequently receives a significant cash flow from the family business. If the business owner desires to pass his or her business to children, arrangements must be made to provide sufficient replacement resources of that cash flow for the benefit of the surviving spouse. Advance planning for the purchase of life insurance, as well as preparation of installment sale notes, private annuities, and self-canceling notes, is therefore essential.

⊁ *How can I make sure my spouse is taken care of from the business after I'm gone?*

There are several ways to do this, ranging from life insurance to non-qualified deferred compensation plans, including:

- Creating a management position guaranteeing an income stream that is not double taxed
- Replacing your income with disability and life insurance proceeds free of tax, and providing for an orderly plan of liquidation
- Providing for the managerial skills of others who can perpetuate the ongoing income stream
- Creating a plan that will provide for a purchaser of the business upon your death or disability

⊁ *What should owners of closely held businesses take into account when they are considering whether or not to allow a key employee to acquire shares of stock?*

Taking on a new owner in a closely held business can involve major business adjustments which require significant deliberation.

Existing shareholders need to assess their feelings about sharing managerial authority while they are still active in the business. After having operated a business for many years, most owners become accustomed to making all the management decisions and otherwise do pretty much as they please on an informal basis. However, when there are other stakeholders involved, the atmosphere is often not conducive to such informality or dominance.

New owners will undoubtedly have the right to participate in dividends and in the election of directors, as well as all other rights which flow from ownership, and these rights must be respected.

⊁ *What kind of ownership plan should I offer my key employees?*

It is important to understand what motivates a particular key employee before offering ownership rights. What does he or she really want? Is the employee interested in financial rewards, or a say in management, or recognition and special status in the company? If financial rewards are the paramount concern, issuing stock may not always be the best solution.

After considering these issues, owners should consult with their professional advisors to explore all the "what if's" that can occur, and all too frequently do, in ill-thought-out business plans. These usually include: What if the employee takes a job with a competitor? What if the employee dies, encounters marital difficulties, files for bankruptcy, gives shares to someone else, and so on? What if the employee has a difference of opinion about the future direction of the business and refuses to cooperate? What if . . . ?

⋊ *Do these same concerns and questions apply to the granting of stock options?*

Yes, they do. Options to acquire shares will eventually result in others owning those shares when the options are exercised.

Tax Considerations

Payment of taxes

⋊ *Are taxes a problem in business succession planning?*

Federal estate taxes are a major problem in conjunction with business continuity planning. Often the family business is a major asset of the estate, and estate taxes are due—in cash—9 months from the date of death (federal estate tax deferral techniques are discussed in Chapter 12).

If the business is typical, it will most probably be difficult to value it, and once the valuation is complete, it is not likely that buyers will easily be found even at a reasonable asking price. In the absence of business continuity planning, there is every likelihood that the business might have to be sold at fire-sale or liquidation pricing.

⋊ *Won't I qualify for the installment payment of estate taxes?*

A business that accounts for 35 percent or more of an estate will generally qualify for the installment payment of estate taxes. However, this exception applies only to the first $1 million of business value, and the tax must nevertheless be paid with interest over a 14-year period. Only interest is paid for the first 4 of the 14 years; thereafter, payments go to reduce principal each year, and interest is charged at the current statutory rate. Before the Taxpayer Relief Act of 1997, the statutory rate was a fixed 4 percent. The act changed the calculation method so that it is now a "floating" rate.

⋈ Are there other requirements that must be met to qualify for installment payments?

The decedent must have owned an interest in a closely held business that qualifies for the special election. To meet this requirement, the decedent must have been one of the following:

- A sole proprietor
- A partner in a partnership with no more than 15 partners, or a partner holding 20 percent or more of the total capital interest in the partnership
- A shareholder owning 20 percent or more of the voting stock of a corporation

Your attorney, together with your CPA, can help you assess whether your closely held business interest will qualify for deferral and whether it would be advisable to take advantage of such.

⋈ Are there problems with unrelated owners?

There can be problems with unrelated business partners and passive owners. When an owner dies, his or her heirs often do not want to own a portion of the business, and the remaining principals do not want the deceased owner's family in the business. Generally, the remaining principals do not have the liquidity necessary to buy the deceased owner's shares, and the respective sides have widely divergent views on the value of the various interests in question.

⋈ Can a fair price be easily established?

Bitter disputes and hurt feelings can result if the terms of a buyout have not been specifically negotiated in advance of the buyout. In addition, an S election can be ruined if transfers of stock are not controlled and proper provisions for its repurchase are not in place.

⋈ If I am unable to sell my closely held business interest before my death, and my heirs run it into the ground, on what amount will my family pay federal estate tax?

Unfortunately, your business will be valued at its date-of-death value or its value 6 months after your death. As a result, the taxes due will be based upon how you ran the business rather than how your heirs mismanaged it.

The small-business estate tax credit

As the owner of a small business, am I better off using my unified credit or the new small-business credit?

The Taxpayer Relief Act of 1997 gives the owner of a small family business or farm the opportunity to shield $1.3 million from federal estate taxes. This opportunity is an alternative to the applicable exclusion amount; only one or the other may be used.

The small-business alternative is not for every family business, because there are a number of qualifications which limit its use, including:

- The value of the business must represent at least one-half of the owner's estate.
- The owner must have actively participated in the operation of the business for at least 10 years before his or her death.
- The business must be left to a family member (or long-time employee) who must continue to operate the business for 10 years.

Won't the small-business estate tax credit decrease in value as the applicable exclusion amount is phased in through 2006?

Yes, it will. Remember, an estate has to choose between using the small-business credit and using the applicable exclusion amount. When the applicable exclusion amount is $1 million, the small-business credit will really be worth only another $300,000. Because of the complexity of using the small-business credit, it may make more sense to use other planning. Other planning may be especially important because, unlike the applicable exclusion amount, the small-business estate tax credit can be used only at death. It may make more sense to transfer all or part of a business during one's life, using all or part of the applicable exclusion amount, rather than relying on the small-business credit.

What happens if my family sells or stops operating the business before the end of the required 10-year period?

If the business does not stay in operation or is sold before the 10-year period ends, your heirs who received the business interest must pay back to the IRS some of the tax savings your estate received from use of the small-business credit. The amount of the payback depends upon how many years they held and operated the business.

The payback penalty can result in unexpected tax liability to your heirs. This must be considered in deciding to take advantage of the small-business credit instead of the unified credit.

🖎 *Is it hard for an estate to qualify for the small-business estate tax credit?*

You bet. The law is very complex. If this provision is to be used, an individual must start planning early so that his or her estate and business will be eligible for this treatment. This is one area in which a great deal of advice and expertise is critical.

Buy-Sell Agreements

🖎 *If I start a corporation with another person, do we need a specific type of buy-sell agreement to protect our respective interests?*

Whenever you have a corporation with multiple owners, you should have a written *buy-sell agreement.* Such an agreement addresses what happens to the shareholders' respective interests in the case of death, disability, divorce, bankruptcy, or an unreconcilable disagreement among the shareholders. A buy-sell agreement can be invaluable and is highly recommended in any privately held corporation.

🖎 *What are the realistic dangers if my fellow shareholders and I fail to prepare a buy-sell agreement and one of us dies?*

Upon the death of a shareholder, that shareholder's shares will pass to others through his or her will or trust or by operation of law. You may end up with new colleagues who do not understand you or the business and who will be looking out for their financial interests through the representation of their lawyers.

🖎 *I already have a buy-sell agreement, but how do I know it contains what it should?*

Does your buy-sell agreement provide for:

- A predictable ownership path
- Control to pass in a way that settles, rather than encourages, arguments
- Ways to settle arguments without your input
- Money if interests need to be bought out or financial obligations need to be secured

In business continuity planning, a good buy-sell agreement settles these questions in advance, smoothing the path for successors to assume the responsibilities of the business. When families are involved in a business, it is especially important to set up a management structure that will function smoothly without an owner's participation in it.

◢ What are the basic types of buy-sell agreements?

The three basic types of buy-sell agreements are stock redemption agreements (entity purchase agreements in the case of a partnership or an LLC), cross-purchase agreements, and hybrid purchase agreements.

◢ What is a stock redemption agreement?

A *stock redemption agreement* is made between the individual shareholders and the corporation. The individual shareholders agree that upon the occurrence of a triggering event such as the death of a shareholder, the decedent's estate is obligated to offer to sell his or her stock ownership to the corporation at a predetermined price and under predetermined conditions of sale. The corporation is likewise obligated to "redeem," or purchase, the stock. The agreement is usually funded by insurance owned by the corporation on the life of each shareholder.

A partnership can buy back a partner's interest through a similar method often referred to as an *entity purchase agreement*. With this type of agreement, the partnership often purchases life insurance on the lives of the partners and is the beneficiary of that insurance. On a partner's death, the partnership purchases the interest of that partner with the funding provided by the insurance. The result is that the partnership is owned by the remaining partners and the deceased partner's family has cash based upon a predetermined value of that partner's interest.

Members of limited liability companies would also follow this planning pattern.

◢ What is a cross-purchase agreement?

A *cross-purchase agreement* is made between the individual shareholders, partners, or LLC members rather than between them and their business entity. With a cross-purchase agreement, upon the death, disability, or retirement of a principal, the remaining principals are personally obligated to purchase the decedent's business interest on a pro rata basis at a predetermined price and under predetermined terms.

In most cross-purchase agreement planning, each principal usually owns a life insurance policy on the lives of the other business principals.

⚜ What are the advantages of a cross-purchase agreement?

The major advantages are:

- The person purchasing the interest gets a new basis in the purchased business interest that is equal to the new price paid, thereby creating income tax (capital gain) savings if that interest is later sold at a higher price.
- The agreement does not generate problems with family attribution rules.
- There are no problems with state law, which may restrict redemptions of stock.

⚜ What are "hybrid" agreements?

Hybrid purchase agreements combine both redemption and cross-purchase features. They are referred to as *wait-and-see agreements* as they enable the remaining shareholders to determine whether the business has sufficient funds to make the purchase or whether the purchase should be made directly by the shareholders.

Life insurance is generally owned by the shareholders, and the selling shareholder or his or her representatives are required to first offer the stock to the corporation. If the corporation declines to make the purchase, the shareholders are then obligated to purchase the stock.

By selecting hybrid agreements, either the business or the business principals can own the life insurance purchased on the life of the shareholder being bought out.

⚜ Which is preferable, a stock redemption (or entity purchase) agreement or a cross-purchase arrangement?

The answer depends on many tax and practical factors. The primary tax issue is that the purchaser should be able to qualify for capital gain taxation rather than ordinary-income treatment on the subsequent sale of his or her business interest. For example:

> In starting a business, Able and Baker each contribute $10,000 for 5000 shares of stock. At the time Able dies, the fair market value of the stock has doubled. If the corporation redeems the stock from Able at his death, Baker will control a $40,000 business but have a tax basis of only $10,000. If a cross-purchase is involved, Baker will purchase the stock at $20,000 and have a $30,000 basis (Baker's $10,000 plus Able's $20,000), which will reduce Baker's subsequent gain when he later sells the stock.

⚸ *In your experience, what determines whether or not a cross-purchase agreement is used?*

Buy-sell agreements are primarily funded with life insurance on the lives of the shareholders or partners. If there are only two shareholders or partners, a cross-purchase agreement can be used, with each owning a life insurance policy on the other. If there are multiple shareholders or partners, it may be simpler for the corporation or other business entity to own the policies.

⚸ *Are there any other determining factors?*

Life insurance owned by a C corporation is subject to the alternative minimum tax, while life insurance owned by individual shareholders is not subject to AMT.

⚸ *What types of events should trigger a buyout under the terms of a buy-sell agreement?*

The death or disability of a business partner or disagreement among business partners should trigger a buyout.

⚸ *What if one of the business owners just wants out of the business?*

This scenario often puts a great deal of financial pressure on the buying partner to find the money to make the deal. Buyouts due to death or disability are often funded through the use of insurance, but no such insurance is normally available when somebody just wants out.

To discourage this situation, a reduction in the formula price for the business is often included in the agreement. Thus, the value that a partner or a partner's estate might receive for his or her ownership interest in the event of his or her death or disability would be reduced by X percent if that partner forces the other partner to buy him or her out.

While this technique has the advantage of discouraging forced sales because of the reduced price, it also gives the remaining principal an opportunity to increase his or her interest in the business at a discounted price.

An agreement does not have to permit forced buyouts. Whether or not it does will depend upon your wishes and the advice of your counsel.

⚸ *What is the relationship between buy-sell agreements and federal estate taxes?*

If a business valuation is properly established, the buy-sell agreement should determine the estate tax value of the business.

In buy-sell agreements involving unrelated principals, the appropriate business valuation used in the agreement will generally avoid an after-death valuation dispute with the IRS.

In buy-sell agreements between related parties, the business valuation will almost always be the subject of close IRS scrutiny to ensure that it does not unreasonably reduce the fair market value of the business interest.

⚜ How does a buy-sell agreement establish a value for estate tax purposes?

In order for the buy-sell agreement to establish the estate tax value of a business, the agreement must be an enforceable and binding agreement established for a valid business purpose.

The agreement must be for a price that is determinable and reasonable at the time the agreement is made. If the agreement represents full and adequate consideration at the time it is made, the price will be upheld even if there is a difference between the agreement price and the fair market value at the time of the triggering event. However, agreements among family members will almost always be scrutinized for reasonableness by the IRS.

In order for the taxpayer to set a business value for federal estate tax purposes, the agreement must be comparable to similar arrangements entered into by persons in an arm's-length transaction rather than a device to avoid federal estate taxes. The burden is on the taxpayer to prove the validity of the valuation.

Transfers to Family Members

⚜ We want our daughter to take over our family business. We cannot afford to give it to her because we need the income it generates for our retirement, and we are reluctant to sell it to her because of the capital gain taxes we'll have to pay. What are our options?

There are a number of planning options you should consider.

INSTALLMENT SALE   An installment sale to your daughter would allow you to transfer the business to her immediately and would provide you with an income stream for the term that you set in the installment note. However, whenever you sell an asset to a family member, you must treat it as an arm's-length transaction; any discounting that you provide your daughter—whether on the price or the interest rate on the installment note—may be construed to be a taxable gift by the IRS if the price is too low or the terms are too good. Under an installment sale you do not avoid the capital gain tax but will be able to defer the tax by paying it over the life of the note.

SELF-CANCELING INSTALLMENT NOTE A self-canceling installment note has a unique additional provision: The obligation is canceled in the event of your death. Thus, you would receive the income stream that you desire, but your estate will not have to pay estate tax on the unpaid portion of the promissory note at the time of your death.

PRIVATE ANNUITY You could sell the business to your daughter in exchange for a private annuity. A private annuity involves a sale to a family member for a number of fixed payments (determined by IRS tables) for the remainder of your life. The obligation to make these payments ends at your death. If you live a short time, your daughter will have acquired the business with very little investment. If you outlive your actuarial life expectancy, your daughter will have paid more than the business was worth.

By using a private annuity, you sell the business to your daughter and receive a set income every year for the rest of your and your spouse's lives. If the asset does not produce an income to cover these payments, this strategy may not be operable because of the demand on your daughter to produce the money to make the payments.

FAMILY LIMITED PARTNERSHIP You can establish a family limited partnership and transfer your business into it. Thereafter, you can give limited-partner interests to your daughter over a period of years at discounts ranging from 30 to 50 percent. As general partner, you will be able to retain control over the management of your business until you feel that your daughter is ready to take over. You can also provide yourself and your spouse with an income stream for as long as you desire for discharging your duties as general partners.

GRANTOR RETAINED ANNUITY TRUST You could create an irrevocable grantor retained annuity trust (GRAT). With this technique, you transfer the business to the GRAT, and the GRAT pays you a percentage of the value of the business over a period of time and at an interest rate that you select. At the end of the payment period, the business belongs to your daughter.

The Internal Revenue Code provides tables that measure the amount of the remainder interest, which constitutes the gift amount upon which you may have to pay gift tax.

The longer the retained income term, the smaller the gift will be; conversely, the shorter the time over which the income payments will be made, the larger the gift will be for federal gift tax purposes. If you die before the expiration of the retained term, the transaction will be treated for federal estate tax purposes as if it never occurred.

Employee Stock Ownership Plans

⧏ *What is an ESOP?*

An *employee stock ownership plan (ESOP)* is a qualified retirement plan which invests in the company's stock; it was created in the Internal Revenue Code. In an ESOP the company makes contributions to the plan for the benefit of its employees, and the contributions to the plan are used to acquire stock in the company, which must be a regular C corporation.

⧏ *Can you explain to me in simple terms how an ESOP works?*

An ESOP is a tax-qualified plan. The employer is allowed to make tax-deductible contributions, of either company stock or cash, to a trust. The employee participants then have the benefit of having stock or cash allocated to them according to a variety of formulas that are identical for practical purposes to any other deferred-compensation plan. When their employment is terminated or when they retire or die, they or their families will receive amounts of cash or stock in the company as distributions from the ESOP.

From the company's perspective, an ESOP can generate meaningful income tax deductions if stock rather than cash is being contributed to the plan. It can also create a wonderful market for stock which might otherwise not be very marketable at all.

⧏ *What are the uses of an ESOP in estate and business planning?*

The adoption of an ESOP by a corporation has several potential advantages:

- It allows majority shareholders to get money out of their corporations that would otherwise be trapped in retained earnings.
- Provided that an ESOP owns 30 percent of the stock after the initial purchase or transfer of shares to it, the selling shareholder can take cash he or she has received, reinvest that cash into *qualified replacement property (QRP)*—essentially U.S. stocks or bonds—

within 1 year, and not recognize any gain on the transaction. As long as the selling shareholder retains the QRP, there is no capital gain recognition. When the QRP is sold, the capital gain will be recognized, but there is a carryover of the basis from the original stock to the QRP.

≥\ Can an ESOP be coupled with an FLP?

A unique planning opportunity exists when the shareholder who is selling stock to an ESOP first transfers the stock to a family limited partnership that he or she creates. The reason for this additional transfer to the FLP is that the value of the partnership interest can be discounted at the death of the shareholder for estate tax purposes and can also receive a step-up in basis for income tax purposes if the proper election is filed at the death of the partnership owner.

≥\ Are there different ways that an ESOP can receive company stock?

There are three ways that an ESOP can receive company stock:

- It can receive stock directly from the shareholder through a purchase with cash or borrowed funds.
- It can purchase the stock from the corporation with cash or borrowed funds.
- The corporation can contribute stock to the ESOP.

≥\ What is a typical situation in which an ESOP might be used?

At some point, closely held company founders often wish to receive cash for all or part of their stock without selling to a third party or taking the company public. They frequently think highly of their employees and are desirous of rewarding key people within their organizations. This is a situation that is ripe for an ESOP.

≥\ Are there additional benefits of an ESOP?

An ESOP gives employees a vested interest in their company, providing additional motivation to make the company and its shareholders more successful. To the extent that the corporation contributes cash or stock to the ESOP, the corporation can deduct the contributions dollar for dollar, in effect making paper contributions to generate bottom-line cash deductions.

◊ Can you give me a "benefit overview" of an ESOP?

A corporation can contribute cash to an ESOP on a tax-deductible basis. The cash can then be used to acquire the stock of a majority shareholder.

It is usually difficult for corporate founders to find someone in the open market who will buy their stock. And, even if they find a buyer, they will not generally be willing to sell a controlling interest in the company. Unless they are willing to sell a majority interest in the company, it is highly unlikely that anyone will want to purchase their stock. With an ESOP, a majority shareholder can sell less than a majority interest in his or her stock to the ESOP and defer or eliminate capital gain taxes. ESOP planning provides an ideal way for a majority shareholder to find a "marketplace" for his or her stock. With the proper use of an ESOP, the business owner can even continue to effectively control the company.

◊ What is a leveraged ESOP?

A *leveraged ESOP (LESOP)* is an ESOP that borrows money either from the corporation or from a bank and uses the funds to purchase the shares. For this transaction to work, however, the selling shareholder will undoubtedly be required by the lending institution to guarantee the note.

◊ Are banks willing to make loans to ESOPs?

Until the 1996 tax act, banks were more than willing to enter into this type of transaction since they were able to exclude from their taxable income 50 percent of the income they received from the transaction. This exclusion for banks no longer applies, so institutions are not as anxious to make this type of loan.

◊ My company has a well-funded profit-sharing plan. Can I use it to facilitate the purchase of my stock?

Most profit-sharing plans have been drafted to permit the purchase of a life insurance policy on the life of the majority owner of a corporation. If your profit-sharing plan purchases a life insurance policy on your life and retains it as a general asset of the plan, with a death benefit equal to 25 percent of the fair market value of the corporation at the time of your death, the profit-sharing plan could be converted into an ESOP with the proceeds of the life insurance policy being used to purchase stock from your estate.

Life Insurance in Continuity Planning

✎ *How can I provide liquidity to pay for my obligations?*

If your spouse is to continue your business, its value will be included in his or her estate. If liquidity is not otherwise provided, the business may have to be sold or heavily leveraged to cover the resulting federal estate tax obligation. In such cases, life insurance planning is usually discussed early on to alleviate the ravages of potentially disastrous estate and generation-skipping taxes.

✎ *Can I purchase life insurance in an irrevocable trust and then let my family liquidate the family business?*

This is a meaningful—but often overlooked—alternative. If you do not have partners or key people whom you wish to have the business upon your death, the combination of life insurance and liquidation could be your best alternative. To implement this strategy, you would make gifts to an irrevocable life insurance trust that purchases life insurance on your life equal to the value of your closely held business interest. Upon your death, the proceeds will be available for your spouse and children and will pass tax-free to your children upon your spouse's subsequent death.

With this approach, your family members can liquidate your business interest and add the proceeds to the insurance benefits they have already received. The tax on the liquidated value of your business interests will be directly proportionate to their liquidated value and might place your estate into significantly lower brackets.

✎ *How do I value my business for buy-sell purposes?*

The fair market value of your interest in the business will be included in your estate for federal estate, state estate, generation-skipping, and inheritance tax purposes. Thus, if you and your co-owners artificially inflate the value of your respective business interests, up to 55 percent of that value could pass directly to the government due to federal estate tax.

Assuming that the other owners of the business are not family members, one recommendation would be to put the lowest possible value on the business interest, especially if the buyout is to be funded by life insurance. Assume that your interest in the business is worth between $750,000 and $1 million. If the other owners agree to buy your interest at your death for $1 million, they can ensure that interest with life insurance. Your business interest will be included in your gross estate at a value of $1 million. At potential federal estate tax rates of 55 percent, your family members may end up getting as little as $450,000.

If, however, you value your interest at $750,000, the federal estate tax savings will be $138,000. The money saved by funding the buyout with $750,000 of life insurance rather than $1 million of life insurance could be used to purchase a second insurance policy on your life in the amount of $250,000. This second life insurance policy would be for the benefit of your family, and it would be owned by an irrevocable trust referred to as an ILIT or wealth replacement trust. The ILIT will be the beneficiary, and the benefits will not be subject to estate taxation. Thus, your family will receive all $250,000 of the proceeds from the second life insurance policy.

In the end, by valuing your business interest at $750,000 instead of $1 million and by utilizing an ILIT, your family will receive $587,500 ($337,500 from the buyout plus $250,000 from the ILIT) rather than $450,000—an additional benefit of $137,500 without a dime of additional cost.

⚒ *Are premiums paid on business life insurance deductible?*

The Internal Revenue Code does not allow a deduction for premiums paid on life insurance.

⚒ *Are life insurance death proceeds exempt from income tax?*

Life insurance proceeds are exempt from income taxes. However, if an existing policy is sold or otherwise "transferred for value," the proceeds may be subject to federal income tax.

⚒ *Are life insurance proceeds payable to a corporation subject to the alternative minimum tax?*

If the corporation is an S corporation, the proceeds received are not subject to the AMT. If it is a regular corporation, however, the proceeds are subject to the AMT.

⚒ *In a stock redemption or buy-sell agreement, are there any tax ramifications if a regular corporation is the beneficiary of the life insurance?*

If life insurance is purchased on the life of each shareholder, the corporation is not the best choice as beneficiary because:

- The cash surrender value and proceeds of the policy will be included in the corporation's adjusted current earnings for purposes of computing the alternative minimum tax.
- If the corporation distributes the proceeds of the life insurance policy to a retiring shareholder, the distribution is considered a dividend and is subject to double taxation.
- When the policy is distributed, the corporation must recognize the gain—the difference between the value of the policy and its adjusted basis—and the shareholder must recognize dividend income.

✑ How can double taxation be avoided in the above situation?

The corporation could sell the insurance policy to the shareholder or an entity controlled by the shareholder, but in doing so care must be taken to avoid the *transfer-for-value* rules. However, if a corporation sells a life insurance policy to an individual shareholder or legal entity for its fair market value at the time of sale, the purchaser could incur an income tax liability on the policy income accrued after the sale.

✑ If I have existing policies that I want to transfer to a limited liability company, are there income tax consequences I should consider?

The transfer-for-value rules do not apply when a life insurance contract is transferred to the insured or to a partner or partnership. An LLC can be a partnership for purposes of federal taxes. Therefore, the insurance proceeds are excluded from income and are tax-free to the partners or LLC members.

With an LLC, there are no problems with retained incidents of ownership. An LLC allows for centralization of management to ensure proper maintenance of the policy and payments of premiums. However, if an LLC is set up and has an insurance policy as its only asset, there may be the question of whether it has an appropriate business purpose.

SALE OF A BUSINESS

✑ Is it better to do my estate planning before or after the sale of my business?

You would be wise to have a complete *wealth strategies* plan before entering into a contract to sell your business.

☙ *What can I do to prepare my business for sale?*

Look at your business through a buyer's eyes. What key issues would a buyer be concerned about, and how could you present them in the best possible light to impress a buyer?

A buyer will usually want to purchase the assets of the business rather than the business entity itself. Purchasing the business entity may result in the purchase of hidden liabilities of the selling entity. A purchase of the old entity's assets allows the buyer to start anew without the liabilities of the predecessor business.

With this fact in mind, it should be clear that one of the things you can do to improve the marketability of your business is to literally clean up its assets. Whether it be the accounts receivable, rolling stock, equipment, inventory, or goodwill, you can significantly heighten its value by preparing the assets for sale. For instance, improving the length of time it takes to collect your accounts receivable improves the value of the remaining accounts receivable. Cleaning and improving the outward appearance of your equipment is another easy way to improve the value of the assets.

The financial records of the business will need to be reviewed and brought up to date. The buyer will want to review at least 5 years of business tax returns. The financial statements should be reviewed and prepared according to generally accepted accounting principles. You would be wise not to overstate or misstate the financial condition of your business, as statements of this sort generally lead to future litigation based upon claims of fraud and misrepresentation.

While it is important that you prepare accurate financial information, it is also important to prepare information about past financial decisions. For instance, in year-end planning for regular corporations, many accountants will recommend that the profit of the company be spent to prepurchase supplies or equipment. This decision means that the profit will be spent solely to avoid taxation at the corporate level. Additionally, the value of improvements and equipment may be reflected only at the book value and not the true fair market value of the asset. These decisions result in reducing the profit of the corporation so that the financial statements do not accurately reflect the financial situation of the business.

It is important for you to prepare emotionally for the sale process and not be thin-skinned, as buyers may be critical of the business or the assets in order to negotiate a lower purchase price. Thick skin and patience are important factors for a seller. Being prepared to walk away from a sale helps keep the price higher and contract terms more favorable.

It is also important to evaluate the type of business you are selling. A business that is based upon a niche market is easier to sell and worth more money than a business that is relationship-based. A business that has failed to modernize or to retool is not as marketable as a business that is on the cutting edge of technology. The more difficult it is to replicate the business, the more valuable the business is.

If the business is a corporation, the minutes and corporate books should be reviewed and updated if they are not already complete. The buyer will likely ask for this information because it can provide insight into the history of the business.

If you are thinking of selling your business, you should plan on consulting with your attorney, accountant, financial planner, and other advisors. They can help structure your business for sale and prepare you for the process. A little time, energy, and advice should produce a higher price at better terms from a greater number of potential buyers.

⋈ When is the best time to sell a business?

Usually the best time to sell a business is when your particular industry is doing well and you do not need to sell it.

⋈ What factors should I consider before I sell my business?

Knowing when to sell a business is an art, not a science. Factors to consider are:

1. Is your industry expanding or contracting?
2. Is your competition increasing or decreasing?
3. Are your children interested in your business?
4. Do you have a key employee or competitor who would want to buy your business?
5. Will your business require a large infusion of capital in the near future?
6. What is the state of your and your family's health?
7. What would you do with the proceeds of the sale? (Would you be able to invest them after paying the taxes and costs of sale and still get a satisfactory return on your money?)
8. What would you do with your newfound idle time?

If I sell on terms, what should I look for in a potential buyer?

Look into the creditworthiness of your buyer and into a past history of successes and failures in running similar businesses.

How do I find a buyer for my business?

The best way to find a buyer for your business is to look at your competition. Is there a competitor in a nearby city or on the other side of town who is in an expansion mode? Competitors know your industry, and you should have a pretty good idea of their ability to perform and *repay* the financing you may be carrying as part of the transaction.

Most likely there are trade journals that apply to your industry or business; classified ads in these publications are usually inexpensive and provide you with broad exposure to potential qualified buyers.

Your accountant or attorney may have clients who are interested in buying a business such as yours. You can also hire a business broker.

Should I consider using a business broker?

A business broker will charge you a fee ranging from 6 to 12 percent of the purchase price. Experience shows that professional brokers earn their money.

What else can a business broker do for me?

A business broker will typically help structure, negotiate, and close the transaction. He or she will help determine the value of the business, help you put the business in sellable condition, and, of course, look for appropriate buyers. He or she may also arrange financing if the buyer requires it.

Should I sell assets or stock?

It is easiest to sell stock, but buyers would rather purchase assets because they can start new depreciation schedules.

Is there a good way to sell my business to key managers?

The company can enter into a nonqualified deferred-compensation plan, which obligates it to pay you a fixed amount of compensation for a certain number of years. Such an arrangement will guarantee you an annual income stream for years after the sale is made while decreasing the value of the company; it will also justify a lower sales price between you and your key people.

⫷ *How can I be sure that my estate will receive the balance of the money owed to me on my death?*

Generally, the key-person shareholders are required to purchase life insurance policies on the selling shareholder's life equal to the remaining value of the purchase obligation. Since the obligation liquidates over time, decreasing term insurance is generally purchased that follows the debt schedule.

VALUATIONS FOR
BUSINESS PLANNING

Reasons for Valuations

⫷ *How important is the valuation of assets in the estate planning process?*

The valuation of assets for gift and estate tax purposes is critical. If effective discount planning is implemented with valuation planning, it is possible to achieve a situation where "the sum of the parts does not equal the whole." To achieve this result, it is essential to form a *valuation team*. This is a team of advisors consisting of an attorney, tax advisor, financial planner, and business valuation appraiser. These professionals must develop and provide the evidence supporting the valuation of the business and any discounting that may be appropriate.

The fair market value methodology of valuing businesses continues to be effective. The tax concept of "fair market value" requires that both the taxpayer and the government determine the value of a business according to a hypothetical, free-market standard in which the hypothetical "willing buyer" and "willing seller" are considered at arm's length.

For business valuation, the family relationship of the parties is irrelevant. This is to the advantage of families seeking to share wealth on a multigenerational basis.

As part of the Revenue Reconciliation Act of 1990, Congress confirmed the viability of "fragmented-ownership" discounts by recognizing that the courts generally approve corporate and partnership equity discounts (lack of control and nonmarketability minority interests) often aggregating 30 to 50 percent in relation to underlying business or asset values.

By using a combination of the business valuation discounts available to them, a married couple, using their combined unified credit of $1.25 million in 1998, might be able to transfer upward of $2.5 million in assets free of federal gift or estate tax to their children.

❧ Why are business valuations important for buy-sell agreements?

A bona fide business valuation is important before commencing any gifting program. Even a $10,000-per-year annual exclusion gifting program may be ineffective if appropriate business valuations are not prepared.

Business valuations establish fair market value for gift and estate tax purposes. The Internal Revenue Code provides a substantial penalty for a material understatement of value. If the value claimed is less than its proper value, there is a 20 percent penalty on the underpayment if it exceeds $5000. There is a 40 percent penalty if the value is 25 percent less than its proper value. However, penalties will not apply if there is reasonable cause for underpayment and the taxpayer acted in good faith with respect to the underpayment.

Taxpayers should remember that the burden of proof for establishing a correct business valuation is on them. Arguably, an independent, professionally conducted business valuation would meet the good-faith test to avoid the underpayment penalty. However, the good-faith test will not alleviate the interest which accrues for underpayments of federal gift tax.

❧ In general, what does the business valuation process involve?

The basic IRS pronouncement on valuations is Revenue Ruling 59-60. This ruling requires consideration of:

- The nature of the business and history of the enterprise
- The general economic outlook and the outlook for the particular industry
- The book value of the stock and the financial condition of the business
- The earning capacity of the company
- The dividend-paying capacity of the company
- Whether or not the enterprise has goodwill or other intangible value
- Past sales of the stock
- The market price of comparable stocks

⅍ Can the value of a business be determined on future earnings?

The value of a business is often based upon its future earnings. Determining future earnings involves a four-step process:

1. *Adjust prior earnings to reflect economic reality.* This involves making adjustments to items such as the business owner's high salary and benefits and one-time expenses, adjusting the inventory accounting system from LIFO to FIFO, and correcting improper accounting methods.

2. *Attempt to find comparable public and private companies upon which to make comparisons in order to determine the business value.* Although a necessary step, finding comparable companies is often difficult and at times impossible.

3. *Use prior financial statements over a 5-year period to project future earnings.* Two popular methods for determining future earnings include the averaging of prior earnings on both a weighted and an unweighted basis. If the business is experiencing financial difficulty, the value of the business could be determined on the basis of its liquidation or net asset value.

4. *Capitalize the business earnings.*

⅍ How do I capitalize earnings for valuation purposes?

A *capitalization,* or *yield, rate* is selected on the basis of a safe rate and a risk rate. The *safe rate* is frequently the interest rate on a long-term or intermediate-term Treasury bond. The *risk rate* is additional compensation to the investor for investing in a particular business. In other words, the more volatile and unpredictable the business, the higher the rate of return the investor must earn to compensate for the additional risk. Considerations of the risk rate include:

- Evaluation of the economy and specific industry outlook
- Whether the business is diversified in its products and customers
- The ability and depth of management
- The profitability and stability of earnings
- Consideration of the financial ratios of the business and comparison of the ratios to those of the industry

For small, closely held businesses the risk premiums can be approximately 15 to 30 percent in addition to the safe rate.

Once the capitalization rate is determined, it is applied to the appropriate valuation method. The primary valuation methods are adjusted net assets, capitalization of earnings, comparison of the price-earnings ratio of comparable businesses, excess earnings, and discounted earnings dividend. For example, using the capitalization of earnings method with average earnings of $100,000 and a capitalization rate of 25 percent, the value would be $400,000 (i.e., $400,000 would be required to yield $100,000 at a capitalization rate of 25 percent).

⩕ *My industry uses "rules of thumb" to value businesses. If I can prove that this is how businesses are bought and sold, will the IRS go along with me?*

Although generalized *rules of thumb* might be used in various industries to arrive at a sales price (e.g., earnings times a specified factor), rules of thumb are not accepted as being accurate for formal appraisals.

Once the value of the business has been determined, the valuation is subject to adjustments for either the payment of a premium based upon the ability to control the business ownership (control premium) or discounts for the inability to control the business (minority discount) and the lack of marketability of shares of a closely owned business (marketability discount). The marketability discount can also be affected by a restrictive buy-sell agreement.

⩕ *Are there IRS guidelines in this area?*

Revenue Ruling 59-60 requires that the appraiser consider all alternatives and select the most appropriate method. Averaging and weighting the results of the various methods is basically not acceptable. A professionally written report meeting IRS and professional standards is necessary to withstand IRS scrutiny. The comprehensiveness and professionalism of the report may well be a factor in whether the IRS desires to question the valuation.

⩕ *Are there additional considerations I should know about in trying to establish a presale value for my business?*

Here are some additional considerations:

- Ask yourself, "How important am I to the success of the business?" If the business is based on your skills or your contacts, you must be willing to stay on and train the buyer and/or ensure the continuity of the base business or you will not realize the full value for your business.

- The identical business in a neighboring market may be worth more or less than your business depending on market factors over which you have no control.
- If your industry has just a few key players, your business may be strategically worth more money to one of your competitors than to others. Selling to a competitor gives that company the opportunity to buy market share. Competitors often buy a business without changing its name.
- Your business is worth more if it does repeat business with several key customers rather than constantly looking for new customers. On the other hand, doing a great deal of your volume with a single customer or a handful of customers can have a negative impact on the value of your business.
- Consider that one of your major customers could be an excellent candidate as a potential buyer of your business.
- Determine how important the location of your business is to a potential buyer.

⩔ Do buy-sell agreement business valuation formulas stand the test of time?

The problem with using formulas or certificates of value is that they represent a methodology for determining value at a given moment in time. The formula that is current when a business is new is probably not correct in later stages of the business life cycle.

⩔ Is there a surefire way of establishing a buy-sell value for closely held business interests on the death of an owner?

The IRS will accept the value set forth in the buy-sell agreement for estate tax purposes if the following criteria are met:

- The price is final or determinable by a formula.
- The estate of the decedent is obligated to sell the decedent's shares, and the surviving shareholders of the company are obligated to purchase the shares.
- The decedent's shares could not have been disposed of during his or her lifetime without first offering the shares to the company or the other shareholders at a price no higher than that fixed for the purchase at death.
- The buy-sell agreement constitutes a bona fide business arrangement and does not serve as a testamentary substitute.

Valuation Discounts

Can you explain valuation discounts in lay terms and tell me how they work?

There are two viable types of discounts: lack of marketability and minority interests. Together, these discounts provide a donor with the opportunity to leverage the transfer of assets during his or her lifetime or upon death.

A *lack-of-marketability discount* is created by restricting the right of an owner to transfer his or her interest in an entity. By making the business interest virtually unmarketable, the holder of the business interest cannot transfer his or her ownership without first complying with the terms and conditions of the agreement. These restrictions, coupled with a restriction of the price to be paid for the business interest if the business or its other owners buy it back, create the lack-of-marketability discount.

A *minority-interest discount* is created by breaking up a block of majority ownership into smaller minority interests. In a death situation, the value of the interest transferred will be based upon the holdings of the decedent at the time of his or her death. A willing buyer will demand a discount from the value of any minority interest because such an interest does not provide the buyer with any means or method of controlling the entity whose units are being purchased.

Minority-discount planning works as well for federal estate tax planning as it does for gift tax planning. If the business owner holds a controlling interest in a business at death, the value of that interest is not subject to a minority discount. But if the business owner holds only a minority interest in the business, the value of that interest may be eligible for a large minority discount.

While transfers at death are valued upon the interest transferred by the decedent, lifetime transfers are valued based upon the interest received by each individual recipient. Minority discounts are possible even though the gifts in question are to members of a single family. If, however, one individual receives a control block as a lump-sum gift, no minority discount will apply. Gifts of noncontrolling interests will usually be eligible for the minority discount.

While the Internal Revenue Service no longer applies the family attribution doctrine—this doctrine attributes ownership by related family members to the family patriarch or matriarch for purposes of denying an otherwise justified minority discount—issues of "form over substance" and "actual value" may prevent application of a minority discount. If the IRS can show that the underlying transfer was clearly designed to avoid income taxes, a minority discount will be denied.

A tremendous opportunity exists in the use of discounts in estate planning. However, it is critical that the attorney, accountant, financial planner, and appraiser work together to properly structure the business agreements necessary to obtain the appropriate discounts.

☙ What is the Internal Revenue Service's response to the use of discounts?

The IRS doesn't like them, but it has been ineffective in fighting them in the courts.

☙ What qualifications should an appraiser have to substantiate the discounts claimed?

It is critical to the valuation discounting process that the professional drafting the organizational documentation for the business has a thorough working knowledge of valuation discounts and what planning will affect the bottom-line evaluation by subsequent appraisers.

It is even more critical that the appraiser be experienced in business appraisals, with an in-depth knowledge in the valuation and discount processes, to be able to carefully and meticulously document the factors affecting the bottom line of the valuation.

Appraisers who do not do their homework will not produce appraisals that will support meaningful discounts that will be approved by the Internal Revenue Service. Nevertheless, quality appraisals will result in substantial federal estate and gift tax savings for the clients.

☙ Do I need more than one appraiser?

When it comes to valuation discounts, two types of appraisers are typically required. The first is the *substantive appraiser,* who can properly value the worth of a particular asset as a specialist in that kind of asset—for example, a farm specialist for valuing farms, a commercial real estate specialist for valuing commercial real estate, or a fast-food-franchise specialist for valuing a fast-food franchise. The substantive appraiser must be followed by a *business valuation specialist,* who then values the discounts that will enure to minority-ownership interests in the assets or businesses.

Valuing Particular Assets

⌇ *How is real estate that is used in my business or my family farm valued?*

Real estate used either in a farming operation or by a closely held business is generally valued at its fair market value, which is often a much higher value than its book, adjusted book, or assessed value. For purposes of valuing such real estate, the IRS allows a *special-use valuation election* so that an executor may, if all qualifications are met, elect to value the real estate based on its actual use as a business or farm property rather than at its fair market value. For such an election, the following requirements must be met:

- The real property must pass to or be acquired by a qualified heir of the estate. (A *qualified heir* is defined as a member of the decedent's family—including the decedent's spouse, parents, children, and stepchildren and the spouses and lineal descendants of those individuals—or a trust for the exclusive benefit of these persons.)
- The decedent, or a member of the decedent's family, must have owned the property and have materially participated in the operation of the farm or business for 5 out of the 8 years preceding the earlier of the date of death, the date on which the decedent became disabled, or the date on which the decedent began receiving Social Security benefits.
- The real property must have been used as a farm or in a trade or business on the date of the decedent's death, and for 5 out of the 8 years before the decedent's death.
- The adjusted value of the real property must make up 25 percent or more of the adjusted value of the decedent's gross estate. (The adjusted value of the real estate is the fair market value of the real estate less any unpaid mortgages.)

Your accounting advisor, together with your attorney, can advise you on whether your real estate qualifies for the special election and whether you should plan to take advantage of it.

PART FOUR

Planning for
Later Years

Chapter 10: Retirement Planning

The questions and answers in Chapter 10 focus on the benefits, control, and taxation of various types of retirement plans rather than on the technical requirements of maintaining and administering the plans. This is not surprising, since they were submitted by attorneys who focus much more on planning than on the mechanics of plan operation. These questions and answers offer insights into the practicalities of plan participation, which are critical in an estate planning practice.

Some of the contributing authors treated individual retirement accounts and qualified plans as separate and distinct topics; others combined them. Because of the different points of view, we thought it might be helpful to the reader to see both approaches. That is why some of the information on individual retirement accounts and other qualified plans is much the same as the information dealing with individual retirement accounts only.

The labyrinth of legal and regulatory retirement complexities made Chapter 10 particularly challenging to edit. The result is a

461

chapter filled with practical information and suggestions about planning for qualified retirement plans and IRAs.

Chapter 11: Elder Law Planning

Elder law is one of the fastest-growing estate planning areas. As the United States makes a demographic leap to a society consisting of more people in older age brackets and more people living longer, the issues of protecting, planning, and helping the elderly are taking on enormous significance.

While many aspects of elder law have historically been of specific concern to lower-income and lower-net-worth individuals and couples, they are now becoming more indigenous in society. People in their forties, fifties, and even sixties are facing the prospect of supporting their parents, and they are increasingly interested in determining the best courses of action for protecting their parents and their parents' assets, as well as ensuring that their parents qualify for available government programs.

These same people are vitally interested in their own well-being and care as they age. With congressional emphasis on deficit reduction, decreasing opportunities for people to retire on solid company pension plans, and the change in public sentiment toward welfare and other social programs, planning for old age must begin earlier. Steps taken early in life can avoid a great deal of emotional and financial stress in the future.

Chapter 11's questions and answers on elder law provide innovative planning solutions in an area that traditionally does not offer much professional maneuvering room. This chapter is must reading for anyone who has an aging parent or who feels the need to plan for his or her own old age. It serves as an excellent primer in elder law and planning strategy.

chapter 10

Retirement Planning

THE IMPORTANCE
OF RETIREMENT PLANNING

⤚ *Why is retirement planning advantageous?*

Qualified retirement plans and deductible IRAs are important ways to save for retirement because they are funded with pre-income tax dollars. The earnings are also exempt from federal income tax until withdrawn.

⤚ *I have spent my life accumulating assets in my retirement plans. What goals should I have in planning for significant or large retirement plan proceeds?*

Once your IRA or qualified retirement plan becomes a substantial asset of your estate, the natural instinct of preservation begins to alter your philosophy with regard to planning strategies. There are two worthy goals for starting and maintaining an IRA or qualified retirement plan:

- The account might serve to support you, your spouse, and dependents upon your death or disability. You should begin to coordinate the effects of income and estate taxes on the account as you begin to make the required withdrawals or as you prepare for lump-sum distributions.
- You should also plan for controlling the use, investment, and distri-

butions of the account upon your death or disability without jeopardizing its income tax–deferred or estate tax–deferred qualities.

QUALIFIED RETIREMENT PLANS

✥ *What are qualified retirement plans?*

The government, as a matter of policy, has decided to encourage everyone to save for retirement. As a supplement to, or perhaps a replacement for, Social Security benefits, the government has created a system of special tax rules under Section 401 of the Internal Revenue Code to encourage the establishment of so-called qualified retirement plans.

The primary types of *qualified retirement plans* are pension plans and profit-sharing plans. There are three types of *pension plans:*

- Defined-benefit plans
- Money purchase plans
- Target-benefit plans

Profit-sharing plans are also generally put into three groups:

- Corporate/business-entity profit-sharing plans
- Section 401(k) plans
- Stock bonus plans

SEP-IRAS

✥ *What is a SEP-IRA?*

SEP-IRAs are *simplified employee pension* arrangements that allow self-employed persons to make IRA contributions for themselves and their employees. SEP rules permit employer contributions for each employee (including a contribution for the self-employed business owner) of up to 15 percent of an employee's compensation or $30,000, whichever is less.

SEP plans may also include an election by the employee to have part of his or her pay contributed to the SEP-IRA.

Employers who participate in SEPs are subject to time limits, employee inclusion or exclusion rules, and contribution limits.

INDIVIDUAL
RETIREMENT ACCOUNTS

❧ *What is an individual retirement account?*

An *individual retirement account (IRA)* is a nonqualified retirement plan. It is nonqualified because it is not described in Section 401 of the Internal Revenue Code. IRAs are generally not subject to the Employee Retirement Income Security Act (ERISA) of 1974 because they are not employee benefit plans.

Even though IRA participants do not enjoy the protections offered by ERISA, most retirement assets end up in an individual participant's IRA because of the flexibility of IRAs.

Earnings such as interest and dividends and capital gains on the assets inside the IRA are not taxed until you withdraw the funds. This can provide years of income tax–free compounding which will result in increased retirement savings.

IRAs are widely available from banks, insurance companies, mutual fund management companies, brokerage houses, and other sellers of investment products that can be used to fund such an account. An IRA must be in the form of a written trust or custodial account held for the exclusive benefit of the trust maker.

IRAs can be any of three types:

1. Those that are established by an individual with a bank, brokerage firm, or similar company that acts as a trustee of the investments
2. IRAs in the form of annuities or endowment contracts purchased by individuals from insurance companies
3. Plans that are established by employers and employee associations that qualify as IRAs

Deductible IRA

❧ *Would you summarize the features of the traditional deductible IRA?*

■ Generally, you can contribute up to $2000 each year provided that your earned income is at least that amount.

■ You receive an annual income tax deduction, up to certain limits, when you contribute money to the IRA.

- Earnings, such as interest and dividends and capital gains on the assets inside the IRA, are not taxed until you withdraw the funds.
- You pay ordinary income tax on both your contributions and the accumulated earnings when you withdraw them from the IRA.
- You cannot make withdrawals without penalty before age 59½ unless certain conditions are met.
- You must begin taking distributions by age 70½.
- You cannot make contributions after age 70½.

Roth IRA

⋨ *What is the difference between the traditional IRA and the new Roth IRA?*

The Taxpayer Relief Act of 1997 created a new IRA called the *Roth IRA Plus,* or *Roth IRA,* named after the author of the bill, Senator William Roth.

- The Roth IRA is nondeductible. This means funds you contribute to a Roth IRA are *not* deductible on your income tax return. In that sense it's not as advantageous as a deductible IRA.
- However, the Roth IRA has higher income eligibility limitations than those for traditional IRAs.
- Like the traditional IRA, earnings accumulate income tax–free.
- Because contributions to a Roth IRA are made with after-tax dollars, you are able to make withdrawals of contributions income tax–free.
- You can withdraw your contributions at any time without an early-withdrawal penalty.
- Most withdrawals of earnings after 59½ and more than 5 years after the establishment of the Roth IRA will also be completely free of income tax.
- You are not required to begin taking minimum distributions by age 70½. In fact, you do not have to take any distributions during your lifetime, and you can continue to make contributions after age 70½.

Contributions to IRAs

⋨ *What is the maximum annual contribution to an IRA?*

The maximum annual contribution to all types of IRAs, Roth or tra-

TABLE 10-1 Deductible IRA: Income Limits

| Year | AGI limits for contributions | |
	Single individuals	Married couples
1998	$30,000	$50,000
1999	31,000	51,000
2000	32,000	52,000
2001	33,000	53,000
2002	34,000	54,000
2003	40,000	60,000
2004	45,000	65,000
2005	50,000	70,000
2006	50,000	75,000
2007 & beyond	50,000	80,000

ditional, is $2000 assuming you meet the income tests for each type. This annual $2000 limit applies whether the contributions to the account are made by the individual or by his or her employer. If a spouse has no earnings, the other spouse may be able to contribute a full $2000 for the nonearning spouse.

⌲ Who is eligible to establish an IRA and make contributions?

Under certain income limitations, anyone who is paid earned income may establish an IRA. *Earned income* includes wages, compensation for services, salaries, commissions, or professional fees. It does not include investment income, such as interest, certain partnership distributions, dividends, or capital gains from investments, and it does not include amounts received as a pension or an annuity. A married person who qualifies for an IRA may also be able to set up and contribute to an IRA for his or her spouse if the spouse has no earned income.

You are eligible to make deductible contributions to traditional deductible IRAs if your adjusted gross income does not exceed the new schedule of limitations, as shown in Table 10-1.

If you are not eligible to make deductible contributions to an IRA, you may be eligible to make nondeductible contributions to a Roth

TABLE 10-2   Roth IRA: Income Limits and Contributions

| AGI limits for contributions | | Contribution |
Individual	Married filing jointly	
Less than $95,000	Less than $150,000	$2,000*
$95,000 to $110,000	$150,000 to $160,000	Use formula†
Over $110,000	Over $160,000	–0–

*Less any contributions you've made to other IRAs that year.

†Formula for individuals:
    AGI – $95,000 ÷ 5 = contribution that year (round to nearest $200)
 Formula for married couple filing joint return:
    AGI – $150,000 ÷ 5 = contribution that year (round to nearest $200)

IRA. The exact amount of the contributions, not to exceed $2000 in any tax year, that you are allowed to make to a Roth IRA will depend upon your adjusted gross income (AGI) for the year in which you make the contribution. Table 10-2 shows the AGI limitations for the Roth IRA. Your ability to contribute to a Roth IRA is determined only by these AGI limitations, regardless of whether you or your spouse is covered by a company-sponsored plan.

If I am covered by a qualified retirement plan sponsored by my employer, under what circumstances are my contributions to an IRA deductible?

If one spouse is covered under an employer's retirement plan, both spouses may be able to make tax-deductible contributions to IRAs, subject to certain restrictions that apply to the spouse who is in the employer's plan.

The AGI limits for deductible IRA contributions for individuals who are active participants in a qualified plan are shown in Table 10-3.

If I can't make a deductible contribution to an IRA, can I make a nondeductible contribution?

Individuals who are not entitled to a deduction are still permitted to make contributions to an IRA of up to $2000 ($4000 for a regular and a spousal IRA combined) or 100 percent of compensation, whichever is less. Although these contributions are not tax-deductible, as long as

TABLE 10-3   Deductible IRA: Income Limits for Participants in Qualified Plans

| Year | AGI limits for contributions* | |
	Individual	Married filing jointly
1998	$30,000–40,000	$50,000–60,000
1999	31,000–41,000	51,000–61,000
2000	32,000–42,000	52,000–62,000
2001	33,000–43,000	53,000–63,000
2002	34,000–44,000	54,000–64,000
2003	40,000–50,000	60,000–70,000
2004	45,000–55,000	65,000–75,000
2005	50,000–60,000	70,000–80,000
2006	50,000–60,000	75,000–85,000
2007	50,000–60,000	80,000–100,000

*A full deduction is available when AGI is below the lower dollar amount for each year. There is no deduction when AGI is above the upper dollar amount.

the contributions are within the allowed contributory limits, the earnings in the account will be tax-deferred until withdrawn.

✍ *What types of assets can be used for contributions to an IRA?*

All contributions to an IRA must be made in cash or negotiable instruments. IRA deductions are not allowed for contributions of property other than cash. Noncash contributions will not disqualify an IRA but will be considered excess contributions subject to a 6 percent annual excise tax.

✍ *When do contributions have to be made?*

Contributions to an IRA for a particular year must be made no later than the date the contributor's tax return is due for that year, typically April 15. Extensions of the filing of an income tax return do not extend the contribution date.

⁂ *At what age can one start making contributions?*

Deductions are available for any contributions made by an IRA participant who is between the age of birth and 70½ years at the end of the taxable year for which the contribution is made.

⁂ *Can I roll over my traditional IRA to a Roth IRA, and is there any advantage to doing so?*

The Taxpayer Relief Act of 1997 allows a person to execute a rollover of funds from a traditional IRA (but not from non-IRA qualified retirement plans) to a Roth IRA. Such a rollover, called a "Rothified" IRA by *Forbes* magazine, can be a powerful wealth-building vehicle for your family. The rollover is considered a "distribution" to the participant, and he or she must pay income tax on the distribution. However, the 10 percent penalty on early withdrawals before age 59½ does not apply.

To qualify for a rollover to a Roth IRA, the participant's adjusted gross income cannot exceed $100,000, whether filing single or married filing jointly. Nonrequired distributions from an IRA or qualified retirement plan will not count toward the AGI limitation. For example, say that you are 65 and your AGI without any distributions from your IRA is $85,000. You want to "Rothify" $125,000 of your traditional IRA. You meet the AGI test since none of the $125,000 distributed to you when you Rothify your traditional IRA will count as AGI.

For rollovers to Roth IRAs before December 31, 1998, the income tax caused by the rollover can be spread equally over 4 years: 1998, 1999, 2000, and 2001. To qualify for this 4-year tax spread, your adjusted gross income cannot exceed $100,000 in 1998, whether filing single or married filing jointly. Under the IRS Restructuring and Reform Act of 1998, if taxpayers rolled over traditional IRAs to Roth IRAs before December 31, 1998, in order to qualify for the 4-year tax spread, and then determine that their 1998 AGI is over the $100,000 limit, they have until their 1998 tax filing date, with extensions, to cancel the rollovers.

Once you have Rothified, a 10 percent penalty will apply to withdrawals of the converted amount if made within a 5-year period beginning with the first taxable year in which you made the conversion. Once you are past the 5-year holding requirement and you meet the other rules for qualification, you're subject to the same withdrawal rules as those that apply for new contributions to a Roth IRA.

A surviving spouse can roll over a Roth IRA of a decedent spouse and have tax-free withdrawals for life. Your children can inherit a Roth IRA, and their withdrawals can also be tax-free.

IRAs and Prohibited Transactions

⚜ *What specific acts are generally considered prohibited transactions between the IRA owner and the account?*

- Borrowing money from the IRA
- Selling property, real or personal, to the IRA
- Having the IRA invest in certain collectibles and other tangible personal property
- Using the IRA as collateral or security for a loan
- Using IRA funds to purchase property for personal use
- Paying the IRA owner for management of the IRA or paying third parties excessively for such services

⚜ *What types of additional penalties, beyond regular taxes, accrue for using IRA funds in prohibited transactions?*

Excise taxes and penalties ranging from 5 to 100 percent of the prohibited transaction amount or distribution may be levied against the owner or the owner's beneficiary if the owner or owner's beneficiary engages in a prohibited transaction.

Disadvantages of IRAs

⚜ *What are some of the disadvantages of IRAs?*

As discussed later in this chapter, IRAs may sometimes be subject to creditors' claims.

Two main additional disadvantages are that no loan can be made from an IRA to the owner, under Section 408(e)(2) of the Internal Revenue Code, and that, upon withdrawal of the funds, there is no special tax averaging available to the owner.

DISTRIBUTIONS FROM IRAS AND QUALIFIED PLANS

Before Reaching Age 59½

⚜ *Can I incur additional taxes over and above the income taxes that I will pay upon taking distributions from my IRA or qualified plan?*

Yes. There is generally a 10 percent penalty on distributions taken before age 59½.

🔊 *Are there any exceptions to the 10 percent penalty for taking withdrawals from a traditional IRA before age 59½?*

Yes, the following distributions are not subject to the 10 percent penalty:

- Distributions made to a beneficiary or participant's estate on or after the participant's death
- Distributions related to disability or mental incompetency
- A withdrawal of up to $10,000 during the participant's lifetime if the funds are being used for expenses of buying a first home within 120 days from the date of distribution (This first-time home-buyer exception was created by the Taxpayer Relief Act of 1997.)
- Unlimited withdrawals for higher-education expenses for the participant and his or her spouse, children, and grandchildren (This exception, also created by the Taxpayer Relief Act of 1997, covers expenses for tuition, fees, books, supplies, equipment, and room and board if required in order to attend.)
- With certain qualifications, withdrawals if the participant is unemployed
- Distributions made in substantially equal annual payments, similar to an annuity, over the participant's lifetime or life expectancy or the joint lifetimes or life expectancies of the participant and the beneficiary
- A qualified rollover to another plan or IRA.

🔊 *What are the rules for taking distributions from a Roth IRA?*

You are permitted to withdraw income tax–free at any time an amount equal to your basis (the amount that you contributed).

During the first 5 years after the original contribution, if you make withdrawals in excess of your basis—that is, withdrawals of earnings—they are taxable, and the total withdrawal is subject to the 10 percent early-withdrawal penalty if you are under age 59½.

🔊 *What are the exceptions to the 10 percent penalty for the Roth IRA?*

You can take a penalty-free distribution from your Roth IRA if it is considered a "qualified distribution." A distribution is qualified if it is made 5 or more years after the first tax year in which you establish the Roth IRA *and* it meets one of the following requirements:

- It is made after you reach age 59½.
- It is made after your death to your beneficiary.
- It is made because you are disabled.
- It is used for expenses directly incurred for the purchase of a principal residence, as a first-time home buyer, for you, your spouse, or your or your spouse's ancestors, children, or grandchildren. The maximum distribution to cover such acquisition expenses cannot exceed the lifetime limit of $10,000 and the distribution must be used within 120 days.
- It is a qualified rollover—a rollover to another Roth IRA will not trigger the 10 percent tax.

⋙ When am I allowed to take money out of my 401(k) without the penalty?

You are allowed to withdraw funds from your 401(k) plan before you are 59½ under the following circumstances:

- Upon death, disability, retirement, or termination of employment
- If the company cancels the 401(k) and doesn't replace it with another type of plan
- If the company sells all or substantially all of its assets to a corporation or sells or disposes of a subsidiary
- On the date of sale if you continue to work for the company that was sold (The purchasing entity must not be a partnership to allow this method of withdrawal.)
- When you can show a hardship that requires the distribution of funds from the plan
- With substantially equal payments under Internal Revenue Code Section 72(t)
- By a qualified rollover to another qualified retirement plan or IRA

⋙ What are the basic rules for making substantially equal annual payments?

1. The substantially equal periodic payments generally must be received for at least 5 years.
2. The method of distribution cannot be changed before age 59½.

Unless a distribution change was because of the intervening death, disability, or mental incompetency of the participant, he or she must wait at least 5 years to change the distribution method even if he or she turns 59½ before the end of that 5-year period.

⚜ How can the substantially equal payment requirement be met?

There are three methods of distribution that meet the substantially equal payment requirement:

1. An annual distribution of the required minimum amount, based on the life expectancy of the participant
2. An annual distribution of the required minimum amount, based on either the life expectancy of the participant or the joint life expectancies of the participant and a designated beneficiary
3. Dividing the plan balance by an annuity factor derived by using a reasonable mortality table at an interest rate which does not exceed a reasonable interest rate on the date that payments commence

⚜ Can you give me an example of how these three methods are actually computed?

Table 10-4 presents the results of the three methods for a person age 50 with a 50-year-old spouse and a $100,000 retirement plan balance averaging a 10 percent yearly investment return that had no new contributions. (The so-called annuity exception allows you to receive substantially equal payments over your life expectancy or over the lives of you and your beneficiary or your joint life expectancy as set forth in IRS Publication 590, Appendix E, Life Expectancy Tables I, II, and III.)

Distributions at Required Beginning Date

⚜ When is the latest date that I can begin taking distributions from my traditional IRA or qualified plan?

Distributions to a participant must begin by the participant's required beginning date, which is generally April 1 of the year following the calendar year in which the participant becomes 70½ years of age. (Should the participant die before age 70½, the required beginning date is the date of death.) Distributions must be paid over one of the following periods:

1. The lifetime of the participant

TABLE 10-4   IRA Distributions under Substantially Equal Payment Requirement

	Single life expectancy method	Joint life expectancy method	Amortization withdrawal method
Account balance beginning year 1	$100,000	$100,000	$100,000
Life expectancy	33.1	39.2	
Annuity factor	—	—	33.1 (constant)
Penalty-free amount to withdraw year 1	$3,021	$2,551	$10,445
Add investment buildup	$9,698	$9,745	
Account balance beginning year 2	$106,677	$107,194	$99,555
Life expectancy	32.2	38.2	
Annuity factor	—	—	
Penalty-free amount to withdraw year 2	$3,313	$2,806	$10,445
Add investment buildup	$10,336	$10,439	
Account balance beginning year 3	$113,700	$114,827	$99,065

2. The lifetimes of the participant and a designated beneficiary
3. A period which may be a term certain, not extending beyond the table of life expectancy set forth in IRS tables for the participant or for a combination of the participant and his or her last designated survivor beneficiary

The minimum number of distributions that is required is equal to the total plan benefit divided by the participant's life expectancy or the joint life expectancy of the participant and a designated beneficiary.

The result of using joint life expectancy is that the distributions from a plan are less each year than they would be if only the participant's life expectancy is used. By distributing less each year, income taxes are deferred as long as possible.

⋊ *Once I reach my required beginning date, how are my required minimum distributions determined?*

Once you reach your required beginning date (RBD), you can select one of two calculation methods to determine your required minimum distributions (RMD): the recalculation method or the nonrecalculation method.

If you select the *recalculation method,* your life expectancy is recalculated each year after your required beginning date to determine your minimum distributions. If you select the *nonrecalculation method,* or "fixed-term" method, your life expectancy is calculated when you take your first minimum distribution. All subsequent distributions are based on that initial calculation. It is imperative that you plan before your RBD because the calculation method you select is irrevocable after your RBD.

⋊ *Which calculation method is the best to choose?*

The calculation method you choose depends upon your planning goals. Before December 31, 1996, you might have incurred a 15 percent distribution penalty if you withdrew too much in a given year. The Taxpayer Relief Act of 1997 removed this penalty tax.

The minimum distribution rules determine only the minimum amount which you must withdraw each year. You are always free to withdraw more, without tax penalty. However, keep in mind that the amount you withdraw will normally be taxable income to you and you will lose the future income tax deferral on that money.

This is important to understand. If you wish to maximize the continued tax-deferral benefit of your qualified retirement plan or IRA, the smaller the amount of money you take out in required minimum distributions, the more will remain in the retirement account, growing tax-free, for a longer period of time. The power of tax deferral on an investment is incredible.

Since you can always take out more than the required minimum amount in any year, but not less than the RMD, the joint life expectancy option offers the most flexibility because you can use it to establish the lower RMD and then take out more if you need it.

The recalculation method almost always results in slightly smaller distributions during your life; however, on death your life expectancy will be reduced to zero for your beneficiaries. If you choose the nonrecalculation (fixed-term) method, your required minimum distributions will be slightly larger during your life, but on death your life expectancy will not be reduced to zero for your beneficiaries. Instead, your beneficiaries will continue to receive your required minimum distributions for the balance of the fixed term.

It is important to discuss the options with a qualified estate planning attorney to determine which method will be best in order to reach your planning goals.

BENEFICIARIES OF IRAS AND QUALIFIED PLANS

Primary Death Beneficiary

How will my qualified retirement plan and IRA proceeds be distributed after my death?

Qualified retirement plans and IRAs are contractual agreements that usually allow you to name the person who will receive the remaining proceeds at your death. You accomplish this by filling out a beneficiary designation form at the time you establish your plan account or IRA.

If you fail to name a beneficiary, or if all of your beneficiaries die before you, there are provisions in the document that will dictate who receives the proceeds. In many documents this "default" beneficiary is your estate.

Drafting the beneficiary designation is extremely important, especially as it relates to your estate plan. A mistake in drafting can cause serious estate tax problems including the loss of the marital deduction for assets in the qualified plan or IRA at your death.

Be careful when using standard forms for naming your beneficiary. It is wise to have these forms reviewed by your attorney, accountant, and other estate planning professionals.

Can I name anyone I want as death beneficiary of my IRA?

Unless the IRA document provides otherwise, you may choose anyone as the beneficiary of your IRA. You may choose your spouse, your children, your living trust, a testamentary trust, or an irrevocable trust as your beneficiary.

The consequences of your beneficiary choice, however, vary greatly, so you should name your beneficiary only after careful analysis.

⚮   *Can I name anyone I want as death beneficiary of my qualified retirement plan?*

If the retirement plan is a pension plan or a profit-sharing plan, the Retirement Equity Act of 1984 (REA 84) requires (1) that your spouse consent if you are choosing any RMD payout method other than a qualified joint-and-survivor annuity, or (2) that the death benefits be made payable to someone other than your surviving spouse.

If you plan to name as a beneficiary of your qualified plan someone other than your spouse, your spouse must sign a consent to the new beneficiary designation.

Again, the consequences of whom you choose to be your death beneficiary can have a significant effect on your financial and estate planning goals, so you should make the decision only after careful analysis.

⚮   *Once I name a beneficiary of my qualified retirement plan or IRA, can I change that beneficiary?*

Unless your plan or IRA provides otherwise, you can always change who will inherit the balance of your retirement proceeds at your death.

A spouse as beneficiary

⚮   *What happens if I die before age 70½ and my spouse is the beneficiary of my IRA or qualified retirement plan?*

If your spouse is the beneficiary of your IRA or qualified retirement plan, he or she will have an additional option that is usually not available to any other beneficiary. Your spouse may be able to request a lump-sum distribution from the plan and roll the benefits into his or her own IRA. This is referred to in the Internal Revenue Code as the *spousal rollover.*

If your spouse does choose the spousal rollover, distributions are not required until April 1 after your spouse reaches age 70½. If your spouse does not elect the spousal rollover, the plan benefits are generally required to be distributed over his or her life expectancy, commencing on December 31 of the year following the year of your death.

⚮   *What happens if I die after I reach age 70½ and my spouse is the beneficiary of my IRA or qualified retirement plan?*

If your spouse is your death beneficiary at your required beginning date, your retirement plan benefits are generally distributed over the joint life expectancy of you and your spouse. If you die after the required distributions have commenced and you are recalculating your life expectancy for minimum distribution requirements, the retirement plan benefits are required to be distributed over your surviving spouse's life expectancy.

If you are not recalculating, the distributions would continue as they were before your death.

⚜ *Don't I lose control by naming my spouse as my beneficiary?*

By allowing your spouse the opportunity to elect the spousal rollover, you may gain maximum tax deferral. However, you lose control over a substantial portion of your estate. Once your spouse chooses the spousal rollover, he or she may then choose how the plan proceeds are to be distributed on his or her subsequent death.

You will not be able to give what you have to whom you want, the way you want, and when you want, and you may not be able to save every last federal estate tax dollar possible because you may have insufficient assets outside the qualified plan or IRA to fully fund your family subtrust. In addition, your trust or will-planning probate estate may have insufficient assets to fully utilize your unified credit; therefore, you may not qualify for the federal estate tax savings available through a fully funded family subtrust.

A nonspouse as beneficiary

⚜ *What happens if I die before 70½ and an individual other than my surviving spouse is the primary death beneficiary of my IRA or qualified retirement plan?*

If you name an individual other than your surviving spouse as the beneficiary of your IRA or qualified retirement plan, the plan benefits generally must be distributed to that individual by December 31 following the fifth anniversary of the date of your death. If your plan allows, however, the beneficiary may receive distributions over his or her life expectancy.

An estate as beneficiary

⚜ *What happens if I name my estate as the beneficiary of my IRA or qualified retirement plan?*

You should avoid naming your estate as the beneficiary of your retirement plan benefits. If you name your estate as the beneficiary, you take a nonprobate asset and subject it to the probate process. The proceeds are subject to the claims of creditors, as well as the cost, publicity, and delay associated with the probate process. In addition, your estate will be required to receive all of your retirement benefits no later than December 31 following the fifth anniversary of the date of your death.

Under this planning situation, your advisor and your spouse will have no opportunity to maximize income tax savings by deferring the income tax on your retirement plan benefits past the December 31 following the fifth anniversary of the year of your death.

A living trust as beneficiary

⚑ *Why should I choose to name my living trust as the beneficiary of my IRA or qualified retirement plans?*

You may want to name your living trust as the beneficiary of your IRA or qualified retirement plan so that you will be able to control who receives the proceeds and how they are spent. A living trust may also protect your retirement plan assets—after they are distributed—from your beneficiaries' creditors or from claims of a spouse in the event of a later divorce.

Also, if you name your living trust as beneficiary, your trustee will have the opportunity to obtain the maximum federal estate tax savings possible by utilizing each spouse's unified credit. However, when plan benefits or IRA funds are used to fund a family trust, it may possibly result in the loss of maximum deferral of income tax on the plan proceeds.

⚑ *Can I name my trust as the beneficiary of my retirement plan if I have charitable beneficiaries of my trust?*

Yes, your trust can be the beneficiary of your retirement plan even if you have charitable beneficiaries. However, having charitable beneficiaries may make it difficult to qualify your trust as a "designated beneficiary" for tax purposes. A trust that qualifies as a designated beneficiary receives special tax treatment.

⚑ *How can I know in advance whether to name my spouse or my living trust as the beneficiary of my retirement plan benefits?*

The bad news here is that you can't. This is because even if you could know the date of your death in advance, you can't know what the tax law will be on that date, let alone what the balance of your retirement plan or the size of your estate will be. The good news is that you don't have to know these things. There is another way to "hedge your bets."

As you are probably aware, you can name both primary and contingent beneficiaries for your retirement plan benefits. By naming both your trust and your spouse as potential beneficiaries of your plan, the final decision can be deferred until the date that it is ultimately needed.

Through a technique called a *disclaimer* your advisors and family can decide after your death what the best course of action will be. A disclaimer is a legal "no thank you." It is a simple, but powerful, document that allows the recipient of property to refuse acceptance. Under the law, when a disclaimer is exercised, the intended recipient is considered to have never received the property involved. Therefore, with a disclaimer, the primary beneficiary can either accept the property (your retirement plan benefits) or sign the disclaimer and allow the benefits to be paid to the contingent beneficiary.

To make this strategy work, however, care should be taken to include special provisions in your revocable living trust and to have the beneficiary-designation paperwork through your retirement plan administrator completed correctly.

Under all circumstances, you and your advisors should meet when you turn 69 years old so that all alternatives can be explored on the basis of your then-current financial and estate status.

Designated Beneficiary

⇗ *What is the importance of a designated beneficiary?*

Whom you name as designated beneficiary may affect your required minimum distribution.

If you are planning to use the joint life expectancy option in order to take a lower required minimum distribution amount each year, thereby allowing more money to remain in your qualified retirement plan or IRA, you must name a designated beneficiary. You cannot use the joint life expectancy option without a designated beneficiary.

⇗ *Who may be the designated beneficiary of my IRA or qualified retirement plan?*

Under the Internal Revenue Code, only an individual or a *"qualified" trust* can be a designated beneficiary. On December 29, 1997, the IRS issued new proposed regulations which provide that a trust named as a primary beneficiary can be the designated beneficiary if it meets certain requirements:

1. The trust must be valid under state law.
2. All beneficiaries of the trust must be individuals.
3. The beneficiary of the trust must be identifiable from the trust document.
4. A copy of the trust instrument (or certain selected information about the trust) must be provided to the plan administrator 9 months from your date of death or on your required beginning date, whichever comes first.
5. The trust must be irrevocable on death.

An estate, a nonqualified trust, or a charity *cannot* be a designated beneficiary.

ᴥ *Is the beneficiary named on my qualified retirement plan or IRA a "designated beneficiary"?*

It depends. *Designated beneficiary* is defined by the Internal Revenue Code and has a particular meaning for required minimum distributions. The beneficiary whom you have named to receive your retirement proceeds upon your death may or may not meet the definition of designated beneficiary under the Code.

ᴥ *What happens if I named death beneficiaries but did not name a designated beneficiary?*

If you named more than one person as primary beneficiary, but no designated beneficiary, the rules require that the oldest person, that is, the one with the shortest life expectancy, will be the designated beneficiary for calculating the required minimum distribution.

ᴥ *I've heard that if I want to name my revocable living trust as a beneficiary of my qualified plan or IRA, the trust must be irrevocable. Is this true?*

Before December 29, 1997, in order to qualify your revocable living trust as a designated beneficiary, it had to be irrevocable as of your date of death or your required beginning date, whichever occurred first. In essence, this meant that your trust had to be irrevocable by your RBD.

However, the IRS changed its proposed regulations. Now your revocable living trust does not have to be irrevocable until your death, even if that is after your required beginning date.

I've named a trust as the designated beneficiary of my IRA. Do I have to provide a full copy of the trust to the financial institution?

No, but for practical purposes it is required. The law has been amended to say that you may provide a form to the IRS listing all the beneficiaries of the trust. Because a broadly worded trust will provide for "contingent beneficiaries," some of whom may not even be born yet, it's possible—even probable—that you or your advisor will omit the name of a future beneficiary. It is uncertain at this time whether liability may attach to you because of this omission, even if you made a good-faith effort to list all beneficiaries. For this reason providing a full copy of the trust to the institution is probably the safest course of action.

What happens if I die before age 70½ and my living trust is the beneficiary of my IRA or qualified retirement plan?

If your living trust is your beneficiary, it will qualify as a designated beneficiary. The qualified retirement plan is then required to make minimum distributions of your plan benefits over the life expectancy of the oldest beneficiary of your trust. If you are married, this beneficiary is usually your spouse.

RETIREMENT PLANS AND TAXES

Estate Taxes

Are IRAs and qualified plans included in the participant's gross estate and subject to federal estate tax?

Yes, with very limited exceptions. At one time, certain qualified plans and IRAs paid after the participant's death were entirely exempt from federal estate taxes. However, the law has changed a number of times.

IRAs The unlimited estate tax exemption for IRA proceeds now applies only if the IRA owner had elected the method of distributions and was receiving them before January 1, 1983. No matter when the owner dies, the proceeds will not be included in his or her estate.

There is a $100,000 exemption available for IRA proceeds for an owner who had elected the method of distributions before July 18, 1984, and was receiving them before January 1, 1985. This exemption applies to those proceeds no matter when the owner dies.

All other IRA proceeds are subject to federal estate tax.

QUALIFIED PLANS   The unlimited estate tax exemption for qualified plan proceeds applies only if the participant separated from service before January 1, 1983, and has not changed the method of distributions since that date. No matter when the participant dies, the proceeds will not be included in his or her estate.

There is a $100,000 exemption available for qualified plan proceeds for a participant who separated from service between January 1, 1983, and January 1, 1985, and has not changed the method of distribution since January 1, 1985. This exemption applies to those proceeds no matter when the participant dies.

All other qualified plan proceeds are subject to federal estate tax.

Because of the law changes affecting the federal estate taxation of qualified plan proceeds, anyone who was part of a qualified plan before 1985 should know when and if he or she separated from service. If either the unlimited or the $100,000 exclusion is available, no change in the method of distribution should be made. A change will cause a loss of those exclusions.

I have $1 million in my IRA and understand that it may be worth as little as $270,000 at my death, due to income and estate taxes. I do not need the IRA proceeds during my lifetime. What can I do to make sure that my heirs receive more than $270,000?

One alternative would be to terminate your IRA now. You would have to pay income taxes of approximately $400,000 (40 percent), leaving you with a net distribution of $600,000. Since the Taxpayer Relief Act of 1997 repealed the 15 percent penalty tax on excess distributions, this is no longer a factor in the calculation. If you place the remaining $600,000 in an irrevocable life insurance trust to fund a last-to-die policy covering the lives of both you and your spouse (assuming that you both are age 70 and in good health), the second-to-die policy will pay your heirs approximately $2.5 million on the basis of current investment, expense, and mortality assumptions. This strategy enables you to increase the value of your retirement assets to your heirs to nine times the current after-tax value. Alternatively, you can pay for the second-to-die policy using discretionary IRA withdrawals or your mandatory minimum IRA distributions each year after age 70½.

Excise Taxes

⍕ *What happens if I accumulate too much in my IRA or qualified retirement plan during my lifetime?*

Under prior law, the amount distributed annually in excess of $150,000 was subject to a 15 percent excess distribution tax. In addition, a lump-sum distribution was subject to the 15 percent excess tax if the distribution exceeded $750,000.

The Taxpayer Relief Act of 1997 repealed the 15 percent penalty tax on excess distributions from IRAs and qualified retirement plans, effective January 1, 1997. The act also repealed the 15 percent estate tax penalty on excess accumulations at death, effective for estates of decedents dying after 1996.

⍕ *Does the repeal of the 15 percent excise tax provide new planning opportunities?*

Individuals whose only available source of liquid funds is a large qualified plan balance can now withdraw additional amounts from their plans to fund other estate planning strategies without exposure to the penalty tax on excess distributions. Thus, qualified plan funds can now be liquidated and be used to take advantage of maximum annual-exclusion giving or the unified credit or generation-skipping tax exemption by making large gifts to a dynasty ILIT to create substantial death benefits for heirs.

Income Taxes: Income in Respect of a Decedent

⍕ *What is income in respect of a decedent?*

Income in respect of a decedent (IRD) is a term that the Internal Revenue Code uses to refer to the income from an asset which is included in a person's gross estate and which he or she did not pay income taxes on during lifetime. Typical IRD items include nonqualified deferred compensation plans, qualified retirement plan benefits, IRAs, and royalties.

TABLE 10-5 Effect of Taxes on Qualified Plan Benefits*

Gross qualified plan benefit		$1,000,000
less: Estate tax (assume 55% marginal tax rate)		550,000
Net qualified plan benefit after estate tax		$ 450,000
less: Income tax:		
Gross taxable income	$1,000,000	
less: Deduction for federal estate taxes paid	550,000	
Net IRD	$ 450,000	
Income tax rate (assume 40%)	× .40	
Income tax on IRD		180,000
Net plan benefits to beneficiaries		$ 270,000

**Assumptions:* $5 million gross estate, including a $1 million qualified retirement plan benefit; age on date of death: 65.

Having IRD items in your estate may be very costly to your beneficiaries. Why? In the event of your death, not only are federal estate taxes due, but your beneficiaries are required to pay income taxes on your IRD items. The calculation in Table 10-5 shows what can happen to a $1 million qualified retirement plan. As the table indicates, as a result of having an IRD item in your estate at your death, you can lose approximately 73 percent of your qualified retirement plan benefits to estate and income taxes.

What can I do to avoid the IRD on my retirement plan benefits?

To avoid the income tax on your retirement plan benefits at your death, you may want to consider naming a charitable remainder trust as the beneficiary of your retirement plan. If your spouse is the income beneficiary of the charitable remainder trust, your retirement plan will not be subject to IRD or estate taxes.

Why? On your death, the IRA or qualified retirement plan benefits will be paid to the charitable remainder trust. The trust is considered a tax-exempt charitable organization for income tax purposes. Also, on your death, there will be no estate tax because of the marital and charitable deductions.

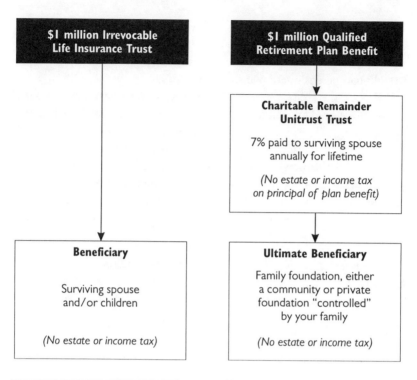

Figure 10-1 *Combined strategy to control estate and income taxes.*

You might consider combining the above strategy of naming the charitable remainder trust as the beneficiary of your retirement plan benefits with the strategy of purchasing a life insurance policy owned by an irrevocable life insurance trust. By combining these two strategies, you will be able to pass on 100 percent of your IRA or qualified retirement plan benefits to charity and an equal amount to your family free of federal estate tax. This approach is illustrated in Figure 10-1.

✒ *Our savings are almost exclusively in my IRA. I've read that if I name a trust as the beneficiary of this account, my spouse will pay a substantial income tax at my death. Is there any way to avoid this?*

Yes. With proper planning, you may benefit fully from your IRA during your lifetime and thereafter leave the proceeds to a credit shelter trust for the benefit of your spouse without incurring significantly more income tax than would be due if you leave the proceeds directly to your spouse, and you can avoid federal estate tax on your IRA assets as they pass to children. This planning requires case-by-case analysis by a thoroughly competent estate planning professional.

Briefly, the strategy works like this: After your death, rather than being distributed and subject to immediate taxation, your IRA account remains intact. The trustee of your credit shelter trust must make annual minimum distributions based on the life expectancy of your spouse. More can be withdrawn at any time by the trustee should the beneficiary require additional income. It is important to remember that just as during your life, these withdrawals will be subject to personal income tax, and the tax will be paid at the beneficiary's income tax rate.

⚜ *I understand all of my beneficiary alternatives. However, my professional advisors still insist there are negative tax consequences to naming my revocable trust as the beneficiary of my retirement plan. Are you sure this is a good idea?*

If satisfying the definition of estate planning is your goal, then naming your revocable living trust as your beneficiary makes sense. Most of the legal and financial world operates on the assumption that income tax planning is all that counts. In addition, most advisors make decisions for clients about tax issues without involving the client. Nowhere is this more evident than in the process of handling beneficiary-designation planning for retirement plans.

Your other advisors are correct when they say that income taxes will be due when the assets are paid to your trust. They are not, however, disclosing the whole picture to you! Retirement plan assets, as you know, are tax-favored investments. Generally, no tax is due when assets are deposited into the plans, and the tax is deferred on the earnings until they are withdrawn. Withdrawals can occur during your lifetime or after your death. Eventually, however, the deferred income taxes *will* become due.

Most advisors only address income tax issues upon the death of the trust maker/retirement plan participant when they talk with clients on this subject. They do not talk about the impact of the estate tax system on retirement plan assets. They also do not, in general, discuss the implications of the client's decision in this area on his or her personal planning instructions.

The advice most commonly given to a married couple is to name the nonparticipant spouse as the beneficiary of the retirement plan dollars. This spouse can receive the benefits and, if received within 60 days of the date of the participant spouse's death, can add the funds to his or her own IRA account. This is known as a *spousal rollover*, or *spousal continuation*, IRA. If the transfer is made within the time frame allowed, no income tax is due.

This advice, in a vacuum, seems sound; however, what if the surviving spouse is involved in a second marriage? Are these advisors so certain that this is the correct course of action? As you can see, the surviving spouse has total control of the assets because he or she can name the beneficiary of the rollover IRA. Individuals in this situation often do *not* place tax concerns above people concerns. And who should make this decision? We believe strongly that only the participant spouse can make this judgment call.

In addition, what are the estate tax effects if the common approach is utilized? The value of the account is included in the estate of the survivor for estate tax purposes. Eventually the deferred income taxes will be due. Finally, if the participant spouse does not have sufficient assets outside the qualified retirement plan or IRA, the result of a spousal rollover is deferred income tax and dramatically increased federal estate tax at the surviving spouse's death.

When these taxes are added together, a huge percentage of the fund can be confiscated by the IRS. In these circumstances, the assumption that the spousal rollover is the only proper course of action can be financially disastrous.

⚜ Can my children continue to defer the income tax from my IRA?

Yes, with proper planning. The deferral is a limited deferral, but it can be substantial over time. This planning technique requires analysis and advice by competent planning professionals.

As beneficiaries, your children must take minimum distributions from the IRA account. If you die before your required beginning date, these distributions are based on the life expectancy of your oldest child unless you created a separate IRA for each child, in which case each child's age would then be used.

The beneficiaries may always take more than the required minimum but must pay ordinary-income taxes on the distributions they receive.

If you die after your RBD, your beneficiaries' minimum distributions are determined by the elections you made for your required beginning date. If you chose the option based on the joint life expectancy of yourself and your oldest child, and the nonrecalculation method, a fixed term was established for minimum distributions.

For example, suppose you name your 42-year-old child as designated beneficiary when you reach your required beginning date of 70½. Your joint life expectancy is 41 years, and because you named a nonspouse as designated beneficiary, your minimum withdrawals will be based on a special IRS table called the MDIB table. (See IRS Publication 590.) You also chose the nonrecalculation method. If you died 10 years later at age 80 and there is still money in your IRA, your children, as your death beneficiaries, may continue to take minimum distributions over the remaining 31 years of the original 41-year term. This is very important, because the minimum distributions are likely to be less than the rate of growth of the plan balance for some time. Thus, your children are deferring not only income tax but the tax on the growth of the balance.

As a result of this planning, your IRA balance might increase substantially even after your death. The cumulative annual distributions received by your children may be several times the original value of the IRA at your death. Under very specific circumstances, you may also choose to make these distributions to a trust for your children. In this way you retain all the benefits of trust planning with the income tax advantages of estate planning IRA distributions.

DIFFERENCES BETWEEN IRAS
AND QUALIFIED RETIREMENT PLANS

⚑ *Are IRAs and qualified retirement plans subject to the claims of creditors?*

Most qualified plans are exempt from the claims of creditors under the 1992 Supreme Court case of *Patterson v. Shumate.* In this case, the Court held that ERISA, the law governing qualified retirement plans, overrides bankruptcy law in terms of the availability of qualified plan assets to creditors. Before this case, the lower courts differed on this issue.

One of the biggest problems with IRAs is that they are not covered by ERISA's favorable creditor protection rules, so they are subject to the claims of creditors unless there is an exclusion granted under state law.

Many states now grant exemptions for IRAs to make them creditor-proof, but you must ask your attorney what the law is in your state.

≥ *Are there any major differences between an IRA and a qualified retirement plan that might affect my estate and tax planning?*

There are two very important differences you must keep in mind when planning for an IRA or a qualified retirement plan. First, to name someone other than your spouse as beneficiary of your qualified retirement plan, you must obtain written and notarized permission from your spouse to do so. This spousal permission is not required with an IRA.

Second, a qualified retirement plan is written and created by an employer to fit the situation and circumstances of that employer. Consequently, each qualified retirement plan is different and, for the most part, unalterable. This means that you and your advisors must be extremely cautious when planning and drafting documents that may affect the administration or qualification of the qualified retirement plan. An employer may not be willing to change the plan to fit your needs. IRAs are extremely flexible and for the most part can be changed or amended to fit your particular estate planning needs.

ROLLOVERS

≥ *What is a "rollover," and how is it accomplished?*

As long as amounts distributed from a qualified retirement plan are rolled over into an IRA within 60 days of receipt by the recipient, they will retain their tax-deferred status. There is a 20 percent withholding for taxes, however, on distributions that are not made directly from a qualified plan to an IRA or from one IRA to another.

≥ *Why do most assets in qualified plans end up in IRAs?*

Most retirement plan assets end up in IRAs because most of these assets are accumulated in qualified retirement plans during the working years. When an employee retires, he or she usually rolls over his or her qualified plan assets into an IRA.

Section 401(c) permits rollovers from qualified plans to IRAs and allows the assets to retain their tax-free status until taken out of the IRA by the owner or beneficiary. Moreover, any distribution to an employee or an employee's surviving spouse, which is includable in the income of the employee or employee's spouse, may be rolled over into an IRA and retain the tax-deferred status.

There are three exceptions to this tax-free rollover:

1. Cases where a minimum required distribution is necessary
2. Distributions made over a term certain of 10 years or more
3. Distributions made over life or life expectancy under Section 402(c)(4)(9)

⚑ *Why is there a tendency for most employees, upon retirement or termination, to roll over their qualified plan assets into an IRA?*

While it is sometimes possible for an employee to leave funds in a qualified plan and not roll them over into an IRA, there is an increasing tendency among qualified plans to not permit the employee to leave the money in the plan after retirement or after termination of employment. This is because it costs the employer money to administer nonemployees' or retired employees' money that is left in the qualified plan.

If an employee does not want to roll over his or her funds to an IRA, the only options remaining are to take the total balance out in a lump sum or a set number of installment payments or to accept an annuity under the terms required by the Internal Revenue Code. Many participants do not like the annuity option because they want to have access to the principal and do not want to rely on a fixed annuity for the rest of their lives. Thus they opt for a self-directed IRA.

An IRA is attractive because it offers the same types of payout possibilities as does a qualified plan (the annuity, lump-sum payments, or installment payments). Thus, the IRA gives greater flexibility to the departing employee. Since the investments in an IRA are not limited to the options provided in the original employer's plan, an IRA may offer some attractive diversification or investment alternatives. The IRA owner is permitted a wide latitude in choosing his or her investments. The exceptions are insurance policies and certain collectibles and other tangible personal property.

The bottom line is that the former employee-participant has greater control over the assets when they are in an IRA rather than in a qualified plan.

chapter 11

Elder Law Planning

ELDER LAW

⚓ *What is elder law?*

Elder law is a special area of legal practice that focuses on issues of particular relevance to senior citizens. Elder law attorneys typically advise their clients on their eligibility for Social Security, Medicare, Medicaid, and other government services. They also consult on long-term-care insurance and all aspects of retirement benefits. They pursue legal claims on behalf of their clients when fiduciaries fail to perform properly and when there are deficiencies in supervised care.

⚓ *Should I seek out an attorney who specializes in elder law?*

Yes. Elder law is a distinct specialty that requires enormous knowledge with regard to the nuances of federal and state statutes and compliance regulations.

⚓ *Are elder law and estate planning the same thing?*

Elder law is a subspecialty of estate planning that often becomes a specialty of its own.

⚮ *What is your definition of "elderly"?*

Generally speaking, a person 65 years old or older can be arbitrarily classed as elderly. However, many people prefer the term "senior citizen" rather than "elderly" because the latter term has come to be popularly—but incorrectly—interpreted as meaning persons who are not only over 65 but also sick or frail.

⚮ *Who will assume responsibility for our senior citizens?*

The answer appears to be nursing homes, but there is a growing fear that many elderly persons will be unable to afford nursing home care and will also not be cared for by their families.

More than one in five citizens will be age 65 or older by the year 2025, effectively doubling our 65-plus population. Given the increasing number of qualifications on Medicaid, many senior citizens are of the opinion that the government is also abandoning them.

⚮ *Won't there always be a government program to pay for my care?*

There have been several legislative attempts to limit and cut back senior citizen programs. Given the emphasis on attempting to balance the federal budget, it is not unreasonable to expect that fewer, rather than more, resources will be made available to these programs in the new millennium.

⚮ *I'm concerned about how the cost of care during a long-term illness or nursing home stay will affect my assets. Is this a legitimate concern?*

It is a legitimate and important concern. Recent statistics indicate that 50 percent of all women and 30 percent of all men who live to age 65 will enter a nursing home at some point in their lives. One-quarter of these will remain in a home for over a year. Obviously, many others will choose to receive in-home care, which only increases the likelihood of higher expenses.

Costs for nursing home care vary widely from state to state, but the average seems to be around $36,000 per year. In-home care can easily run more than $10,000 annually for only three nursing visits per week. Moreover, these costs are increasing at a rate faster than the inflation rate.

⚮ *Can a lawyer meet with family members other than the senior citizen in proceeding to complete various estate planning documents on the senior citizen's behalf?*

An attorney's assistance is often sought after the senior citizen is disabled or seriously or terminally ill. In most situations, the family member who initiates contact with an elder law attorney has the best interests of the senior citizen in mind. However, there are often situations where the family member wishes to gain control over the senior citizen's assets.

In such a case, an attorney has clear-cut ethical standards to follow. He or she must ask: "Who is my client? Do I represent the senior citizen or one or more of the other family members?"

While an initial consultation with family members outside the presence of the senior citizen is generally acceptable, the attorney should meet directly with the senior citizen client in a one-on-one setting whenever appropriate. When an elderly couple has children from prior marriages, it is generally advisable for each to retain separate counsel. If, however, it is appropriate for an attorney to prepare estate planning documentation for both spouses, each should sign a document acknowledging that counsel was independently and freely chosen and that each waives any conflict of interest the attorney might otherwise have.

MEDICAID

⅍ *What is Medicaid?*

Medicaid is an outgrowth of Title XIX of the Social Security Act of 1965. It is a joint federal and state medical assistance program for the aged, blind, and disabled.

A Medicaid recipient does not actually receive direct cash benefits but, rather, receives benefits by way of payments made directly to his or her health care providers, such as doctors, hospitals, nursing homes, medical testing facilities, pharmacies, and dentists.

⅍ *What are the major differences between Social Security, Medicare, and Medicaid?*

Social Security is a federal program that provides retirement, disability, and survivor benefits to wage earners and their spouses, former spouses, widows and widowers, and children. A wage earner's eligibility for retirement benefits is based upon his or her work history—the years during which the wage earner paid taxes into the Social Security trust fund. The amount of monthly retirement benefits Social Security pays is a function of a variety of factors, including the number of years of past work and the amount of earnings.

Medicare provides health care benefits for (1) persons age 65 or older, and certain disabled persons under age 65; (2) certain spouses, divorced spouses, and widows and widowers of certain wage earners; (3) disabled children of certain wage earners; and (4) those with permanent kidney failure. Within the Medicare program, there is Part A Medicare and Part B Medicare. Part A is the Medicare hospital insurance program; Part B is the Medicare medical (nonhospital care) insurance program. Part B is optional, partly because it requires a monthly premium.

Medicaid is run by each state and provides health care benefits for persons with limited or no means. The federal government provides funding assistance for each state's Medicaid program, but each state makes its own eligibility rules. Medicaid assists with the cost of long-term nursing home care for those who qualify. It covers certain inpatient care requiring skilled nursing care for limited periods, but it is not intended to cover nursing home care as such.

⚓ *Who qualifies for Medicaid?*

A person qualifies for Medicaid if he or she is determined to be categorically or medically needy. Persons who are *categorically needy* are eligible only because they meet requirements relating to old age, blindness, or disability and are below certain asset and income levels. *Medically needy* persons qualify for eligibility only because they have high medical bills and their remaining income and other resources are insufficient to meet them.

⚓ *How is the Medicaid program administered?*

Medicaid is administered by each state's welfare agency, such as the Department of Human Services. Approved care and services under Medicaid are funded almost equally by the federal government and each state. While Congress has created federal guidelines for the administration of many programs which may assist the elderly, each state, and even local communities, can alter the general rules and regulations. Specific services and payment rates are established by each welfare agency, which reviews and periodically adjusts them. It is essential that you check with competent professional advisors to determine how the law in your state and community affects a particular program's benefits as they would apply to your situation.

⚖ *What services are available if I qualify for Medicaid?*

Medicaid provides adult care home or nursing facility care, including custodial care and health insurance as a last resort if there is no other coverage (including Medicare) to low-income, blind, or disabled persons of any age. It also provides payment to enrolled providers of comprehensive medical care for services furnished by them.

Your state agency is responsible for completing an assessment of your needs. The purpose of the assessment is to determine what services you need and, if possible, to refer you to home- and community-based services so that you may avoid having to enter a nursing facility, hospital, or state institution.

Your state's Department on Aging provides the assessment service if you enter a nursing facility from the local community. If you enter a nursing facility from a hospital, the hospital performs the assessment.

This assessment determines the level of assistance you need in performing activities of daily living predicated on your medical records. Although services are to be provided on the basis of personal need, priorities are based on a point system which rates your functional level, age, informal support system, and recent hospitalization and medical needs. As a result of the Senior Care Act, your state welfare agency or Department on Aging may be able to help you with homemaking chores in addition to the medical services you may need.

⚖ *If I need to be in a nursing facility, will Medicaid pay the cost?*

Residential (custodial) long-term care is covered. *Residential care* is defined as supervised, nonmedical care in a residence which has been assessed, licensed, or registered by the appropriate state agency.

The facility is to provide care that matches the individual's needs, limitations, and abilities. Care includes assistance with making and keeping appointments for regular or emergency medical care, meeting nutritional needs, taking medications, contacting and maintaining relationships with family and friends, and gaining access to recreational, social, religious, and other community activities. Laundry services and necessary transportation are also included. Each of these services is in addition to assistance with the necessary activities of daily living.

MEDICARE

△ Doesn't Medicare cover the cost of nursing home care?

The misconception that Medicare covers all the costs associated with long-term nursing home care is, unfortunately, commonly held. The basis for this misconception may be the fact that Medicare provides federal health insurance for all persons over the age of 65 who are otherwise entitled to monthly Social Security or Railroad Retirement benefits.

As for Medicare paying the costs of a nursing home, the reality is: Don't count on it. At best, Medicare will pay the costs of a nursing home for a limited period of time only: the first 20 days can be paid in full and, according to 1995 figures, an additional 80 days may be paid—after you pay $89.50 per day.

Even during the 100-day limited-coverage period, certain qualifications must be met in order to receive any Medicare benefits. For example, the care received by the nursing home resident must be "skilled"; the nursing home patient must have spent at least 3 days in a hospital with similar treatments to those being received at the nursing home; the patient must be assigned to a bed that is Medicare-certified for reimbursement; and the nursing home must be Medicare-approved.

To make matters worse, there are often disagreements as to the definition of "skilled care," and they frequently result in disputes over whether the patient qualifies for Medicare during the initial 20- and 80-day periods.

It cannot be overemphasized that, as a general rule, Medicare is *not* an available resource for paying the costs associated with nursing home care.

△ How are long-term-care expenses usually paid?

Contrary to popular belief, Medicare pays very little of these expenses. Studies have consistently shown that the portion of such expenses covered by Medicare averages less than 2 percent. Private long-term-care

insurance is covering a growing proportion of the expenses (an estimated 4 to 5 percent today). The two most common sources of payment, however, remain payment from individuals' own assets and payment by the Medicaid system. Medicaid has become known as the
"payer of last resort." In recent years, assisting clients with qualification
for Medicaid benefits has been a growth industry.

Through a strategy of planned transfers, a family can qualify for
Medicaid benefits while preserving some of its assets. In 1993 Congress
passed OBRA to restrict many of these strategies, particularly those
involving the use of trusts.

In stark contrast to earlier views, both Congress and the state governments have begun to develop incentives encouraging the use of privately purchased long-term-care insurance.

MEDICAID PLANNING

⅍ *Why should I plan for my long-term care or disability?*

Let's start with some statistics to evaluate the likelihood that you may
need assistance with long-term care. Today, the average life expectancy
for a man who reaches the age of 65 is 85 years. For women who reach
the age of 65, the average life expectancy is 89 years. Men who reach
age 65 have about a 30 percent chance of entering a nursing home, and
women have a 50 percent chance. However, only 25 percent of the
individuals who enter nursing homes stay longer than 1 year.

Home health care has become a burgeoning industry primarily
because it tends to be about one-half the cost of nursing home care.
The effect this cost differential will have in coming years is hard to
estimate, although it is likely that the number of people entering nursing homes will decrease as more and more people seek assistance in their
own homes.

A study published by the American Health Care Association in
1993 stated that the average cost of nursing home care was about
$36,000 per year, but in some areas the average was more than twice
that amount. The best nursing homes can cost $100,000 or more per
year, and the cost is going up at about 5 percent each year.

If you are destitute and qualify for public assistance through Medicaid, your alternatives are limited to making sure that appropriate ex-

emptions have been provided and planned for. If you are among those who would not immediately qualify for benefits, you have the choice of divesting yourself of your assets in order to qualify or doing whatever you can to provide for your own care through financial planning and the acquisition of long-term-care insurance.

❧ What is Medicaid planning, and how does it relate to my estate plan?

Medicaid planning involves the structuring of an individual's income and assets to attempt to ensure eligibility for benefits available under Medicaid.

Each state, as well as the federal government, sets limits on the assets and income one can own and still remain eligible for Medicaid. When one's assets exceed Medicaid's limits, they must either be properly disposed of or be used to pay for expenses Medicaid otherwise would cover.

When nonexempt assets render individuals ineligible for Medicaid assistance, these people must "spend down" their assets until they have few enough remaining to meet the eligibility requirements. Medicaid planning invokes a variety of strategies to reduce a person's assets—often years before illness or death—to achieve Medicaid eligibility.

❧ Why should I include Medicaid planning as part of the estate planning process?

Medicaid's eligibility requirements—and the related implementing rules imposed by each state—are complex, far-reaching, and very limiting. More important, they are often inconsistent with estate planning strategies that might be employed in the absence of a goal of establishing Medicaid eligibility. Medicaid planning contemplates, in large part, reducing your estate long before you might need long-term health care. Estate planning contemplates, generally, control of most of your assets during your lifetime and the dispersal of your assets on your death.

People with substantial wealth will be able to afford whatever long-term-care expenses they incur. For such people, there is no reason to structure their affairs so that they will qualify for Medicaid benefits. Some are reluctant, on ethical grounds, to accept Medicaid benefits to pay for services that they could afford without Medicaid eligibility planning. For others, however, ensuring access to Medicaid is an important planning goal.

Whether Medicaid planning is appropriate for you depends on a consideration of many factors, including your age when planning is considered; your health; the assets you anticipate being able to apply to any long-term care you may eventually need; the range of possible long-term care costs; the cost of appropriate long-term-care insurance, if available; other insurance and benefit plans such as employee benefit plans, which might provide you with financial support if you should require long-term care; and the eligibility criteria of the state in which you reside.

Keep in mind that there is continuing political pressure to reduce government benefits in general. Medicaid eligibility rules frequently change, and there can be no guarantee that Medicaid benefits will continue to be available indefinitely in their present form.

How do I begin my Medicaid planning?

You should begin by analyzing your income and income-producing assets to determine whether or not you have sufficient income to provide for your own needs in the event that you do need assistance. You should also determine your cash shortfall on a monthly basis in case you, your spouse, or both of you need assistance. Then you should consider ways to enhance income.

Your planning options include long-term-care insurance (nursing home insurance), life insurance with long-term-care or loan/cash value provisions, annuities, and turning non-income-producing assets into income-producing assets

What are some commonly used strategies?

Making asset transfers more than 36 months before an application for Medicaid is the most common planning technique relied upon by practitioners. In some states divorce is used as a strategy to maximize the assets that the healthy—divorced—spouse may use and enjoy.

Income trusts, limited liability companies, and revocable living trusts can also be effective planning tools.

What is an income trust?

An *income trust* is applicable only to individuals who require nursing home care and whose monthly income exceeds the amount necessary to qualify for Medicaid. It must be an irrevocable trust.

⅍ *How does an income trust work?*

The purpose of an income trust is to reduce an individual's income below that required to qualify for Medicaid. The sole beneficiary of the income trust is the individual, during his or her life. All income received by the trust must be made available to pay for the individual's cost of care each month, with the exception of a monthly fee not to exceed $30, as a trust maintenance fee for trustee compensation, maintenance of a bank account, and preparation of tax returns and $30 per month as a personal-needs allowance to the individual.

The state welfare agency and the Estate Recovery Unit are the beneficiaries after the death of the individual, and the trust must provide that the state's Estate Recovery Unit will be compensated for the amount of medical assistance paid on the individual's behalf from any amount remaining in the trust at the time of the individual's death.

⅍ *If we create a limited liability company and place our personal assets into it, will this be an effective Medicaid planning tool?*

The answer is "maybe."

Limited liability companies (LLCs) have been adopted as a separate form of legal entity in most states. The primary benefit of an LLC is that it acts as a protective device by shielding assets from creditors. If you create an LLC properly and place your assets into the LLC, as a general rule your assets will be protected from creditors. This concept may be effective in protecting your assets, while also allowing you to qualify for Medicaid, presumably after having otherwise met the state's 36-month ineligibility period.

Under your state's laws it may be possible for you to place all or selected assets into an LLC. Your children could be the members, or owners, of the LLC interests and could receive most or all of the income generated by its assets. Further, if properly designed, the children could receive the assets upon the death of the senior citizen who created it.

It is possible for the senior citizen to retain control of the assets in the LLC yet retain no ownership interest.

Although still untested because of the relative newness of the LLC as a form of legal entity, assets placed into an LLC may be protected from nursing home costs after your state's ineligibility period has been met. However, LLCs have largely not been tested as Medicaid qualification vehicles. Your attorney will advise you on your state's laws.

⚮ Is using a revocable living trust the right strategy for persons who are concerned about Medicaid eligibility?

This strategy is not always the best for purposes of alleviating Medicaid concerns. It sometimes happens that the community spouse predeceases the institutionalized spouse. In this situation, a testamentary "sprinkling" trust, established in a will, may best meet the goal of providing supplemental benefits for the institutionalized spouse without having the community spouse's assets disappear into the maw of Medicaid. However, through more sophisticated planning, it may be possible to use a fully funded revocable living trust which could achieve the same result. You should consult with a qualified estate planning attorney if you are concerned about Medicaid eligibility.

⚮ Will the look-back period be a problem for me if I use a living trust?

Transfers *to* a revocable living trust are ignored because the assets are still available to the transferor. Transfers *out* of a revocable living trust are subject to a 60-month look-back period. The standard 36-month period applies to transfers to an irrevocable trust.

Exceptions to the rules regarding look-back periods for transfers of assets include the following permissible non-fair market transfers:

- A home transferred to a spouse, minor, or disabled child
- Assets transferred to or from the applicant's spouse
- Assets transferred to a trust for support of a disabled person under the age of 65 years
- Assets transferred for (or to a trust for) the support of a blind or disabled child
- Asset transfers that were unknowingly made without fair consideration or that were not deliberately made as a means of qualifying for Medicaid benefits
- Asset transfers that were reversed

There may also be an exception if the state determines that the ineligibility penalty would work an undue hardship.

I'm worried that as I get older, I may need someone to handle my finances for me. What is the best way to prepare for this situation?

The safest way for you to handle the possibility that you may become unable to act on your own behalf is to use the protections afforded with a revocable living trust.

You can designate one or more cotrustees whom you can authorize to act for you in the event you become unable to handle your affairs. They can be individuals or institutions, or a combination of both.

You can give them a broad range of authority to cover foreseeable problems that may arise, including authority to make decisions concerning your living arrangements, finances, legal matters, and medical care. You can also authorize them to give directions to your physicians as to whether you should be given life-sustaining measures in the event of serious illness and whether artificial life-sustaining measures should be maintained or withdrawn.

Your trustees can act alone or in conjunction with government administrators and private ombudsmen to ensure you receive all the benefits and services for which you are eligible.

Does it matter what state I live in at the time I do my Medicaid planning?

When Medicaid qualification for long-term care is a part of your plans, the plans should be valid in every state, although the details of each state's Medicaid will be different.

If you plan to move to another state before you qualify for Medicaid, you should review your plans with that specific state's rules in mind. For purposes of Medicaid, every state operates under the same federal rules, but peculiarities of local jurisdictions should be checked with local counsel, especially if you are considering changing your domicile.

LONG-TERM CARE

What is long-term care?

Long-term care is defined as a stay of more than 30 consecutive days in an establishment where food and shelter are furnished to four or more persons unrelated to the owner or operator and where some treatments or services are provided which meet some need beyond the basic provision of food and shelter.

Such care may be provided by adult care homes, hospitals, psychiatric facilities, licensed nonmedical residential care facilities, and other facilities which meet the provisions in the definition of long-term care.

What is a prudent way to plan for mature years if we have assets between $250,000 and $1 million?

The first line of defense is to purchase long-term-care insurance while you are in your forties or fifties, when the cost is manageable. In your fifties or sixties, you should consider putting your name on one or more waiting lists at a continuing-care retirement community *(CCRC)*.

The biggest mistake people make is not putting their names on a list or lists just as if they were applying to one or more colleges. Applying is not a commitment to move to the facility. It simply involves paying a nonrefundable processing fee, typically $250, and leaving a refundable deposit, typically $1000, which means that the cost of creating an option on a future residency is essentially the interest lost on the $1000 each year.

It may be wise for you to put your name on all internal lists of the CCRC you qualify for. For example, you and your spouse might sign up on the one-bedroom as well as the two-bedroom lists. Time passes: the wait at an assisted-living center may be 2 to 3 years for a studio apartment, 4 to 5 years for a one-bedroom apartment, and 7 to 9 years for a two-bedroom apartment.

One day you receive a telephone call and are told that an apartment is available. You then have three options: (1) "No, I'm not ready yet," (2) "I'm ready, so go forward with the application," or (3) "I'm not interested; please give me my $1000 back."

If you choose option 1, most CCRCs will allow you to remain at the top of the list and will take the person next in line. In this way, you can make a future move on relatively short notice without facing years of waiting for the community of your choice.

If, during the waiting period, your health has deteriorated to the extent that admission is denied, there is still the protection afforded by the long-term-care insurance. If you are admitted to a CCRC but with a health care exclusion for the costs of care for a preexisting condition, you will still be covered by your long-term-care insurance.

One planning tip to keep in mind: If you are in a hurry to gain admittance, seek the unit with the shortest waiting time and get under contract with its health care guarantees. Once you gain admittance to the CCRC, you will be able to move to a larger unit when it becomes available. And in the hiatus your health situation will be covered.

⚄ What are my options for remaining in my home and receiving care there if I need it?

In response to the desire of many Americans to age at home, a new type of CCRC—called *continuing care at home*—has been developed. There are many similarities to a conventional CCRC, although there is no waiting list because you provide the housing as well as the meals (unless you are otherwise receiving benefits). Consequently, the entry fee and monthly fee are much lower. However, a prospective member must still meet health and financial requirements to gain admission.

Some CCRCs offer a Type B contract with an entry fee, a monthly fee, and partial or full entry-fee refund provisions. This type of contract costs more than the Type A contract, with the extra money being invested to eventually produce the refund. A few CCRCs offer a Type C contract, which essentially is a monthly rental arrangement without a separate entry fee.

In looking at any contract, you should determine whether the monthly fee stays constant, whether you need an assisted-living or a skilled-nursing level of care, and whether the monthly fee increases with increases in the level of care.

Care is provided in the member's home until the cost exceeds the cost of providing care in one of the nursing homes under the plan. At that point, the member must select and move to one of the nursing homes on a designated list unless he or she wants to pay the excess cost, in which case the plan will keep the member at home.

⚄ What is long-term-care insurance?

Long-term-care insurance has become increasingly popular as the cost of nursing home care and other extended-care alternatives has steadily increased. It covers part or all of the insured's cost of home care, nursing home care, or similar extended care should it become necessary. It is important to understand that long-term-care insurance is not provided by Medicare, Medicaid, Social Security, or Medicare supplementary insurance.

Some states are permitting holders of long-term insurance policies to treat their policy proceeds as exempt from consideration for Medicaid eligibility purposes. These programs create additional incentive for obtaining such coverage.

Long-term-care insurance is one of the few alternatives to self-paying the costs of long-term care. This type of insurance generally provides an amount of money per day for a fixed period of time or for the remainder of the insured's life.

A long-term-care policy can include an escalation feature which automatically increases the amount that will be paid annually, thus keeping up with inflationary pressures. This escalation feature can provide for a fixed percentage increase each year or an increase that is tied to the consumer price index. A problem with many escalation clauses is that nursing home costs have risen steeply over the years and the future escalation in such costs may exceed the consumer price index.

⋟ What are some of the features of long-term-care insurance?

How you structure your policy will obviously affect its cost. Premiums are generally level, meaning a fixed amount per year. Most policies do not provide guarantees that the premiums will not be increased but do provide that your premium can be increased only if rates are raised for everyone in your state carrying the same policy.

The major advantages of funding your potential long-term costs through insurance are simplicity and control. Having your own dollars to spend the way you want gives you power over your circumstances. You can let your loved ones know, and direct in your estate planning documents, how you want your affairs conducted if a major disability strikes. With long-term-care insurance you will not be subject to the whims of government. You can go to the facility of your choosing and get the level of care you want and desire.

Because the Medicaid system does not reimburse nursing homes at the same rate that a private patient pays, there is always a risk that the quality of care received will not be the same if you rely on the Medicaid system to pay your way. By "paying the freight" yourself, you'll have better peace of mind that you'll get the care you expect and desire.

⋟ What is the difference between long-term-care insurance and disability insurance?

Long-term-care insurance is the "flip side" of disability insurance. Disability insurance is typically purchased during one's active working career to protect against income loss. The cost of disability insurance depends on how much the monthly benefit is, how long the insured is willing to wait before receiving benefits, and how long the benefits last.

These same considerations apply to long-term-care insurance. The cost is dependent on the amount of monthly benefit (with an escalation or inflation provision being advisable), the waiting period before benefits begin (e.g., up to 6 months), and the duration of benefits (with 5 years covering more than 95 percent of the cases). Some policies specify a maximum dollar coverage, and when this amount is spent, the coverage ends.

Older policies required at least a 3-day hospital stay to trigger benefits, which is harder to achieve in this day and age and rather impossible to achieve if Alzheimer's is the triggering event. Modern policies speak in terms of inability to perform one or more activities of daily living (ADLs), such as eating, toileting, bathing, dressing, and transferring from bed to a chair. The impairment of two or more ADLs generally triggers coverage either in a nursing home or an assisted-living facility or at home with home health aids provided to help overcome the deficiencies.

With the rise of managed care, more and more long-term-care insurers are providing case management to reduce costs.

One innovation in this area is to combine disability insurance, which speaks of inability to carry on one's own occupation from the standpoint of a medical assessment, and long-term insurance based on loss of ADLs. Such a policy recognizes that disability is a more likely occurrence than death for people until they reach their late thirties. Moreover, disability does not stop at age 65 but becomes an increasing hazard until age 85. As a group, senior citizens are the fastest-growing segment of our population; there is almost a 50-50 chance that a person will become disabled after reaching the age of 85.

➤ *Doesn't my health insurance or Medicare cover long-term-care costs?*

In most circumstances the answer is no, and it often comes as a surprise to people that such an important part of their care has not been covered.

Some private insurance plans will pay for a maximum amount or a maximum number of days in a convalescent care facility.

If you have been hospitalized for a period of 3 days and your doctor has prescribed medical care that must take place each day, Medicare will pay for skilled care for a period of up to 100 days following the hospitalization. If you are on Medicare, the first 60 days are fully paid, and the next 30 days are paid by Medicare on a co-insurance basis (you pay part of the cost). You may also use your lifetime reserve of 10 days for further care to be paid by Medicare. You can qualify for further care, but only with a new illness and a new hospital stay.

Long-term-care needs that do not include medical procedures are not covered by Medicare. In almost all long-term situations, private health insurance and Medicare do not cover a long-term stay.

I've heard that long-term-care insurance is not such a good deal. How do I know if my agent is telling me the right things?

Long-term-care insurance is a relatively new product. The policies have improved greatly in the last few years. Some of the stories you may have heard about unscrupulous agents and poor-quality products may well be true. Because of the tremendous need in this area, however, state governments have begun taking an active role in assisting consumers with information and counseling regarding long-term care.

Every state government has set up some sort of counseling system from which you can benefit. Call your state's Department of Insurance to find out how the program works in your state. The state counselors can assist in determining your needs and can generically describe the background of the type of agent you're looking for. Your other professional advisors can also assist you in locating a skilled professional long-term-care agent.

A very helpful brochure is *A Shopper's Guide to Long-Term Care Insurance*. You can get it from your insurance professional or contact the National Association of Insurance Commissioners, 120 West 12th Street, Suite 1100, Kansas City, MO 64105-1925.

Should long-term care insurance be included in my estate plan?

Your possible need for long-term care should be considered an important component of your estate plan.

What are the main concerns people have about long-term-care policies?

The two biggest concerns are field underwriting and policy gatekeepers. *Field underwriting* is a business practice in which the agent takes health information from the proposed insured directly, and the company issues a contract with little or no review of the client's actual medical records. When the policyholder applies for benefits under the policy, the company then conducts an in-depth review of his or her health situation. In such cases, the company is sometimes able to claim that the original information provided on the application was incomplete or even misleading. In these situations it is not uncommon for the company to deny a claim.

Policy gatekeepers are provisions included in a policy to make it difficult for the policyholder to ever receive benefits. For example, a gatekeeper provision might specify qualification by level of care. Early long-term-care policies provide that a policyholder must receive skilled care, typically in a hospital, before applying for custodial care benefits under the policy. Skilled care is care aimed at rehabilitating a client. Direct entry into a nursing home, therefore, would almost never be covered. Another more direct example is a provision that requires transfer from a hospital to the nursing home. Again, direct entry to the home would not be covered.

⚜ How do I protect against these problems?

The best way to protect yourself is to obtain information from your state's Department of Insurance and, most importantly, to select a qualified agent.

⚜ Is there a way to combine the purchase of long-term-care insurance with other planning strategies?

One of the most common and effective strategies being used under the current Medicaid rules is to have an estate plan prepared which utilizes a revocable living trust and a special durable power of attorney and to purchase long-term-care insurance for a benefit period long enough to cover the Medicaid 36-month look-back period.

In this way, a person can pay for a period of time from his or her assets and have all the benefits of control, including selection of facility. If the need for assistance turns out to be long-term, the person has positioned his or her trustees and agents to make the transfers necessary to preserve assets without having to spend down personal funds beyond the cost of the premiums for the long-term-care policy.

A drawback of this strategy is that the person will eventually be dependent upon the whims of government, but it seems to be a popular "middle ground" because of the difference in the premiums for policies providing 3 or 4 years of benefits and for those providing lifetime benefits.

One caution with this type of planning is that the federal government may, at any time, increase the look-back period to longer than 36 months. If this happens, there may be a shortfall in coverage. This potential problem should be discussed in detail before you use this approach.

⚜ *I have a nursing home policy for long-term care. How will payments from this affect my eligibility for Medicaid?*

Insurance coverage is available to help pay the cost of long-term care. Generally, most of the policies allow for payments to be made either to the individual or to the nursing facility. The benefits are counted as income and either cover the monthly cost of long-term care or are applied toward it with Medicaid paying the difference. Thus, the long-term-care insurance is treated as a third-party resource which does not adversely affect eligibility for Medicaid.

SOCIAL SECURITY

⚜ *How do I find out what my Social Security benefits will be?*

Your income from Social Security will depend on your work history. Social Security makes it easy for you to find out what work history has been reported in your name. You can obtain a Request for Earnings and Benefit Estimate Statement (SSA-7004) from your local Social Security office. After you have completed the form, mail it to Social Security Administration, P.O. Box 3600, Wilkes-Barre, PA 18767-3600. You will receive a copy of your work history and an estimate of your benefits when you retire. If you have access to the Internet, you can request the information from the Social Security Administration at www.ssa.gov.

⚜ *How does early retirement affect my ability to receive Social Security benefits?*

Difficult social and economic issues face many older workers when they are forced to take early retirement by companies that are either downsizing or going out of business. Many of these workers believe that early retirement includes the right to begin receiving Social Security retirement benefits, but these benefits are not available until people reach the age of 62. Moreover, if a person elects to begin receiving benefits at 62, the amount of the benefits is reduced.

In order to receive full benefits from Social Security, you must be 65 years of age. The advantage of taking reduced benefits 3 years early is neutralized by about age 86. After that, you would have been better off financially to have waited to age 65 before starting benefits.

Individuals and couples planning for retirement should understand that there is pending legislation that proposes to increase the age at which Social Security benefits will be paid. This potential change in the Social Security system may have a substantial financial impact on many retirees and should be considered as part of an overall retirement plan.

PART FIVE

Administering Estates

Of all the statistics that we have heard, the one that is the most telling is that we all have a 100 percent chance of dying. All of our planning—or lack of it—must someday be put to the test, and after-death administration is the process of implementing and supervising that planning.

There are practical as well as administrative and tax considerations when a family member or other loved one dies. Survivors have to face the grief of loss as well as the practical tasks of memorial services and funeral arrangements and a myriad of other concerns. After the personal responsibilities have been fulfilled, financial aspects must be addressed.

There may be very real concerns about how a family can survive if the assets of the family's provider are tied up in probate. There may be issues of what the decedent owned and who his or her creditors are. The list can seem endless at times.

There has not been a great deal written for the public about issues that one faces after the death of a loved one. Our contributing authors have provided an excellent overview of many of these points and practical advice on how you should approach them. Chapter 12 serves as a useful checklist of these after-death issues.

chapter 12

After-Death Administration

IMMEDIATE ACTION STEPS
UPON THE DEATH OF
A FAMILY MEMBER

✎ *What immediate actions do we need to take on the death of a family member?*

Upon the death of a loved one, the most important thing to understand is that there are usually no emergencies. There will be plenty of time in the days ahead to handle the necessary business and legal matters. Initially, it is most important to take care of yourself and to satisfy the needs of others as together you grieve your loss.

✎ *When my grandmother died, I called her lawyer and asked for a prompt appointment to take important papers to him so that he could act immediately. The attorney was courteous, but scheduled the appointment for* after *the memorial service. Why didn't he act more quickly?*

A skilled estate planning attorney attends first to emotional and spiritual needs of the family and second to its financial affairs. If the attorney foresaw no need for an immediate conference, it was proper to defer the conference to a more suitable date.

515

⚴ *What are some of the first legal steps that should be taken upon the death of a family member?*

After a loved one is buried, and after appropriate time is devoted to personal grieving, the following actions should be taken:

- Important legal papers, most particularly the decedent's will or trust, should be located.
- The attorney who drafted the documents should be contacted and an appointment set. If the attorney cannot be ascertained or if the decedent did not have an estate planning attorney, the person or institution named as trustee of the decedent's living trust or as personal representative of the decedent's will should retain a competent attorney.
- If there are assets that will be passing under a will, the personal representative named in the will should, with the help of legal counsel, proceed to see that the will is probated.
- An inventory of all assets should be made, and assets which need immediate attention should be reviewed. These assets include life insurance policies, stock options, and retirement plans.
- If the decedent was a principal in a business enterprise, care should be taken to determine what obligations and responsibilities the trustees have to continue its operation. A review of business succession planning documents detailing the ownership, operation, and control of the business should be undertaken immediately.
- If probate is necessary, the estate's attorney may have to petition the court to take swift action in areas such as selling assets that are perishable or that are time-sensitive and subject to sharp fluctuations in value (e.g., stock options).

⚴ *What immediate legal actions do we need to take if a living trust was utilized?*

If the decedent left a living trust–centered estate plan, the transition is normally orderly and simple. The successor trustee can take over the management of the trust affairs without interruption or delay. No court proceedings are required, and business and financial affairs can continue in the customary fashion.

⚴ *Should we pay outstanding bills if a living trust was utilized?*

Bills should not be paid until complete inventories of assets and debts have been made along with a list of all the decedent's creditors.

🔖 *If a will names me as the estate's personal representative, am I empowered to act on its behalf?*

No. Before you have any authority to act, you must file a petition with the probate court to request that it appoint you to act as personal representative. This will entail the court's acceptance of the will as valid.

Ultimately, the probate court will enter an order which gives you or some other person the power to act. It is the probate court's order which empowers you to act, not the decedent's will.

🔖 *What happens if an individual dies without leaving a will?*

When a person dies without a will, that person dies *intestate*. If the individual is married and his or her spouse is living, all property that was owned as joint tenants with right of survivorship or as tenants by the entirety passes to the surviving spouse without any court process.

If the decedent owned assets individually, a court proceeding called an *administration* must be started by a family member, friend, or next of kin. An administration is similar to a probate proceeding, but there are additional steps. The court will appoint an *administrator,* or personal representative. For the most part, the administration proceeding request is initiated through a legal document called a *petition* that calls for the naming of an administrator. In the administration process, unhappy relatives or other interested persons, such as creditors of the decedent, can challenge the petitions of would-be administrators.

Once appointed by the court, the administrator generally must post a bond equal to the value of the gross estate. In addition to other duties, the administrator must prove where the decedent resided and who the decedent's heirs are, because the decedent's domicile will determine which heirs receive his or her property.

🔖 *How does the government know when a person dies?*

In most states, the professionals handling the funeral or memorial arrangements or the physician who pronounces death is required by law to notify the State Department of Vital Statistics.

THE NEED FOR A LAWYER

🔖 *Is legal counsel needed if the deceased had a fully funded living trust or properly designated beneficiaries on life insurance contracts or retirement plans?*

Yes. In every instance, a decedent's family, the personal representative of the decedent's estate, any trustees of the decedent's trust, the decedent's life insurance agent, and the company benefits counselor, if any, should meet with an experienced estate planning attorney to review the status of the decedent's plan and assets.

Any estate plan is based on the financial, tax, and family situations that were envisioned at the time it was prepared. It will need to be analyzed in light of current conditions, as there may be opportunities to reduce taxes or optimize other planning strategies on an after-death basis.

⚜ If there are problems with the plan, can actions be taken to correct it?

There are opportunities under the laws to change the estate plan of a person by having potential recipients of the property "disclaim" their various interests. In other situations, elections under the estate planning documents may be made which would alter previously envisioned tax consequences. These potential opportunities should be carefully reviewed with legal counsel and family members who will be affected by the decisions.

⚜ Dad died last year and now Mom has just died, and my sisters and I are successor trustees under their trust. Should we meet with a lawyer?

We recommend strongly that you and the family have a meeting with the lawyer who prepared your parents' estate plan. Even though the trust—if properly funded—will avoid probate, there are still matters that have to be accomplished:

- Issues regarding income and estate tax returns need to be discussed.
- Your mother's assets need to be valued.
- Insurance claims need to be made.
- Retirement plan options and elections need to be analyzed and discussed.
- Debts and expenses need to be scrutinized and paid.
- Tax returns need to be prepared and filed.
- Finally, assets have to be distributed according to the instructions of your mother and father.

⚜ If I hire an attorney to help me administer my spouse's trust, whom does that attorney represent?

In most situations, an attorney is retained to represent the trustee on behalf of the trust, so the attorney does not represent the beneficiaries in their individual capacities. The trustee has a fiduciary obligation to the beneficiaries, and the attorney must advise the trustee on how to carry out the duties involved. The beneficiaries should retain their own attorneys if they believe the fiduciary obligation has been compromised by the trustee.

When the surviving spouse is a trustee *and* a beneficiary of a deceased spouse's trust, conflicts may arise. This is especially true if the surviving spouse is not the only beneficiary and is a sole trustee or a cotrustee with persons he or she controls, because this situation may lead to disputes over the proper valuation and distribution of the trust assets.

It is important that a surviving spouse who is both a trustee and a beneficiary under the same document resolve the question of whom the attorney represents before any administration of the trust begins.

PROBATE ADMINISTRATION

⋈ *What is the probate process?*

In a nutshell, the *probate process* is a court proceeding that establishes the validity of a will and provides legal oversight to ensure accuracy in accounting for a decedent's assets, fairness in the treatment of heirs, and protection for the rights of the decedent's creditors.

Each state provides, by statute and rule of court, various time limits and procedural steps to properly probate an estate. The process begins with the presentation of the will for probate. The probate process can take anywhere from a few months to many years, depending on the complexity of the estate and on whether there are any challenges to the validity of the will.

There are filing fees to the designated court, as well as attorney fees for the duration of the probate process.

The probate process is more fully discussed in Chapter 1.

⋈ *What assets have to go through death probate?*

Assets which are titled in the decedent's name alone must go through probate in order to be retitled into the name of his or her heirs. As an example, if I own some General Motors stock and only my name appears on the certificate, the only way my spouse or my children can gain ownership and control of that stock at my death is through probate. The probate court would actually issue an order assigning the ownership of the probate asset to my heirs. Pursuant to that order, the stock transfer agent would retire the certificate which had my name on it and reissue a certificate in the name of my heirs.

In contrast, assets which are owned by two or more persons as joint owners with right of survivorship do not go through death probate, as long as there is a surviving joint owner. Assets such as life insurance contracts that name specific individuals as beneficiaries also do not go through probate. And assets which are titled in a revocable living trust are not probated when the trust maker dies because they are titled in the name of the revocable trust, not in the name of the individual.

⚚ Are probate assets readily available to the family?

No. One of the major problems with probate is that the assets are—for the most part—tied up until the process is completed. There are some statutory allowances available for a widow, dependent children, and other family members. These allowances are meager at best and certainly cannot compare to what a family is used to in terms of having complete control over and access to all of a decedent's assets.

Duties of an Executor or Personal Representative

⚚ What are the differences between an executor, personal representative, and administrator?

All these terms refer to the person a court appoints to administer an estate. When the law refers to a "person," the term includes bank trust departments and other corporate fiduciaries.

Executor or *executrix* (the legal term for a female executor) is the traditional term for a person named in a will and subsequently approved by the probate court to administer and distribute the property of a person who has died with a will. We inherited this term from England. *Personal representative* is the modern term for "executor" and is without gender. Many states have adopted statutes that replace the term "executor" with the term "personal representative."

An *administrator* or *administratrix* is the person appointed by a court to administer and distribute the property of a person who has died without a will (intestate).

For all but the most technical purposes, these terms can be used interchangeably.

↛ *If I am named as an executor, what do I have to do with the decedent's assets?*

As executor, you have the responsibility of gathering all the decedent's assets and reporting to the court by preparing and submitting an inventory. You recommend and the court appoints an appraiser to value real estate and anything else that doesn't have a readily ascertainable value. The due date of the completed inventory is governed by state law.

You must then take possession of the assets, usually for several months, in order for creditors' claims to be filed and satisfied according to state law. After you have paid the decedent's debts, claims, and taxes from the probate assets, you can distribute the remaining property to the decedent's heirs as provided in the will. You then must prepare a final accounting and submit it to the probate court for approval.

↛ *As attorneys, what techniques do you use to determine a decedent's assets?*

If a decedent has a previously prepared schedule of assets, this job is much simpler. If there is no schedule of assets, we normally attempt to locate as many of the deceased's financial documents as we possibly can, such as statements from financial institutions (e.g., bank accounts, brokerage accounts, IRA statements). We also attempt to locate deeds and mortgages, stock certificates, and life insurance policies in the decedent's name. Federal and state tax returns can be helpful in ascertaining a decedent's assets. We may also contact the decedent's accountant and other attorneys, if possible, as they may have a clearer picture of the decedent's estate.

↛ *I have been appointed as personal representative to probate the estate of my great aunt. What are some of the most easily overlooked assets?*

Easily overlooked assets include:

- Income tax refunds
- Overpayment of bills
- Prepaid deposits (damage deposits for rental property or utility deposits)

- Collections (coins, stamps, etc.)
- Antiques whose values are not recognized because they are thought to be junk
- Jewelry, precious gems, precious metals
- Corporate share certificates
- Time-share contracts for recreation properties in other states
- Real property in other counties, states, or countries
- Life insurance benefits and disability insurance benefits that are incidental to credit card accounts and savings accounts
- Old life insurance policies for small amounts
- Property entrusted by the decedent to someone else
- Monies owed to the decedent under fixed obligations such as mortgages
- Monies owed under obligations which are in dispute
- Monies held by a state agency under an "escheat" statute if the decedent did not make deposits or withdrawals in bank accounts over a long period of time
- Money lent to loved ones on oral agreements for repayment (The personal representative may have to go through many previous years of the decedent's canceled checks to learn of such loans and to calculate the unpaid amounts owing at death.)
- Rights to reimbursements under medical insurance policies and long-term-care contracts

⚜ *What should I do with the bank books and checking accounts?*

Bank accounts which were in the decedent's individual name will have to be secured. If necessary, an emergency motion for appointment of a temporary executor will have to be filed in the probate court so that the named fiduciary can obtain immediate authority to act on behalf of the decedent. Until a fiduciary is authorized to act on behalf of the decedent, the bank account—not generally accessible–will be vulnerable to abuse.

Banking institutions will not provide information to either the attorney or the named fiduciary until a formal appointment has been made.

⚜ *What about household furnishings?*

Your attorney should be able to recommend a qualified appraiser who will perform a room-by-room appraisal of the household furnishings.

⅍ *I have a funded living trust but have a $2500 account in my name. Will probate be required?*

For small amounts of personal property that have not been funded into a living trust, your heirs might consider a *voluntary administration,* or *small-estate* or *informal* probate, which is allowed by statute in most states. A voluntary administration is not a formal probate; it is an informal probate for modest estates. To qualify, an estate must, as a rule, consist of only personal property valued under a specified statutory amount. If the estate qualifies, the voluntary administrator is not obligated to file a bond or to file an inventory or annual accounting.

If it appears that a voluntary administration will meet your intent and will save the fees and delay of a formal probate, your heirs should consider it.

⅍ *What should we do with our parents' home?*

This question is commonly asked by surviving children. Often, in moderate-size estates, the home is the estate's largest asset and should be immediately secured from vandalism.

If anyone continues to reside at the premises, you must ascertain that he or she is rightfully in possession. You should also contact the homeowner's insurance company and make sure there is sufficient insurance on the residence to cover any liability or loss in case of a catastrophe such as a fire.

You should have the value of the home appraised, and the appraisers should also provide a room-by-room inventory and appraisal of the household furnishings and their fair market values that can be filed with the probate court.

⅍ *I have been appointed by the court as the personal representative of my mother's probate estate. How do I transfer her real estate?*

You prepare a personal representative's or executor's deed from you as personal representative or executor to the designated heir.

⅍ *How do I sell her stocks and bonds and mutual funds?*

You can sell these assets through a stockbroker or directly through the company's transfer agent. The broker or agent will ask for proof of your authority to act, which is confirmed by certified copies of your "letters testamentary" or order from the court.

⊠ *Who will handle the distribution of out-of-state property to my heirs?*

If you die with real property titled in your name and located in another state, your personal representative will have to arrange for an ancillary administration in the probate court of the county and state in which it is located in addition to the state of your residence. Out-of-state personal property such as bank accounts can usually be collected without opening an ancillary probate.

Certified copies of the will and other filings from your home state's probate court are sent to a law firm in the other state so that the firm can complete the probate process under its state's procedure. Your heirs can receive their property when this out-of-state proceeding is completed.

⊠ *What problems will arise if we leave property in different states?*

Probate can be required in every jurisdiction in which you own real property. Your fiduciary will have to deal with different judicial systems over long distances and through attorneys licensed to practice in those jurisdictions.

Ancillary probate can be particularly frustrating in situations where low-valued property requires relatively high fees because of regional red tape.

⊠ *I am the personal representative for the estate of my grandfather. My search for assets has disclosed a $400,000 savings account held jointly by my grandfather and the woman who was attending to his living needs. I've asked her to turn over the money in this account, but she refuses. I want to sue her. Will I win?*

Whether you would win the lawsuit depends upon the answers to a number of questions:

- Does the law of your state raise a presumption that a nonspouse named as the surviving owner of a joint account holds that account as trustee for the estate of your grandfather?
- Does the law of your state raise the presumption that the joint account was intended only to permit lifetime withdrawals by the caretaker for the benefit of your grandfather and was not intended to give beneficial ownership to the caretaker upon your grandfather's death?
- Was your grandfather competent when he created the joint account?

- Did the caretaker assert undue influence over your grandfather to get him to create the joint account?
- When your grandfather created the joint account, did the caretaker orally assure him that after his death she would hold and apply the joint account as a trustee for some other person or for some other purpose?
- Would such an oral trust agreement be enforceable under the law of your state?

The attorney representing you as the personal representative of your grandfather's estate will conduct a preliminary investigation and perform preliminary legal research to form an opinion on which you may act. You should not be surprised if your claim against the caretaker is settled for a fraction of the joint account.

Payment of a Decedent's Liabilities

Is a personal representative personally liable to the estate's creditors?

In all states, the personal representative must wait until after the publication of notice to creditors or the expiration of a "nonclaim" period (generally 3 to 9 months, depending on state law) to distribute the estate's assets.

If a personal representative does not wait the requisite period of time to distribute the assets of the estate, the decedent's creditors may commence a cause of action against the personal representative for failing to adequately provide for them.

When should I pay any bills?

The fiduciary handling the estate must make a clear determination of the value of the estate before paying any of the estate's debts. Once the value of the estate is completely determined, if there are sufficient assets to pay all the claims, including any estate taxes that are incurred as a result of the death, claims are paid.

Generally, the majority of creditor payments are made only after the state's nonclaim period has run. If the assets are more than sufficient to cover miscellaneous claims, the fiduciary is instructed to withhold a reasonable amount in escrow until the nonclaim period has run and to pay bills as they come due.

⚜ *What should the personal representative consider before paying the decedent's debts?*

Is the obligation bona fide and legally enforceable? If the obligation is not legally enforceable, such as a charitable pledge, the representative should definitely not give it equal standing with enforceable claims. The representative should also determine whether an obligation contains a provision extinguishing the indebtedness upon death.

⚜ *Are there priorities for the payment of a decedent's debts?*

Yes. They are provided in your state's probate statute. Generally, first priority is given to administration expenses provided the expenses are reasonable and proper. Funeral expenses as well as those of the decedent's final illness receive second priority. They are followed by state and federal taxes, secured creditors, and, finally, unsecured creditors.

The personal representative should note that bequests cannot be safely paid until the time for presenting claims in accordance with state law has expired or lapsed.

⚜ *What procedure must estate creditors follow to protect their rights?*

The procedure varies from state to state. Typically, a creditor of an estate must send a notice of claim within a specified time period—usually from 3 to 6 months, depending upon the state—personally or by certified mail with return receipt requested, to the personal representative of the estate at his or her place of residence or to the clerk of the probate court.

⚜ *If a creditor has not filed a notice of claim in a timely manner, may the personal representative distribute the estate assets?*

Generally, yes. If the personal representative distributes estate assets in good faith after the nonclaim period, he or she is not liable to creditors even if, for some reason, they may successfully receive a subsequent judgment against the estate.

⚜ *After the beneficiaries have received the funds from an estate, can they still be sued by the decedent's creditors?*

If the statute of limitations has not run, the answer is yes. The beneficiaries of an estate are liable to the decedent's creditors for up to the sum of money they received as a distribution from the estate until the statute of limitations has run.

> ➤ *If a friend of the decedent threatens to file a lawsuit against the estate for services rendered to the decedent, how does that threat affect the administration of the estate?*

The personal representative must resolve every claim against the estate. If the matter cannot be settled or compromised, a hearing can be set by the court and the matter handled like any other lawsuit. The person making the threat or claim must prove that the services claimed were actually performed and that a contract was entered into for which payment was clearly to be made.

Sometimes a friend may take care of a sick person, without payment, expecting an inheritance after the sick person's death. If the inheritance is not received or it is lower than expected, hard feelings occur. The outcome will differ depending upon the facts.

AFTER-DEATH
TRUST ADMINISTRATION

> ➤ *My spouse and I have a fully funded joint revocable living trust. When one of us dies, what will have to be done?*

When the first trust maker dies, there is very little that the surviving spouse must do if all of the decedent's assets have been transferred to the trust. Probate is eliminated, although the deceased spouse's pour-over will should be filed with the probate court. If the deceased spouse had minor children, the pour-over will would have to be filed with the probate court in order to determine their guardians.

The successor death trustees will become the primary trustees of the trust. *Affidavits of successor trustee,* which are legal documents stating that successor trustees have assumed the trusteeship, should be sent to all financial institutions so that these trustees have signatures on file and their authority to act on behalf of the trust is recognized.

If the assets of the deceased spouse are worth the applicable exclusion amount available in the year of death (e.g., $650,000 in 1999), a federal estate tax return must be filed and the assets must be allocated between the marital and family trusts. In states that have an estate or inheritance tax, a return may have to be filed based upon the state's requirements. Final state and federal income tax returns must also be prepared. The trustee may have to obtain a separate taxpayer identification number for the trust.

Specific bequests and distributions required by the trust should be made and final bills paid.

≫ What if my spouse and I have separate revocable living trusts and my spouse dies?

If your spouse's revocable trust was fully funded, the procedures are almost identical to those required for a joint living trust.

≫ Is there usually a fee for utilizing an attorney to settle my trust?

Yes. In almost all circumstances there will be attorney's fees upon the death or disability of the trust maker. Hiring the attorney is necessary to ensure that the estate plan will do what it is supposed to do. Typically, these fees will almost always be far less than the fees associated with the probate process.

≫ In our joint revocable living trust, there are provisions for a marital trust and a family trust. After one of us dies, how exactly are assets put into those trusts?

If provisions have been made in your trust for marital and family subtrusts, they must be established as separate trusts. Typically, the trustee will have to physically transfer the assets to each trust or make "book" entries between the various subtrusts. Accounting records can be set up which account for each trust. The value of each trust and how assets are allocated to each trust are set forth in your trust document in a *formula clause*.

In many cases, the decedent's maximum applicable exclusion amount for the year of death is allocated by a book entry to the family trust, with the balance of the assets being allocated to the marital trust. This will provide for optimum estate tax planning on the death of the second spouse.

If you both had separate trusts, the process would be almost exactly the same.

Duties of a Trustee

≫ What obligation does a trustee of a revocable living trust have to account to the decedent's beneficiaries?

Although the administration of a trust is usually accomplished outside the review of the probate court, certain rules still apply and these rules may be enforced by trust beneficiaries. Accordingly, the prudent trustee will notify, in writing, all the beneficiaries named in the trust, including any contingent beneficiaries, of the existence of the trust and the death of the trust maker.

Unless otherwise prohibited by the trust document, it is wise to supply all beneficiaries with a copy of the trust and to inform them that they have the right to seek and employ legal counsel if that is their wish.

In most jurisdictions, the trustee will have a duty to report and account to the beneficiaries named in the decedent's trust at least once a year. This requirement may generally be waived by the consent of the beneficiaries or by express waiver granted in the decedent's trust instrument. However, good practice dictates a full accounting of all trust activity by the trustee to the named beneficiaries at frequent intervals to avoid any misunderstandings among them.

After a maker of a revocable living trust dies, how can a loved one get access to his or her safety deposit box?

Upon the death of a trust maker, his or her living trust becomes irrevocable. A new trustee (or trustees) steps into the shoes of the trust maker. If the safety deposit box is titled in the name of the trust, the new trustee simply goes to the bank and shows proof of the trust maker's death, typically by showing a certified copy of the death certificate and either an affidavit of successor trustee or a copy of the part of the living trust that discusses successor trustees. After showing identification, the new trustee signs a new agreement allowing access to the box.

If the safety deposit box is not in the name of the trust, it is likely that a probate will have to be initiated in order for the bank to allow someone to have access to it.

Of course, it helps greatly if the trust maker has kept his or her records up to date. A properly drafted living trust plan will include a portfolio of documents, which should include a list of where to find important documents and items such as safety deposit box keys.

Payment of a trust maker's liabilities

If a decedent placed his or her assets in a living trust, are the assets beyond the reach of his or her creditors?

Upon a trust maker's death, a living trust, in many states, completely cuts off the claims of the maker's unsecured creditors. At least seven states—California, Massachusetts, Michigan, New Jersey, New York, Oregon, and Florida—do not follow this general rule of severing creditors' claims. These states allow a trust maker's creditors to reach the assets held in the maker's trust to satisfy debts owed to them by the maker.

≥ℷ *I am the successor trustee under my mother's revocable living trust. Just how far do I have to go in searching for persons who might have claims against my mother or against her trust?*

If you live in a state whose law permits creditors to enforce their claims against such a living trust, the U.S. Supreme Court has made it clear that you must search diligently for creditors. Also, if the trust instrument itself requires that you pay creditors, you must search diligently for creditors.

If you fail to make diligent search and you distribute trust assets to beneficiaries, a successful claim may subject you to liability not only to the creditor but also to the beneficiaries against whom the creditor may seek remedy.

Your fiduciary duties as trustee obligate you to exercise care, skill, and diligence in ascertaining the validity and enforceability of claims. If necessary, you are required to deny payment of a claim and to defend the denial in court.

You should find out from your attorney whether the law of your state permits you to publish notice to creditors as a part of the due-diligence process. Publication is one way that you can demonstrate that you have been diligent in searching for unknown creditors.

≥ℷ *What are some good ways for me, as trustee, to find out who the trust maker's creditors are?*

In your search for creditors, you should examine the maker's canceled checks, previously paid bills, pending unpaid bills, correspondence files, and unopened mail. You should ask liability insurers whether there is any known pending claim against the trust maker or against the trust itself.

Beware of creditors who falsely assert that they are entitled to accelerated payment of a debt not due; always insist that you or fiduciary counsel examine all written documentation to ascertain if amounts are really due.

If the maker was active in business, it is generally prudent to inquire whether claims for breaches of warranties or other contracts may reasonably be expected. If the maker was a partner, shareholder, or member in a partnership, corporation, or limited liability company, reasonable inquiry should be made of the other partners, shareholders, or members as to potential claims or debts.

To uncover potential debts or claims, consider sending a letter requesting verification *that all bills have been previously paid.* For claims that are actually made, verify the balance due, the amount of each current monthly payment, the absence of default by the maker, and other relevant aspects of the particular indebtedness.

✒ *What steps should I take if I find a claim that I do not believe is valid?*

Seek legal advice if you plan to reject a claim.

Consider deferring distribution to beneficiaries of an amount that may be held as a contingency fund to cover unresolved claims.

If you are in doubt about whether a significant claim should be paid, consider asking a court for instruction so that you are protected from future personal liability to a creditor or to a beneficiary.

✒ *I am the trustee under my deceased father's trust. The trust owns a note secured by a mortgage. The borrower is in default. My lawyer says that the lawsuit to foreclose the mortgage will take 2 years and that the value of the land is only half the amount of the expected foreclosure judgment. My brothers and sisters, as beneficiaries of the trust, are clamoring for distribution. I believe that I have paid all creditors to whom my father or his trust owed money. There is no death tax. What are my choices?*

Here are your choices:

1. Under state law, you, as trustee, can ask for instructions from a court, but the time, expense, and uncertainty in getting instructions may dissuade you from this course of action.
2. You may distribute the note and all of your rights under a pending foreclosure action in fractional shares to the beneficiaries of the trust, allowing all the beneficiaries to band together to pursue the foreclosure action.
3. You may tell your brothers and sisters to "cool it" while you press

the foreclosure action to conclusion, but this may result in their going to court to ask the judge to instruct you otherwise.

4. You may negotiate with one of more of your brothers or sisters to get an agreement by which the distributive share of one or more of them may include the note and the mortgage at an adjusted, or "discounted," value. These beneficiaries may then take a gamble to try to recover more than the "half" forecast by the estate's attorney.

I am the sole successor trustee for my deceased mother's trust. How do I transfer or sell her real estate?

The trust is still the owner of the property, so you would prepare and sign a deed granting the property to the buyer or the beneficiary. You would sign this deed as "Maria Jones, sole trustee under the Jones Trust, dated January 1, 1999," or words to that effect. Just be sure the signature section includes the information that you are the sole trustee, the name of the trust, and the date it was established.

How do I sell her stocks and bonds and mutual funds?

Contact her stockbroker, her mutual fund company, or the transfer agent for the company whose stock she holds. All will be able to give you detailed instructions. In almost every case, they will ask for a certified copy of her death certificate; proof of the trust and your position as successor trustee, such as an affidavit of trust or copies of the trust itself; your instructions to them; and your signature on the instructions with a Medallion guarantee. A *Medallion guarantee* is a signature guarantee under the Medallion Program, which was set up to ensure the validity of signatures in such cases. Persons authorized to give Medallion guarantees usually include bank officers, officers of trust departments, and stockbrokers.

Distributions to beneficiaries

Does my trustee have to sell all my property before making distributions?

No, the trust agreement can and should provide that the trustee can exercise discretion as to when to sell property before making distribution and when to make distribution of assets in kind.

You can, of course, also provide in the trust for distribution of specific assets to specific beneficiaries.

✍ *As a trustee, how do I make distributions from the trust and protect myself?*

If you hold property for another's benefit as trustee, you are held to the highest standard of care. This standard of care is called a *fiduciary duty.* You may have personal liability if you are negligent in the handling of trust assets and liabilities.

You must maintain accurate records regarding trust property, including additions of principal and income. Liabilities are even more critical because if an unexpected obligation pops up after you have distributed assets to the beneficiaries, it is difficult to retrieve the funds or assets. You could become personally liable if you distributed funds without properly paying all creditors.

For these reasons it is always a good idea to hold funds or assets back for a year or more in order to allow plenty of time for any adjustments to income and estate tax returns that you filed or for any final medical bills. It is safe to make final distributions to the beneficiaries only when you are certain that all liabilities have been assessed and covered.

✍ *What if I am the surviving spouse and I need some of the money from the family trust?*

You can have direct access to the family trust in accordance with its provisions. If someone other than you is acting as trustee of the family trust, that trustee may have the discretion to make distributions of principal to you.

However, your spouse's family trust may have been drafted very liberally on your behalf. It may provide, for example:

1. That all the income is payable to you
2. That you can have the right to withdraw chunks of principal each year in the greater of $5000 or 5 percent of the trust property (This means that if there is $650,000 in the family trust, you can take out $32,500 to use for whatever you want—such as a trip around the world on the *Queen Elizabeth II.*)
3. That you can distribute to yourself as beneficiary additional principal under the "ascertainable standard" of maintenance, education, support, and health (Since at least "maintenance" and "support" are fairly broad terms, the strings on the property are not particularly onerous.)

≫   *Is it true that the trustee of my living trust is allowed to distribute its assets to my beneficiaries within a few days after my death?*

Your trustee must follow your trust's instructions. Those instructions usually require that your legitimate debts, income taxes, and death taxes be paid and that distributions be made to your beneficiaries. Since your trustee may be personally liable if he or she makes distributions to beneficiaries and then does not have enough money or property left in the trust to pay debts and taxes, your trustee must determine which debts and taxes should be paid from trust assets. This may take some time.

A well-advised trustee will consider partial distributions while the trustee retains assets sufficient to meet the contingencies for unsettled claims and undetermined taxes.

≫   *I am the trustee of my unmarried sister's living trust. On her death, does the trust property immediately belong to her beneficiaries?*

The same applies in your situation as in the previous answer. As trustee, you would first determine the extent of the trust provisions that contain your sister's instructions. As her fiduciary, your job is to follow them to the letter, which may require keeping funds in trust, distributing certain funds in certain ways, or a myriad of other alternatives.

Termination of a living trust after the maker's death

≫   *Does my trust have to continue after I die?*

No, it does not. Your trust will continue as an "administrative trust" only for a period of time that ensures that your trustee pays your debts and your taxes and gets the assets ready to make distributions.

≫   *Are there reasons to continue a trust for a period of time?*

Absolutely. Many trust makers choose to have their trusts continue long after death so that the trustees can carry out their instructions for the benefit of children, grandchildren, and other beneficiaries.

It may be that beneficiaries, in the opinion of the trust maker, are not ready to handle assets that otherwise might be given to them outright. A well-drafted living trust enables its maker to lay out loving instructions for each beneficiary.

⚛ *How can I be sure that my trust does not continue far past its usefulness, when in good sense it should be terminated?*

A skillfully drafted living trust may contain permission for your trustee to terminate the trust when the trustee determines that the trust agreement has become uneconomical to administer due to the high cost of administration relative to the value of the trust property.

State law may also allow the trustee to terminate the trust if continuance of the trust would defeat or substantially impair the accomplishment of the purposes of the trust.

A trustee should always seek legal counsel before terminating a trust to avoid violating state law or the terms of the trust agreement.

⚛ *What happens to the assets in the trust when the trust is terminated early?*

If the trustee terminates the trust under the authority stated in the trust instrument, the instrument should also spell out who gets the trust assets. Often, early termination gives the assets to the trust maker if he or she is living or to the trust maker's spouse if the spouse is a beneficiary of the trust. If neither of them is living, other beneficiaries will be listed.

QUALIFIED DISCLAIMERS

⚛ *What is a disclaimer?*

A *disclaimer* is an irrevocable and unqualified refusal to accept an interest in property. The effect of a disclaimer is as if no transfer was made to or from the person making the disclaimer. Most states have statutes that allow disclaimers and set forth how they are to be made.

⚛ *What is a qualified disclaimer?*

A disclaimer is "qualified" if it meets the requirements of Section 2518 of the Internal Revenue Code. These requirements are:

- The disclaimer must be in writing.
- The disclaimer must be delivered to the person who is attempting to transfer the interest, to his or her legal representative, or to the holder of the legal title to the property interest.
- The disclaimer must be delivered not later than 9 months after the

date of the transfer creating the interest or 9 months after the person making the disclaimer becomes 21.

■   The person making the disclaimer must not have accepted the interest or any of its benefits.

■   As a result of the disclaimer, the property must pass, without any direction on the part of the person making the disclaimer, either to the spouse of the person making the transfer or to someone other than the person making the disclaimer.

⬥ *Why would anyone wish to disclaim an interest in property left to him or her by a decedent?*

Generally, disclaimers are exercised to redirect property to another person either for tax purposes or as a reallocation of assets for nontax purposes. For example, if a parent died leaving all his or her property to the parent's two children or their issue and one of the children is terminally ill, it may be to the advantage of that terminally ill child to disclaim the property that he or she would receive from his or her parent. The property will then pass automatically to the terminally ill child's children without being included in the estate of the terminally ill child.

The same result may be desirable in the case of a child whose estate is already substantial. That child may prefer to have the property pass directly to his or her children as long as it qualifies for the GST tax exemption.

As another example, if property was left to two children or to the survivor of the children and one of the children feels that his or her sibling should receive that property, that child could disclaim his or her interest in the property in favor of the sibling.

There are a variety of situations in which a disclaimer of an interest can be particularly useful in planning for family members. Individuals should obtain counsel before deciding to accept or reject property to determine if disclaimers may be appropriate in specific situations.

⬥ *My husband just died, and I don't need the $500,000 that he left me. I tried to talk my husband into leaving the $500,000 directly to our children, but he said that his attorney had told him that I could divert the $500,000 to them by a disclaimer. Can I do that?*

Whether a disclaimer can be used to divert the $500,000 to your children depends upon the manner in which you are receiving the inheritance:

- If it comes to you under a joint and survivor account that you and your husband created, your disclaimer will most probably force it through the courts before it can get to your children.
- If it comes to you under a trust or a will that provides for your children, it will successfully pass to them in accordance with that document's provisions.
- If your husband's trust or will provides that the $500,000 goes to someone *other than your children* if you should disclaim, you would be foolish to exercise your disclaimer because you are not permitted to say who receives the disclaimed property.

If a disclaimer technique is not available to you, you can receive your inheritance and give it to your children by using your annual exclusion gifts over a period of years. You can also use a portion of your applicable exclusion tax-free amount (e.g., $650,000 in 1999) to give it to them any time you wish. For example, if you have three children and they have an opportunity to use the $500,000 now to purchase an asset that is expected to rise rapidly in value before your death, you might use $470,000 of your applicable exclusion amount combined with a $10,000 annual exclusion gift to each child in the current year.

The appreciated, or increased, value of the asset at your death will be excluded from your taxable estate, but the threshold at which you will pay taxes on your estate at your death will be lowered by $470,000.

What happens if my spouse disclaims her interest under the marital trust?

The marital deduction would be lost, and any amounts over the applicable exclusion amount threshold will be subject to federal estate tax.

What are the consequences if, after my death, my spouse disclaims all her rights under the family trust?

There are no tax consequences if she does so, and the trustee may make a distribution to the other beneficiaries in accordance with the terms and provisions of the trust.

I may receive an inheritance from my parents after they are both deceased, but I would rather have it pass to my children. Is there

*a way that I can get the property to my children without incur-
ring gift taxes?*

This is a perfect situation for using a qualified disclaimer. If you disclaim your inheritance after your parents are deceased, the assets will
pass as if you were deceased at the time of your surviving parent's death.
The recipient of those assets in this event will be determined by the
terms of your surviving parent's will or trust. If the document provides
that in the event of your death, your share will pass to your children in
equal shares, then your children will receive the assets which you have
disclaimed. You will not be deemed to have made a gift to your children
for gift tax purposes.

Please remember, however, that these assets may still be subject to
federal estate taxation in your parent's estate. The disclaimer will eliminate disclaimed assets from your estate and allow them to pass to your
children free of gift tax, but the assets will be included in the estate of
the last one of your parents to die.

The disclaimer is an incredibly useful tool for leveraging the
amount of gifts which you can make during your lifetime without gift
tax liability. There is no limit on the amount you can disclaim, and all
assets which you disclaim to your children will escape estate taxes upon
your death. There may, however, be generation-skipping transfer taxes
in your surviving parent's estate if the amount going to your children
is greater than the then-available exemption for generation-skipping
transfers.

Generation-skipping transfer taxes should be discussed with your
estate planning attorney before you make any disclaimer decisions. In
fact, because of all the limitations and traps that exist around disclaimers, it is critical that you consult an estate planning attorney immediately
after you become aware of your right to any asset which you may want
to disclaim.

⤍ *Can jointly owned property between spouses be disclaimed?*

Yes, jointly owned property may be disclaimed. However, state law
controls the starting point for the surviving spouse's ability to disclaim
his or her survivorship interest.

The *survivorship interest,* which is the survivor's right to the property held jointly, may be disclaimed by the surviving spouse if the joint
tenancy can be severed or partitioned under state law. Phrased another
way, if the surviving spouse had the absolute right to take his or her

share of the property during life by partitioning (splitting up) the property without the other spouse's consent, the surviving spouse has 9 months from the date of his or her spouse's death to execute a qualified disclaimer.

Your attorney will look to state law as to whether an interest may be severed by either spouse during life. This is especially true for real property which is owned in tenancy by the entirety. In one case in Maryland, the IRS denied an attempted disclaimer of a real-property interest within 9 months after the first joint tenant's death. The IRS determined that under Maryland law, tenancy-by-the-entirety property can be partitioned only with the consent of both parties. Because both parties were required to partition the property, the survivorship interest was created when title to the property was originally taken, not at the death of the first joint tenant. The disclaimer had to be made within 9 months of the transfer of the property into tenancy by the entirety to be effective rather than within 9 months after the date of the death of a joint tenant.

THE SPOUSAL ELECTION

⚰ *What is the spousal election?*

In almost all states, a surviving spouse who has not inherited a certain minimum amount provided by state law has a right to take a share of the deceased spouse's estate. This right is known as the *spousal election,* or the surviving spouse's right of election.

States differ regarding not only the amount of this election but also what property the election applies to. In some states, the spousal election is one-third of the deceased spouse's estate. In others, it is one-half or more.

⚰ *What assets are subject to the spousal election?*

This varies from state to state. In many states, these assets include:

- All assets titled in the name of the deceased spouse
- Assets that were given as gifts by the deceased spouse in anticipation of his or her death
- Any property interests transferred by the deceased spouse to or for the benefit of another person within 1 year of his or her death for

which the deceased spouse did not receive adequate and full consideration

- Bank accounts in joint names and payable on death
- Money in savings accounts in the name of the decedent in trust for another person
- Any interest in property that is subject to a general power of appointment by the decedent
- Pension benefits and stock bonus or profit-sharing plans

⊠ How do I claim my spousal elective rights?

The spousal election statutes are generally highly technical and impose strict time limits for claiming the elective share. These statutes vary from state to state and may be amended from time to time. You should consult an attorney with regard to your rights in a particular state immediately after the death of a spouse.

Spousal elective rights must be asserted within specific time limits after the death of an individual. The elective rights are considered a personal right of the surviving spouse and in some states cannot be claimed by children or others acting on behalf of the surviving spouse unless specific written authorization is given to make the claim.

⊠ I am in a second marriage, and I have a will that excludes my present spouse and transfers all my assets to my children from my first marriage. Can my present spouse still take part of my probate estate?

Most likely the answer is yes. Most states allow a spousal election for a surviving spouse. If your spouse does not like the terms of your will, he or she can elect to receive that portion of your estate that is allowed by state law.

⊠ What if I signed a prenuptial agreement waiving my right to an elective share of my spouse's estate?

In most states, a spousal election can be waived through the use of a valid prenuptial agreement. But if you have concerns about yours, you should have your attorney review your prenuptial agreement for its validity and should ask if your state allows the waiver of the spousal election in a prenuptial agreement.

INCOME TAXES AFTER DEATH

A Decedent's Final Income Tax Return

🔊 *Why must an income tax return be filed after the death of an individual?*

During the portion of a tax year that a decedent was alive, income was received under his or her own Social Security number. That income was reported to the state and federal governments along with appropriate tax withholdings. A final return must be filed with the federal, state, and local governments after the death of an individual in order to pay any remaining taxes or to claim refunds for this tax period.

In the case of a married individual, the final return may be part of a joint return with the surviving spouse.

🔊 *What items should be reported on a decedent's final income tax return?*

Any income actually received on a cash basis as well as any expenses that were actually paid should be reported on a decedent's final 1040 return. The tax period between the beginning of a person's taxable year (almost always January 1) and the date of his or her death is treated as the tax period for which Form 1040 and the state income tax return must be filed.

🔊 *Can a joint income tax return be filed in the year that a spouse dies?*

Yes. A joint return may be filed with the decedent's surviving spouse provided that spouse does not remarry before the close of the tax year. The return must include the surviving spouse's income for the entire tax year. The decedent's personal exemption can be used.

Authorization for the personal representative or trustee to file a joint return should be stated in the decedent's will or trust document.

This option should always be explored because a joint return may well reduce total tax liability.

🔊 *My brother recently died, and I am the executor of his estate. He lived in a nursing home for years and has never filed an income tax return. What should I do?*

You should promptly seek the advice of a tax preparer who can examine all the information that you can make available for the purpose of determining whether, in fact, your brother should have filed income tax returns. If your brother should have filed income tax returns, you should now consider filing returns for prior years and pay any necessary tax from estate assets or trust assets as the case may be.

As executor of your brother's estate, your failure to file a return can make you individually liable for tax to the extent of the value of the estate assets or the trust assets under your control. You can find yourself in troubled waters if you ignore your duty to file income tax returns and pay taxes but, instead, distribute assets to your brother's heirs.

Income Received
after the Decedent's Death

⚞ *How is income that is received after the decedent's date of death reported?*

Any income received after the decedent's death is reported on one of the following: the decedent's final income tax return, the estate's income tax return, the trust's income tax return (if the decedent had a living trust), or the returns of the beneficiaries who received income.

⚞ *When my mother died, she had some U.S. savings bonds. Who must report this income?*

The income can be reported on your mother's final income tax return or on her estate's tax return, or, under some circumstances, the heirs can report it.

Determining who should report the income is based on a number of factors such as the tax brackets of your mother, the estate, and the beneficiaries. If there is more than one beneficiary, the income may be divided by the number of beneficiaries receiving it; this may result in insufficient income to place the beneficiary in a higher tax bracket.

In addition, since it is possible to deduct certain expenses on either a federal estate tax return or the decedent's final income tax return, the determination as to who shall pay income taxes on the interest will be affected by which return reflects the expenses.

A prudent trustee or executor will consult with a knowledgeable advisor to determine the existence of a decedent's income. He or she will also consult with the beneficiaries to determine the most beneficial place to report such items.

Income Received in a Living Trust after the Maker's Death

⚜ *Who pays tax on the income generated after the death of a trust maker who had a fully funded revocable living trust?*

If a living trust can be terminated quickly after the death of the trust maker, and preferably within the same tax year as his or her death, the trustee will pass the income to be reported directly to the beneficiaries who receive the income.

If distributions are made to another trust, such as a marital or family trust, the income may have to be reported on that trust's income tax return.

If it appears that the trust cannot be terminated quickly, the trustee creates an *administrative trust* with its own taxpayer identification number. An administrative trust is much like a probate estate in that it has its own income tax bracket. The administrative trust reports the income.

⚜ *If the trust is in order and the assets are easy to distribute, why would a trustee create an administrative trust?*

The primary reason for creating an administrative trust is to allow the trustee sufficient time to review his or her duties and to make sure that all prudent decisions and elections are made. An administrative trust also gives the trustee and the beneficiaries the time to:

- Decide whether disclaimers should be made and then make such disclaimers.
- Make decisions concerning valuation and alternate valuation of assets.
- Determine on which income tax return income should be reported and deductions taken.

Unless there are few income-producing assets and none of the above considerations apply, the better approach is to establish an administrative trust and allow sufficient time to properly evaluate the trust and the correct course of action for complete distribution.

⚜ *Does the administrative trust pay income tax estimates?*

Most trusts must pay quarterly estimates, but under Section 6654(1)(2)(B) of the Internal Revenue Code, an administrative trust whose purpose is to complete the trust in a reasonable time will qualify for a 2-year exemption from quarterly estimates.

After-Death Income Tax Considerations

⅏ *What issues should be considered when electing a tax year for a trust or a probate estate?*

An executor of an estate may elect a fiscal tax year. The first year can be a full 12-month period or can be a short year followed by a 12-month period. For example, if the decedent dies on March 2, the executor may decide that he or she would like to have a tax year that begins on June 1. A short-year income tax return would then be filed for the probate estate income and expenses for the period from March 2 through May 31. Thereafter, the tax year for the probate estate would be from June 1 through May 31.

The successor trustee of a trust has no such option. A calendar year must be used. In the above example, the trust's first tax year would begin on March 2 and end on December 31. Thereafter, the trust's tax year would be a calendar year.

⅏ *Why did the attorney for my spouse's probate estate specify the close of the tax year for the estate as April 30?*

In selecting the ending date for the tax year of an estate, the requirement is that the first tax year end on a date which is at the end of any month and within 12 months of the date of death. For this reason, the first tax year of the estate will usually be less than a full 12 months. Any initial tax year of less than 12 months may be chosen and usually an ending date other than December 31 is selected. An early to midyear ending date for the estate's tax year presents more opportunity for shifting income into a different calendar tax year for the beneficiaries.

The attorney was not simply requiring that an extra tax return be filed. Each estate is required to file a tax return reporting any income that it has received; it may also use that tax return to report expenses and losses allocated to the beneficiaries of the estate for deduction purposes. By selecting a tax year with an ending date other than December 31, the estate has some flexibility in timing the distribution of assets. If the estate sells an asset of the decedent at a gain over date-of-death values, the recognition of gain by the beneficiary may be deferred to a later year if the estate's tax year ends in the next calendar year. The gain on that sale may be distributed to the beneficiary and reported for a tax year in which the beneficiary is in a lower income tax bracket. For instance, if the surviving spouse will receive less income in the next calendar year because the decedent's earnings are no longer available, the surviving spouse may be in a lower tax bracket. If the capital gain on the sale of an asset is carried forward and reported as distributed to the surviving spouse in the later calendar year, a tax savings may result because the surviving spouse is in a lower tax bracket. This income-shifting technique could occur between any two years during the administration of the estate to reduce income taxes.

❧ Is this deferral technique always effective?

One of the problems of deferring income into other tax years is that "bunching" can occur. Bunching means that income is deferred into another year that has high income. This creates taxation at a higher tax bracket because 2 years' worth of income is bunched into 1 year. It is not uncommon in an estate for bunching to occur in the year the estate is closed. That is why great care must be taken when using a fiscal year to defer income; deferral has a habit of biting back!

❧ Are there any tax reasons why I should be paid as personal representative of my father's estate?

Every personal representative performs duties and bears responsibilities which justify the payment of a fee. However, the personal representative is not required to accept a fee. Any fees received are taxable income for local, state, and federal purposes.

If a personal representative is also an heir of the estate, it may be that an estate distribution which is not subject to income tax would produce a greater benefit to the beneficiary/executor.

The income tax on a fee may be avoided only if the fee is waived. To effectively waive the fee, the personal representative should make an early written statement disclaiming the intent to receive the fee. The Internal Revenue Service and some state revenue departments may impose a tax on an imputed fee to the personal representative if the disclaimer is not made early and in a sufficiently definite form.

This tax trap is of more significance in large estates with potentially substantial fees. Attorneys representing estates should place the waiver-of-fees issue near the top of their administration checklist so that it can be discussed and decided upon at the earliest possible time.

↭ Should the personal representative retain income in the estate during the administration or distribute it to the beneficiaries?

Retaining income in a decedent's estate is always a concern because the income tax rates on estates are very compressed and very oppressive. If it appears that the deductible expenses will not zero out the taxable income, it is usually wise to distribute the income to the estate beneficiaries because such a distribution is deductible and avoids payment of income tax at the estate level on the income distributed.

The individual beneficiary who receives the income distribution will pay the income tax on it at typically a much more favorable income tax rate. However, the probate court's permission may be required for such a distribution, and it will be necessary to show that there is sufficient liquidity in the estate to pay any anticipated expenses.

Income Tax of Distributions

↭ Are my children taxed on distributions they receive from a trust?

The answer depends on what type of distributions—income or principal—they receive. Most trusts generate income from investments, and income is always taxed. Beneficiaries usually pay tax at their personal income tax rates on income withdrawn from a trust. The principal of a trust share is not taxed when beneficiaries take distributions.

↭ Do children have to pay tax on distributions from a family trust when both parents are deceased?

They do not have to pay estate taxes when they receive the funds after the death of their surviving parent. The money in the trust has been subject to tax (even if no tax was owed); as a result, the estate tax does not apply again.

Any income created by funds in the trust will be subject to income tax, which must be paid by the individual when he or she receives it. If the income is kept in the trust, the trust pays the income tax.

When the children sell the property they received, they will have to pay a capital gain tax on the difference between the sales price and the value of the property when it was placed in the trust at the death of the first parent.

FEDERAL ESTATE TAXES

The Federal Estate Tax Return

When must a federal estate tax return be filed?

A federal estate tax return (Form 706) must be filed and tax paid 9 months after the decedent's death. If it is impossible or impracticable for the estate tax return to be filed within 9 months, the IRS may grant a reasonable extension of time for filing. Nevertheless, the tax is still due within 9 months unless an extension to pay the tax is authorized as an exception in the Internal Revenue Code.

Who must file an estate tax return?

A federal estate tax return is required if a decedent's gross estate is valued at or more than the applicable exclusion amount in the year of death ($650,000 in 1999; $675,000 in 2000 and 2001; $700,000 in 2002 and 2003; $850,000 in 2004; $950,000 in 2005; and $1 million in 2006). If a person made lifetime taxable gifts that resulted in his or her estate being less than the applicable exclusion amount in the year of death, these gifts must be added back into the value of the estate. If, after adding them back, the decedent's gross estate is at or more than the applicable exclusion amount in the year of death, a federal estate tax return is required, even if no tax is due.

Are there any formal requirements for resident non-U.S. citizens with regard to their U.S.-based properties at death?

Yes, resident non-U.S. citizens must file an estate tax return within 9 months of death just like U.S. citizens. Form 706NA is required for every noncitizen resident whose U.S.-based assets exceed $60,000 at the time of his or her death.

All of the decedent's U.S.-based assets must be disclosed on the estate tax return. In addition, if the estate intends to claim deductions against the gross estate situated within the United States, the return must disclose the decedent's worldwide estate.

The return must be filed by the executor of the estate. If there is no executor or qualified individual in the United States to file such a return, the individual in possession of the property must prepare and file the estate tax return. If the decedent died testate, a certified copy of the will (translated into English) must be attached to the estate tax return.

⚒ *How will my estate be valued at the time of my death?*

Generally, your estate will be valued at the fair market value of all the assets as of the time of your death. If a property is encumbered, the value will be its net equity. Certain property such as farm property or real property used in a closely held business may be valued for estate tax purposes according to special rules. *Fair market value* is generally defined as the price that would be paid between a willing seller and a willing buyer when neither party is under pressure to complete the transaction.

Some assets are easily valued, such as marketable securities listed on an established securities exchange. Other assets, such as real property or partnership interests, may require appraisals to establish value. Since the Internal Revenue Service is not required to accept your appraisals, and in fact can hire its own appraisers in the event of a dispute, hiring recognized and qualified appraisers is important. The cost of qualified appraisers is well worth any additional expense.

Not all assets are valued at liquidation prices. For example, interests in a limited partnership may be valued at less than liquidation price because, in a limited partnership situation, no one partner has authority to liquidate the partnership. Further, the restrictions in the partnership agreement, resulting in lack of control and lack of marketability, often cause an appraiser to conclude that the value of the partnership interest must be decreased from liquidation value. Would you rather own 100 percent of a property worth $100 or 50 percent of a partnership which owns a similar property worth $200? Understanding these valuation principles is the foundation for solid and effective estate planning that can reduce taxes and meet other family goals.

⚒ *Who will be responsible for valuing my assets after my death?*

Assets that have readily ascertainable values, such as CDs and bank accounts, do not have to be appraised in order to determine their value. Assets such as real estate or business interests should be appraised because their fair market values are sometimes subjective and thus subject to IRS challenge.

In probate, the court will appoint either an appraiser recommended by the personal representative or a person from a list the court maintains. If you have done trust planning, your trustee will hire certified appraisers to value your property as needed.

⩍ *How are U.S. Series EE and H bonds valued for federal estate tax purposes?*

They are valued at their redemption value on the applicable valuation date.

Alternate Valuation Date

⩍ *What happens if the value of my assets plummets soon after I die? It doesn't seem fair to make my estate pay taxes on the value of my assets on the date of my death if the assets are worth much less by the time my estate actually pays the taxes.*

The general rule is that assets are valued for estate tax purposes at their fair market values on the date of the decedent's death. But if certain conditions are met, the assets can be valued on the *alternate valuation date* rather than on the date of death. The alternate valuation date is the date that is 6 months after the date of death. However, if the estate sells some assets within that 6-month period, then, for those assets that were sold, the alternate valuation date is the date of the sale.

For example, assume that you die on January 1 owning a car and some General Motors stock. Also assume that the personal representative of your estate sells your GM stock on March 1 but does not sell your car. If your estate elects to value your property on the alternate valuation date, your GM stock will be valued on March 1 and your car will be valued on July 1.

You cannot value some assets on the date of death and other assets on the alternate valuation date. You must value all assets on one or the other date.

⩍ *Why would I use the alternate valuation date?*

Perhaps your estate contains securities and the stock market has a major swing in value between the two dates. Your representative or trustee can make the election to value the estate at a time that is most advantageous to the estate. For example, a lower value might reduce estate taxes, while a higher value might eliminate capital gain taxes on the sale of securities. What election your representative makes will depend on the circumstances, but it is critically important that an informed decision be made before selecting the valuation date.

⩗ *What are the requirements for electing to use the alternate valuation date?*

There are three requirements that must be met to be eligible to choose the alternate valuation date:

1. The total value of the decedent's gross estate must decrease by using the alternate valuation date.
2. The amount of the estate taxes must decrease by using the alternate valuation date.
3. The person who files the decedent's estate tax return must make the proper election on the return.

⩗ *Is there any disadvantage if a death trustee of a revocable living trust distributes depreciating assets before 6 months after the date of death?*

The alternate valuation of assets for calculating federal estate tax is available only in the event that a reduction in tax is ultimately realized. The date of disposition of an asset determines its value for tax purposes. Accordingly, if an asset is depreciating in value or is likely to further depreciate in value during the 6 months after a decedent's death, the prudent trustee will wait until the 6-month period elapses. Any distribution or sale made before that time will "arrest" the value as of the date of disposition, while the additional passage of time may have allowed the trustee to take advantage of an additional depreciated value.

Election for Qualified Terminable Interest Property

⩗ *What does the estate tax QTIP election do?*

QTIP stands for "qualified terminable interest property." A QTIP election must be made on the federal estate tax return to ensure that qualified terminable interest property qualifies for the marital deduction.

⩗ *How does my personal representative or trustee make the election to treat the property I leave for my spouse as QTIP property?*

When you die, the person who is responsible for administering your estate (your personal representative or trustee) must file an estate tax return (Form 706) with the IRS. All property that is part of your gross estate must be listed. This includes all the property which is being transferred to your surviving spouse and for which your estate is to receive an estate tax marital deduction.

Your representative makes the election to treat certain property as QTIP property simply by listing that property on Schedule M of Form 706.

For the election to be valid, the estate tax return must be filed on time. Also, the election must be made on the first estate tax return to be filed—it cannot be made on an amended return. Furthermore, once the election has been made, it cannot be revoked.

Payment of Federal Estate Taxes

   Is there any way to arrange installment payments of federal estate taxes?

Yes. If a substantial portion of your wealth consists of an interest in a farm or a closely held business, your estate may not have enough liquid funds to pay the estate taxes attributable to that farm or closely held business. Unless your estate can postpone the payment of some of the estate taxes, your estate might be forced to sell the farm or business interest at a distressed price in order to pay the estate taxes within 9 months after your death.

The Internal Revenue Code contains an exception to the 9-month rule for estates which consist largely of a farm or business interest. If certain requirements are met, your estate can elect to defer the payment of the estate tax for 14 years. For the first 4 years, your estate will have to pay only interest on the deferred taxes.

Not all of your estate taxes can be paid in installments. Only that portion of your estate taxes which is attributable to your farm or business interest can be paid in installments.

To be eligible for installment payments, the following requirements must be met:

- The decedent must have been a U.S. citizen.
- The value of the farm or business interest must be more than 35 percent of the decedent's adjusted gross estate.

- The person who files the decedent's estate tax return must make an election on the return to pay the taxes in installments.

Special-Use Valuation

꿈 I heard that if I own a farm or a small business, I might be able to avoid some estate taxes. Is that true?

The Internal Revenue Code contains a *special-use valuation* provision by which the land on which a farm or a small business is operated can be valued for estate tax purposes at an amount well below its fair market value.

Generally, land is valued at its highest-and-best-use value, meaning that if the property would be worth more if you had been using it in a different way, then the property is valued at a higher value as though you had been using it in that different and more valuable way. For instance, assume that you owned a building in the middle of downtown in which you rented apartments. If valued as an apartment building, that building may be worth $500,000, but if you had been renting out office space in that building, rather than apartments, the building would be worth $600,000. The building is valued for estate tax purposes at its highest-and-best-use value—$600,000—even though you were not using it for its highest and best use.

Farmers and owners of small businesses are typically hardest hit by this highest-and-best-use rule. There can be a huge difference between the value of land used for farming and the value of the same land if it were subdivided and developed into a new neighborhood. Also, land often is the primary asset of farmers and small-business owners. So, in order to meet the high estate taxes attributable to the land, farmers and small-business owners might have to sell the land, usually at distress prices.

Recognizing that this result is often inequitable, Congress amended the Internal Revenue Code to permit farmers and small-business owners to value their land at its special-use value rather than at its highest-and-best-use value. The total decrease in value, from the highest-and-best-use value to the special-use value, cannot exceed $750,000.

Numerous detailed requirements must be met to be eligible for special-use valuation. These requirements can be summarized as follows:

- The land must be located in the United States.
- The decedent or a member of the decedent's family must have

owned the land for 5 out of the 8 years immediately preceding the decedent's death.

■ The decedent or a member of the decedent's family must have used the land as a farm or in another business for 5 out of the 8 years immediately preceding the decedent's death.

■ The decedent or a member of the decedent's family must have actively participated in the farming or other business for 5 out of the 8 years immediately preceding the decedent's death.

■ Fifty percent or more of the adjusted value of the decedent's estate (valued at its highest-and-best-use value) must consist of the adjusted value of the land and personal property that was used for the farm or business. The *adjusted value* is the value of the land or personal property reduced by any debt that is secured by the land or personal property.

■ Twenty-five percent or more of the adjusted value of the decedent's estate must consist of the adjusted value of the land that was used for the farm or business.

■ The land must pass from the decedent's estate to members of the decedent's family, and the members of the decedent's family who receive the land must agree to continue to operate the farm or business on the property for at least 10 years after the decedent's death.

Flower Bonds

⅍ *What are flower bonds, and why did my attorney include a reference to them in my trust?*

Flower bonds are specifically designated pre-1971 U.S. Treasury securities which may be useful in reducing federal estate taxes. These U.S. Treasury bonds bear low interest rates and trade on the open market at a discount from their face value. If such bonds are held by the decedent at the date of death, they may be used for the payment of federal estate taxes at their face value.

These bonds are said to "flower" because they then have an added, untaxed value for the estate. The bonds themselves, of course, are estate assets and are taxable at their market value.

The savings to the estate result because the bonds are redeemable at the higher face value if they are surrendered to pay federal estate taxes even though they were purchased at a discount. Your trustee under a revocable living trust should be authorized to use such bonds on your behalf to make this benefit available to your estate.

Section 303 Redemptions

⋈ *What is a Section 303 redemption, and when is it used?*

Internal Revenue Code Section 303 allows a C or S corporation to make a distribution in partial redemption of stock from the decedent's estate. There are generally no income tax consequences to the estate because of the step-up-in-basis rules.

A Section 303 redemption is used to allow the estate to keep control of the family corporation and redeem stock to meet the estate's death taxes and other administrative and funeral costs.

appendix A

Finding an Estate Planning Attorney

The inability to find the *right* estate planning attorney is an often-expressed frustration of many people. It is difficult for nonprofessionals to know what degree of legal sophistication an attorney should have to plan their estates. People often take on faith that "any attorney" is competent to plan an estate, and this misplaced confidence most often works to their and their families' detriment. Competent estate planning attorneys often voice their disappointment that potential clients yield to the temptation of shopping for price rather than quality when it comes to legal services.

In our experience, attorneys have varying degrees of skill in the law they practice; they are no different from physicians, athletes, or other paid professionals. The fee an attorney charges is certainly one of the many relevant factors that should be measured in making the appropriate "hiring decision," but it is not—by any means—the only factor.

An attorney-client relationship should be based on a bond of trust and understanding that is developed by open and honest communication. It should necessitate a mutual commitment on the part of both the client and the attorney to help each other in maintaining this bond of trust and respect.

Our contributing authors were very concerned about the entire aspect of choosing and working with a qualified attorney. They went to great lengths to describe all the criteria by which an attorney should be assessed. The result is a comprehensive discussion of the competence

555

needed for an attorney to be able to design, draft, and implement a superior plan.

We found the questions regarding the use of estate planning software to create one's own estate plan particularly interesting. Technology has certainly changed the lives of Americans and has given us more access to more information than at any time in history. Whether this wealth of new information has helped or hindered the search for knowledge is a topic that will be debated for years, but the exposure to the information has certainly expanded the horizons for all of us.

Technology, and the information that goes with it, does not grant instant understanding or expertise. It merely allows us to become broader generalists who can know just enough to ask the right questions.

This appendix is must reading for anyone who is concerned with or confused about how to find a competent estate planning attorney and how to work successfully within the attorney-client relationship. It answers many tough questions about fees and the quality of services that people should expect. We hope that you enjoy the perspectives found in this appendix as much as we did in editing them.

PROPER PLANNING

I recently attended an estate planning seminar sponsored and presented by nonattorneys. I thought only attorneys could prepare estate plans?

Many insurance agents, certified financial planners, stockbrokers, bank trust officers, and accountants hold seminars in their communities extolling the virtues of proper estate planning and the use of living trusts. These professionals provide a valuable educational service and often are highly knowledgeable and thoroughly professional. But they are not licensed to practice law, they cannot draft the documentation that would put their words into action, and they cannot be held ultimately accountable for their words by a disgruntled client or client's family.

Often, they find a struggling attorney and refer clients to him or her in the hope that he or she will "rubber-stamp" whatever they *together* recommended to the "mutual" clients. This practice is not in the best interest of the clients, nor is it compatible with the ethics of any profession.

The best presentations involve the collaboration of many professionals, including a licensed and skilled legal practitioner.

⋈ *I am working with a financial planner in whom I have a great
deal of confidence. Why can't she prepare my estate plan?*

A competent financial planner can provide you with a wide variety of
professional and educational services. Depending upon the planner's
level of expertise, qualifications, and certification, he or she may perform
comprehensive financial planning/analysis; assist in the creation, development, and implementation of short- and long-range financial planning goals; act as the registered broker/dealer for purposes of purchasing
investments; recommend estate planning concepts; and act as a sounding board regarding the performance of investments.

Despite all these beneficial services, there is one service that a
financial planner cannot legally provide: He or she cannot practice law.

The only professional who can assist you in drafting your estate
planning documents is an attorney. Any person who is not an attorney
and drafts legal documents on behalf of another may be guilty of the
unauthorized practice of law. In most states the unauthorized practice
of law is a crime. Also, if the financial planner does draft documents,
any mistakes will not be covered by errors and omissions insurance,
which doesn't cover the unauthorized practice of law.

Many financial planners are well versed with estate planning matters and work closely with competent attorneys to better serve the needs
of their mutual clients. These financial planners are to be sought after.

⋈ *I was approached by a salesman recently who offered to do my
estate plan for free if I would buy the investment that he was
selling. What do I have to lose?*

You stand to lose everything. Estate planning addresses your well-being,
the well-being of your loved ones, all your assets, your income, and the
taxes and expenses you may or may not incur.

⋈ *Can I have a paralegal or someone other than an attorney prepare my trust?*

By law, paralegals are allowed to assist attorneys and laypersons in filling
out paperwork, but they are not licensed to practice law.

⋈ *What about estate planning packages sold by companies?*

Estate planning documents prepared by nonattorneys often create major problems for loved ones, including:

- They may not work in your state because they may have been prepared under another state's law.
- They are pure boilerplate and not likely to meet your planning situation.
- They may cause you unnecessary taxes and expenses.
- Even if drawn properly, they most likely will not work unless they have been funded properly as well.
- Their many mistakes or deficiencies will not come to light until after your death.

One commentator's wry observation on will and living trust hucksters says it all: "There is no reason to buy anything from anybody who comes to the door unless they are about four feet tall and selling Girl Scout cookies."

People should not shy away from living trusts and other estate planning tools just because they are being improperly sold but, rather, should seek out the advice of qualified attorneys with regard to them.

✒ Aren't you being a little hard on the nonlegal professions?

No. It is illegal for a person who is not licensed to practice law to perform legal services, and the preparation of estate planning documents is the practice of law.

✒ If that is so, how come there are so many people selling estate planning materials?

There are many businesses and salespeople masquerading as estate planning professionals. They offer to sell estate planning documents such as wills, revocable living trusts, or irrevocable life insurance trusts without involving an attorney in the design or drafting of the estate planning documents on the pretense that it will be "cheaper" for the clients. In truth, they are in the business of deceiving consumers.

Florida, Iowa, Kansas, Minnesota, Maine, Massachusetts, Nebraska, New Mexico, Ohio, Texas, and Wisconsin, to name a few states, have brought legal proceedings against companies allegedly using scare tactics to sell boilerplate living trusts for thousands of dollars more than they are worth.

Invariably the boilerplate documents create major problems, and by the time these problems ultimately surface, both the companies and their salespeople will have disappeared.

⚂ *Can the staff attorneys in my bank's trust department prepare a revocable living trust document for me if I name the bank as trustee?*

It is common and often advantageous to name an institutional or professional trustee in estate planning documents. For many trust makers, naming a bank trust department makes a great deal of sense because the bank has a highly trained staff of trust specialists who have ongoing, daily experience with the administration of trusts.

However, a bank trust department should, at no time, create trust or estate planning documents. This activity is unauthorized in the law—even if the documents are prepared by bank attorneys—because legal ethics require that an attorney must be independent and represent only the client. An attorney employed by a trust department represents the bank, not its customers, and as a result an inherent and unethical conflict of interest is created.

A bank trust officer should be utilized as a valuable member of your estate planning team. Working with your independent counsel, he or she can be helpful in designing various terms and provisions of the trust.

DO-IT-YOURSELF ESTATE PLANNING

⚂ *I see various will and trust kits advertised in the media. Can I do my own estate planning?*

Legally you certainly can.

Interestingly, we have prepared estate plans for a great many attorneys who do not specialize in estate planning. They follow the adage, "An attorney who has himself or herself for a client has a fool for a client," and instead hire us. The law is highly technical and complicated, and unless the practitioner possesses a high degree of professional training, a great deal of harm can be innocently done. It would be foolish for uneducated, inexperienced, and unlicensed people to plan their estates and equally foolish for educated, experienced, and licensed people to plan their own estates as well.

A *Wall Street Journal* article once observed that proper estate planning is like brain surgery: *it is not a hobby.*

Planning kits are not innocent attempts at saving money; they are potential weapons that can do serious damage to a family. The peace of mind that you seek for yourself and your family in knowing that your planning is properly completed is best achieved by having a competent and experienced attorney assist you in the preparation of your estate planning documents.

⚜ *I have seen living trust software programs for less than $100. Why shouldn't I do my own?*

Software programs typically provide only very general or generic tax advice; they are not likely to address relevant personal and local law issues.

Even good software—without the training to use it—is no different from the issues we have already discussed. This is particularly true in planning for taxable estates that require sophisticated knowledge of estate and gift tax statutes. Innocent mistakes or oversights in tax planning can disqualify major exemptions, deductions, and credits.

Forms, whether they are preprinted or programmed software, are no substitute for experience, judgment, and legal training.

⚜ *Aren't you overstating your case just to promote attorneys?*

Unfortunately, we don't think so. Laws that recognize the validity or invalidity of a will or trust document are complicated and follow constantly changing local and federal law. If you fail to follow the exact requirements set out in the law, your documentation may be held invalid. This could be catastrophic in terms of your assets and loved ones.

Although it is not illegal for you to draft your own estate plan, you might put your talents to better use; simply filling in blanks can be extraordinarily dangerous to your and your family's fortunes.

⚜ *What's wrong with using reputable forms from reputable sources?*

A client of my father used a popular book with trust forms to create a family living trust. He saved over $2000 by doing it himself. When his wife predeceased him, which he never thought would happen, the trust contained an improper marital deduction clause costing the family over $235,000 in estate taxes. All the taxes could have been avoided by having an experienced attorney draft the documents.

When you seek the services of an attorney, you are paying not just for the forms but for the knowledge and experience of knowing which "form" is proper in any given situation.

⚑ *Would your answer be different if I told you that I am very intelligent and have some legal training?*

Many of our Network members are law professors, and they agree, with an overwhelming consensus, that even their best law students do not turn out workable estate plans on their first attempts. Unfortunately, your lay competency will not be challenged until after your disability or death.

⚑ *Can I get an attorney to review and correct the plan I drafted myself?*

Most attorneys cannot afford—mentally or physically—the time and expense involved in explaining the seemingly endless reasons why an amateurish attempt does not work. They prefer to keep both their sanity and their clients' legal fees within reason by starting a professional plan afresh.

⚑ *Why can't I buy some forms and pay an attorney by the hour to review the forms? Wouldn't this give me the best of both worlds?*

Most attorneys would charge less money to tailor an estate plan just for you than they would to retailor one that doesn't remotely fit you. Adopting or placing any "seal of approval" on someone else's work product, even another attorney's, or on a computer-generated work product subjects an attorney to future malpractice suits if something goes wrong—a possibility that most attorneys are greatly concerned about.

ONE-SIZE-FITS-ALL ESTATE PLANNING

⚑ *Isn't the preparation of a trust agreement really a "fill-in-the-blank" exercise for attorneys?*

It is not uncommon to see advertisements touting low-cost wills or trust documents that do precisely what your question implies. Unfortunately, the attorneys who place these ads do not, in the main, possess estate planning expertise; they are simply trying to participate financially in the popularity of estate planning. This has led to a dangerous misconception by many people that a "one-size-fits-all" trust agreement is a reasonable solution to effective estate planning.

In reality, nothing could be further from the truth. Proper planning and use of revocable living trust–centered estate planning techniques require detailed analysis of the client's assets and personal financial situation, as well as his or her individual hopes, plans, dreams, and ambitions. A true estate planning professional will make certain that the trust document is individually tailored and designed to satisfy the intensely personal concerns and goals of each client.

➷ Don't even great attorneys use forms?

Yes, they do, but compare two attorneys:

- Attorney A started practicing right out of law school and took every legal matter that came his way; he has no particular estate planning experience, but he does have a few *very good forms* he collected from books and documents over the years.
- Attorney B has specialized or limited her practice to estate planning law throughout her 25-year career; she has attended hundreds of professional symposia, lectured to bar groups, and written articles and books on the subject. She, too, has forms—thousands and thousands of them—upon which she has labored tens of thousands of hours over the years.

In which practitioner's forms would you have the greatest confidence?

➷ What if lawyer A had lawyer B's forms?

Knowing which wording to place where, and in what relationship to other wording within a document, is the art of the competent practitioner. Professionals who have limited resources—forms or otherwise—are like pharmacists who have a sparse selection of drugs.

It seems to us that physicians are trained to diagnose and prescribe; pharmacists are trained to fill those prescriptions; attorneys are trained to do both; and clients are trained to do neither.

➷ Why are some trusts so inexpensive?

An inexpensive trust is likely to be what is called a "bare-bones trust." Bare-bones living trusts are designed only to avoid probate. They have little personalized instruction. They are boilerplate documents on which the drafter fills in the blanks with your name, address, and the like.

A proper estate plan goes far beyond a bare-bones living trust by adding your personalized instructions. It contains your hopes, dreams, and desires as to the care of you and your loved ones.

A proper estate plan takes advantage, and avoids the pitfalls, of the ever-changing tax laws. A cheap bare-bones trust may be decades old and may trigger unwanted and avoidable taxes in the future.

⍒ *How can I tell if I have a one-size-fits-all trust?*

Price is one way to tell. If you feel you got the cheapest trust in town, you probably have a one-size-fits-all trust.

Look at the bottom of the pages. If you see a form number and edition date, you have a one-size-fits-all trust. If the printing of your name and address looks out of place or is in a different typeface, you have a one-size-fits-all trust. If there are places left blank or you are asked to "fill in the blanks," you have a one-size-fits-all trust.

⍒ *Why should I consult with a specialist and pay higher fees when I can have my general-practitioner attorney prepare the documents for far less?*

There is truth in the proverbial phrase, "You get what you pay for." Estate planning may not be rocket science, but it is very much like surgery: you hope the professional with the scalpel knows what he or she is doing.

Attorneys who concentrate either solely or predominantly on an estate planning specialty are worth higher fees because they can spot more potential problems and provide enhanced techniques that will legitimately save your beneficiaries probate expenses and gift, estate, income, and capital gain taxes.

⍒ *What can a specialist practitioner do for me that a good generalist can't do?*

Specialists spend a great deal of their time going to advanced seminars on tax planning techniques that will enable them to help their clients:

- Pass on their estates to their heirs with built-in creditor protection.
- Reduce and potentially eliminate all estate taxes over and above the traditional unified credit amount.
- Avoid paying higher income taxes or capital gain taxes.
- Keep total control of their estates both during their lifetimes and after their deaths.
- Avoid paying unnecessary and confiscatory intergenerational generation-skipping taxes.

⚜ *I believe in keeping matters as simple as possible. Why aren't shorter documents better than thick ones that always seem to cost more?*

I sat with an elderly father and his two adult children recently. His wife of 55 years had just died, and we were discussing how the estate plan that we had created just a few days earlier was going to work now that Mother was gone. His first question was, "Why is this trust so many pages and so complicated? My sister had a will that was only five pages long and very simple."

My answer was a question: "Did it work?" He replied, "We had to pay thousands of dollars in probate fees, and no one got anything for 2 years!" He had answered his own question.

⚜ *I went to a seminar and was told that the presenters could do my trust for $500. Why should I pay you $2500?*

A low price is a good indication that you are headed for a one-size-fits-all trust. You will get what you pay for.

ATTORNEYS QUALIFIED TO DO ESTATE PLANNING

⚜ *Can any attorney prepare a living trust plan?*

Unfortunately, yes. Any attorney who is licensed to practice law can legally prepare estate planning documents, including revocable living trust–centered plans. A generalization that holds much truth is that attorneys who have dedicated themselves to continuing education and specialized practice generally possess the requisite skills to accomplish better-than-journeyman estate planning.

An article in *Elder Law Forum* (January–February 1995) alerted its readers to the problems that can arise from the practice of an unskilled and untrained attorney: Three hundred people in Oregon and northern California were put at risk because of flawed documents created by the ineptitude of one, now-disbarred, attorney.

⚜ *Is my general practitioner qualified to do my will and trust planning?*

It depends upon the general practitioner. GPs handle several different areas of law. Some are barely capable of writing a will; others have significant planning expertise. You will have to interview your attorney to determine if he or she is honestly able to meet the planning complexities your situation warrants.

◄ Are there established standards of practice for qualified estate planning attorneys?

Unfortunately, there are no national standards. Some law schools, such as the University of Miami and the University of Denver, offer Master of Law degrees in estate planning, but they are the exception. A few states certify practitioners as specialists in estate planning, but they are by far in the minority.

There is some movement in the American Bar Association to establish a national certification program for qualified estate planning attorneys. However, the standards have yet to be set and the proposal has yet to be adopted.

There are two major national organizations which recognize attorneys with expertise in the estate planning field. These are the American College of Trusts and Estates Counsel and the National Network of Estate Planning Attorneys. Members of these two organizations are committed to excellence in estate planning, and membership in them is a recognition of these attorneys' serious commitment to their clients and their individual professionalism.

◄ What should I look for in an attorney who is qualified to plan my estate?

Following are some of the characteristics that a qualified estate planning attorney will undoubtedly possess:

- An attitude that puts the client's well-being ahead of everything else
- A good reputation for the highest levels of honesty, integrity, and ethical propriety
- Discipline and diligence in staying legally current through constant study, research, reading, and interaction with other specialized members of the profession
- Organizational methods and technological systems which allow him or her to provide superior legal services and documents in a timely manner
- The ability to freely acknowledge when a matter is beyond his or her experience or expertise

- Relationships that enable him or her to enlist the aid of specialized colleagues or advisors in situations that call for that expertise
- A cadre of clients who are pleased with his or her legal services

⚠ *What type of attorney should I look for to set up my estate plan?*

When selecting an attorney to prepare your estate plan, you want someone who focuses on counseling clients. Estate planning is not just drafting technical documents; it also involves spending time with clients to counsel them on how to create, implement, and maintain an effective estate plan that will achieve their planning objectives.

⚠ *How can I determine if an attorney is qualified to do my plan?*

The questions to ask should center around the following:

- Does the lawyer practice estate planning exclusively? If not, how many other areas does he or she handle? You are *not* looking for a jack-of-all trades.
- What estate planning associations, councils, forums, and so on, are in his or her credentials?
- How many continuing education events does the attorney attend per year? (For example, the National Network of Estate Planning Attorneys holds semiannual 3-day collegia for continuing education and presents over fifty 2- to 6-day specialized workshops each year. It conducts monthly national telephone conferences and maintains an Internet bulletin board for exchange of ideas and information among the member attorneys. In addition, the members in each state hold forum meetings that address local technicalities.)
- How many estate plans does the lawyer do per year? Does he or she have a sample plan that I can review? (An attorney who tends to specialize should prepare a minimum of five plans per month and be proud enough of his or her work to show you a sample plan upon request.)

⚠ *Are there any specific approaches that qualified estate planning attorneys take in their practices?*

Qualified estate planning attorneys generally share a number of important approaches in their work:

- They are willing to discuss fees openly and reach an agreement before beginning work.

- They offer and adhere to a reasonable turnaround time for the preparation of clients' estate plans. (Unless your situation is unusually complex, the drafting of your plan should be accomplished within 2 to 6 weeks.)
- They create efficiency by using state-of-the-art technology.
- They discuss the pros and cons of various estate planning tools but let their clients decide which strategies are best for them.
- They focus on the goals, desires, concerns, and expectations of their clients rather than their own.

What standards of practice should I look for in an estate planning attorney?

INTEGRITY Integrity includes full disclosure regarding the qualifications of the attorney, written confirmation of the work that has been engaged, and clarity regarding what is expected of both you and the attorney. The standard of integrity precludes misrepresentations regarding tax savings and other results of estate planning strategies.

SERVICE ORIENTATION An estate planning attorney should provide you with the highest standard of service. This includes ensuring that you clearly understand the strategies to be used in the implementation of the estate plan and furnishing documentation in a punctual and accurate manner.

FULL FEE DISCLOSURE This standard demands the use of written engagement letters which fully disclose all fees, costs, and expenses associated with the scope of work to be performed.

AVOIDANCE OF CONFLICT OF INTEREST The attorney should not place you in a position that would put your well-being in conflict with other considerations.

What not-so-obvious skills should I be looking for in an estate planning attorney?

- The ability to *listen* and *question* effectively
- The willingness to determine your objectives, desires, dreams, concerns, and fears
- The tenacity and thoroughness to learn about your family situation, assets, and special needs

An attorney who listens carefully can make an accurate diagnosis of your estate planning needs by fully understanding your situation, goals, and objectives. An attorney who listens poorly and misdiagnoses your situation can do great harm to you and your family.

FEES AND COSTS OF ESTATE PLANNING

⋈ *Why do attorneys charge so much?*

Abraham Lincoln is attributed with saying, "An attorney's time and advice are his stock in trade." In our experience his statement still holds true, even in this era of advanced information systems and computers.

An attorney not only must complete a minimum of 7 years of schooling past high school but must continue his or her education throughout all of his or her practice years. Because of this educational commitment, not all of an attorney's time can be spent producing results for his or her clients. In our experience, an established and experienced attorney who can convert 50 percent of his or her time to collectible hours is working very hard and responsibly.

While a fee may sometimes seem large, its size in relation to the value of the service and to the methodology employed in achieving a particular result is generally relatively small.

⋈ *We hear of so many varied and different prices being charged for living trusts. What causes this difference in fees?*

A living trust is only one piece of a complete estate plan, which would also include a pour-over will, health care powers of attorney, durable funding powers of attorney, a property agreement, memorial and funeral instructions, a living will or directive to physician, and provisions for division of personal property.

Depending upon the size of the estate, a complete plan might also include generation-skipping tax provisions, charitable remainder trusts, charitable lead trusts, irrevocable life insurance trusts, family limited partnerships, limited liability companies, S corporations, and offshore trusts, all of which will need to be customized to fit your and your family's particular needs.

Some attorneys are more talented than others—like fine artists, their canvases command higher prices than those of their less skilled colleagues.

Attorneys are free to run their businesses as they see fit as long as they observe the ethics of the profession. Some choose to cut corners and spend as little time with a client or his or her documentation as possible, and they reflect this preference in a billing system that emphasizes reduced or even cheap legal fees.

However, most attorneys take great pride in their work, and they work diligently to make sure it is the best effort they can produce in meeting the client's needs. Their prices will generally be significantly higher than those of their cost-cutting brethren.

⅍ Why does it cost so little to get a will done?

Most attorneys have been reluctant to charge adequate fees for wills because they generally put very little effort into drafting them. Their work, and corresponding fees, begins upon your disability or death, when the probate process begins.

This "don't pay me now, but pay me later" situation is changing. Many practitioners, and the profession as a whole, are moving toward living trust–centered estate planning that avoids probate. Because this planning requires a great deal more effort on the part of the attorney, the fees are higher initially but much lower later on. A detailed comparison between will-planning probate and living trust–centered estate planning can be found in *The Living Trust Revolution,* by Robert Esperti and Renno Peterson (Viking-Penguin, 1992). In general, their research found that living trust–centered estate planning saved 75 percent of total fees.

What would you be willing to pay your attorney if he or she was able to demonstrate to your satisfaction that a properly conceived and written living trust–centered estate plan could save you and your family $258,500 in federal estate taxes and $40,000 in probate fees compared to your current estate plan? What would you be willing to pay if the tax and expense savings were double, triple, or ten times these amounts?

⅍ What types of fee arrangements are used by attorneys?

Attorneys use various types of billing methods, including:

THE HOURLY RATE   Time is billed by the hour. Progress billings are usually sent out monthly. Time records are typically kept in increments of one-tenth of an hour (i.e., 6-minute segments).

VALUE-ADDED BILLING   In addition to standard hourly billing, the client is billed for any significant or unusual value that is added by the attorney's efforts. This type of billing is generally used when an attorney comes up with a particularly innovative solution that has great economic value to the client.

CONTINGENCY FEES   The amount of the attorney's fee is contingent upon successful results being achieved for the client in the particular matter, such as a settlement or jury verdict. The amount of the fee is expressed as a percentage of the amount of the client's recovery or the savings generated by the attorney's efforts. The types of cases where contingency fees are appropriate are specified in the ethical rules that attorneys must follow. Contingency fees generally have no place in the estate planning area.

FLAT OR FIXED FEES   The attorney and client agree—in advance—on the amount that will be charged for the particular matter regardless of the time spent or the results achieved. Flat fees are very popular with clients because the client knows the final fee in advance. Attorneys are able to quote flat fees because they know, through experience, how long and how much effort it will take to get the particular matter completed.

COMBINATION FEES   Typically an hourly rate or contingency fee is charged in addition to a fixed fee for incidental items such as transferring assets to a plan already covered by the fee quotes.

RETAINER   The attorney charges a fixed amount for undertaking representation. Depending on the circumstances, the amount of the retainer can either be nonrefundable or be applied against another billing method agreed upon by the attorney and the client.

What is your candid opinion of the pros and cons of the various billing methods?

THE HOURLY RATE   If fees were based on time alone, the most inefficient attorneys would be paid the highest fees. Even the world's greatest performers don't get paid unless they perform. The hourly rate is a wonderful incentive to never finish anything—it should be used only as a last resort by attorneys and clients alike.

CONTINGENCY FEE   Attorneys who generate substantial tax and expense savings for their clients like contingent fees, which are usually calculated on the present dollar value of all savings generated for a client. Contingent fees can be popular with wealthy entrepreneurial clients, but they are not suitable for most estate planning clients.

FLAT FEES   Flat fees encourage attorneys to work quickly, and they protect clients from future "surprise" billings. They work well for specialist practitioners who can estimate accurately what resources, expertise, and time a project will most likely take. They work poorly for nonspecialist attorneys who have little or no idea what they are going to encounter in working on an unfamiliar project. In our experience, most clients prefer this billing method over all others.

Value-added billing   Although this is a very popular billing method with some attorneys, it is a very unpopular billing method with most (but not all) clients, who want to know up front what their approximate costs are going to be.

Combination fees   This arrangement is very suitable for living trust–centered planning, where the attorney may quote a flat fee for the documentation but an hourly rate for funding the trust. In our experience, combination fees are a highly popular method of billing with both attorneys and their clients.

⚐ *What do you think about an attorney's taking a percentage of the projected tax savings?*

A value-added approach to billing that takes a percentage of the savings generated on behalf of a client is not inappropriate as long as it is discussed up front with the client, put in writing, and seen by the client as being fair and reasonable. However, this approach is not commonly used as an accepted standard estate planning practice, and it should be thoroughly considered before signing an agreement.

⚐ *Do estate planning attorneys charge an hourly rate?*

Attorneys have standard hourly rates based upon their qualifications, experience, and the difficulty of the service to be rendered. Typically, hourly rates are quoted when it is difficult to estimate the amount of time that it will take to complete the task. Most attorneys do not use hourly-rate billing for estate planning work. However, there may be components of an estate plan for which an hourly rate may be appropriate. For example, the work that goes into funding a revocable living trust is usually accomplished on an hourly basis.

⚐ *Why do estate planning attorneys quote fees rather than charge by the hour?*

Hourly-rate billing is not conducive to this area of the law. It penalizes the brilliant planner who knows the law and how to quickly present it, and it rewards the less than brilliant, ponderous practitioner who learns at his or her clients' expense.

⚹ *What factors will an attorney take into account in establishing his or her fee for my estate plan?*

Fees are often determined by some or all of the following factors:

Cost of doing business   The amount of overhead and other expenses involved in running the practice are usually considered. (In our experience, there are few attorneys who can keep their true overhead below 50 percent of their gross fees.)

Credentials   The attorney's level of expertise, reputation, and achievements usually affect billing.

Time requirements   Emergencies and unusually quick time-lines almost always generate higher fees.

Responsibility and liability   The degree of responsibility and liability that must be assumed by the attorney plays a huge role in determining the fee. Because malpractice insurance rates are raging upward, this is a sensitive issue with most attorneys.

Value of the estate   The complexity, nature, and value of the assets that make up the estate are generally always taken into consideration.

Results and benefits   The economic value resulting from the avoidance of probate and ancillary administration and the dollar value of saving estate, gift, income, capital gain, and excise taxes are always taken into consideration in determining the appropriate billing.

Complexity   The involvement of extraordinary legal, financial, or business issues is important in the billing decision.

Novelty   The novelty of the issues presented and the question, "Are the issues routine or uniquely difficult?" play a large part in the billing decision.

Service   The speed and the overall level of service provided throughout the relationship are important to many attorneys. If the attorney determines that a particular client demands *right-now service,* the billing will usually be higher.

Time   How much time did the attorney spend on the matter that could not be spent on other equally or more profitable matters?

⩗ *How do you determine your fee?*

We refer to the above criteria and attempt to arrive at a charge or fee which is reasonable to all parties, including our firm, and which we feel good about from the perspectives of fairness, morality, and good ongoing relationships with our clients.

⩗ *Will an attorney tell me how he or she calculated my estate planning fees?*

You will most probably need to ask your attorney this question directly. Most attorneys are unbelievably bashful about and hesitant to discuss the details of their fees unless you ask.

⩗ *How do I discuss fees with an estate planning attorney?*

Openly, honestly, and with respect. If you make your inquiries in this manner, you will receive wonderful information in an equally open, honest, and respectful manner.

⩗ *When should I discuss fees with my attorney?*

You can discuss fees at any time, but it is preferable to do so as early as possible in your relationship—and always before giving your attorney the go-ahead to do any work.

Be careful about comparing the relative value between attorneys solely on the basis of their fees or their fee structures. You will generally be far better off comparing the value that each attorney is likely to provide you with and comparing the values of their respective services—less the amount of their fees—one to the other, on an apples-to-apples basis.

⩗ *Should I expect my attorney to enter into a written agreement with me in which he puts his fee in writing?*

Not necessarily. Some practitioners do this as a matter of personal preference; others do it because their jurisdiction requires it. Many attorneys consider this practice unprofessional and rely solely on the integrity of their word, and that of their clients, in verbally coming to an agreement.

⩗ *Given the pros and cons of a written fee agreement, is it necessary to have one or not?*

Whether required by law or not, fee agreements are beneficial to both you and your attorney. If you are uncomfortable dealing with an attorney on a handshake basis, request that your agreement be put in writing to protect both parties. In our experience, the attorney will gladly comply and will not be offended.

⅏ What further billing questions should I consider asking?

We recommend that you ask the following:

- What documents will be included?
- From the time of our first meeting until the time that I sign my estate planning documents, will I be charged for telephone calls or brief meetings with my attorney?
- If I have questions after the signing of my estate planning documents, will I be charged for my telephone inquiries?
- Will there be a separate charge if I ask questions of a legal assistant or paralegal?
- If I change my mind regarding a matter during the drafting of my estate planning documents, will additional charges be incurred? If so, what will they be?
- If I wish to include another family member in my planning process and have that family member meet with my attorney, will this cost extra?
- Will the quoted fee include any necessary transfer of title to my assets?
- Will I need a yearly review of my trust plan, and if so, what will the charge be?

⅏ What else do I need to know about fee arrangements?

Some attorneys require a refundable or nonrefundable retainer. If the attorney uses the client's retainer to offset subsequent hourly or flat fees for work and returns the unused portion to the client, the retainer is *refundable*. If the attorney does not return the unused portion of the retainer, it is considered *nonrefundable*.

⅏ What other items of expense might I have in working with an estate planning attorney?

Costs not usually included in the fee you pay to the attorney for his or her professional services generally include expenses such as:

- Fees to county clerks or registrars of deeds for filing deeds
- Appraisals of real estate, personal property, or other assets for purposes of making gifts or for establishing values in closely held cor-

porations, family limited partnerships, and limited liability companies

- Out-of-state counsel fees for assisting in the preparation and filing of deeds for out-of-state property
- Agency expenses for transferring vehicles to a trust
- Mortgage companies' administrative fees for placing the identity of the trust of record in the mortgage department
- Out-of-pocket costs for photocopying, fax transmissions, long-distance telephone calls, online research, and other direct expenses

Are there any annual or additional costs of keeping the trust plan updated?

A revocable living trust–centered plan does not require annual minutes or memoranda of meetings held by directors or members, as might be the custom with corporations, partnerships, and limited liability companies. The routine conduct of transactions with your trust will not require you to change or amend the trust documents. Putting assets into the trust and taking assets from the trust generally do not require you to change or amend the trust documents. One of the characteristics of a well-prepared estate plan is that amendments can be made without major redrafting of the entire trust document and at relatively reasonable cost.

However, significant changes in your family makeup, events in the lives of the individual members of your family, changes in the way you want assets distributed at death, or substantial changes in your overall tax plan are events that will likely generate higher fees to amend or restate your trust.

It is considered good practice for you to consult and review your overall estate plan on some predetermined regular interval with your estate planning advisors and attorney. We suggest that you have a general-review meeting with your attorney and your other advisors *at least* every 3 to 5 years.

Are there reasons why I should or shouldn't get multiple fee quotes?

If you wish to go to the time and expense of doing so, you may certainly obtain multiple fee quotes from numerous estate planning attorneys. Doing so, however, will require quite a bit of your time and may needlessly impose on the courtesy of an initial complimentary consultation that many attorneys offer. Each professional will be basing his or her quote on your perceived needs and on his or her expertise, and each will certainly have different opinions as to how your needs should be addressed.

⚜ *Do you have any general observations about estate planning fees?*

When it comes to legal fees, we believe that you almost always get what you pay for. In our collective experience you would be well advised, especially over the long run, to spend more money for a highly qualified attorney than to spend less money for someone less capable or experienced. The fee for a comprehensive plan will be based upon its complexity and will vary with every case and every family. Typically, the larger the estate is, the more planning is needed to effectively protect it from confiscatory taxes. More planning requires more attorney time, more expertise, and a greater variety of planning tools.

Very simple estate plans might generate fees in the hundreds or low thousands of dollars; complicated multimillion-dollar plans will generate fees in the tens of thousands; and very large estates could generate fees in the hundreds of thousands of dollars. A plan that makes use of a combination of revocable living trusts, irrevocable life insurance trusts, family limited partnerships, charitable trusts, offshore asset protection trusts, grantor retained annuity trusts, and so on, may require fees in the hundreds of thousands of dollars and will likely save millions of dollars of taxes and expenses.

Regardless of the size and complexity of the estate, the amount spent for legal fees should pale in comparison to the tax and cost savings generated for the family.

⚜ *Can you make any further general observations on fees?*

To determine how much you ought to pay an attorney for estate planning services, you first need to determine, in your own mind, what you perceive the value of estate planning to be for you and your family. We believe that people are only willing to pay legal fees commensurate with the value they place on the work product.

If person A believes the planning is critical to his happiness and his family's well-being, he will gladly pay far more than person B, who sees little, if any, value in the exercise. This is true even if person B receives a far greater objective result than person A.

⚜ *Is it appropriate for me to negotiate an attorney's fee?*

It depends upon the attorney, but in our experience, the majority of skilled and experienced attorneys not only do not negotiate their fees but will be offended by an attempt to do so. We suggest that if you are concerned about the fee, you instead make an honest inquiry as to how your attorney determined it.

⋌ Is it accepted practice to make payments over a period of time for estate planning services?

Most attorneys wish to be paid as they complete their work. However, if you have a compelling reason for paying a fee over time, we believe that you will find a high level of compassion in most estate planning attorneys and that they would be willing to accommodate you.

⋌ Is there anything I can do to reduce my legal fees?

In order to render competent legal advice, it is critical that your estate planning attorney have a detailed inventory of all your financial assets and holdings and copies of all your relevant legal documents.

Most qualified estate planning attorneys will request that you provide them with this personal, financial, and legal information before your first strategy meeting. If you are thorough in your preparation, you will save the attorney significant time and effort, which should reflect itself in your bill or fee quote.

You can also facilitate the estate planning process by familiarizing yourself with basic estate planning concepts before meeting with your attorney. The ideas and concepts contained in this book should adequately prepare you to be an active participant in the estate planning process, resulting in faster and more enjoyable communication with your attorney and potential cost savings to you.

The participation of your accountant, financial planner, stockbroker, and insurance professional in your planning process will greatly assist your attorney and should also result in reduced billing.

THE TEAM APPROACH TO ESTATE PLANNING

⋌ Should I rely solely on my estate planning attorney for his or her advice in planning my estate?

If your estate is of a low to moderate value, chances are that your estate planning attorney can accommodate your estate planning needs alone or with minor coordination with your life insurance agent. As an estate gets more complicated, a closer affiliation between advisors will be necessary.

⚑ *What are the advantages of using a team of advisors for the development of a comprehensive estate plan?*

Over the last two decades, it has become apparent that for many types of complex matters, a client's interests are best served by a multidisciplinary approach which combines the talents and skills of qualified attorneys, CPAs, trust officers, and financial planners.

The advantages of such professional affiliations lie in the quality and cost of the interrelated service to the client. Many people prefer to work with affiliated groups because they are cost-effective in providing axillary nonlegal services and often offer access to talented professionals in a nonlegal capacity who might not otherwise have been available to the client for matters of the same type.

⚑ *What type of professionals do I need to design and implement an effective estate plan?*

To develop the most efficient and effective estate plan, the advice and counsel of several highly skilled professionals including an attorney, accountant, life insurance agent, trust officer, and investment counselor should be utilized.

⚑ *Has the team approach been used historically?*

The traditional estate planning team was composed of the client's lawyer, accountant, trust officer, stockbroker, and insurance professional (the financial planner is of recent vintage). It was a group that was highly touted by estate planning councils, but in practice the members seldom worked together on behalf of mutual clients.

Today, the picture has changed. With the blurring of distinctions between the various estate planning disciplines, it is much more common to have a team of professionals working together to assist the client. This is particularly true of the closely held business estate, which demands more sophisticated design strategies.

⚑ *How do attorneys view working with other professionals?*

A qualified attorney will welcome input from your other advisors and, if circumstances warrant it, will initiate putting the team together on your behalf. For example, you may need a charitable trust or an irrevocable life insurance arrangement, and implementing these more sophisticated techniques requires the services of individuals who are experienced in those areas. The resulting synergy of a properly conceived team tends to prove the adage, "The whole is greater than the sum of its parts."

⚜️ *How can my other advisors become meaningfully involved in my estate plan?*

Either you or your attorney should invite your other advisors to participate in the planning of your estate.

⚜️ *Aren't all these people just so many fees on a shovel?*

It will cost you far less to have them working together on your behalf than to have each one working for you independently. Without a team approach, advisors spend unnecessary time working in ignorance of each other's efforts and tripping over each other's work.

⚜️ *How can I find additional advisors for my estate planning team?*

Knowledgeable professionals know other knowledgeable professionals and are enormously reliable referral sources.

HOW TO BEGIN
THE ESTATE PLANNING PROCESS

Finding Qualified Attorneys

⚜️ *How do I find an attorney who specializes in estate planning?*

Ascertaining the type of professional organizations to which your attorney belongs is usually a good indication of whether he or she concentrates on estate planning. Keep in mind that few organizations require that their members demonstrate a minimum level of professional expertise and that membership in a professional organization does not always equate with professional competence.

A number of sources provide meaningful referrals to competent counsel:

- *Friends, relatives, and business associates who have had their estate planning done:* There is nothing like a satisfied client. A recommendation from one of these people to his or her attorney is definitely worth pursuing.
- *Non-estate planning attorneys:* Attorneys you know who do not emphasize estate planning in their own practices will usually be able to refer you to an attorney who specializes in estate planning.

- *Accountants, financial planners, insurance professionals, and stockbrokers:* These professionals work with estate planning attorneys frequently. When they refer their clients to attorneys, they make it their business to know how well the attorneys perform. Most advisors can thoughtfully refer you to estate planning attorneys whom they respect personally and professionally.

- *Bank trust departments and private trust companies:* These institutions are in the trust business and undoubtedly know the most competent professionals in their communities. If asked, they will be pleased to give you a number of names.

- *Your local estate planning council:* Estate planning councils include lawyers, accountants, life insurance agents, financial planners, and bank trust officers who meet regularly to discuss estate planning trends and new ideas. There are councils in most major metropolitan areas, and they are listed in local telephone directories. They will be pleased to provide you with a list of their members, which should give you some good leads.

- *The American College of Trusts and Estates Counsel and the National Network of Estate Planning Attorneys:* These organizations are committed to excellence in estate planning, and membership in them is a recognition of that commitment. A copy of each one's state membership roster should be of assistance. You can contact the National Network of Estate Planning Attorneys at 410 17th Street, Suite 1260, Denver, Colorado 80202. There are over 1400 Network attorneys in forty-nine states (there are currently none in Louisiana).

- *The Martindale-Hubbell Law Digest:* This directory can be found in any legal library and in many public libraries. It describes attorneys by geographic location, with credentials and ratings by their colleagues. As you peruse the listings, ask yourself: What does his or her listing tell me? How has he or she been rated by colleagues? What credentials are special or missing?

⚱ *Should I call the local bar association for a recommendation?*

In our collective experience, bar associations cannot make qualitative judgments. They will simply give you the next few names on their referral list; these lists ensure nothing other than the attorney's interest in receiving referrals.

⚱ *Should I check advertisements in newspapers or the Yellow Pages?*

Advertising in newspapers, the Yellow Pages, or other media is less an indication of legal expertise than of a willingness to buy advertising.

  I've seen advertisements in the newspaper for estate planning seminars. Should I go to one of these seminars before making an appointment with an attorney?

Attending one or more seminars can only heighten your knowledge. The more information you can acquire on the estate planning process, the better position you will be in to talk knowingly to the attorney you ultimately select to accomplish your planning.

If you attend an educational seminar, be attuned to whether the seminar turns into a sales pitch for a particular product or service. A seminar should be, first and foremost, dedicated to providing information and education. The host of the seminar should never attempt to give specific legal advice to you or anyone else in the audience. If you are invited to participate with the host or one of his or her associates one on one after the seminar, be sure that doing so is on a no-cost, no-obligation basis. You should always know what you are buying before committing to anything.

  I've found some hesitation on the part of my corporate attorney to recommend an estate planning attorney. Why the hesitation?

Since most attorneys recognize their limited areas of expertise, they should not hesitate to refer clients to other qualified attorneys. However, some attorneys hesitate to refer their clients to other attorneys because they fear losing their clients.

  Is my present attorney the right one to do my estate planning?

Read the balance of this appendix and put your attorney through the same scrutiny. If there is a good possibility that he or she will qualify, set a meeting and ask the questions we give you here.

  I know and trust two attorneys: one has a will-planning probate practice and the other does a lot of living trust–centered planning. The will-probate attorney tells me that wills are cheaper and are not difficult to probate. What do you recommend I do?

Obtain as much practical information about estate planning as possible so that the decision you make will be based upon your common sense and your personal knowledge of the planning experiences of others. Skim and read good books on the subject. In addition to this text, we recommend *Loving Trust* (Viking-Penguin, 1994), *The Living Trust Revolution* (Viking-Penguin, 1992), and *Protect Your Estate* (McGraw-Hill, 1993), all written by attorneys Robert A. Esperti and Renno L. Peterson.

These texts directly address the major issues you need to address and will help you make a wise decision.

✍ *Can I use an out-of-state attorney for my estate plan?*

Each state has different laws which may affect your estate plan. An attorney from another state will most likely be unfamiliar with the laws of your state and will need to rely on local counsel.

The National Network of Estate Planning Attorneys was created in part to solve this conundrum. Its members help each other as part of a national collaboration.

✍ *I am near retirement and want to prepare a comprehensive estate plan. Should my attorney be someone near my age?*

The age of the attorney who will be completing your estate plan is, for the most part, irrelevant. What is important is the attorney's expertise.

There are many older attorneys who have taken the time to stay current and flexible within an ever-growing and changing body of law. They have remained knowledgeable regarding the multitude of estate planning vehicles that are available to assist their clients in the estate planning arena and have the advantage of years of practice that their juniors have yet to experience.

However, many clients nearing retirement age have a strong preference for working with an attorney who is 10 to 20 years younger than they are, since such an attorney is *likely to be around* to counsel their children and grandchildren.

✍ *Should I shop for an attorney who is younger than I?*

The estate plan designed by your attorney will leave specific instructions to your trustee and heirs as to the administration and disposition of your estate. These instructions should be written clearly enough so that any experienced estate planning attorney can assist your trustee and heirs. Therefore, it is not necessary for you to make this a factor in hiring an attorney.

Questions to Ask

✍ *What is the best way to contact an attorney?*

Telephone his or her office and state your business (you will almost always get a secretary or an assistant). Ask for an appointment, inquire how long you should spend together, and ask whether or not there will be a charge for the first meeting.

≈ *Should I have to pay an attorney for an initial consultation?*

Some attorneys charge for initial consultations; others do not. It is entirely dependent upon each attorney's billing policies.

≈ *I am very busy, and it's extremely hard to get away from work. Can I ask if the estate planning attorney could come to my home after hours or if I could schedule an appointment on weekends?*

There are always exceptions based on a variety of reasons, but the general rule is that most attorneys prefer to meet in their offices because they have all their resources available to them there. When you telephone to set up an appointment, you can certainly ask what the attorney's policy is regarding location and times of meetings.

≈ *If I can talk with prospective attorneys on the telephone, what other questions should I ask?*

Tell the attorneys you want an estate plan which includes a living trust as its foundation. If they attempt to talk you out of a such a plan, suggest only a will, or tell you that your estate is not large enough to need a living trust–centered estate plan, you should be on your guard or find someone else.

Consider asking:

- How long has the attorney been preparing estate plans?
- How many has he or she completed?
- What kind of clientele does the attorney have?
- What is the size of his or her average client's estate?
- Does the attorney belong to estate planning–oriented organizations or have any specialized degrees or training?
- How long will it take to complete the process? (If an attorney is not willing to commit to a reasonable schedule for completing your plan, you might try another attorney.)
- Is the attorney a member of a large firm? If so, who in the firm will supervise and be responsible for his or her work?

If a call is positive from your perspective, ask if you may make an appointment and inquire about the charge for that first meeting.

≈ *Should I ask about specific types of experience?*

Your attorney must have broad estate planning experience (in addition to will and probate experience). He or she must have reasonable experience in drafting all types of fully funded revocable living trusts and irrevocable trusts including:

- Life insurance trusts
- 2503(c) minor's trusts
- Qualified personal residence trusts
- Charitable remainder and charitable lead trusts
- Grantor retained annuity trusts
- Testamentary private foundations

In addition, you should look for a practitioner who has experience in creating family limited partnerships and limited liability companies, as well as in business continuity planning if you have a family business.

⅍ *Can I expect to receive a fee quote over the telephone?*

Attorneys do not quote their fees over the telephone, nor do they give advice to people they do not know. They wish to practice law the old-fashioned way, in that they wish to:

- Meet with the client to determine if representation would be appropriate.
- Ascertain the client's legal needs by taking the time to carefully diagnose the client's situation.
- Familiarize and make the client comfortable with the laws and strategies that are relevant to his or her situation and the legal documentation that will be necessary.
- Prepare the needed documents on a tailored basis, and execute them only after thoroughly explaining them to the client.
- Prepare all ancillary documents, and initiate funding procedures for whatever trusts or other planning entities have been created.

⅍ *How do I get ready for the first meeting with the attorney?*

Preparing for the first meeting involves a four-step process:

1. *Get organized.* Begin with your personal financial statement and a statement of your goals and objectives. Include everything you "own" on your financial statement, and put your life insurance in at face value. Your advisors will need this information to evaluate the best course of action for you to take.
2. *Be informed regarding the transfer tax system.* Learn everything you can about federal estate and gift taxes.

3. *Evaluate your needs and what you wish to accomplish.* Consider your feelings and desires regarding your spouse, children, grandchildren, and favorite charities.

4. *Consider appropriate strategies to accomplish your estate planning goals.* Read all you can, and seek the advice of professionals who will share their knowledge gracefully with you.

⅍ *What will my spouse and I need for the first meeting with our estate planning attorney?*

A qualified estate planning practitioner will have some sort of intake form for you to complete that will outline in detail the specifics of your finances for his or her review. The attorney will also have an information sheet which will ask you to provide a list of all the assets you own, including real estate, bank and investment accounts, life insurance, motor vehicles, business interests, and so on, and the way you hold title to each of the assets—individually, jointly, tenancy in common, tenancy by the entirety, or community property—on your financial statement.

You should have a reasonably accurate idea of the fair market value of each of your assets and the amounts of the indebtedness against them.

Both you and your spouse should attend the first meeting with your attorney and be prepared to discuss, at least in general terms, how your property and assets should be administered if one or both of you should become disabled, how they should be administered and distributed after one of you dies, and how they should be administered and distributed after both of you have died. During the meeting, your attorney will be able to help you define your very specific goals and objectives to an extent that you might not have been able to do in advance of the meeting.

⅍ *What else do I need to bring to the first planning session?*

It would be very helpful to your attorney if you would bring the following items with you (the attorney's assistant will be glad to make copies of them for the attorney's files):

1. Any prior wills, trusts, or other estate planning documents
2. Deeds to real estate
3. Life insurance policies showing owner, insured, and beneficiaries
4. Statements from savings accounts, certificates of deposit, checking accounts, and other bank accounts

5. Certificates of title for motor vehicles
6. Stock certificates and any other bonds or negotiable instruments, or a brokerage account statement
7. Copies of stock certificates for private corporate ownership, copies of shareholder or other corporate agreements, and partnership and limited partnership agreements
8. Notes receivable and trust deeds or mortgages or other documents representing security for the notes
9. IRA trust agreements and other retirement plan documents
10. Information regarding names, birth dates, and other facts you deem pertinent concerning you and your family

⚜ *How long does the planning process take?*

There are essentially three blocks of time that will be required of you during the estate planning process:

- The first block constitutes the time in which detailed information is accumulated and shared with the estate planning attorney in setting forth your hopes, dreams, aspirations, and planning expectations.
- The second block of time will be when you meet with the attorney to help design the specifics of your plan and to ultimately review and sign the estate planning documentation that he or she prepared on your behalf.
- The third block of time involves transferring the ownership of your assets into your various trust and planning vehicles.

The amount of time needed for the first and last blocks is largely dependent on the number of assets you own and the degree of organization that exists before the planning process.

Generally speaking, for most clients the initial meeting with the attorney is accomplished in 1 to 4 hours; the review and signing of the estate planning documents is usually accomplished in 1 to 4 hours; and the process of transferring the assets ("funding") is a function of how well organized the trust maker is and how rapidly he or she wishes to go about funding assets into the trust.

⚜ *How much of my confidential information must I disclose to my attorney?*

Communications between an attorney and his or her client are privileged, and the attorney must keep all client information confidential.

In order to do a complete job of estate planning, the attorney must be given total information rather than incomplete facts or untruths. If you keep important matters to yourself, your estate plan will generally suffer as a result.

⊀ *Why do I need to provide detailed information about my assets to my attorney just to have a will or living trust prepared?*

A beautifully designed and drafted estate plan can completely fail if the underlying assets are titled incorrectly. The type of assets and how title is held to them is critical in determining how to establish, design, and implement an estate plan.

Just as a doctor needs a patient's medical history before prescribing a treatment, so too an estate planning attorney needs detailed information about the client's assets before preparing an estate plan. Full disclosure of assets is beneficial to the development of a comprehensive estate plan to meet the client's needs, goals, and objectives.

⊀ *Why is it necessary to give detailed financial information to an attorney if my spouse and I do not have a taxable estate?*

It is usual for clients to think that their estate consists of only their home, automobiles, bank accounts, stocks, bonds, and miscellaneous possessions such as a fishing boat, motor home, or time-share vacation home.

However, after investigation, planning professionals often find that clients have other very valuable assets, such as 401(k) plans, individual retirement accounts, and insurance policies. In many instances, these assets bring an estate to or above a taxable threshold. When the client's life expectancy is considered along with even modest appreciation along the way, many nontaxable estates hit that threshold.

Determining if
You Chose the Right Attorney

⊀ *How do I know if a qualified estate planning attorney is the right one for me?*

You should choose an attorney who not only is qualified but is a person you like. A good attorney will be your advisor: he or she will counsel you rather than talk down to you.

Credentials are important—very important—but they do not reveal anything about how the attorney might treat you or how you might react to his or her personality.

⋈ *What should happen after my first meeting with an attorney?*

Evaluate the meeting. Was the attorney prompt, courteous, organized, and knowledgeable? Did he or she speak in plain and understandable language and fully answer your questions? Did he or she seem genuinely interested in you and your family?

Trust your instincts. If you feel good about the experience, you should proceed, but do not forget to determine the cost up front. If something just does not feel right, you should probably look for another attorney because it is likely that you will find a practitioner not only who will meet all of your qualifications and criteria but whose company you enjoy as well.

⋈ *What additional criteria should I use in deciding if this attorney is the one to hire to complete my estate plan?*

One of the most important criteria is the "creation of a relationship" between you and your estate planning attorney. If an attorney fails to show genuine interest in you, your family, and your affairs or is discourteous to you in any way, it is unlikely that he or she will have the necessary ability and personality to create a plan with which you will be comfortable.

Any attorney you select should be well aware of your goals, wishes, and aspirations as they pertain to your family background, assets, and estate planning objectives. This personal knowledge will be a direct by-product of a positive working relationship and can result only from the attorney's asking you the right kinds of questions in a kind tone and polite manner.

Make sure that you do not permit any attorney to think that he or she has been retained by you until you receive a well-defined indication of how your estate plan will be designed. You should know the specifics regarding the number and type of documents and the charge for them.

⋈ *How else should I evaluate the attorney?*

Ask yourself these questions:

- Does the attorney communicate well with me, and do I communicate well with him or her?
- While in the attorney's presence, do I feel secure and trusting, or do I feel nervous and ill at ease?
- Will my family like or dislike the attorney's personality?
- Has he or she demonstrated specialized skill?

- Are the attorney's fees commensurate with the value that he or she will provide to me and my family?

⚜ As attorneys, what would you look for in another attorney?

We would ask ourselves whether the attorney seems to be:

- The kind of person we could enjoy talking with for hours, someone with whom we would feel comfortable sharing our most intimate thoughts and secrets that relate to the planning at hand
- A respectful and good listener who strives to understand our concerns and needs
- Enjoying what he or she does
- Focused in his or her estate and tax planning practice
- Evidencing a strong commitment to serve our family
- Able to provide us with quality work in a timely manner
- Attending significant numbers of ongoing specialized continuing legal education programs
- Comfortable in explaining his or her fees and costs

⚜ How can I determine if I am getting a high-quality living trust plan?

There are several factors that distinguish a comprehensive, high-quality living trust plan from a run-of-the-mill or inadequate plan. A quality living trust–centered estate plan is:

- *Prepared by an attorney who emphasizes estate planning in his or her practice:* Usually, attorneys who devote substantially all of their practices to estate planning attend extensive continuing legal education courses devoted to estate planning and are best-suited to draft plans that most accurately capture their clients' needs.
- *Prepared in a "user-friendly" manner:* Many attorneys feel that it is necessary to draft trusts in legalese to make their clients feel that they are getting their money's worth. Actually, the main goal of an estate planning attorney is to draft documents so that the client's objectives are met and the client can understand what his or her documents say and do not say. The mark of a caring attorney is his or her zeal to incorporate easy-to-read instructions into the living trust plan that explain for the family and the trust maker's fiduciaries—trustees and personal representatives—how the plan works upon the death or incapacity of its maker.
- *Funded with the appropriate assets after the documents are made op-*

erational: All too often we see plans for which the attorneys did not take the appropriate steps to ensure that the clients' assets were transferred into the trusts. Vehicles without fuel do not work very well, nor do trusts without assets.

■ *Prepared by an attorney who has a desire to maintain a continuing relationship with the family.* After the preparation of a trust plan, it is essential that the clients have access to the attorney and his or her staff for interpreting matters concerning the plan.

⚔ *How do I evaluate an attorney's fee quote?*

To evaluate your attorney's fee quote, you might consider:

■ The value to you of the services to be provided
■ The time the attorney must spend to take on and complete the project
■ The skill that went into the result as compared to the skill levels of others
■ The dollar savings of costs, expenses, and taxes generated by his or her advice and work
■ The speed with which the result may be obtained
■ Your confidence in the attorney

⚔ *How do I determine if my attorney is charging me a fair fee for preparing my estate plan?*

The quantum test is to ask yourself this question: *Am I getting value equal to or greater than the cost of the services being rendered on my behalf?*

You should take into consideration the experience of the attorney and a host of other factors including the size of your estate, the number and complexity of trusts and other documents that are being created within the plan, whether or not the attorney is funding your various entities and trusts, whether there are multiple marriages and "his," "hers," and "our" children, whether any of the beneficiaries require special needs, and so on.

The best advice we know is to seek a well-known attorney who practices exclusively in the estate planning area and whom you like and trust.

appendix B

Contributing Authors

George R. Adams, J.D., MBA
Attorney and Counselor at Law
4611 Western Avenue, NW, Suite 33
Washington, D.C. 20016-4339
202-363-9168 Fax: 202-362-7254

Karl W. Adler, J.D.
Adler, Tolar & Adler
1700 NE 26th Street, Suite 4
Fort Lauderdale, FL 33305
954-566-3237 Fax: 954-566-3239

DeWayne E. Allen, J.D.
Allen & Associates
1718 South Cheyenne
Tulsa, OK 74119
918-587-7773 Fax: 918-592-1999

Rock W. Allen, J.D.
Rock W. Allen & Associates
541 Main Street
Longmont, CO 80501
303-774-1976 Fax: 303-682-9633
email: rock.allen.law@internetmci.com

David C. Anderson, J.D.
David C. Anderson, APC
404 Camino del Rio South, Suite 605
San Diego, CA 92108
619-220-8688 Fax: 619-220-8788
email: davidanderson@sprynet.com

David B. Atkins, J.D.
David B. Atkins & Associates
1023 East Hyde Park
Chicago, IL 60615
773-493-8554 Fax: 773-874-1109

Ronald J. Axelrod, J.D.
Adair Law Firm
30 Corporate Woods
Rochester, NY 14623
716-272-7820 Fax: 716-272-8280
email: ronaxelrod@aol.com

David F. Bacon, J.D.
Roth Bacon Young
50 Court Street
Upper Sandusky, OH 43351
419-294-2232 Fax: 419-294-2488

Jerry D. Balentine, J.D.
Jerry D. Balentine, P.C. and Associates
6303 North Portland, Suite 305
Oklahoma City, OK 73112
405-946-4500 Fax: 405-946-4757
email: jbal625@aol.com

Michael R. Bascom, J.D.
Coyle, Bascom & Bergman, P.C.
1000 Cambridge Square, Suite C
Alpharetta, GA 30004
770-650-9670 Fax: 770-650-6670
email: mbascom@mindspring.com

Thomas F. Bean, J.D.
Thomas F. Bean Co., L.P.A.
34950 Chardon Road, Suite 210
Willoughby Hills, OH 44094
440-953-1151 Fax: 440-953-1962

Shelton M. Binstock, J.D., LL.M., CPA
Law Offices of Binstock, Torchinsky and Associates, P.C.
Barlow Building
5454 Wisconsin Avenue, Suite 1340
Chevy Chase, MD 20815
301-657-5555 Fax: 301-657-9871

James T. Blazek, J.D.
Emery & Blazek
11580 West Dodge Road
Omaha, NE 68154
402-496-3432 Fax: 402-496-4519

Robert M. Bly, J.D.
Robert M. Bly, Attorney & Counsellor at Law
9111 Cross Park Drive, D-200
Knoxville, TN 37923
423-694-3868 Fax: 423-694-0848

Gary J. Boecker, J.D.
Boecker & Co., L.P.A.
395 Springside Drive, Suite 100
Fairlawn, OH 44333
330-665-5000 Fax: 330-665-4365

Robert E. Bourne, J.D.
Robert E. Bourne, P.C.
412 Ashman
Midland, MI 48640
517-835-6511 Fax: 517-835-6521
email: rbourne@voyager.net

William R. Brereton, J.D., CLU
Brereton Kraus & Myers, Inc.
5811 Pelican Bay Boulevard, Suite 203
Naples, FL 34108
941-592-6306 Fax: 941-592-6304
email: bkm@sprintmail.com

Chris L. Brisendine, J.D.
The Brisendine Law Firm, P.C.
205 Corporate Center Drive, Suite B
Stockbridge, GA 30281
770-507-8818 Fax: 770-506-6880
email: kbrisendine@minspring.com

and
One Live Oak Center
3475 Lenox Road, NE, Suite 400
Atlanta, GA 30326
404-238-0567

Philip J. Bryce, J.D., CPA
Bryce, Crandall & Coleman, PLLC
212 South Peters Road, Suite 101
Knoxville, TN 37923
423-690-5566 Fax: 423-690-4967

Charles C. Case, Jr., J.D.
Case & Rapp, LLP, Attorneys and Counsellors atLaw
1645 Falmouth Road, Suite 1E
Centerville, MA 02632
508-771-3400 Fax: 508-778-1700
email: caserapp@capecod.net

William M. Casey, J.D.
The Casey Law Firm
8014 Menaul Boulevard NE
Albuquerque, NM 87110
505-291-1225 Fax: 505-298-4491

C. David Clauss, J.D.
P.O. Box 1172
25 South Gros Ventre Street
Jackson, WY 83001
307-733-1191 Fax: 307-733-4718

Nathaniel E. Clement, J.D., MBA
Nathaniel E. Clement
100 Europa Drive, Suite 403
Chapel Hill, NC 27514
919-929-9298 Fax: 919-929-9221
email: nclement@intrex.net

William A. Conway, J.D.
Law Offices of William A. Conway
1300 Chain Bridge Road, Suite 250
McLean, VA 22101
703-448-7575 Fax: 703-448-0059

Stephen W. Dale, J.D., LL.M.
1901 Olympic Boulevard, Suite 230
Walnut Creek, CA 94596
510-280-0172 Fax: 510-280-0177
email: sdale@jps.net

Steven E. Davidson, J.D.
Davidson & Sheehan
11 Embarcadero West, Suite 134
Oakland, CA 94607
510-839-5500 Fax: 510-839-5599
email: stevedav@best.com

Justin Dituri, J.D.
4141 Arapahoe Avenue, Suite 100
Boulder, CO 80303
303-415-0900 Fax: 303-402-0458
email: jdituri@sprynet.com

Austin J. Doyle, J.D., CPA
Doyle Law Firm
3201 New Mexico Avenue, NW
Washington D.C., 20016
202-785-8900 Fax: 202-244-5660
email: adoyle@westlake.com

Jeffrey R. Dundon, J.D., LL.M.
7026 Corporate Way
Centerville, OH 45459
937-438-3122 Fax: 937-291-5491
email: jrdundon@erinet.com

Brian A. Eagle, J.D.
Eagle & Fein
8500 Keystone Crossing, Suite 555
Indianapolis, IN 46240
317-726-1714 Fax: 317-475-1270
email: BAElegal@aol.com

Sidney Eagle, J.D., LL.M.
Eagle & Fein
342 Madison Avenue, Suite 1712
New York, NY 10173
212-986-3211 Fax: 212-986-3219

William L. Eaton, J.D., LL.M.
Woodman & Eaton, P.C.
801 Main Street
Concord, MA 01742
978-369-0960 Fax: 978-371-1343
email: wepclaw@aol.com

Marie Mirro Edmonds, J.D.
Marie Mirro Edmonds Co., L.P.A.
807 E Washington Street, Suite 200
Medina, OH 44256
330-725-5297 Fax: 330-722-5932
email: mmecolpa@ohio.net

Richard Egner, Jr., J.D., LL.M.
1550 NW Eastman Parkway, Suite 150
Gresham, OR 97030
503-665-4186 Fax: 503-665-2038
email: regner@worldnet.att.net

Edward J. Enichen, J.D.
Guyer & Enichen, P.C.
202 W State Street, Suite 400
Rockford, IL 61101
815-965-8775 Fax: 815-965-8784

Robert D. Epple, J.D.
Law Office of Robert D. Epple
16446 Woodruff Avenue
Bellflower, CA 90706
562-804-9555 Fax: 562-920-2737

Robert A. Esperti, Cochairman
National Network Incorporated
Post Office Box 3224
125 South King Street
Jackson, WY 83001
307-733-6952 Fax: 307-739-9191

Isauro Fernandez, J.D.
99-06 Metropolitan Avenue
Forest Hills, NY 11375
718-520-9788 Fax: 718-520-9788
email: ferlaw@aol.com

Richard L. Ferris, J.D., LL.M.
Ferris & Associates
460 McLaws Circle, Suite 105
Williamsburg, VA 23185
757-220-8114 Fax: 757-220-8029
email: ferris@widomaker.com

Marvin J. Frank, J.D., CPA
Frank & Kraft, A Professional
  Corporation
135 North Pennsylvania Street, Suite
  1100
Indianapolis, IN 46204
317-684-1100 Fax: 317-684-6111

Jon B. Gandelot, J.D.
Jon B. Gandelot, P.C.
19251 Mack Avenue, Suite 580
Grosse Pointe Woods, MI 48236
313-885-9100 Fax: 313-885-9152
email: jbg@gandelot.com

Guy B. Garner III, J.D.
Guy B. Garner, III, P.C.
1101 W Randol Mill Road
Arlington, TX 76012
817-261-5222 Fax: 817-277-6424
email: ggarner@ix.netcom.com

Frederick H. Goldinov, J.D., LL.M.
Law Offices of Frederick H. Goldinov
6619 North Scottsdale Road
Scottsdale, AZ 85250
email: FHG111@aol.com
602-948-6713 Fax: 602-948-6775

Robert A. Goldman, J.D., CPA
Goldman & Associates
600 California Street, Suite 1350
San Francisco, CA 94108
415-956-4245 Fax: 415-956-7637
email: rgoldman@bpminc.com

Carol H. Gonnella, J.D.
Gonnella and Sullivan
350 E Broadway
P.O. Box 1226
Jackson, WY 83001
307-733-5890 Fax: 307-734-0544
email: cgonnella@blissnet.com

Timothy D. Good, J.D.
Good & Good, P.C.
7720 East Belleview Avenue, Suite 205
Englewood, CO 80111
303-773-9889 Fax: 303-773-0305

Richard H. Gregory III, J.D., LL.M.
Samuel Staples, Jr., House
Five Benefit Street
Providence, RI 02904
401-331-5050 Fax: 401-454-4209
email: rgregory@ids.net

Scott Hamilton, J.D.
Law Offices of Scott J. Hamilton
P.O. Box 119
Newtown, CT 06470
888-680-6500 Fax: 203-426-1855
email: scott_hamilton@snet.net

Lewis B. Hampton, J.D.
Hagen, Dye, Hirschy & DiLorenzo, P.C.
888 S.W. Fifth Avenue, 10th Floor
Portland, OR 97204
503-222-1812 Fax: 503-274-7979

Darrel E. Johnson, J.D.
White and Johnson, L.L.P.
701 Vilymaca
P.O. Box 450
Elkhart, KS 67950
316-697-2163 Fax: 316-697-2165

Peter R. Johnson, J.D.
Woodman & Eaton, P.C.
801 Main Street
Concord, MA 01742
978-369-0960 Fax: 978-371-1343

Willard A. Johnson, J.D.
Law Offices of Willard A. Johnson
5640 Southwyck Boulevard, Suite 1-E
Toledo, OH 43614
419-865-6586 Fax: 419-865-7241
email: wjohnson@glasscity.net

Steven D. Kaestner, J.D., CPA
Steven D. Kaestner, P.C.
2601 NW Expressway, Suite 405W
Oklahoma City, OK 73112
405-842-3555 Fax: 405-842-3492

Stuart B. Kalb, J.D., LL.M.
Kalb & Peck. P.L.L.C.
5728 LBJ Freeway, Suite 400
Dallas, TX 75240
972-490-8383 Fax: 972-490-8390
email: kalbs@airmail.net

Kenneth T. Kelley, J.D.
Kenneth T. Kelley Law Associates
2307 Silas Dean Highway
Rocky Hill, CT 06067
860-257-1679 Fax: 860-257-1795
email: kel.ham@worldnet.att.net

David L. Kelly, J.D.
Kelly & Pauly
3300 Douglas Boulevard, Suite 120
Roseville, CA 95661
916-782-8100 Fax: 916-782-8121

Mark A. Kemp, J.D.
Mark A. Kemp, P.C.
1771 East Flamingo Road, Suite 119-B
Las Vegas, NV 89119
702-794-2821 Fax: 702-794-2775
email: mark1pc@aol.com

Yung Mo Kim, J.D., Ph.D.
Law Offices of Yung Mo Kim
6470 Main Street, Suite 6
Williamsville, NY 14221
716-631-2300 Fax: 716-631-2316

Paul A. Kraft, J.D.
Frank & Kraft, A Professional
 Corporation
135 North Pennsylvania Street, Suite
 1100
Indianapolis, IN 46204
317-684-1100 Fax: 317-684-6111

Jay H. Krall, J.D.
Law Offices of Jay H. Krall
96 State Street
Augusta, ME 04330
207-626-3330 Fax: 207-622-9115
email: jhkrall@mint.net

Howard M. Lang, J.D.
Law Offices of Howard M. Lang
700 Florsheim Drive
Libertyville, IL 60048
847-367-4460 Fax: 847-367-0090

Tim J. Larson, J.D.
Larson & Schainost, L.L.C.
727 North Waco, Suite 255
Wichita, KS 67203
316-262-3066 Fax: 316-262-7408

Richard Alan Lehrman, J.D.
Law Offices of Richard Alan Lehrman
777 Arthur Godfrey Road, Fourth Floor
Miami Beach, FL 33140
305-534-1323 Fax: 305-531-0314

Stephen J. Livens, J.D., CPA, MBA
The Livens Law Firm
2516 Harwood Road
Bedford, TX 76021
817-545-3425 Fax: 817-545-9847
email: trustlwyr@aol.com

Con P. Lynch, J.D.
336 Leslie Street SE
Salem, OR 97301
503-378-1048 Fax: 503-371-2959

Anthony J. Madonia, J.D., C.P.A.
Anthony J. Madonia & Associates, Ltd.
150 North Wacker Drive, Suite 900
Chicago, IL 60606-1605
312-578-9300 Fax: 312-578-9303
email: tony@madonia.com

Carol E. Magett, J.D.
Magett & Associates
381 Park Avenue South, Suite 601
New York, NY 10016
212-684-1911 Fax: 212-213-1092

Raymond E. Makowski, J.D.
Raymond E. Makowski, P.A.
Post Office Box 49291
Jacksonville Beach, FL 32240-9291
904-246-5050 Fax: 904-246-8649

Howard Mandelcorn, J.D., B.C.L., LL.B., LL.M.
Hutchings, Barsamian & Levy, P.C.
110 Cedar Street
Wellesley, MA 02481
781-431-2231 Fax: 781-431-8726
email: hmm@hblattys.com

Grant R. Markuson, J.D., LL.M.
Markuson & Kalb
One Lincoln Centre, Suite 1050
Oakbrook Terrace, IL 60181
630-261-1490 Fax: 630-261-1494

William J. Maxam, J.D.
The Law Offices of William J. Maxam
404 Camino del Rio South, Suite 605
San Diego, CA 92108
619-220-8666 Fax: 619-220-8788
email: maxamlaw@aol.com

John E. McCullough, J.D.
Law Offices of John E. McCullough,
P.L.C.
1737 King Street
Alexandria, VA 22314
703-548-4990 Fax: 703-824-0666
email: jmccullough@tidalwave.net

Edward D. McGuire, Jr., J.D.
Stein, Sperling, Bennett, DeJong,
Driscoll, Greenfeig & Metro, P.C.
25 West Middle Lane
Rockville, MD 20850
301-838-3227 Fax: 301-340-8217
and
4306 Evergreen Lane, Suite 104
Annandale, VA 22003-3217
703-941-3620
email: emcguire@steinsperling.com

James T. McKenzie, J.D.
McKenzie & Associates, Ltd.
1005 West Wise Road, Second Floor
Schaumburg, IL 60193
847-895-3989 Fax: 847-895-4123

Susan Wolff McMakin, J.D., LL.M., CLU, ChFC
Susan Wolff McMakin, P.C. Attorney &
Counsellor at Law
8002 Discovery Drive, Suite 101
Richmond, VA 23229
804-285-3807 Fax: 804-285-8209

John J. McQueen, J.D., CPA
John J. McQueen
2250 E 73rd Street, Suite 650
Tulsa, OK 74136
918-494-2929 (ext. 11) Fax:
918-492-5433

Gretchen R. Morris, J.D., LL.M.
Gretchen R. Morris, P.C., Attorney &
Counselor at Law
810 SW Madison Avenue
Corvallis, OR 97333
541-754-1411 Fax: 541-754-1413

Ellen Gay Moser, J.D.
E.G. Moser & Associates, P.C.
1112 South Washington Street, Suite
117
Naperville, IL 60540
630-355-6064 Fax: 630-355-7808

Ketra A. Mytich, J.D.
Ketra A. Mytich, Ltd.
416 Main Street, Suite 815
Commerce Bank Building
Peoria, IL 61602-1103
309-673-1805 Fax: 309-673-3700
email: kam@est-planning.com
website: www.est-planning.com

Lucas R. Nardini, J.D.
Nardini & Sheehan, P.C.
31 W Miner Street
West Chester, PA 19382
610-431-6700 Fax: 610-431-9502

Peter J. Parenti, J.D., LL.M.
Peter J. Parenti, A Professional
Corporation
8122 Datapoint Drive, Suite 800
San Antonio, TX 78229
210-614-7766 Fax: 210-692-9066
email: pparenti@swbell.net

Arthur J. Pauly, Jr., J.D., AIC
Kelly & Pauly
3300 Douglas Boulevard, Suite 120
Roseville, CA 95661
916-782-8100 Fax: 916-784-8338

Laurie S. Peck, J.D.
Kalb & Peck. P.L.L.C.
5728 LBJ Freeway, Suite 400
Dallas, TX 75240
972-490-8383 Fax: 972-490-8390
email: lspeck1@airmail.net

Renno L. Peterson, Cochairman
National Network Incorporated
2 North Tamiami Trail, Suite 606
Sarasota, FL 34236
941-365-4819 Fax: 941-366-5347

John S. Pfarr, J.D.
Law Offices of John S. Pfarr
120 Wayland Avenue
Providence, RI 02906
401-274-4100 Fax: 401-831-3837
email: jpfarr@idt.net

Chester M. Przybylo, J.D., MBA
Law Offices of Przybylo and
Kubiatowski
5339 North Milwaukee Avenue
Chicago, IL 60630
773-631-2525 Fax: 773-631-7101
email: trustnow@mcs.net

Donald Joseph Purser, J.D.
Donald Joseph Purser & Associates, P.C.
Kinavy Mansion
236 South Third East
Salt Lake City, UT 84111
801-532-3555 Fax: 801-537-1212
email: purserlaw@aol.com

Kevin D. Quinn, J.D., MBA
Kevin D. Quinn Attorney at Law
30 Hannum Brook Drive
Easthampton, MA 01027
413-527-0517 Fax: 413-529-8027
email: kdqplan@worldnet.att.com

**Gerald J. Rachelson, J.D., CPA, CFP,
LL.M., MPA**
Law Office of Gerald J. Rachelson
12330 Clairmonte Avenue
Alpharetta, GA 30004
770-619-9007 Fax: 770-619-9003

David H. Radcliff, J.D.
Cherewka & Radcliff, L.L.P.
3905 North Front Street
Harrisburg, PA 17110
717-236-9318 Fax: 717-232-4774
email: dhr@cherradlaw.com

Richard L. Randall, J.D.
Randall & Galbraith, P.C.
10333 North Meridian Street, Suite 375
Indianapolis, IN 46290
317-574-9911 Fax: 317-574-9922
email: randall_law@iquest.net

Stuart W. Rapp, J.D.
Case & Rapp, LLP, Attorneys and
Counsellors atLaw
1645 Falmouth Road, Suite 1E
Centerville, MA 02632
508-771-3400 Fax: 508-778-1700

F. David Resch, J.D.
F. David Resch, Esq.
2715 Tuller Parkway
Dublin, OH 43017
614-889-0990 Fax: 614-889-5250

Robert E. Ridgway, Jr., B.B.A., J.D.
93 Chandler Center
P.O. Box 710
Hartwell, GA 30643
706-376-3991 Fax: 706-376-1155
email: ridglaw@hartcom.net

Steven P. Riley, J.D.
Law Offices of Steven P. Riley, P.A.
3333 Henderson Boulevard, Suite 150
Tampa, FL 33609
813-877-4357 Fax: 813-875-2013
email: rileylaw@aol.com

Mark S. Roberts, J.D.
Mark Roberts & Associates, APLC
1440 North Harbor, Suite 900
Fullerton, CA 92835
714-449-3353 Fax: 714-680-0906

Thomas Rogers, J.D., CPA
Tillman Rogers Tansey
900 Fox Valley Drive, Suite 102
Longwood, FL 32779
407-869-4163 Fax: 407-862-0185
email: thom@netpass.com

William K. Root, J.D.
William K. Root & Associates, L.L.C.
2715 Tuller Parkway, Suite 102
Dublin, OH 43017
614-889-0990 Fax: 614-889-5250
email: wroot@netwalk.com

Jeffrey P. Roth, J.D.
Roth Bacon Young
50 Court Street
Upper Sandusky, OH 43351
419-294-2232 Fax: 419-294-2488

Merek S. Rubin, J.D., LL.M.
Rubin, Hay & Gould, P.C.
205 Newbury Street
Framingham, MA 01701
508-875-5222 Fax: 508-879-6803

Robert J. Saalfeld, J.D.
Saalfeld, Griggs, Gorsuch, Alexander &
Emerick, P.C.
250 Church Street SE, Suite 300
P.O. Box 470
Salem, OR 97308
503-399-1070 Fax: 503-371-2927
email: RSaalfeld@SaalfeldLaw.com

Gary A. Sargent, J.D.
Backman, Clark & Marsh
68 South Main Street, Suite 800
Salt Lake City, UT 84101
801-531-8300 Fax: 801-363-2420

Jeanie L. Schainost, J.D.
Larson & Schainost, L.L.C.
7180 W 107th, Suite 20
Overland Park, KS 66212
800-590-0645 Fax: 785-448-3237
email: shiney@kanza.net

Duke Schneider, J.D., M.B.A.
MacElree, Harvey
17 West Miner Street
P.O. Box 660
West Chester, PA 19381-0660
610-436-0100 Fax: 610-429-4486
email: macelree@dca.net

John J. Schneider, J.D.
Weinstein, Schneider & Kannebecker
104 W High Street
Milford, PA 18337
717-296-6471 Fax: 717-296-2653
email: wsklawfirm@pikeonline.net

Daniel L. Sheehan, J.D.
Davidson & Sheehan
11 Embarcadero West, Suite 134
Oakland, CA 94607
510-839-5500 Fax: 510-839-5599
email: estatelaw@yahoo.com

Arnold L. Slavet, J.D.
60 State Street, Suite 700
Boston, MA 02109
781-894-1022 Fax: 781-647-1436
email: arnoldslavet@worlnet.att.net

David A. Straus, J.D., LL.M., CPA
Law Offices of David A. Straus
900 Rancho Lane
Las Vegas, NV 89106
702-474-4500 Fax 702-474-4510
and
1325 Airmotive Way, Suite 175
Reno, NV 89502
702-324-4400 Fax 702-786-4451
email: dstraus@bigplanet.com

Andrew A. Strauss, J.D.
77 Central Avenue
Asheville, NC 28801
704-258-0994 Fax: 704-252-4921

Joseph J. Strazzeri, J.D.
Law Offices of Joseph J. Strazzeri, APC
404 Camino del Rio South, Suite 605
San Diego, CA 92108
619-220-8688 Fax: 619-220-8788
email: strazzeri@page.metrocall.com

Jeffrey B. Strouse, J.D.
Jeffrey B. Strouse & Associates, P.A.
200 Pierce Street
Tampa, Fl 33602
813-226-0074 Fax: 813-224-9153
email: strouselaw@aol.com

Daniel P. Stuenzi, J.D.
Stuenzi & Associates
7105 Virginia Road, Suite 20
Crystal Lake, IL 60014
815-477-5515 Fax: 815-356-7724

Thomas C. Sturgill, J.D.
Elam & Miller, P.S.C.
2401 Regency Road, Suite 201
Lexington, KY 40503
606-277-4849 Fax: 606-278-2207
email: tomstur@ix.netcom.com

**Dennis B. Sullivan, J.D., LL.M.,
    M.Sc., CPA**
Global Design Collaborative, L.L.C.
888 Worcester Street
Wellesley, MA 02482
781-237-0816 Fax: 781-237-3141
email: globaldesign@wealthstrategy.com

Samuel T. Swansen, J.D.
640 Sentry Parkway, Suite 104
Blue Bell, PA 19422
610-834-9810 Fax: 610-834-9812
email: sam@samswansen.com
webpage: www.samswansen.com

Daniel S. Swinton, J.D.
Daniel S. Swinton - Counsellor at Law
95 Westfield Avenue
Clark, NJ 07066
732-381-3838 Fax: 732-381-3445
email: swinton1@aol.com

Michael Tillman, J.D.
5346 SW 91st Terrace
Gainseville, FL 32608
352-376-8600 Fax: 352-376-0026
email: tillman@post.harvard.edu

David B. Torchinsky, J.D., CPA
Law Offices of Binstock, Torchinsky
    and Associates, P.C.
Barlow Building
5454 Wisconsin Avenue, Suite 1340
Chevy Chase, MD 20815
301-657-5555 Fax: 301-657-9871

William G. Touret, J.D.
Law Offices of William G. Touret
One Washington Mall, 5th Floor
Boston, MA 02108-2695
800-345-0080 Fax: 617-523-4876
email: plandesign@ibm.net

Daniel P. Trump, J.D., LL.M.
Trump, Alioto, Trump & Prescott,
    L.L.P.
2280 Union Street
San Francisco, CA 94123
415-563-7200 Fax: 415-346-0679
email: dptofsf@aol.com

I. Michael Tucker, J.D.
Law Office of I. Michael Tucker
498 Palm Springs Drive, Suite 100
Altamonte Springs, FL 32701
407-977-8836 Fax: 407-977-5252

T.A. "Rusty" Ward, Jr., J.D.
2243 W 42nd Street
Casper, WY 82604
307-472-4544 Fax: 307-472-4544

Edward L. Weidenfeld, J.D.
The Weidenfeld Law Firm, P.C.
1899 L Street NW, Suite 500
Washington, D.C. 20036
202-785-2143 Fax: 202-452-8938
email: eweidenf@aol.com

**William T. Whittenberg, Jr., J.D.,
LL.M.**
Whittenberg & Associates
200 Broadway, Suite 306
Lynnfield, MA 01940
781-599-4000 Fax: 781-581-2650
email: wtwllm@aol.com

Arnold Fitger Williams, J.D., M.B.A.
Counselor at Law
800 Wilshire Boulevard, Twelfth Floor
Los Angeles, CA 90017
213-688-7523 Fax: 213-688-2771
email: afwilliams@counsellor.com

Scott A. Williams, J.D.
Scott A. Williams and Associates
398 W Bagley Road, Suite 14
Berea, OH 44017
888-891-7526 Fax: 440-891-9633

Wayne W. Wilson, Jr., J.D.
Wilson Law Group, L.L.C.
7633 Ganser Way
Madison, WI 53719
608-833-4001 Fax: 608-833-1212
email: wwwilson@execpc.com

Addison E. "Bob" Winter, J.D.
The Winter Law Firm
205 South Broadway
Riverton, WY 82501
307-856-1929 Fax: 307-856-4456

William T. "Bill" Winter, J.D.
The Winter Law Firm
205 South Broadway
Riverton, WY 82501
307-856-1929 Fax: 307-856-4456

Eric H. Witlin, J.D.
Law Offices of Eric H. Witlin
1177 High Ridge Road
Stamford, CT 06905
203-975-0885 Fax: 203-461-8515
email: ehwitlin@netaxis.com

Byron E. Woodman, Jr., J.D., LL.M.
Woodman & Eaton, P.C.
801 Main Street
Concord, MA 01742
978-369-0960 Fax: 978-371-1343
email: wepclaw@aol.com

Mark W. Worthington, J.D.
49 Midgley Lane
Worcester, MA 01609
508-757-1140 Fax: 508-795-1636
email: markintosh@aol.com

Guy R. Youman, J.D.
Law Offices of Rupp & Youman
4306F W Crystal Lake Road
McHenry, IL 60050
815-385-7444 Fax: 815-385-7480

John G. W. Zacker, J.D.
Attorney at Law
64 Weir Lane
Locust Valley, NY 11560
516-674-2261 Fax: 516-674-8319

index